Schizophrenia and Related Syndromes

P.J. McKenna
Consultant Psychiatrist, Fulbourn Hospital and A
University of Cambridge

D1494613

PSYCHOLOGY PRESS
ALERE FLAMMAM
· Taylor & Francis Group ·

Hardback edition previously published by Oxford University Press Inc,
New York, 1994

Reprinted in paperback 1997 and 2002
by Psychology Press Ltd
27 Church Road, Hove, East Sussex BN3 2FA

www.psypress.co.uk

© 1997 by Psychology Press Ltd

Psychology Press is part of the Taylor & Francis Group

British Library Cataloguing in Publication Data
A catalogue record for this book is available from the British Library

ISBN 0–86377–790–2 (pbk)

Printed and bound in the UK by Biddles Ltd, Guildford and King's Lynn

Preface

In 1896 a professor of psychiatry published the fifth edition of a previously unremarkable textbook of psychiatry. The same year he gave a lecture at a meeting of the association of psychiatrists to which he belonged. In both these he annnounced that he had come to the conclusion that a frighteningly large number of patients in insane asylums suffered from a single form of mental disorder. This conclusion derived ultimately from the writings of an earlier psychiatrist whose ideas were so offbeat that he had had to publish them at his own expense. It was also based on a study he had been carrying out, which involved summarizing his patients' clinical details on file cards and collating the information during the academic vacations. In some ways, it even grew out of what seemed to be an increasingly natural way of organizing the chapter headings in successive editions of his textbook. The psychiatrist's name was Kraepelin and the form of insanity he was referring to he called dementia praecox.

History does not record the response of the audience at Kraepelin's lecture, but elsewhere his proposal was met with what he termed lively resistance, and what in some quarters amounted to derision. Within a few years, however, the concept of dementia praecox had become accepted all over the world. To some extent this success was attributable to the work of another psychiatrist who had adopted Kraepelin's ideas early on. This psychiatrist was Bleuler, and he produced an exceptionally well-written book on the subject incorporating some of the ideas of psychoanalysis, which was just becoming fashionable. Bleuler also coined the term schizophrenia as a less clumsy and potentially less misleading alternative to dementia praecox.

Both the concept and the term were to prove enduring. Schizophrenia has survived attempts to narrow it down almost to the point of non-existence; to broaden it until it became a synonym for any serious psychiatric disturbance, and sometimes for none; and to wish it away altogether. Many psychiatrists have argued that the disorder is an aggregate of several disorders which will eventually be shown to be aetiologically different. Conversely, a number of attempts have been made to demonstrate that the disorder has no real point of demarcation from other forms of functional psychosis, especially manic-depressive psychosis. Nevertheless, in present-day psychiatry large numbers of patients are still routinely given the diagnosis of schizophrenia—a striking if grim tribute to the intellectual achievement of Kraepelin and Bleuler.

Although the literature on schizophrenia has become huge, there has only been one further English language textbook on the subject which has been written by a single author from the clinical point of view. This was Fish's *Schizophrenia*, first published in 1962. Although revised and updated by Hamilton twice in an exemplary way, Fish's account of schizophrenia has inevitably become dated. The aim of this book was originally—and still is—to follow in Fish's footsteps and provide a clinically oriented account of schizophrenia suitable for the general psychiatrist, particularly the trainee psychiatrist. The book covers the clinical aspects of schizophrenia in some detail, and tries to cut a path through the large body of research into the disorder. The approach of the book is conditioned by the author's background in experimental psychology, where it is considered essential not just to convey findings, but to describe and criticize the research on which they are based; it is hoped that this is not at the price of sacrificing readability. As it was being written, the book also took on a distinctly historical slant. To some extent this was deliberate, an attempt to communicate the feel of a great deal of high quality work that has been carried out over the years—some of which has been neglected or distorted. Also, and less consciously, it has undoubtedly been a reflection of the renewed sense of respect with which descriptive psychiatry has begun to regard itself in recent years.

June 1993   P.J.M.
Cambridge

Acknowledgements

Without the unwitting help of four of my teachers, it is most unlikely that this book would have been written. These are Thomas Powell, Eve Johnstone, David Cunningham Owens, and Philip Snaith.

I would like to thank a number of people who have given comments on chapters, provided references, or otherwise made constructive suggestions. These include Paul Bailey, Peter Bentham, Paul Calloway, John Cutting, Carol Gregory, Ann Mortimer, Richard Mindham, Michelle Turner, Christopher Ward, and especially Linda Clare. I would also like to thank Philip Ball who drew many of the figures in the book. I am also indebted to Michael Todd-Jones who obtained numerous obscure articles, arranged for the translation of some of these, and turned a blind eye to several very prolonged book loans. I am similarly indebted to Patricia Allderidge who gave up time to discuss the cases of the artists described in Chapter 10. I am grateful for the secretarial assistance (and also encouragement) of Shirley Easton and Jacqueline Waller. I would also like to thank my editors at Oxford University Press for guidance in developing the idea of the book, and for extreme patience in its execution. On many occasions I was fortunate to be able to access the vast historical knowledge of German Berrios, whose contribution to this book is wholly inadequately reflected in the references to his published work.

Finally, a special debt of gratitude is owed to my wife, Kay.

Acknowledgements for tables, figures, and quotations of text

The following are reproduced by permission of the Royal College of Psychiatrists: Material in Fig. 1.3 from Benson, D.F. (1973). Psychiatric aspects of aphasia. *British Journal of Psychiatry*, **123**, 555–66. Fig. 1.5 from Mellor, C.S. (1970). First-rank symptoms of schizophrenia. *British Journal of Psychiatry*, **117**, 15–23. Material in Fig. 4.2 from Kendell, R.E. and Gourlay, J. (1970). The clinical distinction between the affective psychoses and schizophrenia. *British Journal of Psychiatry*, **117**, 261–6. Material in Fig. 4.2 from Brockington, I.F., Kendell, R.E., Wainwright, S., Hillier, V.F., and Walker, J. (1979). The distinction between the affective psychoses and schizophrenia. *British Journal of Psychiatry*, **135**, 243–8. Fig. 7.2 from Owens, D.G.C. and Johnstone, E.C. (1980). The disabilities of chronic schizophrenia – their nature and the factors contributing to their development. *British Journal of Psychiatry*, **136**, 384–93. Table 7.4 from Buhrich, N., Crow, T.J., Johnstone, E.C., and Owens, D.G.C. (1988). Age disorientation in chronic schizophrenia is not associated with pre-morbid

viii   *Acknowledgements*

intellectual impairment or past physical treatments. *British Journal of Psychiatry*, **152**, 466–9. Table 8.1 from Goldberg, S.C., Klerman, G.L., and Cole, J.O. (1965). Changes in schizophrenic psychopathology and ward behaviour as a function of phenothiazine treatment. *British Journal of Psychiatry*, **111**, 120–33. Table 9.2 from Kavanagh, D.J. (1992). Recent developments in expressed emotion and schizophrenia. *British Journal of Psychiatry*, **160**, 601–20. Material in Fig. 9.2 from Vaughn, C.E. and Leff, J.P. (1976). The influence of family and social factors on the course of psychiatric illness. *British Journal of Psychiatry*, **129**, 125–37. Material in Fig. 9.2 from MacMillan, J.F., Gold, A., Crow, T.J., Johnson, A.L., and Johnstone, E.C. (1986). The Northwick Park study of first episodes of schizophrenia IV. Expressed emotion and relapse. *British Journal of Psychiatry*, **148**, 133–43. Fig. 12.1 and Table 12.2 from Davison, K. and Bagley, C.R. (1969). Schizophrenia-like psychoses associated with organic disorders of the central nervous system: a review. *British Journal of Psychiatry, Special Publication*, **4**, 113–83. Table 12.4 from Cutting, J. (1987). The phenomenology of acute organic psychoses: comparison with acute schizophrenia. *British Journal of Psychiatry*, **151**, 324–32.

The following are reproduced by permission of Cambridge University Press: quotations of text on pages 2–4 from Wing, J.K., Cooper, J.E., and Sartorius, N. (1974). *The measurement and classification of psychiatric symptoms*. Fig. 5.2 from Hirsch, S.R. and Leff, J.P. (1971). Parental abnormalities of verbal communication in the transmission of schizophrenia. *Psychological Medicine*, **1**, 118–27. Table 5.5 from Owens, D.G.C., Johnstone, E.C., Crow, T.J., Frith, C.D., Jagoe, J.R., and Kreel, L. (1985). Lateral ventricular size in schizophrenia: relationship to the disease process and its clinical manifestations. *Psychological Medicine*, **15**, 27–41. Table 7.6 from Shallice, T., Burgess, P.W., and Frith, C.D. (1991). Can the neuropsychological case-study approach be applied to schizophrenia. *Psychological Medicine*, **21**, 661–73. Table 12.3 from Ron, M.A. and Logsdail, S.J. (1989). Psychiatric morbidity in multiple sclerosis: a clinical and MRI study. *Psychological Medicine*, **19**, 887–96. Table 13.4 from Tantam, D. (1991). Asperger syndrome in adulthood. In *Autism and Asperger Syndrome* (ed. U. Frith), pp. 147–183.

The following are reproduced by permission of the American Medical Association: quotations of text on pages 14–16 from Andreasen, N.C. (1979). Thought, language and communication disorders: I. Clinical assessment, definition of terms and evaluation of their reliability. *Archives of General Psychiatry*, **36**, 1315–21. Fig. 2.1 from Carpenter, W.T., Bartko, J.J., Carpenter, C.L., and Strauss, J.L. (1976). Another view of schizophrenic subtypes. *Archives of General Psychiatry*, **33**, 508–16. Table 4.2 from Koehler, K., Guth, W., and Grimm, G. (1977). First rank symptoms in Schneider-oriented German centers. *Archives of General Psychiatry*, **34**, 810–13. Table 5.4 from Andreasen, N.C., Swayze, V.M., Flaum, M., Yates, W.R., Arndt, S., and McChesney, C. (1990). Ventricular enlargement in schizophrenia evaluated with computed tomographic scanning. *Archives of General Psychiatry*, **47**, 1008–15. Fig. 7.4 from Saykin, A.J., Gur, R.C., Gur, R.E., Mozley, P.D., Mozley, L.H., Resnick, S.M., *et al.* (1991). Neuropsychological function in schizophrenia: selective impairment in memory and learning. *Archives of General Psychiatry*, **48**, 618–24. Fig. 10.4 and Table 10.4 from Kendler, K.S. (1980). The nosologic validity of paranoia (simple delusional disorder). *Archives of General Psychiatry*, **37**, 699–706. Table 11.1 from Pope, H.G. and Lipinski, J.F. (1978). Diagnosis in schizophrenia and manic-depressive illness: a re-assessment of the specificity of 'schizophrenic' symptoms in the light of current research. *Archives of General Psychiatry*, **35**, 811–28. Table 13.1 and 13.2 from Rumsey, J., Andreasen, N.C., and Rapaport, J. (1986). Thought, language, communication, and affective flattening in autistic adults. *Archives of General Psychiatry*, **43**, 771–7.

The following are reprinted by permission: Fig. 6.2 from Peroutka, S.J., and Synder, S.H. (1980). Relationship of neuroleptic drug effects at brain dopamine, serotonin, alpha-adrenergic, and histamine receptors to clinical potency. *American Journal of Psychiatry*, **137**, 1518–22. © 1980, the American Psychiatric Association. Table 7.5 from Faber, R., Abrams, R., Taylor, M.A., Kasprison, A., Morris, C., and Weisz, R. (1983). Comparison of schizophrenic patients with formal thought disorder and neurologically impaired patients with aphasia. *American Journal of Psychiatry*, **140**, 1348–51, © 1983, the American Psychiatric Association. Fig. 5.3 from *Schizophrenia genesis: the origins of madness*, by Irving I. Gottesman. © 1991 by Irving I. Gottesman. Reprinted with permission of W.H. Freeman and Company. Fig. 5.4 from Smith, G.N. and Iacono, W.G. (1986). Lateral ventricular size in schizophrenia and choice of control group. *Lancet*, **i**, 1450, © the Lancet Ltd. Fig. 6.3 from Johnstone, E.C., Crow, T.J., Frith, C.D., Carney, M.W.P., and Price, J.S. (1978). Mechanism of the antipsychotic effect in the treatment of acute schizophrenia. *Lancet*, **i**, 848–51, © the Lancet Ltd. Fig. 9.1 from Taylor, P. and Fleminger, J.J. (1980). ECT for schizophrenia. *Lancet*, **i**, 1380–2, © the Lancet Ltd. Table 2.1 from WHO (1973). *The international pilot study of schizophrenia*. World Health Organization (WHO offset publication, no. 2.), Geneva, Fig. 4.1 from Laing, R.D. and Esterson, A. (1964). *Sanity, madness and the family* (2nd edn), Tavistock publications, London.

Permission has been granted for the following: Material in Fig. 1.3 from Rochester, S. and Martin, J.R. (1979). *Crazy talk: a study of the discourse of schizophrenic speakers*. © Plenum Publishing Corp., New York. Material in Fig. 1.3 from Neale, J.M. and Oltmanns, T.F. (1980). *Schizophrenia*. © John Wiley & Sons Inc., New York. Material in Fig. 1.3 from Harrow, M. and Quinlan, D.M. (1985). *Disordered thinking and schizophrenic psychopathology*. Gardner Press, New York. © Williams & Wilkins. Fig. 3.1 from Bleuler, M. (1978). *The schizophrenic disorders: long-term patient and family studies* (trans. S.M. Clemens). © Yale University Press, New Haven. Fig. 4.3 and Fig. 11.5 from Spitzer, R.L., Endicott, J., and Robins, E. (1978). *Research diagnostic criteria for a selected group of functional disorders*. Biometric Research, New York State Psychiatric Institute, New York. Table 5.1 from Bebbington, P. and Kuipers, L. (1988). Social influences on schizophrenia. In *Schizophrenia: the Major Issues* (ed. P. Bebbington and P. McGuffin), pp. 201–25. Heinemann/Mental Health Foundation, Oxford. © Butterworth-Heinemann Ltd. Table 5.2 from Slater, E. (1968). A review of earlier evidence on genetic factors in schizophrenia. In *The Transmission of Schizophrenia* (ed. D. Rosenthal and S.S. Kety) pp. 15–26. Pergamon, Oxford. Table 5.7 from Tyrer, P., Casey, P., and Ferguson, B. (1988). Personality disorder and mental illness. In *Personality disorders: diagnosis, management and course* (ed. P. Tyrer), pp. 93–104. Wright, London. © Butterworth-Heinemann Ltd. Fig. 6.1 from Hyttel, J., Larsen, J-J., Christensen, A.V., and Arnt, J. (1985). Receptor-binding profiles of neuroleptics. In *Dyskinesia— research and treatment*, Psychopharmacology Supplementum, No. 2 (ed. D.E. Casey, T.W. Chase, A.V. Christensen, and J. Gerlach), pp. 9–18. © Springer-Verlag GmbH & Co. KG, Berlin. Fig. 6.4 reprinted by permission of Elsevier Science Inc. from Angrist, B.M. and Gershon, S. (1970). The phenomenology of experimentally induced amphetamine psychosis— preliminary observations. *Biological Psychiatry*, **2**, 95–107, © the Society for Biological Psychiatry. Figs 6.5 and 8.2 from Seeman, P. (1987). Dopamine receptors and the dopamine hypothesis of schizophrenia. *Synapse*, **1**, 133–52, © *Synapse*, 1987. Reprinted by permission of John Wiley & Sons, Inc. Fig. 7.1 from Gould, L.N. (1949). Auditory hallucinations and subvocal speech. *Journal of Nervous and Mental Disease*, **109**, 418–27, © Williams and Wilkins. Table 7.3 from Payne, R.W. (1973). In *Handbook of abnormal psychology* (ed. H.J. Eysenck), pp. 420–83. Pitman, London. © Churchill Livingstone. Table 8.2 from Davis, J.M. (1985). Antipsychotic drugs. In *Comprehensive Textbook of Psychiatry*, 4th edn (ed. H.I. Kaplan and B.J. Sadock). Williams and Wilkins, Baltimore. © Harold I. Kaplan, M.D. Table 10.2 from Bridge, T.P. and Wyatt, R.J. (1980). Paraphrenia: paranoid states of late life. *Journal of the American Geriatrics Society*, **28**, 193–205, © Williams & Wilkins. Table

10.3, Table 10.5, and Fig. 11.1 from Hamilton, M. (1984). *Fish's schizophrenia* (3rd edn). Wright, Bristol. © Butterworth-Heinemann Ltd. Table 11.2 from Grossman, L.S., Harrow, M., Fudala, J.H., and Meltzer, H.Y. (1984). The longitudinal course of schizoaffective disorders. *Journal of Nervous and Mental Disease*, **172**, 140-9, © Williams and Wilkins. Fig. 11.3 from Perris, C. (1974). A study of cycloid psychosis. *Acta Psychiatrica Scandinavica*, supplement **253**, 1-76, © Munksgaard International Publishers Ltd. Fig. 11.4 from Brockington, I.F., Perris, C., Meltzer, H. (1982). Cycloid psychoses: diagnostic and heuristic value. *Journal of Nervous and Mental Disease*, **170**, 651-6, © Williams and Wilkins. Fig. 11.6 from Kendell, R.E. (1986). The relationship of schizoaffective illness to schizophrenic and affective disorders. In *Schizoaffective psychoses* (ed. A. Marneros and M.T. Tsuang), pp. 18-30. © Springer-Verlag GmbH & Co. KG, Berlin.

Although every effort has been made to trace and contact copyright holders, in a few instances this has not been possible. If notified the publishers will be pleased to rectify any omissions in future editions. Permission has been sought for the following: Table 3.4, Table 4.1, and material in Fig. 4.2 from WHO (1979). *Schizophrenia: an international follow-up study*. Wiley, Geneva. Table 13.3 from Victor, G. *The riddle of autism*. Lexington Books, Lexington.

Contents

1

The cardinal symptoms of schizophrenia

Schizophrenia confronts the clinician with a range of symptoms which is remarkably diverse and disconcertingly large. The symptoms themselves are very variable from patient to patient, not to mention being frequently bizarre, sometimes extraordinary, and on occasion downright unbelievable. In such circumstances their description and classification might be considered to present something of a daunting task.

To a considerable extent this task was accomplished by Kraepelin (1913a) and Bleuler (1911) in the original accounts of schizophrenia. With an eloquence which has never been equalled, they delineated the full range of symptoms seen in the disorder, brought them to life with examples, and constructed a framework for classifying them which has governed all subsequent thinking. Succeeding decades saw only minor modifications to their scheme, the most important of which was the isolation by Schneider (1958) of a set of 'first rank' symptoms, which he considered to be pathognomonic of schizophrenia. Some further refinement has been achieved in the contemporary era with the development of standardized methods for assessment of psychiatric symptoms. A particularly influential contribution in this area has been made by the Present State Examination of Wing *et al.* (1974), which has provided a rich and phenomenologically rigorous source of definitions of many schizophrenic symptoms.

The symptoms detailed in this chapter consist of those which would be generally regarded as psychotic rather than neurotic, which would be considered unexceptional in established schizophrenia, and which would, if they occurred in isolation, raise the distinct possibility of schizophrenia being the diagnosis. These are divided along conventional lines into categories of *abnormal ideas; abnormal perceptions; formal thought disorder; motor, volitional, and behavioural disorders*; and *emotional disorders*. Some members of each category have come to be regarded as prominent, striking, or especially characteristic of schizophrenia and so are singled out as *cardinal symptoms*. Other more minor or non-specific phenomena are grouped together as *miscellaneous symptoms*. Finally, there are *the first rank symptoms of Schneider*, which are given a category of their own.

Abnormal ideas

The cardinal abnormal idea of schizophrenia is of course delusion. This is defined as a belief which is judged to be erroneous; which is held with fixed, intense conviction; which is incorrigible to argument; and which is out of keeping with the individual's social, educational, and cultural background. Delusions are also usually fantastic, patently absurd, or at least inherently unlikely (Feighner *et al.* 1972); typically they are also justified by the patient in a peculiarly illogical way (Sims 1988). Abnormal ideas which are not delusions are undoubtedly also seen in schizophrenia, but are very much a mixed bag of individually uncommon phenomena.

Delusions

Classically, delusions have been considered the hallmark of insanity. Kraepelin (1913*a*) drew attention to the extraordinary frequency with which delusions of many types developed in schizophrenia, transitorily or permanently. Bleuler (1911) observed that schizophrenic delusions characteristically lacked systematization and logical integration. In almost all cases ideas which were obviously inconsistent with one another were simultaneously entertained; often there was a whole series of senseless and completely contradictory beliefs; occasionally this amounted to what could only be described as a 'delusional chaos'. Both authors considered persecutory and grandiose delusions to be particularly common but sexual, hypochondriacal, referential, and guilty delusions could also be seen.

Contemporarily, delusions are accepted as forming a commonplace, though variable part of the clinical picture of schizophrenia. They may be florid, multiple, and shifting; or alternatively sparse, only elicited on questioning, but persisting in the background for years. The rich variety in the content of schizophrenic delusions continues to be noted (Fish 1962/ Hamilton 1984); nevertheless it is striking how regularly particular themes recur. The most detailed classification of delusions according to content is that in the Present State Examination of Wing *et al.* (1974). This is reproduced in a slightly condensed form and with a few minor modifications below.

Delusional mood: Here the subject feels that his familiar surroundings have changed in a puzzling way which he may be unable to describe, but which seems to be especially significant for him. Everything feels odd, strange, and uncanny, something suspicious is afoot, events are charged with new meaning. This may be experienced as ominous or threatening, or there may simply be puzzlement. The state typically precedes the development of full delusions: the patient may fluctuate between acceptance and rejection of various delusional explanations, or the experience may suddenly crystallize into a clear, fully formed delusional idea.

Delusions of reference, misinterpretation, and misidentification: The central experience of this class of delusion is that all kinds of neutral events acquire special significance and refer to the patient personally, but in a more definite way than in delusional mood. What is said has a double meaning, someone makes a gesture which is construed as a deliberate message, the whole neighbourhood may be gossiping about the patient, far beyond the bounds of possibility. He may see references to himself on the television, radio, and in newspapers; or feel he is being followed; that his movements are observed; and that what he says is tape recorded. The same phenomenon can extend beyond gestures and words to many other aspects of the environment, so that situations appear to be created and people seem to be acting in ways which have a special meaning. Circumstances appear to the patient to be arranged to test him out, objects are placed in particular positions to convey a meaning to him, whole armies of people are deployed to discover what he is doing or to convey some information to him. The patient sees people he knew from the distant past planted in his way to remind him of something; there are people about in disguise; patients on the ward are not what they seem to be.

Delusions of persecution: Here the patient believes that someone, some organization, some force or power is trying to harm him in some way, to damage his reputation, to cause him bodily injury, to drive him mad, etc. The symptom may take many forms from the simple belief that people are hunting him down, to complex and bizarre plots incorporating all kinds of science fiction. *Delusions of assistance* are a variant of the same phenomenon in which the patient believes the same forces, powers, and organizations are endeavouring to help him in surreptitious ways—to direct his life, to enable him to become a better person and so on.

Grandiose delusions: These can be separated into *delusions of grandiose ability*, *delusions of grandiose identity*, and *religious delusions*. In *delusions of grandiose ability* the subject thinks he has unusual talents, he is much cleverer than others, he has invented things, composed music, or solved mathematical problems beyond most people's comprehension. Because of these talents he may feel he has a special mission or that he is particularly suited to helping people. The patient with *delusions of grandiose identity* believes he is famous, rich, titled; or is related to royalty or to other prominent people. Although not all *religious delusions* are grandiose, grandiose delusions commonly have a religious colouring: patients may believe they have a divine purpose, they are saints, angels, even God.

Hypochondriacal delusions: At its purest, this term is applied to an individual's belief that his body is unhealthy, rotten, or diseased; the bizarre complaints of bodily change and malfunction in schizophrenia, however, frequently go far beyond that which can be attributed to imaginary disease. Schizophrenic patients may describe that their tongue is made of iron, that their lungs are dried up, their body is full of wax, their flesh is coming away from their bones (Kraepelin 1913*a*). One patient considered that his semen travelled up his vertebral column to his head, where it was laid out in sheets (Sims 1988).

Sexual, fantastic, and related delusions: Sexual delusions are by no means uncommon in schizophrenia. Sometimes they are intimately bound up with hallucinatory sensations, for example in the genitals; in other cases, however, there are beliefs — of pregnancy, in a fantasy lover, that one's sex is changing — which cannot be attributed to abnormal perceptions. In *fantastic delusions*, the notable bizarre quality of schizophrenic delusions comes to violate common sense at its most elementary. Patients describe giving birth to thousands of children, walking all over the moon, having hundreds of people inside their body, and so on. One form of *delusional memory* consists of clearly recalled experiences of past events which equally clearly did not take place. These commonly have a fantastic quality, for instance a patient's recollection that he came to earth on a silver star or that members of the Royal Family were present at his birth. In other instances, genuine memories become distorted by delusional significance in much the same way as do current events in referential delusions; for example, a patient realized he was of royal descent when he remembered that the fork he had used as a child had a crown on it (Fish 1962/Hamilton 1984). *Delusional confabulation* is a rare phenomenon in which delusions — often fantastic delusions and delusional memories — appear to be made up on the spot and shift, change, and become more elaborate as the patient is questioned about them. An example is shown in Fig. 1.1.

Miscellaneous abnormal ideas

Partial delusions: It is a common clinical observation that schizophrenic patients express ideas which are not held with complete conviction but which are so bizarre that to entertain them at all has to be regarded as abnormal. Although they fail to meet the criterion of fixity, these ideas closely resemble delusions, for example by virtue of having typical referential, persecutory, or grandiose content. Jaspers (1959), the authority on delusions, criticized the standard definition on a number of counts, one of which was degree of conviction. It was, however, Wing *et al.* (1974) who took the step of extending the concept of delusion to include what they called partially held delusions. The presence of these seemed to have much the same diagnostic value as full delusions.

Delusional confabulation

Extract from an interview with a 32-year-old woman with schizophrenia who held a number of fixed delusions, including one that she had a twin sister.

Interviewer: Could you tell me about your twin?

Patient: Her name is Elizabeth Pamela Margaret Jones.

Interviewer: And what's your name?

Patient: My name is Elizabeth Pamela Robertson.

Interviewer: Why have you both got the same name?

Patient: We haven't.

Interviewer: You're both called Elizabeth.

Patient: Yes, I don't know why we're both called Elizabeth.

Interviewer: And where is she now?

Patient: I haven't got a clue, I don't know. She's done a baby murder, she killed a baby and then she disappeared and blamed it on me and Mum. Me and Mum were put in prison and in this psychiatric home—28 years, we've been here.

Interviewer: Have you?

Patient: She did the murder, she murdered a little girl—called Emma Richards—and she blamed it on me and Mum. She cut her throat to cover up her own evidence. She is bad. She is two and a half years old in her mind, and when she saw 'The Merchant Of Venice' it turned her mind. The police are after her, she is named as a murderess. She uses a plastic mac and she's got long red hair—henna'd hair. I'm telling the truth, I don't see why I should lie.

Interviewer: Let's move off this topic, because it's obviously upsetting.

Patient: It's not upsetting. It's just that me and Mum were going on holiday to Felixstowe. The police came and took Mum away in a Black Maria (police van). They came for me and took me to—hospital later on that night. My sister has gone somewhere she can hide, someone is hiding her.

Fig. 1.1

Obsessions: Repetitive, intrusive ideas which are recognized by the patient as senseless are an established, but uncommon finding in schizophrenia. According to Fish (Fish 1962/Hamilton 1984) around 3 per cent of schizophrenic patients experience obsessional symptoms at some point: typically they appear at the beginning of the illness and tend to continue unchanged in content and severity after the diagnosis becomes established. Sometimes obsessions appearing at the onset of schizophrenia transform into delusions (Bleuler 1911). Occasionally, schizophrenic delusions (and also hallucinations) assume a repetitive, intrusive quality, but these lack the other phenomenological attributes of obsessions (Lewis 1936).

Over-valued ideas: This term refers to isolated, preoccupying abnormal beliefs which, unlike obsessions, are not resisted or considered senseless by the patient, and which at the same time seem to lack the bizarre, qualitatively abnormal conviction of delusions (McKenna 1984). The content of the idea may revolve around an alleged injustice, marital infidelity, hypochondriasis, or a number of other themes. The aetiological settings in which over-valued ideas develop are diverse, but they have been regularly described in schizophrenia. Usually, but not always, they appear as the earliest sign of illness; as the diagnosis becomes obvious, the idea may transform into a delusion, or become lost among other psychotic symptoms.

Abnormal perceptions

The cardinal phenomenon of this class of abnormality is hallucination, although there are a variety of other perceptual experiences which make a significant contribution to the clinical picture of schizophrenia. As originally defined by Esquirol (1838), a hallucination is a perception without an object. Other authors have added that hallucinations occur simultaneously with and alongside real perceptions, that they have the force and impact of real perceptions, and that they are outside voluntary control (Jaspers 1959; Slade 1976a; Sims 1988). Hallucinations may occur in any sensory modality; however, those of hearing are especially prominent in schizophrenia and are treated separately from the rest.

Auditory hallucinations

The phenomenon of verbal auditory hallucinosis — hearing voices — was singled out as the characteristic hallucinatory experience of schizophrenia by Kraepelin (1913a) and Bleuler (1911), both of whom also emphasized the almost limitless variety of this symptom. Summing up years of clinical observation, Mayer-Gross *et al.* (1969) pointed out that auditory hallucinations could be the first sign of schizophrenia, or be absent until chronicity is established. They might appear only on a single occasion or persist for years, overwhelming, directing, and tormenting the patient every waking moment. In character they could vary from an indistinct muttering to elaborate conversations involving several parties. Their source could be unlocatable, they could be felt to come from all sides, to emanate from a particular point in space, or to originate within the head or body. Commonly derogatory, schizophrenic voices could also be neutral, observing, reassuring, encouraging, or praising. One of the very few verbatim examples of the content of auditory hallucinations is illustrated in Fig. 1.2.

Currently, auditory hallucinations maintain their primacy among schizophrenic abnormal perceptions. They are usually considered to be the commonest symptom of schizophrenia with few patients failing to exhibit them at some stage (Fish 1962/Hamilton 1984). Despite their great variability, certain forms of auditory hallucination occur with regularity and are worth distinguishing for phenomenological and diagnostic purposes. The following classification is combined from the accounts of Fish (Fish 1962/Hamilton 1984), Wing *et al.* (1974), and Sims (1988).

Elementary (non-verbal) hallucinations: Relatively uncommonly, schizophrenic patients report hearing noises like tapping, scuffling, banging, car engines, or occasionally music. Such experiences are frequently given a delusional interpretation, for instance as a machine being turned on, or as burglars moving around outside the house. Also included in this category by Wing *et al.* (1974) is indistinct whispering, muttering, or mumbling where no words can be made out.

Third person and commenting hallucinations: A hallucinating schizophrenic patient may describe hearing a voice or voices speaking about him and accordingly referring to him in the third person. Typically, two or more voices discuss the patient with one another. In the most extreme expression of this phenomenon, one or more voices keep up a continuous commentary on the patient's every thought and action. Such experiences form one class of *first rank symptom.*

Imperative hallucinations: These are voices which quite simply command the patient to carry out actions. They are said to be not very common (Fish 1962/Hamilton 1984) and usually they are easily ignored. Occasionally, however, the patient obeys with grave or horrific consequences.

Functional hallucinations: In this rare phenomenon the patient hears voices superimposed on and developing out of real environmental noises, such as leaves rustling, water running from a tap, cars revving up, etc.

What schizophrenic voices say
(from Kraepelin 1913a)

Notes made by a patient of what he heard. Statements in parentheses are questions inwardly directed by the patient to his voices.

(Why are you speaking in me?)
'You must eat blood. A. must laugh at you. Because we are poor blockheads. Asylum. We'll bring you later to an asylum. Oh my dear genius! Because we are hypochondriacs. I am your poor marmot. We are the mistresses of the German whipping-club. We inhale you.'

(Why do you torment me?)
'Have you a fate! We think the best of you. Taraxacum! Taraxacum! We thrash Dr S.'s bones bloody for he has become surety for you. Because we are frightfully fond of you. What am I to do? We weep laughing tears. We are differently developed. Oh you my darling little Jesus. Because we ourselves are tormented. Because we morally act perversely. We have christian catholic morality. Every human being must laugh at you. You are mentally ill. Yes, it is so. Because we have to fear your brain grease. Oh wild sheikh Almagro! Whom one loves, one torments. We have no implements of handicraft. You are in many things an absolute child, an absolute fool. We torment you as moral rapscallions.'

(What is your real object?)
'We wish to kill you. You have offended divine providence. Our object is morally irrelevant. M. must laugh at you. Our object is your cleansing. But Absalom! We love and hate you. Our object is terrible establishment of women's regiment. We are silly.'

(Are you human beings or spirits?)
'We are human beings, old topswine. Oh that needs an insane patience! I will show you my last aims. We weep about you. You have been very prudent. We are climbing up Ararat. Now then, little spirits! Little folk, brownies! You are fundamentally insanely deep!'

(Are you near?)
'No, far away. What shall we do contrary to your interests? No, in the middle of your head.'

Fig. 1.2

Extracampine hallucinations: These hallucinations (which may occur in other modalities besides the auditory) are identified by the patient as originating from beyond the limits of normal perception. For example, a patient may describe hearing the screams of children being tortured in another city or hear himself being discussed by his relatives who are several miles away.

Other hallucinations

Hallucinations have been described in all other sensory modalities in schizophrenia. Their frequency is uncertain but they are generally regarded as considerably less common than auditory hallucinations.

Visual hallucinations: Phenomena ranging from spots, rays and plays of colour, through human figures, to panoramic or apocalyptic scenes, were considered by Kraepelin (1913*a*) to be common enough, if rather inconspicuous in schizophrenia. Bleuler (1911, 1926) described visual hallucinations as being frequent and lively in the acute stages, but otherwise rare. Subsequently, visual hallucinations came to be regarded as rare by Fish (Fish 1962/Hamilton 1984), although he accepted that complex visions and scenic hallucinations could be fairly convincingly described in a few cases.

Somatic hallucinations: These were given somewhat more prominence by Kraepelin and Bleuler. They described sensations of being touched, tickled, and pricked (*haptic hallucinations*); of heat and cold (*thermic hallucinations*); wetness (*hygric hallucinations*); and movement and joint position (*kinaesthetic hallucinations*). Patients also complained of pain and sexual sensations, as well as more incomprehensible electric, vibratory, rolling, moving, and sliding experiences inside the body. Somatic hallucinations continue to be regarded as quite common in schizophrenia (Fish 1962/ Hamilton 1984; Sims 1988). It has been observed (Berrios 1982) that such experiences are not usually reported simply, but are invariably combined with a degree of delusional elaboration—the relative contributions of hallucination and delusion to the bizarre bodily complaints of schizophrenic patients are often impossible to disentangle.

Olfactory and gustatory hallucinations: Sometimes simple, or sometimes bound up with delusional interpretations, these were considered to be encountered with approximately the same frequency as somatic hallucinations by Kraepelin and Bleuler. Their occurrence, with or without delusional elaboration, continues to be documented in schizophrenia, although how commonly is uncertain.

Miscellaneous abnormal perceptions

Perceptual distortions: McGhie and Chapman (1961) gave the first detailed account of a variety of perceptual changes which a sizeable minority of schizophrenic patients reported experiencing in the early stages of illness. These took the form of transient alterations in the size, distance, and shape of objects, and heightening or dulling of colour, brightness, or contrast; analogous changes could also be found in the auditory sphere. Subsequent studies have supported these findings (for example Cutting and Dunne 1989), although the impression is that they are minor aspects of the clinical picture which have to be elicited by questioning rather than being described spontaneously. Similar phenomena are also sometimes encountered in schizophrenic patients with established illnesses.

Pseudohallucinations: This term refers to perceptual experiences which are similar to hallucinations in the sense of being vivid, compelling, and involuntary, but which are localized by the individual to inner subjective space (that is heard 'inside the head', seen 'with the mind's eye'). The term has unfortunately acquired different shades of meaning (Hare 1973), and an enduring controversy surrounds the issue of whether pseudohallucinations are perceived as 'real' by the patient (see Sims 1988). Schizophrenic verbal auditory hallucinations commonly take the form of pseudohallucinations; true and pseudo-auditory hallucinations, however, may also co-exist in the same patient (Wing *et al.* 1974). According to Fish (Fish 1962/ Hamilton 1984) many schizophrenic visual experiences turn out to be pseudohallucinatory in nature when the patient is questioned closely.

Altered self-perception: The 'as if' phenomena of depersonalization and derealization have been considered to be common in schizophrenia, especially in the early stages (Sedman 1970; Sims 1988). In established, usually florid schizophrenia these symptoms may acquire a delusional interpretation—becoming what Wing *et al.* (1974) refer to as *delusions of depersonalization*. The patient states with full conviction that he has no brain, no thoughts, there is a hollow in his skull, his body is a shadow, or that he cannot see himself in the mirror. Cotard's syndrome of nihilistic and other delusions is sometimes considered to be the most flamboyantly psychotic expression of depersonalization; this is occasionally seen in schizophrenia as well as in its more familiar setting of depressive psychosis (Enoch and Trethowan 1979).

Formal thought disorder

The 'formal' of formal thought disorder refers to disturbances in the *form* of thinking—that is, its structure, organization, and coherence—which manifest themselves as a loss of intelligibility of speech; the listener becomes unable to follow what is being said. The term undoubtedly encompasses a number of quite disparate abnormalities which may occur in more or less pure form or in erratic combinations (Andreasen 1979*a*). Perhaps most commonly it is the moment-to-moment, logical sequencing of ideas which is at fault. At other times, the mechanisms of language production themselves appear to be disturbed, so that the meaning of individual words and phrases is obscured. At still other times, the fault seems to be at the level of discourse: individual words, sentences, and sequences of thought make sense, but there is no discernible thread to longer verbal productions.

Of the many descriptive abnormalities that have been proposed to underlie formal thought disorder in schizophrenia, a relatively small number have come to be regarded as accounting for a disproportionate amount of the phenomenon. These are designated here as the cardinal elements of formal thought disorder. Some of the remainder are less specific for schizophrenia, or specific but uncommon; these are grouped together as miscellaneous aspects of formal thought disorder.

Cardinal elements of formal thought disorder

Attempts to define what it was that made schizophrenic speech sometimes difficult to follow largely began, once again, with Kraepelin and Bleuler. Kraepelin (1913*a*) considered that there was a central process of *derailment*, a continual tendency to be deflected from the point, to glide off into more or less closely related areas. He hypothesized that, operating at different levels, derailment could give rise to a range of abnormalities: a lack of connectedness in the train of ideas; a disturbance in the construction of individual sentences; even a peculiarity of word selection to the point of invention of entirely new words or *neologisms*. Bleuler (1911) proposed a somewhat different unifying explanation. In his view the fundamental disturbances were *associative loosening* and *loss of the central determining idea*: while thought continued to be subordinated to some sort of general idea, it was no longer governed by any precise purpose or goal.

Other classical authors built on Kraepelin's and Bleuler's explanatory constructs and made contributions of their own. C. Schneider (1930) enlarged on Kraepelin's idea of *derailment* in the train of thought, proposing additional derangements like *fusion*, where there was a blending together of completely unrelated ideas, and *omission*, in which there was a dropping out of part of the train of thought crucial for the whole to be understood. Schilder (1920) correspondingly elaborated on Bleuler's concept of *loss of central determining idea*, speculating that in the absence of conscious goal-directedness, Freudian unconscious 'primary process' mechanisms might come to determine the flow of ideas. The most significant contribution during this era, however, was that of Kleist (1914, 1960), who argued that dysphasia-like abnormalities were discernible in thought-disordered schizophrenic speech, particularly when it was severe. In addition to *neologisms*, which were also a feature of dysphasias, he claimed he could find evidence of other dysphasic phenomena, including *paraphasias* (erroneous words phonetically or semantically related to the target word), *agrammatism* (a simplification and coarsening of sentence structure), and *paragrammatism* (fluent speech which features multiple grammatical misuses).

Bridging the classical and contemporary eras were two influential studies which sharpened existing concepts and added important new ones. In an analysis of schizophrenic formal thought disorder which seems to have been carried out largely in ignorance of previous work, Cameron (1938, 1944) concluded that three important abnormalities stood out. In *asyndetic thinking*, a tendency to use loose clusters of related ideas rather than well-knit sequences of concepts, he essentially redescribed *loss of central determining idea*. *Metonymic distortion* (word approximation), in which imprecise verbal constructions are substituted for commonplace words or phrases was, however, the first succinct identification of a phenomenon which had previously only been referred to obliquely. The eloquent term *interpenetration of themes* described an inability to keep the topic of speech and inner preoccupations apart. Somewhat later, Wing and colleagues (Wing and Brown 1970; Wing *et al.* 1974) evolved the concept of *poverty of content of speech* out of rather elusive earlier traditions of *alogia* and *woolliness of thought*. This described speech which was free and normal in quantity, but which was so vague and contained so little information as to produce an impression of complete emptiness.

In the last two decades these strands have been woven together into a reasonably coherent account of formal thought disorder. Partly, this has been a result of the drive to make the diagnosis of schizophrenia and other psychiatric disorders more objective (see Chapter 4). More importantly, it is due to the work of Andreasen (1979*a*), who pooled classical descriptions of what she termed thought, language, and communication disorders, extracted their common themes, and developed a reliable system for assessing them.

Formal thought disorder is a relatively uncommon finding in acute schizophrenia, although in subtle or subclinical forms it has been claimed to be present in a substantial majority of cases (Harrow and Quinlan 1985). Most authorities agree that it becomes more frequent among chronic schizophrenic patients. The following classification of schizophrenic formal thought disorder is a composite of those of Wing *et al.* (1974), and Andreasen (1979*a*); except where otherwise stated, the definitions are those of Andreasen. The scheme is also broadly in line with those in DSM III and DSM IIIR. The terms in brackets refer to generally older descriptions which are synonymous or at least partially overlapping. Some examples are given in Fig. 1.3.

Examples of formal thought disorder

Derailment

Interviewer: (Tells the donkey and the salt story and asks patient to tell it in his own words.)

Patient: A donkey was carrying salt and he went through a river, and he decided to go for a swim. And his salt started dissolving off him into the water, and it did, it left him hanging there, so he crawled out on the other side and became a mastodon. . . . It gets unfrozen, it's up in the Arctic right now; it's a block of ice, the block of ice gets planted. . . . It's forced into a square, right? Ever studied that sort of formation, block of ice in the ground? Well it fights the perma frost; it pushes it away and lets things go up around it. You can see they're like, they're almost like a pattern with a flower; they start from the middle and it's like a submerged ice cube that's frozen into the soil afterwards.

(Rochester and Martin 1979)

Incoherence

Interviewer: (Asks patient to interpret the proverb 'don't change horses in mid-stream'.)

Patient: That's wish-bell double vision. Like walking across a person's eye and reflecting personality. It works on you like dying and going into the spiritual world but landing in the vella world.

(Harrow and Quinlan 1985)

Interviewer: Have you been nervous or tense lately?

Patient: No, I got a head of lettuce.

Interviewer: You got a head of lettuce? I don't understand. Tell me about lettuce.

Patient: Well, lettuce is a transformation of a dead cougar that suffered a relapse on the lion's toe. And he swallowed the lion and something happened. The . . . see, the . . . Gloria and Tommy, they're two heads and they're not whales. But they escaped with herds of vomit, and things like that.

(Neale and Oltmanns 1980)

Poverty of content of speech

Interviewer: Are you feeling unwell?

Patient: It's hard to live on your own in this society. I get fears of violence and death — feeling that I'm all negative inside — you know — I always have a clash with authority. They have too much power to incarcerate me and you. The alternative is death; I would have done myself in. There's no love in an empty flat . . .

(author's own example)

Fig. 1.3 (Material from Neale and Oltmanns reproduced by permission of John Wiley & Sons, Inc.)

Interviewer: Do you ever get the feeling that everybody knows your thoughts?

Patient: Yes, I was thinking that just before I came in here, actually I have the feeling, which I feel is just a sort of creation of myself and I've created, I've formed, a person which is the character, the part of me which is ordinary, the other self which I've shaped as an onlooker, as Fred, or John, or Allan and so on, people I know, and I converse with them a lot of the time.'

(Benson 1973)

Stilted speech
Interviewer: (Asks patient to interpret the proverb 'discretion is the better part of valour'.)

Patient: Pliant rectitude is a trait more appropriate for successful living than hot-headedness, which is either stubborn or crusady.

(Harrow and Quinlan 1985)

Neologisms, word approximations, and idiosyncratic use of words
Neologisms: *Vella* world, stubborn or *crusady*, God's *tarn-harn*

(Harrow and Quinlan 1985; Wing *et al*. 1974)

Technical neologisms: *Snortie*—to talk through walls; *Trominoes*—tiny people who live in one's body; *Split-kippered*—to be simultaneously alive in Lancashire and dead in Yorkshire.

(Bleuler 1911; author's own examples)

Word approximations: *Daily reflector*—mirror, *suction device*—cigarette, *handshoe*—glove. 'My tongue is *exceeding* my mouth'—patient describing acute dystonic reaction.

(Fish 1962/Hamilton 1984; author's own examples)

Idiosyncratic use of words: 'Well, there is a *frequenting of clairvoyance*.', 'It's a *conservative stream* if it never rises above its peak.'

(Wing *et al*. 1974; Harrow and Quinlan 1985)

Fig. 1.3   *contd.*

Derailment (loosening of associations, asyndetic thinking, knight's move thinking): This describes a pattern of spontaneous speech in which the ideas slip off the track onto another one which is clearly but obliquely related, or onto one which is completely unrelated. Things may be said in juxtaposition which lack a meaningful relationship, or the patient may shift idosyncratically from one frame of reference to another. In what is perhaps the commonest manifestation of this disorder, there is a slow, steady slippage, with no single derailment being particularly severe, so that the speaker gets farther and farther from the point. The related term *tangentiality* has been partially redefined by Andreasen (1979*a*) to refer to replies to questions which are oblique, off the point, or irrelevant from the outset.

Loss of goal (lack of central determining idea, loosening of associations, asyndetic thinking): This refers to a failure to follow a train of thought through to its conclusion, usually manifested in speech that begins with a particular subject, wanders away from this, and never returns to it. The abnormality often occurs in association with *derailment*, but sometimes no clear-cut instances of this can be demonstrated.

Incoherence (drivelling, word salad, paragrammatism, 'schizophasia'): This describes a severe disorder where the pattern of speech is essentially incomprehensible at times. Several different mechanisms may contribute, all of which may occur simultaneously. Sometimes the disturbance appears to be at a semantic level so that words are substituted in a phrase or sentence in a way which distorts or destroys the meaning; the word choice may seem to be totally random or may appear to have some oblique connection with the context. Sometimes portions of coherent sentences may be observed in the midst of a sentence that is incoherent as a whole. Sometimes the rules of grammar and syntax are ignored, and a series of words or phrases seem to be joined together arbitrarily and at random.

Neologisms and related abnormalities: Neologisms are completely new words or phrases whose derivation usually cannot be understood. Occasionally patients coin words or phrases to describe otherwise indescribable experiences; this phenomenon is referred to as *technical neologism* (Fish 1962/Hamilton 1984). In *idiosyncratic use of words* (Wing *et al.* 1974), phrases are used which are composed of ordinary words, but which are incomprehensible as a whole. *Word approximations* are also idiosyncratic uses of words but here the meaning is evident even though the usage seems peculiar, stilted, or bizarre. All these abnormalities tend to make a prominent contribution to *incoherence.*

Poverty of content of speech (woolliness of thought, alogia, empty speech): Here, although replies are long enough for speech to be adequate in amount, they convey little information. Answers to questions tend to be vague, often over-abstract or over-concrete, repetitive, and stereotyped. The interviewer may recognize the abnormality only by observing that the patient has spoken at some length but has not given sufficient information to answer the question. Sometimes the speech can be best characterized as 'empty philosophizing'.

Miscellaneous aspects of formal thought disorder

Circumstantiality: This is defined as a pattern of speech which is very indirect and delayed in reaching its goal idea (Andreasen 1979*a*). In replying to a question, the speaker brings in a welter of unnecessary detail and explores all sorts of unnecessary avenues before returning to the point. The disorder differs from *derailment* and *loss of goal* in that the unnecessary details are clearly related to the main theme, and that the goal idea is eventually reached. Circumstantiality is perhaps the best example of an abnormality in thought form which is found in schizophrenia, but which is by no means specific to it. It has been described in some patients with epilepsy, in chronic organic states, and in mental subnormality. It is also by no means rare among normal individuals (Sims 1988).

Vorbeireden: This rare phenomenon (literally talking past the point) is also known as *approximate answers* or *paralogia*. It has also been referred to as *Ganserism* as it is the pre-eminent feature of the Ganser syndrome (Whitlock 1967). The patient gives replies to questions which are incorrect, but in a way which betrays that the correct answer is known. Sometimes the answers are truly approximate, for instance, a cow is said to have three legs, a pack of cards five suits, etc.; more commonly, however, they are random or absurd. When asked the difference between a fence and a wall, a patient replied 'well, a wall's made out of wood, isn't it'; some of his further verbal productions are illustrated in Fig. 1.4.

Stilted speech: Occasionally in patients with schizophrenia, speech appears excessively formal, ornate, or pompous. The stilted quality may be a consequence of excessive use of polysyllabic rather than monosyllabic words, over-polite phraseology, or stiff and over-formal syntax (Andreasen 1979*a*). This abnormality overlaps to a considerable extent with the catatonic phenomenon of *speech mannerism*.

Concrete thinking: This term was introduced by Goldstein (1944) to describe an inability to generalize, grasp the essential rather than literal meaning of a statement, and keep in mind different aspects of the situation — in short, to think abstractly. Originally intending it to explain some aspects of schizophrenic thought disorder, Goldstein recognized that concrete thinking occurred in organic brain syndromes as well — his application of the concept to schizophrenic thinking was in fact somewhat convoluted (Fish 1962/Hamilton 1984). Currently, concrete thinking is considered a sign of dementia and some other chronic organic states and is not thought to be indicative of schizophrenia, except perhaps in chronic, severe illness.

DEPARTMENT OF CLINICAL PSYCHOLOGY
REPORT

Date	Name: BARRY XXXXXXXXX	Age: 24 YEARS
	Hospital Number: xxxxx	Referred by xxxxx

GENERAL COMMENTS

Barry was first seen cn Monday 26th November when he was accompanied by his parents. He slumped into his chair and maintained an inane smile expressing absence of concern for the proceedings. After brief preliminaries the parents responded to my request that they leave and after a further brief period during which I attempted to achieve satisfactory rapport, but with only partial success, the WAIS proceedure was commenced. Barry's reactions to this were reminiscent of the classical dementia praecox - bizarre illogical answers, silences, and inappropriate laughter.

Examples

Information - 8.   Weeks in year? "Twenty four" (laughter).

Information - 1   Average Height of women? "Three foot six".

How tall is your mcther? "Over five foot"

Is your mcther tall, short or average? "About average".
Then what is the average height of English women?

"three foot six".

(c) Capital of "Italy"? "Spain".
Comprehension - 3. Envelope - "Lick and stick it on" Repeated. "Take it home. What would you do with it? "Keep it".

(d) Similarities -

1. Orange-Banana "Both red". Repeated. "Both yellow".
2. Coat-dress "Green". Repeated - "Clothes".

Numbers 3 and 4 were correct.
5. North-West "It's like a compass isn't it?
6. Eye-Ear. "Parts of human body".
7. Air-water. It's a balloon.
8. Table-Chair. "Both stools aren't they".

At this point testing was temporarily discontinued.

Fig. 1.4 Vorbeireden in a schizophrenic patient.

Motor, volitional, and behavioural disorders

Peculiarities of movement, bizarre behaviour, and alterations in the overall level of activity are part and parcel of the clinical picture of schizophrenia. The cardinal symptoms of this class are those which have, somewhat arbitrarily, acquired the designation of catatonic. In addition, there are a variety of other abnormalities which are less striking, but which are on the whole considerably more common.

The term catatonic has not been defined, except in a roundabout way: Jaspers (1959) stated that when purely neurological motor disorders and those understandable as an expression of psychic events were left aside, a large number of surprising phenomena still remained. Some of these phenomena are simple, some are complex, and some are distinctly esoteric. Their underlying nature is also variable. Sometimes the abnormality appears to be primarily motor; at other times it appears to lie in the volition behind the act rather than in the act itself; perhaps most characteristically the relative contributions made by movement and volition are impossible to disentangle.

Catatonic phenomena

Kahlbaum (1874) gave the first account of catatonia, describing many of the individual symptoms which were later subsumed under the term. Incorporating catatonia into schizophrenia, Kraepelin (1913*a*) detailed an even wider range of abnormalities. It was, however, Bleuler (1911) who provided the first systematic description and classification of 'peculiar forms of motility, stupor, mutism, stereotypy, mannerism, negativism, command-automaticity, spontaneous automatism and impulsivity'. As well as presenting in frequent combination in catatonic schizophrenia, Bleuler observed that more than half of institutionalized patients developed isolated examples of such symptoms, transitorily or permanently. Classical descriptions were supplemented by Kleist (1943, 1960) whose particular contribution was to enlarge the category of simple motor abnormalities in schizophrenia.

Of late, catatonia has come to be considered an uncommon feature of schizophrenia. As a bald statement, this is misleading and a more accurate view would be that while acute presentations dominated by catatonic phenomena appear to have declined in frequency, there is good evidence that individual catatonic phenomena are still prevalent among chronic patients (see Rogers 1985; Lund *et al.* 1991). Until recently, the description of catatonic symptoms consisted of Fish's classificatory scheme (Fish 1962/Hamilton 1984), which essentially combined the accounts of Bleuler and Kleist. In the last few years, however, there has been a significant degree of re-appraisal at the hands of neurologists and neuropsychiatrists, including notably Marsden *et al.* (1975), Lees (1985), Rogers (1985, 1992), and Lohr and Wisniewski (1987). The following account therefore brings together that of Fish with these more recent authors; for the sake of convenience, the disorders are separated into *simple disorders of movement, more complex disorders of volition*, and *very complex disorders of overall behaviour*, although, in reality, these categories overlap with one another.

Simple disorders of movement: The commonest representatives of this class of abnormality are *stereotypies, mannerisms*, and *posturing. Stereotypies* are defined as more or less purposeless motor acts which are carried out repetitively and with a high degree of uniformity. They include simple movements like rocking, rubbing hands, and tapping objects, as well as more complicated, 'gymnastic' or 'contortionist' phenomena. In *mannerisms*, everyday goal-directed acts such as washing, dressing, and eating come to be executed in idiosyncratic ways; for example, while eating a patient may hold the spoon by the wrong end, put his hand round the back of his head to bring the food to his mouth, or drop the food back on to the plate several times between each mouthful. *Manneristic gaits*, have mincing, over-precise, or alternatively extravagant qualities and sometimes incorporate stooping, twisting, grotesque limb movements, walking on the toes, interpolated actions, etc.. *Posturing* is the modern term for stereotypies and mannerisms of posture: patients sit hunched and constrained, often in a way which seems to express a turning away from the world; in some cases bizarre, statuesque, 'pharaonic' poses are adopted (Sims 1988).

In practice, it is usually difficult to separate *stereotypies, mannerisms*, and *posturing* from one another: patients show motor behaviour which is abnormal by virtue of varying degrees of repetitiveness, purposelessness, and stiltedness of execution. Exactly analogous motor abnormalities may affect facial expression and are collectively referred to as *grimacing*.

Other catatonic abnormalities at this level take the form of impairments rather than embellishments of movement. In *blocking* and *freezing*, a purposive act becomes interrupted in mid-sequence; the final movement may become fixed or the limb may gradually sink back to a resting position. In *waxy flexibility* (catalepsy) the patient allows his limbs or torso to be placed in any position, which is then maintained for minutes or occasionally much longer. This disorder is rare but maintenance of uncomfortable positions for a few seconds (*Haltungsverharren*) and so-called *psychological pillow* where the patient lies with his head two to three inches off the bed, can be quite commonly observed among chronically hospitalized patients.

More complex disorders of volition: Although expressed in relatively simple motor acts, these abnormalities appear to involve a disturbance in the will behind the movement rather than in the movement itself; at the same time the disorders give the compelling impression of being outside conscious control. Figuring prominently at this level are disorders of co-operation, including *negativism* and a variety of abnormalities characterized by over-responsiveness and excessive compliance which have been grouped together by Lohr and Wisniewski (1987) as *positivism*.

According to Bleuler (1911) the term *negativism* encompasses a spectrum of phenomena. At the simple, motor end of this is the phenomenon of *gegenhalten (opposition)*, where the patient resists all passive movements with exactly the same degree of force as that exerted by the examiner. At a more complex, volitional level, patients do the reverse of whatever is asked of them; they hold their breath when asked to breathe deeply, violently resist attempts to get them to stand up, only to continue to resist when it is desired that they lie down.

The term *positivism* conveniently groups a number of phenomena previously separated into *mitgehen, automatic obedience*, and *echophenomena*. In *mitgehen*, the patient appears to wish to anticipate the intention of the examiner. There is scarcely any resistance to passive changes of posture, and limbs elevate themselves at the slightest touch like an anglepoise lamp. Requests to move are complied with abrupt, exaggerated movements which may overshoot the mark or even unbalance the patient. When requested to perform a particular act, the patient continues to do so unnecessarily, or copies one limb movement with another. Such phenomena shade into *automatic obedience* where any and every suggestion (even one that is merely implied) is mindlessly obeyed; and *echopraxia*, where gestures and actions are copied, sometimes with a certain amount of modification.

Other volitional catatonic phenomena include *ambitendence*, where a patient appears to simultaneously try to and prevent himself from carrying out actions: he may move his hand from his body with obvious intent, then stop, start, and stop again until finally giving up altogether. In *handling* and *intertwining* the patient touches and manipulates everything within reach, kneads objects, and continually adjusts his clothes.

Very complex disorders of overall behaviour: At this level, the drives which underlie behaviour as a whole become disturbed in ways which carry the pointless, bizarre stamp of catatonia. Some *sterotypies* and *mannerisms* were considered by Bleuler to be expressed at this level: the patient's whole daily routine may assume a monotonous rhythmicity, every action being carried out with an almost photographic sameness. Gestures and demeanour may become affected, pompous, a caricature of some cultural or subcultural style. Similarly, *negativism*, according to Bleuler, gives way by degrees into an all-pervading contrariness of attitude: patients insist on staying in bed when they should be getting up and *vice versa*; they resist going for a meal and then refuse to leave the table once they had been taken there; they demand baths at unconventional temperatures and then complain that attempts are being made to scald or freeze them. The converse phenomenon of *positivism* probably also has its corresponding higher echelons: Fish (Fish 1962/Hamilton 1984) described *advertence* where the patient always turns to the examiner when approached and begins talking, usually nonsense, until he is cut short by walking away.

Catatonic stupor, excitement, and impulsiveness also affect the patient's entire behaviour. In *catatonic stupor* the patient sits or lies motionless, expressionless, mute and often incontinent, perhaps in a contorted posture. Typically the state is associated with other catatonic phenomena like grimacing, waxy flexibility, and gegenhalten; occasionally the patient can be lifted up bodily without any alteration in position. Although unresponsive, there is evidence that the patient is aware of his surroundings; he may tense or blush when people enter the room, or follow their movements with his eyes.

Catatonic excitement consists of aimless overactivity, destructiveness and violence, from which the patient seems strangely disengaged and out of contact with the environment. Such patients run about naked, masturbate openly, bite crockery, destroy furniture, strip beds, embrace and kiss other patients only to violently assault them a second later. Manneristic and stereotyped actions, often of a complicated kind, are typically also incorported into the presentation.

Catatonic impulsiveness refers to sudden, incomprehensible, and often very violent acts for which the patient is unable to give any more than a facile explanation. Often in a setting of stupor, the patient will suddenly rouse himself, knock over furniture, throw objects, strike another patient, set fire to his hair. Explanations like 'I had a sort of feeling to do that', and 'because it was desired' are given, or none at all.

Catatonic speech disorders: Speech, like any other motor activity, can become distorted by catatonic phenomena, and once again the abnormalities can range from the simple to the highly complicated. In the simplest cases, speech may be interrupted by hawking, grunting, or other vocalizations. Or it may be *aprosodic*, normal delivery being replaced by a flat monotone, peculiar scanning, affected or telegrammatic intonations. Speech *stereotypies and mannerisms* are also seen: a word or phrase may be repeated over and over again (*palilalia*), the patient may speak in all kinds of accents, in infinitives and diminutives, or add -ism or -io to every word. In *verbigeration*, speech is replaced by more or less incomprehensible mumblings, amongst which a few repetitive words and phrases can be made out. *Echolalia* is the verbal counterpart of *echopraxia*. Finally, *mutism* often accompanies other catatonic symptoms; conversely occasional patients speak at great length without a listener being present.

Miscellaneous motor, volitional, and behavioural disorders

Parakinesia: This was the term used by Kleist (1943, 1960) to describe the occurrence in catatonic schizophrenic patients of motor activity which is reminiscent of, but somehow different from chorea, athetosis, and tics. Such patients grimace, twitch, and jerk continuously, carry out voluntary movements in an abrupt way, and speak in short, sharp, disjointed bursts (Fish 1962/Hamilton 1984). In contrast to extrapyramidal involuntary movements, parakinesia gives the appearance of having a certain emotional colouring, a motivated quality not ordinarily seen.

Extrapyramidal movement disorders: In his description of catatonia, Kahlbaum (1874) included various spasmodic phenomena which would nowadays be classified as chorea, athetosis, and dystonia. Kraepelin (1913*a*) also thought that some schizophrenic patients showed 'peculiar, sprawling, irregular, choreiform, outspreading movements'. Initially, Bleuler (1911), considered chorea and athetosis to be rarely if ever seen in schizophrenia, but by 1930 (cited by Rogers 1992) he had come round to the view that there were some schizophrenic symptoms 'which are likewise found in various diseases of the basal ganglia'. Other descriptions made before the introduction of neuroleptic drugs (reviewed by Waddington 1984; Rogers 1985, 1992; McKenna *et al.* 1991) have strongly suggested that extrapyramidal signs, both hyper- and hypokinetic, can be found in some schizophrenic patients, unrelated to treatment. Most recently, Owens *et al.* (1982) were able to find among a population of chronically hospitalized patients 47 who met strict diagnostic criteria for schizophrenia, but who had ostensibly never been exposed to treatment. The prevalence of tardive dyskinesia-like involuntary movements in these patients was found to be only slightly lower than that in the neuroleptic-treated patients.

Lack of volition: Kraepelin (1913*a*) described a 'permanent weakening in the mainsprings of volition' as one of the main elements of the state of deterioration to which schizophrenic patients progressed. Currently, lack of volition is considered to be one of the key negative symptoms of the disorder (see Chapter 2). Patients showing the phenomenon get up late, go to bed early, and do very little in between. They no longer bother to wash or shave, and change their clothes only sporadically; in extreme cases they become filthy and infested. There is no inclination to socialize, to follow former pursuits, and particularly to work—unemployment is the rule in chronic schizophrenia. *Poverty of speech* (Wing 1978; Andreasen 1982) can be regarded as the same disorder affecting verbal output. Affected patients answer questions readily enough but use only the minimum necessary number of words; they do not elaborate on their replies and make few spontaneous comments.

Non-specific abnormal behaviours: As graphically described by Fish (Fish 1962/Hamilton 1984), many chronic patients show patterns of behaviour which, while not sufficiently striking or specific to be classified as catatonic, are nevertheless characteristically schizophrenic. *Collecting* and *hoarding* are common examples: useless items like old newspapers, pieces of stale food, grass, stones, and dead insects are stuffed in pockets and handbags; sometimes the preferred articles, for instance hymn books or bicycles, are more difficult to come by and have to be stolen. *Wandering* is another well known occurrence; at least a third of vagrants and those without a permanent address are chronic schizophrenics (Priest 1976).

Emotional disorders

In psychiatric parlance, the rather sweeping term emotion is broken down into affect and mood. *Affects* are moment-to-moment, specific, differentiated emotional responses, which also carry a connotation of objectivity — they refer to the emotional state as inferred on the basis of facial expressions, gestures, posture, and tone of voice. *Moods* are longer lasting, prevailing feeling states which tend to colour the whole of mental life. Judgements about mood rely principally on the individual's subjective description supplemented by questioning (Jaspers 1959; Owens and Maxmen 1979; Sims 1988). Disorders of both affect and mood are recognized in schizophrenia; as affective flattening and inappropriateness, the former are particularly important and so are given the status of cardinal symptoms here.

Affective flattening and inappropriateness

Affective flattening, the core affective disorder in schizophrenia, eludes easy definition. According to Sims (1988), the subtleties of an individual's emotional state are constantly being signalled to others, largely unconsciously, by facial expression, tone of voice, gesture, posture, and 'body language'. The registration and interpretation of these signals by an observer also takes place more or less without conscious awareness, and is responded to in the same way, so that a kind of emotional dialogue accompanies verbal interaction. It is this that becomes diminished, lost, or altered in schizophrenia. When mild, the effect is noticeable, if intangible: there is, as Jaspers (1959) put it, 'something queer, cold, rigid and petrified there'. When more marked, a definite lack of responsiveness to emotive topics can be pinpointed: the patient may discuss unpleasant and even horrific experiences casually and matter-of-factly. When the disorder is severe, all emotional expression becomes impoverished and the patient exhibits an obviously indifferent, withdrawn, stiff, or peculiar manner.

Affective flattening first assumed major significance as a symptom when

Hecker described hebephrenia in 1871 (see Sedler 1985). Hebephrenia was absorbed into schizophrenia by Kraepelin, who continued to place particular emphasis on the emotional dullness which developed as part of the deterioration of the disorder (Kraepelin 1913*a*). Bleuler (1911) elevated affective flattening to the status of a fundamental symptom, that is one present to some extent in all cases (see Chapter 4). In their descriptions both these authors were at pains to point out that affective flattening had a variety of different manifestations. These included coldness, indifference, shallowness, loss of delicacy of feeling, and lack of conviction when emotions were expressed.

Complicating and interrupting affective flattening, Kraepelin and Bleuler noted the appearance of sudden, intense emotional states, which were out of keeping with events or completely causeless. Patients would fall into uncontrollable laughter or become inconsolably sad for no reason; they would laugh while recounting suicide attempts; become miserable or irritated on occasions for happiness; sometimes they appeared to be able to laugh and cry simultaneously.

The subsequent career of affective flattening and inappropriateness has been nothing if not chequered. As a Bleulerian fundamental symptoms, they were first accorded unprecedented diagnostic significance. Somewhat later they came to be disparaged as thoroughly untrustworthy (see Chapter 4). In recent years they have been rehabilitated, and are currently considered to be important symptoms whose presence can be detected with a reasonable degree of accuracy. Affective flattening has been found to be present in between one-third to two-thirds of acute schizophrenic patients (Andreasen 1979*b*; Boeringa and Castellani 1979); inappropriateness of affect, however, is uncommon. Both become considerably more common in chronic schizophrenic patients. Authors interested in the reliability and validity of assessment of affective flattening have also rediscovered the point made by classical authors, that the phenomenonon is multifaceted (Abrams and Taylor 1978; Andreasen and Olsen 1982; Mortimer *et al*. 1989). Based on the studies of the patterns of associations shown by various schizophrenic symptoms (discussed further in Chapter 2) the following tentative dissection of schizophrenic affective abnormality is offered.

Affective unresponsiveness: Perhaps the most important element of affective flattening, this refers to a narrowing or constriction in the range of emotions expressed during normal conversation or in the course of an interview. The patient fails to smile in response to social cues; other facial expressions, gestures, and expressive postures are reduced in range or absent; an apparent indifference to emotive topics is distinctly evident. Typically, the symptom is reckoned to be unmistakeably present when a patient relates what would normally be distressing delusions or hallucinations without concern.

Emotional withdrawal: This was repeatedly alluded to by classical authors and describes a aloofness which is easily recognizable but difficult to describe. Sometimes there is nothing more than a certain lack of the normal rapport which is established when two people converse. When more severe, the patient seems wrapped up in his own concerns, distracted, or alternatively cold and detached. This disorder tends to be seen in association with *affective unresponsiveness.*

Inappropriate affect: This describes a tendency to express emotions incompatible with the subject under discussion. In practice it almost always takes the form of smiling or laughing whilst discussing distressing topics, such as persecutory delusions, derogatory auditory hallucinations, or suicidal ideas. The term is often also extended to include unprovoked, causeless laughter. The available evidence indicates that inappropriate affect occurs independently of *affective unresponsiveness* and *emotional withdrawal.*

Shallowness, coarsening, and blunting of affect: This term groups together, largely for convenience, disorders where emotional expression lacks subtlety, refinement, and sensitivity, or appears to be without depth or conviction. As pointed out by Sims (1988), this type of phenomenon is conceptually quite different from *affective unresponsiveness.* There are some suggestions, however, that it tends to be seen in association with *inappropriate affect.*

Retardation of affect: This was originally described by Bleuler (1911), and the similar term *stiffening of affect* was used by Fish (Fish 1962/Hamilton 1984) to describe a slowing of changes in emotional expression and the maintenance of any given affect for too long. This affective disorder has since been largely neglected in the literature; this may be because it is uncommon.

Miscellaneous abnormalities of mood

Mood colourings: Making the distinction from affective flattening, Bleuler (1911) described the occurrence of certain 'basic moods'. These were seen particularly in chronic patients and took the form of a monotonous bonhomie, moroseness, irritability, querulousness or some other emotion, which formed a backdrop against which all other symptoms were expressed. The moods could be fairly transient, but generally tended to persist without much variation for years or decades. Inevitably, the prevailing mood was one of depression or elation in a proportion of cases. In such cases, however, Bleuler maintained that the quality of the mood change could be distinguished from that seen in manic-depressive psychosis. The question of just how far depression and elation can be considered to form part of schizophrenia is discussed further in Chapter 10.

Perplexity: This is typically seen in schizophrenia at the beginning of an acute exacerbation. The patient appears bemused, this sometimes being tinged with anxiousness, suspiciousness, or rapture, and searches the environment restlessly asking repetitive questions. The disorder is closely associated with delusional mood and has been argued to be the objective counterpart of this (delusional mood can, however, be described by a patient without there being any obvious evidence of perplexity). Perplexity is not specific to schizophrenia and can occur in organic confusional states, manic-depressive psychosis, depressed type, and also in normal individuals following exposure to severe emotional stress (Jaspers 1959).

Anhedonia: This state of inability to experience pleasure was originally proposed as a theoretical counterpart to analgesia, the inability to experience pain (see Snaith 1992). Anhedonia was first assigned psychiatric significance by Schneider (1958) who regarded it as a characteristic symptom of manic-depressive psychosis, depressed type. Its application to schizophrenia arose in America, where psychodynamically oriented authors, notably Meehl (1962), argued that inability to feel pleasure was present as a lifelong trait in individuals who became schizophrenic. This hypothesis has never, it should be noted, been put to any proper experimental test. Anhedonia is a subjective experience, and is thus quite different from affective flattening and lack of volition which is observed objectively and of which the patient is usually blithely unaware. (The term *anhedonia/ asociality* has, confusingly, been used by Andreasen (1982) to denote objectively discernible symptoms characterized by loss of interest in sex, friendships, family life, and recreational activities.)

The first rank symptoms of Schneider

Among the many abnormal experiences of schizophrenia, Schneider (1958) put eight in the 'first rank of importance'. These were *audible thoughts*; *voices heard arguing*; *voices heard commenting on one's actions*; *the experience of influences playing on the body (somatic passivity experiences)*; *thought withdrawal and other interferences with thought*; *diffusion of thought*; *delusional perception*; and *all feelings, impulses (drives), and volitional acts that are experienced by the patient as the work or influence of others*. Schneider made no claim that these symptoms were new (many of them had in fact already been described by Kraepelin and Bleuler). Nor, in his view, did they have any particular contribution to make to the understanding of schizophrenia. Rather, their value was diagnostic: in the absence of any physical cause, Schneider considered the presence of any one of them to be decisive evidence for a psychosis being schizophrenic.

Schneider speculated that some first rank symptoms might have a common phenomenological basis in a 'lowering of the barrier between the self and the surrounding world'. This idea has been taken up by Fish (Fish 1962/Hamilton 1984) and particularly by Sims (1988), who argue that an invasion, blurring, or loss of ego boundaries is one of, perhaps, the fundamental experience of schizophrenic patients. Such a concept can be readily applied to some first rank symptoms, such as passivity and interferences with thought; but not very easily to others, especially special forms of auditory hallucination and delusional perception. Concepts of what constitute first rank symptoms and how they should be classified, have also evolved and changed since Schneider's description (see Koehler 1979). The following account is a synthesis of the descriptions of Mellor (1970), Wing *et al.* (1974), and Sims (1988). Some examples, which are taken from Mellor (1970), are illustrated in Fig. 1.5.

Special forms of auditory hallucination

Audible thoughts (gedankenlautwerden, echo de la pensée, thought echo) are auditory hallucinations which speak the patient's thoughts out loud. The phenomenon may precede, occur simultaneously with, or follow the thought, but the content of each are the same; phenomena such as voices answering thoughts, talking about them or saying the opposite of them may, however, additionally be present. In *voices arguing*, two or more voices discuss the patient. In *thought commentary* one or a number of voices comment on the patient's actions, describing them as they occur, often providing a running commentary with derogatory asides. The patient is usually, but not necessarily, referred to in the third person.

Passivity experiences (made experiences, delusions of control)

Somatic passivity is Schneider's experience of influences playing on the body. The patient describes bodily sensations, heat, pain, sexual excitement, etc., as being imposed on him by some external agency in an immediate and vivid way. The same phenomenon can apply to emotions, as *made feelings*, to irresistible urges as *made impulses*, and most importantly to movements and speech as *made volitional acts*. Schneider considered all these experiences to be first rank in nature, but not all subsequent authors have agreed (see Koehler 1979). As *delusions of control*, Wing *et al.* (1974) emphasize *made volitional acts* which they also broaden to include the experience of being under the direct influence of someone else's will.

Examples of First Rank Symptoms
(from Mellor 1970)

Special forms of auditory hallucination
Patient who heard a quiet voice with an Oxford accent and immediately experienced whatever the voice was saying as his own thoughts. When he read the newspaper the voice would speak aloud whatever his eyes fell on (*audible thoughts*). One voice, deep in pitch, repeatedly said to a patient 'G.T. is a bloody paradox'. Another, higher in pitch said 'He is that, he should be locked up'. A female voice occasionally interrupted, saying 'He is not, he is a lovely man' (*voices arguing*). Patient who heard a voice from across the road describing everything she was doing in a flat monotone. 'She is peeling potatoes, got hold of the peeler, she does not want that potato, she is putting it back because she thinks it has a knobble like a penis, she has a dirty mind.' (*thought commentary*).

Passivity experiences
Patient who felt X-rays entering his neck, passing down his back and disappearing into his pelvis. These were accompanied by warmth, tingling, and then coldness and prevented him from getting an erection (*somatic passivity*). Patient who felt that others were projecting unhappiness and other emotions onto her brain (*made feelings*). Patient who stated 'when I reach my hand for the comb it is my hand and arm which move and my fingers pick up the pen, but I don't control them. I sit there watching them move, and they are quite independent ... I am just a puppet who is manipulated by cosmic strings' (*made volitional acts*).

Alienation of thought
Patient who felt that Eamonn Andrews (a British TV personality) treated her mind like a screen and flashed his thoughts on to it 'like you flash a picture' (*thought insertion*). Patient who stated, 'I am thinking about my mother, and suddenly my thoughts are sucked out of my head by a phrenological vacuum cleaner, and there is nothing in my mind, it is empty' (*thought withdrawal*). Patient who said, 'As I think, my thoughts leave my head on a type of mental ticker-tape. Everyone around has only to pass the tape through their mind and they know my thoughts' (*thought broadcasting*).

Delusional perception
At breakfast, a patient felt a sense of unease, that something was going to happen. One of his fellow lodgers pushed the salt cellar towards him, and as it reached him he realised that he must return home 'to greet the Pope who is visiting Ireland, to see his family and reward them because Our Lord is going to be born again to one of the women. And because of this they are all born different with their private parts back to front'.

Fig. 1.5

Interference with thought (thought alienation, disorders of the possession of thought)

It is misleading to refer to these subjectively described experiences as 'schizophrenic thought disorder' as they are quite different from objectively observable *formal thought disorder*. In *thought withdrawal*, the subject feels that his thoughts are being taken from his mind, typically leaving it completely empty. Wing *et al*. (1974) consider this symptom to be a delusional interpretation of another symptom of first rank importance, *thought block*, in which the patient reports that all thinking suddenly and unexpectedly comes to a halt for seconds, minutes, or even longer. *Thought insertion* refers to the experiencing of thoughts which lack the quality of being one's own. Usually, but not always, some outside agency is invoked to account for this. *Thought broadcasting, diffusion, or sharing* describes a patient's feeling that his thoughts are not contained within his mind, that they are made public and often that they are projected over a wide area. The symptom differs from the more commonplace *delusion of thoughts being read* by being indiscriminate—the patient feels that his thoughts are freely available to all and sundry. In many cases the phenomenon appears to be a delusional explanation of *audible thoughts*.

Delusional perception

Schneider (1949, 1958) applied this term to a variety of experiences in which abnormal, self-referential significance became attached to environmental events, amongst which he clearly included delusions of reference and misinterpretation. As these phenomena are not generally accepted as being diagnostic of schizophrenia, various refinements of his definition have been proposed with the aim of making it more restrictive. In one such attempt, it has been argued that in a delusion of reference significance is triggered off by an environmental event and is only loosely linked to this. In delusional perception, on the other hand, the significance is somehow contained within the perception itself (see Koehler 1979). As this argument is difficult to follow by anyone other than German psychopathologists, a more mundane alternative has been developed by British psychiatrists (Fish 1962/ Hamilton 1984; Mellor 1970; Wing *et al.* 1974). They suggest that the sense of meaning, which is vague and unspecified in delusions of reference, becomes explicit and immediate in delusional perception. On perceiving a neutral event, a delusional interpretation of it, which is usually elaborate, suddenly crystallizes, dropping, as it were, fully formed into the patient's head.

Conclusion

This listing of schizophrenic symptoms is far from exhaustive. There are special forms of delusion, for instance the Capgras syndrome, and a variety of abnormalities in perception—of the body, of self, and of time—which are found more or less exclusively in schizophrenia but which it is not possible to do justice to in a single chapter. In addition to psychotic phenomena, a wealth of neurotic, depressive, and non-specific symptoms are commonplace among schizophrenic patients and form an important source of their suffering. A more detailed account of these other symptoms can be found in textbooks on psychopathology, notably that by Sims (1988).

The ways in which schizophrenic symptoms combine with each other are just as erratic and complicated as the phenomena themselves. Virtually any symptom may occur in complete (or perhaps more accurately almost complete) isolation. Alternatively, there are undoubtedly patients who can be found to be experiencing an exceptionally wide range of delusions and hallucinations, who also exhibit significant formal thought disorder, affective flattening, and even a smattering of catatonic phenomena. While it is probably safe to assume that any particular schizophrenic symptom can be seen in association with any other, certain groupings nevertheless appear with regularity. It is these recurring themes in the clinical presentation of schizophrenia which form the subject of the next chapter.

2

The clinical pictures
of schizophrenia

Schizophrenia, as it was first delineated by Kraepelin in 1896, came into being as the end result of three converging lines of argument. First, Kraepelin made the observation that three existing forms of insanity, catatonia (described by Kahlbaum in 1874), hebephrenia (described by Kahlbaum's follower, Hecker in 1871), and dementia paranoides (described by Kraepelin himself) were all characterized by a course which led inexorably to deterioration. Secondly, he pointed out that the initial presenting features of these three disorders were not sharply demarcated from one another and transitional forms could regularly be seen. Finally, he noted that the conditions had other features in common: they all tended to develop in early adult life, there was no marked depression or elation of mood, and indicators of the ultimate poor outcome were present from the earliest stages. Kraepelin therefore concluded that the three states should be brought together as paranoid, hebephrenic, and catatonic forms of a single disorder, *dementia praecox*, a series of outwardly divergent states which led to a peculiar destruction of the personality.

Renaming dementia praecox as schizophrenia, Bleuler (1911) felt that the diversity of its presentations was so great that it might be more proper to speak of a group of schizophrenias. Possibly as an attempt to reconcile this wide range of symptomatology with the concept of a unitary disorder, he went out of his way to devise a series of subdivisions of the clinical picture. To the paranoid, hebephrenic, and catatonic forms distinguished by Kraepelin, he added a fourth variety, simple schizophrenia (which had also previously been described as a separate disorder, simple dementia). He highlighted the fact that the course could be chronic or marked by intermittent attacks, and described these latter in detail. Most significantly, he proposed that schizophrenic symptoms themselves were divisible into two types, *fundamental symptoms*, which were always present and specific for schizophrenia, and *accessory symptoms*, which could come and go and were seen in other psychoses as well.

Contained in Kraepelin's and Bleuler's accounts were the seeds of all later approaches to the subclassification of schizophrenia. The distinction between intermittent attacks and the development of permanent disability has been preserved as *acute and chronic schizophrenia*. The differentiation of paranoid, hebephrenic, catatonic, and simple forms of schizophrenia has, with a circuitous series of modifications, survived as the *classical subtypes of schizophrenia*. Finally, it is not stretching the truth too far to maintain that Bleuler's proposal of a broad division of fundamental and accessory symptoms has as its legacy the contemporary *positive : negative dichotomy* in schizophrenia.

Acute and chronic schizophrenia

Viewing schizophrenia from a longitudinal perspective, Kraepelin (1913*a*) and Bleuler (1911) felt that only two statements could be made with certainty. The first of these was that in many cases the disorder began with a discrete attack of symptoms which was followed by improvement and then further exacerbations. The second was that sooner or later a state of permanent, relatively immutable deterioration was reached. Acute exacerbations tended to be more common in the first few years, although they were not unknown later in the course. Signs of deterioration became, in the majority of cases, unmistakeable within two to three years. It was in this rather uncertain way, hedged with reservations and qualifications, that the distinction between acute and chronic phases of schizophrenia was first drawn.

Acute schizophrenia

This was given its first description by Bleuler (1911). Under the heading of acute syndromes, he detailed a series of presentations of new symptoms or exacerbations of existing ones. These episodes could set in out of the blue or after a prodrome of non-specific symptoms. They could last from as little as a few hours to as long as several years. Symptoms could develop in pure form or in combinations. Most commonly the states were characterized by the appearance or worsening of delusions and hallucinations. Sometimes these were accompanied by pronounced mood colourings, florid formal thought disorder, and catatonic phenomena especially of a hypo- or hyperkinetic kind. Rather less frequently the picture was predominantly one of dreaminess, abstraction, clouding, or torpor. Occasionally, an episode could consist of little more than fits of anger or attacks of screaming.

The term acute schizophrenia, and closely related terms such as exacerbations, thrusts, shifts, and phases soon became part of the vocabulary of schizophrenia. The connotation of development of new symptoms or worsening of pre-existing ones was retained, and the implication of fairly recent onset of illness became virtually a prerequisite. But beyond this the concept of acute schizophrenia remained rather nebulous. Clinicians were familiar with the clinical pictures encountered, but descriptions of them were sparse, insubstantial, and hardly changed from the time of Bleuler. More than anything else acute schizophrenia became a convenient label for any change in a patient's condition which required treatment or hospitalization.

In the 1970s, however, a formal re-assessment of the meaning of acute schizophrenia was made. This was, as it were, as a by-product of a large scale investigation, the International Pilot Study of Schizophrenia (WHO 1973), which was undertaken to determine whether schizophrenia existed and could be reliably diagnosed across different cultures (this study is discussed in detail in Chapter 4). In this study over 1200 referrals to hospital psychiatric services received an extremely detailed clinical assessment using a version of the Present State Examination. Eight hundred and eleven of these were given a consensus diagnosis of schizophrenia. All of the patients were required to have had an onset of illness within the last five years, to have experienced persistent symptoms for less than three years, and to have spent less than two years in hospital.

In this group of operationally defined cases of acute schizophrenia, virtually every class of schizophrenic symptom was found. Particularly common were delusions and 'predelusional' symptoms such as delusional mood; and also flattening of affect and auditory hallucinations. Non-specific symptoms like derealization, disturbance of mood, lack of insight, or poor rapport were equally or even more common. Schneiderian first rank symptoms were slightly less commonly found, none of them being among the ten most frequent symptoms. Formal thought disorder and incongruity of affect were relatively uncommon, and catatonic symptoms were exceptional. The fifteen most frequent symptoms in the patients are shown in Table 2.1.

In short, the typical patient with acute schizophrenia is likely to be in the relatively early stages of his or her illness, and presents most commonly with delusions, especially persecutory, and hallucinations, especially auditory. These tend to develop in a setting of suspiciousness, flattening of affect, and poor rapport and may be accompanied by non-psychotic symptoms such as anxiety, derealization, and mood change. Formal thought disorder and incongruity of affect are uncommon features, and catatonic phenomena make only an occasional and then usually minor contribution to the overall picture.

Chronic schizophrenia

If credit for the description of acute schizophrenia belongs to Bleuler, that for chronic schizophrenia has to be given to Kraepelin (1913a), who provided what has proved to be the only detailed account of the presentation. He specified a number of different schizophrenic end states on the basis of their severity and special characteristics. While he considered that these

Table 2.1 15 most frequent symptoms in 811 acute schizophrenic patients (from WHO 1973)

Symptom	Frequency found (%)
Lack of insight	84.1
Inadequate description	64.5
Suspiciousness	60.2
Unwilling to co-operate	57.5
Ideas of reference	54.8
Flatness of affect	51.9
Delusions of persecution	51.8
Delusions of reference	49.6
Delusional mood	48.7
Poor rapport	47.0
Auditory hallucinations	42.3
Verbal hallucinations	38.0
Voices speaking to patient	35.6
Thought alienation	34.2
Gloomy thoughts	32.9

were to some extent separable, and he hoped that their classification would prove to have scientific usefulness, he recognized that all kinds of transitional forms could be seen, and that in individual cases transformations from milder to more severe states sometimes took place.

The mildest form of chronic schizophrenia Kraepelin termed *simple weak-mindedness*. After the florid phenomena of an acute episode had subsided, the patient was left odd, stiff, constrained, awkward, and sometimes eccentric in manner. A degree of affective flattening was noticeable and this was often overlaid with mood colourings of suspiciousness, moroseness, irritability, etc.. Lack of volition showed itself in an inability to manage at a previous occupation or a disinclination to do work of any kind; there could also be poverty of speech. Thinking became narrowed, impoverished, and a certain weakness of judgement manifested itself when complicated decisions had to be made.

In *hallucinatory and paranoid weak-mindedness*, the above changes were complicated by the continuing presence of hallucinations, delusions, or both. These, however, tended to be much less preoccupying and disturbing than during the acute phase. Thus, patients would no longer speak openly about their voices, and complaints of persecution would become monotonous and unelaborated. Peculiarly stoic, indifferent, or inconsequential attitudes became adopted to symptoms which would, in the normal course of events, be highly distressing.

More severe chronic states were grouped together as *drivelling, dull, silly, manneristic*, and *negativistic dementia*. All of these forms merged into each other and their common denominator was a marked affective flattening and impairment of volition, coupled with a striking impoverishment of all mental life. Such patients showed complete emotional indifference, interrupted only by causeless, silly laughter, tearfulness, fits of anger, and so on. Many, if left to themselves, would do nothing or lie in bed all day. Others might be temporarily rousable to carry out some kind of simple work, but would soon sink back into a state of apathy. Many were mute or nearly so. A minority of cases appeared relatively unimpaired superficially, but demonstrated no ability to use any skills they had previously learned, and failed spectacularly when given any task requiring independent thought.

Although not always present, delusions, hallucinations, and formal thought disorder were a frequent complication of these severe states of deterioration. These symptoms could be far in the background, or make only a minor contribution to the overall clinical picture. More characteristically, however, they took a very florid form, patients expressing a wealth of fantastic and nonsensical beliefs, hearing a profusion of voices, or displaying an extraordinary degree of incoherence of speech. Invariably, catatonic symptoms also made an appearance to a more or less marked degree, especially stereotypies, mannerisms, echopraxia, and disorders of compliance.

More recent accounts of chronic schizophrenia are decidly thin on the ground. In one short account, Mayer-Gross *et al.* (1969) described the schizophrenic patient coming, as the years went by, to an arrangement with his illness. As a degree of stability was achieved, apathy, flattening of affect, and mannerisms grew to rule the clinical picture, and behaviour, thought, and attitudes became narrow and inflexible. Delusions and hallucinations, if they did not fade away altogether, became colourless, repetitive, and lost much of their emotional impact on the patient. Formal thought disorder, on the other hand, tended to become more prominent. Wing (1978), in what seems to be the only other contemporary description, considered that chronic schizophrenic patients came to show one or other of two prominent syndromes, or perhaps a combination of both. One of these was formal thought disorder. The other was composed of a series of behaviours—affective flattening, slowness of thought and movement, under-activity, lack of drive, poverty of speech, and social withdrawal— which tended to cluster together to form a 'clinical poverty' syndrome.

These modern descriptions fail to do justice to the marked variability which is one of the hallmarks of patients with severe, chronic illness.

Among the long-stay population of any psychiatric hospital, patients can be encountered who, rather than showing a withdrawn, apathetic picture are continually overactive, pace around, wander restlessly, or leave the hospital grounds every day. Others give the impression of having typical lack of volition, until it is learnt that they attend occupational therapy every day, or keep busy doing chores around the ward in a conscientious way. Still others, although generally deteriorated, pay careful attention to some aspect of self care and grooming, make a point of wearing a tie, etc. Conversely, some patients appear quite well dressed and are pleasant and amiable, but when their carers are questioned about them it becomes clear that they spend all day sitting in front of the television not taking it in and are frequently incontinent. In some chronically hospitalized patients the presentation consists almost entirely of unrelenting, extremely florid delusions, tormenting hallucinations, and marked formal thought disorder which are accompanied by only the subtlest evidence of affective flattening, lack of volition, and deterioration in standards of self care. At the other extreme there are patients who need assistance to wash, dress, and maintain minimal personal hygiene, and who would not bother to eat unless led to the table and fed. Exceptionally, there are chronically hospitalized patients who, just as described by Kraepelin (1913a), are free from all active psychotic symptoms and exhibit no more signs of deterioration than many patients out of hospital, but whose disabilities are in the realm of judgement: they are unable to carry out any tasks requiring planning and if not closely supervised behave completely irresponsibly and get into all kinds of trouble.

Some objective confirmation of the picture of chronic schizophrenia comes, once again, from the International Pilot Study of Schizophrenia. Two years after the initial survey, 543 of the original 811 schizophrenic patients were re-examined (WHO 1979). Although the interval between the two assessments was relatively short, clear differences in the pattern of symptoms had emerged. The fifteen most common symptoms at this time are shown in Table 2.2. The frequency of delusions, auditory hallucinations, and first rank symptoms was significantly lower. Four symptoms which were present at initial evaluation had dropped out of the list. Three of these, delusional mood, voices speaking to the patient, and thought alienation, were florid symptoms; the fourth was gloomy thoughts. These were replaced by four new symptoms, three of which, apathy, restricted speech, and autism (emotional withdrawal) corresponded to a picture of evolving deterioration.

The common theme uniting the various presentations of chronic schizophrenia is that of development of deficits. The typical chronic schizophrenic patient shows 'clinical poverty' symptoms which, however, may vary in severity from a minor degree of lack of volition and flattening of

Table 2.2 15 most frequent symptoms in 543 schizophrenic
patients 2 years after acute presentation (from WHO 1979)

Symptom	Frequency found (%)
Lack of insight	42.5
Flatness of affect	27.1
Poor rapport	26.3
Inadequate description	25.2
Suspiciousness	25.2
Unwilling to co-operate	24.5
Apathy	18.8
Ideas of reference	18.0
Delusions of reference	14.2
Restricted speech	12.9
Autism (emotional withdrawal)	12.7
Delusions of persecution	12.7
Hypochondriacal/neurasthenic complaints	12.7
Auditory hallucinations	11.6
Verbal hallucinations	10.7

(Absolute rates for symptoms are lower than for acute patients because of the high
proportion with few or no symptoms of any kind.)

affect to very marked apathy, emotional impoverishment, and impaired self
care. Sometimes but not always continuing florid symptomatology in the
shape of delusions, hallucinations, and particularly formal thought disorder
is superimposed on this state, and once again this ranges from the mild to
the very severe. To some extent the severity of the latter symptoms tends
to be a function of the severity of the former so that it is the patients with
the worst degrees of deterioration who are prone to show the most fantastic
delusions, the most tormenting hallucinations, and the most incoherent
speech.

The classical subtypes of schizophrenia

Schizophrenia was the outcome of a merger between four disorders previously thought to be independent, dementia paranoides, hebephrenia,
catatonia, and simple dementia. One of the principal reasons these could
be combined into paranoid, hebephrenic, catatonic, and simple forms of
schizophrenia was, according to Kraepelin (1907) and Bleuler (1911), that
transitional forms were seen at least as often as pure forms of each disorder.
In addition, each form had the potential to transform into another, a case

which started out as paranoid, for example, becoming hebephrenic later on. Nevertheless, both authors felt that a sizeable proportion of cases of schizophrenia retained a paranoid, hebephrenic, catatonic, or simple stamp throughout their whole course. This distinctiveness was typically most marked at initial presentation, but it remained apparent in the manner of progression, and was even discernible as subtle differences in the severity and character of the terminal state.

The following descriptions of the classical subtypes of schizophrenia are based on those of Kraepelin (1907, 1913*a*) and Bleuler (1911) which remain unmatched in richness of detail. Following their format an idealized form of each subtype is presented first and this is followed by some of the variants which tend to be met with in practice. (It should be remembered that the symptoms and courses are those of schizophrenia as unmodified by treatment.)

Paranoid schizophrenia

In this form, delusions and hallucinations are to the forefront of the clinical picture continuously or for long periods of time.

The typical first sign is a feeling of change which may or may not amount to delusional mood. This gives way to suspiciousness and ill-formed persecutory and grandiose delusions. Gradually or suddenly, these then go on to acquire complete conviction. Later, derogatory verbal auditory hallucinations set in; these become incorporated into what by this time is a complex delusional system involving plots, conspiracies, and the like. Other hallucinations, particularly somatic hallucinations, may follow. The patient becomes increasingly withdrawn and isolated and he may not dare to leave his home; alternatively he may move repeatedly on the basis of imagined persecution.

Sooner or later general behavioural disturbance, squalid living conditions, or a violent act based on delusions precipitates admission to hospital. The persecutory delusions are by now very florid and hallucinations may be present in all modalities. Formal thought disorder can also be a prominent feature at this stage.

Once the patient is in hospital improvement begins to take place. The florid symptoms clear up completely or nearly completely and there appears to be little in the way of residual handicaps. Nevertheless, after discharge the patient does not manage outside hospital for very long. Attempts to get re-established in work fail: the patient may be unable to apply himself, or fail to turn up regularly, or simply no longer get along with co-workers. Active symptoms recur at some point and further hospitalization becomes necessary. This time recovery is slower. The delusions and hallucinations do not recede completely, and signs of lack of volition become more apparent.

Ultimately a more or less stable terminal state is reached. The overall severity of this may vary dramatically, but is most commonly one of mild or moderate deterioration. The patient's delusions lose their force and no longer exert any influence over his behaviour. Lack of volition and self neglect are generally obvious, but affective changes may only be slight. Typically, the patient is indifferent, apathetic, and lives from day to day without goals. He may manage to carry on some work in hospital, but only mechanically and without initiative. In favourable circumstances he may even maintain himself outside hospital. Just occasionally, the chronic state is marked mainly by persistent delusions and hallucinations, with any deterioration so far in the background that the patient remains capable of steady work, even, it is said, notable achievements.

Commonly, this pattern is not adhered to and a more irregular course is followed. Florid symptoms may appear suddenly, out of the blue, or emerge only after a prolonged prodromal phase of non-specific symptoms. Rather than there being a more or less smooth development of symptoms, the course may be one of swings and oscillations with returns to near normality in between. The delusions may be predominantly grandiose, religious, or hypochondriacal rather than persecutory. Instead of being relatively fixed they can be fluid and constantly changing. Some patients experience only delusions, others only hallucinations. Catatonic phenomena of every kind can intrude into the clinical picture.

Hebephrenic schizophrenia

In this form the leading symptoms are formal thought disorder and affective flattening and incongruity, which become superimposed upon a particularly severe deterioration.

In most cases symptoms develop gradually, even insidiously over many years; in a minority the onset is acute or subacute. The first symptoms tend to be vague: absentmindedness, dreaminess, or forgetfulness are noticed; there are complaints of lassitude, nervousness, irritability; performance at school or work falls off. More serious abnormalities then appear: the patient stands around, stares into space, talks to himself. His behaviour becomes bizarre, money is squandered, all kinds of pointless and childish pranks are engaged in.

Sooner or later the diagnosis is clarified by the appearance of delusions which tend to be multiple, ill formed, poorly sustained, and often fantastic. Hallucinations are usually only present to a minor degree and may be absent altogether; they are commonly visual or somatic, rather than auditory. Formal thought disorder, on the other hand, is a prominent feature, especially poverty of content of speech and stilted speech. Catatonic phenomena may complicate the picture, but generally only in a minor way.

In a few cases this form of schizophrenia follows a fluctuating course punctuated by periods of considerable improvement. In the majority, however, there is a more or less smooth progression to a state of deterioration which is usually more severe than that of paranoid schizophrenia and against the background of which formal thought disorder, inappropriate affect, and bizarre behaviour continue to be evident. Some cases, however, merely show a uniform emotional dullness; in others catatonic phenomena become more prominent. Few of these patients are able to survive outside hospital, and hebephrenic end states are commonplace among the institutionalized populations of mental hospitals.

Hebephrenic schizophrenia was originally characterized as appearing particularly early, at around the time of puberty. Age, however, did not figure in Kraepelin's later descriptions and was dismissed as irrelevant by Bleuler. Bleuler also extended the concept of hebephrenia to include virtually all cases which did not carry a distinct paranoid or catatonic colouring. According to his view, hebephrenic schizophrenia was characterized by deterioration where hallucinations, delusions, formal thought disorder, and even catatonic symptoms could complicate the clinical picture without ever dominating it.

Catatonic schizophrenia

This form of schizophrenia is characterized, quite simply, by a predominance of motor and volitional disorders, which almost invariably occur in a setting of stupor, excitement, or alternations between the two.

Catatonic schizophrenia may commence abruptly, evolve over weeks or months, or have a more insidious onset. In the latter cases an essentially non-specific prodrome of quietness, withdrawal, absentmindedness, etc. is followed by the development of florid delusions, hallucinations, and formal thought disorder. At this stage peculiarities of behaviour, bizarre actions, or severe self-neglect are frequently disproportionately prominent.

The catatonic nature of the disorder then declares itself by the appearance of stupor or excitement. This often has an abrupt onset, but stupor may evolve quite slowly. Stupor and excitement tend to alternate, but in an irregular way; sometimes one or the other phase may be no more than a brief interlude; occasionally a mixed state of stupor and excitement is seen, as in patients who dance about mute or lie motionless singing. As well as the entire range of individual catatonic phenomena, extravagant delusions, hallucinations of all types, and formal thought disorder of an extreme kind may be incorporated into the clinical picture.

At some point, often unexpectedly, improvement sets in. The excited patient becomes quiet, the stuporose patient gradually takes up activities again. At this stage the outcome can be favourable with some patients showing degrees of improvement approximating to full recovery. In other cases an otherwise excellent remission is spoilt by the continuing presence of minor stereotypies and mannerisms. But in at least half of all cases the remission is clearly incomplete.

Subsequently, sometimes only after several years have elapsed, further attacks follow. After one of these attacks, signs of deterioration become obvious and go on to worsen with each subsequent episode. The terminal state is one of severe deterioration — the most profound of any of the classical subtypes according to Kraepelin — in which remnants of stereotypies and mannerisms can be discerned and which are often pervaded by a continuous mild stupor or excitement. Interrupting this from time to time may be spontaneous transitory worsenings in which patients rage, insult, vilify, smear faeces, etc.

For Kraepelin, catatonic schizophrenia invariably featured stupor, excitement, or a conjunction of the two, even though the hypo- or hyperkinesia could be quite subtle. Bleuler, however, included presentations which had a catatonic flavour from the outset, but in which stupor or excitement did not figure. In these cases the illness was ushered in by peculiarities of behaviour and bizarre actions which became steadily more frequent and finally gave way to negativism, mutism, and other clear-cut catatonic phenomena, out of which a state of severe deterioration usually evolved.

Simple schizophrenia

This form, which did not form part of Kraepelin's original concept of schizophrenia, but was included by Bleuler, consists essentially of a slowly progressive impoverishment of mental life without development of florid symptoms.

The onset can often be traced to adolescence; occasionally it seems to go back even earlier. The leading sign is a fall-off in capacity which becomes more and more noticeable: a student begins to fail incomprehensibly, an officer leaves the army to start a string of unsuccessful businesses, a well-qualified teacher takes up a succession of temporary positions and engages in disastrous financial dealings. Hand in hand, a change in temperament appears in the direction of depression, irritability, or hypochondriasis. There is a narrowing of interests, and the patient becomes cold, unsympathetic, and estranged from his family. As the disorder evolves work becomes impossible. The patient sits around for days on end, whiles away his time in bars, and makes no plans for the future. Some patients wander, become vagrants, or fall into alcoholism, prostitution, or petty crime.

The course of this type of schizophrenia invariably extends over several years, if not decades. There may be clinical standstills as well as more or less sudden exacerbations. The ultimate outcomes varies greatly. At one extreme there may be only a slight decline accompanied by minor peculiarities of conduct, which is perceptible only by the contrast to the individual's former self. At the other, there is obvious deterioration with gross lack of volition, flattening of affect, poverty of speech, and self neglect. Kraepelin considered that progression to a really profound dementia did not occur, but Bleuler described some patients who became completely apathetic and required long-term hospital care. Sometimes the diagnosis is only confirmed when, after several years, florid symptoms flare up briefly and are then followed by more severe deterioration.

The likelihood of subclinical and variant forms of simple schizophrenia was recognized by both Kraepelin and Bleuler. Kraepelin speculated about individuals who, without ever coming to psychiatric attention, failed to live up to their potential and, if they worked at all, ended up holding a position far below their abilities. Bleuler considered that there were many simple schizophrenics among eccentrics, philosophers, world reformers, and vexatious litigants. He also gave the example of an intelligent woman who married at twenty and lived happily for more than five years. She then gradually become increasingly irritable, gesticulated whilst talking, quarrelled with neighbours incessantly, and became unbearably demanding at home. The suspicion of schizophrenia was raised by her complete indifference to her children and the fact that she had become unable to manage her household, making all kinds of silly mistakes and useless purchases.

Kraepelin's and Bleuler's four-way classification of schizophrenia was never intended to be sacrosanct. Bleuler (1911) felt that it was largely of practical usefulness and could only reflect true aetiological groupings in the broadest and crudest way. Kraepelin (1913a), came to consider the classification unsatisfactory and ultimately increased the number of subtypes to eleven. Paranoid schizophrenia was divided into two groups with mild and severe outcomes. Five new groups were added in which depression, elation, or alternations between the two were prominent features and which progressively approximated to catatonic schizophrenia. A final group was added consisting of a small number of cases which, after an unremarkable development with delusions and hallucinations, gave way to a stable state characterized by severe formal thought disorder against a background of unusually well preserved behaviour and ability to work.

Given this latitude, later authors had no qualms in making major alterations to the subtype classification of schizophrenia. A massive expansion was undertaken by Kleist and his follower Leonhard (see Fish 1957, 1958a; Leonhard 1979). In their view, as schizophrenia evolved towards chronicity, its initially rather amorphous presentations crystallized into a large number of stable states—19 in Leonhard's classification—which were individually distinctive and which did not overlap with each other to any significant degree. In each form the picture was dominated by one or a few symptoms, such as formal thought disorder, affective flattening, or one type of catatonic phenomenon. Kleist, Leonhard, and several other authors claimed to be able to categorize chronic schizophrenic patients according to this scheme (for example, Fish 1958*b*; Astrup 1979). It is clear from their writings, however, that the individual subtypes were at best seen in less than pure form, and at worst the fit appeared distinctly procrustean. But whatever its validity, such a minute, rigid dissection of the clinical picture of chronic schizophrenia simply failed to find favour with the majority of clinicians. It is now only of historical interest.

Other moves were made in the direction of simplification. In the 1940s a selection of alternative classifictions were proposed based on three subtypes; these have been described by Fish (Fish 1962/Hamilton 1984). These inititiatives, though, were quite idiosyncratic and did not have a wide impact. In the USA, the classification of schizophrenia was often collapsed into paranoid and non-paranoid types. This grew out of procedures adopted by psychologists in order to facilitate research, and it made little clinical impression. Some countries such as France (Pichot 1982) and the USSR (Calloway 1993) developed their own, quite individualistic approaches to subtype classification.

For better or worse, it has been the original classification of schizophrenia into paranoid, hebephrenic, catatonic, and simple subtypes which has survived. Beyond standing the test of time, however, its validity remains uncertain. Only one determined attempt to examine this issue has been made, and this was by Carpenter *et al.* (1976), who made use of the large body of detailed clinical information gathered in the International Pilot Study of Schizophrenia (WHO 1973).

In the first part of their study, Carpenter *et al.* took patients who had been given a clinical diagnosis of paranoid schizophrenia (325 patients), hebephrenic schizophrenia (87 patients), catatonic schizophrenia (53 patients), and simple schizophrenia (31 patients). For each group, they averaged the ratings on 27 types of symptom and plotted the scores to form a 'profile'. When these were inspected it was apparent that they were all roughly similar in pattern and levels of psychopathology. The differences between the paranoid and hebephrenic profiles were minimal, although they were in the expected direction: paranoid schizophrenics had higher scores on persecutory, but not other delusions, and lower scores on the items relating to affective flattening. In the catatonic and simple groups the differences from paranoid schizophrenics were more substantial, but still modest overall. The four profiles are illustrated in Fig. 2.1.

Carpenter *et al.* then went on to apply cluster analysis to the data. This mathematical technique (discussed further in Chapter 4) has the effect of partitioning the sample into groups of patients showing the most homogeneity of their symptoms. For this they used 600 schizophrenic patients with subtype diagnoses of paranoid, hebephrenic, catatonic, and simple (and also acute and schizoaffective) schizophrenia. They found that four clusters accounted for almost all the patients. The first cluster was

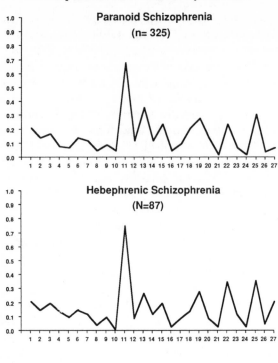

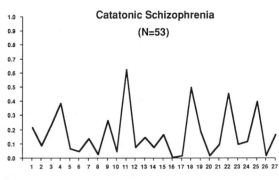

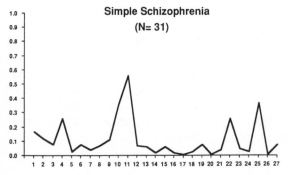

characterized by poor insight, persecutory delusions, auditory hallucinations, passivity, flattened affect, and social withdrawal. The other three clusters shared many of the characteristics of the first, but were distinguished by additional features. In the second cluster there was aberrant, agitated, or bizarre behaviour, incomprehensibility of speech, unkempt appearance, and incongruent and flattened affect. Cluster three was characterized by neurotic symptoms and more preservation of insight, as well as delusions and hallucinations. The final cluster was characterized by high ratings on somatic concerns, neurotic symptoms, and visual hallucinations. Clusters one and two are reminiscent of paranoid and hebephrenic schizophrenia, but the remaining two show little correspondence to catatonic and simple schizophrenia.

The interpretation that has to be drawn from this work is that schizophrenia does not divide into subtypes in any very clear-cut way. It is, however, an open question whether subgroups exist at all. Cluster analysis suggests that this is the case, but the finding of a positive result has to be balanced against the fact that this technique will generate clusters even in samples which are known to contain no significant heterogeneity. A reasonable conclusion might be that schizophrenia does divide up into clinically meaningful subgroups, but that the paranoid, hebephrenic, catatonic, and simple classification does not carve the disorder particularly close to its natural joints.

The positive:negative dichotomy

According to Berrios (1985), the concept of positive and negative symptoms originated in 1857 when Reynolds, a physician, used the terms to divide neurological phenomena into two classes. Symptoms such as spasms and convulsions could be considered as 'the excess or alteration of vital properties'. In contrast, others such as paralysis and anaesthesia were understandable as the 'the negation of vital properties'. The application of this

---

Fig. 2.1 Symptom profiles for the classical subtypes of schizophrenia (from Carpenter *et al.* 1976). (1, depression; 2, anxiety; 3, restlessness; 4, psychomotor retardation; 5, hypomania/mania; 6, somatic concerns; 7, belligerence; 8, obsessions; 9, unkempt appearance; 10, disorientation; 11, lack of insight; 12, depersonalization/derealization; 13, paranoid delusions; 14, grandiose delusions; 15, delusions of control; 16, depressive and nihilistic delusions; 17, other delusions; 18, visual hallucinations; 19, auditory hallucinations; 20, other hallucinations; 21, bizarre behaviour; 22, withdrawal; 23, incomprehensibility; 24, non-social speech; 25, restricted affect; 26, labile affect; 27, incongruous affect.)

distinction to the symptoms of insanity was made somewhat later by the distinguished neurologist Hughlings Jackson. However, in his hands the terms underwent more than a little modification and lost much of their simple clinical 'productive' and 'deficit' senses.

While it predated the description of schizophrenia, the concept of positive and negative symptoms is not known to have had any direct influence on Kraepelin and Bleuler. Nevertheless, somewhat similar ideas ran through their thinking. In order to define schizophrenia, Kraepelin (1896; 1913a) essentially separated and then coupled together a set of florid symptoms and a characteristic deterioration. Bleuler (1911) explicitly distinguished what he termed the accessory symptoms of schizophrenia, which included most florid symptoms, from the fundamental symptoms, some but not all of which were deficits. He considered this distinction to be of crucial diagnostic and aetiological importance, but any purely phenomenological considerations were lost in a wealth of theoretical speculation.

The separation of classes of symptoms which, even though they might co-exist in the same patient, were in some way conceptually distinct came to seem increasingly natural over subsequent decades. It was perhaps Schneider's (1958) influence which more than anything else focused attention on the florid symptoms of schizophrenia, especially those which were seen in acute episodes. Interest in the deficits of schizophrenia—those symptoms which found their fullest expression in the chronic stage—also increased, though somewhat more erratically. Jilek (1968) was the first author to construct a full catalogue of residual or defect state symptoms. He placed these under four general headings: impairment in ability to work, lessened drive and initiative, impaired emotional modulation, and impoverishment of interpersonal relationships. These encompassed major and fairly specific symptoms such as lack of volition and flattened affect, as well as milder and less tangible changes such as poverty of ideas, lowering of aspirations, and narrowing of interests.

During this period the terms positive and negative were sporadically applied to schizophrenia (de Clérambault 1942; Ey 1952; Mayer-Gross *et al.* 1954; Fish 1962), but the usage was casual, haphazard, and lacked any attempt to specify what the essential features of each were. It was Wing, who, in a series of papers culminating in Wing and Brown (1970), was responsible for distilling these traditions into the modern concept of positive and negative symptoms. Arguing along a number of lines of evidence he concluded that the intrinsic symptoms of chronic schizophrenia (that is, those which could not be understood as arising as a reaction to being ill or in response to the unfavourable social consequences of illness) fell into two independent clusters. Florid or positive symptoms included delusions, hallucinations, formal thought disorder, overactivity, and various forms of odd behaviour. His clinical poverty syndrome—which he now referred to as negative symptoms — consisted of social withdrawal, affective flattening, lack of volition and poverty of speech, and also slowness and underactivity. Subsequent authors (Strauss *et al.* 1974; Crow 1980; Andreasen 1982) added the finishing touches to the concept by giving formal definitions of positive and negative symptoms: positive symptoms were those distinguished by the presence of an abnormal phenomenon, whereas negative symptoms were characterized by the absence or diminution of a normal function.

In its original form the proposal of positive and negative symptoms merely alleged the existence of two separate constellations of symptoms in schizophrenia. However, it rapidly came to be realized that the distinction had potentially wide implications. Positive symptoms appeared to come and go and were closely bound up with acute episodes. Negative symptoms, on the other hand, seemed to be relatively enduring and appeared to underlie much of the chronic disability of schizophrenia. It thus became suspected that positive and negative symptoms had differing prognostic implications. There were also strong suggestions that the two types of symptom responded differentially to neuroleptic drug treatment (see Chapter 8). Finally, in an influential paper, Crow (1980) proposed that positive and negative symptoms might have different aetiologies, the former being due to a dopamine excess and the latter being the manifestation of an irreversible destructive process in the brain.

The positive:negative dichotomy currently casts its shadow across almost all areas of theory and research in schizophrenia. At its heart, nevertheless, the distinction is a clinical one, and it is on phenomenological grounds that its validity must be judged. A considerable literature has accumulated on the clinical status of the concept. Much of the work has employed the statistical approach of analysis of correlations: if positive and negative symptoms represent separate syndromes, then in groups of patients presence of one positive symptom should be associated with presence of other positive symptoms. The same should also be true for negative symptoms. Positive and negative symptoms, however, should be uncorrelated with each other.

Intercorrelations among negative symptoms

Several studies (Andreasen and Olsen 1982; Bilder *et al.* 1985; Kulhara *et al.* 1986; Mortimer *et al.* 1989) have rated negative symptoms, using a variety of scales, in groups of schizophrenic patients ranging from 32 to 100 in number. These studies all found that negative symptoms including lack of volition, affective flattening, poverty of speech, impoverishment of thought, and self neglect were intercorrelated to a statistically significant extent, usually highly so. Further supporting evidence was provided in two studies (Andreasen and Olsen 1982; Kay *et al.* 1986), which found that negative symptoms had a high internal consistency, using a special statistical measure of this (Cronbach's alpha).

Intercorrelations among positive symptoms

In three of the above studies (Andreasen and Olsen 1982; Kulhara *et al.* 1986; Mortimer *et al.* 1990) the interrelationships of delusions, hallucinations and formal thought disorder were examined. Strong positive correlations were found between delusions and hallucinations. The correlations of formal thought disorder with these two symptoms, however, appeared more variable, ranging from being barely significant to being somewhat more weakly significant than that between delusions and hallucinations. Bizarre behaviour (Andreasen and Olsen 1982; Kulhara *et al.* 1986) and catatonic symptoms (Mortimer *et al.* 1990) were found to be significantly correlated with formal thought disorder, but only marginally correlated or uncorrelated with delusions and hallucinations. The internal consistency of positive symptoms was found to be modest in one study (Andreasen and Olsen 1982) but high in a second (Kay *et al.* 1986).

Some symptoms do not seem to fit into the positive:negative framework very well. For example, inappropriate affect was found to be associated with neither negative symptoms nor positive symptoms by Mortimer *et al.* (1989). Poverty of content of speech, considered on theoretical grounds to be a negative symptom by Andreasen (1979*a*, 1982), seems empirically to be more closely aligned to positive symptoms: it has been found to correlate poorly with other negative symptoms while being significantly associated with delusions, hallucinations, and other aspects of formal thought disorder (Andreasen and Olsen 1982; Mortimer *et al.* 1990).

Correlations between positive and negative symptoms

This question has been examined at least eight times (Owens and Johnstone 1980; Andreasen and Olsen 1982; Lewine *et al.* 1983; Rosen *et al.* 1984; Pogue-Geile and Harrow 1985; Kay *et al.* 1986; Kulhara *et al.* 1986; Mortimer *et al.* 1990). The study populations have comprised acute, chronic, or mixed cases; the numbers have varied from 32 to over 500; positive and negative symptoms have been rated individually or in some cases summed to form overall syndrome scores. Without exception, these studies have found no correlations between positive and negative symptoms. Two studies (Andreasen and Olsen 1982; Kulhara *et al.* 1986) in fact found moderate inverse correlations between individually rated positive and negative symptoms.

The study of Mortimer *et al.* (1990) also suggested that the positive: negative dichotomy might extend to encompass a greater breadth of symptoms than it is customarily applied to. The large category of thought, language, and communication disorders, which includes formal thought disorder and also poverty of speech was found to separate unequivocally into positive and negative components. There were indications that catatonic phenomena could be similarly subdivided into abnormalities characterized by the presence of an abnormality, such as stereotypies, mannerisms, and excitement, and those where there was the absence or diminution of a normal function, such as slowness, blocking, and stupor.

Factor analysis (which is described in detail in Chapter 4) provides another way of testing the hypothesis that positive symptoms associate with other positive symptoms, negative symptoms with other negative symptoms, but that the two syndromes are independent of each other. This has been carried out in a number of studies (for example, Kulhara *et al.* 1986; Liddle 1987; Mortimer *et al.* 1990; Arndt *et al.* 1991). Each time clear-cut negative and positive factors have been isolated and have accounted for the two largest proportions of the variance respectively. Unexpectedly, though, a third factor has also emerged in every study; this has invariably been smaller but has still accounted for a significant proportion of the variance. Although somewhat variable this third factor tends to include inappropriate affect, poverty of content of speech, other elements of formal thought disorder, and sometimes bizarre behaviour (see Table 2.3).

It has to be concluded from these studies that the validity of the positive: negative dichotomy is established beyond any reasonable doubt. In schizophrenia, there are two separate constellations of symptoms which, although they may be simultaneously present in a particular patient at a particular time, are entirely unrelated to each other in the likelihood with which they occur. At the same time, what initially appeared to be minor irregularities concerning the correlations of inappropriate affect and poverty of content of speech have come to assume major significance with the application of factor analysis. One interpretation of these findings is that there exists a third syndrome in schizophrenia, which Liddle (1987) has termed the 'disorganisation' syndrome. There is certainly a precedent for this, in that both Kraepelin (1913a) and Bleuler (1911) considered that a splitting and fragmentation of mental functions was an important part of the clinical picture of schizophrenia. Alternatively, as suggested by Mortimer *et al.* (1990), it could be that, while negative symptoms form a tightly knit, 'core' of symptoms in schizophrenia, there are other clusters of symptoms such as delusions, hallucinations, and 'positive' formal thought disorder which have in common an independence from negative symptoms but which are only loosely associated with one another. At the present time there seems to be no way to choose between these alternatives.

Conclusion

One of the most enduring controversies surrounding schizophrenia has been whether it should be considered one or a group of disorders. The clear message of this chapter is that schizophrenia resists sharp divisions of any

Table 2.3   Factor analyses of symptoms in groups of schizophrenic patients

Factor 1	Factor 2	Factor 3
Liddle (1987) *45 patients*		
Poverty of speech	Voices speaking to	Inappropriate affect
Decreased spontaneous	patient	Poverty of content of
movement	Delusions of	speech
Unchanging facial	persecution	Tangentiality
expression	Delusions of	Derailment
Paucity of expressive	reference	Pressure of speech
gestures		Distractibility
Affective non-responsivity		
Lack of vocal inflection		
Mortimer et al. (1990) *62 patients*		
Neglected appearance	Delusions of control	Inappropriate affect
Lack of movement/	Thought alienation	Poverty of content of
gestures	Persecutory ideas	speech
Poverty of speech	Grandiose ideas	Incoherent speech
Impoverished thought	Auditory	Other delusions
Flattening of affect	hallucinations	
Lack of volition		
Arndt. et al. (1991) *207 patients*		
Affective flattening	Hallucinations	Formal thought disorder
Alogia	Delusions	Bizarre behaviour
Avolition		
Anhedonia		
Attentional impairment		
Frith et al. (unpublished) *329 patients*		
Retardation of movement	Hallucinations	Inappropriate affect
Mutism	Delusions	Incoherence of speech
Flattening of affect		

kind. There are certainly genuine differences between acute and chronic schizophrenia, but it would be foolhardy to suggest that the two were somehow separate—the latter simply represents the later evolution of the former. The classical subtypes of schizophrenia, if they are worth distinguishing at all, have to be considered as nothing more than particularly conspicuous points along a continuum of presentations. The most robust clinical distinction in schizophrenia is the positive:negative dichotomy. This, however, applies to groups of symptoms rather than groups of patients; most patients show some combination of both syndromes and there are few who can be referred to as 'positive symptom' or 'negative symptom' schizophrenics. As yet, it has not become possible, as Bleuler hoped, to speak of the group of schizophrenias.

A corollary to this conclusion is that the different ways of subcategorizing schizophrenia are in some tantalizing and as yet ill-understood way complementary. The concepts of acute and chronic schizophrenia overlap with those of positive and negative symptoms, which in turn have some kind of connection with the paranoid and simple subtypes of the disorder. In the same way, hebephrenia is conceptually related to the disorganization syndrome, and their common theme of splitting and fragmentation of mental functions is at the heart of Bleuler's idea of fundamental symptoms. But at present, a way of weaving these strands together to form a coherent and comprehensive account remains elusive.

3

The natural history
of schizophrenia

The basic epidemiological facts about schizophrenia are reasonably well established. As reviewed by Hare (1982) and Shur (1988), the incidence of the disorder lies between the limits of 13 and 70 per 100 000 of the population. Its prevalence is somewhere in the region of 1 to 7 per 1000. The lifetime risk of developing the disorder is of the order of 0.7 per cent to 2 per cent. Some of the variability of these figures may be attributable to methodological differences in the studies which have been carried out, and some of it in all probability reflects fluctuations in the occurrence of schizophrenia in different parts of the world. In any event, when rigorous diagnostic criteria are applied, the variation is markedly reduced and the frequency of the core schizophrenic syndrome becomes fairly uniform worldwide (Jablensky 1987).

The demographics of schizophrenia are also well understood. The disorder develops most commonly in early adult life, its frequency decreasing steadily in both directions outside the age bracket of twenty to thirty-five. Broadly speaking, men and women are affected equally, but the age distribution differs so that the peak age of onset is five to ten years later for women compared with men (Lewine 1980). Schizophrenia is associated with single status and reduced rates of reproduction, and is also disproportionately represented among lower socio-economic classes. The available evidence suggests that these latter findings are consequences of the disorder rather than being of causal significance (Shur 1988).

An area where hard data are, however, conspicuously lacking concerns the course of schizophrenia. In spite of follow-up studies which can be numbered in the hundreds, and reviews of these which have appeared at regular intervals, what the future holds for an individual who has been diagnosed as schizophrenic remains uncertain and often a matter of dispute. A degree of order can be brought to the large and somewhat ramshackle literature on this issue by breaking it down into its three constituent parts. These are *the pattern of course of schizophrenia, its long-term outcome*, and *its prognosis*.

The pattern of course of schizophrenia

Whilst maintaining that the trajectory of schizophrenia was always towards deterioration, Kraepelin and Bleuler were the first to acknowledge the variety of routes the disorder could take in its downhill course. Kraepelin (1913*a*) observed that some cases progressed slowly and insidiously to result in a profound, if outwardly not very striking, destruction of the personality. In other cases, symptoms broke out suddenly and were followed by a severe decline which became evident within a few months. But most typically, the course was interrupted by remissions of greater or lesser completeness, which could last days, weeks, months, sometimes years, and occasionally decades. According to Bleuler (1911), advances, halts, exacerbations, and remissions were seen at all stages. The evolution of symptoms could be smooth, along a regular flat curve, or take place via an irregular series of thrusts. Deterioration could progress relentlessly, take place in a series of steps, or develop all at once; sometimes it supervened early and sometimes late in the course of the disease.

The detailed cataloguing of the various patterns of evolution of schizophrenia fell to later investigators. These studies (reviewed by WHO 1979; see also Ciompi 1980; Harding 1988) all arrived at remarkably similar conclusions. One of them, however, stands head and shoulders above the others. This is the monumental personal follow-up of 208 schizophrenic patients which Manfred Bleuler (Bleuler's son) carried on for over 20 years (Bleuler 1974, 1978).

In Bleuler's study, the diagnosis of schizophrenia was made in a rigorous and fair-minded way which anticipated present day criterion-based approaches. He considered that, by virtue of their showing at least three different classes of symptoms, 185 of his patients would also be likely to be diagnosed as schizophrenic by other schools of psychiatry. Of the 23 in whom the diagnosis might be open to debate, nine had 'serious manic-depressive manifestations'; in three the illness began at the age of 60; and in nine alcoholic hallucinosis, reactive psychosis, or paranoid psychosis was a realistic differential diagnosis.

The method of follow-up was thorough. What Bleuler termed 'objective and complete' data were obtained on the patients' further hospitalizations, their functioning outside hospital, their domestic circumstances, whether and how successfully they were employed, how well relatives and carers judged them to be, and also how well Bleuler himself judged them to be. 'Non-objective and incomplete' information was also gathered: this consisted of impressions that were gained about the patients' relationships with their relatives, how these relationships were affected by the patient's illness, and the influence of various life events on the patients' mental state and functioning.

On the basis of this work, Bleuler came to three broad conclusions. The first was that, in the sense of activity of the disease process, schizophrenia tended to run a very prolonged course. Years and even decades after they became ill, patients still occasionally underwent acute exacerbations of florid symptoms. Sometimes, in addition, they became generally more agitated or tranquil, or abnormalities in dressing, eating, personal hygiene, etc. developed or subsided. Not infrequently, there were also more gradual trends towards overall improvement or further deterioration.

Bleuler's second conclusion was that, notwithstanding this, a substantial majority of cases eventually reached a certain stability in their condition. Twenty years after the follow-up began, three-quarters of the 208 patients had reached a position where their clinical state had persisted relatively unchanged for at least five years. In such patients it was rare to encounter any marked change subsequently, although minor fluctuations could and did take place.

Finally, Bleuler came to the conclusion that schizophrenia could not be considered to be a progressive disorder in the strict sense of the term. A more accurate view would be that it was a disorder which evolved over a period of around five years, and afterwards showed no further deterioration and, if anything, a tendency to improve. Even this statement was only true in the statistical sense: after five years nearly a third of the sample continued to experience worsenings of their condition, but these were matched by an equivalent number who showed improvement. There was, as it were, a dynamic equilibrium, so that the ratio of improved to unimproved patients was the same at 20 years as it was at five years, although the improved and unimproved groups would not contain all the same patients.

In addition to these general conclusions, Bleuler found that in over 90 per cent of cases the course of schizophrenia followed one of seven patterns. Typically, the course that was going to be taken became established within a few years; although one course could change into another, such conversions were the exception rather than the rule. The different courses could be conveniently classified into two main types, simple (continuous) and undulating (intermittent), each of which had a number of subtypes. A small minority fell into a third, atypical or miscellaneous category. These disease courses are described below, and are illustrated schematically in Fig. 3.1.

Simple (continuous) courses

Psychoses in this group could begin abruptly or insidiously, but were characterized by a steady progression with little or no remission.

Acute onset leading to severe, moderate, or mild end states: These included so-called catastrophic illnesses, which were very uncommon and accounted for only 1 per cent of cases. Cases which began abruptly and proceeded

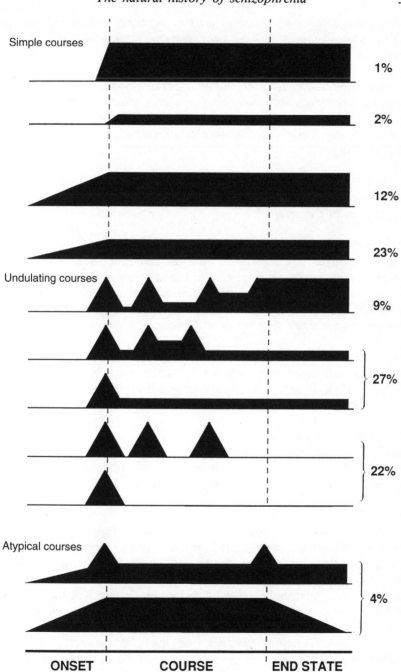

Fig. 3.1 The disease courses of schizophrenia (from Bleuler 1978).

rapidly and without remission to mild or moderate end states were only slightly more frequent at 2 per cent. Generally, such patients had hebephrenic or sometimes catatonic presentations.

Chronic onset leading to severe end states: These accounted for 12 per cent of cases. These patients' illnesses evolved slowly and smoothly to chronic severe terminal states. They consisted principally of hebephrenic, paranoid, and simple schizophrenics, but some catatonic patients also followed this type of course.

Chronic onset leading to mild and moderate end states: This group consisted principally of late onset paranoid schizophrenias and accounted for 23 per cent of the sample.

Undulating (intermittent) courses

These comprised psychoses with more or less acute onsets which were followed by incomplete recovery, or complete recovery followed by further episodes with incomplete recovery. There was also a significant number of cases showing one or more acute episodes from which a complete recovery was made each time.

Undulating course leading to mild, moderate, and severe end states: These psychoses were made up of hebephrenic, catatonic, and paranoid schizophrenics. They accounted for 9 per cent of cases (progressing to severe end states) and 27 per cent (progressing to moderate or mild end states).

Undulating courses leading to recovery: These 'benign' or 'phasic' psychoses were composed principally of acute catatonias, schizoaffective presentations, and states presenting with 'acute delirious' features. At 22 per cent of cases they were not at all uncommon.

Atypical courses

In addition to the above six types, various other types of evolution were occasionally seen. These accounted for less than 5 per cent of cases overall, and they tended to be individually variable. The most common example was the patient who started to experience acute exacerbations after a previous prolonged simple chronic course. A less common type was the patient in whom substantial improvement gradually took place after a chronic state had existed for many years.

One further finding of Bleuler's study deserves comment. This was a tendency towards late improvement in schizophrenia, a phenomenon which was seen especially among chronically hospitalized patients. Some patients, who had not uttered coherent sentences for years, were observed to start to speak normally on certain occasions. Others took up social activities when they had previously always been apathetic. Still others would suddenly begin to behave in a normal way on leave, during hospital entertainments, or whilst suffering from a physical illness. Occasionally, despite years of unrelenting illness, something approximating to recovery could be seen. Examples included a woman who, after 28 years of illness culminating in chronic hospitalization, improved to the point where the diagnosis of schizophrenia was no longer considered applicable; she was left, however, with a moderate memory impairment. Twenty-one years after his illness began, and after he had developed severe deterioration accompanied by stereotypies, a male patient began to take interest in many things, read the newspapers, speak to his relatives, and attend church. From the age of 30 a female patient gradually became more and more deluded and developed increasingly disturbed behaviour until she required institutional care. At the age of 65 she unexpectedly improved, showed no trace of self-neglect, and became devoted to her grandchildren. Nevertheless she remained in hospital and showed no insight into her illness. Two patients with more episodic illnesses also showed prolonged remissions after stormy courses. One showed a spectacular response to neuroleptic treatment after fourteen years of chronic hospitalization, and thereafter continued to improve to a point where he was regarded as being better than he was before he became ill.

The outcome of schizophrenia

While Kraepelin and Bleuler regarded schizophrenia as a disorder which led inexorably to deterioration, at the same time they recognized that the ultimate degree of this could vary from the slight to the very profound. On the question of whether full recovery ever took place, their views were marked by equivocation and paradox: Kraepelin (1913*a*) found spontaneous improvement to the point where the patient could be regarded as 'completely well without reservation' in 16 (about 3 per cent) of his patients. This lasted longer than 5 years in four of these cases; in one it lasted 29 years; but in each case there was ultimately a return of symptoms followed by the development of deterioration. He therefore preferred to talk of remissions rather than recovery. Nevertheless, he felt that if the disease process could remain quiescent for nearly thirty years the possibility of permanent recovery could not be denied. Bleuler (1911) stated flatly that he had never released a patient in whom distinct signs of the disorder were not still present. However, in describing what he referred to as far-reaching improvements, he gave examples of patients who between episodes became poets, judges, and academics; one patient qualified as a doctor, another maintained an international scientific reputation.

Kraepelin (1913*a*), in particular, was at pains to point out the pitfalls associated with trying to establish the recovery rate of schizophrenia. When patients who appeared to have been cured were found, there was always a lingering doubt about the diagnosis, especially if there had only been a single episode of active symptoms. Another problem was defining what exactly was meant by recovery. The dividing line between complete mental well being and a personality change which might be missed on casual examination but which was obvious to the patient's relatives, and between this and mild but definite deterioration, was not always clear and might, in the final analysis, be arbitrary. Conversely, abnormalities that might have been present before a patient became ill could later be wrongly ascribed to the effects of the illness. Finally, the length of the follow-up period was a crucial factor. If this was too short an artificially favourable picture would be painted.

There have been a very large number of formal follow-up studies of schizophrenia which, despite being subjected to several critical reviews (for example, Blair 1940; Stephens 1978; WHO 1979; Ram *et al.* 1992), have produced no consensus on the figures for outcome. Possibly their most important result has been to clarify what the requirements for such studies are — often by not fulfilling them themselves. The ground rules that have emerged seem to comprise the following.

1. A sample size which is large enough to permit meaningful analysis needs to be used.

2. The patients need to be representative of schizophrenia as a whole, and should not, for example, consist only of patients who have achieved discharge from hospital.

3. The diagnosis should not just be taken from the hospital case-notes, official records, and the like, but should be made independently and in a critical way.

4. The ascertainment of cases should be made early in the course of the illness. This is to ensure that the diagnosis is really made on the basis of the presenting clinical picture and is contaminated as little as possible by information about the course subsequently pursued.

5. The follow-up should be by personal interview with the patients in as many cases as possible, and at the very least in all those who are not chronically hospitalized. The use of labour saving devices such as postal questionnaires (and more recently telephone interviews) is grounds for immediate disqualification of a study.

If only studies which meet these minimal requirements are selected, their numbers are reduced to a handful. The studies described below all had the following features in common. They included at least 100 patients at the point of entry. The sample was based on patients admitted to hospital, a procedure which can reasonably be assumed to capture the vast majority of patients who develop schizophrenia. While making allowances for changes in diagnostic fashion, the diagnosis was made independently and based on the presence of florid symptoms in a way consistent with modern concepts of schizophrenia. Finally, the follow-up was by personal interview, at least of those patients who were out of hospital. In addition, it would have been desirable to restrict the study population to first admissions. This is not included as a requirement because it has been criticized as impracticable (for example by Bleuler 1978). Instead the stipulation has been made either that the studies stated (or at least implied) that their patients were early in the course of their illness, or that they examined a subgroup of first admissions separately.

The studies selected fall naturally into three groups according to the time period in which they were carried out. The first group comprises those dating from the period before the introduction of neuroleptic drugs. The second consists of one study which bridges the preneuroleptic and neuroleptic eras. The third group consists essentially of contemporary studies in which neuroleptic drug treatment, criterion-based diagnosis, and prospective design have become a fact of life. The results of all the studies are summarized in Table 3.1.

Studies from the preneuroleptic era

Two very early investigations are included here: Langfeldt's (1937) study of 100 patients followed-up for 7–10 years, and Malamud and Render's (1938) study of 177 patients followed-up for 6–8 years. Out of a series of large-scale studies by Astrup and co-workers, that of Holmboe and Astrup (1957) is selected as the simplest, and the one from which overall outcome figures can be most easily extracted. Finally, the careful study of Johanson (1958) is included even though it was restricted to male patients.

In these studies the diagnosis of schizophrenia was generally based on Bleulerian fundamental symptoms, although the presence of florid symptoms such as delusions and hallucinations was also explicitly or implicitly required. All the patients in each study were diagnosed by a single individual, either one of the study investigators or the director of the hospital at the time. In each of the studies attempts were made to exclude diagnostically doubtful cases and cases with organic disorders; Johanson, however, included some patients with low intelligence. The patients in the studies of Holmboe and Astrup and Johanson were all first admissions, but there was an implication of lack of chronicity in the other two studies.

Two studies which have regularly featured in other reviews are not included here. The study of Mayer-Gross (1932) is excluded because nearly half the sample died of starvation in the First World War, which intervened during the follow-up period (Stephens 1978). The often-cited study of

Schizophrenia and Related Syndromes

Table 3.1 Outcome studies in schizophrenia

	Percentage rates			
	Complete recovery	Social recovery	Improved	Unimproved or worse
Preneuroleptic era				
Langfeldt (1937) 100 followed-up 7–10 years	17	4	13	66
Malamud and Render (1938) 160 followed-up 5–10 years	15	9	12	64
Holmboe and Astrup (1957) 255 followed-up 6–18 years	29	9	20	42
Johanson (1958) 82 followed-up 10–18 years	2	9	26	63
Bridging neuroleptic era				
Bleuler (1978) 152 reached stable end-state 20 years	← 20 →		33	47
Neuroleptic era				
WHO (1979) 543 followed-up 2 years	26	25	20	29
WHO (Sartorius *et al.* 1987) 513 followed-up 5–7 years (preliminary results)	← 61 →		← 39 →	
Shepherd *et al.* (1989) 107 followed-up 5 years	16	32	9	43

The outcome groups are somewhat variable between studies, but typically include some or all of the following.

Complete recovery: No active symptoms, no signs of deterioration, working at previous level, no or minimal social impairment, only one episode of illness.

Social recovery: No or minimal active symptoms, minimal signs of deterioration, for example in affect, working, no severe social impairment, may have been more than one episode of illness.

Improved: Ongoing active symptoms and/or obvious signs of deterioration, may or may not be able to work at lower level, out of hospital.

Unimproved or worse: Moderate or severe ongoing active symptoms and signs of deterioration, unable to work, may or may not require long-term hospitalization.

Eitinger, Laane, and Langfeldt (1958) separated the patient sample into 'schizophrenic' and 'schizophreniform' groups in a way which did not permit their recombination.

The findings of two of the studies, Langfeldt's (1937) and Malamud and Render's (1938) are in close agreement. In both, slightly over one-fifth of the patients fell into the two best outcome groups, with a large majority being in the completely recovered category. Similarly, in both studies somewhere in the region of two-thirds were found to be unimproved or worse, with most of these requiring chronic hospitalization. The other two studies found somewhat differing percentages of patients in the worst outcome groups, and they diverged considerably on the proportion showing a good outcome. In Holmboe and Astrup's study over one-third of patients were considered to have made complete or nearly complete recoveries. In Johanson's, the corresponding figure was 11 per cent, and most of these patients were not completely well.

In spite of these differences, it can be concluded that in the days before any effective treatments for schizophrenia were available, the outlook was not nearly as gloomy as Kraepelin and Bleuler thought. After several years of illness, 20 per cent of patients – plus or minus 10 per cent – can expect to present a picture of full, or at least social recovery.

Studies bridging the preneuroleptic and neuroleptic eras

Of the studies carried out during this period, the outstanding example is that of Manfred Bleuler described above. His diagnostic criteria were ahead of their time. All the patients were diagnosed by Bleuler himself and followed-up by him personally. Not all of his sample of 208 patients were first admissions – in fact some had long prior durations of illness – however, he separately examined 68 patients who entered the study at the time of their first hospitalization. Many of the patients had been treated with neuroleptics, but Bleuler stated that in all cases this was only on an intermittent basis, when they were actively psychotic.

Several other studies date to this era, but are excluded from consideration for one reason or another. The study of Huber *et al.* (1975, 1980) is simply too difficult to evaluate: these authors employed an idiosyncratic method of categorizing outcome and it is difficult to be sure what they meant by remission. Much of the detail of this study is also not available in English. In the study of Stephens (Stephens and Astrup 1965; Stephens 1970, 1978) the sample was based on patients discharged from hospital, and so suffers from ascertainment bias. The diagnosis was taken from the case-notes, and it was not specified in what proportion of cases the follow-up was made by personal interview. The study of Tsuang and Dempsey (1979) has also been excluded, but this is essentially for technical reasons: because of the very long duration of follow-up (30–40 years), personal interview was only possible for 93 of the 186 patients. Also, the patients were divided into only three outcome groups, recovered, improved, and unimproved.

In Bleuler's study, it was considered that 152 of the 208 patients had reached a stable end state of at least five years duration by the end of the 20 year follow-up period. Of these, 20 per cent fell into his recovered category, which corresponds to the complete and social recovery groups of earlier studies. Nearly half were in the two worst outcome groups. The findings in 68 patients who entered the study at the time of their first hospital admission were slightly better but not markedly different.

These results are much the same as those of the studies carried out earlier. Particularly striking was the finding that the same proportion, one-fifth of cases, was either fully or socially recovered. This is despite the longer follow-up period in Bleuler's study, and the availability of neuroleptic treatment for some of the time.

Studies in the neuroleptic era

Recent work on the outcome of schizophrenia is dominated by the very large-scale, diagnostically sophisticated, and prospective 2 and 5-7 year follow-ups undertaken as part of the International Pilot Study of Schizophrenia (WHO 1979; Sartorius *et al.* 1987). The only other study which can be included is the smaller, but otherwise equally rigorous 5 year follow-up of Shepherd *et al.* (1989).

A number of studies have been excluded. The study of Bland and Orn (1978) was too small to be included, consisting of only 50 patients, of whom seven were not be traced. The study of Biehl *et al.* (1986) was methodologically superior, but likewise too small at 70 patients at the point of entry. Small numbers and other methodological idiosyncrasies also make some other recent studies unusable (Carone *et al.* 1991; Breier *et al.* 1991; Marengo *et al.* 1991). Perhaps the most surprising omission is the study of Brown *et al.* (1966). Although this followed large numbers of patients and was meticulous in design, the focus was on social outcome to the exclusion of all else: the follow-up interviews were carried out by a social worker rather than a psychiatrist, who interviewed a relative in preference to the patient.

In both the International Pilot Study of Schizophrenia and the study of Shepherd *et al.* the diagnosis of schizophrenia was made on clinical grounds, but with the benefit of very detailed mental state information from the Present State Examination. Neither study was restricted to first admissions. However, the International Pilot Study included only patients with a duration of symptoms of 5 years or less, and Shepherd *et al.* analysed the outcome separately for their 49 first admissions. In contrast to earlier studies, formal ratings of clinical and social outcome were made, and these were combined according to a fixed scheme to arrive at overall outcome groups.

The results of the two studies were highly consistent. In the International Pilot Study 51 per cent of the patients at 2 years, rising to 61 per cent at 5 years were in the best two outcome groups. In the Shepherd *et al.* study 48 per cent were in the best two outcome groups (this rose to 55 per cent if only first admissions were considered). The two poor outcome groups are not strictly comparable because of methodological differences in the studies, but there is a measure of agreement between them that there was a corresponding shift of outcome away from the most severe end of the spectrum.

On the face of it, schizophrenia seems to have undergone a substantial lessening in severity over the last 20 to 30 years, with the proportion of patients showing a good or excellent outcome appearing to have at least doubled. It is not likely that this difference is merely a function of shorter follow-up period in the later studies. The two studies from the preneuroleptic era which had the most consistent results both had follow-up periods ranging from 5–10 years. It does not seem credible that recovery rates could fall so precipitously over the second 5 years as compared to the first (particularly in view of Bleuler's conclusion referred to earlier, that the evolution of schizophrenia tends to come to a halt after an average of about 5 years).

A more important difference that the International Pilot Study and the study of Shepherd *et al.* show from earlier studies lies in the way in which the outcome figures were derived. Both studies employed structured interviews covering symptoms and social function, which were combined according to a set of rules to arrive at an outcome categorization. In the earlier studies, the assessments were made according to clinical impression, which although it was independent and anchored to objective variables such as employment and lack of hospital admissions, still relied heavily on unquantifiable factors such as judgement and experience. Johnstone (personal communication) has suggested that some or all of the apparent improvement in outcome may be attributable to two different senses of the term recovery that these two methods entail—on the one hand describing the patient who shows, in Bleuler's (1911) phrase, a full *restitutio ad intregrum*, and on the the the other, the patient who is free of symptoms and shows good occupational and social adjustment, but who may have fallen a long way from his or her previous level of functioning. Johnston (1991) recently completed her own 5–10 year follow-up of 328 patients with schizophrenia. This study cannot be used to calculate outcome figures, but some of the findings tell their own story. Less than 20 per cent of the patients were in full time work, less than 50 per cent were regarded as fully independent by their relatives, 60 per cent were single, 60 per cent had no confiding relationship, and many lived alone, with their parents, or with other supporting relatives.

If there has been a genuine improvement in the outcome of schizophrenia, there are two strong candidates for the explanation of this. The first is that the disorder itself has undergone a change in severity, evolving over decades into a more attenuated form. This was postulated to be the case by Manfred Bleuler who concluded from his own observations that there had been a decline in the frequency of 'catastrophic' presentations of schizophrenia in the first half of the century. However, this view is not easy to reconcile with the finding of almost exactly similar rates of recovery in the two earliest outcome studies and Bleuler's own study carried out thirty years later. The other explanation is that an effective treatment for schizophrenia has become available. This is highly plausible and fits with the timing of the improvement in outcome; otherwise, however, it lacks any definitive support. These issues are discussed further by Harrison and Mason (1993).

The prognosis of schizophrenia

It is clear from the preceding two sections that schizophrenia pursues an erratic course to issue ultimately in anything from complete recovery to profound incapacity. In such circumstances, it would be desirable to be able to make predictions about the long term course from features present at the early stages. Research into prognostic factors in schizophrenia has certainly been sustained and intense, but it is far less clear that it has had any great success. The literature is perhaps most easily considered in the three successive stages it can be regarded as having fallen into.

The era of clinical impression

Although informed chiefly by the authoritative views of Kraepelin and Bleuler, these authors were, in fact, uncharacteristically reticent on the matter of prognosis in schizophrenia. Kraepelin (1913a) singled out a number of symptoms, the appearance of which often announced the beginning of the end for hope of improvement. These included flattening of affect, fixed mannerisms and stereotypies, especially when simple, and the appearance of abrupt episodes of excitement or moodiness. He also believed that the subtype diagnosis had prognostic implications, but that the relationships were complex. As described in Chapter 2, catatonic schizophrenics showed the highest rates of remission, but also had the highest frequency of severe deteriorations. Paranoid patients, on the other hand, hardly ever had full remissions, but in general they did not go on to develop the most severe forms of deterioration. Hebephrenic patients had an outcome which was intermediate between the other two types. Regarding general factors, only insidious onset stood out as definitely unfavourable. Age and sex affected the outcome only indirectly: being female and having a later age of onset predisposed to paranoid presentations, and hence to development of a less severe terminal state.

Bleuler (1911) had little to add on the prognostic value of individual symptoms. He agreed that affective flattening conferred a poor prognosis, as did catatonic symptoms, although not all of them — waxy flexibility and negativism were not necessarily sinister signs in his experience. Grandiose delusions were also often but not always a sign of poor outcome. Bleuler also considered that patients with a schizoid premorbid personality tended to have a poor outcome, and he thought that those with a family history of mental illness underwent the greatest deterioration (cited by Langfeldt 1937). Bleuler's main contribution, though, was to examine the the the way in which subtype diagnosis affected the prognosis in a systematic way. He found that paranoid schizophrenics had the best outcome, showing a high frequency of mild deterioration (65 per cent) and a low frequency of severe deterioration (19 per cent). Hebephrenics were next in order, showing slightly less in the way of mild deterioration (58 per cent but no difference in the rate of severe deterioration (20 per cent). Catatonic schizophrenics showed the worst outcome: the rate of mild deterioration was much the same as for hebephrenics (57 per cent), but severe deterioration was considerably more common (30 per cent). Overall, it was noteworthy how small the differences were.

The era of schizophreniform psychosis

The second and longest phase of prognostic thinking was ushered in by Langfeldt (1937). As part of the follow-up study of schizophrenia described above, Langfeldt took the trouble to examine the initial presentation of each of the patients as it had been documented in the case-notes. In addition to paranoid, hebephrenic, and catatonic cases and those showing combinations of these, he found 13 cases which were difficult to classify. In all of these patients the diagnosis was 'unmistakeable schizophrenia', and all had florid symptoms, showing one or more of delusions, auditory hallucinations, and catatonic phenomena. Nevertheless, the picture tended to be distinctive. In several, although it would have been difficult to construe the overall presentation as affective, there was a pronounced expansive, religious, guilty, or nihilistic theme to the psychosis; sometimes both grandiose and depressive delusions were simultaneously present. Typically, the delusions had a vague and shifting character and the hallucinations lacked a 'massive' (that is bizarre and alien) quality. A degree of clouding of consciousness was present in some cases. In a few there were hysterical or hypochondriacal features.

On follow-up 7–10 years later, 11 out of these 13 atypical cases were found to fall into the 'fully recovered' category. The other two were considered to be 'cured with defects'. This was in contrast to the 87 typical patients, of whom only six could be regarded as completely recovered and two cured with defects. The outcome of the atypical patients was so radically different from the rest that it almost seemed as if schizophrenia contained a small group of patients who were quite different from the majority, both in terms of presenting symptoms and long term prognosis. Langfeldt coined the term schizophreniform psychosis to describe this group of patients. A description of one of his original cases is reproduced in Fig. 3.2.

Very shortly afterwards, Kant (1940, 1941a, b), working independently, reached similar conclusions to Langfeldt. A number of other studies of the same kind were reviewed by Vaillant (1962), who likewise concluded that schizophrenic patients with good and poor prognosis appeared to be distinguishable at the time of their initial presentation. According to Vaillant, some or all of six features were repeatedly associated with recovery in these studies: family history of affective psychosis (usually depression), normal rather than schizoid premorbid personality, acute or relatively acute onset, presence of a precipitating event, presence of confusion or disorientation during the episode of illness, and presence of affective symptoms, particularly depression. These, along with Langfeldt's lack of 'massiveness' of the delusions and hallucinations (which became converted into a concept of 'understandability'), became the defining characteristics of schizophreniform, or good prognosis schizophrenia.

This work left unsettled the nature of the relationship between schizophreniform psychosis and schizophrenia proper. The strong view, which was implied by Langfeldt but only stated openly by Robins and Guze (1970), was that they were separate disorders. Others, including Vaillant (1962) and also Langfeldt himself in his later work (for example Langfeldt 1956), adopted a more cautious position. They made statements to the effect that, while as a group the features of schizophreniform psychosis appeared to separate recovered from non-recovered schizophrenics to a considerable degree, none of them possessed great specificity in the individual case.

These competing interpretations are of course susceptible to testing. All that is necessary is to identify clear-cut cases of schizophrenia and schizophreniform psychosis at the time of their initial presentation, and then to follow their subsequent progress. If the two disorders are distinct, then their separation at follow-up should remain absolute (or nearly absolute as the initial clinical differentiation can not be expected to be perfect): most of the schizophreniform patients should show recovery, or at worst minor residual symptoms, whereas the schizophrenic group should show a wider spectrum of outcome, though always with some degree of deterioration being detectable. If on the other hand schizophreniform psychosis merely represents a cluster of individually unrelated prognostic variables, then the

One of Langfeldt's schizophreniform cases
(from Langfeldt 1937)

Case G.K. born 7/4/1890. Admitted 4/4/28. Discharged home 17/4/28.

Family: The mother has had a depressive illness.
Temperament and character in childhood and youth: Sociable, gentle, chatty, liked to associate with people. Often strikingly excited, conceited.

Onset of the disease: 7 years prior to admission to the Clinic he became depressed, anxious, frightened of people, nervous about the future, now and again wished he had never been born, but was not suicidal. The last three years did practically no work, went about in a continual state of restlessness and was somewhat fearful.

At the Psychiatric Clinic: Orientated, quite clear and easy to deal with. Hears whispers a long way off. Various fancies come to him, e.g. that he has been loved by an unmarried woman in the district. He fights on two flanks against powers of good and evil. Often afraid of being poisoned. Has had a feeling that someone followed him in the lanes with the intention of maiming him. Felt he was being libelled. The whispering voices say both good and bad things. Has, inter alia, conceived the idea that he is to preach the word of God. States that since the age of 20 he has had periods of despondency. During the past 7 years he has nearly always been despondent, had some religious doubts accompanied to some extent with ideas of eternal death. Says that he has seen many strange things during these years. 'There was something from the other side which he saw in a dream'. During his stay he showed no sign of hallucination or feeling of passivity. The ideas that people wished to injure him completely disappeared, he believed that they only wished to keep an eye on him if they could.

Further course: The patient himself writes on 20/5/33. 'I am much better. The nervousness with which I was afflicted has disappeared. I have worked practically every day for two years.' The County Medical Officer writes that since the patient ceased to be under public care on 15/8/31 he has been quite well.

Mental state in 1936 (at home): Quite open and approachable, talkative. Full insight into the period of his disease which he remembers very well. Believes that to a great extent the cause of his illness lies in financial worry during the past years. He began to worry and became sleepless. Remembers that he had an aversion to mixing with people and that he had a feeling that people followed him. Remembers that he believed people wished to do him harm. During the past 4–5 years he has been quite rid of these thoughts. But now and again he has brief periods in which he is deprimated. He now works as a master builder and has more than enough to do.

Fig. 3.2

At the mental examination he appeared somewhat dull in thinking, his memory was also slightly weakened. Moreover, it proved somewhat difficult for him to interpret proverbs, but he showed no disorder in thinking otherwise. Apart from this he revealed no mental defects.

Fig. 3.2   *contd.*

two groups should show considerable overlap, with the range of outcomes in schizophreniform psychosis being merely shifted towards recovery.

Several such studies have been carried out, most of which have been reviewed by Stephens (1978). The results of those whose methodology approximates to that of the outcome studies described earlier are summarized in Table 3.2. It is clear that the second rather than the first hypothesis is supported. Patients designated as 'schizophreniform', 'reactive', or 'good prognosis schizophrenia' at an early stage invariably fare better in the long term than those considered to show 'true', 'process', or 'poor prognosis' schizophrenia. However, in every study the differences are relative rather than absolute and in all cases a significant proportion of schizophreniform patients are found in the 'unimproved' category.

The era of empirical investigation

This third and current phase can also be considered to have begun with Langfeldt, whose 1937 study also contained the first formal examination of various factors which had been held to be of prognostic significance by Kraepelin, Bleuler, and other classical authors. Langfeldt was able to confirm the unfavourability of insidious onset, presence of catatonic symptoms, and pre-morbid schizoid personality. Age of onset was found to show complex interactions with outcome. Presence or absence of a family history of psychosis was, however, found to be irrelevant.

Later, in a replication and extension of this study, Langfeldt (1956) found that the relationship of prognosis in schizophrenia to a number of factors such as age, sex, intelligence, previous personality, family history of schizophrenia, rapidity of onset, precipitating stress, and individual symptoms was, in almost every case, less clear-cut than he had originally thought. At around the same time Astrup and co-workers (Holmboe and Astrup 1957; Astrup *et al.* 1962; Astrup and Noreik 1966) were coming to similar conclusions in a series of studies of their own. A number of other studies had findings which pointed in the same direction (Schofield *et al.* 1954; Simon and Wirt 1961).

With the schizophrenic:schizophreniform distinction having indicated

Table 3.2 Outcome in patients designated as schizophrenic and schizophreniform at initial presentation

	Percentage rates							
	Schizophreniform				Schizophrenia			
	Recovered	Improved	Unimproved		Recovered	Improved	Unimproved	
Achte (1967) (n = 57 and 89)	70	21	9		15	30	55	
Eitinger et al. (1958) (n = 44 and 110)	75	14	11		2	10	88	
Astrup and Noreik (1966) (n = 304 and 271)	26	46	28		6	10	84	
Stephens (1970) (n = 116 and 90)	35	61	4		7	39	54	

that predictions about outcome could be made in schizophrenia, but with the search for individual prognostic factors proving to be frustrating, the need was apparent for a thorough re-appraisal using modern diagnostic techniques and a prospective design. The opportunity for this has been afforded, once again, by the International Pilot Study of Schizophrenia (WHO 1979). This study had the benefit of large numbers (over 500 patients) and the advantage that the initial evaluation and re-evaluation was detailed and standardized. Its main disadvantage has been that so far only an analysis of the 2 year follow-up data has been made.

Initially, a set of 47 'predictor variables' was examined, which the previous literature had suggested might be of prognostic importance. These covered sociodemographic factors such as age, sex, and educational level; history factors, including mental illness in relatives, and preceding physical and psychiatric illness; and a number of factors pertaining to the illness at the time of initial evaluation, including type of onset and the broad characterization of clinical presentation.

The main finding was that no single factor, nor any combination of them accounted for the variation in course and outcome. Even when the factors which individually had the greatest predictive power were combined, only 26 per cent of the outcome variance could be explained. Addition of other predictors resulted in relatively small gains. These best predictors of 2 year outcome are given in Table 3.3.

Because this general approach proved to be unenlightening, the predictive power of the initial clinical picture was then focused on in more detail. This time the amount of outcome variance which could be explained rose to 68 per cent, indicating that patients with the best and worst outcomes at two years had patterns of presenting symptoms which were, to a considerable extent, distinguishable. Individual symptoms which were found to be predictive of good outcome at two years included some which were obvious concomitants of acute, florid presentations: perplexity, overactivity, derealization, and affective symptoms, especially depression. Some of those predicting poor outcome were associated with insidious onset and suggested a picture dominated by negative symptoms: flatness of affect, haughtiness, personality change, changes in interests and sexual behaviour, and social withdrawal. Some delusions, for example delusions of persecution were associated with a good outcome; others, for example fantastic delusions, were associated with poor outcome. Hallucinations showed no obvious affiliations, nor did first rank symptoms — some types of each were represented among the good and poor predictors. Some of the best predictors among symptoms are shown in Table 3.4, from which it is clear no immediately recognizable pattern emerges.

Overall, thinking on prognosis in schizophrenia appears to have gone round in a circle. From a small number of rather guarded statements by

Table 3.3 Best predictors of two year outcome in schizophrenia (general) (from WHO 1979)

Sociodemographic characteristics
Social isolation (poor)
High educational level (poor)
Widowed, divorced, or separated (poor)
Professional, managerial, or clerical occupation (good)

Past history characteristics
Past psychiatric treatment (poor)
Poor psychosexual adjustment (poor)
History of behaviour symptoms (poor)
Unfavourable environment (poor)
Previous contact with other agencies with psychiatric problems (good)

Characteristics of inclusion episode
Long prior duration of episode (poor)
Insidious onset (poor)
High score on flatness of affect (poor)
High score on psychophysical symptoms (good)
High score on indications of personality change (poor)

Table 3.4 Best predictors of two year outcome in schizophrenia (clinical) (from WHO 1979)

Good outcome	Poor outcome
Early waking	Suicidal thoughts
Overactivity	Flatness of affect
Ambivalence	Worries
Negativism	Change in sex behaviour
Derealization	Mutism
Speech impediments	Repetitive movements
Mannerisms	Fantastic delusions
Lability of affect	Speech dissociation
Delusions of persecution	Situational anxiety
	Haughtiness
	Social withdrawal

Kraepelin and Bleuler, it has progressed through a series of extravagant claims for the existence of a subgroup of good prognosis cases, to the current position where there seems to be good evidence that prognosis can be determined from the initial presentation, but that it is controlled by a hotchpotch of variables.

Conclusion

The message of this chapter is that, so far as its course is concerned, schizophrenia follows no rules but its own. Cases in which several acute episodes have been followed by full recovery cannot be relied on to remain free of deterioration indefinitely. Conversely, in cases which seem to have become hopeless, substantial improvement may later take place. To put it another way, a number of misconceptions about the natural history of schizophrenia need to be avoided. The first of these is that schizophrenia is a progressive disorder. The work of Manfred Bleuler makes it clear that a much more sophisticated view needs to be taken, one which may, in fact, have no parallels in the rest of medicine.

A second pitfall to be wary of is the concept of recovery in schizophrenia. Figures like 20 per cent 'recovered' or one-third who 'do well' always include patients who, while they may have no active psychotic symptoms, are able to work and function socially, and seem quite normal to their doctors, have undergone an unquestionable decline — which their relatives will often touchingly describe. With the recovery figures of 50 per cent and 60 per cent quoted in the most recent outcome studies, it is possible to wonder just how much astute clinical judgment about well being has been sacrificed to the objectivity of rating scales.

But it is in the area of prognosis that the most caution has to be exercised. It is sobering to realize how insubstantial terms like 'benign', 'good-prognosis', 'reactive', and 'schizophreniform' turn out to be when they are subjected to close scrutiny. The International Pilot Study of Schizophrenia makes it clear just how frustrating an exercise it can be to try to pin down the prognostic factors which are undoubtedly there.

4

The diagnosis of schizophrenia

Identifying diseases by means of their characteristic symptoms and signs is one of the cornerstones of medicine whose value is usually taken for granted. It therefore comes as something of a surprise to find that all those who have given the matter any thought have concluded that the concepts of disease and diagnosis are fraught with difficulties and uncertainties (see Kendell 1975; Clare 1980). Every attempt to capture the essential nature of disease – as suffering, as presence of a lesion, as biological disadvantage, etc. – has been found to be unsatisfactory; like health, disease eludes easy definition. Diagnosis is also a rather less straightforward process than it might appear. Theoretically, the classification of diseases into diagnostic categories, as with the classification of natural phenomena generally, is always less than perfect. The practical act of making diagnoses is of course less perfect still, being subject to human error and suffering rather more than might be wished from the vagaries of medical fashion.

In most branches of medicine, any such reservations about disease and diagnosis are easily brushed aside. In psychiatry, however, they cannot be ignored. The concept of disease begins to show signs of strain when it is applied to depression, anxiety, and personality disorder, and it falters badly when faced with conditions such as alcoholism and sexual deviation. The process of psychiatric diagnosis is complicated by the need to rely on a set of symptoms which do not lend themselves to accurate description. Worse still, making a psychiatric diagnosis tends not to have the clear-cut implications it does in the rest of medicine. In any functional disorder, the prognosis can be counted on to range from complete recovery to permanent disability, and treatment all too often runs the gamut of psychotherapy, tranquillizers, neuroleptics, antidepressants, and ECT. Psychiatry runs the risk of – and is regularly accused of – merely attaching labels which are meaningless or even pejorative.

It is schizophrenia, more than any other psychiatric disorder, at which such criticisms have been levelled. The reasons for this are not hard to find: its symptoms are legion, its presentations are diverse, its cause is unknown, and its response to treatment is unsatisfactory. In the 1960s and 1970s these criticisms reached extraordinary heights, when as the 'sacred symbol of psychiatry', schizophrenia was singled out for particular vilification and attack. This antipsychiatry movement ran its course and abated, but it left a legacy of disquiet about the nature of the disorder, its status as a distinct entity, and the foundations on which its diagnosis was based. One way of considering the issues that have been raised is to ask three questions, which need to be addressed in order. These are: *Does schizophrenia exist?*; *Is it separable from manic-depressive psychosis?*; and *Can it be diagnosed cross-sectionally?*

Does schizophrenia exist?

In the half-century or so after its introduction, the reputation of schizophrenia made the transition from comfortable respectability to distinct unsavouriness. The reasons for this decline are difficult to reconstruct, and were undoubtedly multiple. They ranged from purely academic concerns about the lack of clear boundaries from other psychotic disorders to, at the other extreme, a social and political stand against what was perceived as the incarceration and barbaric treatment applied to individuals who deviated from society's norms.

But perhaps the most important factor was historical, in the shape of an extraordinary sequence of events that unfolded in the USA. As documented by Blashfield (1984), in this country psychoanalysis and the psychodynamic tradition became the mainstream of psychiatric thought. With the assistance of influential figures such as Meyer and Menninger, the medical model of mental disorders was more or less openly rejected, diagnosis on the basis of presenting symptoms was disdained, and clinical decision-making, so far as there was any, was based on intuition and interpretations of patterns of interpersonal relationships. The diagnostic category of schizophrenia, in particular, was retained, but it was broadened drastically. This was apparently on the basis of an opinion expressed in passing by Bleuler (1911), that individuals with latent forms of schizophrenia, who showed far less in the way of manifest symptoms, were many times more frequent than fully developed cases. The concept of schizophrenia became so loose that it could be diagnosed in virtually anyone.

Eventually the credulity of some was strained too far and attempts were made to put American diagnostic practice to the test. In one study (Katz *et al.* 1969), an audience of American and British psychiatrists were shown a filmed interview with a young woman who described symptoms of anxiety and depression; she also gave an account of difficulties in relationships and the frustrations of attempting to become an actress. A third of the American psychiatrists, but none of the British, felt able to make a diagnosis of schizophrenia. In another study (Rosenhan 1973) eight volunteers posed as patients and sought admission to American psychiatric hospitals of varying prestigiousness. Each complained of a single symptom — hearing voices saying single words like 'empty', 'thud', and 'hollow' — and, apart from falsifying their names and employment, they gave an otherwise entirely truthful history. They all gained admission to hospital without difficulty, whereupon they behaved as normally as they could; at first they took notes secretly, but soon were able to do this openly as it became clear that no interest was being shown in this activity. In 11 of the 12 cases, the 'pseudopatients' were given a diagnosis of schizophrenia; one received a diagnosis of manic-depressive psychosis. In no cases was the deception detected by the hospital staff. On the other hand, 35 out of a total of 118 patients on the same wards made statements like 'you're not crazy', 'you're a journalist', 'you're a professor', and 'you're checking up on the hospital'.

In the wake of fiascos like these, a general uneasiness began to be felt about the way schizophrenia was diagnosed, and how responsibly psychiatrists were acting. The opposition which built up can perhaps best be described as taking strong and weak forms. In the strong form, the whole concept of schizophrenia was attacked by the antipsychiatry movement. Authors such as Laing (1964, 1965, 1967) and Szasz (1960, 1971), as well as others (for example Sarbin and Mancuso 1980) argued passionately that schizophrenia did not in fact exist, that it was an invention, a myth. To diagnose an individual as schizophrenic was a spurious attempt to 'medicalize' patterns of behaviour which were better understood in social or cultural terms. In the extreme expression of these views, diagnosis was an essentially political act, designed to marginalize, victimize, and persecute someone who was merely reacting understandably to the ills and hypocrisies of contemporary society.

The antipsychiatry position on schizophrenia cannot be done justice here; a detailed and balanced account is given by Clare (1980) and a flavour of it can be conveyed in Fig. 4.1. The important point to realize, however, is that the claims it made are not scientific in nature. They are not susceptible to any kind of confirmation or refutation, no formal alternative hypotheses are presented, and no testable predictions are offered. The arguments advanced by the authors in favour of their positions are polemical (particularly in the case of Laing), one-sided (clearly apparent in the work of Szasz), or sometimes just uninformed (this applies particularly to the book by Sarbin and Mancuso).

The weak form of the argument against the existence of schizophrenia, as exemplified by Boyle (1990), requires more serious consideration. This accepts that mental suffering should be considered as illness, but maintains that it is not legitimate to split off some of this into a category of schizophrenia. Put more formally, it is argued that the diagnosis of schizophrenia is so lacking in reliability and validity that it should be abandoned altogether. Such a view is also more amenable to investigation. From the 1930s onwards, a number of studies of the reliability of psychiatric diagnosis were carried out (see Kendell 1975; Blashfield 1984). There have

---

The antipsychiatry position on schizophrenia
(from Laing and Esterson 1964)

When a psychiatrist diagnoses schizophrenia, he means that the patient's experience and behaviour are disturbed *because* there is something the matter with the patient that causes the disturbed behaviour he observes. He calls this something schizophrenia, and he then must ask what causes the schizophrenia.

We jumped off this line of reasoning at the beginning. In our view it is an assumption, a theory, a hypothesis, but not a *fact*, that anyone suffers from a condition called 'schizophrenia'. No one can deny us the right to disbelieve in the fact of schizophrenia. We did not say, even, that we do *not* believe in schizophrenia.

If anyone believes that 'schizophrenia' is a fact, he would do well to read critically the literature on 'schizophrenia' from its inventor Bleuler to the present day. After much disbelief in the new disease more and more psychiatrists adopted the term, though few English or American psychiatrists knew what it meant, since Bleuler's monograph, published in 1911, was not available in English till 1950. But though the term has now been generally adopted and psychiatrists trained in its application, the fact it is supposed to denote remains elusive. Even two psychiatrists from the same medical school cannot agree on who is schizophrenic independently of each other more than eight out of ten times at best; agreement is less than that between different schools, and less again between different countries. These figures are not in dispute. But when psychiatrists dispute the diagnosis there is no court of appeal. There are at present no objective, reliable, quantifiable criteria — behavioural or neurophysiological or biochemical — to appeal to when psychiatrists differ.

We do not accept 'schizophrenia' as being a biochemical, neurophysiological, psychological fact, and we regard it as palpable error, in the present state of the evidence, to take it to be a fact. Nor do we assume its existence. Nor do we adopt it as a hypothesis. We propose no model of it.

Fig. 4.1

---

also been a few attempts to test the validity of psychiatric diagnosis over the same period. Of all the studies, however, one, the International Pilot Study of Schizophrenia (WHO 1973, 1979), stands out as being the largest, as the most thorough, as covering both reliability and validity in a systematic way, and also of course as being devoted specifically to schizophrenia. Accordingly, this study is focused on here, and its findings are described in detail.

Reliability

Although it does not in itself establish validity, the demonstration that clinicians can agree on diagnosis is customarily regarded as a prerequisite for this.

The first phase of the International Pilot Study of Schizophrenia (WHO 1973) consisted of an examination of 1202 patients who had been referred to psychiatric services in nine different countries. Patients were included only if they showed abnormalities of mental state or behaviour which raised the possibility of functional psychosis being present. All patients were subjected to detailed history-taking and mental state examination (using a version of the Present State Examination), and this information was used to arrive at a clinical diagnosis, according to the International Classification of Diseases (ICD-9).

As part of the study, all participating psychiatrists interviewed a number of patients in pairs, and then made their diagnoses independently. These diagnoses were then compared with each other. This procedure was carried out on 190 patients altogether, 122 of whom were subsequently given a consensus diagnosis of schizophrenia. There was found to be complete diagnostic agreement in 131 (69 per cent) of the 190. In almost all of the cases where there was disagreement this was between one or another psychotic category; the disputes involved particularly 19 patients diagnosed as 'schizoaffective' by one of the pair. In only five cases was there a disagreement over a psychotic or a non-psychotic diagnosis.

This degree of inter-rater reliability may not appear outstandingly high, but it compares favourably to those of earlier, more general reliability studies (see Kendell 1975). If it is accepted that differences within the overall category of functional psychosis are less important than those between psychotic and non-psychotic categories, then the level of serious disagreement falls to less than 3 per cent.

Validity

Of the many approaches to establishing validity, the psychologist Zubin (1967) has enumerated four which are particularly appropriate to psychiatric diagnosis. *Content validity* merely requires that diagnosis relies on the clinical features which are alleged to define the condition, rather than being made on the basis of some other factor such as overall severity. *Concurrent validity* is the demonstration that clinical diagnosis is corroborated by methods other than the clinical, for example scores on a rating scale or a psychological test. *Construct validity* is similar to concurrent validity, but here it is necessary to show that the clinical diagnosis is associated with some objectively measurable variable—an example would be indices of autonomic arousal in anxiety states. *Predictive validity*, which is by far the most important type, consists of determining that diagnosis is borne out by a particular outcome, as measured by prognosis, mortality, response to a particular treatment, etc..

The concept of construct validity cannot be applied to schizophrenia, since no reliable marker for the disorder, biological or otherwise, is known to exist. However, some findings from the International Pilot Study (WHO 1973, 1979) can be brought to bear on the remaining three aspects of validity, if it is accepted that the fit is at times a little forced.

Content validity: Of the 1202 potentially psychotic patients examined in the International Pilot Study, 811 received a diagnosis of schizophrenia. In these patients the most common symptoms found (as described in Chapter 2) were lack of insight, suspiciousness, flatness of affect, poor rapport, together with ideas and delusions of reference, delusions of persecution, auditory hallucinations, especially verbal, and thought alienation. Much the same pattern was observed in each of the nine centres in different countries. The distribution of symptoms in patients given diagnoses of mania and depression was quite different.

The diagnosis of schizophrenia thus appeared to be firmly based on the presence of the cardinal symptoms of the disorder. While this conclusion might appear somewhat circular, it has to be remembered that the psychiatrists taking part were under no obligation to follow any particular set of rules when making a diagnosis of schizophrenia; they could and did make significant numbers of diagnoses of simple, latent, residual, and schizoaffective schizophrenia.

Concurrent validity: The requirement here, that independent methods of assessment converge to give the same diagnosis, is not easy to fulfil: no means of diagnosing schizophrenia other than by clinical interview has yet been devised. An approximation to this ideal was achieved in the International Pilot Study by comparing the clinical diagnoses with those generated by a computer programme, CATEGO. This programme applied a standard set of rules to information from the mental state examination in order to arrive at an overall diagnostic classification. The procedure comprised, first combining individual ratings of symptoms into 'syndromes' of intuitively related phenomena (for example delusions, first rank symptoms, simple depression). The syndromes themselves were then combined into descriptive categories (for example simple depression + depressive delusions = psychotic depression). Finally, by assigning differential weights and utilizing priorities, the descriptive categories were transformed into an overall diagnostic category for each patient.

Of 876 patients with a clinical diagnoses of schizophrenia or paranoid psychosis, 786 were also assigned by the CATEGO computer programme to one of the schizophrenic groups, giving a concordance of 89.7 per cent.

The agreement between clinical diagnosis and a method which simulated the diagnostic process in a fixed way was thus extremely high.

Predictive validity: In the absence of firm aetiological knowledge or of an outstanding response to treatment, the aspect of schizophrenia by which the diagnosis stands or falls is its tendency to poor outcome. Even this approach faces difficulties, as psychiatric outcome is not very easy to measure and the differences between various disorders are not especially great. This aspect of validity was examined by the International Pilot Study of Schizophrenia (WHO 1979) in a two year follow-up study of the original cohort of patients. This paid attention to what might be referred to as both the quantitative and qualitative elements of outcome.

Quantitatively, social functioning was assessed at the end of the two year follow-up period, as were a number of clinical course measures such as percentage of follow-up period spent in psychosis, frequency of active psychotic symptoms at re-examination, and numbers of patients still actively psychotic at the end of the follow-up period. It proved possible to re-examine 585 of the 811 patients with an initial diagnosis of schizophrenia in this way. Twenty-three per cent were found to show severe social impairment, more than twice the rate seen in any other diagnostic group. All the course measures likewise clearly distinguished the schizophrenics from those with other diagnoses: between 26 and 37 per cent failed to achieve any kind of sustained remission of symptoms, once again twice the rate seen for patients with mania or psychotic depression. It is difficult to escape the conclusion that patients diagnosed as schizophrenic tend to fare more badly than those with other diagnoses.

Qualitatively, patients with schizophrenia should be expected to show not just evidence of decline from a previous level of functioning, but a particular kind of deterioration not seen in other diagnostic groups. Re-examination of 543 of the original 811 schizophrenic patients after two years revealed that symptom scores were in general quite low. There was a low level, in particular, of positive symptomatology in the form of delusions, verbal hallucinations, and formal thought disorder. The symptoms which tended to be prominent were negative symptoms, notably flatness of affect, or non-specific symptoms, for example lack of insight and poor co-operation with interview. The fifteen most common symptoms at follow-up for the schizophrenic patients and those with mania or depression are shown in Table 4.1, from which it can be seen that the pattern is different in each case. It thus appears that patients diagnosed as schizophrenic, but not others, are liable two years later to develop a clinical picture instantly recognizable as chronic schizophrenia.

In one way, however, the predictive validity of schizophrenia was found to leave something to be desired. During the two year follow-up period,

Table 4.1 15 commonest symptoms at 2 year follow-up in patients initially diagnosed as schizophrenic, depressed and manic (from WHO 1979)

	Frequency of symptom (%)	
Schizophrenia	Depression	Mania
Lack of insight (42.5)	Worse in morning (30.6)	Lack of insight (27.4)
Flatness of affect (27.1)	Lack of insight (19.4)	Elated thoughts (19.6)
Poor rapport (26.3)	Early waking (16.3)	Early waking (19.6)
Suspiciousness (25.2)	Gloomy thoughts (15.3)	Elated mood (15.7)
Inadequate description (25.2)	Hypochondriacal (15.3)	Worse in morning (13.7)
Unwilling to co-operate (24.5)	Hopelessness (13.9)	Ideas of reference (11.8)
Apathy (18.8)	Situational anxiety (13.9)	Self depreciation (11.8)
Ideas of reference (18.0)	Lability of affect (13.9)	Verbal hallucinations (11.8)
Delusions of reference (14.2)	Obsessive thoughts (9.2)	Voices speak to patient (11.8)
Restricted speech (12.9)	Delusional mood (8.3)	Auditory hallucinations (11.8)
Delusions of persecution (12.7)	Anxiety (8.3)	Depressed mood (11.8)
Hypochondriacal (12.7)	Sleep problems (8.3)	Sleep problems (11.8)
Autism (12.7)	Inadequate description (8.3)	Unwilling to co-operate (11.8)
Auditory hallucinations (11.6)	Flatness of affect (8.3)	Flight of ideas (9.8)
Verbal hallucinations (10.7)	Social withdrawal (8.3)	Pressure of speech (9.8)

177 of the patients with an initial diagnosis of schizophrenia were noted to have experienced one or more subsequent episodes of illness. While the vast majority of these episodes could be characterized as schizophrenic or probably schizophrenic, in 16 per cent of cases the form taken was that of depression or mania. Thus, in a small but significant minority of patients diagnosed as schizophrenic, the course does not always seem to run true.

In summary, having been subjected to very close scrutiny in the International Pilot Study, the reality of schizophrenia emerges as clearly established. The diagnosis can be made reliably, and it shows strong evidence of validity in all of the admittedly rather limited ways that can be devised to test this. There is only one reservation to this conclusion: a minority of patients diagnosed as schizophrenic will have later relapses which are manic-depressive rather than schizophrenic in character.

Can schizophrenia be separated from manic-depressive psychosis?

As important as the controversy about its existence was, most psychiatrists were never in any doubt that patients showing the typical symptoms of schizophrenia were very much in evidence. A far more significant and arguably less sterile debate has been whether schizophrenia is a distinct clinical entity, or whether it represents an artificial attempt to isolate a group of cases from what is in reality a continuously varying spectrum of functional psychosis. As the other main variety of functional psychosis is manic-depressive psychosis, this question reduces to whether the two disorders are separate or whether they lie at opposite poles of a continuum with no sharp demarcation between them.

This issue is by no means new. In the nineteenth century (and traceable back even earlier), one school of psychiatric thought held that there was only one type of insanity—*Einheitpsychose*—which took endlessly varying forms in different individuals (see Berrios and Beer 1994). After the distinction of schizophrenia and manic-depressive psychosis by Kraepelin, the concept of unitary pschosis was eclipsed, but it never completely disappeared. A version of it has provided a longstanding undercurrent to discussions about the status of schizoaffective psychosis (see Chapter 10). More recently, it has surfaced with an aetiological emphasis in the 'continuum of psychosis' hypothesis of Crow (1986).

Debates on where schizophrenia and manic-depressive psychosis stand in relation to one another have invariably had recourse not only to their presenting symptoms, but also to their course, their outcome, their family history, and even their treatment (for example see Kerr and McCelland 1991). Such a blunderbuss approach, however, is probably unnecessary. Since the separation of the two forms of psychosis arose originally and continues to be made on purely clinical grounds, it is on these grounds, above all, that it needs to be judged.

The distinction between the symptom patterns of schizophrenia and manic-depressive psychosis can be examined in a relatively straightforward way by applying the techniques of multivariate statistical analysis. This requires, first the collection of a sample of patients with both disorders, which should be large and unselected. Next, all the patients' symptoms need to be rated, preferably in detail and when they are acutely ill. The symptom scores can then be subjected to factor, cluster, or discriminant function analysis. If schizophrenia and manic-depressive psychosis are separate entities, two corresponding patterns should emerge; if they are not, this will fail to happen. In practice, a number of obstacles lie in the way of achieving this aim. One of these is the shortcomings of the techniques themselves — factor and cluster analysis are regarded as distinctly shady by mathematicians. In addition, many of the relevant studies in the area are also less than ideal for examining this issue, most commonly because they have not restricted themselves just to functionally psychotic patients. The best of them are described below.

Factor analytic studies

This set of related techniques (see Kendell 1975; Blashfield 1984) work by mathematically transforming a large number of variables which show all degrees of correlation with each other, into a series of new variables, or factors, which are uncorrelated with each other. These factors have 'loadings' of +1 to −1 on the original variables, and a few of them tend to account for a substantial proportion of the original variance of the sample. As applied to psychiatric classification, the original variables are scores on different symptoms, and the factors translate into syndromes — items with heavy loadings on a particular factor representing highly associated constellations of symptoms. It is accepted (though often seemingly forgotten by psychiatrists) that there is no necessity for the number of factors isolated to correspond to the number of hypothetical underlying sources of variation, that is the syndromes themselves should not be taken as intrinsically meaningful. It should also be borne in mind that factor analysis can only isolate groups of related symptoms and not groups of patients, and so its bearing on the separation of schizophrenia and manic-depressive psychosis is somewhat indirect.

The most exhaustive application of factor analysis to functionally psychotic patients has been in the work of Lorr and co-workers (1963). Reviewing previous studies including their own, they concluded that between 5 and 11 factors tended to be isolated, of which 10 seemed to have validity across studies. The loadings on these factors suggested the following syndromes of psychosis: *excitement* (conforming closely to manic symptoms), *hostile belligerence* (essentially the attitudes and behaviours of hostility), *paranoid projection* (persecutory, referential, and other delusions), *grandiose expansiveness* (grandiose ideas, delusions, and behaviours), *perceptual distortion* (mainly various modalities of hallucination), *anxious intropunitiveness* (a constellation of depressive symptoms), *retardation and apathy* (objective signs of retardation), *motor disturbances* (principally catatonic phenomena), *conceptual disorganization*, (formal thought disorder) and *disorientation* (as commonly understood).

Lorr *et al.* then proceeded to factor analyse the ten factors themselves to produce a set of second-order factors. When this was done, three factors emerged: one was a bipolar factor containing all the first-order factors which might be expected to be associated with manic-depressive psychosis, with the exception of *grandiose expansiveness*. The second factor loaded on *grandiose expansiveness* and on the two delusion and hallucination factors, and was considered to correspond fairly closely to paranoid schizophrenia. The third second-order factor, which loaded on *disorientation, motor disturbances, conceptual disorganization*, and *retardation and apathy*, was considered to combine elements of hebephrenic and catatonic schizophrenia.

Remembering that the groupings are of symptoms and not patients, and that there is no necessity for the number of factors isolated to correspond to the number of hypothetical underlying sources of variation, these findings provide a surprisingly close approximation to the separation of schizophrenia and manic-depressive psychosis. The first-order factors are all recognizable as intuitively clinically meaningful constellations of symptoms. Repeating the process to produce superordinate syndromes results in a separation which is almost entirely along conventional lines. Schizophrenia ends up as two syndromes; but the distinction of paranoid and non-paranoid forms is hardly counterintuitive. Grandiosity fails to segregate with the bipolar factor, but then this syndrome is common to both schizophrenia and mania.

Cluster analytic studies

This disparate group of techniques (over 150 methods have been developed) aims to subdivide heterogeneous populations into more homogeneous subgroups of its members (Kendell 1975; Blashfield 1984). In principle, the individual members of the sample are partitioned and re-partitioned into groups of varying size, which are then examined according to some criterion of within-group similarity or between-group dissimilarity until an optimum is reached. In practice, many short-cuts have to be employed because of the huge scale of the calculations involved. Cluster analysis has advantages over factor analysis for psychiatric classification because it addresses similarities between patients rather than the association of their symptoms—

for each patient, clinical diagnosis and cluster membership can be directly compared. However, cluster analysis faces its own set of difficulties. One of the most important of these is that a hierarchy of solutions is always generated, from a single cluster which takes in the whole population to one which has a cluster for each individual member. An intermediate solution must be chosen from between these extremes, either intuitively or on the basis of a variety of mathematical devices, none of which is without its critics.

Cluster analysis in one or other of its forms has been applied to functional psychotic patients many times (see Blashfield 1984). Unfortunately many of the studies have used inappropriate material (for example scores on psychological tests), or had other obvious shortcomings. Only three studies stand out as being of a high standard methodologically, and even these for one reason or another are not ideal.

Lorr *et al.* (1966) clustered profiles of symptoms in 547 acute admissions to hospital, almost all of whom had a clinical diagnosis of schizophrenic or affective 'reaction'. The cluster analysis was carried out independently on males and females. Nine clusters were isolated, of which seven met the authors' criterion of validity, being common to both men and women. No direct comparison with clinical diagnosis was made (which was probably a good idea in the USA in the 1960s); however, one cluster seemed clearly to consist of patients with mania, and another of those with depression, with and without psychotic features. Four 'paranoid' clusters were identified, containing patients with persecutory delusions variously in combination with grandiose delusions, hallucinations, or disturbed behaviour. Other clusters, containing patients with disorientation, motor abnormalities, and anxiety accompanied by psychotic phenomena had no obvious clinical counterparts.

Everitt *et al.* (1971) used detailed history and mental state data obtained from two samples of 250 in-patient admissions. The clinical diagnoses were made by a single research team and encompassed not only schizophrenia (163 cases, including 17 schizoaffective schizophrenics) and manic-depressive psychosis (146 cases) but also, unfortunately for the present purposes, neuroses, alcoholism, drug dependency, and other diagnoses. Two forms of cluster analysis were applied to each of the samples, and the results of the four analyses were similar enough to justify a common interpretation. In each case there was a small group composed predominantly of manic patients (64–86 per cent of clinically diagnosed cases), another small group composed mainly of patients with depressive psychosis (53–88 per cent of clinically diagnosed cases), and a third group made up of paranoid and other types of schizophrenia (70–94 per cent of clinically diagnosed cases). A less clear-cut fourth group contained an excess of chronic, residual, and other schizophrenics (56–82 per cent of clinically diagnosed cases). In all the analyses, however, over 60 per cent of the sample remained in other clusters which were poorly defined and contained repesentatives of all diagnostic groups.

A cluster analysis was also carried out as part of the International Pilot Study of Schizophrenia (WHO 1973). This was performed on all 1202 patients most, but not all of whom had been given a diagnosis of functional psychosis. Centre by centre, the solutions were fairly similar and it was possible to accomplish an analysis of all patients combined. A 10 cluster solution was chosen as the one which seemed both the mathematically best structured and most clinically interesting. The results were much less clear than those of Everitt *et al.*: essentially clinically diagnosed schizophrenic and manic-depressive patients were found to be distributed across all 10 clusters. This distribution, however, was highly significantly non-random ($P < 0.005$) and patients with particular clinical diagnoses were overrepresented in a small number of clusters.

These three studies all had some degree of success in distinguishing schizophrenic from manic and depressed patients. However, this was minimal in the International Pilot Study, and while it was much more pronounced in the studies of Lorr *et al.* and Everitt *et al.*, their results are vitiated by the substantial numbers of patients who remained outside any clinically recognizable clusters.

Discriminant function analysis

This technique, which is described in detail by Kendell (1975), is conceptually rather different from factor and cluster analysis. It is carried out in a number of stages. First, a sample (that is psychotic patients) consisting of two identified subpopulations (that is those with schizophrenia and manic-depressive psychosis) are rated on a set of variables which are considered relevant to the distinction between them (that is symptoms believed to be discriminatory). Next, a way of weighting each of these variables is calculated which achieves the maximum possible degree of separation of the two alleged subpopulations. In the final stage, the scores on all the weighted variables are summed for each individual and the results plotted as a histogram. If the two subpopulations are genuinely distinct a bimodal distribution with well separated means will be the result; if not the distribution will be unimodal. Discriminant function analysis is a powerful technique for investigating the distinction of functional psychoses, and it avoids many of the problems of factor and cluster analysis. Probably its most important difficulty lies in the determination of whether the final distribution is bimodal or not: the decision rests ultimately on visual inspection of the histogram, in which a central 'point of rarity' is sought. This can be supplemented by one of several mathematical validators, but the superiority of these is debatable.

Discriminant function analysis has been applied to the distinction between schizophrenia and manic-depressive psychosis only twice, but both times in large scale and rigorous studies. The first of these was the series of investigations carried out by Kendell and co-workers, and the second was as part of the International Pilot Study of Schizophrenia.

Kendell and Gourlay (1970) selected 146 patients with a diagnosis of schizophrenia and compared them with 146 with a diagnosis of affective psychosis; these included both manic and depressed patients. In all cases the diagnosis had been made by the same team, on the basis of detailed history and mental state information. Ninety clinical items were found to differ in frequency of occurrence between the groups of patients, and of these 14 history and 24 mental state items were selected as the best potential discriminators. Some of these like 'blunting of affect' and 'hears voices nearly every day' followed clinical intuition; others like 'difficulty relaxing' and 'always nervous or highly strung' (and also age and sex) were more surprising choices. The discriminant function revealed a distribution which was not unimodal, but which appeared trimodal rather than bimodal. A repeat of the same analysis on an independent sample of patients resulted in a distribution which was neither trimodal nor clearly bimodal, and was not significantly different from a normal distribution.

Some years later, Brockington *et al*. (1979) carried out a further analysis on the original sample of patients, this time including follow-up information. In this study the distribution obtained was unequivocally bimodal. The findings of both studies are shown in Fig. 4.2.

In the International Pilot Study of Schizophrenia (WHO 1979) a series of discriminant function analyses were carried out on groups of over 500 patients. These differed from the studies of Kendell and co-workers in that patients diagnosed as schizophrenic were compared separately with those diagnosed as manic and with those diagnosed as depressed. The most important analyses were those in which patients with clinical diagnoses of schizophrenia and mania or depression were compared on the basis of the symptoms they exhibited at initial presentation. Both for schizophrenia and mania, and for schizophrenia and depression, the distributions were clearly bimodal, and the overlap between the two groups of patients was small. The discriminant functions that were obtained are also shown in Fig. 4.2.

The initial results of Kendell and co-workers were viewed by the authors themselves as equivocal. Their later findings, which incorporated follow-up information, yielded, however, a clear-cut separation of schizophrenia and manic-depressive psychosis. To some extent this difference may have reflected these author's decision to treat mania and depression as a single disorder, which must inevitably have placed the burden of discrimination on the longitudinal course, rather than the cross-sectional clinical picture of the two disorders. The findings of the International Pilot Study, which

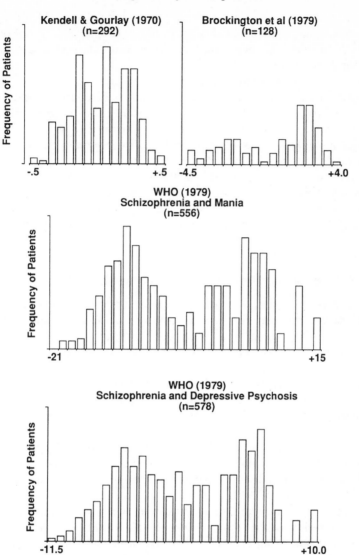

Fig. 4.2 Discriminant function analysis of groups of schizophrenic and manic-depressive patients.

concentrated firmly on cross-sectional symptomatology, on the other hand, are unqualified: the clinical classification of patients as schizophrenic as opposed to manic or depressed reflects measurable differences in their patterns of symptoms.

Taken overall, the evidence from these different statistical approaches converges on the minimal conclusion that schizophrenia and manic-depressive psychosis cannot be treated as a single disorder. Even the weakest cluster analytic study resulted in functionally psychotic patients showing a highly significantly non-random distribution of cluster membership. Given the limitations of factor analysis, it is surprising how closely the syndromes that emerge are identifiable with those in schizophrenia and manic-depressive psychosis. Finally, when discriminant function analysis, the most powerful tool of all, is employed, the degree of separation between the two disorders can, with only minor reservations, be regarded as convincing.

Can schizophrenia be diagnosed cross-sectionally?

At the heart of the definition of schizophrenia is the coupling of a characteristic clinical picture with a distinctive course. As a concept of disease, this is entirely legitimate. As an approach to diagnosis, however, it contains more than a hint of tautology: schizophrenia, a disorder defined in part by a deteriorating course, can only be said with certainty to be present when signs of deterioration become apparent. If the diagnosis of schizophrenia is not to be confounded with one of its main purposes, that of making prognostic predictions, it follows that it should be capable of being made at an early stage, as it were cross-sectionally rather than longitudinally.

It has always been accepted that the diagnosis of schizophrenia from other disorders is not always easy to make at initial presentation, and by far the greatest difficulties involve its differentiation from manic-depressive psychosis. Kraepelin (1913a) believed that no single symptom could ever differentiate the two, and sometimes even the whole picture could not be interpreted with certainty. Schizophrenia could be accompanied by pronounced mood colourings; conversely, florid delusions and hallucinations could complicate manic-depressive psychosis. Difficulties could also arise when patients presented principally with formal thought disorder or behavioural disturbance; or when there were few symptoms of any kind to go on.

The first attempt to articulate a set of principles for the foolproof diagnosis of schizophrenia was made by Bleuler (1911), quite possibly unintentionally. He isolated a number of what he termed fundamental symptoms which he considered were 'present in every case and at every period of the illness'. These comprised *association disturbance*, or formal thought disorder; *affective disturbance*, especially flattening and inappropriateness; *autism*, the tendency to consider inner life more real than the outside world; and less clearly *ambivalence*, the apparent ability of patients to hold completely contradictory feelings, wishes, and beliefs simultaneously.

Bleuler was himself noticeably ambivalent about the extent to which fundamental symptoms could be used in the service of diagnosis. Nevertheless, they were seized on for this purpose, to some extent in Europe (see Hoenig 1983), but above all in the USA. As psychiatrists in the USA broadened the concept of schizophrenia to the point that it became virtually meaningless, it was on the alleged presence of mild fundamental symptoms that the diagnosis came to be made. After the collapse of this approach, as described above, fundamental symptoms were widely perceived as being too soft and subjective to be diagnostically useful; unlike delusions and hallucinations, they rarely presented unambiguously and were not sharply demarcated from normal phenomena. Even though these claims seem in retrospect overstated (see Chapter 1), it had become abundantly clear that basing the diagnosis of schizophrenia on fundamental symptoms would always render it liable to serious abuse.

Two other approaches to the cross-sectional diagnosis of schizophrenia have risen out of the failure of fundamental symptoms. The first was the attempt by Schneider (1958) to identify a set of pathognomonic, or first rank symptoms. The second approach is that which underlies contemporary criterion-based diagnostic schemes; this can be referred to as the concept of schizophrenia as non-affective functional psychosis.

Schneider's first rank symptoms

Recognizing that psychiatric diagnosis 'must be based on the presenting situation and not on the course taken by the illness', Schneider (1958) proposed that certain symptoms were of special diagnostic importance for schizophrenia. As described in Chapter 1, these were certain types of auditory hallucinations; thought withdrawal, insertion, and broadcasting; passivity experiences; and delusional perception. These symptoms were not always present in schizophrenic patients, but when they were and there was no evidence of organic brain disease, the diagnosis could be made with certainty. In their absence, diagnosis had to rest on symptoms of second rank importance—other delusions and hallucinations, affective flattening, exceptionally the presence of formal thought disorder alone.

Schneider's concept of first rank symptoms was arrived at from his own experience and their usefulness was supported only by his clinical authority. It was left to subsequent investigators to determine how useful they were in practice, or to put it another way, to establish their sensitivity and specificity for schizophrenia.

The sensitivity of first rank symptoms can be assessed from a swathe of studies of their prevalence among schizophrenic patients that have been carried out. These have been reviewed by Koehler *et al.* (1977) (see Table 4.2). It is clear that first rank symptoms are far from universal in schizophrenia; at most 72 per cent of patients will exhibit one or more such phenomena at any given point in their illness, with around 50 per cent being a more realistic figure. First rank symptoms are clearly relatively insensitive as a means of diagnosing schizophrenia cross-sectionally.

If they were specific to schizophrenia, first rank symptoms would nevertheless still be a valuable aid to diagnosis. Two studies, however, have suggested that this is not the case. Taylor and Abrams (1973) and Carpenter *et al.* (1973) examined patients with well established diagnoses of affective psychosis and found that between 11 per cent and 23 per cent appeared to exhibit one or more first rank symptoms. The conclusion of these studies, that first rank symptoms can be found in manic-depressive psychosis, have become well known; both, however, are open to criticism. Taylor and Abrams employed their own diagnostic criteria for mania which are generally regarded as being loose. None of the patients with first rank symptoms had been given a clinical diagnosis of mania and a significant proportion also displayed catatonic phenomena. Carpenter *et al.*'s findings are weakened somewhat by the fact that an unspecified number of patients with diagnoses of neurosis or personality disorder were also said to show first rank symptoms, a finding that few psychiatrists would find believable.

Table 4.2 Frequencies of first rank symptoms in schizophrenia (from Koehler *et al.* 1977)

Type of study	Number of patients	Percentage with first rank symptoms
Case record		
Huber (1967)	195	72
Taylor (1972)	78	28
Abrams and Taylor (1973)	71	34
Koehler *et al.* (1977)	210	33
Prospective		
Mellor (1970)	166	72
Carpenter *et al.* (1973)	103	51
Carpenter and Strauss (1974)	811	57

A more definitive examination was made by Wing and Nixon (1975). They found that, of the 1202 patients in the International Pilot Study of Schizophrenia, between 93 per cent and 97 per cent who showed one or another first rank symptom had been assigned a clinical diagnosis of schizophrenia. The frequency of first rank symptoms among other diagnostic groups was 7.5 per cent overall, and it was only in manic patients that the numbers were anything like substantial (13 of 79 cases). When the mental state interviews for these 13 patients were examined, it was also found that in all cases the identification of the first rank symptom was inadequately justified, entirely unsubstantiated, or in some cases just plain wrong. Wing and Nixon's findings are shown in Table 4.3.

A reasonable synthesis of these findings might be that, providing first rank symptoms are defined with phenomenological rigour, they are highly discriminatory for schizophrenia. They are not, however, entirely specific, being found in a small minority of patients in whom affective psychosis is a realistic differential diagnosis. Some of these latter patients will also show other schizophrenic symptoms such as catatonic phenomena, but whether all of them can be subsumed under a category of 'schizoaffective' is a question that remains unanswered. This was essentially the conclusion reached by O'Grady (1990) in a recent thorough study of first rank symptoms in patients with psychiatric diagnoses of all types.

Schizophrenia as non-affective functional psychosis

In this approach, diagnosis is achieved, quite simply, by weighing up the various aspects of the clinical picture as it appears at the time of initial presentation. When longitudinal course is disregarded in this way, the differentiation of schizophrenia from manic-depressive psychosis turns on whether or not there is a significant mood alteration, whether this has the qualities of manic-depressive affective change, and whether it is present to a degree which can account for the rest of the clinical picture. If a functional psychotic state is encountered in the absence of these, then the disorder must, by default, be schizophrenia.

The origins of this method of diagnosis can probably be traced back to Kraepelin (1913a), who felt that while no individual symptom was characteristic of schizophrenia, the composition of the entire picture was often, though not always decisive. Schneider (1958) took a similar position when he stated that in the absence of first rank symptoms, diagnosis had to depend wholly on the coherence of the rest of the clinical presentation. But by far the most important influence on the development of this approach was the so-called neo-Kraepelinian movement in American psychiatry which has been charted by Blashfield (1984) (see also Wilson, 1993).

In the 1960s a number of psychiatrists took stock of the appalling diagnostic disarray in USA, and in a rather conspiratorial way, undertook the

Table 4.3 First rank symptoms in various diagnostic groups (from Wing and Nixon 1975)

Clinical diagnosis	Presence of first rank symptoms			
	Two or more	One	'Partial' only	Absent
Schizophrenia (n = 810)	233 (29%)	144 (18%)	44 (5%)	389 (48%)
Paranoid psychosis (n = 68)	13 (19%)	10 (15%)	2 (3%)	43 (63%)
Mania (n = 79)	5 (6%)	5 (6%)	3 (4%)	66 (84%)
Depression (n = 176)	3 (2%)	4 (2%)	2 (1%)	167 (95%)
Neuroses and personality disorder (n = 53)	0 (0%)	1 (2%)	0 (0%)	52 (98%)

task of re-establishing psychiatric diagnosis on the basis of symptoms and signs. The first step was the devising of operational criteria for several disorders by Feighner *et al.* (1972); this was ostensibly for the purposes of research. Then a more refined and elaborate version of these, the Research Diagnostic Criteria (RDC) of Spitzer *et al.* (1978), were developed. By this time, although research was the stated purpose, it was clear that classification issues were beginning to be confronted for their own sake. With the incorporation of Feighner *et al.*'s and Spitzer *et al.*'s approach into the production of the third edition of a previously rather nondescript diagnostic manual, the psychodynamic establishment was infiltrated and overthrown. DSM III, which appeared in 1980, was closely modelled on the RDC, and represented a landmark in American psychiatry which was met with, as its authors put it, 'interest, alarm, despair, excitement and joy'.

The approach to the diagnosis of schizophrenia is much the same in the Feighner *et al.*, RDC, and DSM III approaches. The presence of at least two different types of florid symptom is required, and there must be an absence of significant evidence of manic-depressive mood change. Differential significance is attached to different classes of schizophrenic symptom, so that those which are hard to assess (for example formal thought disorder), are given a low weighting, whereas those which are traditionally considered characteristic (for example delusions and hallucinations, especially when both are present) are valued more highly. First rank symptoms are also incorporated into the scheme, where they are given overriding or near-overriding importance. The requirement of absence of elation or depression of mood can be made to accommodate schizophrenic mood colourings by stipulating the exclusion only of mood changes which are accompanied by the specific concomitants of mania (increased vitality accompanied by overactivity, overspending, decreased need for sleep, etc.) and depression (anhedonia, biological symptoms, self depreciation, etc.). As a final fillip, in some of the classifications, the course of the disorder up to the time of evaluation is taken into consideration, an insidious decline prior to development of florid symptoms adding weight to the diagnosis of schizophrenia. This dilutes the cross-sectionality of the diagnosis, but is a legitimate manoeuvre for what is after all a practical procedure. The Research Diagnostic Criteria for schizophrenia, the purest example of the overall approach, are shown in Fig. 4.3.

The criterion-based approach is currently the fashionable method of diagnosing schizophrenia, but its success needs to be judged as much as that of its predecessors, first rank symptoms and for that matter fundamental symptoms. This, however, presents problems. It is immediately clear that the approach is not susceptible to any kind of sensitivity and specificity analysis. After some thought, it also becomes apparent that the only way of avoiding circularities is to demonstrate that patients diagnosed as

Research Diagnostic Criteria for schizophrenia
(from Spitzer et al. 1978)

A through C are required for the period of illness being considered.

A. During an active phase of the illness (may or may not now be present) at least two of the following are required for definite and one for probable:

(1) Thought broadcasting, insertion, or withdrawal (as defined in this manual).

(2) Delusions of being controlled (or influenced), other bizarre delusions, or multiple delusions (as defined in this manual).

(3) Somatic, grandiose, religious, nihilistic, or other delusions without persecutory or jealous content lasting at least one week.

(4) Delusions of any type if accompanied by hallucinations of any type for at least one week.

(5) Auditory hallucinations in which either a voice keeps up a running commentary on the subject's behaviour or thoughts as they occur, or two or more voices converse with each other.

(6) Non-affective verbal hallucinations (as defined in this manual) spoken to the subject.

(7) Hallucinations of any type throughout the day for several days or intermittently for at least one month.

(8) Definite instances of marked formal thought disorder (as defined in this manual) accompanied by either blunted or inappropriate affect, delusions or hallucinations of any type, or grossly disorganized behaviour.

B. Signs of the illness have lasted at least two weeks from the onset of a noticeable change in the subject's usual condition (current signs of the illness may not now meet criterion A and may be residual symptoms only, such as extreme social withdrawal, blunted or inappropriate affect, mild formal thought disorder, or unusual thoughts or perceptual experiences).

C. At no time during the *active* period (delusions, hallucinations, marked formal thought disorder, bizarre behaviour, etc.) of illness being considered did the subject meet the full criteria for either probable or definite manic or depressive syndrome (criteria A and B under Major Depressive or Manic Disorders) to such a degree that it was a *prominent* part of the illness. (See criteria for Depressive Syndrome Superimposed on Residual Schizophrenia.)

Fig. 4.3

schizophrenic using purely cross-sectional criteria subsequently go on to develop the typical picture of chronic schizophrenia as frequently as patients diagnosed in the normal clinical way, taking both cross-sectional and longitudinal information into account. Until the marathon exercise of evaluating DSM III is carried out, the only work that comes close to fulfilling this requirement is the series of investigations by Brockington and co-workers (Brockington *et al.* 1978*a*; Kendell *et al.* 1979) in which the predictive validity of different ways of diagnosing schizophrenia was examined.

Utilizing detailed history and mental state data gathered on 134 patients with functional psychosis, these authors made diagnoses of schizophrenia according to several different definitions. The *clinical diagnosis* was based on all the available information, both the presenting symptoms and the course of the illness up to the time of assessment. The diagnosis according to the *Research Diagnostic Criteria* of Spitzer *et al.* (1978) depended exclusively on the clinical picture at the time of examination. Diagnosis was also made on the basis of whether *first rank symptoms* were present. A number of other diagnostic approaches were included as well.

On average 6.5 years later, as many as possible of the 134 patients were traced and re-interviewed by an investigator unaware of the original diagnosis. Ratings of symptomatology and social functioning were made, and corroborative information from hospital records and interviews with relatives and carers was obtained where possible. On the basis of these data a follow-up clinical diagnosis was formulated for all patients, which was made blind to the original diagnosis.

The results for patients given clinical and RDC diagnoses, and also for those diagnosed according to presence of first rank symptoms, are shown in Table 4.4. It was found that diagnosing schizophrenia according to the RDC was as good or better than diagnosing it clinically in terms of predicting incomplete recovery, persistent delusions and hallucinations, development of a defect state, and social isolation. Both systems also misdiagnosed patients to much the same extent: just over 10 per cent of cases diagnosed as schizophrenic clinically or by RDC, subsequently turned out to show features more consistent with manic-depressive psychosis. Perhaps the most important finding, however, was the lack of any marked differences between any of the diagnostic approaches employed — whether clinical or criterion-based, cross-sectional or longitudinal, dependent on or independent of first rank symptoms — there appeared little to choose between any of them. It was true that considerably more patients were classified as schizophrenic clinically than with any of the formal systems, but this was largely due to the inclusion of patients with residual schizophrenia (that is without active symptoms at initial evaluation); when these were excluded the numbers became comparable.

Table 4.4   Predictive validity of different diagnostic systems in schizophrenia (from Brockington *et al.* 1978; Kendell *et al.* 1979)

Outcome measure	Clinical diagnosis (*n* = 45)	Research Diagnostic Criteria (*n* = 34)	First rank symptoms (*n* = 38)
Incomplete recovery	22 (49%)	19 (56%)	16 (42%)
Persistent delusions and hallucinations	15 (33%)	14 (41%)	13 (34%)
Defect state	8 (18%)	8 (23%)	7 (18%)
Social isolation	25 (49%)	22 (65%)	22 (58%)
Outcome diagnosis of affective psychosis	5 (11%)	4 (12%)	8 (21%)

These findings suggest rather compellingly that making a diagnosis of schizophrenia according to the simple formula, presence of psychotic symptoms plus absence of manic-depressive mood shift, is on the whole as accurate as a more judicious weighing of all relevant mental state and history information. Incorporation of the latter undoubtedly allows cases of schizophrenia to be picked up which would otherwise be missed; but even so the gains are relatively minor.

Conclusion

The term diagnosis has two quite different meanings. In its theoretical sense, it refers to a method of classifying a disease according to a scheme which may or may not be valid. In its practical sense, it describes an act of clinical decision-making; this cannot be valid or invalid, it can only be done with greater or lesser degrees of acumen. It seems possible that the uncertainty and controversy which has surrounded the diagnosis of schizophrenia might, more than anything else, be a consequence of a confusion between these two usages of the term.

At the theoretical level, it is difficult to see what all the fuss over the diagnosis of schizophrenia was about. The alleged disease entity of schizophrenia seems to have emerged from a very searching examination as both valid as a disease and valid as an entity. In the practical sense of the term, it is clear that the record of psychiatrists in diagnosing schizophrenia (and other psychiatric disorders) has not always been very good. However, the important question here is not whether schizophrenia *is* diagnosed reliably, but whether reasonable levels of reliability *can* be achieved. The evidence reviewed in this chapter suggests that it is possible to make the diagnosis of schizophrenia with an acceptable degree of accuracy, and also that this can be done before it becomes a self-fulfilling prophecy.

A minor anomaly remains in that a small number of patients with functional psychosis — something in the region of 10 per cent — stubbornly resist being diagnosed as either schizophrenic or manic-depressive the time of presentation, or fail to stay in their designated category as their illness evolves. The question of how these patients who do not respect the rules of diagnosis should be regarded is discussed at length in Chapter 11.

5

Aetiological factors
in schizophrenia

After nearly a century, the fact is that the cause or causes of schizophrenia remain unknown. The disorder itself, as Bleuler (1911) pointed out, gives few clues as to where its origins might lie. Schizophrenia shows no obvious signs of having an underlying physical pathology; there is nothing to be found at post-mortem. Nor has there ever been much to suggest that it is connected in any very direct way with emotional trauma, childhood deprivation, or any of the other vicissitudes of life. While, over the years many lines of investigation have been pursued and a handful of positive findings have been thrown up, the leads have generally turned out to be slender and there has often been dispute, if not about the findings themselves then about the construction that can be placed on them.

A second fact which is abundantly clear is that the aetiology of schizophrenia is a battleground, disputed territory over which long and bitter campaigns have been fought. The two sides in this struggle have consisted quite simply of those who believe schizophrenia to be a biological brain disorder, and those who maintain that it can only properly be understood psychologically, as a manifestation of the self's inner conflicts or in terms of the individual's relationship to others. One or other of these camps has held the upper hand for decades at a time whilst the other has been forced underground and has only been able to engage in guerilla tactics. Although there have been attempts at reconciliation, the relationship between the two sides continues to be much more of a stand-off than an accommodation.

The most obvious result of the sizeable, protracted, and well-diversified research effort in schizophrenia has been the accumulation of a forbidding body of literature. It is not possible to weave this into any kind of a coherent synthesis—this is a futile quest in the present state of ignorance. Nor is it possible to review the evidence in a way which does justice to all the avenues which have been or are currently being explored with promising results—this cannot be done in a chapter, perhaps not even in a whole book. Instead the aim of this chapter is to take a critical look at the overall status of the psychodynamic and biological schools of thought as applied to schizophrenia, a strategy which ensures that the main themes of research over the last thirty years will be touched on.

Psychodynamic approaches

Psychodynamic psychiatry began with Freud and it is to him that all interpretative theories of schizophrenia can be traced. Freud himself paid comparatively little attention to the psychoses and it was left to his immediate circle of followers to produce the first orthodox psychoanalytic accounts of schizophrenia. Over the course of time these have undergone considerable change and evolution, as of course has the psychoanalytic tradition as a whole. Nevertheless, within the many variations a constant theme has been the emphasis on development of personality and the understanding of schizophrenic symptoms by interpretation. These approaches can be referred to as *individual theories* of schizophrenia.

The history of psychodynamic psychiatry has also been one of schism, rivalry, and the setting up of schools which have strayed far from Freud's original individually based approach. One result of this was the emergence in the 1940s of a movement which shifted the emphasis away from the individual to the family. This gave rise to a number of theories about schizophrenia which had largely independent origins and which were couched in quite different terminologies, but which as a group came to exercise unprecedented influence over psychiatric thought. These are usually referred to collectively as *family theories* of schizophrenia.

Individual theories

Arieti (1974), in one of the few scholarly overviews of the field, considered that three figures had made outstanding contributions to the psychoanalytic understanding of schizophrenia. The first of these was of course Freud. He originated a key explanatory principle behind delusions and other classes of what would now be called positive symptoms. This was the mental mechanism of projection, whereby the individual's own unbearable sexual ideas and wishes became displaced on to others in an inverted or otherwise disguised form. He also explained what would now be called negative symptoms as being due to a withdrawal of the libidinal energy which is normally invested in people and the outside world. Later, he applied his formulation of ego psychology to schizophrenia. The central idea here was that in the face of an intolerable conflict regression to a very early (pre-oral) stage of development took place. This allowed the unconscious id to become able to intrude into consciousness and partially usurp the rational functions of the ego with its irrational, childlike mode of functioning.

The two other psychiatrists who exerted a major influence departed somewhat from the strict Freudian tradition. Jung also believed that under stress or prolonged conflict the unconscious started to overwhelm normal conscious life. However, he was more concerned to try and make sense of the bizarre world of the schizophrenic. He argued that the alien, autonomous quality of florid symptoms was a consequence of a process he called complex formation, in which a set of emotionally charged ideas were removed from consciousness and took up a more or less independent existence in the unconscious. Such complexes subsequently re-entered consciousness in an uncontrolled and uncorrectable way as delusions, hallucinations, and other symptoms. Jung was also struck by the primitive, often mythic themes which dominated schizophrenic experiences, and it was this which led him to his well-known theory of the existence of a collective unconscious.

Sullivan's contribution was to establish the importance of interpersonal relationships in schizophrenia. He argued that the alteration which Freud believed took place between the individual and the world was specifically a change in the individual's relationship with people in the world. According to Sullivan, all thoughts and fantasies were to do with people, real and imaginary, which were built up in childhood from what he termed the reflected appraisals of parents or parent figures. In a roughly similar way to Freud and Jung he believed that traumatic experiences—but interpersonal ones causing blows to self-regard—were excluded from consciousness. These then went on to distort interpretations of other experiences with people, causing a vicious circle of interpersonal difficulties. A series of 'not-me' processes was set up outside consciousness which ultimately returned to consciousness and gave rise to schizophrenic symptoms.

As is the way of psychodynamic psychiatry, these theories are not notable for their scientific rigour, or even for being framed in a way which permits testable hypotheses to be extracted. Taken as a group, however, they do share a current of thought which places them within reach of the scientific method. A key proposition in all of the theories is that psychological stress, by causing a regression to take place or by overburdening already strained coping mechanisms, triggers a sequence of internal changes whose outward expression is the development of psychotic symptoms. The stress itself may be more of a prolonged conflict than a single disturbing experience; or it may be objectively minor but have special psychological implications for the individual; or it might exert its effect by virtue of acting on an already abnormal personality structure. But there is no getting away from the principle that stressful events precipitate schizophrenic breakdown. This can be construed as a prediction, one which can be tested quite easily by examining the frequency of stressful life events in patients over the weeks and months before they become schizophrenic.

The first and most famous study of life events in schizophrenia was carried out by Brown and Birley (Brown and Birley 1968; Birley and Brown 1970). They established a set of eight classes of events which seemed likely on common sense grounds to provoke emotional reactions, either of a positive or negative kind. The events selected were typically personal, concerning the individual or his close relatives, and involved danger, significant changes in health, status, or way of life, the promise of these, or important fulfillments or disappointments. For the purpose of the study Brown and Birley only included events which could be dated with accuracy, and those which were not obviously a result of the individual's own actions – for example losing a job because of strange behaviour at work. As a further safeguard, the events were broken down further into those which were 'definitely independent' and 'possibly independent'.

Fifty patients with acute schizophrenia were selected by screening admissions to a number of psychiatric hospitals and interviewing them with a forerunner of the Present State Examination. Only patients with an acute onset of symptoms were included in the study. This was defined as a sudden and marked change in behaviour accompanied by the public expression of schizophrenic symptoms, which had to be dateable to within one week as judged by the patient's own and independent accounts. Life events were rated over the three month period prior to onset in the 50 patients, and also in a control group of 325 normal individuals who were roughly similar in age and sex distribution.

The results were clear-cut. The patients had experienced on average 1.74 life events in the three month period before they became ill, compared with 0.96 for the controls, a near doubling of the rate which was highly statistically significant. An excess number of objectively defined stressful events had been demonstrated in a methodologically scrupulous study, and the hypothesis of stress as an aetiological factor in schizophrenia was thus supported.

Or was it? In the first place, the finding was not as strong as it might have been. A marked difference in the occurrence of life events was only found for the small minority of 'possibly independent' events; an increase in the considerably larger number of 'definitely independent' events was evident but did not reach statistical significance. The differences were also noted to be confined to the three weeks immediately prior to onset; for the bulk of the three month period the rates were the same in the schizophrenics and the controls. Secondly, it was not altogether clear how far the life events could be regarded as causal. The majority of the sample consisted not of patients who were developing schizophrenia for the first time, but of those with established illnesses who were undergoing a relapse: only 24 of the 50 patients were first admissions and only 15 of these were experiencing their first episode. Thirdly, it was questionable whether the life events rated always preceded the development of schizophrenia. In 15 patients the onset was not onset of illness but a move from mild to severe schizophrenic symptoms; in 8 more it was change from non-specific symptoms such as depression or withdrawal to florid psychosis.

Five further studies of life events which had reasonably adequate methodologies and which permit conclusions about schizophrenia to be drawn have been reviewed by Bebbington and Kuipers (1988); Bebbington *et al.* (1993) have also provided a further study. As is clear from Table 5.1, any hopes that the shortcomings of the study of Brown and Birley have been overcome are quickly dashed. The patient numbers were in all cases small or relatively small, ranging from 24 to 62. Most of the studies defined onset similarly to Brown and Birley, including exacerbations as well as first appearance of symptoms; one (Canton and Fraccon 1985) used a highly dubious criterion of onset, equating this with admission to hospital. In four of the studies not all of the patients were first admissions. In another (Chung *et al.* 1986) it was not specified whether any of the patients were first admissions. Even so the findings are not strong. Only one of four studies with designs which, if not better than those of Brown and Birley are certainly no worse, found any increase in independent life events.

Family theories

The way in which the view developed of schizophrenia as the outcome of abnormal parent–child interaction has been traced by Hirsch and Leff (1975). Speculation along these lines began with the orthodox psychoanalyst, Hadju-Gaines (1940) who, in the course of analysing four schizophrenic patients, concluded that they had in common the experience of a cold, rigorous, sadistically aggressive mother and a soft, indifferent, passive father. A few years later Fromm-Reichmann (1948) coined the term 'schizophrenogenic mother'. In the 1950s, a number of authors, working more or less independently, elaborated these ideas into thoroughly worked-out theories of schizophrenia. These were chronologically: Bateson (Bateson *et al.* 1956), who proposed the double-bind hypothesis; Lidz and co-workers (Lidz *et al.* 1957*a, b*) who conceptualized the abnormal parental relationships as marital skew and marital schism; Wynne and Singer (Wynne *et al.* 1958; Wynne and Singer 1963) who argued for a central role of abnormalities in communication in the parents; and, most famously, Laing and colleagues (Laing 1964, 1965; Laing and Esterson 1964) who placed a composite of these ideas within the framework of existential philosophy.

The theme which runs through all these theories is that schizophrenia is a way of thinking and behaving inculcated during childhood, usually by the sufferer's parents. According to Bateson, a parental tendency to communicate ambiguous and conflicting messages had enduring effects on the child's capacity to focus attention and extract the meaning of what was being said. In Lidz's theory, coldness in the parent–child relationship provided a model which the child later adopted in his interactions with others outside the family. In a similar way, the parents' ambivalence laid the groundwork for a distorted perception of logic. Wynne and Singer argued that it was the parents' abnormal mode of speech which communicated itself to the child, affecting his or her pattern of thinking and interacting as an adult. For Laing, these and other abnormalities in the family relationship undermined the child's sense of self until he or she was no longer able to maintain any sense of being in the world.

Explanations of symptoms like formal thought disorder, delusions, and affective flattening flow naturally from such accounts. It is also easy to see how social withdrawal would be a natural reaction to the interpersonal difficulties that resulted. The theories can even explain why schizophrenia tends to develop in early adult life—this is the time when an individual's relationships with family members begin to be replaced with significant relationships with other adults.

The formal investigation of the parents of schizophrenic patients has been, by the standards of psychodynamic psychiatry, surprisingly thorough. The first study was carried out in the 1930s, and investigation continued until, to all intents and purposes, it came to a halt in the 1970s. In a definitive review of the field, Hirsch and Leff (1975) concluded that, although methodologies tended to be flawed and the findings were frequently contradictory, a number of statements could be made which were reasonably well supported by evidence. These are summarized in Fig. 5.1. Briefly, there was no evidence that the mothers of schizophrenic patients

---

What can be considered established about the parent-child relationship in schizophrenia
(from Hirsch and Leff 1975)

1. More parents of schizophrenic patients are psychiatrically disturbed than parents of normal children and more of the mothers are 'schizoid'.
2. There is a link between 'allusive thinking' in the parents of schizophrenics and in their children, but this is also true of normal people in whom it occurs less frequently.
3. The parents of schizophrenics show more conflict and disharmony than the parents of other psychiatric patients.
4. The pre-schizophrenic child more frequently manifests physical ill health or mild disability early in life than the normal child.
5. Mothers of schizophrenics show more concern and protectiveness than mother of normals, both in the current situation and in their attitudes to their children before they fell ill.

Fig. 5.1

Table 5.1 Studies of life events in schizophrenia (from Bebbington and Kuipers 1988)

Study	Subjects	Diagnostic criteria	Stage of illness	Definition of onset	Period of analysis	Findings
Jacobs and Myers (1976)	62 patients 62 controls	Authors' own (similar to RDC)	First and readmissions	Emergence or exacerbation of symptoms; change in social functioning	12 months	Significant excess for all life events, but not for independent events
Malzacher *et al.* (1981)	33 patients 33 controls	Clinical	First admissions	Emergence of psychotic symptoms	6 months	No excess of life events
Canton and Fracon (1985)	54 patients 54 controls	DSM III	Not all first admissions	Not given	6 months	Significant excess of life events in 3 out 10 categories
Al Khani *et al.* (1986)	48 patients 62 controls	PSE/Catego	Not all first admissions	Normal to psychotic; neurotic to psychotic; minor to major psychotic	6 months	No excess of life events

| Chung et al. (1986) | 24 patients 24 controls | DSM III | Not clear if any first admissions | Normal to psychotic; normal to prodromal; residual to psychotic | 6 months | No excess of life events; significant excess of threatening events in schizophreniform pts |
| Bebbington et al. (1993) | 52 patients 207 controls | DSM III | Unspecified number were not first admissions | Normal to psychotic; neurotic to psychotic; exacerbation of psychotic symptoms | 6 months | Significant excess of life events, including definitely independent events |

were aloof, cold, or rejecting, or that fathers of schizophrenic patients were abnormal in any way. There was, however, evidence that the mothers of schizophrenics tended to be more concerned, protective, and possibly more intrusive than mothers of normal children. Both parents showed a tendency to be psychiatrically abnormal, with mothers, in particular, being identifiably more schizoid than parents of non-schizophrenic children.

Hirsch and Leff also noted that one set of results stood out from this welter of unimpressive findings. Singer and Wynne carried out a series of careful studies to examine their proposal that the parents of schizophrenic patients showed abnormalities in communication. In the first of these (Singer and Wynne 1965), transcripts of the speech of the parents of 20 schizophrenic patients, 6 neurotic patients, and 9 patients with a diagnosis of borderline personality were rated for abnormalities in language and style of communication under blind conditions. Based purely on these analyses made on the *parents*, the correct diagnosis could be assigned to the *child* in 17 of 20 of the schizophrenic cases, 4 out of 6 of the neurotic cases, and 7 of the 9 borderlines. It also proved possible to predict the thinking style of the schizophrenic offspring and the severity of what was termed their ego disorganization. Subsequently, using a manual for scoring communication deviances, the authors (Singer and Wynne 1966; Wynne 1968, 1971) were able to demonstrate that parents of schizophrenic patients invariably achieved a range of scores which were higher than and showed little overlap with those of the parents of normal and neurotic patients—no more than 22 per cent of normals scored above a cutoff for communication deviance defined as the lowest score for any of the schizophrenic parents.

As Hirsch and Leff (1975) put it, the magnitude of Wynne and Singer's accomplishment in these studies was truly remarkable. For this reason, they undertook to replicate their findings (Hirsch and Leff 1971, 1975). They first collected a group of 20 patients with acute schizophrenia, diagnosed using the Present State Examination, and a group of 20 patients with neurotic illnesses, who were closely matched for age, sex, and social class. Next, the parents of both groups were interviewed under blind conditions. Their speech output was rated using the manual developed by Wynne and Singer, and strenuous efforts were made to ensure that interviewing and scoring was carried out in the same way (this included close liaison with Wynne's group throughout the study). When the deviance scores of the two sets of parents were compared it was found that the schizophrenics' were significantly higher. However, as shown in Fig. 5.2, it was also clear (a) that the degree of overlap between the two groups was great; (b) that a large proportion in both groups showed very little or no abnormality of speech; and (c) that the difference was almost entirely accounted for by five of the 40 parents of the schizophrenic patients who showed exceptionally high scores. On further analysis it emerged that the parents of the schizophrenics

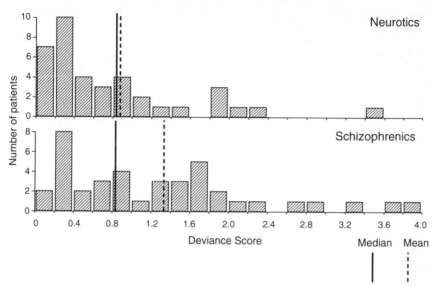

Fig. 5.2 Communication deviance scores for the parents of schizophrenic patients and neurotic controls (from Hirsch and Leff 1971).

used significantly more words than the parents of the neurotics. When this was corrected for, the difference between the groups disappeared. The compelling conclusion was that the parents of the schizophrenic patients exhibited garrulousness rather than any more sinister abnormality.

The psychodynamic approach to schizophrenia has a seductive appeal and, as described in Chapter 4, held sway over psychiatric thinking for a long period of time. This stands in sharp contrast to its experimental support, which has never been anything but faint. As concluded by Day (1981), life events may be part of the pool of causal factors associated with the onset of acute schizophrenic episodes, but there is little to suggest that the association is a necessary or direct one. To this it might be added that there is still less to suggest that there is an association with the onset of a first episode of schizophrenia. Exploration along the avenue of abnormal family interactions in schizophrenia was effectively brought to an end by Hirsch and Leff's failure to replicate what appeared to be the most robust of all the findings in this area. At this point it became clear to many that, while the parents of schizophrenics may show psychiatric abnormalities intriguingly similar to those of the patients themselves, any attempt to build a psychological bridge from one to the other would be doomed to failure.

Biological approaches

The earliest aetiological hypothesis advanced about schizophrenia was that it was an organic brain disease. Kraepelin (for example 1913*a*) expressed this view emphatically in his writings, and it was under his direction that the first genetic and neuropathological studies of the disorder were undertaken. A somewhat watered down organic position was also taken by Bleuler (1911): after concluding that hereditary, age, sex, constitution, infection, and structural brain abnormality were of definite but limited significance, he expressed some sympathy for the view that a toxic-metabolic disorder was the root cause of the condition.

Subsequently, biological research in schizophrenia has not exactly proceeded apace, and at times it has moved forward in a distinctly meandering way. For several decades the rate of advance was slowed by the relatively crude methods available for studying the brain in life. For nearly as long a period progress was held up by the ascendancy of psychodynamic psychiatry, particularly in America. A turning point was the discovery of chlorpromazine and other antipsychotic drugs, which pointed rather plainly to the possibility that some of the symptoms of schizophrenia might be biologically determined. Later, the development of brain imaging techniques added to the momentum, the making-up of lost time being ironically most evident in America. Leaving aside biochemical research, which is given a chapter to itself, the two most productive areas have been genetics and neuroimaging; these are discussed at some length below. A number of other lines of investigation have been followed which have resulted in only minor, equivocal or contested findings; these are relegated to the final section of this chapter.

The genetics of schizophrenia

The first study of the familial occurrence of schizophrenia was undertaken by Rudin (1916) in Kraepelin's department. Investigations of the parents, twins, siblings, children, and other relatives of schizophrenic patients have since formed the main output of some of the most distinguished of several generations of schizophrenia researchers. This work has been reviewed and updated many times, first by the daughter of Rudin (Zerbin-Rudin, cited by Slater 1968); and later by many other authors (for example Kallman 1938; Slater 1968; Gottesman and Shields 1982; McGuffin 1988). However, possibly the best and certainly the most readable of these accounts is that of Gottesman (1991), and what follows covers the same ground, with a few embellishments and changes of emphasis.

By pooling the results of around 40 of the better studies carried out in Britain, Europe, and Scandinavia (but not the USA) between 1920 and 1987, Gottesman was able to produce a table of risks for developing schizophrenia in first-degree, second-degree, and third-degree relatives of patients with the disorder. His summary of these findings is reproduced in Fig. 5.3. It is clear that the risk rises more or less steadily with increasing consanguinity to reach a peak of nearly 50 per cent in monozygotic twins and the children of two schizophrenic parents. It is equally clear that even when the relative is genetically identical (that is a monozygotic twin), the chance of developing schizophrenia falls far short of 100 per cent.

It does not take long to realize that while these findings are suggestive, they do not by themselves establish that a hereditary factor operates in schizophrenia. Demonstrating familiality does not necessarily demonstrate genetic transmission, because families have a notable tendency to share a common environment as well as common genes. As Gottesman pointed out, juvenile delinquency and adult criminality show significant degrees of familial clustering, and measles has a high rate of concordance in monozygotic twins; yet these are disorders whose genetic basis few would care to defend. To exclude a spurious reason for the familiality of schizophrenia it is clearly necessary to disentangle the part played by genetics from the part played by environment; to try and do this two strategies have been employed.

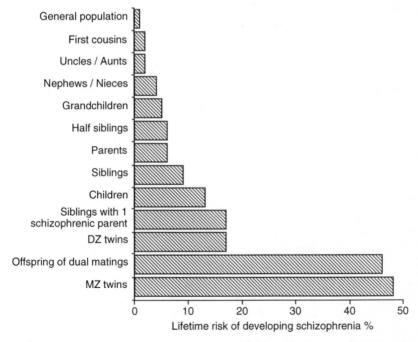

Fig. 5.3 Pooled data for occurrence of schizophrenic in increasingly consanguinous relatives of schizophrenic patients (modified from Gottesman 1991).

The first method is to compare the concordance rates for monzygotic and dizygotic twins. The genetic differences between the two are substantial (the former are genetically identical whereas the latter are no more closely related than siblings); on the other hand the environmental influences would be expected to be similar in both. The results of ten studies in twin pairs with one schizophrenic member are summarized in Table 5.2, which is based on the reviews of Slater (1968) and Gottesman (1991). All the studies show a higher concordance rate in monozygotic twins, supporting the genetic hypothesis. One further study (Tienari 1963) originally provided an exception, finding a concordance of zero in 16 monozygotic twin pairs. However, on following-up the pairs up a decade later (Tienari 1975), it turned out merely to prove the rule—by this time the monozygotic concordance rates had become a respectable 36 per cent, with that for dizygotic twins being 14 per cent.

The second way of unconfounding the familiality findings is to examine children with a schizophrenic parent who have not been brought up by their families. The classic study of this type was carried out by Heston (1966). He traced and interviewed the adult offspring of 47 women who had been hospitalized with a diagnosis of schizophrenia; all of them, in accordance with the laws of the time, had been separated from their mothers within three days of birth and raised in orphanages or with non-maternal relatives. Heston also traced and interviewed a control group of 50 children of normal mothers adopted way under similar circumstances. According to the consensus diagnosis of three clinicians, 5 (10.4 per cent) of the schizophrenic mothers' offspring were found to be suffering from schizophrenia; this was in contrast to none of the controls. Another 22 of the children of schizophrenic mothers had other psychiatric disorders, with sociopathic personality and episodic depression and anxiety featuring especially prominently. A further interesting finding was the impression that several of the schizophrenic mothers' children were more spontaneous when interviewed, had more colourful life histories, and had more creative occupations and imaginative hobbies.

These studies placed the existence of a significant genetic contribution to the causation of schizophrenia beyond reasonable doubt. Or did they? Their credibility hinges on the way the diagnosis of schizophrenia was made; but, as documented in Chapter 4, at the time the key genetic studies were being carried out psychiatric diagnosis was reaching the peak of its unreliability. Index cases of schizophrenia were invariably diagnosed clinically, and even where safeguards were built in, for instance requiring a consensus between two or more clinicians, some patients would have undoubtedly been included who would not meet modern diagnostic criteria for the disorder. When it came to diagnosing the relatives, there was a widespread tendency to include as schizophrenic 'borderline', 'latent', and 'pseudoneurotic' cases; one or two studies made a point of also including individuals who were psychiatrically abnormal but clearly not psychotic – those with so-called schizophrenia spectrum disorders. Could, as Gottesman put it, the earlier overwhelming evidence for familial clustering have been generated merely by biased psychiatrists, making unreliable clinical judgements, and operating under non-blind conditions?

This suspicion remained largely unvoiced until it was finally brought out into the open by an attempt to repeat Heston's study on the adopted-away offspring of schizophrenic parents. This study was carried out by Rosenthal *et al.* (1968, 1971), ostensibly with meticulous attention to detail, and it produced results which were broadly in line with those of Heston. Then, several years later it was singled out for attack by Lidz and co-workers (Lidz *et al.* 1981; Lidz and Blatt 1983), an attack which was as effective as it was vitriolic. First, Lidz *et al.* made the point that Rosenthal *et al.* seemed to have little interest in drawing a distinction betweeen schizophrenia and schizophrenia spectrum diagnoses among the relatives – the two were lumped together as an implicit conceptual unity. However, when the data were re-analyzed considering only cases where the agreed diagnosis was schizophrenia, the rate among the offspring became negligible. Secondly, Rosenthal *et al.* included a number of patients with a diagnosis of manic-depressive psychosis in their index group. While it was reasonable to do this in the interests of comparison, the two groups were not, in fact, kept separate in the analysis but were muddled together in a way which was by any standards sloppy.

On the heels of Lidz *et al.*'s critiques, two studies (Pope *et al.* 1982; Abrams and Taylor 1983) appeared which examined the familial tendency of schizophrenia diagnosed according to the newly introduced Research Diagnostic Criteria and DSM III. These both found substantial rates of psychiatric ill health among the first degree relatives of schizophrenic patients; however, the rates for schizophrenia were exceptionally low at 0 per cent and 2.8 per cent respectively. The authors of both of these studies had a reputation for challenging conventional dogma and it is likely that they were aiming to be provocative rather than wishing to be seen as having mounted definitive investigations. In fact, Pope *et al.*'s study relied exclusively on family history information which was available in the patients' case notes, and Abrams and Taylor were only able to contact less than half of their patients' relatives, many of whom they interviewed over the telephone.

Soon, a series of fresh family studies followed which diagnosed schizophrenia according to contemporary standards. The results of five of these are summarized in Table 5.3. The risk of schizophrenia in the first degree relatives of schizophrenics ranged from around 3 per cent to just over 8 per cent. In all cases this was greater than the general population risk; where

Table 5.2 Twin studies in schizophrenia
Classical studies (from Slater 1968)

	Number of pairs	Monozygotic percentage concordance*	Dizygotic percentage concordance*
Luxenburger (1928)	19 MZ 13 DZ	58	0
Rosanoff *et al.* (1934)	41 MZ 53 DZ	61	13
Essen-Moller (1941)	11 MZ 27 DZ	64	15
Kallman (1946)	174 MZ 296 DZ	69	11
Slater (1953)	37 MZ 58 DZ	65	14
Inouye (1961)	55 MZ 11 DZ	60	18

*Concordance calculated pairwise.

Contemporary studies [from Gottesman 1991]

	Number of pairs	Monozygotic percentage concordance*	Dizygotic percentage concordance*
Gottesman and Shields (1966)	22 MZ 33 DZ	58	15
Kringlen (1967)	55 MZ 90 DZ	45	15
Pollin *et al.* (1969)	164 MZ 277 DZ	31	6
Fischer (1973)	21 MZ 41 DZ	56	27

*Concordance calculated probandwise, which gives higher rates.

Table 5.3   Family history studies of schizophrenia using diagnostic criteria

	Numbers	Diagnostic criteria	Percentage of 1st degree relatives affected	
			Patients	Controls
Tsuang *et al.* (1980)	200 patients/ 375 relatives 160 controls/ 543 relatives	Feighner	5.3	0.6
Guze *et al.* (1983)	44 patients/ 111 relatives	Feighner	8.1	–
Baron *et al.* (1985)	90 patients/ 376 relatives 90 controls/ 374 relatives	RDC	5.8	0.6
Kendler *et al.* (1985)	253 patients/ 723 relatives 261 controls/ 1056 relatives	DSM III	3.7	0.2
Frangos *et al.* (1985)	116 patients/ 572 relatives 116 controls/ 694 relatives	DSM III	4.5	0.9

the rates were lower than previously found, the rates in the control groups were also lower. In addition, a re-analysis of one of the series of twins (McGuffin *et al.* 1984; Farmer *et al.* 1987) has also been carried out with the application of various diagnostic criteria under blind conditions. When DSM III criteria were applied, the concordance rates for monozygotic twins was found to be 48 per cent and that for dizygotic twins 10 per cent.

After a series of twists and turns, it finally seems safe to conclude that there is a genetic component to the aetiology of schizophrenia. At the same time this conclusion needs to be placed in perspective. At the end of his review of the genetics of schizophrenia, Gottesman pointed out that 89 per cent of patients will have parents who are not schizophrenic, 81 per cent will have no affected first degree relatives, and 63 per cent will show no family history of the disorder whatsoever. At most, therefore, only a predisposition to develop schizophrenia can be inherited. This and the lack of 100 per cent concordance in identical twins underline the point that some additional factor must be involved. In fact, the pattern of familiality of schizophrenia aligns it closely with disorders like diabetes mellitus, disseminated sclerosis, and pernicious anaemia, in which genetics are considered to form merely a background to some unknown environmental agent.

Structural brain abnormality in schizophrenia

So convinced was Kraepelin that schizophrenia was an organic disease of the brain that he persuaded a psychiatric colleague to apply himself to uncovering the neuropathology of the disorder. This soon revealed that that there were no obvious abnormalities, at least at a macroscopic level (Kraepelin's colleague, whose name was Alzheimer, went on to have more success with another disorder). From 1918 onwards it was also possible to examine the structure of the brain during life using the technique of air encephalography. Although these studies (see Haug 1962) gave hints that the brain was not normal in schizophrenia, the findings were not consistent and made little impression on mainstream psychiatric thought.

In the mid-1970s the languid pace of research in this field changed abruptly. Johnstone *et al.* (1976), using one of the two CT scanners which existed at the time, reported that a sample of 13 chronically hospitalized schizophrenic patients had significantly larger lateral ventricles than 8 controls; in some cases the enlargement appeared to be gross. An avalanche of replications and extensions of this study followed, in the aftermath of which the consistency of the finding became clear. As reviewed by Andreasen (1990*a*), 35 out of 48 studies which compared schizophrenics and normal individuals under blind conditions found a significant increase in lateral ventricular size. Most of the negative findings were in studies with small sample sizes, or with other shortcomings of design. Firm evidence of brain abnormality in schizophrenia, and hence of a biological aetiology, had finally been found.

Or had it? It was clear from the outset that the degree of ventricular enlargement in schizophrenia was for the most part modest. In the first study with a large sample size (Weinberger *et al.* 1979), 60 per cent of a group of 58 chronic schizophrenic patients were found to have lateral ventricles which were within the control range. In an even higher percentage, the scans were reported by radiologists as being within normal limits. Only in 10 cases could the presence of clinically significant ventricular enlargement be agreed on, and in most cases this was described as mild or borderline. Later, one methodologically rigorous study (Jernigan *et al.* 1982), which used a computer-based method of measurement, reported a failure to find any difference in lateral ventricular size between schizophrenics and controls. This was the first of several negative findings.

Already faltering, the CT scan research in schizophrenia was dealt a body blow in a brief paper by Smith and Iacono (1986). These authors selected, from the studies available at the time, 14 in which significant ventricular enlargement had been found, and also 7 where there were no differences. They then took the mean ventricular size figure (customarily the ventricle: brain ratio or VBR) for the schizophrenics and the controls in each of the two sets of studies and plotted them as a scatter diagram. The results of this manoeuvre are shown in Fig. 5.4. The range of average VBR values for the schizophrenics in the positive studies was closely similar to that in the negative studies. On the other hand, the corresponding values for the controls differed substantially: control subjects in the positive studies generally had smaller VBRs than those in the negative studies. In other words, the finding of significantly larger ventricular size in schizophrenia appeared to be due to the controls having smaller lateral ventricles rather than the schizophrenics having larger ones.

Smith and Iacono's interpretation ran as follows. Almost every study apart from the first by Johnstone *et al.* (1976) drew its control group from CT scans available in radiology files (typical examples included patients who had been investigated for headache with negative results, or the asymptomatic relatives of patients with Huntington's chorea). In these circumstances the decision as to whether or not a scan should be included as a control would have to depend on the radiologist's report. However,

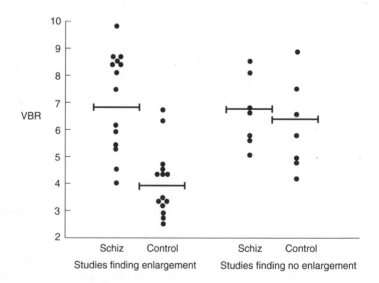

Fig. 5.4 Mean ventricle: brain ratio (VBR) for schizophrenic and control groups in studies reporting ventricular enlargement and no ventricular enlargement respectively (from Smith and Iacono 1986).

because lateral ventricular size is normally distributed through the population, there will always be a few individuals who have very large lateral ventricles merely by virtue of being at the extreme upper end of the normal range. Such individuals then run the risk of being judged as having lateral ventricles which are 'borderline', 'possibly abnormal', or (a particular favourite in Britain) 'larger than expected in an individual of this age'. If these individuals' scans are excluded from a control group, the range and mean will be systematically biased downwards. Put simply, some normal individuals have abnormally large lateral ventricles and it is all too easy for these to fail to find their way into a control group.

Lewis (1990) subsequently reviewed those CT scan studies which compared schizophrenic patients with prospectively ascertained normal volunteers. Of 20 studies, many of which had small sample sizes, only 8 found significant lateral ventricular enlargement, with a further 3 reporting marginal increases.

By this time it was clear that a definitive CT scan study of schizophrenia was urgently required. Such a study has recently been provided: Andreasen *et al.* (1990*a*) compared 108 patients meeting DSM III criteria for schizophrenia with 75 prospectively ascertained normal volunteers. The two groups were matched not only for age and sex, but also height, weight, and level of education. Potential control subjects were interviewed and excluded if they had a history of significant medical illness, head injury, neurological disorder, substance abuse or even psychiatric disorder. The findings of this study are shown in Table 5.4. Lateral ventricular size was found to be greater in the schizophrenic group than in the controls. The magnitude of the difference was small and its significance was relatively weak ($P < 0.04$). When only the patients and controls under the age of 50 were considered, the level of significance became somewhat higher ($P = 0.01$) (ventricular size increases steadily after late middle age which might have obscured any differences between the groups). As found previously, there was a substantial degree of overlap between the two groups: only 29 per cent of the schizophrenic patients were more than one standard deviation above the control group mean, and only 6 per cent more than two standard deviations above it. The most important finding of all, however, was that significant ventricular enlargement was only present in male schizophrenic patients; the distributions for female patients and controls were almost identical. These findings were unaltered by manoeuvres such as excluding the 18 schizophrenic patients with a history of drug or alcohol abuse, excluding the 4 controls with very large ventricular sizes, and stratifying the samples into age bands.

Andreasen *et al.*'s study at last indicates that there is significant lateral ventricular enlargement in schizophrenia. The issue then arises of what this means. One obvious question is whether ventricular enlargement predates the development of schizophrenia or whether it appears as the disorder

Table 5.4   Lateral ventricular size in a methodologically rigorous study of schizophrenics and prospectively ascertained controls (from Andreasen *et al.* 1990*a*)

	Mean VBR		
	Schizophrenic	Control	Significance
Total sample (108 pts; 75 controls	6.6	5.7	$P < 0.05$
Sample under 50 (101 pts; 60 controls)	6.5	5.4	$P < 0.01$
Males under 50 (63 pts; 29 controls)	6.6	4.8	$P < 0.01$
Females under 50 (38 pts; 31 controls)	6.2	5.9	NS

progresses—whether, in current parlance, it is neurodevelopmental or neurodegenerative. Almost all studies (see Lewis 1990) have found no relationship between lateral ventricular size in schizophrenia and factors, such as age and prior duration of illness. Several studies (for example, Weinberger *et al.* 1982; Schultz *et al.* 1983; Turner *et al.* 1986) have also found ventricular enlargement to be present in young patients and those undergoing their first episode of psychosis. This evidence, however, might be considered inadmissable because of the above-described difficulty with control groups; furthermore not all the studies have concurred with such a view (see Woods and Wolf 1983). Five studies have carried out follow-up CT scanning on schizophrenic patients up to nine years after the procedure was originally performed. Four found no change (Nasrallah *et al.* 1986; Illowsky *et al.* 1988; Reveley *et al.* 1988; Sponheim *et al.* 1991), whereas in one (Kemali *et al.* 1989) there was evidence of progression. Although it is clear that ventricular enlargement in schizophrenia does not progress rapidly, it cannot be definitively stated that progression does not take place at all.

Another issue is the relationship of lateral ventricular enlargement to aspects of the clinical picture of schizophrenia. Many studies have examined variables ranging from premorbid adjustment, through various classes of symptoms, to presence or absence of cognitive impairment, neurological signs, and tardive dyskinesia. As a rule the results have been evenly divided between those finding and those failing to find an association with lateral ventricular size (see Lewis 1990). One study, however, stands out from the rest in terms of patient numbers and methodological rigour. Owens *et al.* (1985) examined the relationship of lateral ventricular size to a wide range of clinical variables in 112 chronically hospitalized schizophrenic patients. As can be seen from Table 5.5, the only significant associations were with presence of tardive dyskinesia and impairment of current behaviour—this latter reflecting mainly reduced activity and poor social behaviour. Particularly noteworthy were the lack of any relationship between ventricular enlargement and negative symptoms or intellectual impairment.

Table 5.5 Correlates of lateral ventricular size in schizophrenia (from Owens *et al.* 1985)

Feature	Correlation with VBR	Comment
Positive symptoms	NS	
Negative symptoms	NS	No differences between groups matched for defect state vs no defect state
Abnormal behaviour	$P < 0.05$	Largely due to impaired social function and reduced activity
Intellectual impairment	NS	Curvilinear relationship with excess of impaired patients at both extremes of ventricular size
Academic record	NS	No differences between groups matched for high vs low achievement
Involuntary movements	$P < 0.01$	Found with two different scales and employing various cutoffs for abnormality
Insulin treatment	NS	No differences between groups matched for none vs much
Electroconvulsive therapy	NS	No differences between groups matched for none vs much
Neuroleptic treatment	NS	No differences between groups matched for none vs much

The outcome of 15 years of CT scan studies in schizophrenia has been the demonstration that there is a structural brain abnormality in the shape of lateral ventricular enlargement. Much of the force of this finding, however, is lost among arguments about the meaning of small diferences in wide and overlapping distributions. Perhaps the most telling conclusion is that the difference between the brains of an average schizophrenic and an average normal individual is scarcely greater than that between an average normal man and an average normal woman. Still waiting to be confronted at the present time is the uncomfortable fact that lateral ventricular enlargement only seems to be present in male schizophrenics. Ventricular enlargement has not convincingly emerged as reflecting either a neurodevelopmental or a neurodegenerative process in schizophrenia, nor has it been clearly associated with any clinical variable. It may be that the more sensitive technique of magnetic resonance imaging will resolve some of these questions, but the studies to date remain conflicting (for example, Kelsoe *et al.* 1988; Andreasen *et al.* 1990*b*; Young *et al.* 1991; see also Owens 1992).

Functional brain abnormality in schizophrenia

It is perfectly possible for the function of the brain to be seriously compromised without its structure being affected in any way whatsoever. The detection of abnormalities in the functional state of the brain in schizophrenia, however, presents technical difficulties which are if anything even greater than those associated with the demonstration of structural abnormalities, particularly if these are of comparable subtlety.

The first and until fairly recently the only technique available for investigating abnormal brain activity was electroencephalography (EEG). This tends to show slowing of normal rhythmical activity — the appearance of so called theta and delta waves — in encephalopathies of any origin, although in a somewhat insensitive and even rather capricious way. In addition, so-called paroxysmal abnormalities are found in epilepsy, the most extreme expression of which are the 'spikes' which are pathognomonic of the disorder. A wealth of other EEG phenomena have been described, the vast majority of which have at best dubious claims to pathological significance.

Over the years EEG abnormalities have been reported to be present in up to 80 per cent of patients with schizophrenia. However, it is clear from a critical review of the early literature (Ellingson 1954) and from the results of two more recent surveys (Itil 1977; Shagass 1977), first that the rates of all abnormalities are considerably lower in studies which have employed proper controls, and secondly that the abnormalities seen consist exclusively of nonspecific phenomena, that is those also seen with not substantially less frequency in normal individuals. Put bluntly, EEG studies of schizophrenia have provided no evidence of a functional brain disturbance of the same order as that seen in delirium or dementia, and they have lent precious little support to the view that there is any disturbance at all. (Broadly speaking, a similar conclusion can also be reached about the presence of epileptiform EEG abnormalities in schizophrenia. Here, though, the findings are complicated by a number of claims that a minority of schizophrenic patients, in particular those showing atypical clinical features, have an underlying epileptiform disturbance. This issue is dealt with in Chapter 11.)

About twenty years ago, a potentially much more powerful tool to observe the functional activity of the brain became available: measurement of regional cerebral blood flow and metabolism. The basic principle of the method is to introduce a radioactive substance into the bloodstream and measure the radioactivity emitted from the brain, using detectors placed over different parts of the head. The level of radioactivity will vary according to the blood flow to the brain region concerned, and this is known to be proportional to the metabolic and thus ultimately neuronal activity in the same region. In a variation of the technique radioactively labelled glucose is used, which gives a direct measure of neuronal activity in the region concerned. It has recently become possible to link the output of the detectors to computational software similar to that used in CT scanning, and so construct very detailed images of the brain, but of its metabolic function rather than its structure.

Functional imaging was first applied to schizophrenia in 1974 by Ingvar and Franzen (Ingvar and Franzen 1974). Using a crude technique to measure regional cerebral blood flow, they compared 15 normal controls (actually abstinent alcoholics), 11 patients with dementias of various origins, and two groups of schizophrenic patients. The first of the schizophrenic groups consisted of 9 middle aged or elderly chronically hospitalized patients who showed severe degrees of deterioration. The second was made up of 11 younger patients with more acute clinical pictures. Ingvar and Franzen found that while the demented patients showed significantly reduced cerebral blood flow in all areas compared with the controls, both of the schizophrenic groups had flow rates which were only slightly and not significantly different from normal. Three findings, however, suggested that cerebral blood flow might not be entirely normal in schizophrenia. First, there was evidence in both groups of schizophrenic patients of a changed regional pattern of flow, with a loss of the normal pattern of greater flow in anterior as compared with posterior regions – this has subsequently come to be referred to as 'hypofrontality'. Secondly, there were suggestions of a relationship between symptoms and blood flow, so that patients who were depressed and/or showed negative symptoms had lower rates than those who were excited/showed positive symptoms. Finally, in the controls there was a detectable increase in blood flow when

they performed cognitive tasks, but this was not seen in the schizophrenics —
at least as far as could be judged given the uncertainties as to whether some
of the patients were actually complying with the test instructions.

Something in the region of thirty further functional imaging studies in
schizophrenia have subsequently been carried out. Unfortunately, while
there have been spectacular advances in technological sophistication, these
have not always been matched by corresponding increases in sample size.
Those studies which have employed 12 or more schizophrenic patients are
summarized in Table 5.6. It is apparent from this that Ingvar and Franzen's
principal finding is upheld: general reductions in cerebral blood flow and
metabolism are either not found in schizophrenia or they are small and
usually fail to reach statistical significance. It is also evident that, contrary
to a widely propagated view, the hypofrontality hinted at in Ingvar and
Franzen's study has not been substantiated. None of the studies shown in
Table 5.6 (or any of the smaller ones for that matter) has ever demonstrated
this in an absolute sense, that is as lower flow or metabolism in anterior
compared with posterior regions. Some studies have reported 'relative'
hypofrontality — an anterior:posterior ratio which, while still positive, is
smaller in schizophrenics than normals. A clear majority, however, have
not found this. One study found a tendency to hyperfrontality.

Ingvar and Franzen's two other tentative findings have been followed-up,
somewhat belatedly but in a rather more impressive way. The possibility
that schizophrenic patients, while showing no great differences from
normals in cerebral blood flow under resting conditions, might show a
failure of activation during cognitive task performance was pursued by
Weinberger *et al*. (1986). They examined cerebral blood flow in 20 schizophrenic patients and 25 age- and sex-matched controls, both at rest and
during performance of the Wisconsin Card Sorting Test, an executive
('frontal') neuropsychological task. The schizophrenic patients performed
more poorly than the controls on this task, as expected (see Chapter 7). This
impairment was mirrored in a significantly smaller increase in blood flow
to the prefrontal cortex during the task. No such differences were found
with a control neuropsychological task. The authors went to considerable
lengths to exclude possible confounding factors. They established that the
degree of failure of prefrontal cortex activation correlated with the severity
of the impairment in task performance, and that the differences between
patients and controls were not attributable to drug treatment. However,
attempts to correct for the non-specific effects of task activation resulted
in the effect, which was small in the first place, becoming attenuated to the
point of near disappearance. Weinberger *et al*.'s finding has been replicated
in subsequent studies (Rubin *et al*. 1991; Andreasen *et al*. 1992), but once
again the differences have been small.

Ingvar and Franzen's other suggestion, that schizophrenic patients

Table 5.6 Functional imaging studies in schizophrenia (a) regional cerebral glucose metabolism studies

Study	Numbers	Medication	General reduced metabolism	Hypofrontality (relative)	Comments
Buchsbaum *et al.* (1984)	16 patients 13 controls	Drug free	No	Yes	Anterior:posterior ratio 1.02 in patients, 1.08 in controls
Farkas *et al.* (1984)	13 patients 11 controls	Some drug free	No	?	No significance figures presented
DeLisi *et al.* (1985)	21 patients 21 controls	Drug free	No	Yes	Angerior:posterior ratio 1.04 in patients, 1.11 in controls
Gur *et al.* (1987)	12 patients 12 controls	Drug free	?	No	General reductions, but not significant
Volkow *et al.* (1987)	18 patients 12 controls	All treated	No	Yes	Both patients and controls showed 'absolute' hypofrontality
Cohen *et al.* (1987)	16 patients	Drug free	No	Yes	—
Wolkin *et al.* (1988)	13 patients 8 controls	Drug free	Yes	Yes	Anterior:posterior ratio 1.04 in patients, 1.11 in controls
Szechtman *et al.* (1988)	17 patients 10 controls	Some drug free	—	No	Hyperfrontality found
Siegel *et al.** (1993)	70 patients 30 controls	Drug free	No	No	Anterior:posterior ratios 1.03 for patients v 1.06 in controls, but this was due to high occipital activity rather than low frontal activity

*Includes patients from 2 earlier studies by Buchsbaum and co-workers.

Table 5.6 Functional imaging studies in schizophrenia (b) Regional cerebral blood flow studies

Study	Numbers	Medication	General reduced metabolism	Hypofrontality (relative)	Comments
Mathew *et al.* (1982)	23 patients 18 controls	Some drug free	Yes	No	Significant reductions in 11 out of 16 areas examined
Ariel *et al.* (1983)	29 patients 22 controls	Mostly treated	Yes	Yes	Anterior: posterior difference 0.3 SD in patients, 0.8 SD in controls
Gur *et al.* (1983)	15 patients 25 controls	All treated	No	No	–
Gur *et al.* (1985)	19 patients 19 controls	Drug free	No	No	–
Kurachi *et al.* (1985)	16 patients 20 controls	All treated	No	Yes	Patients also showed increased flow in temporal regions
Weinberger *et al.* (1986)	20 patients 25 controls	Drug free	No	No	Overall tendency to hyperfrontality, but reduced flow in dorsolateral prefrontal cortex
Dousse *et al.* (1988)	27 patients 27 controls	Most treated	Yes	Yes	–

Study	Sample	Drug status			Findings
Mathew *et al.* (1988)	108 patients 108 controls	Some drug free	—	No	Patients had significantly higher flow in temporal and occipital regions bilaterally and in the left central region
Bacj *et al.* (1989)	28 patients 11 controls	All treated	—	No	—
Paulman *et al.* (1990)	40 patients 31 controls	Half drug free	No	No	Patients showed sig. increased general flow. Patients also showed sig. greater proportion of frontal and temporal perfusion deficits on visual inspection
Sagawa *et al.* (1990)	53 patients 32 controls	All treated	—	Yes	—
Rubin *et al.* (1991)	19 patients 7 controls	Most drug free	No	No	Both patients and controls showed a tendency to absolute hypofrontality
Tamminga *et al.* (1992)	12 patients 27 patients	All drug free	—	No	Significant reductions in flow found in hippocampus and anterior cingulate cortex
Andreasen *et al.* (1992)	36 patients 15 controls	13 drug naive 23 drug free	—	No	Both patients and controls showed absolute hypofrontality

showing different patterns of symptoms might show different patterns of cerebral blood flow and metabolism, has been taken several steps further by Liddle *et al.* (1992). He and colleagues carried out cerebral blood flow measurements, combined with sophisticated computer analysis, on 30 chronic schizophrenic patients in whom detailed symptom ratings had also been obtained; there was no control group. Scan appearances were compared between groups of patients exhibiting positive, negative, and disorganization syndromes (see Chapter 2). In practice, this meant contrasting groups of patients with high and low scores on negative symptoms, high and low scores on positive symptoms (defined narrowly as delusions and hallucinations), and high and low scores on disorganization symptoms (that is formal thought disorder, inappropriate affect, and bizarre behaviour). Significantly different patterns of brain activity emerged as associated with each of these syndromes: negative symptoms were associated with decreased flow in the prefrontal cortex, this being more marked on the left than the right. Positive symptoms were associated with increases in the left temporal lobe, particularly the parahippocampal gyrus. Disorganization symptoms were associated with increases in the right anterior cingulate cortex, and also decreases in the right prefrontal cortex and parietal cortex bilaterally. There were also changes in other cortical areas and the basal ganglia which did not follow any simply interpretable pattern.

The main conclusion to be drawn from the functional imaging studies of schizophrenia is that not a great deal has been added to Ingvar and Franzen's original finding that any abnormality is subtle to the point of testing the limits of the technique. It is sobering to reflect that a very deteriorated, wildly disturbed, probably cognitively impaired, and perhaps incontinent schizophrenic patient is unlikely to show any marked deviation from normal when scanned using a technique which is sensitive enough to detect changes when words are spoken or when the eyes are opened! It is possible that a prefrontal cortical dysfunction of a peculiarly subtle kind has been uncovered by Weinberger *et al.*; but their findings are not as yet robust enough to convince sceptics. The work of Liddle *et al.* provides tantalizing glimpses of what the functional architecture of schizophrenic symptoms might turn out to be; but his group have only, it must be remembered, demonstrated differences between patients and patients, and not between patients and normals.

Miscellaneous findings

After the major psychodynamic theories of schizophrenia have been put to the test and the leading biological findings have been subjected to critical scrutiny, there remain a number of areas of research which have yielded positive or at any rate hopeful findings. These results have all been generated as part of the biological initiative in schizophrenia, but it has to be said that on the whole they have provided few clues to the nature of the underlying pathological process: where the link is most direct—as in neuropathological studies—the findings tend to be at their weakest. In at least one case—the relationship of schizophrenia with schizoid personality—a biological explanation is only one of several constructions which can be placed on the association.

Neuropathological abnormalities

While accepting that the brain appeared macroscopically normal in schizophrenia, Kraepelin (1913*a*) interpreted a variety of histological findings made by Alzheimer and Nissl as evidence of severe and widespread cortical disease. Even at the time, and certainly by the standards of contemporary neuropathology, there was reason to suspect that these findings were rather slim and to treat Kraepelin's confident interpretation of them with caution. Subsequent studies of the classical era, which have been reviewed with exceptional clarity by David (1957), made it clear that most or all of the reported abnormalities were minor, widely scattered, and largely non-specific. By the time of the first International Congress of Neuropathology in 1952 schizophrenia had come to be regarded as an unproductive area of investigation, the 'graveyard' of neuropathology.

As part of the subsequent renewal of interest in biological aspects of schizophrenia, and in the wake of the CT scan studies in particular, there has been a spate of recent post-mortem studies (reviewed by Kirch and Weinberger 1986; Lantos 1988; Roberts 1991). Some of these have compared the brains of schizophrenic and normal individuals macroscopically, typically using quantitative methods to search for small differences in the size of cortical and subcortical structures. Claims have been made for decreased brain size; for decreased thickness of the parahippocampal gyrus; and also for reduced size of a number of subcortical structures, including the hippocampus, the amygdala, and basal ganglia nuclei among others. Other studies have attempted to demonstrate abnormalities at the microscopic level. The most well-known finding of this type is that of disarray of the normally regularly arranged hippocampal pyramidal cells, first described by Scheibel and Kovelman (1981). Many other histological changes have also been reported, mainly in the frontal and cingulate cortex.

Unfortunately, despite a steady stream of studies, it is not at all clear that any neuropathological abnormality can be regarded as established in schizophrenia. Post-mortem studies face many potential methodological pitfalls, especially when small, subtle, or quantitative differences are being sought. Some of those which are particularly applicable to studies on schizophrenic brains have been reviewed by Benes (1988): several studies have relied on series of brains collected earlier this century, when even the best clinical information was liable to have been partial and inaccurate. The control groups have not always been appropriate, for instance not matched for the important variable of sex. The cause of death, the duration of the agonal period, the length of post-mortem delay, the amount of time spent in fixative, and numerous other factors can all introduce systematic bias, but in general have not been equated between patient and control groups. Sometimes the volume or area estimations have been unsatisfactory. Even when the studies have seemed sound, their findings have often not been replicated. A good example is the alleged abnormalities found in hippocampal structure in schizophrenia. A significant reduction of the overall size of this structure was reported by Bogerts *et al.* (1985), but was later contradicted by Altschuler *et al.* (1990) and Heckers *et al.* (1990). Scheibel and Kovelman's finding of hippocampal pyramidal cell disarray was not made under blind conditions. Subsequently, these authors found that the abnormality was equally prevalent in normal brains (Altshuler *et al.* 1987), and the result was not replicated by an independent group (Christison *et al.* 1989). Further work by the original authors has recently tended to support the original finding (Conrad *et al.* 1991).

When the contemporary neuropathological research in schizophrenia is compared with that carried out earlier in the century, it is difficult to avoid a feeling of *déjà vu*. The overall impression has to be that no abnormality has been reliably demonstrated, either at the macroscopic or microscopic level, and that some of the initial claims were extravagant. If a positive note can be sounded, it is that the CT scan finding of lateral ventricular enlargement in schizophrenia has recently been confirmed in a post-mortem study (Crow *et al.* 1989).

Early cerebral insult

The idea that injury to the brain *in utero*, at birth, or in the early postnatal period might in some way encourage the later development of schizophrenia is one which has cropped up a number of times in a number of different guises. According to Murray *et al.* (1988) and Lewis (1989), the key stages in the evolution of the idea were, in historical order: (1) early claims, notably by Rosanoff (Rosanoff 1914; Rosanoff *et al.* 1934), that any neuropathological abnormalities in schizophrenia had to represent development aplasia rather than a degenerative atrophy; (2) the observation, first made by Katz (cited in Mednick and Cannon 1991), that patients with schizophrenia seem to have had a high rate of obstetric complications; (3) the suggestions (see above) that ventricular enlargement on CT scan is not progressive and if anything predates the onset of illness; and (4) the appreciation, due to the work of Goldman and Galkin (1978), that the behavioural effects of brain injury in young animals can lie dormant for a long time before becoming apparent.

These disparate strands of evidence were drawn together by authors such as Schulsinger *et al*. (1984) and Weinberger (1987), but especially by Murray and Lewis (see Murray *et al*. 1985, 1988; Lewis 1989), who can be regarded as the principal architects of the neurodevelopmental theory of schizophrenia. Their central hypothesis is that a brain lesion produced around the time of birth remains quiescent until it interacts with normal brain maturational processes around the time of puberty, when it causes the clinical symptoms of schizophrenia to appear. The lesion is not necessarily completely silent in the intervening period, however, and tends to show itself in developmental delays or subtle disturbances in cognitive, emotional, and social functioning.

The obvious test of the hypothesis is whether individuals who have become schizophrenic have experienced more medical complications during their mother's pregnancy, the perinatal period, and early life than those who have not become schizophrenic. A fair number of studies directed to this question have been carried out; these have usually focused on obstetric complications, which are the most susceptible to accurate objective determination. A serious problem still remains, however, in the necessarily retrospective nature of the analysis: either hospital obstetric records or the mothers' recall of her child's birth have been relied on. The former are often of poor quality and in the latter, the mothers will not be oblivious to the presence of mental illness in their children (not to mention the fact that some of the mothers will themselves be psychiatrically ill). On the two occasions these studies have been reviewed, the reviewers have come to diametrically opposed conclusions. Lewis (1989) considered that despite wide methodological differences all but one of eight studies found a significant excess of obstetric complications in the schizophrenic group. Done *et al*. (1991), in contrast, felt that only around half of the same selection of studies could be considered to have shown an association. In these circumstances, perhaps the best course is to let the adversaries speak for themselves through their own studies, which were carried out in full knowledge of the pitfalls of earlier work.

Lewis and Murray (1987) used large numbers and a standardized procedure for rating obstetric complications in order to dilute the effects of variable quality of retrospective information. The case summaries of 1385 first admissions to two pychiatric hospitals were screened for history of birth complications (such information was obtained from relatives as a routine practice). In 955 cases where the information was judged to be adequate, presence of definite obstetric complications was rated according to a fixed scheme under blind conditions. The rate for 207 patients meeting diagnostic criteria for schizophrenia was found to be 17 per cent, compared with 8 per cent for the remaining 745 patients with other psychiatric diagnoses. This difference was significant. Patients with anorexia nervosa had a rate of obstetric complications which was almost as high, but the numbers were small. The rate for patients with manic-depressive psychosis also showed a trend towards significant elevation.

Done *et al.* (1991) avoided the difficulties associated with using obstetric records and/or maternal recollection altogether. They took advantage of the fact that a large scale systematic survey of perinatal mortality and morbidity had been carried out in Britain on a cohort of individuals born in a single week in 1958. Every member of this cohort who subsequently had a psychiatric admission in young adult life was then traced; their case notes were obtained and a diagnosis was applied using a modification of the Present State Examination. Out of 235 cases, a diagnosis of schizophrenia was made in 79 cases. The number of risk factors for perinatal mortality (which approximates closely to the complications of pregnancy and delivery) was found not to differ substantially between those who developed schizophrenia and those who remained psychiatrically well. The odds ratio for the risk ranged from 1.41 for narrowly defined schizophrenia, to 1.50 for broadly defined schizophrenia, to 1.77 for schizophrenia as diagnosed clinically according to the case notes; none of these increases was statistically significant.

At present, these findings remain unreconciled. One possible reason for a false positive finding, suggested by Done *et al.* is that a number of the mothers of the schizophrenics might themselves have been suffering from schizophrenia whilst pregnant and this might have attracted obstetric complications by virtue of poor diet, lack of compliance with antenatal care, etc. Alternatively, one reason for a false negative result could be that counting obstetric complications is too coarse a way of indexing the relevant perinatal event—which could be something as subtle as asymptomatic intracranial bleeding. Overall, the early cerebral insult theory of schizophrenia has to be regarded as *sub judice*.

The season of birth effect

The observation that excessive numbers of patients with schizophrenia appeared to have been born in winter was first made by Tramer in 1929. Since then this finding has been confirmed, repudiated, considered to be established, dismissed as an artefact, and generally picked over up to the present day. That interest in the field has been kept alive is in no small part due to the efforts of Hare (for example 1980), who has repeatedly argued that whilst the effect in itself is no more than a minor irregularity, it might turn out to provide a clue to a more crucial causative factor in schizophrenia.

The evidence for and against the season of birth effect of schizophrenia has been exhaustively reviewed by Bradbury and Miller (1985). They found that around two thirds of 37 studies carried out in the Northern hemisphere reported a seasonal variation. Of these studies, 12 were considered to have avoided major methodological shortcomings; 10 of the 12 reported a seasonality effect, and in 9 this was restricted predominantly or exclusively to the winter months. In the Southern hemisphere, where the seasons are reversed, only 2 of 6 studies found any effect, both reporting excesses in winter; however, neither of these were methodologically sound. Some studies have reported more complicated or even frankly erratic patterns of variation in schizophrenic birth rate which cannot be understood as in any way seasonal. A number of actuarial reasons why the effect might be spurious have been proposed, but there are cogent arguments for not accepting these; three of the studies (two of them in the methodologically rigorous subgroup) continued to find the effect after correcting for these. Bradbury and Miller concluded that the season of birth effect could be regarded as firmly established, but their conclusion has to be qualified by the statement that it is only established for the Northern hemisphere, and in some of the most rigorous studies the effect clearly spills over into spring and even early summer.

Accepting that there is a variation in the season of birth of individuals destined to become schizophrenic, it remains unclear what this means. The effect is small, of the order of a 5–15 per cent excess, and it is probably not restricted just to schizophrenia — Hare *et al.* (1974) also found it in manic-depressive psychosis and there was a nearly significant excess in mental handicap. The most popular explanation involves interuterine or neonatal infection, in particular viral infection — many infections have a peak incidence in winter and early spring. Other theories have invoked obstetric complications and nutritional deficiency. Any role for temperature as such, however, appears to have been excluded. The season of birth effect may be a bona fide phenomenon in schizophrenia, but it is evident that the attempts to account for it are all pure, if plausible, speculation.

Schizoid premorbid personality

Kraepelin (1907) considered that at least 20 per cent of patients who developed schizophrenia had exhibited mental peculiarities from early youth, among which seclusiveness, affectation, and eccentricity figured prominently. Bleuler (1911) went further, claiming that anomalies of character could be uncovered by careful enquiry in more than half of all individuals who later became schizophrenic; all ten of his own childhood acquaintances who became schizophrenic stood out from other children by virtue of, amongst other things, their inability to engage in play.

According to Bleuler's son (Bleuler 1978), it was Bleuler's students who first used the term schizoid to describe individuals who were peculiar in a way reminiscent of schizophrenia whilst not suffering from the disorder itself. Thereafter the concept of schizoid personality pursued two conflicting courses. On the one hand, it was shaped by Schneider (1950) into one of his ten types of abnormal personality: schizoid individuals were characterized by a cluster of traits of emotional coldness, detachment, lack of interest in other people, eccentricity, and introspective fantasy. On the other hand, under the influence of Kretschmer (1925), the concept came to denote something much broader, more intuitive than descriptive, which aimed to capture all the kinds of abnormality seen in schizophrenics before they became ill, and also those encountered in their relatives. The former of these definitions of schizoid pesonality has survived many changes in the classification of personality disorder unscathed, and continues to feature in all current schemes. The fate of the latter definition was summed up by Mayer-Gross *et al.* (1969) as follows: 'The validity of identifying the symptoms of a psychosis leading to personality deterioration with certain superficially similar features in the patient before his illness or in his relatives has not been accepted outside Kretschmer's own school'.

It is widely acknowledged that the majority of individuals with schizoid personalities in the Schneiderian sense of the term do not become schizophrenic, and also that patients with schizophrenia do not necessarily show any evidence of schizoid traits before the onset of their illness. What is uncertain is whether schizoid personality disorder predisposes to development of schizophrenia. Studies on this issue carried out between 1912 and 1978 were reviewed by Cutting (1985), who concluded that between 20 per cent and 30 per cent of patients who became schizophrenic could be described as 'shut in', 'shy and solitary', or 'schizoid'; other abnormal personality traits could be found in a similar proportion again. However, the definition of schizoid personality was neither very rigorous nor very consistent across these studies.

A method of assessing personality objectively and in a detailed way has been developed by Tyrer *et al.* (1988). The Personality Assessment Schedule consists of a battery of questions directed to many different traits which is designed to be administered to patients' relatives or other informants, and also to the patients themselves. The schedule yields 'agnostic' personality groupings, which have been validated by cluster analysis. It also distinguishes more severe 'personality disorders' and less severe 'personality difficulties' or traits. Tyrer *et al.* (1988) used this schedule to assess the premorbid personalities of 109 patients meeting DSM III criteria for schizophrenia, usually by interviewing a relative or other informant, but in a minority of cases administering it only to the patients themselves. The results are shown in Table 5.7. Forty-five per cent of the sample were classified as having a personality disorder. Eighteen per cent fell into the schizoid cluster (schizoid, paranoid, and avoidant personalities). Another 17 per cent were found to have an antisocial personality disorder. The proportion of schizoid personalities in the schizophrenic patients was

Table 5.7 Personality Assessment Schedule classification of 109 schizophrenic patients (from Tyrer et al. 1988)

Personality type	Normal	Personality difficulty	Personality disorder	Combined personality disorder	Severe personality disorder	Gross personality disorder	Total (%)
Normal	38						38 (34.9)
Sociopathic			1		2	1	4 (3.7)
Explosive		1	3	1	4	3	12 (11.0)
Sensitive-aggressive		1	1	1			3 (2.8)
Passive-dependent			3	1	2		6 (5.5)
Histrionic		2	2	1			5 (4.6)
Asthenic			2				2 (1.8)
Anankastic			1	1		1	3 (2.8)
Anxious		2	1	2			5 (4.6)
Hypochondriacal				1			1 (0.9)
Dysthymic			1	2	1	1	5 (4.6)
Schizoid		2	5	1	4	2	14 (12.8)
Avoidant		3	3	2	1		9 (8.3)
Paranoid					1	1	2 (1.8)
Total	38	11	23	13	15	9	109
(%)	(34.9)	(10.1)	(21.1)	(11.9)	(13.8)	(8.3)	(100.0)

significantly higher than that found in 200 normal individuals and 159 patients with anxiety disorders.

Tyrer *et al.*'s conclusion was that, although there was an excess of patients with schizoid personality disorder in schizophrenia, the degree of co-occurrence was not nearly as high as might be expected from clinical impression; the personality abnormalities found also extended well beyond the schizoid category. It should also be noted that Tyrer *et al.*'s findings indicate that around a third of cases of schizophrenia show no abnormalities of personality, and that in another substantial proportion the abnormalities are minor and also commonplace in the normal population.

Conclusion

If anything has been learnt about the cause of schizophrenia, it is more in the way of what is not, than what is of aetiological significance in the disorder. However, in the course of narrowing the range of possibilities and establishing what are the right questions to ask, some findings of undeniable importance have emerged. These have been both of a negative and a positive kind.

The most significant negative finding has undoubtedly been the failure to confirm that schizophrenia has a primarily psychological basis. No matter how plausibly argued and how passionately advocated, psychodynamic theories have conspicuously failed to achieve any significant experimental support—and this has not been for want of trying. After all this time and with the unprecedented effort that has gone into trying to prove the case, absence of evidence can only mean evidence of absence.

The strongest positive finding in schizophrenia research has been the demonstration that there is a genetic contribution to the disorder. Although this has been established beyond any reasonable doubt, it remains to be seen whether what is inherited is a predisposition which is played out in some relatively straightforward biological way; or whether it is merely a vulnerability, which is expressed indirectly via a number of intervening variables—including perhaps personality and psychosocial factors. As regards other areas of biological research, the conclusion has to be that those who view schizophrenia as a brain disease have not so far managed to come up with any evidence which is stronger than that used by their psychodynamically oriented colleagues to support their own position.

6

Pathogenesis: the dopamine hypothesis

Accepting a biological basis for schizophrenia leaves something of a credibility gap in the understanding of the disorder. This is that it is not immediately apparent how an abnormality in brain structure or function might become translated into the many, varied, and changeable symptoms of the disorder, most if not all of which are quite different from the signs of neurological disease. The usual way of bridging this gap has been to postulate an intervening variable in the shape of a disturbance of neurochemical function. Such a disorder could easily be the mode of expression of a genetic fault, for example one affecting the regulation of a neurotransmitter; and it is equally compatible with a structural brain abnormality—for example, insidiously evolving damage might trigger off pathological fluctuations in neurotransmitter levels. Equally, it is not difficult to imagine a chemical disturbance acting to produce a relatively subtle derangement of brain function, which results in disorders that are primarily in the realm of thinking, feeling, and perception.

Precedent certainly exists for the idea of alterations in brain chemistry giving rise to abnormal mental states. From the ancient religious usage of psilocybin and mescaline, through the plagues of ergotism of the middle ages, to the opium-induced pipe dreams of Victorian England, drugs have always been known which have the ability to induce, in clear consciousness, mental changes every bit as remarkable as the symptoms of schizophrenia. However, it was probably the synthesis of LSD in 1947 and its subsequent widespread illicit use which first concentrated the minds of researchers on biochemical hypotheses of schizophrenia. The first wave of these suggested that there might be some inborn error of metabolism—a 'pink spot' in the urine, an aberrant form of the copper transporting enzyme, a tendency to abnormal transmethylation of biogenic amines—which could lead under certain conditions to a chemical being produced which had mind-altering properties. For one reason or another these theories did not stand the test of time (see Iversen 1978; Smythies 1983). Shortly afterwards they were replaced by another biochemical theory which went on to show a remarkable tenacity; this is the hypothesis that some schizophrenic symptoms are due to an excess of brain dopamine.

Every psychiatrist is familiar with the observations on which the dopamine hypothesis of schizophrenia were originally based. Somewhat less well known is the ingenious and resourceful investigation that went into establishing that dopamine rather than any other neurotransmitter played the crucial role in these effects. Perhaps less widely appreciated still has been the methodical series of steps that were then taken to provide a direct test of the dopamine hypothesis, a series of steps which culminated in what can arguably be considered to have been the most important experiment in the history of psychiatry.

Origins of the dopamine hypothesis

The concept of a disorder of brain chemistry in schizophrenia can be traced back to Kraepelin and Bleuler, although only with difficulty. Kraepelin (1907) believed that the underlying brain pathology was potentially and to a limited extent reversible. Bleuler (1911) speculated that some toxic agent — for example an endocrine abnormality or an infectious process — might produce both the symptoms of schizophrenia and then go on to cause permanent changes in the brain.

The nearest thing to an explicit foreshadowing of the dopamine hypothesis appeared in the work of Mettler (Mettler 1955; Mettler and Crandell 1959). He, like a number of other authors (see Chapter 1), was struck by the occurrence in chronic schizophrenic patients of abnormal movements highly reminiscent of those seen in extrapyramidal disease. He therefore speculated that a basal ganglia pathology might underlie the disorder. However, since schizophrenia was a disorder of exacerbations and remissions, it seemed unlikely that the pathological process was one which caused permanent damage to basal ganglia structures. Dopamine having not yet been discovered, Mettler had to fall back on the rather unsatisfactory suggestion of some form of vasospasm which intermittently compromised the function of this part of the brain.

But this was all essentially preamble. The dopamine hypothesis proper emerged suddenly in the 1960s as the result of two symmetrical and more or less contemporaneous observations. The first of these concerned the antipsychotic action of neuroleptic drugs; the second the psychosis-inducing properties of amphetamine and other stimulant drugs.

The antipsychotic effect of neuroleptic drugs

Chlorpromazine was first used for the treatment of schizophrenia in 1952. As described in detail in Chapter 8, the effectiveness of this and a number of other drugs became apparent to clinicians very quickly, and over the next decade or so was placed beyond doubt by a large number of double-blind, placebo-controlled studies.

How neuroleptics exerted their therapeutic effect, however, remained uncertain for considerably longer. Eventually, several lines of evidence converged to suggest that dopamine receptor blockade was the important pharmacological action. These have been reviewed by Seeman (1980), and can be briefly summarized as follows. Various neuroleptic drugs were found to accelerate the metabolic turnover of dopamine. In animal behavioural studies, as well as inducing a state similar to human Parkinsonism, the drugs reversed the effects of dopamine agonist drugs like apomorphine. In neurophysiological experiments, the drugs were found to inhibit the effects of dopamine on the firing rate of neurones in the basal ganglia. Finally, in terms of their molecular structure, it was shown that there was a conformational relationship between different neuroleptic drugs and dopamine.

All this evidence is indirect. Futhermore, the view that neuroleptic drugs exert their antipyschotic effect by virtue of dopamine receptor blockade faces a number of difficulties and inconsistencies. For example, the majority of neuroleptics block not only dopamine and noradrenaline receptors, but also those for serotonin, histamine, and in some cases others as well. Another problem is that, while a great deal of effort has been devoted to developing neuroleptics with more powerful and/or selective actions on dopamine receptors, such drugs have not turned out to have correspondingly greater antipsychotic efficacy. But perhaps the most serious objection is that the neuroleptic treatment of schizophrenia is widely recognized to be far from satisfactory—in such circumstances it is probably a good idea to be cautious about ascribing improvement to one pharmacological action to the exclusion of all others.

What might be referred to as the dopamine hypothesis of neuroleptic action is one of the two pillars of the dopamine hypothesis of schizophrenia, and needs to be shown to rest on secure foundations. To do this, three questions need to be answered in turn. These are: (1) Do all antipsychotic drugs block dopamine receptors? (2) Is their antipsychotic effectiveness related to their dopamine-receptor blocking properties? (3) Can the antipsychotic effect be attributed exclusively to their dopamine antagonist properties, without any additional effects, known or unknown, playing a part?

Do all antipsychotic drugs block dopamine receptors? Since antidopaminergic activity is the pharmacological effect screened for in the in the development of new neuroleptic drugs, the answer to this question hardly needs to be spelled out. The receptor-blocking profiles of different neuroleptics have been reviewed by Hyttel *et al.* (1985), whose diagrammatic representation of these is reproduced in Fig. 6.1. It can be seen that some neuroleptics, such as chlorpromazine, thioridazine, and fluphenazine have blocking effects on multiple receptor types, but these always include

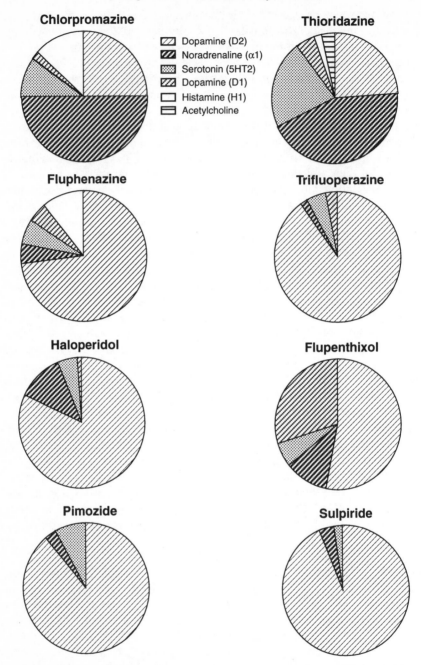

Fig. 6.1 Pie charts showing the receptor blocking profiles of different neuro-leptic drugs (from Hyttel *et al.* 1985).

dopamine. Others, for example haloperidol and trifluoperazine, exert their main effect on dopamine receptors and have only minor actions at other receptor sites. Still others can only be regarded as highly selective for dopamine receptors, a good example being pimozide. Finally, there is one drug, sulpiride, which is to all intents and purposes entirely specific for dopamine receptors. Thus it is clear that, whatever other actions they may have, dopamine receptor blockade is the only pharmacological action that all antipsychotic drugs share.

There are three apparent exceptions to this conclusion. Reserpine is a drug which, while being pharmacologically quite distinct from neuroleptics, has shown clear evidence of therapentic effectiveness in schizophrenia (Kline 1954). However, although reserpine does not block dopamine receptors it has a functionally equivalent effect on dopamine availability, that of depletion of synaptic stores of the transmitter. Promazine, a close chemical relative of chlorpromazine, has a long history of usage in schizophrenia. Its dopamine receptor blocking effects are, however, weak (for example Seeman 1980). This apparent inconsistency is resolved when it is realized that promazine is relatively ineffective compared with other neuroleptics (see Davis 1985). Finally, the atypical neuroleptic clozapine (see Chapter 8) is, it seems clear, clinically more effective than other neuroleptics, whereas its dopamine receptor blocking effects have always been considered unexceptional or even weak (for example Andersen *et al.* 1986). Recently, though, using PET scan technology in human subjects (Farde *et al.* 1989, 1992), it has been shown unequivocally that clozapine occupies brain dopamine receptors to a roughly comparable extent to conventional neuroleptic drugs. All these exceptions, therefore, merely prove the rule that dopamine receptor blockade is a prerequisite for antipsychotic effectiveness.

Is the antipsychotic effectiveness of neuroleptic drugs related to their dopamine receptor blocking effects? The first attempt to demonstrate a quantitative rather than qualitative association between the therapeutic and dopamine-blocking properties of neuroleptic drugs was made in 1967 by Janssen (cited in Iversen 1978). Using a number of neuroleptics, he found that a correlation existed between the average daily dose necessary to control schizophrenic symptoms and the dose necessary to reverse the behavioural effects of dopamine agonist drugs in animals. Later, when a direct assay for dopamine receptors was developed, a similar correlation was found for some neuroleptics, but a major discrepancy became apparent; this concerned the butyrophenone group of drugs, for example haloperidol (see Seeman 1980). In 1976, however, a new, direct, and highly accurate method of assaying dopamine receptor binding was simultaneously applied by two groups of investigators (Creese *et al.* 1976; Seeman *et al.* 1976). Both found that the correlation between the average daily dose of all drugs (including butyrophenones) and their ability to block dopamine receptors was exceptionally high at around 0.9. (It was, in fact, as a result of this experiment that it became clear that there were two types of dopamine receptor, D1 and D2, and that neuroleptics preferentially blocked D2 receptors.) The obvious conclusion was that the antipsychotic effect of neuroleptics was a direct function of their actions at dopamine receptors.

It could still be argued that neuroleptic drugs might show a similar clinical: pharmacological correlation for one or more other classes of receptor. This possibility was investigated by Peroutka and Snyder (1980). Using 22 neuroleptic drugs, they plotted the relationship between average clinical dosage and receptor blocking effects for dopamine (D2), serotonin (5HT2), noradrenaline (alpha), and histamine (H1) receptors. Their findings are shown in Fig. 6.2, from which it is clear that the correlations for all three receptors are either not statistically significant or inverse.

Is the antipsychotic effect of neuroleptics attributable exclusively to dopamine receptor blockade? Although the preceding studies make it clear that the antipsychotic properties of neuroleptic drugs are closely related to their effects at dopamine receptors, they do not establish that dopamine receptor blockade and only dopamine receptor blockade is responsible. Not ruled out is the possibility that blockade of another receptor type—for example blockade of serotonin receptors—makes an additional contribution. Alternatively it could be that the effectiveness of a neuroleptic is related more to the breadth of its actions than to its action on dopamine receptors—the more receptor types affected, the better the antipsychotic effect. A remote chance also exists that a pharmacological action on some as yet undiscovered neurotransmitter system might be responsible for the antipsychotic effect, possibly a system that is coupled to the dopamine system in some way.

These possibilities were put to the test in an elegant study by Johnstone *et al.* (1978). They took advantage of the fact that the neuroleptic flupenthixol exists in two forms, the alpha (*cis*) isomer and the beta (*trans*) isomer. The slight structural difference between the two isomers is enough to confer different biological actions; in particular, the alpha isomer has been shown to have dopamine blocking effects, whereas the beta isomer does not. Otherwise, the receptor blocking profiles of the two drugs are fairly evenly matched (although the beta but not the alpha isomer also lacks serotonin blocking effects). The authors assigned 45 acute schizophrenic patients, randomly and under blind conditions, to treatment with either alpha flupenthixol, beta fluopenthixol, or placebo for four weeks. The findings are shown in Fig. 6.3. All three groups showed some improvement, but only in the alpha flupenthixol-treated group was this significantly greater than with placebo.

This result makes it difficult to argue that anything other than or additional to dopamine receptor blockade underlies the antipsychotic action of neuroleptics. The difference in serotonin receptor blocking capacities could conceivably have played a part, but as Johnstone *et al.* pointed out, there was (and still is) very little independent evidence to implicate serotonin in psychosis and antipsychotic drug effects. To attribute antipsychotic action to some unknown chemical action is just as difficult; it would have to be assumed that alpha flupenthixol just happened to have such an effect whereas beta flupenthixol just happened to lack it.

Taking these three lines of evidence together, the proposition that the antipsychotic effect of neuroleptic drugs is a function of their ability to block dopamine receptors must be regarded as having been established beyond any reasonable doubt. There is very little room for argument about the additional role of blockade of other known receptors, and the possibility that some as yet unknown neurochemical property might underlie their antipsychotic effect has effectively been ruled out by Johnstone *et al.*'s study.

The psychosis-inducing effects of amphetamine and other stimulant drugs

The amphetamines (amphetamine, methamphetamine, methylphenidate, and some other compounds) are a group of drugs which are known to exert their principal pharmacological actions on brain catecholamine neurones (Biel and Bopp 1978; Moore 1978). A wealth of pharmacological evidence has made it clear that they act to cause a functional excess of both dopamine and noradrenaline; this is achieved via a number of mechanisms, including enhancement of synaptic release, blockade of re-uptake, and reduction of degradation by inhibition of monoamine oxidase. The class of drug has little if any effect on serotonin neurones, and is not known to have any other important central nervous system actions.

The first report of a psychosis resembling schizophrenia as a complication of amphetamine administration was made by Young and Scoville (1938), three years after the drug was introduced. Over the next two decades single case reports and small series continued to document the occurrence of psychotic states similar to schizophrenia as a sequel of chronic amphetamine use. The idea that amphetamine might cause psychosis, however, remained controversial. One recurrent issue in the debate was whether what was being seen was merely latent schizophrenia being released, or incipient schizophrenia being hastened in individuals whose predisposition had also led them into drug usage. Another question was whether the

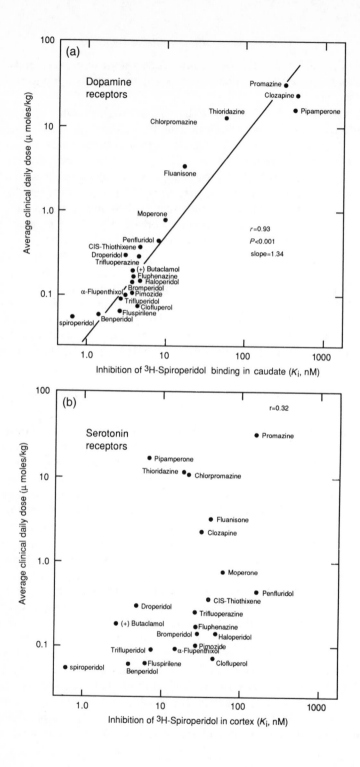

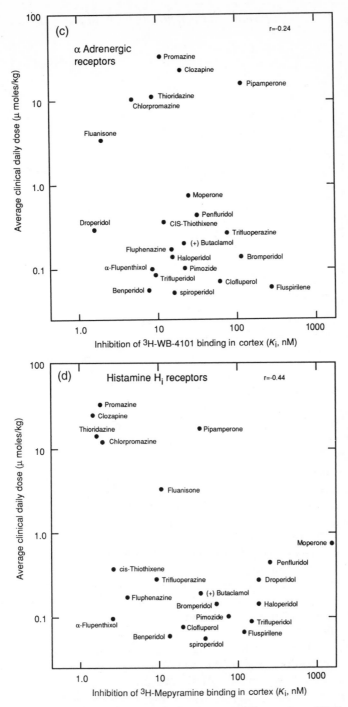

Fig. 6.2 Correlations between clinical potency and receptor affinity for 22 neuroleptic drugs (from Peroutka and Snyder 1980).

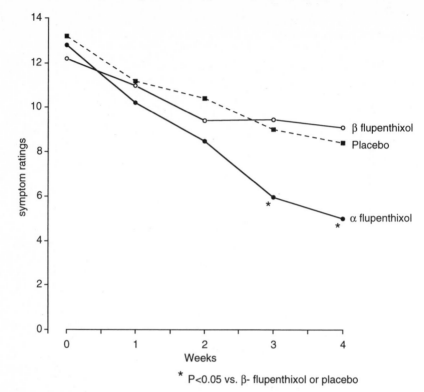

Fig. 6.3 Clinical improvement in acute schizophrenic patients treated with alpha flupenthixol, beta flupenthixol, or placebo (from Johnstone *et al.* 1978).

psychosis occurred in clear consciousness or whether it was really an acute confusional state (see Connell 1958; Rylander 1972).

Perceptions were permanently altered by the publication of two detailed accounts of psychosis associated with stimulant drug abuse. The first of these was by Connell (1958). He collected a series of 42 patients who developed schizophrenia-like states whilst taking amphetamine. Thirty had been taking the drug regularly, but in 8 only a single large dose had been consumed. In the remaining 4 patients amphetamine abuse was superimposed on excessive alcohol intake (another 16 had a previous history of alcohol abuse which did not seem to be a contributory factor at the time of presentation). There was very little to suggest that the patients were predisposed to develop schizophrenia: a fairly thorough assessment of premorbid personality revealed no excess of schizoid traits and a family history of schizophrenia was found in only one case.

The form taken by the psychosis was typically that of a paranoid-hallucinatory state, with delusions of reference and persecution which were accompanied, in some but not in all cases, by auditory hallucinations. Visual hallucinations were uncommon and were never a prominent part of the picture. Occasionally there were hallucinations in other modalities. Formal thought disorder was also evident in some of the cases described in detail, but no reference was made to catatonic phenomena. For the most part, there was a striking absence of signs of clouding of consciousness. Disorientation—for time only—was present in three cases, two of whom had independent reasons for this, for example a recent suicide attempt by drug overdose. It was, however, noted that in several more cases apparent short periods of confusion had been recorded in the case notes.

The duration of the disorder was exceptional in comparison with schizophrenia. In 77 per cent of cases recovery took place within a week; almost all the remaining cases remitted within 2–4 weeks; only two episodes lasted longer than this. In nearly all the cases the psychosis subsequently recurred, but it was not possible to determine whether or not this was in the setting of further abuse.

At around the same time Connell was collecting his case material, Tatetsu in Japan was accumulating a series of patients with psychiatric complications of methamphetamine abuse; this was not published until 1964 (Tatetsu 1964). Out of 492 chronic abusers, 92 per cent showed some form of psychiatric disorder. This was mostly minor, but in 19 per cent it took the form of a schizophrenia-like state. Tatetsu's patients, like those of Connell, exhibited delusions and hallucinations, as well as various first rank symptoms and formal thought disorder. He also noted, however, lack of volition, shallowness of affect, solitariness, and, of particular interest, catatonic phenomena up to and including stupor. On the whole, however, these additional abnormalities were less frequent and less striking than in true schizophrenia.

Tatetsu also described manic- and depressive-like states in association with methamphetamine abuse, the former being considerably more common than the latter. In manic states, however, notable features were diminished spontaneity, superficial expression of feelings, and a tendency to solitude. Depressed states were often accompanied by blunting of affect.

In Tatetsu's series, as in Connell's, improvement tended to take place rapidly after cessation of the drug. In many cases, however, full recovery was not attained, and in his experience after a month any further progress was slow or absent. Only half of his cases could be discharged in less than six months and 14 per cent were still in hospital five years after admission. In some cases active symptoms continued for eight to thirteen years after withdrawal from methamphetamine; others showed autonomous relapses and remissions or fluctuations in severity which could not be attributed to further drug abuse.

Within ten years of Connell's and Tatetsu's pioneering accounts, over two hundred cases of amphetamine psychosis had been reported worldwide (Kalant 1966). It had become clear that schizophrenia-like psychosis was also a complication of abuse of other stimulant drugs including cocaine, phenmetrazine, and methylphenidate, and even the milder ephedrine and diethylpropion (Angrist and Sudilovsky 1978). Abusers themselves gave the informal impression that psychotic symptoms—'speed paranoia'—were a routine hazard to be faced in any period of indulgence (Rylander 1972; Schiorring 1981).

It is thus clear that a class of drugs which acts to produce a functional excess of brain dopamine also regularly gives rise to a psychotic state closely resembling schizophrenia. The evidence for what might be termed the dopamine hypothesis of stimulant drug-induced psychosis so far, however, is not conclusive. In an analogous way to the previous section, three questions need to be answered. These are: (1) Does amphetamine invariably induce psychosis? (2) Is the psychosis specific to amphetamine and other stimulant drugs? (3) Is the psychosis attributable to a functional increase in brain dopamine?

Does amphetamine invariably induce psychosis? There are certainly indications from the studies cited above that amphetamine psychosis is common among abusers, and may develop after only a single exposure to the drug. However, the immediate effects of amphetamine—euphoria, increased alertness and energy, and lack of fatigue—are not those of psychosis. It therefore needs to be established whether schizophrenia-like psychosis is an inevitable, and hence presumably direct pharmacological consequence of taking amphetamine, or whether it develops unpredictably and so might depend on other factors.

The ethically rather delicate task of determining whether amphetamine will sooner or later induce psychotic symptoms in everyone it is administered to has been undertaken in two studies. Griffith *et al.* (1968) gave 10 mg of amphetamine hourly to four volunteers, all of whom were previous illicit users of the drug who had no history of psychosis. In all four cases, after around 50 mg had been given the initial euphoria disappeared and was replaced by depression, lack of interest, hypochondriacal complaints, and 'adoption of dependent attitudes'; from the subjects' retrospective accounts it was also clear that abnormal ideas were being entertained at this time. After between one and five days, psychotic symptoms abruptly manifested themselves in the patients: specifically, paranoid and referential delusions began to be discussed openly. As soon as this occurred the drug administration was terminated. Recovery then followed over a few hours, or three days in one case.

Angrist and Gershon (1970) repeated essentially the same experiment on four similar volunteers. Two developed clear-cut psychotic states, with one showing obvious formal thought disorder. The sequence of mental changes in this latter patient is described in Fig. 6.4. The other two patients, however, showed, at most, only changes in the direction of psychosis, for example becoming hostile and suspicious but not deluded, or experiencing minor hallucinations such as hearing their name being called.

Is the psychosis specific to amphetamine and other stimulant drugs? There are many other drugs besides stimulants which have predominantly central nervous system effects. Some of these drugs induce, as their immediate effects, changes in perception, thinking, and feeling which are much more reminiscent of the symptoms of schizophrenia than the corresponding initial effects of stimulants. It is thus important to make sure that psychosis is not a complication of abuse of other psychoactive drugs, particularly if, as in most cases, their pharmacological actions do not include major effects on dopamine.

The obvious drugs of interest in this respect are LSD and other hallucinogens and cannabis. The remarkable mental changes these drugs, particularly the hallucinogens, produce have been the subject of many fascinating descriptions, particularly by the users themselves (for example Wolfe 1971). These accounts make it clear that, although the experiences induced by these drugs may be vivid, they show only a passing similarity to the symptoms of schizophrenia: delusions, for example, are very uncommon and the perceptual changes consist not of auditory hallucinations, but take the form of heightening of perception, illusions, and kaleidoscopic visual patterns superimposed on the environment or projected on the back of the closed eyelids. It has been claimed that schizophrenia-like psychosis is seen as a complication of repeated use of LSD (Klawans *et al.* 1979; Vardy and Kay 1983). Whilst these claims are convincing, it is not clear how frequently such states occur and the impression is that they are distinctly uncommon.

The question of schizophrenia-like psychosis as a consequence of cannabis use has been reviewed by Rathod (1975) and Thornicroft (1990). Both noted that many alleged cannabis psychoses were in reality acute confusional states brought on by overindulgence, and that there was only weak evidence that long term and heavy users of the drug occasionally developed acute psychoses in clear consciousness. Recently, using questionnaire data from Swedish army conscripts, Andreasson *et al.* (1987) were able to document an increasing risk of developing schizophrenia with increasingly heavy cannabis use. Even so, the risk was small—less than 3 per cent of the heaviest users developed schizophrenia.

The picture is rather different for one further drug of abuse, phencyclidine. This is clearly and unequivocally associated with development of

*Evolution of mental changes with continuous amphetamine
administration*
(from Angrist and Gershon 1970)

Clinical notes recorded during administration of 5–10 mg amphetamine
hourly to a volunteer. The individual concerned abused heroin, which he
regularly dissolved in the contents of an ampoule of methamphetamine.
Although considered to have a personality disorder and subject to chronic
complaints of depression, he had not previously shown psychotic
symptoms.

After 5 hours: Mild pressure of speech,

After 6 hours: Mild grandiosity, 'If I felt this way I'd be a teacher. I've
learned the truth through suffering and pain', etc.

After 7 hours: Slight headache. Talking about manliness and Thomas
Wolfe, 'He had being a man in the palm of his hand. That book was his
guts', etc.

After 8 hours: Emergence of emotional lability and primitive material in
content of speech. Tearfully discusses mother's promiscuity, abandonment
by parents and grandfather, wife's infidelity, and homosexual attacks by
relatives.

After 17 hours: Hostile to nursing staff and feels that their attitude is
disparaging.

After 26 hours: Agitated philosophic diatribe with riddles that make little
sense. 'One man goes to school, the other can't. Then the other cuts out,
says "Fuck you, buddy"'—interpreted to mean there is no brotherhood in
the world.

After 32 hours: Less pressure of speech and irritability. Diminution of
feelings of profundity to ideas.

After 34 hours: Returns from patients' movie after a half-hour,
frightened. Feels he can judge at a glance which patients are dangerous
and 'sensed the presence of danger'.

After 37 hours: Speaking of revelations but is unable to explain what has
been revealed. He 'has received new understanding not given to everyone
in this cycle'.

After 40 hours: Writing and talking excitedly, constantly. 'My
consciousness in the form of what you know as human. My feeling
which I receive from him. I bring the answer to the unknown and yet.
They who do not hear or show laugh or murder my love. In my human
form He might let me act human for the rest must still wonder at my
actions which make them doubt my having been used to enlighten. Every
thought that stops me accepting *all knowledge* more than man has ever
known.'

After 43 hours: Preaching aloud constantly. Content as above.

After 46 hours: Preaching at maximum vocal volume. Content and form as above. Unable to cooperate with interviews or psychological testing. Amphetamine cut.

After 50 hours: Diminution of agitation. Ideation unchanged.

After 54 hours: Feelings of profundity, but coherent. 'Different races are a source of beauty in the world', etc.

After 60 hours: Sleeps five to six hours. Awakes hostile and demanding.

Over next 31 hours: At first depressed and dishevelled but returns to normal.

Fig. 6.4

psychotic states (Dove 1984; Javitt and Zukin 1991). Most commonly, these take the form of acute or subacute confusional states, but schizophrenia-like episodes in clear consciousness have also been described, as well as depression and mania. The frequency with which schizophrenic states are seen is uncertain, but the impression is that it is substantial. Phencyclidine has what is currently believed to be its major effect at glutamate receptors; it also has marked anticholinergic effects, and also effects at opioid and perhaps also serotonin receptors (for example Giannini *et al.* 1987; Johnson 1987). There is, however, evidence from both pharmacological and animal behavioural studies that the drug also has clear-cut dopamine agonist effects as well.

Is amphetamine psychosis attributable to functional dopamine excess?
Because it produces functional increases in both dopamine and noradrenaline, amphetamine psychosis could be attributed to either pharmacological action, or to both. The view that dopamine is the critical neurotransmitter rests on two pieces of evidence, both of which are indirect.

The first line of argument is that in animals most or all of the behavioural effects of amphetamine appear to be due to its actions on dopamine. As described in Chapter 8, amphetamine induces a state of behavioural hyperactivity which is initially accompanied by and eventually gives way to a syndrome of stereotyped motor responses. Pharmacological experiments (see Kokkinides and Anisman 1981; Mason 1984) have established that these effects are also produced by drugs with pure dopamine agonist effects but not by those with noradrenergic agonist effects. Similarly, their effects are reversed by dopamine but not by noradrenaline antagonists. It is, in fact, difficult to provoke any behavioural change at all in animals by manipulation of noradrenaline levels.

Secondly, there is evidence that dopamine agonists other than stimulants can also induce schizophrenia-like psychotic states. Mental changes are a well-known complication of L-DOPA treatment in Parkinson's disease. According to Goodwin (1971) these are found in 30 per cent of cases and, although commonly accompanied by some degree of confusion, it is accepted that psychotic symptoms—typically delusions and/or hallucinations—may occur in clear consciousness. L-DOPA, however, has noradrenergic as well as dopaminergic agonist effects, at least theoretically. The literature on other dopamine agonist drugs is extremely sparse, but it appears that psychotic symptoms are a significant complication of treatment with these in Parkinsonian patients and also in patients with endocrine disorders (for example Stern *et al.* 1984; Turner *et al.* 1984). However, the frequency of psychosis in clear consciousness is low, of the order of 1–4 per cent.

In summary, incriminating dopamine in the psychosis-inducing effects of amphetamine is a less than straightforward exercise. It certainly seems to be true that amphetamine produces a psychosis that is essentially identical to schizophrenia with a fair degree of regularity. It is also possible to dismiss the fact that other drugs of abuse are sometimes associated with psychosis as a red herring, though perhaps not entirely satisfactorily. When it comes to establishing that amphetamine psychosis is due to the dopaminergic effects of the drug, the chain of reasoning becomes quite complicated. While it is likely that the bulk of the effects of amphetamine are due to its dopaminergic rather than its noradrenergic effects, this has not been proved. Why other dopaminergic drugs appear to produce schizophrenia-like states only infrequently remains something of a mystery.

Direct tests of the dopamine hypothesis

The case that neuroleptic drugs exert their therapeutic effect in schizophrenia via blockade of dopamine receptors appears incontestable. The case that dopamine agonist drugs can induce a schizophrenia-like psychosis, if not watertight, is at least presentable. Nevertheless, however strong and convergent the evidence appears, it is circumstantial: it suggests that there may be a functional dopamine excess in the brains of patients with schizophrenia, but this still needs to be confirmed by direct investigation.

A functional excess of brain dopamine can only be brought about in a limited number of ways. One obvious way is via *increased synaptic availability*. Such an increase can theoretically be achieved via increased synthesis of dopamine, increased synaptic release, decreased metabolic degradation, or blockade of neuronal re-uptake, or a combination of these.

All these mechanisms have been shown to cause dopamine increases in pharmacological experiments, but it should be noted that they have no clinical precedent—excesses of neurotransmitters are not known to occur in naturally occurring disease states. If present, the consequences of increased synaptic availability of dopamine should be easily detectable as raised levels of dopamine in dopamine-rich parts of the brain and/or raised levels of the metabolic products of dopamine in the cerebrospinal fluid.

A second mechanism for production of a functional dopamine excess is *post-synaptic receptor supersensitivity*. Here, the effects of normal synaptic release of dopamine become multiplied because there is a greater than normal density of post-synaptic receptors. There is precedent for such a mechanism in the phenomenon of denervation sensitivity, where receptors on the motor end-plate of muscle fibres proliferate after damage to their nerve supply; the same phenomenon is widely believed to occur in the central nervous system under analogous conditions. The pharmacological consequences of dopamine receptor supersensitivity are uncertain, but there is a consensus that this would not necessarily result in any abnormalities in dopamine levels or indices of its turnover.

Other potential ways of inducing a functional dopamine excess exist, all of which revolve around the idea of an *anomalous dopamine agonist*. One possibility is an abnormal substance in the general circulation which gains access to the central nervous system and mimics the action of dopamine or stimulates its release from nerve terminals. Alternatively, it has been suggested (Knight 1982) that there could be an autoantibody to post-synaptic dopamine receptors which, in the same way as in hyperthyroidism, for some reason has stimulatory rather than blocking actions. However, these mechanisms are hypothetical and have not so far attracted any significant experimental investigation.

Increased synaptic availability of dopamine

As described above, the markers of this are increased levels of dopamine in the brain, with or without an accompanying increase in its metabolic products in the cerebrospinal fluid. Dopamine levels themselves can only be measured in post-mortem brain, and such studies present considerable technical difficulties. The metabolic turnover of dopamine can be assessed in life by measuring the level of its principal metabolite, homovanillic acid (HVA), in the cerebrospinal fluid. These studies have the advantage that it is possible to examine untreated patients, but they are not without technical complications of their own. For example, levels of cerebrospinal fluid HVA are generally close to the limit of detectability. HVA levels also reflect dopamine turnover in the basal ganglia to a much greater extent than in limbic and cortical regions.

Comparison of levels of HVA in normal and schizophrenic cerebrospinal

fluid formed the first wave of investigation of increased synaptic availability of dopamine. Studies of this type carried out on drug-free patients
have been reviewed by Heritch (1990), and the findings of the 12 of these
which included 10 or more patients are shown in Table 6.1. In a clear
majority, the schizophrenics failed to show any differences from normal
individuals, or patients with neurological disorders, or patients with a
variety of other psychiatric diagnoses. Four studies reported lower levels
of HVA in the schizophrenic group and one found higher levels than
normal.

Although they lend no support to the view that dopamine turnover is
greater overall in schizophrenia than in normal individuals, these studies
have repeatedly given hints of interesting associations within the schizophrenic group. Beginning with Bowers (1974), there have been claims that
HVA levels in schizophrenia show a pattern of correlations with aspects
of the clinical picture. A recurring theme has been that of a relationship
between high HVA and florid psychotic symptomatology, and low HVA
with withdrawal, negative symptoms, and signs of chronicity. There have
also been suggestions that exacerbations and remisssions of symptoms tend
to be accompanied by increases and decreases of HVA levels respectively.
Finally, in one or two studies the subgroup of patients marked by chronic,
treatment-resistant illnesses have been found to have the lowest levels of
HVA.

Studies which took the more direct approach of measuring brain levels
of dopamine followed somewhat later. These have also been reviewed by
Heritch (1990), whose summary of their results is shown in Table 6.2. Once
again it is evident that the findings are predominantly negative, with most
of the studies reporting no increases in dopamine in most of the brain
regions examined. Nevertheless, all but one of the studies reported a significant elevation of dopamine levels in at least one brain area.

The patients in these post-mortem studies had all been exposed to neuroleptic drug treatment, and few were drug free at the time of death. One
obvious explanation of the inconsistent increases in dopamine levels might
be that they were a function of treatment. However, while neuroleptics are
known to increase the synthesis, release, and degradation of dopamine, at
least when given acutely, it is not at all clear that they affect brain levels
of dopamine (Carlsson 1977). One further finding is also not easy to reconcile with such an explanation. Reynolds (1983) found that dopamine levels
in the amygdala of schizophrenic brains were nearly double the levels found
in normal controls. When this author examined a further series in more
detail, he found that the differences were due to a selective increase in the
left amygdala. It is possible to envisage neuroleptic drugs having asym-
metrical dopaminergic effects in a particular individual (for example,
Parkinsonian side-effects are sometimes more pronounced on one side), but

it is very difficult to see how the left side could be preferentially affected by drugs across a whole series of patients.

In summary, the hypothesis of increased dopamine availability in schizophrenia has not received strong or even lukewarm support. But at the same time the evidence has not been entirely negative; suggestions that there might be a subtle derangement of dopamine metabolism keep cropping up. Given the methodological difficulties faced by cerebrospinal fluid and post-mortem brain studies, this might turn out not to mean very much, but it could also be the tell-tale sign of a dopamine system which is, in the terminology of Siever and Davis (1985), dysregulated by malfunction at another point in the system. The natural place to locate such a dysregulation is at the post-synaptic receptors for dopamine.

Increased dopamine receptor sensitivity

As the lack of any marked abnormality of dopamine metabolism emerged, attention turned to the possibility of post-synaptic receptor supersensitivity as the only remaining candidate for causing the putative functional dopamine excess in schizophrenia. The focus of this research has always been the dopamine D2 receptor, with the D1 receptor receiving consideration only in passing. The reason for this was partly historical: at the time the relevant studies were beginning to be undertaken pharmacologists had persuaded themselves that the D2 receptor was the main mediator of dopamine's post-synaptic effects — quite wrongly as it turned out (see Waddington 1989). But mainly, the emphasis on D2 receptors was for reasons of expedience: a simple and accurate method for measuring D2 receptors had just become available (this was the same method used by Creese *et al.* (1976) and Seeman *et al.* (1976) as described earlier), whereas only indirect and crude assays of D1 receptor activity existed at the time.

The first three studies of dopamine D2 receptor density in post-mortem schizophrenic brain were published in the same year. Two of them (Lee *et al.* 1978; Owen *et al.* 1978) found evidence of substantial increases compared with normal controls; the third (Mackay *et al.* 1978) found no differences, although an increase was subsequently confirmed with a larger sample (Mackay *et al.* 1982). The studies all restricted their examination to the basal ganglia, where the brain dopamine innervation is at its richest. However, the increases were found in all the basal ganglia nuclei studied, including one closely related to the limbic system, the nucleus accumbens. The many subsequent studies of D2 receptors in schizophrenia have been reviewed by Seeman (1987). The finding of increases in the range of 60 per cent to 110 per cent has been almost unanimous, with there being only two dissenting results, both in studies with small sample sizes.

Unfortunately, while these studies provided strong and replicable evidence of a functional dopamine excess in schizophrenia, interpretation of

Table 6.1 Studies of the dopamine metabolite homovanillic acid (HVA) in cerebrospinal fluid of drug-free schizophrenic patients (from Heritch 1990)

	Patients	Controls	HVA levels	Comment
Gottfries et al. (1971)	40 unspecified	60 normal	No difference	—
Rimon et al. (1971)	31 acute	27 psychiatric	No difference	Higher levels in patients with paranoid forms of disorder
Bowers and Van Woert (1972)	23 acute	15 normals 11 depressed 10 Parkinsonian	No difference	Lower levels in Parkinsonian group
Bowers (1974)	17 acute	11 affective	Reduced	Higher levels associated with good outcome
Sedvall et al. (1974)	34 acute	11 manic	Reduced	—
Post et al. (1975)	18 acute	10 normal 19 neurological 98 affective	No difference	—
Kirstein et al. (1976)	9 acute 1 chronic	10 affective	Increased	—
Gattaz et al. (1982)	28 chronic	16 neurological	No difference	Higher levels associated with higher hostility scores
Nyback et al. (1983)	26 acute	43 normal	No difference	—

Gerner *et al.* (1984)	20 chronic	38 normal 41 depressed 15 manic	No difference	No associations with psychopathology scores
Lindstrom (1985)	40 acute	21 normal	Reduced	Higher levels associated with higher social interaction scores Lower levels associated with higher scores for lassitude and slowness
Davidson and Davis (1988)	14 chronic, treatment resistant	14 normal	Reduced	Higher levels associated with higher psychopathology scores

Table 6.2 Studies of dopamine levels in schizophrenic post-mortem brain (from Heritch 1990)

	Caudate nucleus	Putamen	Nucleus accumbens	Olfactory tubercle	Amygdala	Septal area	Hypothalamus
Bird et al. (1977, 1979)	Normal	Normal	Increased	Increased	–	Normal	–
Owen et al. (1978)	Increased	Normal	Increased	–	–	–	–
Crow et al. (1979)	Increased	Increased	Normal	–	Normal	–	–
Mackay et al. (1982)	Increased	–	Increased	–	–	–	–
Toru et al. (1982)	–	–	Normal	–	–	Normal	–
Bird et al. (1984)	Normal	–	Increased	–	Normal	–	–
Bridge et al. (1985)	–	–	Increased	–	–	–	Normal

this as confirmation of the dopamine hypothesis proved to be difficult. The patients who contributed their brains to these post-mortem studies had been treated with neuroleptics, in most cases continuously for up to twenty years. By the time the studies were reported it had also become known that chronic neuroleptic treatment in animals could also cause post-synaptic dopamine receptor supersensitivity, by virtue of producing a functional equivalent of dopamine denervation (Burt *et al.* 1977). Both Owen *et al.*'s (1978) and Lee *et al.*'s (1978) studies contained a handful of patients who had ostensibly not received any drug treatment in life, and these patients were still found to show dopamine receptor increases. However, evidence from the study of Mackay *et al.* (1982) pointed in the opposite direction. They found that increases in dopamine receptor numbers were restricted to those patients who were on drug treatment at the time of death; those who had been drug free for one month or longer before death showed no significant differences from controls.

Valiant attempts to unconfound this issue have been made by Seeman and co-workers. Lee and Seeman (1980) managed to collect a series of 11 brains from schizophrenic patients who had received no or negligible amounts of neuroleptic medication during life. As illustrated in Table 6.3, the D2 receptor densities for these patients were not significantly different from those of 26 treated patients (although they were slightly lower), and they continued to show a highly significant elevation compared with controls. Later, this group (Seeman *et al.* 1984; Seeman 1987) also compared the brains of 91 schizophrenic patients with those of patients with Alzheimer's disease, some but not all of whom had received neuroleptic treatment during life. Their findings are shown in Fig. 6.5. The D2 receptor densities for the schizophrenic patients were elevated overall, but the distribution was bimodal. Whereas unmedicated patients with Alzheimer's disease showed a similar range of D2 receptor densities to the normal controls, Alzheimer's patients who had been treated with neuroleptics showed an increase which was smaller than that for the schizophrenic patients; this contained no hint of bimodality. The clear implication is that neuroleptics cause a modest increase in D2 receptor numbers, but that a considerably larger increase is seen in some schizophrenic patients which cannot be attributed to this factor.

Ingenious though Seeman and co-workers may have been, it was clear that their efforts were doomed to failure. Once it is accepted that neuroleptic drugs can themselves produce dopamine D2 receptor increases, the view that such increases in schizophrenic patients are due to treatment becomes impossible to disprove. Rather inconveniently, the drugs which were largely responsible for generating the dopamine hypothesis of schizophrenia seemed to have made it impossible ever to prove whether or not it is correct.

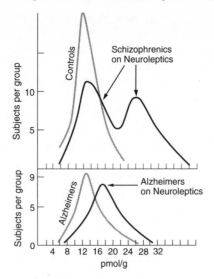

Fig. 6.5 Post-mortem dopamine D2 receptor densities in the basal ganglia of patients with schizophrenia compared with normal controls and patients with Alzheimer's disease, both neuroleptic treated and untreated (reprinted by permission from Seeman 1987).

Table 6.3 Dopamine D2 receptors in treated and untreated schizophrenic post-mortem brain (from Lee and Seeman 1980)

	Mean spiperone binding (fmol/mg protein)		
	Treated patients ($n = 21$–26)	Untreated patients ($n = 8$–11)	Normal controls ($n = 27$–33)
Caudate nucleus	155.6	131.7	101.1
Putamen	159.0	128.8	103.7

	Mean haloperidol binding (fmol/mg protein)		
	Treated patients ($n = 14$–16)	Untreated patients ($n = 5$–7)	Normal controls ($n = 32$)
Caudate nucleus	80.1	74.7	44.1
Putamen	76.9	73.1	47.8

The decisive test of the dopamine hypothesis

At a time when two lines of investigation into the dopamine hypothesis had produced negative or equivocal findings, and the only direct and strong evidence had to be considered irretrievably confounded by the issue of prior neuroleptic treatment, a way out of the impasse was suddenly found. In 1983, Garnett *et al.* combined administration of radioactively labelled L-DOPA with the kind of functional imaging techniques described in the last chapter, and succeeded in producing a visual map of sites of dopamine innervation in the living human brain. It was quickly realized that a simple adaptation of the technique would allow visualization of dopamine D2 receptors, and also their quantitative estimation. A study of dopamine receptors in schizophrenic patients before they had ever been exposed to neuroleptic drugs became a realistic possibility.

In principle, such a study is easy to carry out. All that is necessary is first, to radioactively label a drug which binds to dopamine D2 receptors (that is a neuroleptic); then to inject this into groups of never medicated, 'drug-naive' schizophrenic patients (for example those having their first episode of illness) and a matched group of normal individuals; and finally to scan both groups and compare appropriate brain regions in a quantitative way. In practice, the obstacles are formidable. Current functional imaging techniques only allow resolution of dopamine D2 receptors in the basal ganglia; this is the site where they are at their most abundant, but it is almost certainly not the site of most interest in schizophrenia. Quantification is also far from a straightforward procedure: the best methods, which derive an absolute figure for dopamine receptor density, require that at least two scans be performed on each individual, and even then a number of mathematical assumptions have to be made. Finally, the most sensitive technique, PET scanning, is expensive and complicated.

The net result has been that the crucial experiment to test the dopamine hypothesis has only been carried out twice, at least only twice in the most technologically sophisticated way. The first of these studies was reported by Wong and 16 co-authors (Wong *et al.* 1986) at the Johns Hopkins School of Medicine in America; the second was carried out by Farde and colleagues (Farde *et al.* 1992) at the Karolinska Institute in Sweden.

The Johns Hopkins study (Wong *et al.* 1986)

In this study 10 drug-naive schizophrenic patients and 11 age- and sex-matched controls were compared. The patients were on the whole a rather exceptional group, for whom the statement 'only in America' seems applicable. Generally, they had a long (on average five-year) duration of illness. Most of the patients had expressed longstanding reluctance to accept psychiatric diagnosis or psychotropic medication; some had undergone prolonged investigation for physical complaints, which had all along been delusional; in several, psychotherapy had been the main form of treatment—one patient had been in psychoanalysis for ten years. The symptoms of the patients, however, were typical of chronic schizophrenia and they all met DSM III criteria for the disorder. The absence of any exposure to neuroleptic drugs was carefully established by interview of both patients and relatives.

The labelled neuroleptic used was 3-*N*-methylspiperone, a drug which has significant serotonin receptor blocking actions as well as effects at the dopamine D2 receptor. This drug binds irreversibly to D2 receptors, and on injection continuously accumulates in the basal ganglia without coming to an equilibrium. This means that the rate of increase of radioactivity in the basal ganglia is the only index that can be used, and since this also depends on blood flow to the same brain region, there is a potential confounding factor. The way in which the authors decided to correct for this involved carrying out two PET scans some days apart, the second of which was after administration of a single dose of (unlabelled) haloperidol. Comparison of the two scans enabled the effects of blood flow to be covaried out. Calculation of D2 receptor numbers was based on a complicated mathematical model, which made a considerable number of assumptions.

The findings of Wong *et al.* were clear-cut. The mean density of dopamine D2 receptor binding sites (customarily referred to as B_{max}) for the schizophrenic patients was 41.7 pmol/g of basal ganglia tissue, whereas that for the controls was 16.6 pmol/g—a more than two-fold increase. Over the next few years the authors managed to increase their sample sizes to 20 drug-naive schizophrenics and 14 controls (Tune *et al.* 1992). The increase in D2 receptor numbers has continued to be found, although its magnitude has dropped somewhat (mean B_{max} 33.1 pmol/g for the schizophrenics compared with 14.4 pmol/g for the controls). It has also become evident that there is a great deal of variability, with some patients showing normal dopamine D2 receptor densities but others exhibiting marked increases.

The Karolinska study (Farde *et al.* 1987)

Six months after the study of Wong *et al.* Farde *et al.* published the first results from their study. Their group consisted of 15 patients, all of whom met DSM III criteria for schizophrenia. These were compared with 14 controls who were not significantly different in age and sex distribution. The patients were generally young and, although they had been ill for more than 6 months in every case, were undergoing their first hospital admission. Drug-naivety was accordingly easy to establish.

The radioactively labelled neuroleptic used was raclopride. Unlike 3-*N*-methylspiperone, this is highly specific for dopamine D2 receptors. Raclopride also binds reversibly rather than irreversibly to D2 receptors and this led to a different method of estimating their density. Once again two PET examinations were carried out. In the first, a tracer dose of raclopride was injected and equilibrium was allowed to be reached. Some days later a saturating dose was given. This permitted something approximating to the standard method for determining receptor densities in post-mortem brain to be carried out (the ratios of bound and free drug are obtained at different saturations and then plotted as a 'Scatchard' diagram, the intercept giving the figure for B_{max}). The method of analysis employed was simpler than that employed by Wong *et al.* and also had considerable credibility, having been used extensively in post-mortem studies. However, it had the disadvantage that the Scatchard diagram had to be based on a plot containing only two points, a practice which would be be considered unacceptable in animal studies.

These authors' results were in complete contrast to those of Wong *et al.* The dopamine receptor binding for the schizophrenic patients was 25.1 pmol/g and 24.6 pmol/g for the controls, a difference which was not significant. Subsequently the authors (Farde *et al.* 1990) were able to increase their sample size to 18 patients and 20 controls, with no hint of differences emerging. However, in both Farde *et al.*'s early and later studies it was noted that there was a significant degree of asymmetry in the dopamine receptor densities of the schizophrenic patients, the values being higher on the left than the right; no such differences were observed in the controls. For example, in their 1990 sample, 14 out of the 18 patients had greater D2 receptor densities in the left putamen and in one case the difference was of the order of 40 per cent.

There are three other studies which also need to be taken into consideration. Crawley *et al.* (1986) compared 12 schizophrenic patients and 13 controls using a radioactively labelled spiperone and a relatively crude functional imaging technique. They found an 11 per cent increase in D2 receptor binding in the basal ganglia, a difference which was small but significant. Two patients also showed striking laterality differences, with greater binding on the left. However, only four of their patients were drug-naive; the rest had merely been drug free for six months or longer. Martinot *et al.* (1990) compared 12 patients, all of whom were either drug-naive or who had received only trivial amounts of neuroleptic medication, with 12 controls. They used labelled spiperone and PET; their technique was broadly similar to that of Wong *et al.* but they made no attempt to correct for the confounding factor of blood flow (which they argued was unnecessary using their methodology). They found no differences in D2 receptor densities between patients and controls. Subsequently the same authors (Martinot *et al.* 1991) repeated the study using a different, non-neuroleptic drug which binds to dopamine D2 receptors, and again found no differences. Finally, Pilowsky *et al.* (1994) examined 20 schizophrenic patients

(17 drug-naive and 3 drug-free for at least 5 years) and 20 controls using SPECT, which is less sophisticated than PET, and radiolabelled iodoben-zamide. They found no overall increases in D2 receptor numbers but, as in the study of Farde *et al.*, and also to some extent that of Crawley *et al.*, there was a significant left–right asymmetry of dopamine receptors in the patients but not in the controls.

The decisive test of the dopamine hypothesis has certainly yielded decisive results; unfortunately, in the two principal studies, these have not been consistent with each other. Accordingly, the theory can still cling on to tenability. The findings of Wong *et al.* cannot easily be explained away, and there are broad hints from the asymmetry found in all of the other studies except those of Martinot *et al.* that there is something amiss with basal ganglia dopamine D2 receptors in schizophrenia. As a last resort, it could be argued that the basal ganglia are the wrong place to look for dopamine receptor increases in schizophrenia, the limbic and cortical sites of dopamine innervation being a more likely site of dysfunction. But against this, it is difficult to ignore the fact that the weight of the evidence points to a lack of any marked abnormality of dopamine D2 receptors in schizophrenia.

Conclusion

In the 1990s, the dopamine hypothesis is widely regarded as at best peripheral to the pathogenesis of schizophrenia, and at worst a blind alley that research would do well to abandon. In fact, it is neither. Abnormal dopamine function was originally incriminated in schizophrenia by circum-stantial evidence, and this has become progressively stronger over the course of time. The search for confirmation then led to the most con-sistently reproduced biological abnormality ever found in schizophrenia research—dopamine D2 receptor supersensitivity in post-mortem brain—and while this has been confounded by the issue of neuroleptic treatment it is not disproved by it. The evidence which has emerged from PET scan studies on drug-naive schizophrenic patients is, quite simply, completely contradictory. The dopamine hypothesis is perhaps more properly viewed as being in an acute crisis rather than suffering from a chronic lack of experimental support.

In the trials and tribulations of the dopamine hypothesis a point some-times seems to have been lost sight of, which was originally so obvious that it hardly seemed worth stating. This is that, if schizophrenia has a biological basis, then a neurochemical disturbance of some kind is the only plausible candidate for the pathogenesis of its symptoms. Drugs which alter brain neurochemistry regularly induce phenomena which, if not identical to schizophrenic symptoms, resemble them more closely than anything else. Conversely, the florid symptoms of schizophrenia appear and disappear, wax and wane in intensity, and change unpredictably from one form to another in a way which is difficult to imagine as the consequence of any type of brain dysfunction other than one which is biochemical. If and when a neurochemical disorder is uncovered in schizophrenia, it may not prove to be located primarily in dopamine systems, but it will perhaps be surprising if the dopamine hypothesis turns out to be completely wrong.

7

The psychology and neuropsychology of schizophrenia

It is evident that, whatever ultimately causes schizophrenic symptoms, the pathological process is played out in one or more of the domains of higher cognitive function. Over the years there has been a steady stream of attempts to identify the psychological disturbance or disturbances, within which the application of two broad strategies can be discerned. These might be referred to as, on the one hand, the search for the psychological abnormalities which underlie the clinical picture of schizophrenia, and, on the other, the search for the abnormalities which lie behind it.

The psychological abnormalities underlying the clinical picture of schizophrenia are those which have the power to explain the occurrence of one or more classes of symptom. Attempts to define these derive mainly from cognitive psychology and they are typically theory-driven: they proceed from hypotheses which are formulated a priori, to testing in specially devised experimental procedures which it is hoped will expose differences between schizophrenic patients and normal individuals. Sometimes the theories have been ingenious and powerful. Unfortunately, at least as often they have shown a tendency to be vague, abstruse, and to bear little obvious relationship to the phenomena they have sought to explain.

The abnormalities lying behind the symptoms of schizophrenia are those which turn up when patients are subjected to standard psychological tests. These approaches are on the whole data-driven and are usually neuropsychological in orientation, taking the form of screening schizophrenic patients for impairment on tests of overall intellectual function or of particular faculties such as perception, language, and memory. The difficulty here is that it has been found that schizophrenic patients will perform more poorly than normal individuals on virtually any task that is set them; this applies particularly to chronic schizophrenic patients who often show quite marked cognitive deficits. In these circumstances it becomes difficult to be certain what, if anything, is specifically abnormal in schizophrenia rather than just forming part of a general pattern of poor performance.

Psychological theories of schizophrenia and particular schizophrenic symptoms abound, and there is if anything an embarrassment of abnormal empirical findings on one or another test of psychological function. In order to review this large and sprawling area of research, a fairly ruthless approach needs to be taken. As a first step, discussion is restricted to studies which are concerned with higher cognitive functions; the assumption is made that work on conditioning, arousal, and the like is too far removed from the clinical picture to be able to throw much light on it. In addition, given the credibility problems which have dogged both the cognitive psychological and neuropsychological approaches to schizophrenia, any findings which emerge are required to pass a 'stringency' test to make sure that they are as real and robust as they claim to be.

The cognitive psychology of schizophrenia

Traditionally, the theory-driven experimental psychological approach to schizophrenia has regarded as its province the florid, positive symptoms of the disorder; explanations of negative symptoms, if attempted at all, have usually been tacked on as an afterthought. Both general and specific attacks have been mounted on schizophrenic symptomatology, the former attempting to bring many or all positive symptoms under the umbrella of a single psychological dysfunction, and the latter being directed to one class of symptom such as delusions, hallucinations, or formal thought disorder.

Whether general or specific, psychological theories of schizophrenia, like all theories, are only as good as the experimental support they receive. It is at this point that difficulties often arise. The evidence which is produced for a particular theory invariably consists of a demonstration that schizophrenic patients show impaired performance on some test of the psychological function in question. However, since schizophrenic patients, particularly chronic schizophrenic patients, are liable to perform poorly on any test, it becomes easy to obtain spurious experimental support. In order to avoid this methodological pitfall, therefore, the stringency test that will be adopted is that any alleged abnormal psychological finding should be demonstrable in acute patients, in whom the general tendency to poor performance can reasonably be expected to be at a minimum.

General approaches

There has only ever been one general psychological theory of schizophrenia, or at any rate only one which has generated a significant body of experimental investigation. This is the hypothesis that many of the symptoms of the disorder are the manifestation of a defect in selective attention.

The background to the selective attention account of schizophrenic symptoms was a surge of interest in the various aspects of normal attention that took place in the 1950s. A number of competing theories were developed, the most influential of which was that of Broadbent (1958). He argued that a crucial aspect of the attentional process was the filtering of sensory information: out of the huge amount of perceptual information which continually impinges on the senses only a tiny amount normally enters conscious awareness. Much of the rest of this information, however, is potentially accessible: if desired it is easy to make oneself aware of the watch on one's wrist, the hum of one's word processor, etc.. It follows that there must exist one or more filtering mechanisms which continuously choose a small selection of stimuli for entry into conscious awareness, based presumably on their novelty or their significance to the individual at that particular time. Broadbent and others were soon able to adduce evidence that selective attentional processes of the hypothesized type did operate in normal individuals, although the exact details by which the filtering was achieved became, in the way of experimental psychology, the subject of a debate which is still unresolved.

The possible relevance of selective attention to psychiatric disorders was not lost on psychologists. Although the movement towards a defective filtering theory of schizophrenia took place more or less *en masse*, the contributions of two authors stood out. In the course of eliciting retrospective accounts of the onset of their symptoms from young schizophrenic patients, McGhie (McGhie and Chapman 1961; McGhie 1969) was struck by reports of alterations in the quality of their conscious experience. The changes included increased subjective alertness, heightening of perception, exaggerated awareness of the environment, and the capturing of attention by irrelevant stimuli. In some patients, thoughts would sometimes seem to trigger a whole cascade of associations. In others, everyday actions could no longer be carried out automatically, but had to be thought through consciously, step by step. At around the same time, Payne (see below) was developing the idea that an abnormality of 'overinclusive thinking' could explain some schizophrenic symptoms, principally formal thought disorder. At a conference in 1964, (see Payne 1973) he proposed that as well as conceptual overinclusiveness there might be a corresponding perceptual overinclusiveness: during the performance of cognitive operations, the mechanism which ensures that only essential information (internal or external) is perceived and thought about might become unable to exclude the irrelevant.

The groundwork having been laid, it was Frith (1979) who was largely responsible for parlaying defective selective attention into a fully fledged theory capable of explaining the florid symptoms of schizophrenia. He prefaced his argument with a summary of the distinction between conscious and preconscious information processing. Consciousness is where, in full subjective awareness, the highest, 'executive' level of cognitive operations takes place. Such processes are characterized by a severely limited capacity and the tasks undertaken can by and large only be dealt with one at a time. Conscious processing is called into play for tasks which are novel, complex, and require strategic rather than automatic responses to be made; it is concerned with courses of action rather than individual actions themselves. Preconsciousness, in contrast, describes the much larger numbers of cognitive operations which are being carried on at any given moment outside awareness, 'without thinking'. Preconscious processes may be highly sophisticated, perhaps nearly as sophisticated as conscious ones, but they are automatic and many operations are routinely performed at the same time. The tasks undertaken are those which are more or less routine, and in which strategic decisions are not required most of the time—examples would include driving, copy-typing, and sight-reading music.

If the selective filter that determines which items of information in preconsciousness should enter consciousness were to break down, Frith argued that an individual would continually receive an overload of sensory information which was already highly analysed. Accordingly, he would become aware of different potential interpretations of perceptions. At the same time he would be likely to start experiencing difficulties in selecting and carrying through the right course of action in response to these perceptions. This could give rise to schizophrenic symptoms as follows.

Delusions: In the normal course of events most of the environmental information available to consciousness fails to reach it; it is irrelevant to any executive decisions that may need to be made and so is not noticed. But if a breakdown in filtering were to cause inconsequential items of information to be passed up into conscious awareness, because the arrival of such information normally signals that it is important and needs to be acted upon deliberately, it might therefore acquire a connotation of significance. The seed of an entire class of delusions—referential delusions—could thus be planted. Elaboration into other forms of delusions might take place through the individual's attempts, using normal reasoning, to explain why he has started to notice all sorts of ostensibly significant events. Alternatively, the reasoning process itself might be undermined by the defect in selective attention simultaneously giving rise to formal thought disorder.

Auditory hallucinations: It is reasonable to suppose that when a speech sound is heard, a sequence of hypotheses about its possible interpretation are tested in preconsciousness, before the final result is presented to consciousness as a meaningful message. It also seems inevitable that at least part of the same analysis would have to be carried out on all sounds, with non-speech sounds being rejected at an early stage. In schizophrenia, a defective preconscious:conscious filter could allow the entry of incorrect early interpretations of non-speech sounds as speech into awareness, and these might then be experienced as voices speaking. The assumption has to be made that there is a steady input of non-verbal environmental sounds to provide the substrate for the erroneous interpretations, but as Frith pointed out, under normal conditions it is seldom that this is not the case.

Formal thought disorder: The process of finding the right words to convert what one wishes to say into speech is, like the understanding of speech, likely to involve a complicated search procedure. Various candidate words and phrases will need to be accessed and subjected to scrutiny, this being via a series of operations taking place in preconsciousness. If all of the intermediate steps between thought and its expression were to be consciously perceived, it is only natural that a certain amount of distraction and loss of the thread of conversation would ensue. That there might also be a tendency to slip into using more or less inappropriate words rather than the correct ones could also easily be envisaged. At least some of the abnormalities that contribute to formal thought disorder, like derailment, loss of goal, and neologisms can thereby be accounted for.

In a less thoroughly worked out way, Frith was also able to bring the defective conscious:preconscious filter theory to bear on other schizophrenic phenomena such as catatonic symptoms. The application of the theory to negative symptoms is due primarily to Hemsley (1977). He proposed that schizophrenic patients sooner or later developed one or more deliberate strategies for minimizing their constant overload of information. One way of dealing with the influx of stimuli demanding conscious attention would be to slow the rate at which all decisions were made; the objective manifestation of this would then be slowness of thought and action. Another would be to raise the threshold for making any response at all; in this case poverty of speech and flattening of affect might be the anticipated result. Finally, the patient might endeavour to avoid environmental stimulation of any kind as much as possible. Plausible consequences of this might be withdrawal, apathy, and other aspects of the picture of chronic, deteriorated schizophrenia.

While Frith's and Hemsley's account of schizophrenic symptoms might be viewed as preliminary, incomplete, and perhaps even vulnerable to fairly obvious attack in places, there can be no doubt that overall it has considerable explanatory power. Nevertheless, it is on experimental support rather than theoretical plausibility that it has to be judged. The earliest formal tests of the theory were carried out by McGhie and co-workers (see McGhie 1969), who examined the simple prediction that a breakdown in selective filtering would render schizophrenic patients more vulnerable than normal to distraction. However, when visual or auditory distracting stimuli were introduced during a variety of psychomotor tasks, schizophrenic patients showed no greater deterioration in performance than controls. On tasks designed to test distraction directly, impairments were only found in a few cases and on the whole the differences between the schizophrenic and control groups were small. Payne and Caird (1967) also found it difficult to demonstrate anything more than marginal effects of distraction on schizophrenic patients.

By this time, a particular type of distraction experiment had become the stock-in-trade of psychologists investigating Broadbent's model of selective attention in normal individuals. This was the dichotic listening task in which a message, such as a series of numbers or a passage of prose, is delivered through headphones to one ear, while a different message is delivered to the other ear. The subject's task is to repeat aloud (shadow) one of the messages, efficiency being measured by speed of performance and by the number of errors of intrusion from the other message. A small industry devoted to dichotic listening in schizophrenia quickly sprang up and papers using the technique or variants of it continue to appear. Although the literature (reviewed by Neale and Oltmanns 1980; Cutting 1985) has become substantial, the number of studies which have examined dichotic listening performance in schizophrenics compared with controls, and which have used shadowing rather than some derivative measure such as later recall of the message (making the dubious assumption that memory is intact in schizophrenia) is, however, surprisingly small. Those studies which meet the stringency requirement of using acute schizophrenic patients are summarized in Table 7.1. It is clear that the findings have usually been negative: only two studies found significantly poorer performance in the schizophrenic group. In one of these (Hemsley and Richardson 1980) the task was exceptionally difficult, the subjects being required to distinguish prose passages delivered simultaneously to both ears in the same voice purely on the basis of their content. In the other (Rappaport 1967), half of the patients but none of the controls had been given an injection of sedative medication half an hour before the test!

To sum up, defective selective attention in schizophrenia was a horse which seemed worth backing on theoretical grounds, but which fell at the first experimental hurdle. It remains possible that such a mechanism underlies some but not all classes of symptom, for example hallucinations (see below). Alternatively, the deficit may be of a more sophisticated kind than can be unmasked by dichotic listening studies. Broadbent's original model of selective attention has undergone substantial revision over the years and the possibility that later versions can be applied to schizophrenia has been canvassed (Hemsley 1975; Gray *et al.* 1991), but not so far put to the test. But before too many apologies for the theory are made, it has to be remembered, as pointed out by Cutting (1985), that disorders of attention of any kind have never struck clinicians as forming a conspicuous part of the clinical picture of schizophrenia. In fact, they are much more typical of mania, where distractibility is one of the cardinal symptoms of the disorder.

Table 7.1 Dichotic listening studies in acute schizophrenic patients

Study	Subjects	Diagnosis	Shadowing task	Findings	Comment
Rappaport (1967)	90 acute pts normal controls	Clinical	Digits one vs both ears	Pts significantly worse	Half of the patients had received IM neuroleptic or barbiturate prior to test
Korboot and Damiani (1976)	16 acute pts Neurotic controls	Clinical (rigorous)	Digits/letters different ears	No significant differences	—
Straube and Germer (1979)	24 acute pts psychiatric and normal controls	Clinical	Words different ears	No significant differences	—
Pogue-Geile and Oltmanns (1980)	8 acute pts Psychiatric and normal controls	RDC	Prose passages different ears	No significant differences	Schizophrenics' performance deteriorated slightly
Hemsley and Richardson (1980)	9 acute pts Psychiatric and normal controls	Clinical	Prose passages both ears	Pts significantly worse	Difficult task
Wielgus and Harvey (1988)	20 acute pts Psychiatric and normal controls	DSM III	Prose passages different ears	No significant differences	—

Specific approaches

Leaving aside selective attention, there remains a large and unwieldy body of research on the psychology of schizophrenia, much of which is devoted to specific symptoms. The size of this can be reduced by removing all work which is not cognitive psychological in orientation; and it becomes a lot more manageable when that which does not address itself to the symptoms of schizophrenia is excluded from consideration. Even so, it only becomes possible to steer a route through the literature by courtesy of a few authors who have taken the trouble to review particular areas thoroughly and critically. This applies particularly to the book by Cutting (1985), to that by Slade and Bentall (1988) on hallucinations, and those of Chapman and Chapman (1973) and Rochester and Martin (1979) on formal thought disorder, on which much of what is summarized below draws heavily.

Delusions

Attempts to explain, or even to provide the framework for an explanation of delusions are thin on the ground. Schneider (1949) and Jaspers (1959) provided rigorous delineations of the phenomenology of delusions, but it is clear that there was no pretence at explanation. There have been numerous theories steeped in the traditions of existential philosophy or psychoanalysis; these, however, either severely test the reader's comprehension, or defy rational evaluation, or sometimes both. There have also been a handful of genuine explanatory ventures. Unfortunately, these all date from the classical era of psychiatry, often the last century, and perhaps the most that can be said in their favour is that they have a perennial quality, cropping up in thinly disguised form again and again. These theories have been reviewed by Arthur (1964) and Winters and Neale (1983), who grouped them in the following way.

Delusions as secondary to a disorder of intelligence: Conventionally attributed to nineteenth century authors (Gruhle and Griesinger in particular), this theory proposes that delusions are a consequence of defective intellect, judgment, and powers of reasoning. It is flatly contradicted by clinical experience, which gives no grounds for supposing that delusions are restricted to, or are even especially prominent among schizophrenic patients who are of low IQ, or otherwise intellectually impaired.

Delusions as secondary to perception of change in oneself: This was apparently first put forward as a theory by Janet in the last century, but the theme has been regularly rehearsed by later authors. The basic idea is that, as schizophrenia insidiously develops, the individual becomes aware of a change in himself — in personality, in mood and affective response, or in social interactions—and delusions arise out of his attempts to account for this. Suspiciousness and anxiety are transformed into delusions of persecution; depression and elation into nihilistic and grandiose delusions respectively; and awareness of emotional emptiness and inability to relate socially into referential delusions. This group of theories is of dubious explanatory value and is singularly unable to account for the basic phenomenological characteristics of delusions, that they are fixed, incorrigible, absurd, and so on.

Delusions as secondary to formal thought disorder: This approach was advocated most notably by Bleuler (1911). He argued that loosening of associations, as a fundamental symptom, was invariably present in schizophrenic patients. When coupled with the illogicality of thought that often went with it, fertile ground could be created for the development of abnormal beliefs. Although a more sophisticated theory than the other two, it makes the prediction that delusions should only be seen in the presence of some degree of formal thought disorder, which is far from being the case.

There remains one further class of theory of delusions; this is that delusions are secondary to abnormal perceptions, developing when the normal processes of logical deduction are applied to pathological experiences. Such an approach also has a long tradition; Kraepelin, Bleuler, and Schneider all expressed the view that some delusions were explanations of hallucinations. Unlike the above classical theories, however, it has been translated into a contemporary, formal explanatory account by Maher (Maher 1974; Maher and Ross 1984).

Normal individuals, Maher's account began, react to the perception of new, novel, or unprecedented events in a characteristic way. Initial puzzlement is followed by a search of the immediate environment for related untoward events. This gives way to the formulation of various potential explanatory hypotheses which are then examined in turn against the evidence. Most of these are quickly discarded or else modified. Sooner or later, however, one appears to be able to offer an explanation for the untoward environmental event, and this gives rise to a flash of insight. This initial success is then followed by a phase in which the individual confirms the explanation by devising a series of further tests.

According to Maher, when the environmental events on which this process is focused are abnormal, then the interpretation which is eventually assigned to them must turn out to be abnormal as well—normal cognitive machinery acting on abnormal input can only give rise to abnormal output in the form of a delusional belief. One obvious class of abnormal perceptual input is hallucinations, which would, according to the theory, go on to elicit delusional explanations. Subtler perceptual disorders might result in the appearance of delusions with correspondingly less obvious antecedents.

However, some, perhaps the majority of delusions in schizophrenia are not traceable to any perceptual abnormality, obvious or otherwise. To account for delusions in the absence of any other psychopathology, Maher postulated that there might be a 'central neuropathology' in schizophrenia which gave rise to a free-floating feeling of significance, which could then in turn be elaborated into the various classes of referential delusions and perhaps form the core of more elaborate delusional systems.

Although it has been, at least until very recently, the only formal psychological theory of delusions, Maher's hypothesis has never, in fact, been subjected to any form of experimental test. It is nevertheless vulnerable at a theoretical level to the type of criticisms facing other, earlier theories: for example, it cannot account for the fixity and incorrigibility of delusions, and it predicts that patients with hallucinations should always be deluded, which is not the case. The theory also faces certain difficulties of its own: delusions might be anticipated in individuals who have abnormal perceptions but who are not suffering from schizophrenia. But patients with conditions ranging from tinnitus and the phantom limb syndrome to migraine and epilepsy do not generally develop delusions about their symptoms. Most seriously of all, Maher's account fails to explain why schizophrenic delusions incline to the bizarre, patently absurd, and fantastic—an essentially normal hypothesis-testing machinery should produce explanations which tend to be rational, mundane, and plausible.

Interestingly, Maher's argument works equally well if it is proposed that the cognitive fault underlying delusions lies, not in the input to the cognitive machinery of belief, but in the machinery itself. Just such a possibility has recently been explored by Hemsley and Garety (1986), who argued that patients with delusions might be more prone than normal individuals to draw firm conclusions from equivocal evidence. In a series of studies to test this hypothesis (Huq *et al.* 1988; Garety 1991), schizophrenic patients and controls had to make a decision based on statistical evidence (whether a series of black or white beads had been drawn from jars containing predominantly one or the other colour). It was found that the schizophrenic patients came to a conclusion significantly earlier than the controls, and held onto it more tenaciously in the face of conflicting evidence from further presentations. So far, however, these authors' findings have to be treated with caution as they have not shown that such reasoning biases are restricted to deluded schizophrenics rather than being a feature of schizophrenia in general.

Hallucinations

The psychological study of hallucinations has covered considerably more ground than that of delusions. The relevant literature has been lucidly reviewed by Slade and Bentall (1988), who distinguished three separate lines of attack on the problem (and also a fourth which is not cognitive psychological and so is not considered further). The first two of these, referred to by Slade and Bentall as *cognitive seepage* and *abnormal imagery*, are conventional psychological theories accompanied by experimental findings; the third, *subvocalization*, is perhaps best described as a set of findings in search of a theory.

Cognitive seepage: These theories seek to explain hallucinations in terms of the entry into consciousness of mental activity which would normally remain preconscious. They are thus merely specific versions of the general selective attentional theory of schizophrenic symptoms. Typically, such theories are aimed at understanding auditory hallucinations; one of these has already been described (Frith 1979), and another (Slade 1976*b*) provides a closely similar account. A somewhat over-elaborate version of the same idea has also been developed to be applicable to all types of hallucination (West 1962; 1975).

Although the overall credibility of the defective filtering account of schizophrenic symptoms has to be regarded as seriously dented, it is still feasible that such a disorder might underlie the particular symptom of hallucinations. However, even here experimental support has not been forthcoming. For example, a simple prediction of the Frith/Slade account of auditory hallucinations is that they should vary directly with the level of environmental noise to which the patient is exposed. In fact, in the single study which tested this prediction (Margo *et al.* 1981), increases in both meaningless (for example electronic bleeps) and meaningful (for example pop music) auditory stimulation had complex effects, but tended if anything to reduce the duration, clarity, and loudness of auditory hallucinations. A number of other findings cited by Slade and Bentall have also pointed in the same direction, and these authors concluded that it was unlikely that cognitive seepage/defective filtering could provide a sufficient explanation of hallucinations.

Abnormal imagery: This account proposes essentially that patients who hallucinate are experiencing exaggerated mental images, which have become so vivid that they are difficult to distinguish from real perceptions. Bearing in mind that schizophrenic auditory hallucinations are commonly reported as being heard inside the head, and that the distinction between true and pseudohallucinations has been one of the most troublesome in phenomenology, any approach which maintains that imagery and hallucination might lie on a continuum has a certain immediate appeal.

The relationship of hallucinations and abnormal imagery has been investigated assiduously since as long ago as the last century. In a way which is rather characteristic of experimental psychology, some support for the idea was originally found; subsequently the findings were questioned; then influential reviews criticized the validity of the measures of imagery used. Next, studies with improved methodology were undertaken; these themselves were subjected to further critical scrutiny; and so on to the present day. Slade and Bentall concluded, with more than a hint of exasperation, that it was difficult to know what to make of the findings taken as a whole. Certainly, they have lent no consistent support for a link between mental imagery and hallucinations. As a side issue, it has become less and less clear that abnormal vividness is in anyway related to judgments of whether an image is real or not.

Subvocalization: The foundation of this approach is a curious experimental finding which may or may not be robust, but whose understanding remains sketchy if not completely obscure. In 1949, Gould, an American psychologist, reported a single case study on a chronically hospitalized schizophrenic woman who was continuously auditorily hallucinated and whom he had noticed also made slight lip movements when she was not speaking. When he placed a stethoscope on her larynx, he heard faint sounds. On attaching a microphone to her throat, words could be made out which accompanied her lip movements. These were found to correspond closely to the patient's own account of what her voices had just been saying. Gould's transcript of the patient's subvocalizations are reproduced in Fig. 7.1; they bear a noticeable resemblance to Kraepelin's description of the content of auditory hallucinations shown in Chapter 1.

This finding was investigated further by Gould (1948, 1950), who showed that electromyograhic (EMG) activity in the speech musculature was increased in hallucinating, but not in non-hallucinating patients, and that the timing of these increases correlated significantly with the patients' reports of the onset of hallucinations. On further investigation, the finding has in some ways become weaker: the studies reviewed by Slade and Bentall (1988) have made it clear that only about half of all schizophrenic patients show increased EMG activity when they are experiencing auditory hallucinations, and the temporal relationship of the speech musculature changes to the onset and offset of hallucinations is, to say the least, complex. In other ways, though, it has become tantalizingly stronger: Green and Preston (1981), whilst testing a patient similar to Gould's, amplified his subvocalizations and played them back to him. This led to a progressive increase in the loudness of the subvocalizations until a conversation between the patient and his hallucinated voice could be clearly heard! The most recent, and perhaps the best study (Green and Kinsbourne 1990) has done little to clarify matters, giving esentially inconclusive results.

The inference these findings invite is that the schizophrenic patient who hears voices is actually talking to himself and experiencing some cognitive

Subvocalizations recorded from a schizophrenic woman
(from Gould 1949)

At initial recording

'Something worse than this. . . . No, certainly not. . . . Not a single thing. It certainly is not. Something going on. That's all right. Anything around. Not very much. Something else. Looks like it isn't. It's just what I know. Something funny about it. Anything doing. Anything else. Get near it. Every single thing. No I don't think so. But this one. Society. I don't expect anything.'

At a time when briefer productions were heard on inspiration as well as expiration

Expiration: 'Oh, she is certainly the wisest one in the world.'
Inspiration: 'No, she is not.'
Expiration: 'I don't know if she is on the level.'
Inspiration: 'What is she going to do?'
Expiration: 'I don't know what she is going to do.'

After being given amytal followed by caffeine

'She knows. She's the most wicked thing in the whole wide world. The only voice I hear is hers. He knows everything. She knows all about aviation.'

Fig. 7.1

correlate of this. Such a conclusion becomes all the more intriguing when it is realized that normal individuals may carry on an analogous form of talking to themselves, which may also be consciously experienced as something not entirely dissimilar from a hallucinated voice: it is known that certain types of mental activity such as reading, problem solving, or rehearsing material are often accompanied by covert speech muscle activity (in prelingually deaf individuals similar activity can be recorded in the finger muscles). It is tempting to speculate that subvocalization is closely related to this phenomenon, which is usually termed inner speech; and that a derangement of inner speech is in turn at the heart of auditory hallucinations. As yet, however, the theoretical framework to develop this proposal into a proper cognitive psychological account of auditory hallucinations does not exist.

Formal thought disorder

Formal thought disorder is by far the most extensively studied phenomenon in schizophrenia. Its investigation, unlike that of delusions and to some extent also hallucinations, has taken the form of a fairly orthodox interplay between theory and experiment. Broadly speaking, the literature can be divided into approaches which are more empirical in orientation, which have first and foremost sought to define what the abnormalities in schizophrenic speech are; and into those which are more theoretically oriented, and which have proceeded by hypothesizing an underlying disorder and examining whether it is borne out or not. The latter approaches, in particular, have tended to tackle formal thought disorder piecemeal, tacitly accepting the assumption that it encompasses a range of conceptually quite different disorders (see Chapter 1).

More empirically oriented approaches: These consist essentially of surveys of schizophrenic speech output for their statistical properties and informational content. The findings have been reviewed many times, but to summarize briefly, schizophrenic patients may or may not use more subjects than objects; they show a tendency to repetitiveness which is at most slight; there is some evidence that they have a more restricted vocabulary than normal individuals; and it is quite well established that their speech contains less of the redundancy of normal speech, is less predictable, and contains less information than normal speech (see Maher 1972; Rochester and Martin 1979; Schwartz 1982; Cutting 1985).

As Maher (1972) pointed out, these findings provide a somewhat limited basis for the understanding of psychotic utterances, and it is only the last group of findings which are at all relevant to the question of why schizophrenic speech is difficult to follow. A more important failing of the studies in this area is many of them do not pass the stringency test specified earlier, that the abnormality in question be demonstrable in acute schizophrenic patients, where the confounding effects of general tendency to poor performance are least evident. In many of the studies, in fact, it is not even clear whether the patient samples were even restricted to those showing formal thought disorder.

More theoretically oriented approaches: There have been two of these, which are not mutually exclusive. The first has been Rochester and Martin's (1979) hypothesis of an abnormality in the communicability of discourse — thought-disordered schizophrenic patients fail to abide by the conventions speakers normally use to ensure that what they say is clear to listeners. The second is Payne's (1973) proposal that schizophrenic speech is difficult to make sense of because conceptual thinking is affected by a disorder of overinclusiveness.

Rochester and Martin began by making the point that, just as a lecturer marshalls what he is going to say in order to maximize the intelligibility of his talk, speakers engaged in everyday conversation also routinely employ a ragbag of rules, conventions, and devices to ensure that their message will get across. Stripped of these, speech would merely be a jumble of more or less well-formed ideas, perhaps resembling the above lecturer's preliminary notes. In these circumstances it might well come to be designated as abnormal, that is showing formal thought disorder.

The authors went on to analyse the verbal output of well-diagnosed acute schizophrenic patients: one group of these was rated clinically as showing formal thought disorder, and another showed no evidence of this. A group of normal individuals was also tested. Using techniques which were rigorous but too complicated to summarize (their book provides a lucid account), transcripts of speech were analysed for the presence of various classes of 'cohesive tie'. It was found that the thought-disordered but not the non-thought-disordered schizophrenics used significantly fewer such ties, in particular, there seemed to be an especial lack of ties referring the listener to context. However, it was also evident that lack of cohesive ties provided an incomplete explanation of formal thought disorder, accounting for less than half the variance in clinical ratings of the phenomenon. A recent replication of Rochester and Martin's study (Chaika and Lambe 1989) gave less grounds for confidence: schizophrenics with formal thought disorder differed significantly from normals in only one out of six categories of cohesive tie measured.

The concept of overinclusiveness stems from the work of Cameron (1939, 1944). In addition to giving a descriptive account of various aspects of formal thought disorder (see Chapter 1), he suggested that these might be understood as arising from a single underlying disorder. The central feature of this was overinclusiveness of conceptual thinking, an inability to select, eliminate, and restrict thought to the task in hand, causing concepts to lose their sharp boundaries and closely or even distantly related ideas to merge into one another. Since the mental set of the speaker would no longer correspond to that of the listener, the result would be that thinking itself would appear vague, imprecise, and difficult to follow.

The experimental investigation of overinclusive thinking was undertaken, not by Cameron, but principally by Payne and co-workers (see Payne 1973; Chapman and Chapman 1973) in a careful and thorough series of studies. A number of initial studies attempted to demonstrate overinclusiveness in a variety of ways, for example requiring subjects to sort words or pictures into conceptual categories, or asking them to give synonyms for words. These invariably found that schizophrenics as a group were more overinclusive than normals or other psychiatric control groups. In several cases the findings were replicated in independent studies. Over-inclusiveness was demonstrated in acute schizophrenic patients, and there were suggestions that the phenomenon tended to be seen in patients who were clinically thought-disordered. These findings are summarized in Table 7.2.

Subsequently, the validity of some of the measures of overinclusiveness used was questioned. Also, a number of negative findings were reported in schizophrenia, and conversely overinclusiveness was claimed to be present in patients with other diagnoses besides schizophrenia. Payne's response was to devise a battery of tests of overinclusiveness whose validity was beyond question, and to re-apply this to various patient groups. The results of these 'second generation' studies are shown in Table 7.3. Almost no normal or neurotic patients obtained a combined overinclusiveness score comparable with that of the schizophrenics as a whole, although there was a tendency for some neurotics to be more overinclusive than normals. High overinclusivness scores were not exclusive to schizophrenia, however, also being found in mania and in a small group of patients with organic disorders.

Table 7.2   Tests of overinclusive thinking in schizophrenia (based on Payne 1973)

	Found in schizophrenia	Independently replicated	Found in acute schizophrenics
Verbal tests			
Giving synonyms for words	Yes	Yes	—
Rating words as being in a conceptual category	Yes	Yes	Yes
Giving information about a story	Yes	—	—
Selecting information for a story	Yes	—	—
Interpreting proverbs	Yes	Yes	Yes
Non-verbal tests			
Sorting objects by physical features	Yes	Yes	Yes
Sorting pictures by conceptual category	Yes	Yes	—
Tests of set formation			
Changing set	Yes	No	Yes
Developing a set	Yes	No	—

Table 7.3 Combined overinclusiveness scores in various diagnostic groups (from Payne 1973, reprinted with permission of Churchill Livingstone).

	Mean	Standard deviation	Number of cases
Paranoid schizophrenics	8.7	3.7	38
Non-paranoid schizophrenics	9.0	4.1	55
Acute schizophrenics	10.0	4.5	20
Chronic schizophrenics	5.3	2.4	17
Manics	10.9	4.6	13
Depressives	6.3	3.0	41
Organics	11.6	3.5	7
Alcoholics	8.0	2.9	12
Personality disorders	7.1	2.9	20
Neurotics	7.3	2.9	55
Normals	4.9	1.6	20

The findings were also notable for the fact that chronic schizophrenic patients were no more overinclusive than neurotics, whereas acute schizophrenics contained a sizeable proportion with the highest scores of any group.

Payne's final conclusion was that overinclusive thinking was a relatively uncommon and somewhat elusive phenomenon which was not specific to schizophrenia. However, as noted by Chapman and Chapman (1973), overinclusiveness stands out as the only psychological abnormality which has ever been found to be more characteristic of acute schizophrenics than chronic schizophrenics. While it has to be accepted that the phenomenon is not confined to schizophrenia, the only other functional psychiatric disorder in which it has been found is mania — whose clinical features also include formal thought disorder.

In summary, it has reluctantly to be concluded that the experimental psychological approach has not yet managed to make many inroads into the understanding of schizophrenic symptoms. The only attempt to generate an overall theory, in the shape of defective selective attention, has proved to be completely sterile. Investigation of what underlies particular classes of symptom has been scarcely more productive. Virtually nothing is known about the psychological basis of delusions. The study of auditory hallucinations has yielded, at best, hints of a relationship with inner speech. It is only in the case of formal thought disorder that anything approaching bona fide psychological abnormalities have been uncovered. Yet not much seems to have been done with the discoveries that have been made, particularly the robust finding of overinclusive thinking. Has the neuropsychological approach fared any better?

The neuropsychology of schizophrenia

This approach makes no attempt to shed light on the process of symptom formation in schizophrenia; in fact it is not really concerned with the clinical features of the disorder at all. Instead, what has been learnt about the way higher mental functions are affected in various brain diseases is applied to schizophrenic patients, who are as it were trawled for evidence of similar impairments. Once again, both general and specific approaches can be distinguished. The former is directed to the question of whether there is overall intellectual impairment in schizophrenia. The latter examines the possibility that one or more of a number of particular cognitive functions are impaired.

By virtue of being a largely data-driven enterprise, the stringency tests which need to be applied to any positive findings are necessarily different from those used in the section on cognitive psychology. If poor performance is found on tests of general intellectual function, the obvious requirement is to ensure that the impairment is genuine and not merely attributable to factors such as poor co-operation, lack of motivation, distraction by psychotic symptoms, etc.. If specific deficits are found, it is important to demonstrate that they are present over and above any general intellectual impairment, in other words to show that they are not just part of a pattern of overall poor performance which would show up on any test.

General intellectual function

One seemingly straightforward way to examine the overall level of intellectual functioning of patients with schizophrenia is to measure their intelligence. After IQ tests were developed in the early part of the century, it quickly became more or less standard practice to administer them to all newly admitted psychiatric patients. Numerous surveys of IQ in various diagnostic groups were published up until around 1960, after which, for obscure reasons, the popularity of this type of study declined precipitously.

The most comprehensive review of IQ in schizophrenia is that of Payne (1973), who pooled the results of all previous studies which used the Weschler Adult Intelligence Scale (WAIS). The average IQ of 1284 schizophrenic patients was found to be 96 compared with the normal population mean of 100. The level also varied according to the subtype diagnosis: paranoid schizophrenics showed only a modest reduction (mean IQ = 95); the difference was more substantial for catatonic schizophrenics (mean IQ = 83); and was greater still for hebephrenic schizophrenics (mean IQ = 81).

Payne then went on to try and establish whether patients with schizophrenia showed low IQ as a lifelong trait, or whether this represented a decline from normal levels after the onset of illness. Indirect evidence, based on the fact that some IQ subtests are resistant to intellectual decline whereas others are sensitive, suggested the latter. Direct evidence on this point was also available from three large studies which had been carried out on servicemen who became schizophrenic after they joined the armed forces. When retested on the IQ tests they had originally taken as part of enlistment, all three studies found an average decrease of about 6 IQ points (this may have been an underestimate since the controls in these studies were found to have increased their scores by a similar number of points). These studies were carried out before the introduction of diagnostic criteria for schizophrenia, but the findings, both of low IQ and of IQ decline have been replicated in two contemporary studies which employed these criteria (Nelson *et al.* 1990; Frith *et al.* 1991).

Does this finding of apparent general intellectual deterioration in schizophrenia pass the stringency test stipulated above, that it cannot be attributed to confounding factors? Unfortunately not. IQ testing is a thoroughly unsatisfactory way of indexing neuropsychological impairment: it is a composite of scores on a wide ranging set of subtests which are designed to draw out differences between normal individuals rather than to pick up those who are abnormal. There is a substantial variation in performance with age which is corrected for in deriving the final IQ figure. Some of the subtests are also timed and so mere slowness can lower the overall score. Finally, testing is also a long and a somewhat arduous procedure, in which motivational and attitudinal factors are expected to be taken into consideration. Poor IQ performance by schizophrenic patients could thus be due to any of a number of extraneous reasons, from apathy and slowness, to poor concentration, distraction by psychotic experiences, and distortion of responding by incoherent speech.

A better way of demonstrating intellectual decline is by use of a battery of neuropsychological tests designed to be sensitive to the kinds of impairment found in patients with brain damage. The tests which make up such batteries tend, of necessity, not to place too many demands on the motivation and concentration of the individual, which will often be compromised to some extent. Often, normative data will have been obtained so that thresholds for normal and impaired performance can be derived. Ideally (if not always in reality), the tests will also have been selected so that scoring is independent of the IQ of the patient.

Heaton *et al.* (1978) critically reviewed 94 studies carried out between 1960 and 1975 which compared the performance of neurotic and psychotic patients on one or more neuropsychological tests with that of patients with organic brain disease. They found that groups of acute, mixed, and chronic schizophrenic patients were increasingly difficult to distinguish from organic patients; for the chronic patients a meaningful differentiation was not possible. The authors were sceptical that motivational and attentional factors could explain the chronic schizophrenics' performance and concluded that, whatever the underlying reason, 'groups of unselected institutionalized chronic schizophrenics will appear organic on neuropsychological testing because a significant proportion of them are organic'. (They in fact thought that some of the patients might have been suffering from undiagnosed neurological disease.)

Two more recent studies have applied neuropsychological test batteries to schizophrenic patients diagnosed according to modern diagnostic criteria. Kolb and Whishaw (1983) employed an extensive set of tests which they had validated against neurological patients with a variety of localized brain lesions. The performance of 30 acute admissions meeting DSM III criteria for schizophrenia on this battery was compared with 30 normal controls. Deficits were found in many, but not all of the tests used, particularly those considered to be sensitive to frontal and temporal lobe function. Taylor and Abrams (1984) compared 62 acute hospital admissions meeting their own criteria for schizophrenia and 42 controls using a roughly similar battery of tests. Three quarters of the schizophrenics showed moderate or severe deficits on a composite score, whereas none of the controls showed more than a mild deficit.

Impaired performance on these tests is more difficult to ascribe to poor concentration and uncooperativeness, but there is still a lingering doubt. For example, the length of time required for testing might have been excessively taxing for patients whose vigilance is known to be poor, or particularly poor performance by a few subjects of dubious testability might have exerted a disproportionate influence on the means for the group as a whole.

A simpler way still of assessing intellectual function exists in the screening tests for delirium and dementia that have been evolved by clinicians. These are little more than a formalization of 'bedside' questions used to determine whether or not a patient has intact orientation, memory, language ability, abstract thinking, and so on. While these tests are crude, their brevity and straightforwardness make it difficult to regard deficits when they are found as due to anything other than genuine intellectual impairment.

The largest survey of this type was carried out by Owens and Johnstone (1980) using a relatively lengthy clinically oriented test devised by Withers and Hinton (1971). They examined 510 chronically hospitalized patients meeting stringent diagnostic criteria for schizophrenia, and compared their scores with a control group made up of 33 patients who required chronic institutional care for physical illnesses. Their findings are shown in Fig. 7.2, from which it is evident that while some of the schizophrenic patients scored within the normal range, over half were more than two standard deviations

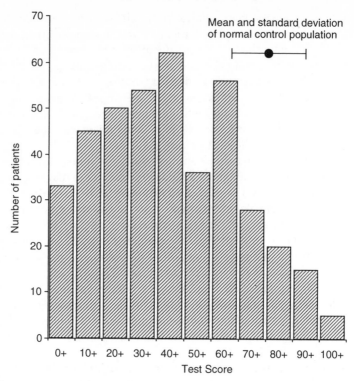

Fig. 7.2 Scores of chronically hospitalized schizophrenic patients on a clinically oriented test of intellectual function (from Owens and Johnstone 1980).

below the control group mean. Fifteen per cent of the sample were only able to achieve scores of 20 or less — spectacularly poor performance on a test where merely being oriented in time, place, and person, and being able to answer elementary general knowledge questions gives a score of 25.

The simplest intellectual test of all is merely to ask the patient questions about his orientation in time and place. Crow and co-workers (Crow and Mitchell 1975; Stevens *et al.* 1978) required chronically hospitalized patients to state their age and found that approximately 25 per cent were wrong, typically underestimating it by five years or more. Age disorientation in schizophrenia has been investigated extensively by this group (Liddle and Crow 1984; Buhrich *et al.* 1988) and it has been established that it is not attributable to lifelong low intelligence, or exposure to various modalities of physical treatment. It is also clear that age disorientation typically forms part of a wider pattern of neuropsychological impairment, which is usually marked. Some illustrations of the phenomenon are shown in Table 7.4.

These last findings cannot be explained away. It is difficult to believe that

Table 7.4 Extracts from casenotes of age-disoriented schizophrenic patients (from Buhrich *et al.* 1988)

Age at admission	Age when cognitive impairment first noted	Comments in casenotes
20	28	'Confused, not oriented in space or time'
20	26	'100 − 7 = 88'
20	46	'Gives age as 17 ... does not appear to understand what is being said'
33	56	'Says she is aged 26 years'
22	34	'Answers questions incorrectly. Gives age as 12 years'
20	26	'Dull ... disoriented'
25	59	'Gives age as 26 years'
22	35	'Dull and confused. Memory shows gross impairment'
28	32	'Very disoriented in time and place'

withdrawal, distraction, or preoccupation with inner experiences can compromise the ability of chronic schizophrenic patients to answer mundane questions and perform simple mental tests in so many cases to such a severe degree. Nor is it credible to maintain that keeping track of one's age is too demanding a task for institutionalized patients.

Taken together, the findings provide compelling evidence that a substantial intellectual decline takes place in schizophrenia. In acute patients this is variable and usually minor, but it can be detected by IQ testing or using neuropsychological test batteries. As the disorder becomes more severe and chronic, impairment becomes widespread and easy to demonstrate. In a proportion of institutionalized cases the degree of impairment amounts to what is to all intents and purposes a dementia.

Specific neuropsychological deficits

While it is not possible to separate higher mental functions absolutely from one another, perception, language, memory, and executive (frontal) function stand out as relatively independent domains, both on intuitive grounds and on the basis of having been so treated by neuropsychology without major difficulties having arisen. The central aspects of motor control also fall within the realm of neuropsychology, but these, with the exception of reaction time, have not been investigated to any significant degree in schizophrenia. As previously, the summary of the work on specific neuropsychological deficits in schizophrenia presented here is heavily dependent on the reviews of other authors, notably Cutting (1985).

Perception

From the neuropsychological standpoint (for example see Ellis and Young 1988) visual perception can be regarded as the construction of a series of increasingly sophisticated representations of the basic retinal image. The ultimate step is the creation of a model of seen objects and surfaces which is independent of the viewer's position and which specifies their real shape and how they are positioned in relation to one another. It is likely that a similar series of steps underlies auditory and tactile perception as well. Beyond these stages are others involving recognition and accessing of information about these complex perceptual configurations, which are necessary for the comprehension of events taking place in the world, and for writing and speech.

A number of aspects of these processes have been studied in schizophrenia and the findings have been reviewed by Frith (1973) and Cutting (1985). As might be anticipated from clinical impression, there is little evidence that the early stages of visual and auditory processing are disturbed. The occasional impairments that have been reported, for example slowness of processing and higher thresholds for detection of sensory stimuli, appear to be readily explainable as secondary to other disorders and not primarily perceptual. At a somewhat higher level of perceptual processing, chronic schizophrenic patients have been found to have difficulties recognizing out of focus pictures, figures embedded in other figures, and ambiguous figures; according to Cutting, however, the methodology of these studies was unsound. At a higher level still, there have been scattered reports that schizophrenics are less accurate than normals in making judgements of the size and distance of objects, and they may have difficulties in judgements of facial expression. Once again, the relevant studies have tended to have methodological shortcomings.

Cutting drew the conclusion from this work that basic perceptual processes were probably normal in schizophrenia, but that there was some evidence of a disorder of perception of form, affecting the way faces and ambiguous stimuli are interpreted. What has not been demonstrated is that any such abnormalities pass the stringency test allotted to studies of specific neuropsychological deficits, that they should be disproportionate to any overall intellectual impairment in schizophrenia. Until this is done, there seems little reason to reject the view that perceptual processes are fundamentally unimpaired in schizophrenia.

Language

The study of normal language is a vast topic, within which it has become customary to recognize a series of subdivisions. One broad division is between the receptive and expressive aspects of speech; another is the separation of phonemic, syntactic, and semantic components of language (to which a fourth category, pragmatics, has recently been added). The investigation of language breakdown in neurological disorders is nearly as complicated; at both the clinical (for example Benson 1979) and neuropsychological levels (for example Ellis and Young 1988), the classification of dysphasias is complex and controversial.

Examination of language in schizophrenia has been complicated by the fact that while many patients show no obvious abnormality, speech is certainly unusual in those who show formal thought disorder, although whether there is an intrinsic abnormality of language is debatable. The ideal way to investigate language in schizophrenia would be to study patients with and without formal thought disorder. In practice, the studies can usually only be separated into those which have examined schizophrenic patients as a whole, and those which have focused on patients exhibiting the severer forms of formal thought disorder. The former have taken the form of more or less systematic searches for subtle, quantitative differences in the phonemic, syntactic, and semantic components of speech; the latter have been more naturalistic and descriptive.

Studies of language in schizophrenic patients as a whole are rather sparse; the available literature has been most thoroughly reviewed by Cutting (1985). To précis his conclusions, there is no evidence of any marked phonemic abnormalities in schizophrenia, either receptive or expressive. Nor has there been much to suggest that there is any abnormality in the appreciation or use of syntax. As far as the semantic aspects of language are concerned, it has been found that schizophrenic patients are able to extract the gist of sentences to the same extent as normals, and that as a rule they show unexceptional patterns of word association. The last conclusion has to be qualified to some extent, because some studies on chronic patients or on those showing formal thought disorder have recorded abnormal word associations; however, these findings are not entirely consistent.

Taking a more utilitarian approach, three studies (DiSimoni *et al.* 1977; Faber and Reichstein 1981; Silverberg-Shalev *et al.* 1981) have examined the performance of unselected groups of schizophrenic patients on dysphasia screening batteries. All found that the patients performed more poorly than normals on comprehension and repetition of speech. However, as none of the studies included any measure of overall intellectual impairment, once again, these studies fail the stringency test of showing a disproportionate deficit.

It remains possible that schizophrenic patients with formal thought disorder exhibit linguistic abnormalities which failed to show up in the above studies as a result of their being swamped by normal function in the majority. In fact, the points of similarity between severe formal thought disorder with incoherence, word approximations and neologisms, and fluent dysphasias has struck numerous authors beginning with Kraepelin and Bleuler, and a common basis for them was argued strenuously by Kleist (1960). Modern study of this issue has been characterized by a polarization of views: on the basis of single case studies, Critchley (1964), a neurologist, concluded that fluent dysphasia and schizophrenic thought disorder were recognizably different; in contrast a linguist, Chaika (1974), argued that several characteristic phonological, syntactical, and semantic features of dysphasia could be discerned in thought-disordered schizophrenic speech.

The debate has continued, quite acrimoniously, but in a way which is not very accessible to anyone without linguistic expertise (see Rochester and Martin 1979). There has only been one attempt to resolve it pragmatically. Faber *et al.* (1983) prepared transcripts of the speech of 14 schizophrenic patients with clearly evident formal thought disorder and 13 patients with dysphasias, which were fluent in 11 cases. The transcripts were carefully edited to remove all potential clues to diagnosis, and then presented under blind conditions to two psychiatrists, two neurologists, and a speech pathologist. Only the speech pathologist came close to discriminating the schizophrenics from the dysphasics perfectly; the psychiatrists did rather less well; and the neurologists failed to score significantly above chance. Most errors derived from misidentifying dyphasic patients as schizophrenic; at the same time, paraphasias—the hallmark of dysphasia—were blindly rated as present by the speech pathologist in over half the schizophrenic patients. This and other findings are shown in Table 7.5. Faber *et al.* concluded that dysphasia and formal thought disorder could be distinguished, although there was considerable overlap in the language abnormalities shown by the two groups. Their findings also provide a rather strong vindication of the rather lonely position taken first by Kleist and later by Chaika.

Memory

The outcome of a massive, and at times highly disputatious investigation of normal memory has been the acceptance that there exist two major distinct stores (see Baddeley 1990). *Short-term or primary memory* holds a small number of items of information (approximately seven) for up to about 30 seconds; *long-term or secondary memory* holds all information required to be stored for any longer than this. It has become useful to

Table 7.5 Language abnormalities rated blindly in dysphasic patients and schizophrenic patients with formal thought disorder (from Faber et al. 1983)

	Dysphasic patients ($n = 13$)	Schizophrenic patients ($n = 14$)	Significance of difference
Paraphasias	8	9	NS
Agrammatism	2	0	NS
Impaired comprehension of speech	5	0	0.04
Anomia/word finding problems	7	0	0.01
Pronoun word problems	4	0	NS
Circumlocutions	1	0	NS
Neologisms	1	3	NS
Word approximations/ idiosyncratic use of words	0	8	0.01
Perseveration	1	4	NS
Incoherence	3	10	NS
Derailment/tangentiality	2	11	0.05
Poverty of content	8	1	0.04
Illogicality	1	5	NS
Clanging	0	3	NS

distinguish several subdivisions of long-term/secondary memory: episodic (memory for personal experience), semantic (memory for general knowledge), and procedural (memory for skills), amongst others. There has never been, however, much evidence to support a compartmentalization of recently and remotely acquired memories within long-term/secondary memory, a distinction which has traditionally been made much of by clinicians.

Although memory was considered to be comparatively little affected in schizophrenia by Kraepelin (1913a) and not to suffer at all by Bleuler (1911), virtually all of a number of early studies found evidence of impairment; on the whole, however, this was not severe. After reviewing these studies, Cutting (1985) concluded that memory remained intact in acute schizophrenic patients, at least superficially, but that poor memory function was common in chronic patients and could sometimes amount to quite marked amnesia.

Since Cutting's review, a number of studies have appeared which have suggested that memory impairment is one of the major neuropsychological deficits seen in schizophrenia. These have found mild but still clear-cut memory impairment in acute patients (for example Calev 1984*a*; Gruzelier *et al*. 1988). In chronic patients, the deficits have been found to be moderate or sometimes severe (Calev 1984*b*; Calev *et al*. 1987*a,b*; Goldberg *et al*. 1989). McKenna *et al*. (1990) found that the memory performance of a mixed group of 60 acute and chronic patients was no better than that of a sample of 176 patients attending a rehabilitation centre for brain injury. Memory impairment was found in three-quarters of the entire sample and was by no means confined to old, chronic, or deteriorated patients; the deficits were sometimes substantial in acute patients.

Memory impairment may have been established as commonplace, even ubiquitous in schizophrenia, but to qualify as a specific neuropsychological deficit it needs to be established that it is disproportionate to the overall level of intellectual impairment. In the study of McKenna *et al*. memory performance was compared with overall intellectual functioning. As shown in Fig. 7.3, it was found that whereas nearly half the sample showed memory scores in the moderately or severely impaired range, a much smaller proportion fell below the threshold scores for presence of general intellectual impairment on two different rating scales for this.

An aside to this researh is the finding that the memory impairment of schizophrenia follows a distinctive pattern. Tamlyn *et al*. (1992) applied the neuropsychological case study approach to five schizophrenic patients who showed memory function in the setting of relatively well preserved overall intellectual performance. They found that in all cases the impairment was restricted to long-term/secondary memory and that short-term/primary memory was spared. This is the pattern which characterizes the so-called classical amnesic syndrome (seen for instance in Korsakoff's psychosis) and is different from that seen in dementia of Alzheimer type, in which both stores are affected from an early stage.

Executive ('frontal lobe') function

A long tradition in neuropsychology has supported the notion of a cognitive system whose main purpose is to orchestrate the function of other systems in the performance of complex tasks such as comprehension, learning, and reasoning. Recently this system has been given a degree of neuropsychological specification as the central executive of Baddeley (1986) and the supervisory attentional system of Norman and Shallice (see Shallice 1988). Both these models embody the concept of a supervisory function, closely identified with consciousness and the control of attention, which integrates information from several sources, schedules its processing according to the needs of the moment, and selects overall strategies of action. The models also offer a promising framework for understanding the distinctive pattern

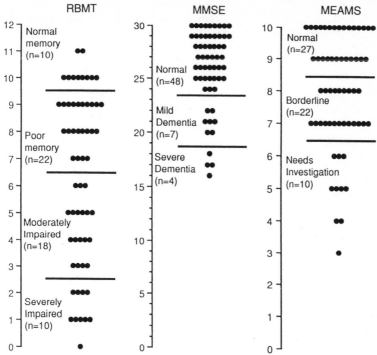

Fig. 7.3 Performance of a mixed group of schizophrenic patients on the Rivermead Behavioural Memory Test (RBMT) and on two tests of general intellectual function, the Mini-Mental State Examination (MMSE), and the Middlesex Elderly Assessment of Mental State (MEAMS) (from Mckenna *et al.* 1990).

of cognitive impairment seen in patients who have sustained injuries to the frontal lobes, in which there are difficulties in the planning, initiation, and execution of complex sequences of behaviour, together with a striking failure to monitor and revise these when they are unsuccessful.

The best known test of executive function is the Wisconsin Card Sorting Test. In this the subject is required to sort cards according to rules which are arbitrarily changed from time to time. Many patients with frontal lobe lesions, while learning the initial sorting principle easily, have difficulty switching to a new rule when this is required of them and tend to make perseverative errors; characteristically, they seem to be aware of these but are unable to correct them. There are numerous other tests, many of which involve strategic decision-making, on which patients with frontal lobe lesions have been found to perform poorly.

In schizophrenia, poor Wisconsin Card Sorting Test performance has been found in a number of studies (see Goldberg *et al.* 1987; Morice 1990).

Table 7.6 Performance of three chronic schizophrenic patients without marked overall intellectual impairment on executive and other neuropsychological tests (modified from Shallice *et al.* 1991)

(a) visuospatial and language tests

	Patient		
	HE (age 44)	HS (age 66)	RS (age 55)
Visual tests			
Figure-ground discrimination	0	0	0
Dot centring	0	0	0
Dot counting	0	0	0
Cube analysis	0	0	0
Unusual views	0	0	3
Usual views	0	0	3
Naming from silhouettes	0	2	2
Copying a figure	0	2	0
Language tests			
Graded spelling	0	0	0
Graded naming	0	0	0
Naming from description	1	0	3
Token test	0	0	3

Impairments have also been demonstrated on a number of other tasks which involve hypothesized executive function and/or are sensitive to frontal lobe lesions (for example Goldberg *et al.* 1988; Liddle and Morris 1991). Although the literature is not very clear on this point, the impression is that the deficits tend to be seen particularly in chronic schizophrenic patients.

When attempts are made, however, to determine whether the executive impairment in schizophrenia is disproportionate to the overall level of intellectual function, serious difficulties are run into. The vast majority of studies of executive function in schizophrenia have paid no attention whatsoever to their patients' general intellectual level. Another problem is that 'frontal lobe' tests as a group are peculiarly prone to difficulties of interpretation, performance being adversely affected by factors such as low IQ, intellectual decline, or presence of other neuropsychological impairments — all of which are to be expected in schizophrenic patients. At the present time, no decisive answer to this question can be provided, and all that can be done is to outline the findings which point one way or the other.

Shallice *et al.* (1991) used the neuropsychological case study approach and subjected five chronically hospitalized schizophrenic patients to an

Table 7.6   (b) tests sensitive to executive impairment

	Patient		
	HE (age 44)	HS (age 66)	RS (age 55)
Wisconsin Card Sorting Test	3	0	3
Object sorting	0	3	0
Cognitive Estimates Test	3	0	3
Motor alternation	0	0	3
Money's Road Map Test	0	3	3
Personal Orientation Test	0	0	3
Self-ordered pointing	0	3	3
Stroop Test: word reading	0	3	3
Stroop Test: colour naming	2	3	0
Trail Making Test (b)	3	2	0
FAS Test (verbal fluency/1 min.)	0	1	2

Scores 0–3 represent impairment indexes derived from normative data on each of the tests. 0, at or above 25th percentile; 1, 10th to 25th percentile; 2, 5th to 10th percentile; 3, below 5th percentile. (NB: performance on memory tests was intermediate between that on perceptual and language tests and that on executive tests.)

extensive battery of tests. These consisted of various general measures, mainly of current and estimated premorbid IQ, together with specific tests of visuospatial function, language, memory, and 12 tests sensitive to executive/frontal lobe impairment. They found that the patients showed a more or less consistent pattern of severe impairment on the executive tests. In two of the patients this was in the setting of preserved IQ and normal performance on tests of visual perception and language, plus only scattered deficits on memory tests. In two more it was part of a pattern of widespread deficits coupled with IQ decline. The last patient performed at a level intermediate between the other two groups. It was argued that impaired executive function was thus the common denominator of schizophrenic neuropsychological impairment, being present against a background of no, some, or a great deal of overall intellectual impairment. The findings in the three of the patients without marked overall deterioration are given in Table 7.6, which highlights the contrast between the performance on frontal tests and that on tests of visual perception and language.

Saykin *et al.* (1991) administered a wide ranging battery of neuropsychological tests to a group of 36 chronic schizophrenic patients and to normal controls. They found that, as expected, the patients performed significantly more poorly than the controls across the board. They then went on to express the schizophrenic patients' scores in a way that reflected the degree to which their performance fell below that of the controls on each test (this employed the technique of Z-transformation in which scores are expressed in terms of the number of standard deviations below the control group mean). As can be seen from Fig. 7.4, it was found that the patients' performance was selectively impaired on the tests of memory, that is these scores were depressed to a much greater extent than those on the rest of the battery. The impairment on a test of executive function was only modest, and not obviously greater than on the remainder of the tests.

In contrast to purely psychological approaches, the neuropsychological approach has yielded strongly positive findings from the outset. Taken overall, the evidence suggests that there are two axes of impairment in schizophrenia: on the one hand there is a tendency to general intellectual impairment which is discernible as a fall in IQ in many patients, and which becomes increasingly clinically apparent with increasing severity and chronicity of the disorder. On the other, there are specific neuropsychological deficits: memory is definitely affected, executive function is somewhat more controversially impaired, and it may be that language is also disturbed in the minority of patients with marked formal thought disorder. Nevertheless, there are considerable numbers of patients, many of whom have acute or mild illnesses, in whom there is no obvious impairment.

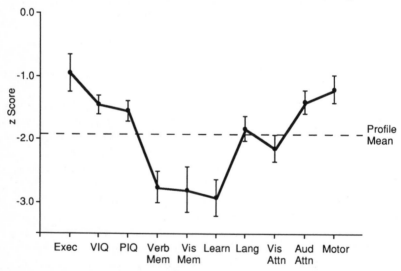

Fig. 7.4 Profile of performance on tests of executive function, memory, and other neuropsychological functions in 36 patients with schizophrenia (from Saykin *et al.* 1991). (Exec, Wisconsin Card Sorting Test; VIQ, verbal IQ; PIQ, performance IQ; Verb Mem, verbal recall memory; Vis Mem, visual recall memory; Learn, verbal learning; Lang, combined scores on a language battery; Vis Attn, visual-motor processing and attention; Aud Attn, auditory processing and attention; Motor, motor tests.)

Conclusion

Attempting to account for the symptoms of schizophrenia in cognitive psychological terms has seen the exercise of much theoretical ingenuity but the generation of few hard facts. The screening of schizophrenic patients for neuropsychological deficits, on the other hand, has yielded a plethora of abnormal findings but little in the way of insights into the mechanisms of symptom formation. The findings of years of experimental psychological investigation of schizophrenia thus appear to have converged to pose a riddle: how can the neuropsychological deficits seen in the disorder be made to account for its symptoms, many of which are anything but deficits?

The currently fashionable way to try and solve this riddle involves combining the cognitive psychological and neuropsychological approaches into what is unsurprisingly referred to as the cognitive neuropsychology of schizophrenia. Frith (1987; Frith and Done 1988) has proposed a theory in which impairment of executive function gives rise to a defect of monitoring of intended actions, which is in turn capable of explaining a variety of positive symptoms. McKenna (1987, 1991) has argued that, rather than impairment, it is necessary to think of schizophrenic symptoms such as delusions, hallucinations, and formal thought disorder in terms of a hyperfunction or a biasing of the function of cognitive systems. Gray *et al.* (1991) have constructed an elaborate neuropsychological model for the control of voluntary action, the framework of which can accommodate a modified selective attentional account of schizophrenic symptoms. Finally, Cutting (1990) has exploited the laterality differences that exist in certain neuropsychological functions to arrive at his own rather different interpretation of schizophrenic symptoms.

These accounts all contain a large pinch of speculation and none of them can be regarded as rigorous within their own psychological terms of reference—they draw on neurochemical, neurophysiological, and neuroanatomical findings, which themselves are sometimes not very firmly established, in a somewhat indiscriminate way. Whether or not this latest generation of theories will prove to be any more productive than their predecessors, only time will tell.

8

Neuroleptic drug treatment

Schizophrenia became a treatable illness in 1952. As reconstructed by Caldwell (1970), the story of the discovery of neuroleptic drugs began with a French surgeon, Laborit, who was investigating the usefulness of various compounds in combating the adverse autonomic and psychological consequences of surgery. In the course of testing an antihistamine, promethazine, he observed that this drug tended to induce a state of calm, quiet, relaxation in volunteers. Attempts to maximize this effect by pharmacological manipulation resulted in the synthesis of chlorpromazine, a drug which reliably produced 'not any loss in consciousness, not any change in the patient's mentality but a slight tendency to sleep and above all "disinterest" for all that goes on around him' (Laborit *et al.* 1952). Laborit immediately recognized the potential usefulness of this effect in psychiatry and managed to persuade some rather reluctant psychiatric colleagues to try it on psychotic patients. Successes in individual cases were quickly followed by the now classic report on a small series of patients by Delay *et al.* (1952).

This version of events does not tell quite the whole story. For centuries rauwolfia root had been used in India as a treatment for severe psychiatric disturbance. Reserpine, the active component of rauwolfia root was also isolated in 1952. A year later Hakim (1953) claimed cures of schizophrenia with rauwolfia, and Kline (1954) in the USA described amelioration of various psychiatric disorders, though not specifically schizophrenia, with reserpine. It was soon noted that the commonest side-effects of both chlorpromazine and reserpine took the form of basal ganglia signs (Steck 1954) and this led Delay and Deniker (1955) to coin, somewhat obscurely, the term neuroleptic. Although the usefulness of reserpine in schizophrenia was accepted, interest in this drug waned; more than anything else it was eclipsed by chlorpromazine, use of which spread explosively.

Beginning with haloperidol, a range of drugs with similar profiles of effect to chlorpromazine was soon developed. The main chemical classes expanded to include the *phenothiazines* (for example chlorpromazine, thioridazine, trifluoperazine, fluphenazine), the *butyrophenones* (for example haloperidol, droperidol), the *thioxanthenes* (for example flupenthixol, clopenthixol, thiothixene), the *diphenylbutylpiperidines* (for example pimozide, fluspirilene) and the *substituted benzamides* (for example sulpiride, remoxipride). Miscellaneous compounds with similar actions were also found, including clozapine, loxapine, molindone, and risperidone. Between them, these drugs have become the treatment of choice in schizophrenia, as well as its mainstay. Their use has now become so wide that it is difficult to locate any patients with established schizophrenia who have not been exposed to them.

The accumulated knowledge on the actions of neuroleptic drugs, whilst far from meagre, remains somewhat piecemeal, a jigsaw puzzle whose clinical and pharmacological pieces do not fit together very well. In this chapter an attempt is made to bring together the available clinical and preclinical information and to integrate these where possible. Such an approach is worthwhile in its own right, and it is a prerequisite for understanding the progress that has been made in the search for new, atypical, and hopefully therapeutically superior neuroleptics.

The therapeutic effect of neuroleptic drugs

Within ten years of the introduction of chlorpromazine, a consensus on neuroleptic drug treatment in schizophrenia had emerged. It was accepted that the drugs provided an excellent means of controlling disturbed behaviour, and as a consequence markedly decreased the need for hospitalization. It was also widely believed that they had a specific therapeutic effect on schizophrenic symptoms, although this was individually quite variable. As Freeman (1978) put it, while the outlook for patients with schizophrenia had not been entirely bleak before the advent of neuroleptics and did not become entirely satisfactory afterwards, the drugs greatly mitigated the distress and suffering caused by the disorder.

Unfortunately, there was a problem. Twenty years before the discovery of neuroleptics, insulin coma therapy had been introduced for schizophrenia in somewhat similar circumstances. Its use had also spread worldwide and numerous studies testified to its effectiveness. But then the value of the treatment was first questioned (Bourne 1953), and then exposed as worthless in a blind study (Ackner *et al.* 1957). Its apparent beneficial effects were revealed as an artefact of selective referral, high staff morale, and the mystique of an intensive and dangerous procedure (see Cramond 1987). The implications for neuroleptic treatment were clear: their effectiveness needed to survive close scrutiny in properly controlled clinical trials.

By 1966 over 40 double-blind, placebo-controlled studies of neuroleptic treatment had been carried out (see Davis 1985). Most of these showed that neuroleptics were significantly superior to placebo, and the minority which failed to do so invariably suffered from a combination of poor design, small sample sizes, low dosage, and short duration regimens. One of the largest and most careful of these studies was carried out by the National Institute of Mental Health (NIMH 1964; Goldberg *et al.* 1965). Three hundred and eighty newly admitted schizophrenic patients, recruited from nine centres, were randomly assigned to treatment with one of three neuroleptics (chlorpromazine, fluphenazine, or thioridazine) or placebo under double-blind conditions for six weeks. The findings are summarized in Fig. 8.1. It can be seen that, whereas the global improvement ratings for patients receiving placebo were fairly evenly distributed above and below 'no change' and 'minimally improved', less than 5 per cent of the neuroleptic-treated patients were rated as 'no change' and 75 per cent showed moderate or marked improvement. These differences between drug and placebo were, in all probability, an underestimate since 36 of the 110 placebo-treated patients dropped out of the trial because of deteriorating clinical condition.

The clinical impression that the effect of neuroleptics went beyond simple tranquillization was also upheld in this study. In the first place, it was evident that quite varied schizophrenic symptoms improved. As shown in Table 8.1, the neuroleptic-treated group showed significant improvement in all the 21 aspects of psychopathology rated, and this was significantly greater than for the placebo group in 13 of these. Secondly, it was noted that the improvement in symptoms such as hostility, agitation, and anxiety — which might be considered the target symptoms of a general tranquillization — was not as great as for other symptoms, such as hebephrenic symptoms, social participation, and self care, which could not be construed in this way. Finally, the investigators asked the question of whether neuroleptics followed and merely amplified the improvement seen

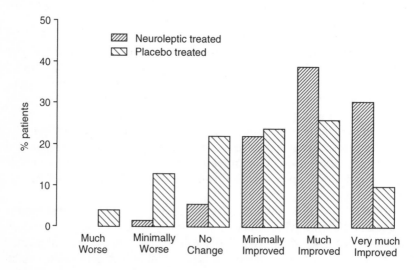

Fig. 8.1 Neuroleptic versus placebo treatment in patients with schizophrenia (from Goldberg *et al.* 1965).

Table 8.1 Changes in symptoms and behaviour as a consequence of neuroleptic treatment (from Goldberg *et al.* 1965)

Symptom/behaviour	Standardized change (drug treatment)	Standardized change (drug − placebo differences)
Resistiveness	0.68**	0.32
Hostility	0.86**	0.58**
Irritability	0.86**	0.79**
Pressure of speech	0.87**	0.46**
Agitation and tension	0.96**	0.68**
Delusions of grandeur	1.04**	0.20
Ideas of persecution	1.13**	0.57**
Auditory hallucinations	1.72**	0.62**
Non-auditory hallucinations	1.66**	0.19
Hebephrenic symptoms	1.44**	1.19**
Incoherent speech	1.47**	0.87**
Slowed speech and movements	0.85**	0.73**
Indifference	1.24**	0.89**
Self care	1.28**	0.93**
Social participation	1.78**	0.99**
Observed sadness	0.67**	0.04
Guilt	0.65**	0.20
Confusion	1.69**	0.98**
Feelings of unreality	1.68**	1.19
Memory deficit	1.90**	0.60
Disorientation	2.06**	0.34

**$P < 0.01$.

on placebo, or whether the pattern was different. To answer this they correlated the changes in symptom scores found on drug treatment and placebo with each other. The correlation between the two was significantly inverse, indicating that the patterns of improvement were quite different.

While studies like that of Goldberg *et al.* (1965) indicated that a wide variety of schizophrenic symptoms were responsive to neuroleptics, clinical impression was giving a somewhat different picture. Initially, it was suspected that it was acute rather than chronic patients who showed the bulk of the improvement. For instance, Letemendia and Harris (1967) started neuroleptic treatment in a number of chronic schizophrenic patients with predominantly withdrawn, apathetic presentations and found an indifferent response. More recently, Johnstone *et al.* (1978), in their study of active and inactive isomers of flupenthixol described in Chapter 6, found that only positive symptoms improved on neuroleptics, negative symptoms (and also non-specific symptoms such as depression and anxiety) showing no significant change over the four week study period. The conclusions of both these studies, however, are open to criticism: Letemendia and Harris used only low doses of neuroleptics for a short period, and in the study of Johnstone *et al.* negative symptoms were at a low level at the beginning of the study, leaving little scope for improvement.

Goldberg (1985) reviewed the findings of several large-scale placebo-controlled studies of neuroleptic drugs with respect to this issue. He noted that, in his own study (Goldberg *et al.* 1965), negative or Bleulerian fundamental symptoms such as indifference to the environment, slowed speech and movements, and poor self care improved on neuroleptic treatment, although this improvement appeared to be less than that for positive or accessory symptoms, such as excitement, ideas of persecution, and incoherence of thought. Of five further studies, all showed a significant effect of treatment on formal thought disorder, two showed an effect on affective flattening, four showed an effect on withdrawal and retardation, and four showed an effect on 'autistic' behaviour.

In conclusion, there is no doubt that neuroleptic drugs are efficacious in schizophrenia. There is also no doubt that they have a specific action on the symptoms of the disorder, rather than exerting some general tranquillizing or other non-specific effect. With regard to the question of whether neuroleptics have an effect on all schizophrenic symptoms, the evidence is inconclusive: while beneficial effects on some negative symptoms seem to be established, whether this is true for all of them and whether it occurs to a comparable degree to that seen for positive symptoms are questions which remain unanswered.

The pharmacological effects of neuroleptic drugs

For over a decade after their introduction, the essential pharmacological effect of neuroleptics remained unknown. Chlorpromazine was found experimentally to have numerous biochemical actions, but this seemed to reflect merely its high lipid solubility and consequent interactions with cell membrane systems (Iversen 1978). It was not until Carlsson and Lindqvist (1963) discovered that chlorpromazine and haloperidol caused acute increases in catecholamine turnover in rat brain that significant progress began to be made: they hypothesized that the likeliest cause of this was blockade of the post-synaptic receptors for these transmitters.

For a further decade it remained unclear whether dopamine, noradrenaline, or both catecholamine receptors were blocked by neuroleptics. Then in 1974 direct evidence for preferential dopamine receptor blockade became available (Seeman *et al.* 1974). As detailed in Chapter 6, the evidence that dopamine receptor blockade is the principal pharmacological effect of neuroleptics, the one which they all have in common, and the one which is responsible for their therapeutic effect has since gradually become incontrovertible.

The basis of neuroleptic antidopaminergic effects next became complicated by the increasing evidence for more than one type of dopamine receptor. By 1980 it was clear that there existed at least two distinct classes of dopamine receptor (Kebabian and Calne 1979; see also Seeman 1980; Joyce 1983), which had quite different pharmacological properties. D1 receptors were the first dopamine receptor to be discovered. Like many other types of receptor, D1 receptors are linked to an intracellular 'second messenger' system involving cyclic AMP, stimulation of the receptor producing increased synthesis of this compound. D2 receptors were originally postulated in order to explain an increasing number of anomalous findings. Subsequently, their existence was confirmed. Stimulation of these receptors by dopamine agonists produces no increase in cyclic AMP, and some evidence points to an inhibition of the cyclic AMP system (for example Seeman 1987).

Dopamine receptor pharmacology continues to be in a state of flux. Shortly after the existence of D1 and D2 receptors was established, it was proposed that there were in reality four different classes of dopamine receptor in the central nervous system. This particular debate was resolved by showing that each of the two receptors could exist in high and low affinity states for dopamine (see Seeman 1987). More recently, the whole field has been thrown into disarray by the discovery, using molecular genetic techniques, of at least three new types of dopamine receptor, D3, D4, and D5 (see Sibley and Monsma 1992; Waddington 1993). Fortunately, at least so far, these seem to fall into two 'families' with D1-like (D1 and D5), and D2-like (D2, D3, and D4) pharmacological properties. For the time being, it remains useful to talk of D1 and D2 dopamine receptors, but how much longer this will be so is uncertain.

The principal effect of neuroleptic drugs on animal behaviour is inhibition of spontaneous motor activity without induction of drowsiness. In rats, the usual animal species studied, the striking change is in locomotor activity, both spontaneous activity and especially the exploration which takes place in a new environment (Kreiskott 1980). At higher doses neuroleptics induce a state of profound immobility often referred to as catalepsy (Joyce 1983; Mason 1984). Though conscious, the animal has difficulty executing any acts and crouches in a hunched posture, passive to all but the strongest external stimuli. If placed in an uncomfortable position, for instance with one hind leg raised on a platform, it will remain in it for many minutes before stepping down. The animal is not, however, paralyzed: under intense adverse conditions (procedures employed have included immersing rats in freezing water or placing them among cats) motor activity temporarily reverts to normal, the animal, however, sinking back into motionlessness as soon as the danger is escaped.

A second, somewhat more esoteric animal neuroleptic effect should be mentioned, since this has become the standard means of screening drugs for antipsychotic action. This is the hyperactivity/stereotypy model (Joyce 1983: Mason 1984). Acute administration of dopamine agonists such as amphetamine or apomorphine to rats induces a state which is in many ways the reverse of catalepsy. An increase in locomotor activity is initially observed which proceeds to become first accompanied by and then completely overshadowed by the syndrome of stereotypy. The range and unpredictability of the animal's behaviour becomes increasingly constrained until eventually it incessantly performs one or a few responses like sniffing and rearing. Neuroleptic drugs characteristically reverse both the hyperactivity and stereotypy components of this dopamine agonist response.

The therapeutic effects of neuroleptic drugs could theoretically be ascribed to blockade of either D1 or D2 receptors, or both. Circumstantial evidence has always implicated D2 receptors: the concentrations of neuroleptics necessary to block D1 receptors have been found to be 100-fold higher than those which reach the blood and cerebrospinal fluid of patients on therapeutic dosages of these drugs. On the other hand, neuroleptics interact with D2 receptors at very low concentrations, well within reach of their therapeutic dose ranges. This hypothesis was elegantly confirmed by Creese *et al.* (1976) and Seeman *et al.* (1976) who demonstrated that the clinical antipsychotic potency of different neuroleptic drugs correlated highly with their affinities at the D2 receptor; later it was shown that there was no correlation with their potency at the D1 receptor (see Seeman 1987). These findings are shown in Fig. 8.2.

The relationship of animal behavioural effects to the therapeutic effect of neuroleptics has never been particularly clear. Based on various lines of evidence (see Costall and Naylor 1981; Iversen and Fray 1982), neuroleptic-induced catalepsy has been considered to be essentially a basal ganglia phenomenon, due to blockade of dopamine receptors at this site. Accordingly, it is widely considered to be an animal model of human Parkinsonian side-effects. Dopamine agonist drug-induced hyperactivity/stereotypy, on the other hand, has come to be regarded as an animal model of psychosis, but it is entirely empirical and few inferences about the basis of antipsychotic action can be drawn from it. Some evidence has suggested that there is an anatomical dissociation between the hyperactivity and stereotypy components of the response, with stereotypy reflecting mainly basal ganglia

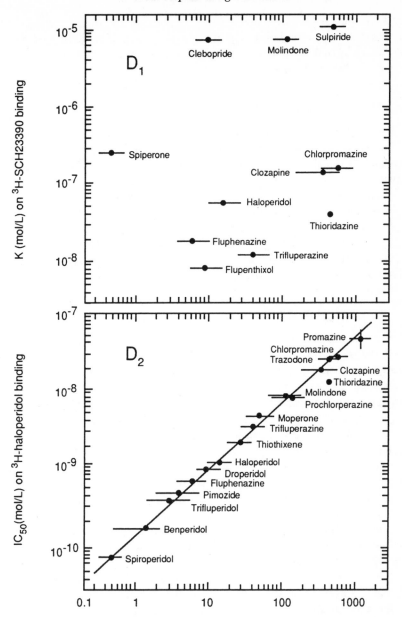

Fig. 8.2 Correlations between clinical potencies of neuroleptic drugs and their affinities at dopamine D1 and D2 receptors (reproduced by permission from Seeman 1987).

stimulation and hyperactivity being the consequence of similar activity in ventral striatal and meolimbic regions. However, any partitioning of such functions is in reality probably considerably more complex than this (see Joyce 1983; Mason 1984).

Side-effects of neuroleptic drugs

Almost as soon as the success of neuroleptic drug treatment in schizophrenia was recognized, it became appreciated that a price frequently had to be paid in the shape of serious side-effects. A number of these shared the striking feature that they were also seen in basal ganglia disease states. They thus became known as the extrapyramidal side-effects of neuroleptics, and soon established themselves as the most troublesome and important complications of neuroleptic treatment. They comprise, in order of the time course of their appearance, *acute dystonic reactions, akathisia, Parkinsonism*, and *tardive dyskinesia*. The rare and life-threatening *neuroleptic malignant syndrome*, is also probably best classed as an at least partly extrapyramidal side-effect.

Acute dystonic reactions

First clearly described by Delay *et al.* (1959) and Sigwald *et al.* (1959*a*), these form the most uncommon extrapyramidal side-effect (apart from neuroleptic malignant syndrome). Early figures (Ayd 1961) suggested a frequency of occurrence of 2–3 per cent; after the introduction of haloperidol and depot neuroleptics the figure climbed to around 10 per cent, with even higher rates sometimes being reported (see Rupniak *et al.* 1986). Acute dystonic reactions have been considered to be commoner in males and in younger patients; the sex differences are, however, not great and tend to equalize with advancing age (see Marsden *et al.* 1975, 1986). Classically, acute dystonic reactions are seen in the earliest stages of neuroleptic treatment: many occur within hours of its initiation and 90 per cent take place within the first 4 days (Ayd 1961; Swett 1975). The rest develop later when treatment is established, typically as a recurrent phenomenon (Owens 1990) which is sometimes but not always attributable to increases in dosage of medication.

The typical acute dystonic reaction has been described by Marsden *et al.* (1975, 1986), Lees (1985), and Owens (1990). The essential feature is remitting or sustained muscular spasms which begin abruptly or evolve stepwise. Attacks can last from seconds to hours and may wax and wane. They are invariably painful and also, surprisingly, highly susceptible to external influences, such as suggestion. Any muscle groups or even the entire body may be involved, but neck and facial contractions are particularly common. Blepharospasm, perioral spasms, and gaze fixations are said to be characteristic, and there may also be trismus, forced mouth opening, and tongue protrusion. Oculogyric crises (originally described in post-encephalitic Parkinsonism) also occur: in the fully developed form of these the patient's eyes become deviated upwards and often also laterally, the neck is hyperextended, the mouth is opened wide, and the tongue is forced out. Acute dystonic reactions can involve the torso with lordosis, scoliosis, tortipelvis, and opisthotonus. Sometimes the limbs are held in distorted positions. Laryngeal and pharyngeal dystonias causing dysphonia and dysphagia are rarely seen (and can be life threatening). The Pisa syndrome (Ekbom *et al.* 1972) is the name given to torsion movements of the trunk which became worse on walking, causing the patient to tilt to one side.

An akathisia-like inner restlessness is commonly described as accompanying acute dystonic reactions, and there may be Parkinsonian signs such as facial immobility, tremor, and salivation. Autonomic signs, including hyperpyrexia, tachycardia, and pallor occur in a few cases and may be severe. Occasionally, instead of being dystonic, the movements are more choreoathetoid in nature (Gerlach 1979; Lees 1985); the movements resemble those of tardive dyskinesia but are said to be somewhat more stereotyped and rhythmical. Rarely, exacerbations of psychosis, waxy flexibility, and other catatonic phenomena are seen (Chiu 1989; Thornton and McKenna 1994).

The course of acute dystonic reactions is generally short and self-limiting: if neuroleptic treatment is withdrawn they invariably remit, and even if it is continued they generally subside, with or without therapeutic intervention, not to recur. Acute dystonic reactions almost always respond promptly to a single intravenous dose of an anticholinergic drug like procyclidine, this being the treatment of choice. From time to time other therapeutic strategies have been advocated, the most effective of which appears to be intravenous diazepam or clonazepam (see Lees 1985).

The pathophysiology of acute dystonic reactions has been the subject of a number of reviews (for example Marsden *et al.* 1975, 1986; Lees 1985; Rupniak *et al.* 1986). Whilst circumstantial evidence has related dystonias in general to both functional increases and decreases in basal ganglia dopamine, in the particular case of neuroleptic-induced dystonia the evidence points clearly to the former mechanism. One species of baboon reliably develops dystonias on neuroleptic administration: pretreatment with drugs which prevent dopamine synthesis and release attenuates or prevents them from occurring. Very little evidence, on the other hand, suggests that these animal dystonias are ameliorated by dopamine-agonist drugs. Marsden and Janner's (1980) plausible suggestion is that early in the course of neuroleptic treatment a preferential blockade of presynaptic dopamine autoreceptors occurs. As these are inhibitory to dopamine synthesis and release, a dopamine excess is produced. This then exerts agonistic effects on post-synaptic dopamine receptors whose blockade is not yet established.

Akathisia

The peculiar phenomenon of mental and motor restlessness leading to an inability to remain seated was originally described in Parkinson's disease, in post-encephalitic Parkinsonism, and as an idiopathic disorder. As a complication of neuroleptic treatment, the same symptom was first noted by Steck (1954). Facing difficulties both in its definition, and in its separation from disorders such as tardive dyskinesia and psychotic agitation, estimates of its frequency have ranged from 6 per cent (NIMH 1964) to 21 per cent (Ayd 1961), or even higher (see Lees 1985). Akathisia occurs at all ages and in both sexes unpreferentially. Its onset is on average later than that of acute dystonias: it is occasionally seen within days of starting treatment; 50 per cent of cases develop with the first month; 90 per cent within the first 10 weeks; and almost all the rest over the first 6 months (Ayd 1961; Lees 1985).

As described by Lees (1985), the core of the clinical syndrome is a subjective feeling of motor unease affecting the legs disproportionately but not exclusively, which leads to an irrestible urge to keep moving, and an inability to sit still. As a consequence, the patient continually taps his feet, moves his legs, or shifts his weight from foot to foot. In more severe forms, he treads on the spot, paces back and forth, breaks into a trot, or may dance, march, climb, or rock repetitiously. Abnormal sensations in the legs are commonly reported, such as pins and needles, cramps, vibration, warmth or formication, but the disorder is currently considered to be distinguishable from Ekbom's syndrome of restless legs.

As well as the subjective feeling of restlessness, there may be mental accompaniments including inability to concentrate, malaise, depression, euphoria, rage, sexual arousal, or exacerbation of psychosis (Van Putten 1975; Lees 1985). It is increasingly recognized that some patients develop a syndrome of objective motor restlessness without any subjective distress — so called tardive akathisia or pseudoakathisia (see Barnes and Braude 1985). This tends to be seen later in the course of treatment and appears to be closely related to the emergence of tardive dyskinesia.

If neuroleptic treatment is continued, akathisia may diminish or disappear over weeks to months. Alternatively, it may persist unchanged and distressing for years; or relapse or remit; or finally begin to lose its subjective component and shade into tardive dyskinesia (Lees 1985; Barnes and Braude 1985). Discontinuation of drugs, if feasible, is usually followed by complete resolution of the symptom, although this may be slow. Active therapeutic interventions are by and large unsatisfactory. Some patients may respond to anticholinerguc drugs or benzodiazepines, but the effect is unpredictable, limited, and generally disappointing. Recently, claims have been made for a favourable response to propranolol (Lipinski *et al*. 1983; Adler *et al*. 1986).

The pathogenesis of akathisia is shrouded in mystery. Since the same phenomenon may complicate Parkinson's disease and post-encephalitic Parkinsonism, as well as sometimes being provoked by dopamine-depleting drug treatment (Marsden and Jenner 1980), it has been suspected that dopamine deficiency is a crucial factor. Akathisia certainly commonly co-exists with Parkinsonism in neuroleptic-treated patients (Marsden *et al.* 1986); at the same time, however, there is no doubt that it is also seen in association with tardive dyskinesia (Barnes and Braude 1985). So far the only theory of akathisia has been that of Marsden and Jenner (1980), who suggested that an imbalance between striatal and cortical dopamine-receptor blockade, with the latter being greater, might underlie the syndrome. In support of this, selective blockade of cortical dopamine receptors has been found to cause a paradoxical increase in locomotor activity in rats. However, beyond this rather tenuous link the hypothesis remains unsupported.

Parkinsonism

Neuroleptic-induced Parkinsonism, also first described by Steck (1954) soon became recognized as the most common side effect of antipsychotic drug treatment. Various prevalence surveys (see Marsden *et al.* 1975, 1986) have concluded that 20–40 per cent of neuroleptic-treated patients show obvious Parkinsonian signs. According to Marsden and Jenner (1980), a considerably higher percentage exhibit subtler but unmistakable akinesia, and they suspected that all patients would develop some evidence of Parkinsonism if given large enough doses of neuroleptics. Neuroleptic-induced Parkinsonism increases in prevalence with age (Ayd 1961) paralleling idiopathic Parkinson's disease. Unlike idiopathic Parkinsonism, however, a female-to-male ratio of 2:1 has been found (Ayd 1961). The time course of appearance of the disorder closely follows that of akathisia: it occasionally appears within days of starting treatment; half to three-quarters develop within a month; and 90 per cent within 10 weeks (Ayd 1961).

The classic accounts of neuroleptic-induced Parkinsonism have been given by Marsden and co-workers (Marsden *et al.* 1975, 1986). Every Parkinsonian sign can be seen, including the classical triad of akinesia, rigidity and tremor, as well as stooped posture, shuffling and festinant gait, sialorrhoea and seborrhoea. In the clustering and sequence of progression of its signs, however, neuroleptic induced Parkinsonism carries its own distinctive stamp. The earliest and most common finding is akinesia which may appear as an entirely isolated phenomenon, even when very marked: the face is expressionless; associated movements, gestures, and arm swing are lost; and voluntary movements become economical, initiated slowly, and executed in a laboured way. Rigidity is less common and tends to develop later; cogwheeling is often absent. The characteristic pill-rolling tremor is said to be even more uncommon and to occur later still. Other, non-specific tremors, particularly affecting the perioral region (the so-called rabbit syndrome) are by no means rare, however.

It is accepted that once established, neuroleptic-induced Parkinsonism tends to resolve spontaneously over weeks or months despite continued treatment (Marsden and Jenner 1980). If neuroleptics are withdrawn, the symptoms disappear, for the most part over a few weeks; occasionally signs persist for longer, and durations of up to 18 months after discontinuation have been recorded. In about 1 per cent of cases, Parkinsonism persists indefinitely after drug withdrawal. According to Marsden and Jenner (1980) such a figure is compatible with neuroleptic treatment revealing sub-clinical idiopathic Parkinson's disease which would ultimately have appeared spontaneously. The responsiveness of neuroleptic-induced Parkinsonism to anticholinergic drugs has become so widely accepted that they form the standard method of treatment. Surprisingly though, the evidence for their effectiveness (exhaustively reviewed by Marsden *et al*. 1986) is less convincing than might be expected. The dopamine agonist drugs, L-DOPA, bromocriptine, and amantidine have also been reported to be effective, but here the literature is marked by conflicting findings. In practice their effect is less than optimal and is frequently complicated by worsening of active psychotic symptoms (Marsden *et al*. 1986).

The pathophysiology of neuroleptic-induced Parkinsonism is naturally assumed to be one of functional striatal dopamine deficiency. The precise mechanism of this deficiency, though, remains far from clearly established. It seems very unlikely that it is a consequence of reduced dopamine availability (as in idiopathic Parkinson's disease), since neuroleptics induce a compensatory increase in dopamine synthesis and release, at least when administered acutely. The other obvious candidate for the pathogenesis of the syndrome, striatal dopamine D2 receptor blockade, is widely accepted (Marsden and Jenner 1980; Marsden *et al*. 1986). Even so some inconsistencies are apparent. First, there is the obvious fact that not all patients taking neuroleptic drugs develop clinical signs of Parkinsonism. Secondly, there is the delay in its appearance as well as its tendency to spontaneous resolution. Early explanations which invoked individual variations in the degree of D2 receptor blockade achieved, or its gradual accumulation for pharmacokinetic reasons are now contradicted by PET scan findings which demonstrate that substantial striatal D2 receptor occupancy takes place almost immediately after commencement of neuroleptic treatment (Farde *et al*. 1989, 1992).

Tardive dyskinesia

A lasting syndrome of involuntary movements developing late in the course of neuroleptic treatment — hence the name tardive — was first properly described by Sigwald *et al.* (1959*b*), although two years previously Schonecker (1957) had reported persistent orofacial movements in three elderly patients after days or weeks of treatment. Subsequently, tardive dyskinesia has emerged as the most important side-effect of neuroleptic treatment. Although, as described in Chapter 1, it is widely accepted that a similar involuntary movement disorder may occur in schizophrenic patients who have not been exposed to neuroleptic drugs, there is a consensus that the probability of its appearance is significantly increased by chronic exposure to neuroleptic agents (Marsden *et al.* 1986).

Estimates of the frequency of occurence of tardive dyskinesia are very wide. Its prevalence has been found to range from 0.5 per cent to 41 per cent (Jus *et al.* 1976), or to be as high as 72 per cent (Smith *et al.* 1979). Its incidence has been quoted at 3–4 per cent per year (Kane and Smith 1982) or at 5–10 per cent per year (Gardos and Cole 1980). The higher of each of these figures is undoubtedly inflated by the use of very sensitive rating scales (clinically obvious tardive dyskinesia is probably present in no more than a third of schizophrenic patients), and the fact that frequency of the disorder increases with age (its prevalence is probably 20 per cent at most in the age range 20–50). Age is the only risk factor for tardive dyskinesia on which there is universal agreement, associations with female sex, prior cerebral damage, and duration and dosage of neuroleptic all having been asserted in some studies and denied in others (APA Task Force 1979; Lees 1985; Marsden *et al.* 1986). There are, however, strong indications that the development of drug-induced Parkinsonism may predispose to later development of tardive dyskinesia (Crane 1972; Gerlach 1978; Kane *et al.* 1985).

Clinically, tardive dyskinesia can be separated into a number of sub-syndromes; all of these, however, overlap and may present in erratic combinations in individual patients.

Orofacial dyskinesias: The most familiar variant of tardive dyskinesia (Lees 1985) has at its core champing, chewing, and lateral jaw movements. These may be accompanied by pursing, smacking, and puckering of the lips, and tongue movements ranging from working and rolling to repetitive reptilian protrusions (the 'flycatcher tongue'). In more severe cases there may also be puffing out of the cheeks, grimacing, and periorbital contractions, gagging, retching, bruxism, and neck movements. Very rarely respiration and swallowing are affected and the disorder can then threaten life. Repetitiveness and stereotypy are notable features: while the sequence of movements is not entirely predictable, there is as it were a recurring theme to them, and they tend to occur rhythmically, with a more or less fixed tempo (Mackay 1982; Lees 1985). This pattern of dyskinesia is most common in patients over the age of 50, where it tends to present in relatively isolated form.

Trunk and limb dyskinesias: These are more common in younger patients and are especially characteristic of tardive dyskinesia in children. Irregular 'guitar playing' finger movements may be accompanied by dystonic posturing of the fingers, wrist movements, and pronating and supinating movements of the forearms (Lees 1985; Marsden *et al*. 1975, 1986). Analogous movements can involve the toes and feet. The trunk may be affected by rocking, torsion movements, and pelvic thrusting (axial hyperkinesia). The quality of the movements has variously been considered to be irregularly repetitive (Simpson *et al*. 1979), nearly repetitive (Marsden *et al*. 1986), or indistinguishable from choreoathetosis (Lees 1985). It is also clear that some authors include more complex and integrated movements as dyskinetic, for instance, caressing and rubbing the face, hair, or thighs, crossing and uncrossing the legs, and 'holokinetic' movements involving large parts of the body (Simpson *et al*. 1979).

Tardive dystonia and tardive Gilles de la Tourette's syndrome: In these uncommon variants of tardive dyskinesia, the movements have a predominantly sustained, dystonic quality, or alternatively take the form of multiple tics and vocalizations (Lees 1985; Owens 1990). The age preferences of these two types are not very clear. Tardive dystonia has been most commonly reported in children and young adults. However, it seems likely that, like tardive dyskinesia, its prevalence increases linearly with age, although it becomes less likely to be severe and generalized in older age groups (Owens 1990). While dystonias or tics are the prominent symptoms respectively, it is clear from the available descriptions that the presentations are not pure and elements of orofacial, trunk and limb dyskinesia are commonly also present (Sacks 1982; Lees 1985).

A number of obstacles stand in the way of investigating the natural history of tardive dyskinesia, but some clinical impressions are backed up by formal studies. That tardive dyskinesia may be irreversible, even if neuroleptics are withdrawn after its development, is universally accepted; at a conservative estimate this happens in up to 50 per cent of cases (APA Task Force 1979). Higher rates of remission may be seen in early cases and in younger patients—in children complete recovery appears to be the rule (Lees 1985). When it does occur, improvement is slow and may continue for months or even years (Marsden *et al*. 1986). For the large majority of schizophrenic patients who require continued neuroleptic treatment, information on the course of tardive dyskinesia is less certain: it is clear that the condition is not commonly progressive and in the majority of cases it remains mild. Some patients improve and up to 40 per cent may become symptom free; in a small minority, though, a slowly worsening course is followed (Lees 1985).

Active therapeutic intervention in tardive dyskinesia is generally unsatisfactory. Of the many pharmacological approaches advocated (reviewed by Marsden *et al*. 1986; Jeste *et al*. 1988), the best results have been found with, in descending order, dopamine antagonists, GABA agonists, and acetylcholine agonists. Many of the studies are methodologically flawed, however, and the improvements are usually not great. Perhaps the most reliable finding is that increasing the dose of neuroleptic generally suppresses tardive dyskinesia to a considerable extent. The benefits gained may be at the expense of Parkinsonism, and after weeks or months the dyskinesia tends to 'break through', sometimes worse than before.

A functional dopamine excess, presumptively affecting the basal ganglia, is widely considered to be the common denominator of choreoathetoid movements in a number of disease states (Klawans and Weiner 1976). That this is also the case for tardive dyskinesia is supported by the powerful circumstantial evidence that the movements are suppressed and enhanced by dopamine antagonist and agonist drugs respectively (Gerlach 1979; Marsden and Jenner 1980). How drugs whose action is to block dopamine receptors might cause a state of functional dopamine excess has been explained as being due to the development of a compensatory receptor supersensitivity, analogous to denervation supersensitivity (Klawans and Weiner 1976; Gerlach 1979). Supporting evidence for this idea has come from animal work (see Lees 1985; Marsden *et al*. 1986). There are, however, also a number of difficulties associated with it (Jeste and Caligiuri 1993). For example, neuroleptic-induced dopamine receptor supersensitivity in animals reverses after a few months off treatment (Marsden and Jenner 1980). Also, it has not been possible to demonstrate differences in receptor numbers in the post-mortem brains of schizophrenic patients with and without tardive dyskinesia (Mackay *et al*. 1982).

Overall, the conclusion reached by a committee of clinicians and scientists reporting on tardive dyskinesia over ten years ago (APA Task Force 1979) remains appropriate: 'Although the aetiology of tardive dyskinesia remains unknown, there is considerable pharmacologic evidence to suggest that a functional over-activity of extrapyramidal mechanisms mediated by dopamine is an important aspect of pathophysiology. An explanation for the prolonged and even irreversible course of many cases of tardive dyskinesia awaits further research'.

Neuroleptic malignant syndrome

This rare and potentially fatal complication of neuroleptic treatment was first described and named by Delay and Deniker (1968). An almost certainly identical disorder was later independently documented by Cohen and

Cohen (1974), who erroneously ascribed it to the combination of treatment with haloperidol and lithium. Since then, many descriptions and reviews of the syndrome have been provided (for example Caroff 1980; Levensen 1985; Shalev and Munitz 1986). Like tardive dyskinesia, it has become increasingly apparent that a disorder showing at least some of the same features as neuroleptic malignant syndrome could be seen in schizophrenic patients in the days before neuroleptic treatment, when it was known as lethal catatonia (see Mann *et al.* 1986; Lohr and Wisniewski 1987). Nevertheless the causal role of neuroleptic drugs in the vast majority of contemporary cases seems beyond dispute. All the information on neuroleptic malignant syndrome has recently been assembled by Addonizio and Susman (1991), and except where otherwise stated, what follows is based on their account.

The incidence of neuroleptic malignant syndrome probably lies somewhere between 0.07 per cent and 1.4 per cent, the latter figure being considerably higher than clinical experience would suggest. While initial reviews suggested that an excess of cases in male patients and among younger age groups, it now appears increasingly clear that the disorder affects both sexes equally and can occur in any age group. Neuroleptic malignant syndrome may develop after the institution of neuroleptic therapy, after switching to a different drug, or after increasing the dosage of the same drug. Typically, it occurs within hours or days of such an event; there is, however, no doubt that a significant number of cases (up to a third) are seen after two weeks to six months of treatment. It is also accepted that, while some cases may develop on small doses of neuroleptics, high or rapidly escalating dosage regimes are a risk factor for occurrence of the syndrome.

The central features of neuroleptic malignant syndrome are Parkinson-like rigidity, clouding of consciousness, fever, tachycardia, and other fluctuating autonomic disturbances, which usually evolve over a period of hours to days. Often in a setting of acutely exacerbated psychosis (which often gives the impression of being particularly florid and accompanied by disturbed behaviour), a state of sluggish unresponsiveness supervenes. Akinesia, bradykinesia, and rigidity become evident; hypersalivation, dysarthria, and dysphagia may also be present. Tremor is seen in about half of cases. Superimposed choreoathetoid or dystonic movements are also described. It is also established beyond doubt that catatonic symptoms, in particular mutism, posturing, and waxy flexibility, may form an integral part of the presentation (Caroff 1980; Abbot and Loizou 1986; see also Mann *et al.* 1986; Lohr and Wisniewski 1987)—hence the overlap with lethal catatonia. The altered consciousness in neuroleptic malignant syndrome has eluded precise description, but it is likely that it usually takes the form of organic confusion and disorientation, which is often accompanied by drowsiness, unresponsiveness, and even coma. Stupor has also been described, and in some cases, conversely, agitation is a prominent feature. The temperature is usually elevated, though not always to hyperpyrexial levels. Tachycardia, tachypnoea, sweating, and raised blood pressure are the main autonomic accompaniments and these characteristically fluctuate. Miscellaneous signs include increased tendon reflexes, upgoing plantars, and seizures. All of these features may wax and wane unpredictably. Different classes of symptom may combine and recombine, partial forms are seen, and there is no consistent order of progression.

The most consistent laboratory abnormality is raised creatine phosphokinase. This is elevated in over 90 per cent of patients, often massively so. This elevation is almost certainly related to muscular rigidity although the exact process underlying it is obscure. A related myoglobinaemia has been found in 75 per cent of patients. In about 70 per cent of cases, the white cell count is raised, with a polymorphonuclear leucocytosis of up to $40\,000/mm^3$. Less consistently found are electrolyte imbalances and raised liver enzymes. Lumbar puncture and CT scan are usually unrevealing; the EEG remains normal or may show diffuse slowing or non-specific changes.

Neuroleptic malignant syndrome has been found to have a mortality of 15–22 per cent, but there are now suggestions that this is decreasing; this almost certainly reflects early diagnosis and institution of vigorous treatment. Perhaps most frequently, death is due to medical complications such as dehydration, chest infection, and rhabdomyolysis leading to renal failure. Cerebral oedema has been found occasionally at post-mortem, and sometimes death is sudden and unexpected, possibly a consequence of cardiac arrest secondary to the autonomic dysfunction. In those patients who survive, the syndrome regresses after discontinuation of neuroleptics within a maximum of 40 days, the average duration being 1–2 weeks. This figure is approximately doubled if patients have been taking depot neuroleptic medication.

The mainstay of treatment is supportive management with cooling and rehydration. Various drug treatments have also been tried: dopamine agonists of all types are commonly used and are usually reported to be beneficial, but decisive evidence that they are effective is lacking. ECT has been recorded as bringing about rapid resolution or being without effect, but in any event is hazardous, mainly due to precipitation of cardiac arrhythmias. Another therapeutic strategy is use of dantrolene, a peripherally acting muscle relaxant. Studies reporting definite, possible. or no therapeutic effect with this treatment are roughly evenly divided.

The pathogenesis of neuroleptic malignant syndrome remains largely conjectural, and two main lines of speculation have been followed. The first of these implicates intense dopamine receptor blockade affecting the striatum and the hypothalamus. Providing circumstantial support for this view are scattered case reports: for instance, one patient with Huntington's chorea developed neuroleptic malignant syndrome when treated with dopamine depleting agents, and a number of patients with Parkinson's disease have developed it on withdrawal of dopamine agonist drugs. The rigidity and other extrapyramidal features seen in neuroleptic malignant syndrome also strongly suggest that there is a hypodopaminergic state. Finally, neuroleptic drugs are know to affect thermal regulation and can produce hyperthermia when injected into the hypothalamus.

The second approach draws on similarities between neuroleptic malignant syndrome and malignant hyperthermia. In this rare, genetically mediated disorder, anaesthetic agents such as halothane induce, via a direct effect on muscle fibres, sustained contractions which lead to rigidity, hyperpyrexia, and rhabdomyolysis. While some evidence has suggested that patients with neuroleptic malignant syndrome show a malignant hyperthermia-like hypermetabolic response to both fluphenazine and halothane, subsequent work has not convincingly replicated this finding.

Finally, the unpredictable development of neuroleptic malignant syndrome suggests a possible role for host factors: an individual who develops the disorder on treatment with a particular neuroleptic may show no recurrence when subsequently re-challenged with the same drug. It may be that susceptibility to neuroleptic malignant syndrome varies at various times according to clinical condition; it may even be the disorder will ultimately be best understood as an iatrogenic form of lethal catatonia (Mann *et al.* 1986).

Atypical neuroleptic drugs

It is clear that neuroleptic drugs, while effective, are a far from satisfactory treatment for schizophrenia. In a sizeable proportion of patients they have little overall effect: for example, in the National Instititute of Mental Health collaborative study described earlier (NIMH 1964; Goldberg *et al.* 1965), around a quarter of cases showed no or only minimal improvement. Many more patients continue to experience exacerbations of symptoms despite good compliance with medication. Finally, negative symptoms remain a formidable clinical problem: perhaps the most typical outcome of neuroleptic treatment is the schizophrenic patient whose florid symptoms are well controlled, but who is permanently handicapped by lack of volition, flattened affect, and poor self care, for which nothing can be offered.

It is also evident that no neuroleptic has therapeutic advantages over any others. This was demonstrated by Davis (1985), who compared the comparative efficacy of different neuroleptics by simply counting the number of studies which found them to be more effective, equally effective, or less effective than a standard drug such as chlorpromazine. His table is reproduced as Table 8.2, from which it is depressingly clear that none of quite a long list of drugs has been found to be superior to chlorpromazine even once.

Obviously, it is not possible to take advantage of differences in the therapeutic effect of neuroleptics and use this as a means for developing new and potentially better drugs. Therefore, the remaining sources of variation between them have had to be exploited. These consist quite simply of the differences in receptor blocking effects shown by the drugs (described in Chapter 6), and the differences in their animal behavioural effects and human side-effects described above. On one or more of these grounds, three drugs have established themselves as atypical, and have raised the hope that this atypicality might extend to their therapeutic properties as well. These drugs are thioridazine, sulpiride, and clozapine.

Thioridazine

This was the first neuroleptic to stand out as in any way unusual. Pharmacologically, it has unexceptional receptor blocking effects; like its close chemical relative chlorpromazine it blocks dopamine D2 receptors, noradrenaline (alpha2), and serotonin (5HT2) receptors. Also like chlorpromazine, it has been found to have dopamine D1 receptor blocking effects only at high concentrations, above those normally achieved by therapeutic doses (the recent work of Farde *et al.* (1989, 1992) using PET in humans, suggests that this may be an oversimplification and the drug

Table 8.2 Studies comparing the effectiveness of various neuroleptic drugs to chlorpromazine (from Davis 1985)

Drug	Compared with chlorpromazine, number of studies in which drug was		
	More effective	As effective	Less effective
Trifluoperazine	0	11	0
Perphenazine	0	6	0
Thioridazine	0	12	0
Fluphenazine	0	9	0
Haloperidol	0	4	0
Loxapine	0	14	1
Promazine	0	2	4
Thiothixene	0	4	0
Molindone	0	6	0
Prochlorperazine	0	10	0
Mesoridazine	0	7	0

may in fact have significant D1 receptor occupancy at therapeutic doses). Its main pharmacological peculiarity is that it shows strong anticholinergic effects.

Thioridazine's animal behavioural effects have also attracted attention. Although cataleptogenic to much the same extent as other neuroleptics, its ability to reverse the dopamine agonist response has been claimed to be restricted to the hyperactivity (putatively non-striatal) component of this. In some studies, however, thioridazine has been found to reverse both hyperactivity and stereotypy to approximately the same degree (see Joyce 1983).

Thioridazine is well known to be relatively free of extrapyramidal side-effects in man, especially Parkinsonism (Herman and Pleasure 1963), but also acute dystonias and perhaps also akathisia. On the basis of a retrospective analysis, the proposal has also been made that thioridazine might not cause tardive dyskinesia (Borison *et al.* 1983). Such a claim has, however, been hotly disputed (Ayd *et al.* 1984) and lacks any support from prospective studies which would make it convincing.

Despite such properties the therapeutic effect of thioridazine has never been considered exceptional: as shown in Table 8.2, it has invariably been found to be no more or less effective than chlorpromazine. Furthermore, the anticholinergic effects of the drug could plausibly account for both its unusual animal behavioural effects and lack of human side-effects — even though the evidence that this is in fact the case remains equivocal (see Crow *et al.* 1977; Joyce 1983). Whatever the truth of the matter, it nevertheless seems clear that the atypical properties of thioridazine are primarily of theoretical interest rather than of practical benefit.

Sulpiride

This substituted benzamide drug was developed in France in the late 1960s, and pharmacologically is characterized by a highly selective blockade of dopamine D2 receptors. It blocks D1 receptors only at extremely high concentrations and shows very few interactions with other neurotransmitter receptors. Even sulpiride's action on D2 receptors may show unusual features: it has been suggested that it binds to a different portion of the receptor than other neuroleptics (see Jenner and Marsden 1984), and that prolonged treatment does not lead to increased dopamine D2 receptor numbers in animals (Rupniak *et al.* 1984).

In animal behavioural models, the striking property of sulpiride is its weak cataleptogenic effect. In a more convincing way than thioridazine, it also preferentially reverses the hyperactivity rather than the stereotypy component of the dopamine agonist response, a finding that cannot be attributed to inherent anticholinergic properties (see Joyce 1983).

In man, claims have been made that sulpiride induces less extrapyramidal side-effects than other neuroleptics. One survey (Alberts *et al.* 1985) found acute dystonic reactions, akathisia, and Parkinsonism to be present in no more than 4 per cent of patients receiving treatment. In other studies however, the differences have been less impressive (Harnryd *et al.* 1984; Gerlach *et al.* 1985). The possibility that sulpiride may not cause tardive dyskinesia has been expressed, but mainly as a hope and with — after a number of years of clinical usage — no clear substantiation as yet.

With these genuinely atypical properties in mind, the therapeutic effectiveness of sulpiride has been subjected to close scrutiny. No work to date has indicated an overall superior effect to other neuroleptics, but some early reports did suggest that the drug might be particularly effective against negative symptoms (Freeman and Soni 1985). In one controlled study (Harnryd *et al.* 1984) sulpiride showed a significantly greater reduction of negative symptom ratings than haloperidol. However, in another study (Gerlach *et al.* 1985) no differences were observed.

Clozapine

This drug was discovered in the 1950s, quickly established itself as an effective neuroleptic, but was then withdrawn from general use after an unacceptably high number of patients developed the potentially fatal side-effect of agranulocytosis. Like classical neuroleptics, clozapine blocks dopamine D2 receptors; this action has, however, been considered to be disproportionately weak (for example Anderson *et al.* 1986). Recent PET scan studies have also indicated that, at therapeutic dosages, clozapine occupies basal ganglia D2 receptors to a somewhat lesser degree than standard neuroleptics, and also occupies D1 receptors to a significantly greater degree than any other drug (Farde *et al.* 1989, 1992). Like sulpiride, prolonged treatment with clozapine does not produce dopamine D2 receptor supersensitivity in animals (Rupniak *et al.* 1984). Clozapine has an otherwise fairly typical profile of receptor interactions, and notably has very strong anticholinergic properties (Hyttel *et al.* 1985).

The animal behavioural effects of clozapine are the most atypical of any neuroleptic: catalepsy is induced only by extremely high doses or when the drug is given intrastriatally (see Coward 1992). In the dopamine agonist model clozapine, like sulpiride, has usually been found to reverse only the hyperactivity component of the response, and even here its effect is unusually weak (see Joyce 1983).

Clozapine's human side-effects are equally atypical. Acute dystonic reactions and akathisia have never been reported, and in various studies Parkinsonism has been documented only to the same extent as with placebo (Casey 1989). None of a large number of patients treated with clozapine alone over periods of years both in the USA (Davis 1985) and Scandinavia (Povlsen *et al.* 1985) appear to have developed tardive dyskinesia (see also Casey 1989).

In early controlled trials, clozapine, unlike any other neuroleptic, was found to be therapeutically superior to chlorpromazine in 6 of 13 studies and superior to haloperidol in 4 out of a 6 further studies (see McKenna and Bailey 1993). This evidence, coupled with anecdotal impressions, led directly to a the large, methodologically rigorous study of its effect in treatment-resistant schizophrenia (Kane *et al.* 1988). Two hundred and sixty eight patients meeting DSM III criteria for schizophrenia were recruited from 16 centres. Before entering the trial they had to fulfil retrospective, cross-sectional, and prospective requirements for treatment resistance. Retrospective criteria revolved around documentation of poor response to multiple periods of treatment with different neuroleptics given in high doses. Cross-sectionally, patients had to show moderate or high ratings on an overall severity scale, and to show some positive symptoms. Prospectively, before entering the trial proper, all patients had to demonstrate no more than minimal improvement with up to six weeks treatment with haloperidol in high doses.

These patients were treated under double-blind conditions for six weeks with flexible dosages of either clozapine or chlorpromazine. Improvement in the clozapine-treated group was found to be significantly greater than for the chlorpromazine-treated group. The advantage for clozapine was evident in terms of total symptom scores, and in subsets of these devoted to positive and negative symptoms. A priori criteria for 'clinically significant improvement' were also defined: 30 per cent of the clozapine-treated patients met these, as opposed to only 4 per cent of those receiving chlorpromazine.

After false starts with thioridazine and sulpiride, the concept of atypical neuroleptics has finally come into its own and revealed the existence of one drug—clozapine—whose extraordinary profile of effects is reflected in a convincing therapeutic superiority. Other drugs are on the verge of entering clinical practice, of which the most important are remoxipride and risperidone. These drugs show pharmacological and animal behavioural effects which are to some extent different from conventional neuroleptics, and their human side-effects may be atypical as well. Whether these drugs will replicate the pattern of clozapine, however, is at present uncertain.

9

The management of schizophrenia

The outlook for the average patient with schizophrenia is not good. He or she will show an incomplete response to treatment and will be prone to flare-ups of florid symptoms from time to time. In addition, enduring deficits will sooner or later develop which may progress, or at any rate change in character over the course of what is likely to be a normal lifespan. These facts conspire to make factors other than neuroleptic drugs loom large in the management of the disorder.

In the face of pessimism and sometimes despair, any and every therapeutic avenue has been explored in schizophrenia. The treatments which have been tried have ranged from psychoanalysis to frontal lobotomy. Despite being enthusiastically advocated in some quarters, neither of these extreme modes of therapy has stood the test of time, and currently it is as uncommon for schizophrenic patients to be referred for psychosurgery as it is for them to be taken on for interpretative psychotherapy (although this does not mean that either practice has died out completely). Other lines of treatment linger on, neither discredited nor universally accepted as being of value. These include other psychotropic drug treatments, electroconvulsive therapy, and various psychological and social interventions. Other therapeutic approaches are not forms of treatment at all, but are merely measures designed to improve the quality of life of the sufferers of a chronic incurable disease. Much of what is termed rehabilitation falls into this category.

This chapter takes the form of a critical review of the more practical, strategic aspects of the treatment of schizophrenia. These are approached in the way they tend to be approached in clinical practice, via a three-way division into the treatment of acute schizophrenia, the prevention of relapse, and the amelioration of chronic disability or rehabilitation. Each of these areas has acquired its own literature, its own preoccupations, and in some cases its own idiosyncrasies as well.

Treatment of acute schizophrenia

As described in Chapter 2, exacerbations of schizophrenia may occur at any stage and tend to be characterized by delusions, hallucinations, formal thought disorder, and other positive symptoms. Because neuroleptic drugs have been established as effective, and because they exert their main effects on positive symptoms, it is these drugs which have become the mainstay of treatment of acute episodes. However, the efficacy of neuroleptic treatment is limited. Schizophrenic patients in relapse may be unmanageable despite neuroleptic drug treatment, or have distressing symptoms which cannot be controlled by this, or the episode may persist for an inordinately long time despite escalations in dosage.

It follows that the management of acute schizophrenia is the management of adjunctive physical treatments, the biological measures that are sometimes needed beyond the fairly straightforward manoeuvre of giving adequate doses of neuroleptic drugs. A wide variety of drug treatments has been advocated and, in the way of clinical practice, these are often used more in the hope than the expectation that they will be of benefit. There are, however, two drugs which have been considered possibly to have genuine therapeutic value rather than just having sedative, tranquillizing, or non-specific effects; these are lithium and carbamazepine. Electroconvulsive therapy has also, over the years, fallen in and out of favour.

Lithium

The story of the introduction of lithium to psychiatry is rich in serendipity. Whilst working in a mental hospital in Australia, Cade (see Cade 1970) decided to investigate mania in a way that was popular at the time, by injecting concentrated urine from patients into guinea pigs. This proved fatal in most cases, and he quickly established that this was due to the presence of urea. It also became apparent that there was considerable variation in the toxicity of the urine, and it seemed possible that this might be related to the amount of uric acid which was also present. The next step was to inject mixtures of urea and uric acid into guinea pigs. Unfortunately a practical problem was encountered at this stage as uric acid is only slightly soluble in water; its least insoluble salt is lithium urate. Injection of lithium urate was found to have the unexpected effect of making the guinea pigs placid and unresponsive to stimuli (in retrospect, this probably reflected lithium toxicity). After administering lithium to himself, Cade took the step of trying the drug on an excited psychotic patient. He selected a man who had been chronically hypomanic for five years. After a few days he wondered if he could see signs of improvement. After another few days there could be no doubt. The patient went on to make a full recovery and was subsequently discharged from hospital.

How lithium made the transition from discovery to first-line treatment for manic-depressive psychosis has been recounted by King (1985), and owes almost everything to the Scandinavian psychiatrist Schou. It might be expected that lithium would also have some effect in schizophrenia, the other main functional psychosis besides manic-depressive psychosis and one with which it shares a considerable number of symptoms. However, a distinctly unfavourable view developed of its usefulness in this disorder. The line taken in most contemporary textbooks and articles has been that it is ineffective, except possibly to a minor extent when mood elevation forms a significant part of the picture.

A thorough review of the use of lithium in schizophrenia has been provided by Delva and Letemendia (1982). They noted that all of seven uncontrolled studies—which were sometimes little more than anecdotal reports—found improvement when lithium was given with or without concurrent neuroleptic medication. In some of these studies it was considered that only mood colourings of elation or depression were affected, but others noted a beneficial effect on a wider range of symptoms, occasionally to the point of their complete disappearance. Three out of four small scale controlled studies, one comparing lithium with placebo, the others using an 'add on' design to neuroleptics, also found an effect; once again this ranged from significant improvement only in excitement to more widespread benefits.

Pooling the data from 14 studies, Delva and Letemendia were able to obtain a total of 157 schizophrenic patients treated with lithium, usually in addition to neuroleptic drugs. Of these, 80 (51 per cent) were rated as improved and 76 (48 per cent) unchanged. Even when all cases described as 'excited schizophrenics' or 'schizophrenics with affective overlay' were excluded, 45 out of 111 (40 per cent) were still rated as improved. Delva and Letemendia concluded that between a third and a half of patients with schizophrenia will benefit from lithium treatment. The response is inferior to that seen with neuroleptics, but the usefulness of the drug is probably not restricted to those patients with mood colourings.

Given this conclusion, a large and rigorous clinical trial of the effects of lithium in schizophrenia would seem to be warranted. Although not specifically devised with this in mind, a study by Johnstone *et al.* (1988) fulfils many of these requirements. These authors' patient sample consisted of 105 acute admissions to hospital who had a diagnosis of functional psychosis of any type; disorders included were schizophrenia, schizoaffective psychosis, mania, and also depression if this was accompanied by psychotic symptoms. The patients were treated for four weeks under double-blind conditions with either lithium, a neuroleptic (pimozide), the combination of both drugs, or neither. The main finding concerning lithium was that it produced a significant reduction in ratings of elevation of mood in the group as a whole, and this was irrespective of diagnosis. In those patients who showed elevation of mood, lithium treatment was also associated with improvement in delusion and hallucination scores, although this did not reach significance. About half of this group had a diagnosis of schizophrenia rather than mania or schizoaffective psychosis. In patients with no elevation or depression of mood—most of whom had a diagnosis of schizophrenia—lithium had no therapeutic effect. (This study is discussed further in Chapter 11.)

Scanty though the available evidence is, it is possible to come to some provisional conclusions about the usefulness of lithium in schizophrenia. It seems clear from Delva and Letemendia's review that lithium has a definite therapeutic role to play; this is almost certainly modest, but even so it seems to have been underestimated. The study of Johnstone *et al.* adds support to this view, and it also suggests a possible resolution of the controversy about whether the drug affects mood disturbance exclusively, or whether it has wider effects. At the risk of overinterpreting their findings, lithium appears to have a beneficial effect on psychotic symptoms such as delusions, hallucinations and formal thought disorder, but only if mood is elevated as well.

Carbamazepine

The wide use of carbamazepine in psychiatry grew mainly out of its use in Japan in psychotic states termed 'atypical' or 'epileptoid' in this country (Post *et al.* 1984; see also Chapter 11). Its apparent beneficial effects in some such patients, together with the observation that the drug often had positive effects on mood and mental functioning in patients with epilepsy (Dalby 1975), led directly to its use in manic-depressive psychosis. In the wake of this significant therapeutic advance, there has followed a wave of interest in the use of carbamazepine in schizophrenia. In Britain, at the present time, it has become common to find acutely exacerbated schizophrenic patients, as well as chronic patients with ongoing florid symptoms, on treatment with this drug.

The use of carbamazepine in schizophrenia was first reported in two small studies. One of these was an open study of violent schizophrenic patients (Hakola and Lauluma 1982) and the other was a controlled study examining the effects of the drug on psychiatric patients with EEG abnormalities, some but not all of whom were schizophrenic (Neppe 1982). Both these studies gave promising results, and they were followed by a spate of controlled clinical trials.

Three controlled studies have evaluated the use of carbamazepine as sole medication in schizophrenia (Sramek *et al.* 1988; Heh *et al.* 1989; Carpenter *et al.* 1991). These uniformly found that it was ineffective. The four double-blind controlled trials of carbamazepine as an adjunctive medication to neuroleptics are summarized in Table 9.1. Only one of the studies found that addition of the drug produced significant improvement; its numbers were small, it did not use a parallel group design, and not all the patients were schizophrenic. One other study found a trend towards significant improvement with carbamazepine, but some of the patients in this study

Table 9.1 Controlled studies of carbamazepine as an adjunctive treatment in schizophrenia

Study	Diagnostic criteria	Design	Number of patients	Duration	Findings	Comment
Neppe (1983)	None	Double-blind Cross over	11	6 weeks	Carbamazepine superior to placebo	All patients had EEG abnormalities. Only 7 of sample were schizophrenic.
Klein *et al.* (1984)	RDC	Double-blind Parallel groups	16	5 weeks	Carbamazepine superior to placebo	Differences only became significant at week 5. Included patients with RDC schizoaffective disorder (mainly schizophrenic).
Kidron *et al.* (1985)	RDC	Double-blind Cross over	9	5 weeks	NSD	Sample made up of chronic patients with positive symptoms.
Dose *et al.* (1987)	DSM III	Double-blind Parallel group	22	5 weeks	?NSD	No significance figures given but both groups improved to a comparable degree.

had a diagnosis of schizoaffective psychosis rather than schizophrenia.

The use of carbamazepine in schizophrenia thus rests on a research base which is to say the least slender. There is no evidence to suggest that the drug is useful on its own, and its use as an adjunctive medication is supported by evidence of a rather dubious kind. In short, its reputation in schizophrenia is undeserved.

Electro-convulsive therapy (ECT)

Convulsive therapy arrived on the psychiatric scene as a treatment for schizophrenia. The events leading up to and following its discovery have been described in some detail by Fink (1984). Based on the 'antagonism' theory of schizophrenia and epilepsy, and following the unsuccessful attempts of others to treat epilepsy by injecting patients with the blood of schizophrenic patients, a Hungarian psychiatrist, von Meduna, conceived the idea of inducing seizures to treat schizophrenia. He found a suitable trial subject in a patient who had been in a catatonic stupor for four years. After five injections of camphor, the patient got out of bed, requested breakfast, and was noted to be interested in everything around him. Later he was discharged and remained well, apparently indefinitely. (Von Meduna's reward was to be hounded out of Hungary by his colleagues who believed that schizophrenia was an incurable heredofamilial disease, and not therefore susceptible to treatment.)

After decades of indiscriminate, and at times gratuitous usage, the only indication for which seemed to be a psychiatric disturbance which was relatively severe, the facts about ECT gradually clarified. As recalled by Rollin (1981), the treatment came to be recognized as effective in depression, particularly in severe cases with retardation and psychotic symptoms, in which it 'worked like a charm'. It also established a niche for itself in the treatment of mania. In addition, until the 1950s ECT was the most popular treatment for schizophrenia, and it was only after the introduction of neuroleptic drugs that the truth sank in that this was the condition for which the treatment was least effective. Even than, the impression remained that, while ECT was of little value in chronic schizophrenia, it was effective in states of acute catatonic stupor and excitement, and that it still had its uses when neuroleptic treatment failed to relieve grossly disturbed behaviour.

As expected given the abundance of patients treated, there has been no shortage of trials of ECT in schizophrenia. The best known, and also one of the largest of these was that of May (1968). He randomly assigned 228 clinically diagnosed schizophrenic patients, who were neither so acute that spontaneous recovery might affect the results nor so chronic that any improvement was unlikely, to treatment with ECT, neuroleptics, analytical psychotherapy, or milieu therapy (that is routine hospital care). Improvement rates, as measured by discharge from hospital and length of stay were significantly better for the ECT-treated group than for the psychotherapy or milieu therapy groups, but not as good as for the neuroleptic-treated group.

Although it is clear that neuroleptic drugs are the preferred treatment of acute schizophrenia, the study of May *et al.* suggests that there is a case to answer for ECT in certain circumstnces, for example in treatment-resistant patients. Two modern studies with rigorous designs have been carried out to assess the usefulness of ECT as an adjunctive treatment to neuroleptic drugs.

Taylor and Fleminger (1980; see also Taylor 1981) gave schizophrenic patients, diagnosed according to the Present State Examination, real or simulated ECT under double-blind conditions. Like May, they selected a 'middle' group, excluding patients with a short history of illness (less than six months) or with clearly chronic illnesses (more than two years continuous hospitalization in the last five years or six of the last twelve months in hospital). If, after two weeks of neuroleptic treatment (or more in some cases), additional treatment was felt to be necessary, ECT was offered. From an initial sample of 55 patients, 20 entered the trial phase and were randomly assigned to real or simulated ECT, receiving between 8 and 12 treatments. Half of each group had high levels of depression, and the groups were otherwise similar in the type and degree of psychopathology shown. As shown in Fig. 9.1, it was found that while both groups showed improvement overall, this was significantly greater in the group that received real ECT; a difference was evident at two weeks (six treatments) and became more pronounced at four weeks. Depressive symptoms were better relieved by ECT than placebo, although the differences showed only a trend towards significance. Scores on ratings of a number of schizophrenic symptoms also improved differentially, this reaching significance for four delusion and hallucination ratings, and also for affective flattening. After the trial period, the differences between the two groups diminished progressively until at three months they were minimal. However, during this period four of the control group were started on (real) ECT, compared with only one of the treatment group.

Brandon *et al.* (1985) reported on 17 patients with schizophrenia who took part in a large-scale trial of real versus simulated ECT in patients of all types. The patients were randomly assigned to eight real or eight simulated treatments over four weeks under double-blind conditions. The results were closely similar to those of Taylor and Fleminger: both groups improved, but after two and four weeks of treatment there was a significant advantage for those receiving real ECT. Once again, the differences in depression ratings between the two groups at the end of the trial were marginal: they were evident only on a visual analogue scale and not on a formal rating scale. As in Taylor and Fleminger's study, after the end of

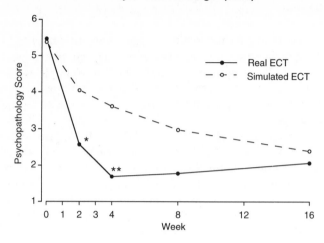

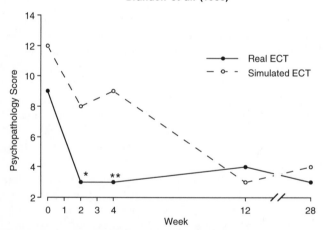

Fig. 9.1 Effect of real versus simulated ECT in schizophrenia (from Taylor and Fleminger 1981; Brandon *et al.* 1985).

the trial, when a free choice of further treatment could be made, the advantage for the real ECT group progressively faded. However, five of the eight patients in the placebo group subsequently had ECT compared with only one of nine in the original real ECT group. Brandon *et al.*'s findings are also shown in Fig. 9.1.

All the studies thus concur in indicating that ECT is of some therapeutic value in schizophrenia, and that this value is not just resticted to — or even accounted for — by relief of any accompanying depression. Although both Taylor and Fleminger and Brandon *et al.* found that the benefits were not sustained, and that the placebo-treated group subsequently 'caught up', different interpretations were given for this result: Taylor (1981) strongly implied that the main effect of ECT was to accelerate improvement that would have taken place with time and neuroleptic treatment anyway. Brandon *et al.* on the other hand, merely contented themselves with pointing out that without adequate control of treatment during the follow-up period it was not possible to comment on the duration of the effect of ECT.

The value of ECT in catatonic schizophrenia remains unresolved. It seems most unlikely that it is of no benefit, given that it was from observation of its effects in such patients that the treatment was originally introduced. In Britain, ECT remains the standard treatment for the psychiatric emergency of catatonic stupor, and this presumably reflects a consistent clinical impression of favourable response. At the same time, several states in the USA face severe obstacles in prescribing ECT, but they nevertheless seem to manage to deal with catatonic stuporose states without disastrous consequences. ECT continues to find a use in some centres for patients with catatonic excitement or who have pictures dominated by catatonic features but without stupor or excitement. It is unknown whether or not this is justified.

Prevention of relapse

Schizophrenia is, particularly in the days of neuroleptic treatment, a disorder of exacerbations and improvements. If physical treatments are the mainstay of treatment of acute episodes, the management of patients after they have achieved their maximum degree of remission is a different and more complex matter. One important element is maintenance neuroleptic drug treatment, whose efficacy has been examined in numerous well designed clinical trials. For reasons to be discussed below, the suspicion has also arisen that social factors might play an important part in the precipitation of relapse, and this has become the subject of a substantial research initiative in the shape of studies of expressed emotion.

Maintenance neuroleptic treatment

In the years after the introduction of neuroleptics, it became apparent that schizophrenic patients tended to relapse when they stopped taking their medication, although this could be delayed for weeks or months. At some point this recognition of a need for continued treatment blurred into a realization that neuroleptic drugs might have a genuine prophylactic effect, reducing the frequency of future relapses (see Davis 1975). One of the first trials of maintenance treatment in schizophrenia to avoid a number of rather serious methodological pitfalls was that of Leff and Wing (1971). They assigned 35 patients who has recently recovered from an acute schizophrenic episode to treatment with oral neuroleptic or placebo and followed their progress for a year. Thirty three per cent of the treated group relapsed, compared with 83 per cent of those receiving placebo.

The many subsequent studies of maintenance medication have been reviewed by Davis (1975, 1985). He pooled the data from 35 double-blind studies comparing neuroleptic with placebo. These all had a duration of more than six weeks, and they were carried out on both out-patients and chronically hospitalized in-patients. Of a total of 3609 patients followed for periods of time of on the whole four to six months, 20 per cent on average relapsed on active medication compared with 53 per cent on placebo. Only four studies found that the relapse rate on placebo was less than twice that on drugs, and all found some advantage over placebo. Virtually all the studies found that the difference was statistically significant, often highly so.

These studies also revealed that schizophrenic patients do not necessarily relapse quickly after discontinuing neuroleptic medication. Davis (1975) reviewed the evidence on this point from two large neuroleptic:placebo maintenance studies. He concluded that the rate of decline of patients who remained well on no medication followed an exponential function, indicating that they tended to relapse at a constant rate over time—somewhere in the range of 8–15 per cent per month. This rate remained the same until up to 18 months. When the patients in these studies who had been maintained on active medication and had not relapsed had their medication stopped, they also began to relapse at much the same rate. The implication is that there is a slow, steady tendency to relapse in schizophrenia which does not seem to alter substantially over quite long periods of time.

The beneficial effect of maintenance treatment has also been established in patients who have only experienced one episode of schizophrenia. In a study with a conventional double-blind, placebo-controlled design, Crow *et al.* (1986) followed 120 such patients for two years or until relapse. Forty six per cent of the patients on active medication relapsed compared with 62 per cent on placebo, a highly significant difference.

The benefits of neuroleptic medication have also, somewhat more surprisingly, been demonstrated in schizophrenic patients who have been stable and whose symptoms have been well controlled for several years. Dencker *et al.* (1980) selected a sample of 32 out-patients who were taking depot neuroleptic medication and who had not had a relapse in the preceding two years; none showed any active psychotic symptoms. These patients' medication was then stopped. Seventeen relapsed in the first six months, a further nine relapsed in the next six months, and four of the remaining six had relapsed by the end of the second year without medication.

The value of maintenance neuroleptic treatment in schizophrenia is established beyond doubt by these studies. As Davis (1975) concluded, it is in fact unusual to find such unanimity in psychiatry. The evidence also suggests rather strongly that patients who have only had a single episode, or who have been well for years should, on the whole, receive continued treatment. At the same time, a substantial proportion of schizophrenic patients relapse despite taking medication. One possible reason behind this phenomenon is discussed in the next section.

Social factors: the role of expressed emotion

According to Brown (1985), the work that led to the famous concept of expressed emotion had humble beginnings in a survey of the social adjustment of male patients who had been discharged from long stay hospital care (Brown *et al.* 1958). This found that schizophrenic patients, but not those with other diagnoses, were more likely to require re-admission to hospital if they returned to live with their parents or wives than if they went to live in lodgings or with brothers or sisters.

This observation led to a second prospective and more rigorous survey (Brown *et al.* 1962). This was designed to examine the hypothesis that something about family relationships affected the rate of relapse in schizophrenia. A series of acute and chronic patients and their relatives were interviewed together just after discharge from hospital and rated on a questionnaire developed to measure various aspects of their emotional interaction. It was found that high levels of emotional involvement on the part of the relatives provided a good predictor of subsequent deterioration in the patients' clinical state.

The third study (Brown *et al.* 1972) was the first in which the term expressed emotion (EE) was used. The patient sample consisted of 101 patients who were diagnosed as schizophrenic according to the Present State Examination. An interview of each of the patient's relatives (spouse or parents) was carried out before discharge from hospital, and the patient was then interviewed with his or her relatives about two weeks after discharge. Various aspects of the relatives' emotional response were assessed. The degree of EE was determined by combining ratings on three variables in the interview schedule: *critical comments* made by the relative about the patient and his or her illness; *hostility*, based on negative emotion or a clear statement of resentment, disapproval, dislike, or rejection; and *over-involvement*, defined as excessive anxiety, overconcern, or overprotectiveness. Based on the combined EE scores, the sample was split so that approximately half the patients were assigned to high and low expressed emotion groups respectively.

The patients and their relatives were re-assessed if they were re-admitted at any time over the next nine months. Relapse was defined in the same way as in the study of Brown and Birley (1968) (see Chapter 5), that is as either a re-emergence of psychotic symptoms or a marked exacerbation of persistent symptoms. Twenty six of 45 (58 per cent) patients with high EE relatives relapsed during the follow-up period, compared with 9 of 56 (16 per cent) of those in the low EE group. This finding was highly significant statistically, and significant differences were also found when critical comments, hostility, and emotional over-involvement were examined separately. Further analyses were used to demonstrate that the association between expressed emotion and relapse was not an artefact of other factors, such as behavioural disturbance or poor compliance with neuroleptic treatment, which were independently associated with relapse.

Beginning with Vaughn and Leff (1976), essentially the same study has been repeated many times and in a number of different countries. The findings of these studies have been reviewed several times, most recently and most thoroughly by Kavanagh (1992). The results are summarized in Table 9.2, from which it is clear that the finding of significantly higher rates of relapse in high EE families has been upheld in a substantial majority of studies. There are also, it should be noted, a number of failures to replicate, which currently stand at 7 out of 24 studies.

Vaughn and Leff (1976) made the additional proposal that EE and maintenance medication interacted in an additive way. By combining their data with that from the study of Brown *et al.* (1972), they were able to produce the diagram shown in Fig. 9.2. This suggested that there was a stepwise increase in relapse rate, from a low level in patients in low EE environments who showed compliance with neuroleptic treatment, to the highest rate of all, which was seen in patients in high EE households who were not taking drugs. Other studies, however, have not confirmed the finding that regular intake of neuroleptics reduces the effects of high EE on relapse. This was demonstrated particularly clearly in the study of MacMillan *et al.* (1986), in which patients were randomly assigned to real or placebo medication under double-blind conditions (this was as part of the study as Crow *et al.* 1986, described earlier). This is also shown in Fig. 9.2.

As a theoretical construct, EE is open to a number of criticisms (see Birchwood *et al.* 1988) and even its proponents accept that high levels may not themselves determine relapse, but instead provide an index of some other factor which is directly related to this (Kuipers and Bebbington, 1988). In such circumstances the acid test of EE to some extent becomes its practical usefulness in the management of schizophrenia. To date, seven studies have examined the effect on relapse of interventions designed to

Table 9.2 Studies of expressed emotion in schizophrenia (from Kavanagh 1992)

Study	9–12 month relapse rate	
	low EE	high EE
	% (N)	% (N)
Vaughn and Leff (1976)	6 (16)	48 (21)**
Vaughn *et al.* (1984)	17 (18)	56 (36)*
Moline *et al.* (1985)	29 (7)	71 (17)
Dulz and Hand (1986)	65 (17)	48 (29)
MacMillan *et al.* (1986)	41 (34)	68 (38)*
Nuechterlein *et al.* (1986)	0 (7)	40 (20)*
Karno *et al.* (1987)	26 (27)	59 (17)*
Leff *et al.* (1987, 1990)	9 (54)	31 (16)*
McCreadie and Phillips (1988)	20 (35)	17 (24)
Parker *et al.* (1988)	60 (15)	48 (42)
Cazzullo *et al.* (1988)	27 (11)	63 (8)*
Gutierrez *et al.* (1988)	10 (21)	54 (11)*
Tarrier *et al.* (1988)	21 (19)	48 (29)
Rostworowska *et al.* (1987)	9 (11)	60 (25)**
Mozny *et al.* (1989)	29 (38)	60 (30)
Montero *et al.* (1990)	19 (36)	33 (24)
Arevalo and Vizcarro (1989)	38 (13)	44 (18)
Ivanovic and Vuletic (1989)	7 (31)	66 (29)**
Buchkremer *et al.* (1991)	28 (40)	37 (59)
Barrelet *et al.* (1990)	0 (0)	33 (24)
Stirling *et al.* (1991)	47 (17)	31 (5)
Vaughan *et al.* (1994)	25 (40)	53 (47)**

$*P < 0.05$; $**P < 0.01$.

lower the level of EE in the relatives of patients with schizophrenia. These have been reviewed by Barrowclough and Tarrier (1992), who noted that five found a significant effect and two failed to do so. These studies varied considerably in factors such as sample size and choice of therapeutic intervention, and it is difficult to draw any clear conclusions from them. Possibly the best strategy, therefore, is to focus on the largest of these studies, which is also among the most methodologically rigorous of them.

Hogarty *et al.* (1986, 1987, 1991) recruited 103 in-patients meeting Research Diagnostic Criteria for schizophrenia or schizoaffective psychosis, who prior to admission has been living with relatives assessed as showing high EE. After discharge, these patients were randomly allocated to one of four treatment groups. A control group received only medication and

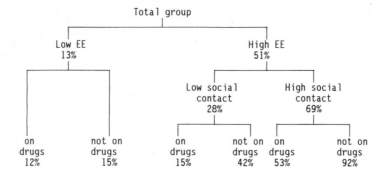

Brown *et al.* (1972) / Vaughn and Leff (1976)
(*n* = 128)

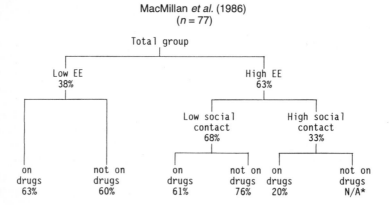

MacMillan *et al.* (1986)
(*n* = 77)

*Based on only 1 patient (who relapsed) in this group.

Fig. 9.2 Interaction of expressed emotion and neuroleptic treatment on relapse rates in schizophrenia.

routine out-patient care. A second group were given social skills training weekly. In a third group, the family were involved in weekly sessions which combined education about schizophrenia with strategies to deal with interpersonal issues. A final group recieved both the preceding treatments. Relapse was defined in much the same way as by Brown *et al.* (1972).

After 12 months, the relapse rates were 41 per cent for the control group, 20 per cent for the social skills training group, 19 per cent for the family management group, and 0 per cent for the combined treatment group. These differences were statistically significant. Even when patients and relatives who had dropped out of the study were included, the same progression was still evident. After two years a similar pattern of relapses was found, although by this time the corresponding figures were 66 per cent, 42 per cent, 32 per cent, and 25 per cent. Follow-up family assessments supported the conclusion that reductions in relapse rate were found in families where there had been a corresponding reduction in the level of EE.

Uncomfortable though it may be to some, the studies of EE provide compelling evidence that psychological factors contribute to exacerbations of schizophrenia. It may not be EE itself which promotes relapse, but rather some unknown factor; this might be some specific aspect of family life, or it might merely be generally high levels of stress and strain. This finding should come as no surprise. Even the most dyed-in-the-wool biological psychiatrist can hardly have failed to notice that schizophrenic patients often relapse when they are, for instance, bereaved, and—anticipating the theme of the next section—that their overall condition tends to improve when their living conditions also improve.

Rehabilitation

As described by Bennett (1983), the roots of psychiatric rehabilitation can be traced back as far as the humanitarian reforms of asylum care in the early and middle parts of the last century. Its particular application to patients with schizophrenia, however, seems to have grown out of three more recent developments. One of these was the introduction of neuroleptic drugs, which as well as producing a sharp increase in the number of patients who were potentially able to leave hospital, also created an atmosphere that emphasized treatment more than custodial care (Davis 1985). Another element was the development of behaviour modification techniques which suggested that quite simple strategies could have useful effects on the behaviour of mentally ill patients (see Birchwood *et al.* 1988). But easily the most important ingredient was a sea change that took place in the philosophy of psychiatric care. As pioneered by Bennett (1978), Wing (1963), Clark (1981), and others, this led to the de-institutionalization of chronic schizophrenic patients and their re-integration into the community.

Broadly speaking, rehabilitation in schizophrenia is targeted at the most chronically ill, seriously disabled patients. These are the ones who tend to fall into the worst two outcome groups in the follow-up studies described in Chapter 3; those who are at risk of becoming permanently hospitalized and who, more often than not, show both severe positive and negative symptoms. Strides in the management of such patients have spawned a large literature, much of which is technical and concentrates on the issues surrounding delivery of services to the exclusion of all else. In these circumstances, it is not easy to unearth and expose to critical scrutiny the work which is considered to have established the credentials of the field. In order to pursue this aim, a leading authority on rehabilitation psychiatry in Britain (Dr G. Shepherd) was consulted and asked to select what he considered to be the key studies of the post-war period. Three of these are desribed below; each covers a different facet of rehabilitation.

Rehabilitation in the hospital setting

The study which is widely considered to have put the overall effectiveness of rehabilitation on a firm scientific footing is that of Wing and Brown (1970). They examined the adverse effects of long term hospitalization on schizophrenic patients, and assessed the effectiveness of attempts to ameliorate these.

Three mental hospitals which differed markedly in their policies of care were investigated. From each, a random sample of 73–120 female in-patients was selected: these patients all had a diagnosis of schizophrenia (made clinically), were less than 60 years old, and had been continuously hospitalized for more than two years. The patients' positive and negative symptoms were rated (it was, in fact, this study which first employed the terms positive and negative symptoms in their current sense—see Chapter 2). Their behaviour on the ward was also assessed. The patients' social circumstances were measured in terms of the number of their personal possessions (for example a toothbrush), the number of hours spent in activities each day, time spent off the ward, and contact with the outside world. Nursing staff were also interviewed and other observations were made, for example about the restrictiveness of the ward regime.

The three hospitals were found to vary considerably in their climates. One showed uniformly high scores on a cluster of 'social impoverishment' ratings: little contact with the outside world, few personal possessions, little constructive occupation, spending much time doing nothing, and being regarded pessimistically by nursing staff. Another received generally low scores on these measures. The third hospital showed an overall intermediate pattern of scores.

It was found that the patients in each of the hospitals showed corresponding clinical differences: the hospital with the highest levels of social impoverishment had significantly more patients rated as moderately or severely ill than that with the lowest levels, and on average higher levels of disturbed behaviour. Patients in the third hospital fell between the other two on both sets of ratings. The findings were most marked on clinical ratings of negative symptoms and behavioural ratings of withdrawal.

The hospitals were visited again four years later. By this time various administrative and social changes had been made, particularly at the hospital with the highest levels of social impoverishment. On this occasion the patient samples were combined and the status of the whole group was compared between the first and second visits. As expected, significant improvement had taken place on all measurements of impoverished social environment. Correspondingly, the patients as a group showed significant clinical improvement. Nearly a third of the patients who had been rated as severely impaired at the time of the original visit had improved by at least one category by the time of the second visit; in some cases the improvement was judged to be marked. In contrast, less than 5 per cent had become worse. Most of the improvement was accounted for by a decrease in social withdrawal, flatness of affect, and other negative symptoms, although florid symptoms, particularly coherently expressed delusions also improved somewhat. Further analysis indicated that clinical improvement was most closely related to an increase in the time spent in activities and occupational therapy and a decrease in the time spent doing nothing. Other social changes, such as increased contact with outside world, more optimism among nursing staff, and an increased supply of personal belongings were less important, but seemed to have a role in reducing secondary handicaps. There was no evidence to suggest that changes in drug treatment were responsible for the improvements seen.

The authors thus provided evidence of a link between social impoverishment in chronically hospitalized patients and severity of clinical symptoms, particularly negative symptoms. The hospital with the richest social milieu also contained patients with the least marked negative symptoms. Furthermore, the introduction of a more stimulating environment — especially occupationally — was successful in bringing about an improvement in these symptoms. The change it proved possible to bring about in chronically hospitalized schizophrenics was sometimes to the extent that they no longer fitted the stereotype of the 'back ward' patient.

Day care

Linn *et al.* (1979) carried out what is probably the best, and certainly the largest study of the value of day centre attendance in the aftercare of schizophrenic patients discharged from hospital. They randomly assigned 162 chronic schizophrenic patients (diagnosed clinically) to either routine out-patient care or attendance at a day centre. Out-patient care consisted essentially of visits to a clinic where the emphasis was on monitoring of neuroleptic medication. The day centres were devoted specifically to chronic patients, and their goals included maintaining or bringing about improvement in family and social interactions, providing a place for patients to socialize and engage in productive activities, and fulfilling the need for a sheltered environment outside hospital. Measures were made of symptoms, social functioning, time spent out of hospital (or prison), and also the patients' attitudes. These were carried out every six months for two years; it was not possible to make the ratings under blind conditions.

No differences were found in the rates of relapse for the two groups. Nor did any differences become evident in the groups' levels of symptoms. Social functioning was, however, significantly better for the day centre attenders from a year onwards. Some of the centres, but not others seemed to be effective in forestalling relapse and reducing overall reductions in level of symptoms, and this seemed to be associated with presence of more recreational and occupational therapy. On the other hand, an emphasis on individual psychotherapy was associated with a higher rate of relapse.

Intensive hostel care

Following suggestions that patients with chronic psychotic illness might be better cared for in a 'ward in a house' than in hospital, Hyde *et al.* (1987) evaluated the success of such a unit. Their sample consisted of 22 patients who had been under in-patient care for longer than six months (the mean duration of the current hospitalization was 3.5 years). All the patients had resisted attempts at resettlement and were considered to need round-the-clock nursing care. In 14 the diagnosis was schizophrenia and the remainder had a variety of other functional and organic disorders.

The patients were randomly chosen either to stay in hospital or to be transferred to a 24-hour staffed hostel in the community. The two groups were fairly well matched in terms of age, sex, duration of illness, and in the nature of their impairments and problem behaviours. In the hostel, the emphasis was on maintaining and/or improving self-care, and acquiring domestic skills such as cooking, cleaning, and shopping. Each patient had their own individual care plan in which problem behaviours were specifically targeted. Nursing was organized along behavioural lines under the supervision of a psychologist, and a reward system operated whereby points could be exchanged for money. The patients were encouraged to pursue leisure activities, and they arranged group outings for themselves. The control group remained in hospital, but had access to a comprehensive range of occupational and social therapies. They were able to use community facilities as they wished.

The patients were assessed six monthly or yearly on a variety of clinical and behavioural measures. As in the study of Linn *et al.* it was not feasible to make these assessments under blind conditions. For the 16 patients who remained in the study at the end of two years, those assigned to the intensive community hostel showed significantly fewer behavioural problems. The differences were most evident in ratings of indifference and non-assertiveness. Domestic skills showed a significant improvement, as did use of social facilities, and time spent on socially constructive behaviours (for example eating, working, and conversing with others). However, no differences were found between the groups in hygiene, self-care, and social and community skills. There were no differences between the groups on any of the clinical measures, although there was a trend towards less negative symptoms among the hostel patients.

Although not suitable for all patients — 3 of the original 11 had to be returned to hospital — Hyde *et al.* concluded that there were certain advantages associated with intensive hostel care. The impression gained was that the patients who were able to survive in such a setting fell into two groups. The first consisted of those who did not show much improvement after the first six months, and who continued to require continuous nursing care. The second group progressively improved in psychosocial functioning and, rather to everyone's surprise, eventually became potentially able to move on to more independent accommodation.

The three studies that have been described here are rather different in character from those in other sections of this chapter. In particular, they could be regarded as producing soft data which are open to other interpretations, and the use of non-blind ratings might be frowned on. However, the message the studies convey most strongly is not in their findings — which are uniformly modest — but in the way they demonstrate that attempting to improve the quality of life of patients with severe, chronic schizophrenia, invariably has a by-product in the form of useful clinical improvement. It is this, perhaps more than anything else that captures the essential quality of rehabilitation.

10

Paraphrenia and paranoia

What terms like paranoia and paranoid should refer to has exercised psychiatry for decades, if not centuries, and is still a vexed question. As a noun, paranoia denotes a disorder which has been argued in and out of existence, and whose clinical features, course, boundaries, and virtually every other aspect of which is controversial. Employed as an adjective, paranoid has become attached to a diverse set of presentations, from paranoid schizophrenia, through paranoid depression, to paranoid personality—not to mention a motley collection of paranoid 'psychoses', 'reactions', and 'states'—and this is to restrict the discussion to functional disorders. Even when abbreviated down to the prefix para-, the term crops up causing trouble as the contentious but stubbornly persistent concept of paraphrenia.

Some of this confusion derives from the different shades of meaning that the adjective paranoid has acquired. In its European sense—which is traceable back to Kraepelin and beyond him to Kahlbaum—paranoid means, quite simply, delusional. This usage is exemplified by paranoid schizophrenia, in which persecutory, grandiose, or other delusions are to the forefront of the clinical picture. In British and American psychiatry, paranoid has come to be used more or less interchangeably with persecutory. This sense of the term is perhaps best illustrated by paranoid personality, a disorder characterized by touchiness, sensitivity, suspiciousness, and a tendency to misconstrue the intentions of others as hostile or contemptuous. In yet another usage, as seen, for example, in contemporary Scandinavian psychiatry, paranoid refers to any disorder where there are delusions and hallucinations.

After subjecting the term paranoid to a thorough historical review, Lewis (1970) concluded that it should be applied to syndromes in which there are delusions, which may be concerned with persecution, grandeur, or any number of other themes, and should carry no implications about presence of hallucinations, or relationship to schizophrenia. When defined in this way, the focus narrows on to two disorders, paraphrenia and paranoia. After these have been tackled, there remain a miscellany of minor disorders which are customarily, but not always very logically, also subsumed under the heading of paranoid.

Paraphrenia

The term paraphrenia was coined by Kahlbaum in 1863 (cited by Berrios 1986). He did not create it to describe any particular clinical entity, but merely to draw attention to the tendency of certain psychiatric disorders to develop at certain periods in life: in his scheme, for example, paraphrenia hebetica was the insanity of adolesence and paraphrenia senilis the insanity of the elderly. As with most of Kahlbaum's ideas, this classification gained little acceptance and came, even within his own lifetime, to be regarded as a historical curiosity.

Kraepelin's paraphrenia

Fifty years after Kahlbaum gave paraphrenia its name, Kraepelin (1913*a*) revived the term to describe a comparatively small group of cases which he had come to conclude resembled schizophrenia, but which deviated from the typical picture in several significant ways. He gave no reason for choosing the name paraphrenia, stating only that it seemed suitable. However, as he alluded to the marked delusional component that all paraphrenic states had in common, it might be inferred that he wished to emphasize a relationship to paranoid schizophrenia on the one hand and paranoia on the other. Beyond this, it is possible to speculate that Kraepelin was acknowledging a general indebtedness to Kahlbaum, who was the major formative influence on his views. What is less clear, as will be seen below, is whether he employed the term in the belief that the disorders were associated with a particular age of onset.

The feature of paraphrenia which led Kraepelin to separate it from schizophrenia was first and foremost its course. This showed a 'far slighter development of the disorders of emotion and volition' that characterized schizophrenia. Despite persistent and sometimes remorselessly progressive florid symptoms, the patient remained lively, accessible, and pleasant to outsiders, and was often able to work; the severer degrees of deterioration never supervened. The other conspicuous feature of paraphrenic states was the presence of a marked paranoid colouring: the clinical picture was dominated by delusions, whose content was often but not always persecutory; and these were accompanied by hallucinations, which were predominantly but not exclusively auditory. Formal thought disorder made at most a minor contribution, and catatonic phenomena were hardly ever encountered.

In his customary way, Kraepelin divided paraphrenia into a number of subgroups, although he considered that these were not sharply demarcated from one another. The largest of these was a slowly evolving form which he termed *paraphrenia systematica*. Two smaller and perhaps related groups were *paraphrenia expansiva* and *paraphrenia confabulans*. Finally he distinguished *paraphrenia phantastica* which was exceptional, not only because of its rarity but also by virtue of its extraordinary clinical features.

Paraphrenia systematica was characterized by the insidious and continuously progressive development of persecutory and referential delusions, to which other delusions and hallucinations later become added.

The disorder typically began with the gradual development of delusions of reference, misinterpretation and misidentification—patients started to believe they were being insulted, jeered at, followed, spied on, etc.—out of which delusions of persecution crystallized and became increasingly elaborate. Subsequently, sometimes only after many years, other delusions appeared, for example with a grandiose, religious, or hypochondriacal content. At some point hallucinations crept into the picture; these were typically auditory, but could be seen less commonly in other modalities. From Kraepelin's description, there is no doubt that first rank symptoms, in the shape of passivity and thought alterations were also commonplace.

Paraphrenia expansiva consisted of the gradual, or occasionally more abrupt, development of grandiose delusions which inclined to the fantastic and which became accompanied by auditory and visual hallucinations.

At the outset, these patients began by expressing grandiose delusions, of exalted religious status, high descent, great wealth, and so on, often against a background of expansiveness or slight excitement. In about half of the cases the presentation was one of erotomania—the belief that a highly placed person was in love with the patient. These ideas frequently went hand in hand with persecutory delusions, and they were invariably accompanied by multiple delusions of reference and misinterpretation. Hallucinations appeared early on, taking the form of voices and visions which often had a religious colouring. Delusional memories, first rank symptoms, and occasionally somatic hallucinations could also form part of the picture. In some cases the state eventually became very florid.

Paraphrenia confabulans was characterized principally by a proliferation of delusions and delusional memories, some of which were fixed while others constantly shifted and changed.

After a prodromal period of brooding and withdrawal, these patients would suddenly start voicing an enormous volume of persecutory, grandiose, and fantastic delusions. Woven into these would be numerous delusional memories which, although they tended to have an adventurous, story-like quality, would be related with complete conviction and precise details: one patient reported to the authorities that he had dug up a human arm and had then been compelled at gunpoint by his neighbour to keep silent about it; this caused a police investigation. Sometimes the delusions were absolutely fixed and repeated again and again in almost exactly the same words, but more typically, on questioning, further details would be added and the stories would undergo a progressive embroidering—the phenomenon of delusional confabulation. In the background were delusions of reference and misinterpretation and verbal auditory hallucinations.

Paraphrenia phantastica was the most florid presentation of all, characterized by, in the words of Kraepelin, 'the luxuriant growth of highly extraordinary, disconnected, changing delusions'.

Typically, the disorder would be ushered in by a period of listlessness, depression, and withdrawal. This was gradually replaced by delusions and auditory hallucinations, which even at this early stage were notably florid. The delusions, in particular, then went on to acquire quite prodigious forms and to be produced in an almost inexhaustible supply: patients would state that their bodies were being melted down and torn apart; that other people, sometimes crowds, were inside them; that thousands or even millions of people were being murdered daily; that they were of multiple royal descent, infinitely rich, owned properties on different planets, and so on. Delusional memories and confabulations also formed a conspicuous part of the picture. Hallucinations, for the most part auditory, might also be present, as could be a degree of formal thought disorder, which typically only became obvious when the patient was describing his delusions.

The age of onset of Kraepelinian paraphrenia clustered between 30 and 50 in the majority of cases, although the disorder could commence in the twenties and in one case it began at the age of 64. Both sexes were affected: overall there was if anything a slight male preponderance; however, almost all cases of paraphrenia expansiva were female.

The course of the four subtypes of paraphrenia showed, according to Kraepelin, more similarities than differences. In general, this was gradually progressive: while there could be fluctuations in the intensity of symptoms, marked improvement was unusual and recovery did not occur. With time, the delusions tended to become more and more nonsensical and fragmented. In some cases formal thought disorder developed, expressing itself in speech which was stilted or verbose, or in use of neologisms and peculiar turns of expression. Stereotypies or oddities of behaviour became a feature in some patients, but these were usually of an isolated kind. However, the most striking feature was the lack of serious evidence of deterioration: the patients remained pleasant, mostly cheerful, and often vivacious. Other than a certain superficiality of emotional expression, affective flattening was the exception rather than the rule. Many patients remained able to work. Typically, the terminal state was milder than even the mildest of those associated with schizophrenia.

The subsequent history of paraphrenia was destined to be short. Kraepelin himself entertained doubts about its validity as a nosological entity: he questioned whether paraphrenia systematica might merely represent a mild form of paranoid schizophrenia; whether paraphrenia expansiva was really a variant of mania; and whether in paraphrenia confabulans and paraphrenia phantastica, he was not just singling out cases of schizophrenia where the picture was dominated by a single, albeit unusual symptom. The concept also came under attack from Kraepelin's contemporaries, who seemed on the whole to have been rather sceptical that paraphrenia was definitely distinguishable from the already broad range of presentations of schizophrenia.

Within a few years a seemingly mortal blow was dealt to paraphrenia. Mayer (1921) followed up 78 of Kraepelin's original paraphrenic patients approximately ten years after Kraepelin described them. At this time he concluded that just over a third (27) could still be considered to show the characteristic features of paraphrenia. In another third (28) the picture had become unequivocally one of schizophrenia. The remaining patients had acquired a collection of revised or additional diagnoses — paranoia, manic-depressive psychosis, or organic brain disease — and in a small minority remissions had taken place. As can be seen from Table 10.1, a substantial proportion of the systematic, expansive, and confabulatory subgroups retained their distinguishing characteristics, but all the cases of paraphenia phantastica appeared to have evolved into schizophenia. Mayer's study lacked detail, the way in which the follow-up was carried out was not specified, and the final diagnoses sometimes seemed contrived or even unsatisfactory. Nevertheless, the findings were fully endorsed by Kraepelin in a commentary on the paper.

Mayer's study revealed that, with the passage of time, patients with paraphrenia tend to merge into the pool of chronic schizophrenic presentations. Perhaps, therefore, the best way to regard paraphrenia is as a fifth subtype of schizophrenia — a special variety whose features of delusions and lack of deterioration, and perhaps also later age of onset, mark it out, but whose differences from schizophrenia proper are quantitative rather than qualitative. Nevertheless, there will always be some 'pure' cases who retain their characteristic paraphrenic features despite years of relentless illness. One possible such example is described in Fig. 10.1. This position appears close to that advocated by Kraepelin in his comments on Mayer's follow-up of his cases of paraphrenia and, while it failed to have much of an impact at the time (paraphrenia largely disappeared as a concept), it was to have important repercussions half a century later.

Late paraphrenia

By the middle of the twentieth century paraphrenia had been relegated to the position of a historical curiosity, a minor nosological excursion whose results had proved to be disappointing. In Britain, and even more so in America, schizophrenia became regarded as a disorder of adolescence and early adult life which rarely if ever appeared for the first time in middle age, and never later than this. When paranoid delusions developed in later

Table 10.1 Results of Mayer's (1921) follow-up study of 78 of Kraepelin's paraphrenic patients

Paraphrenia systematica (n = 45)	Schizophrenia (11) Paranoia (2) Paranoia abortiva* (3) Schizoid reaction in a paranoid personality (1) Evolved into paranoid personality (1) Cyclic psychosis (3) Senile dementia (2) Diagnosis unclear (2) Diagnosis unchanged (17)	Patients who followed a typical paraphrenic course all had an onset at about age 50. Considered that this group was closely to schizophrenia genetically.
Paraphrenia expansiva (n = 13)	Schizophrenia (5) Manic-depressive psychosis (1) Organic brain disease (1) Diagnosis unclear (1) Diagnosis unchanged (5)	Speculated that a combination of schizophrenic and manic-depressive genetic disposition might give rise to symptoms resembling but distinct from those of schizophrenia.
Paraphrenia confabulans (n = 11)	Schizophrenia (5) Complete remission (1) Diagnosis unchanged (5)	
Paraphrenia phantastica (n = 9)	Schizophrenia (9)	All patients showed a picture of deteriorated paranoid schizophrenia.

*According to Kraepelin such cases were in reality suffering from manic-depressive psychosis.

Kraepelinian paraphrenia: the case of Richard Dadd
(from Greysmith 1973; Allderidge 1974)

Richard Dadd (1817–1886) was a leading talent of the Royal Academy Schools where he was a student. While in his twenties he exhibited paintings, received commissions, and was considered to be on the threshold of a promising career. Two of his six siblings became permanently insane and a third 'required an attendant'. Before becoming ill the patient was described as gentle, affectionate, pleasant, and cheerful.

At the age of 25 he accompanied a patron on a journey around Europe and the Middle East. During this he began to feel that his companion was an emissary of the Devil and that people around him were spirits in disguise. After returning to England he was noted to be suspicious, hostile, and at times bizarre in behaviour; at one point he cut out a birthmark believing it had been imprinted on him by the Devil. He came to believe he was subject to the will of the Egyptian god Osiris, and that he had a mission to destroy certain people who were possessed by evil spirits. 'Secret admonitions' (it is not clear whether or not these took the form of voices) urged him to carry out violent acts. Having been persuaded by these that his father was the Devil, he murdered him in a carefully planned way. He then fled to France where he was arrested after trying to murder a stranger in a carriage.

He was admitted to the State Criminal Lunatic Asylum and then to the Bethlem Hospital at the age of 27. He remained an in-patient for the rest of his life, later being transferred to the newly opened Broadmoor Hospital. His delusions remained fixed, but his intellectual capacity was said to have remained practically untouched. For several years he remained dangerous and was liable to attack others without any provocation and then apologize. This was explained as arising from a belief that certain spirits possessed his body and compelled him to act in such a way. He also regarded himself as not being bound by social customs, and could be unpleasant in manner, for example gorging himself till he vomited. However, he could hold an intelligent and interesting conversation as long as his delusions were steered clear of. At the age of 37 he was described as a sensible and agreeable companion, who showed a well educated mind in conversation and who was thoroughly informed in artistic matters. At the age of 43 he was said to associate very little with other patients but was generally civil and well behaved. At the age of 60 he was described by a journalist as simply dressed, courteous, with an unassuming manner. He remained obviously deluded.

He resumed painting some time after his admission to the Bethlem Hospital and continued to paint for the rest of his life. His two best known works, *Contradiction: Oberon and Titania* and *The Fairy Feller's*

Master Stroke were completed in 1858 and 1864, after 14 and 20 years of continuous illness. The quality of his work was of a consistently high standard, sometimes quite extraordinarily so, up to within three years of his death.

Opinions have differed as to whether Dadd's art is great or pedestrian, although it is now widely acknowledged to be of outstanding quality. *Oberon and Titania* has been sold for £1 500 000, and the British Museum bought a recently discovered watercolour for £100 000.

Fig. 10.1

life, the practice was to consider them as a manifestation of underlying organic brain disease, especially dementia (Fish 1960), or of affective disorder, especially depression (Volavka 1985).

Then, in the course of a survey of mental hospital admissions aged 60 or over, Roth and colleagues (Roth and Morrissey 1952; Roth 1955; Kay and Roth 1961) observed a number of patients (approximately 10 per cent of all admissions) who presented with well organized delusions with or without auditory hallucinations. In all of these the disorder had developed after the age of 45, and in many after the age of 60. These patients did not seem to be suffering from affective psychosis, and in the majority of cases there was no evidence of intellectual impairment on examination or underlying brain disease on investigation. Because the patients showed predominantly persecutory delusions with a striking preservation of personality and affect, the authors resurrected Kraepelin's term paraphrenia to describe the disorder, naming it late paraphrenia.

The clinical features of this newly discovered (or rediscovered) clinical entity were subjected to detailed examination in two more or less contemporary studies, both of which came to closely similar conclusions. The first of these was carried out by Kay and Roth (1961) on 99 cases drawn from two centres. The second was the study of Post (1966), who examined a total of 93 patients from his own unit. In both series, patients were excluded whose onset of symptoms occurred before middle or late life (the age cut-offs were 55 and 50 respectively), or who showed paranoid symptoms in the setting of a diagnosable depressive disorder (this was based on clinical judgement, but was rigorous in both studies). Kay and Roth excluded all cases who showed unequivocal evidence of intellectual impairment; Post took a different approach and included such cases, classifying his cases into those with no, doubtful, or definite organic impairment.

Kay and Roth noted that there was a large excess of women in their series (93 per cent and 84 per cent in each of the two centres). Eighty of the

93 (86 per cent) patients in Post's study were also female. In both studies the mean age at admission was 70. Physical health tended to be good, and in many cases terms like 'vigorous' and 'sturdy' were applicable. Kay and Roth found that 40 per cent of their patients showed some degree of hearing impairment, a higher frequency than in other diagnostic groups of comparable age; in Post's study the corresponding figure was 31 per cent. Visual defects were present in a further 15 per cent of Kay and Roth's series, but this rate was not greatly different from that of other patient groups in the same age range. Absence of generalized organic brain disease was a prerequisite of Kay and Roth's study, but they noted that a small proportion had neurological abnormalities which were minor or longstanding, and not obviously related to the onset of psychosis: these included epilepsy, isolated tremors, and mono- or hemiparesis.

As described by Kay and Roth (see also Mayer-Gross *et al*. 1969) the first discernible sign of illness was often an accentuation of previous personality traits; the patient became more irritable, bad tempered, hostile, suspicious, hypochondriacal, or morose than previously. At the same time or soon after, definite abnormalities of behaviour began to appear: the patient would become seclusive, refuse to see callers, begin to pester the police with complaints, write anonymous letters, and so on. The second stage was initiated, often abruptly or dramatically, with the onset of auditory hallucinations and florid delusions, which typically led to disturbed behaviour and brought about admission to hospital.

Both Kay and Roth and Post found essentially similar clinical characteristics among their patients. Delusions were invariable, and usually persecutory; however, the authors noted that there could also be grandiose, depressive, hypochondriacal, or erotic beliefs. The delusions were frequently fantastic, but they tended to be systematized and were often intimately bound up with hallucinations: for example, a patient might hear a voice making threats and therefore believe that someone was intent on murdering her, or smell an odour and believe that gas was being pumped into the room. Another notable feature was the tendency for delusions to revolve around the daily life, anxieties, and unfulfilled wishes of the elderly person: they were focused on the bed, the room, the house, neighbours, and those with whom the patient was in daily contact; the themes revolved around theft, interference with the gas, water, and electricity supplies, etc.. Hallucinations were present in most but not all cases, being absent in 10–20 per cent. Auditory hallucinations were by far the most common and were typically verbal, but elementary hallucinations were also conspicuous. Visual, olfactory, gustatory, and somatic hallucinations, all of a familiar schizophrenic kind, were also encountered. First rank symptoms were evident in the descriptions of Kay and Roth, and were explicitly described by Post in about a third of cases.

Other symptoms figured much less prominently. Although Kay and Roth alluded to verbosity, circumstantiality, and irrelevance in 30 per cent of their cases, more obvious formal thought disorder was considered unusual. According to Post, formal thought disorder was never recognized with certainty. Catatonic phenomena were also conspicuous by their absence: stupor was described as rare by Kay and Roth, and Post noted only occasional isolated stereotypies and mannerisms. Kay and Roth stated that while a degree of flattening or incongruity was quite common, gross affective abnormalities were not seen. Mood colourings, of fear, anger, euphoria, depression, and occasionally excitement were, however, commonplace. Post drew attention to the frequency of subjective depression, which he found in over half his cases — not infrequently there was a depressive syndrome complete enough to raise the possibility of an alternative diagnosis of manic-depressive psychosis, depressed type.

According to both sets of investigators, late paraphrenia typically took a chronic course. Among Kay and Roth's series, temporary remissions occurred spontaneously or were achieved with treatment in about a quarter of cases, and in the rest there was no great improvement. Even with treatment, the vast majority were found to be ill at five year follow-up, and in at least half of the cases indefinite hospitalization had proved necessary. (Post, however, found a considerably better response to treatment, as described below.) The clinical changes that took place with time resembled to some extent those described by Kraepelin and Mayer for paraphrenia: after years of illness many patients remained clean, tidy, normally motivated, and showed no pronounced deterioration in personality. Some, however, developed increasing affective flattening or incongruity, and others ended up mute, inaccessible, withdrawn, and preoccupied, or alternatively periodically incoherent, hostile, and negativistic. In a few the disorder eventually seemed to 'burn out', leaving a simple defect state similar to that seen in schizophrenia proper.

Kay and Roth argued that the incidence of dementia in late paraphrenia was no higher than that in the corresponding age group of the general population — about 20 per cent of both their late paraphrenic patients and those with other psychiatric diagnoses went on to develop either dementia or signs of focal brain disease. At the same time, these authors observed that as time went by memory tended to fail in a proportion of cases, and episodes of disorientation sometimes occurred, for which a cause could not always be established. In Post's study, 2 of the 44 patients who showed no evidence of organic brain disease at the time of diagnosis died within the three year follow-up period, one of bronchopneumonia and the other in a road traffic accident. A further two had developed evidence of intellectual impairment, which was mild in both cases. In contrast, the mortality was much higher in his group of late paraphrenic patients with definite organic brain disease at the time of initial presentation: 8 out of 13 of these patients had died within the three year period, and in at least 5 of these the presence of generalized brain disease was confirmed at post-mortem.

Two subsequent studies have suggested that the natural history of the disorder is more complicated than the simple picture painted by Kay and Roth. Holden (1987) retrospectively identified 37 patients who met both Kay and Roth's and Post's definitions of late paraphrenia, and in whom cognitive impairment could be confidently excluded at the time of initial presentation. He traced these patients ten years later, personally interviewing them where possible and obtaining supplementary information from surviving relatives and medical records. Thirteen of the 37 (35 per cent) appeared to have progressed to dementia within three years of diagnosis, and two more were found to be demented at 10 years. In a similar study, Hymas *et al.* (1989) followed-up a group of 42 prospectively identified, rigorously diagnosed late paraphrenic patients three to five years later. Of the 31 who were still alive, only two had developed a global intellectual decline suggestive of dementia clinically. However, a cognitive state examination had been included as part of the initial evaluation, and it was found that a further 9 (32.5 per cent) had undergone a significant deterioration in performance: these patients all showed serious difficulties in recall of a name and address and some of them had obvious deficits in time and place orientation. The findings were much worse than in a control group of age- and sex-matched normal individuals, only one of whom had developed any degree of intellectual deterioration.

There can be little doubt from these studies that, in a cross-sectional sense, late paraphrenia exists. Patients showing the typical features of paraphrenia as originally described by Kraepelin, and who are not depressed or demented at the time of initial presentation are by no means rare in clinical practice. As with Kraepelinian paraphrenia, it is also clear that the disorder is a type, a variant, or at the very least a close affiliate of schizophrenia: all the cardinal features of schizophrenia proper can either be seen at presentation or turn up at a later stage, if only as a minor aspect of the clinical picture. In terms of its natural history, however, late paraphrenia presents a more complex picture. It seems highly likely that patients with the disorder progress to a state resembling dementia more frequently than expected, and certainly more frequently than orginally claimed by Roth and co-workers. Whether this means that there is an association with standard causes of dementia such as Alzheimer's disease and cerebral arteriosclerosis, or whether late paraphrenics merely follow an accelerated route to the state of 'schizophrenic' intellectual impairment described in Chapter 7, is an unresolved question (see Almeida *et al.* 1992). Nevertheless, again as with Kraepelinian paraphrenia, many cases of late paraphrenia show a characteristic clinical picture in which decline is only a very late feature. One such case is the artist and illustrator Louis Wain who became permanently psychotic in his late fifties but showed little in the way of deterioration and continued to be artistically productive until very near the end of his life. This is summarized in Fig. 10.2.

Aetiological factors in paraphrenia

In the absence of any firm knowledge about the aetiology and pathogenesis of schizophrenia, it is only possible to examine to what extent the general aetiological factors which emerged as reasonably firmly established in Chapter 5, are also operative in paraphrenia. These are genetic predisposition, lateral ventricular enlargement, and abnormal premorbid personality. In addition, three factors specific to paraphrenia stand out as demanding explanation. These are its apparent later age of onset, its female sex preponderance, and the relationship with sensory impairment, especially deafness.

Genetic predisposition: This has been examined in late paraphrenia by a number of investigators, beginning with Roth and co-workers (Kay 1959, 1963; Kay and Roth 1961) who reported a risk of 3.4 per cent among siblings and children. This and later studies have been reviewed by Bridge and Wyatt (1980), Grahame (1982), and more recently by Hassett *et al.* (1992). Their results are summarized in Table 10.2: it is clear that the risk is higher than that for the general population (of 0.8 per cent) but less than for first degree relatives of patients with schizophrenia (of around 10 per cent). These findings clearly suggest a genetic loading, but they make it unlikely that precisely the same hereditary factors operate in both disorders. It was initially suggested by Kay and Roth that late paraphrenia shows a tendency to 'breed true', in the sense that schizophrenia in affected relatives also frequently has a late age of onset. However, this was not replicated in a subsequent study (Kay 1963).

Lateral ventricular enlargement: Two CT scan studies have been carried out in late paraphrenia. Rabins *et al.* (1987) scanned 29 patients with a mean age of 73, who met DSM III criteria for schizophrenia except that their age of onset was at age 45 or greater. These were compared with 23 age-matched normal volunteers. The paraphrenics showed significantly larger lateral ventricles, the mean ventricle:brain ratio (VBR) being nearly double that of the patients (13.3 ± 3.4 versus 8.6 ± 5.2). Naguib and Levy (1987) compared 43 patients with a mean age of 75 who had developed typical paraphrenic symptoms for the first time from the age of 60, with 40 age-matched normal volunteers. They also found evidence of significant lateral ventricular enlargement, with the mean VBR being 13.1 ± 4.3 for the patients and 9.7 ± 4.3 for the controls; 6 (14 per cent) of the paraphrenic

Late paraphrenia: the case of Louis Wain
(from Dale 1991)

For much of his adult life, Louis Wain (1860–1939) was famous in Britain for his cartoons, drawings and paintings of cats. However, demand for his work fell off in his later years.

He was an imaginative solitary child, who did poorly academically and truanted from school. As an adult he was regarded as a social oddity. He held cranky ideas about science, and tried to patent several unlikely mechanical devices; one contemporary described him as being 'as eccentric as they come'. At the age of 54 he fell off a bus and was unconscious or semi-conscious for several days. However, he made a full recovery and returned to work, ignoring doctors' advice to take six months off. One sister suffered from what was almost certainly schizophrenia which developed in early adult life.

From around the age of 58, he became more and more hostile to his sisters, although to outsiders he appeared normal. By the age of 61 he was writing at great length about various theories, in the course of which he alluded to ideas about being full of electricity and being influenced by spirits. He came to believe that his living sisters were responsible for another sister's death from influenza, and that they were stealing cheques and personal effects from him. He also became preoccupied with the idea of breeding spotted cats.

He was admitted to the Bethlem hospital at the age of 64. This was after he had become obviously behaviourally disturbed, endlessly rearranging furniture, wandering the streets in the middle of the night, writing abusive letters about his sisters, and being violent towards them. On examination he was found to be floridly deluded, believing that his sisters were maltreating him and claiming to have powers of healing by virtue of electricity imprisoned inside him. He believed that ether was the source of all evil and was present in his food. Later, he also came to believe that he was influenced by icicles. He appeared quaint and eccentric in manner, as he always had, but was quiet, co-operative, and courteous.

He continued to draw and paint in hospital, giving the impression of working at close to his earlier standards. However, particularly in later years, his work was sometimes crude. Although somewhat reclusive, he was described as reasonable, responsive to questions, and retaining his sense of humour. A letter written in 1929, five years after admission, was stilted and showed evidence of poverty of content of speech.

In 1930, at the age of seventy, he was transferred to Napsbury Hospital. By this time his behaviour had become obviously bizarre. He insisted on wearing many layers of clothes, even in summer, and avoided washing, bathing, shaving, and undressing. He was inordinately fond of drinking liquid paraffin, and also took to rubbing this in his hair. He spoke in a rambling incoherent way. He was also noted to be physically feeble and may have showed some signs of intellectual impairment. Even so, he was able to appreciate his pleasant surroundings and his art was reported as having lost none of its skill. Over the next few years he developed signs of arteriosclerosis and at the age of 76 he suffered a stroke. After this he became increasingly withdrawn and incoherent, and was hostile when approached. He died at the age of 78 of renal failure.

Fig. 10.2

patients had ventricular:brain ratios which were two standard deviations or greater than the control mean. The degree of enlargement was much less than that reported in patients with dementia, but was considered to be comparable to the degree of enlargement found in schizophrenia. As in schizophrenia, ventricular enlargement in paraphrenia has also been found to be unrelated to prior duration of illness or to outcome three years later (Hymas *et al.* 1989).

Abnormal premorbid personality: Roth and co-workers (Kay and Roth 1961; see also Mayer-Gross *et al.* 1969) considered this to be the rule in late paraphrenia. The patients' relatives frequently described them as having been narrow-minded, quarrelsome, unsociable, sensitive, or cold-hearted; commonly they made statements such as '(she is) not ill but exaggeratedly herself' or 'I always expected this to happen' when the patient became ill. The patients tended to live in isolation, were often unmarried, and several belonged to obscure religious sects. These observations were backed up in two formal studies (Kay *et al.* 1976; Herbert and Jacobson 1967) which both found a high rate of schizoid or paranoid traits. Kay and Roth, however, made the point that simplistic statements did not fully capture the quality of the personalities of many of their late paraphrenic patients, who showed positive as well as negative attributes, and had strengths as well as vulnerabilities.

The late age of onset: Although it seems likely that paraphrenia should be regarded as a form of schizophrenia, the question remains as to why the disorder should take such a form with increasing age of onset. No definite answer can be given, but the point can be made that this is part of a larger issue of age-related differences in the presentation of schizophrenia.

Bleuler (1911) regarded it as well accepted that individuals who developed schizophrenia in adolesence or early adult life were for the most part hebephrenics and catatonics, whereas those becoming ill later showed a tendency to take the paranoid form of the disorder. This view was

Table 10.2 Rates of schizophrenia in the relatives of patients with late paraphrenia (from Bridge and Wyatt 1980)

Study	Number of patients	Age range of patients	Prevalence in		
			Parents (%)	Siblings (%)	Children (%)
Funding (1961)	7	>50	1.0	2.5	1.4
Kay (1963)	57	>65	2.1	4.9	7.3
Herbert and Jacobson (1967)	46	>65	4.3	13.0	–

NB: rates in relatives are those for schizophrenia and paraphrenia combined.

formalized by Fish (Fish 1962/Hamilton 1984) who, as illustrated in Table 10.3, showed unequivocally that as age of onset increases paranoid presentations become more common at the expense of hebephrenic and catatonic forms. Thus, with increasing age, two trends are discernible: on the one hand there is a shift of symptoms, with catatonic phenomena, affective abnormality, and formal thought disorder dropping out as delusions and hallucinations become more prominent; on the other, the severity of the deterioration becomes progressively less marked. Paraphrenia can easily be viewed as a continuation of this trend, with delusions and hallucinations coming to take up almost all of the clinical picture while the development of deterioration becomes attenuated and delayed.

The female sex preponderance: Although there was no excess of female cases in Kraepelinian paraphrenia (except in one subtype, paraphrenia expansiva), this has been very marked in all the series of late paraphrenics. As with the age of onset, there is reason to believe that this key feature of paraphrenia is recognizable as an exaggeration of a trend which is detectable in schizophrenia as it occurs in older age groups.

The relevant observation was, once again, first made by Bleuler (1911). Quoting figures from his own hospital, he found that schizophrenia showed a slight male predominance at the youngest ages of onset. The sex ratio equalized at a point between the ages of 30 and 40. After this an excess of female cases became progressively more evident until all of the small number of cases beginning at the age of 50 or older were women. This

Table 10.3 Age of onset of classical subtypes in 110 chronic schizophrenic patients (from Fish 1962/Hamilton 1984)

Age group (years)	Hebephrenic	Catatonic	Paranoid
Up to 19	4	7	—
20–24	2	7	8
25–29	7	8	10
30–34	4	7	7
35–39	—	5	11
40–44	—	1	7
45–49	1	—	4
50–54	—	—	6
55–59	—	—	3
Over 60	—	—	1

finding has been amply confirmed in later studies (reviewed by Lewine 1980; Gold 1984).

The association with deafness: Initially noted by Roth and co-workers, a high prevalence of deafness among late paraphrenics has been found in all subsequent studies (see Grahame 1982, Hassett *et al*. 1992). Only one study has investigated this apparent association further; this was carried out by Cooper *et al*. (1974).

These authors compared 54 patients with paranoid psychoses (not otherwise specified) and 57 age- and sex-matched patients with manic-depressive psychosis; in both groups the onset was at the age of 50 or older. The paranoid patients showed greater hearing loss than the affective patients for all sound frequencies, although the differences were significant in only four out of the six comparisons made. In the affective patients, the rates of deafness were only marginally above the general population rates, whereas in the paranoid patients it was three times higher. Other analyses strongly suggested that the deafness antedated the onset of psychosis in a high proportion of the paranoid but not the affective patients.

The association of late paraphrenia with deafness is thus robust, but the reason for it remains conjectural. For a number of years the leading, in fact the only, explanatory hypothesis has been that deafness conspires with a predisposed personality to produce social isolation, and that this then paves the way for development of psychotic symptoms. If nothing else, this idea must now be regarded as dated.

Treatment of paraphrenia

All authorities are agreed that, as expected, late paraphrenia responds to neuroleptic drugs. This was convincingly, if rather informally, demontrated by Post (1966): his study spanned the introduction of neuroleptic drugs, allowing him to compare a group of 20 untreated patients with a later group of 71 patients which was treated. None of the first group lost their symptoms, in contrast to 40 (56 per cent) who showed partial remissions and 22 (31 per cent) complete remissions of active symptoms. The vast majority of patients, however, did not gain insight, and over half of the whole group showed some symptoms or remained actively psychotic during the follow-up period.

According to Post (1966) the dosage of neuroleptics required to control symptoms was unexceptional or even low (thioridazine 75–600 mg/day or trifluoperazine 15–30 mg/day). Roth and co-workers (see Mayer-Gross *et al*. 1969) took a different view, commenting that sometimes very high doses were needed. Other treatments have only been advocated as adjuncts to neuroleptics. ECT was recommended by Post (1966) and Herbert and

Jacobson (1967); this was felt to be most helpful when depressive symptoms were prominent.

Paranoia

The history of the term paranoia, as recounted by Lewis (1970), is long and troubled. The term was current in ancient Greece where it had a wide range of meanings, being used in a medical sense for dementia and delirium, and also colloquially to denote madness, folly, or going astray. Paranoia was re-introduced as a concept in the eighteenth century; the term initially had the strict connotation of dementia, but its use rapidly widened to include virtually any abnormal mental state. The term was re-introduced twice more in the nineteenth century, first by Heinroth, and later and more successfully by Kahlbaum; in both cases it was used to refer to states characterized largely or solely by delusions. Kahlbaum's particular contribution was to identify paranoia as an essentially stable disorder, in contrast to most other psychotic disorders which he considered to pass through various stages and culminate in dementia. Once again the term quickly became debased: over the next 50 years, although the core meaning of delusional remained, its application became so wide that as many as half of all mental hospital patients were considered to be suffering from some form of paranoid state.

Kraepelinian paranoia

Once again it was Kraepelin (1913*b*) who delimited the modern concept of paranoia. He came to the conclusion, largely out of necessity, that no matter how disorders presenting with delusions were classified – into those with and without hallucinations, those with or without an identifiable organic basis, or those pursuing a schizophrenic or a paraphrenic course – there remained a small group of awkward exceptions. The essential feature of these cases was the insidious development of a system of delusions which were logical, well integrated, and without gross internal contradictions. This system remained essentially unchanged for years or decades. Finally, the disorder left large areas of mental life untouched or nearly so: thinking was sensible, behaviour was reasonable, and the personality remained perfectly preserved.

In the Kraepelinian sense paranoia was a rare disorder: it accounted for less than 1 per cent of hospital admissions, although this undoubtedly underestimated the true frequency, as many cases did not require institutional care. From the limited figures he had available, the onset was most frequently between the ages of 30 and 40. Sometimes it was later than this, and occasionally the beginning of the symptoms could be traced back to early adult life or adolescence. There seemed to be a preponderance of male cases, with the male-to-female ratio being just over two to one.

The disorder developed mostly, but not always, very gradually, so that as a rule the onset could be dated only approximately. Sometimes there was a prodromal period in which abnormal ideas emerged in partial form and then disappeared or were forgotten about. Typically, the first sign was the development of delusions of reference, misinterpretation, and misidentification which became increasingly pervasive and related to each other in intricate ways: a movement of the hand, a shrug of the shoulders, the glances of passers-by would all seem to have mysterious meanings; remarks at a neighbouring table contained hidden allusions or pointed to some dimly perceived secret; there would be references to the patient in plays, books, and newspapers; his clothes were being copied by numerous people; he would keep meeting the same individuals, who must be watching him. These beliefs often came to be accompanied by delusional memories. Sometimes these merely took the form of false constructions which were placed on real past events, as in patients who recalled intimations of their future destiny that were given to them in childhood, or traced back suspicious observations to many years ago. But in other cases events which were clearly wholly fictitious would be described, for instance meetings with prominent individuals.

Eventually—sometimes suddenly, sometimes maturing over years—an explanation of all that had been happening would form in the patient's mind and crystallize into a central unshakeable delusion. This was invariably either persecutory or grandiose in nature. Although this explanation would be extremely unlikely and have only the flimsiest justification, characteristically it would not contain any absolute impossibilities. To a certain extent it could even be considered to be an understandable, if pathological, realization of the fears, wishes, and hopes of many individuals. (This important feature of paranoia was later to become important as the 'non-bizarre' quality of the delusions). Thereafter, a tightly-knit delusional system developed where the central abnormal belief and surrounding referential delusions supported and reinforced each other, and contradictions and unclear points would be thought through laboriously until they were resolved.

Other symptoms were inconspicuous or absent. In particular, auditory hallucinations never occurred. Visual experiences, on the other hand, were not uncommon. Typically, these took the form of isolated visionary experiences, of stars, shining figures, divine apparitions, often occurring at night. In some cases these could be construed as illusions (for example a cloud taking on the form of an apocalyptic animal), or as having taken place during a dream-like state; in others the experience could not be disentangled from delusional memories (as in a patient who stated that she saw Heaven open at the age of four). Affect was objectively normal, although there could be mood colourings in keeping with the content of the central delusion, for example suspiciousness or exaggerated self-confidence. Some patients became withdrawn, or took to writing obscure documents, or moved around from place to place, but in general behaviour remained surprisingly normal; many patients continued to work.

At some point the clinical development would reach a standstill. The central delusion would be elaborated no further and the referential delusions which supported and nourished it would abate to some extent. It could sometimes be observed that the abnormal ideas became less preoccupying, or no longer seemed to have the emotional investment they once had. Often, the delusions themselves and what they were believed to be founded on became indistinct. But beyond this, deterioration to even the mildest degree did not occur.

Kraepelin subdivided paranoia into three subtypes based on the content of the central delusion. The *persecutory form* was the most common type: in the face of continual observation the patient came to believe that he was being conspired against by a person or organization, a sister-in-law, a colleague, the mayor, the freemasons, etc.. In the *jealous form*, the same kinds of experiences were seized on as evidence of a partner's infidelity; in this form delusional memories often figured prominently. Subsumed under the *grandiose form* were patients who believed they had invented things — typically useless and sometimes already in existence — and the supporting referential delusions often revolved around machinations to suppress or steal these. There could also be delusions of high descent, where the patient found that he was continually being subjected to tests of his worthiness for his future position, conspired against by the rest of the aristocracy, etc.; religious delusions, of being a prophet or saint; and finally erotomania. Kraepelin also alluded to a hypochondriacal form of paranoia. However, he stated that, while hypochondriacal beliefs were often voiced by patients with paranoia, he was unable to find any cases where the theme of the central belief was exclusively hypochondriacal in nature.

None of these subtypes departed in any significant way from the general account given above; in particular, the association of the central delusion with multiple, clear-cut delusions of reference, misinterpretation, and misidentification was described in each case. Kraepelin was ambivalent about the inclusion of a fifth disorder under the heading of paranoia. This was the querulous paranoid state, where a patient became preoccupied by a real or supposed wrong and pursued his case vigorously and determinedly, usually dragging it through a succession of courts. Originally, he included it as a 'secondary form' of paranoia (Kraepelin 1905), but by 1913 (Kraepelin 1913*b*), he had decided that it was more closely allied to other disorders. The querulous paranoid state is discussed further below.

Kraepelin was never entirely happy with the concept of paranoia. As described by Kendler (1988), he conceded that a number of disorders could exhibit a similar picture, particularly in their early stages, and so paranoia should be diagnosed reluctantly, after everything else had been excluded. Later, he considered whether the disorder was in reality a form of schizophrenia running a particularly slow and mild course, but seemed to have decided that this was not the case. This latter difficulty, in particular, refused to go away and was widely discussed as 'the paranoia question'. Bleuler (1911) succinctly stated the central clinical uncertainty: '. . . it may be possible that paranoia is an entirely chronic schizophenia which is so mild that it could just about lead to delusional ideas; its less striking symptoms, however, are so lacking in prominence that we cannot demonstrate them. I would consider this extremely probable if it were more common that an originally pure paranoia at a later stage also develops schizophrenic symptoms. Only in a very few cases have we been forced to change our diagnosis from paranoia to schizophrenia and among these there were none that were not right from the start suspected of being schizophrenic. Unfortunately, such experiences are not sufficient proof for the basic difference between the two diseases since paranoia is very rare among hospital patients.'

Clearly, the stage was set for the kind of follow-up study carried out by Mayer in paraphrenia. This eventually appeared when Kolle (1931) followed-up (or rather re-examined the case notes of) 19 patients diagnosed as suffering from paranoia by Kraepelin and his colleagues. This was done between 4 and 22 years after the diagnosis was originally made. Kolle excluded two cases in which Kraepelin had added 'manic predisposition' or 'possible manic-depressive psychosis' to the diagnosis. Of the remaining 17 cases he excluded 7 more on various grounds: one had experienced ecstatic visionary experiences and later in the course of her illness was prone to talk incoherently about Hitler. Another developed bizarre delusions of being affected by radiation and described imaginary blows to his chest. Another had a history of alcoholism and his paranoid delusion followed in the wake of an admission for delirium tremens. Another ultimately became withdrawn and lived a hermit-like existence. In the rest, the reasons for exclusion were not specified.

The remaining 10 cases fitted without difficulty into the definition of paranoia according to Kraepelin. However, Kolle argued that in all these cases the delusion showed some of the phenomenological characteristics of true, primary, or schizophrenic delusions. It is possible to construe from his lengthy argument on this point that the delusions lacked the characteristics of non-absurdity, systematization, and logical development specified by Kraepelin. This would be, however, to oversimplify a tortuous and largely impenetrable foray into the minutiae of German psychopathology. In any event, Kolle's conclusion was that primary delusions were diagnostic of schizophrenia and hence paranoia was a subtype of schizophrenia.

Apart from its relationship to schizophrenia, the concept of paranoia faced another difficulty. This was exemplified by the querulous paranoid state described above. Having originally classed this with paranoia, Kraepelin came to feel that it was different, being struck by its precipitation by external causes rather than arising gradually through an internal change, and by the fact that it did not seem to have such far-reaching effects as other forms of paranoia. However, it was not at all clear that querulous paranoid patients adhered to either Kraepelin's first or second classifications. As Bleuler (1911) stated: 'We find numerous transitions from simply unbearable people to the paranoid litigants with marked delusions. The best solution perhaps is to draw a line somewhere in the middle of the scale and place the half that do not have real delusions there and count the others as paranoid.' The scope of the problem was widened by Jaspers (1959) who argued that exactly the same point could be made about individuals with morbid jealousy, as well as probably applying to other groups such as cranky inventors and world reformers. It seemed that any definition of paranoia would inevitably encompass some individuals who were not obviously psychotic, and perhaps not even ill in any meaningful sense of the term.

As with paraphrenia but more so, Kraepelin's concept of paranoia was vulnerable to attack. Yet, despite Kolle's argument that the disorder was not distinct from schizophrenia, and notwithstanding other serious nosological uncertainties, at the end of the classical period there were many who believed that it was a genuine clinical entity (see Fish 1962/Hamilton 1984). This undoubtedly reflected the fact that, in spite of its rarity, clear-cut examples of patients with the disorder could be documented. A famous, and absolutely characteristic case of Kraepelinian paranoia is described in Fig. 10.3.

Contemporary paranoia

In the years leading up to the introduction of criterion-based approaches to psychiatric diagnosis, the concept of paranoia lapsed into much the same terminological inexactitude as it had done a century earlier. As described by Lewis (1970) and Kendler and Tsuang (1981), in Europe there continued to be controversy over whether the disorder was a form of schizophrenia or whether some cases at least were an independent entity. The lingering question of how far the definition of paranoia should include forms which were understandable as the response of a predisposed personality to adverse events led, in America, to a very loose usage of the diagnosis. British psychiatrists generally recognized that a series of paranoid 'states' existed which, if they had to commit themselves, they considered were probably more closely related to each other than to schizophrenia.

The relationship of paranoia to schizophrenia was thoroughly examined

Paranoia: the case of Ernst Wagner
(from Gaupp 1914, 1938)

Ernst Wagner was a teacher who, in 1913, committed what was at the time a sensational mass-murder. Two of his mother's brothers were mentally ill, one with delusions of persecution. A brother drank heavily. His mother was impulsive and unstable, and also litigious. The patient was described as lively and somewhat self-conscious, imaginative but with a tendency to arrogance and cynicism. He was also said to have a fanatical regard for the truth.

At the age of 27, whilst working as a teacher and at a time of sexual frustration, he committed some form of sexual act with animals (he never revealed the precise details). The next day he believed that others could tell what he had done by looking at him. Before long, he noticed that people were making remarks about him and pointing at him behind his back. He came to believe that groups of people standing together were laughing and jeering at him, that obscene remarks were being passed about him, and that he was an object of general derision. He took to carrying a loaded gun with him at all times so that he could shoot himself in case the police came for him.

After he married and moved to another village, his ideas did not develop further, although when he returned to his previous place of residence he still noticed all the previous mockery. Eventually, however, he began to notice friends and colleagues making remarks which showed that they knew about his abnormal sexual practices. He requested a transfer, but after this the same thing happened. By the age of 35 he had worked out a plan to murder the residents of the places he had lived in and then to kill himself. He also came to the conclusion that he should kill his family, as his children might carry the germ of the same or even worse sexual deviations. This caused him to postpone carrying out his plan.

At the age of 41 he cut the throats of his wife and children while they slept and then travelled to the village of his birth where he set fire to houses, shot dead eight men and severely wounded 16 others. It was clear from letters that he had posted just before the event that he intended to kill himself as well, but he was apprehended before he could do so.

When examined in custody, he was temporarily shaken that no one knew anything about his sexual misdemeanours, but soon returned to his belief that he had been persecuted for years. He tried unsuccessfully to have his case re-opened so that he could be proved mentally healthy and be sentenced to death. Apart from the above delusion, and a belief that bestiality was a worse crime than murder, he remained an intelligent individual whose judgement in many matters was shrewd and accurate. His delusion fluctuated, subsiding only to flare up again—for instance when a patient who made animal noises to himself was admitted. In later years he wrote poems and several plays. He developed the belief that one of his plays was plagiarized and conducted an extended legal action about this, which he lost.

In 1932, over 30 years after the onset of his illness, the patient was presented at a meeting of psychiatrists and he spoke for two hours. According to Gaupp, it was concluded at this meeting that he showed no signs of schizophrenia. He remained interested in current affairs which he followed attentively through newspapers and the radio. A year before his death at the age of 64 he was reported to be well-informed about everything and to show excellent judgment. However he still believed that everyone in the asylum was talking about his bestiality.

Fig. 10.3

by Kendler (1980). First, following the example of DSM III, he renamed paranoia simple delusional disorder and established a set of criteria for it. These are shown in Fig. 10.4. The central requirements were presence of persecutory, grandiose, hypochondriacal, jealous delusions or other delusions, or pervasive delusions of reference (Kendler actually used the term ideas of reference). Hallucinations, a full affective syndrome, or symptoms suggestive of schizophrenia had to be absent. It was also specified that the delusions should be 'non-bizarre', an acknowledgment of Kraepelin's stipulation that the beliefs in paranoia should be logically constructed and not utterly impossibe. He then proceeded to subject the various follow-up studies of paranoid disorders which had been undertaken over the years to a critical, patient (and to anyone familiar with the stultifying effects of such an endeavour, even Herculean) review.

After sifting through the literature, Kendler was able to identify four follow-up studies of paranoia which met his criteria. The findings of these are shown in Table 10.4. After follow-up periods ranging from a few months to twenty years, the proportion of patients who had developed schizophrenia ranged from 3–13 per cent; one study suggested a higher proportion, but this was based on a sample of nine patients, two of whom became schizophrenic. Somewhat surprisingly, two of the studies indicated that a small minority of cases with paranoia (3 per cent and 6 per cent) evolved into affective psychosis over time; one of these, however, did not rigorously exclude affective symptoms at initial presentation. Most but not all patients meeting strict diagnostic criteria for paranoia thus showed diagnostic consistency over time. These studies also found that around three quarters of their patients were out of hospital at follow-up, two thirds had worked much of the time since their index admission, and about a third had had no further hospitalizations. Some of this last group showed improvement which could amount to social recovery.

Kendler's criteria for delusional disorder (paranoia)
(from Kendler 1980)

1. Onset of illness before age 60.
2. Nonbizarre delusions of any type (that is persecutory, grandiose, somatic, jealousy, etc.) and/or persistent, pervasive ideas of reference are present. These delusions are usually of a fairly systematized kind.
3. The symptoms have been present for a minimum of two weeks.
4. Persistent hallucinations of any kind are absent.
5. A full affective syndrome, either depressive or manic, is absent when the patient is delusional.
6. There are no symptoms suggestive of schizophrenia including prominent thought disorder, inappropriate affect, patently bizarre delusions, and first rank symptoms.
7. Symptoms suggestive of an acute or chronic brain syndrome are absent.

Fig. 10.4

The majority of patients who develop states characterized purely by delusions thus go on to follow a course similar to that outlined by Kraepelin for paranoia. Kendler therefore concluded that this evidence supported the view that the two disorders are independent. A small number of cases do evolve into schizophrenia, but this is still compatible with such a conclusion—as noted above, Kraepelin considered that the diagnosis of paranoia was essentially impossible to make cross-sectionally. More unexpectedly, some patients with paranoia may later develop manic-depressive psychosis. This finding remains unexplained, although it is possible that it is one facet of the perplexing issue of schizoaffective psychosis (see Chapter 11).

The question of the demarcation of paranoia from certain conditions which are only uncomfortably regarded as psychotic has not been answered nearly as clearly. There are patients who develop what are undoubtedly abnormal beliefs, which are circumscribed and persistent, and which are sometimes, but by no means always persecutory. The course is typically chronic and the outcome is often unfavourable. The prototypical example is, as mentioned above, the querulous paranoid state. One of the very few examples of this disorder is described in Fig. 10.5. Other English-language accounts of this rare disorder have been provided by Rowlands (1988) and Ungvari and Hollokoi (1993). The essential problem is that this state fulfils definitions of paranoia in all respects, even the strict criteria of Kendler, but it somehow seems to be fundamentally different from the Kraepelinian

Table 10.4 Outcome studies of paranoia/simple delusional disorder (from Kendler 1980)

Study	Numbers of patients	Follow-up period	Diagnosis unchanged	Diagnosis changed	Comment
Faergeman (1963)	9	5 years	7 (78%)	2 (22%) schizophrenia	Uncertain cases and cases presenting with bizarre delusions excluded by Kendler.
Johanson (1964)	52	Few months to 4½ years	46 (88%)	6 (12%) schizophrenia	No systematic follow-up. No follow-up diagnoses other than schizophrenia found.
Retterstol (1966, 1670)	163	5–15 years	132 (81%)	21 (13%) schizoprenia 10 (6%) ?manic-depressive	Good systematic follow-up. Some evidence that 6% of patients had affective disorder at follow-up.
Winokur (1977)	25	Few months to 20 years	23 (93%)	1 (4%) schizophrenia 1 (4%) ?manic-depressive	For 86% follow-up was longer than 6 months, for 34% longer than 2 years.

The querulous paranoid state
(from Kraepelin 1905)

A 38-year-old master tailor had previously become insolvent and at that time had fought out a fierce lawsuit with a creditor. Three years later he again fell into debt and, in the course of trying to prevent a creditor and a bailiff removing his furniture, he locked both of them up in his house while he lodged a complaint in court. The patient was tried for this and found guilty of false imprisonment.

A short, humorously treated account of the affair, which contained inaccuracies, appeared in a newspaper. The patient became angry and wrote a correction, only part of which was printed. A further enraged letter to the editor was responded to by publication of a full report of the proceedings. In this, the words 'master tailor' were printed in large type; the patient took offence at this and brought three legal actions against the newspaper. These actions were all rejected in the courts. The patient was not satisfied and gradually set in motion a series of appeals through higher and higher courts, eventually petitioning the Ministry of Justice, the Ministry of State, the Grand Duke, and the Emperor. After these failed the patient tried the experiment of complaining to the heads of the courts, appealed to the public, and was considering proposing disciplinary proceedings against the Public Prosecutor.

On examination, the patient was coherent and able to give a clear account of the history of events. On the subject of his court actions he expressed himself volubly and showed increased self-confidence and superiority, a certain satisfaction and readiness for battle. He was also exceedingly touchy—if pressed on whether he might have been mistaken in his interpretation of events, he immediately became mistrustful and raised the suspicion that the interviewer supported his opponents. He was never at a loss for an answer to objections, which he justified by quoting minutiae of the law; in prolonged conversation a wearisome diffuseness crept into his narrative. The patient believed that an attorney involved for the plaintiff in his original bankruptcy proceedings was the real source of his misfortunes. This was because, when he first wanted to bring an action against the editor of the newspaper, the clerk of the court dissuaded him from doing so, referring to this earlier proceedings—he believed that this attorney had prejudiced the clerk of the court against him, and also wished to ruin him. As a result, the clerk did not draw up the accusation properly; the Public Prosecutor gained an erroneous impression from it; the judges of several courts did not want to reverse verdicts once agreed to; and they were as a body prejudiced. He believed that the whole system of law had been obstructed via a conspiracy involving Freemasonry. He also believed that Jewish financiers played a part in the conspiracy as the newspaper which wrote about him was supported by them; and that the press was associated with the attorney in question. He believed that a whole

series of individuals were working together secretly to bring about his
ruin.

As a consequence of his incessant pestering of the authorities, the patient
was eventually pronounced to be mentally deranged, against which
opinion he adopted every possible legal means of redress. Meanwhile he
continued to carry on his business, and apart from writing innumerable
petitions, did not appear strange or troublesome. Because of his course
of action he had brought his family deeper and deeper into misfortune.
Nevertheless, in spite of every failure, he expected a happy outcome to his
case.

Fig. 10.5

paranoid patient who shows multiple delusions of reference, misinterpretation, and misidentification similar to those seen in schizophrenia.

There has been no empirical investigation of this issue, but there have
been two attempts to deal with it at a conceptual level. The first owes
much to the work of Jaspers (1959) who, originally in connection with
morbid jealousy, drew a distinction between abnormal beliefs which were
due to *process* and *development*. In the former case, a belief appears
which is essentially the first sign of an evolving psychosis (usually schizophrenia). The belief cannot be seen as arising comprehensibly from personality and experience; like delusions in general, its nature is ultimately
'un-understandable'. The psychosis may eventually manifest more florid
symptoms, but there is no absolute necessity for this to happen—the process
may arrest or spontaneously remit. The latter form of abnormal belief is
the outcome of an interaction between the individual and his environment
which brings a focus to his or her life and results in the development of
an idea which is certainly pathological, but always understandable—it is a
'hypertrophy' of an already abnormal personality in reaction to adverse
events. The contrasting features of processes and personality developments
as summarized by Fish (Fish 1962/Hamilton 1984) are shown in Table 10.5.

The main shortcoming of this approach is its fallibility in practice.
Whilst, theoretically, the distinction has a great deal of intuitive plausibility
and is backed by the intellectual weight of Jaspers, when it is applied to
any particular patient it depends ultimately on an evaluation of what is
understandable given the personality, background, experiences, and current
situation of the individual concerned. This is inevitably highly subjective,
and, as pointed out by Fish (Fish 1962/Hamilton 1984), clinicians vary considerably in what they will accept as understandable: some psychiatrists are
always ready to go to extraordinary lengths to construe obviously bizarre
experiences as comprehensible, whereas others take a distinctly narrow view

Table 10.5 Summary of differences between personality development and process (from Fish 1962/Hamilton 1984)

Personality development	Psychic process
Slow, gradual change analogous to the development of a child.	A new development that begins at a definite point in time.
Acute events do not signify a lasting change. The *status quo ante* is restored again.	Acute events signify a change which is not reversible (although the process can arrest).
The whole course of life can be understood from the predisposition of the personality	When an attempt is made to derive the changes from the personality a limit is found at a given point in time where something new appeared.
	There is a definite regularity of development and course of the changed personality, which can be understood in the same way as the normal events of psychic life and which possesses a new unity.

of what is normal and abnormal and confidently diagnose early schizophrenia, only to find themselves waiting a very long time for the full blown
syndrome to declare itself.

The second approach focuses not on the individual with the abnormal
belief, but on the phenomenological characteristics of the belief itself. The
proposal is that two quite different types can be distinguished. The first of
these, seen in schizophrenia and Kraepelinian paranoia, is *delusion proper*.
As described briefly in Chapter 1, and discussed more fully by Jaspers
(1959), Sims (1988), and Walker (1991), such delusions are essentially qualitatively different from normal beliefs. They are held in a way which seems
alien and quite different to the beliefs of normal individuals, and they are
justified by the patient in a characteristic, self-evidently illogical fashion.
It may be added that a delusion proper is rarely encountered as a solitary
phenomenon but is generally accompanied by other psychotic symptoms,
even if these are only delusions of reference and misinterpretation.

The second form of abnormal belief is *the overvalued idea*, a term which
was introduced by Wernicke, was elaborated on by Jaspers, and has been
given its only contemporary account by McKenna (1984). The overvalued
idea is a preoccupying abnormal belief which often appears following a key
event and which comes to single-mindedly preoccupy an individual, often
indefinitely. According to all definitions the idea is solitary, that is, it is
not accompanied by delusions of reference and misinterpretation or other
delusions. Phenomenologically, the nature of the belief seems different
from that of delusion proper, resembling more than anything else a quantitative exaggeration of the passionate political, religious, and ethical beliefs
of normal individuals. Overvalued ideas most commonly arise in the setting
of abnormal personality, though they can sometimes be seen in manic-
depressive psychosis, and occasionally as the prodrome to schizophrenia
or an organic state. The disorder in which the concept of the overvalued
idea is classically encountered is, in fact, the querulous paranoid state. The
term has also been considered to be applicable to one form of morbid
jealousy, to hypochondriasis and dysmorphophobia (and also, according to
McKenna, to anorexia nervosa).

The phenomenological concept of the overvalued idea places the debate
about the scope of the concept of paranoia on a clinical footing and avoids
the necessity of dragging in what are essentially speculative arguments
about the factors involved in the development of a belief. It also has the
advantage of a certain objectivity — the rule of thumb is that beliefs which
are delusions will always be accompanied by delusions of reference and
misinterpretation (or other obviously psychotic symptoms), whereas if the
belief is entirely isolated it is likely to be an overvalued idea. The difficulty
with this approach to the partitioning of paranoia is that its simplicity is
more apparent than real: sometimes patients with established schizophrenia

show delusions which are overwhelmingly preoccupying and solitary. In other cases the evolution of an abnormal belief does not seem to follow any simple rules, with abnormal personality, earlier periods of psychosis, and perhaps even organic factors all needing to be taken into consideration.

Paranoia is clearly a resilient disorder and one which has not proved to be easy to dismantle into smaller parts. Perhaps the best way to regard it is as having a core that cannot be explained away, but which can never be defined perfectly. This core of paranoia is the disorder described by Kraepelin, consisting of the development of multiple delusions of reference supporting a central explanatory delusion. The central delusion tends not to be bizarre and the network of referential delusions tend to be intricate, but their difference from more florid delusions, and hence from schizophrenia, is a only matter of degree. The vast majority of individuals who develop such states will not go on to develop a wider range of schizophrenic symptoms, or deterioration, or other psychiatric disorders. However, diagnosis in psychiatry being what it is, paranoia will inevitably describe some initial presentations which, in the fullness of time, reveal themselves to be schizophrenic, schizoaffective, or manic-depressive in nature; it will also apply to some states whose 'process' or genuinely delusional quality is be open to question.

The aetiology of paranoia

The discussion here is restricted exclusively to paranoia in its principal, psychotic, 'process' sense. The findings and conclusions are mainly taken from Kendler's (1980) review. An account of the scanty knowledge on the development of other forms of paranoia can be found in McKenna (1984).

Family history: Three studies were considered suitable for inclusion by Kendler (Kolle 1931; Debray 1975; Winokur 1977). These found frequencies of schizophrenia in first degree relatives of between 2.4 per cent and 3.2 per cent. This risk is clearly higher than that for the general population of 0.8 per cent, but much lower than that of around 10 per cent for the first degree relatives of schizophrenic patients. All three studies also found appreciable rates of affective disorder in the relatives, of between 1.1 per cent, 2.4 per cent, and 5 per cent; in the last of these studies, however, the frequency was no higher than in a control group of normal individuals.

Two of these three studies also found a clustering of 'pathological personalities' (5.7 per cent) or 'soft paranoid syndromes' (2.4 per cent) in the relatives of paranoid patients. A significant excess of paranoid personality disorder in the relatives of patients was the only one of the above findings to be replicated in a subsequent family study of paranoia which used diagnostic criteria (Kendler *et al.* 1985).

Premorbid personality: Although the retrospective determination of pre-morbid personality faces methodological difficulties, three studies have provided worthwhile information by comparing patients with paranoia with those with schizophrenia. These (Bonner 1951; Johanson 1964; Retterstol 1966) all found that patients with paranoia were less likely to be schizoid, introverted, or submissive than schizophrenic patients; two (Bonner 1951; Retterstol 1966) also suggested an increased frequency of extraverted, dominant, or oversensitive traits. Perhaps the strongest con-clusion that can be drawn from such findings is that the association with premorbid schizoid disposition found in schizophrenia (see Chapter 5) is absent in paranoia.

Other aetiological factors

The slight sex preponderance of males found by Kraepelin has found little support subsequently. As reviewed by Kendler (1980), two substantial series (Kolle 1931; Retterstol 1966) found rates of 47.5 per cent and 53 per cent for men.

Four studies, however, did suggest, in line with Kraepelin, that paranoia had a significantly later age of onset than schizophrenia. Two of these (Bonner 1951; Rimon *et al.* 1965) recorded a mean age of onset of 46; two other studies (Kolle 1931; Retterstol 1966) pointed towards a peak age of onset between the ages of 35 and 50.

Treatment of paranoia

Surprisingly little has been written about this subject, no doubt reflecting to some extent the lack of clarity about the boundaries of the disorder. Once again, the best evidence comes from Kendler's (1980) review. The studies reviewed were generally poor (for instance, lacking controls), but it could be concluded that at least a subgroup of patients show a response to neuro-leptics. One open trial of ECT in a small group of patients with paranoia found that the response was comparatively poor (Huston and Locher 1948).

Other paranoid disorders

Paranoid depression

In the course of describing a number of subtypes of manic-depressive psychosis (see Chapter 11), Kraepelin (1913*b*) singled out a particular form which he called paranoid melancholia. Such patients showed a depressed mood which was often associated with retardation, agitation, ideas or delu-sions of hopelessness, or guilt. At the same time they exhibited persecutory and referential delusions, that they were being watched, spied on, threat-ened with murder, etc.. These beliefs were accompanied in some cases by auditory hallucinations of a derogatory kind.

The definitive study of paranoid delusions in depressive psychosis was carried out by Lewis (1934) as part of a survey of 61 cases of melancholia (as described in more detail in Chapter 11, his cases conformed closely to modern definitions of manic-depressive psychosis, depressed type). Persecutory and referential ideas, ranging from mere impressions of contempt, jeering, or hostility on the part of others, to full delusions of being poisoned, followed about, shot at, tormented etc., were found in 43 out of the 61 patients. Lewis went on to consider the prevailing view that such beliefs were not truly persecutory, but were an elaboration of depressive self-depreciation and self-blame, according to the formula, 'I'm worthless; others know it; they treat me accordingly; they put slights on me, they persecute me.' On examination of his patients' beliefs, he found that 17 thought they were getting their just desserts, although this conclusion had to be qualified in some cases. Seven patients expressed resentment or hostility about their persecution in their words or behaviour. Another eight, while conceding their sinfulness or wrongdoing, also described persecution which they could not account for. Finally, 11 patients felt they should take no blame whatsoever for what they were experiencing. Lewis concluded that the received wisdom that the paranoid ideas and delusions seen in depression were understandable in terms of the mood disturbance was 'to make the matter very simple, simpler than the data permit'.

Since Lewis' survey, there has been almost total silence on the topic of paranoid depression, at least in the English-language literature. Just about the only contemporary author to discuss the matter has been Fish (Fish 1962/Hamilton 1984). He proposed that some persecutory delusions in depression were an exaggerated form of lifelong paranoid personality traits. He also made a case for premorbid obsessional traits or morbid anxiety becoming transformed into persecutory ideas in the context of depression; here though, the arguments became decidely convoluted. Ultimately, he conceded that in some cases the delusions of paranoid depression went considerably beyond anything that was understandable.

The occurrence of persecutory and referential delusions which are not mood-congruent in manic-depressive psychosis is currently tacitly accepted. Such patients are not easily understood as suffering from a variety of schizoaffective disorder, since, in terms of other episodes, outcome and response to treatment, their illnesses can be entirely typical of affective disorder.

The sensitive delusion of reference

This term was coined by Kretschmer (1927) and has become enshrined in the British and European literature on paranoia. It is usually considered (for example Sims 1988) to describe individuals with a personality characterized by shyness and certain other traits, who, in the face of a stigma such as illegitimacy or physical deformity, or following some humiliating experience, develop self-torturing ruminations. These eventually become held with a delusion-like intensity and fixity. The important point is that the belief is not a delusion proper but is understandable in terms of the sufferer's personality and experiences, and that the resultant state is not psychotic in the strict sense of the term. In contrast to true paranoia, there are reasonable prospects for recovery.

It is instructive to read Kretschmer's (1927) original account of the sensitive delusion of reference, parts of which are available in English translation (Hirsch and Shepherd 1974). As part of his own, sowewhat idiosyncratic classification of personality, Kretschmer described a 'sensitive' type. This referred to individuals with gentle, insecure natures who were ethically or spiritually inclined, and who, while appearing quiet and reserved, felt experiences deeply to the extent of being consumed by them. When the delicate emotional life of these individuals was subjected to forms of conflict with which they could not cope, the sensitive delusion of reference was liable to develop. He described a number of examples, of which two were translated.

The first case was a 29-year-old woman who had previously experienced a prolonged grief reaction following the death of her mother. She became sexually attracted to a fellow worker but at the same time tried to suppress her feelings; this developed into a continual struggle. Eventually she confided in a relative who became exasperated and shouted about the matter by an open window. After this the patient began to believe that remarks were being passed about her, and started to notice indications in the newspapers that the police were coming to arrest her. Over the next two to three years she became more and more psychotic, showing persecutory and referential delusions, auditory and perhaps also visual hallucinations, all in the setting of depression, anxiety, and self-reproach. After another five to seven years she improved and was discharged from hospital. A few years later she relapsed and was re-admitted. After a further 12 years she made a full recovery, returned to work, and on follow-up showed no sign of schizophrenic deterioration.

The second case concerned a middle aged man who shortly after being passed over for promotion at work, developed fluctuating feelings of listlessness and restlessness. These developed into a state characterized by nervousness, excitability and agitation, accompanied by sleep disturbance, loss of appetite, and constipation. At a later point he became suspicious, believed that he had stared too long at the wife of the colleague who had been promoted over him, and elaborated this idea until he believed that she was at the centre of a conspiracy to drive him from his job and destroy him; this involved the police and a whole army of adversaries, including his own wife. This state improved over several weeks. He returned to work, but the same symptoms recurred, first a few months later and then again after a further two years. Afterwards he remained well until his death some years later.

While both these cases could certainly be considered unusual, it is clear that neither of them conform to the present day stereotype of an isolated, easily understandable persecutory belief developing in a thin-skinned individual. The first case had a florid, relapsing illness in which there were both schizophrenic symptoms and a full affective syndrome. The second would seem to be classifiable as a case of paranoid depression.

Etats passionnels

French psychiatry has traditionally recognized a much larger number of paranoid disorders than anywhere else in the world. One reason for this was the sway that Magnan, a contemporary of Kraepelin's, and his followers Capgras and Serieux exerted (and seemingly continue to exert) over the classification of psychotic disorders in this country. They insisted on a much narrower definition of schizophrenia than elsewhere, and correspondingly developed a wider and more detailed classification of paraphrenia-like and purely delusional states (see Pichot 1982).

The other reason was the somewhat maverick influence of de Clérambault, who postulated the existence of what he called *états passionels*. De Clérambault distinguished three types of presentation of this disorder: the querulous paranoid state, morbid jealousy, and particularly erotomania, with which his name has become synonymous. In all three conditions, but most strenuously in the last (see de Clérambault 1942; Baruk 1959), he argued that the nature of the belief was isolated, preoccupying, and phenomenologically distinct from the delusions of paranoia and schizophrenia. The patient with an *état passionnel*, he stated, was in a state of constant striving and advanced to his goal consciously and determinedly; there was a 'hypersthenic' quality about this behaviour which extended to the point of hypomania. He acknowledged that some cases eventually gave way to schizophrenia, but pointed out that when this happened the quality of the belief also changed to one that was more obviously delusional. While de Clérambault's views echo what has already been stated about the querulous paranoid state and they are in sympathy with many accounts of morbid jealousy (see Cobb 1979), as applied to erotomania, ironically they have been largely forgotten. The existence of erotomania as a pure, not frankly, psychotic disorder is currently regarded as, at best, controversial (Enoch and Trethowan 1979).

The concept of the *état passionnel* is clearly closely similar to that of the overvalued idea and the clinical forms such disorders are alleged to take obviously overlap. It is also noteworthy that both concepts embody elements of the process:personality development distinction advocated by Jaspers and Fish.

Monosymptomatic hypochondriacal psychosis

Kraepelin (1913*b*) stated that he had not been able to find an unequivocal case of paranoia which was characterized only, or at least predominantly, by a hypochondriacal delusion. When Kolle (1931, cited by Lewis 1970) later enumerated the different forms that the delusions of paranoia could take, he included persecution, grandeur, litigation, jealousy, love, envy, hate, honour, and the supernatural; bodily illness was noticeably absent from the list. More recent studies have done little to change this view: for example, Winokur (1977) did not find hypochondriasis to be the major theme in any of his 29 cases, and subsidiary hypochondriacal delusions were found in only 3.

The concept of hypochondriacal paranoia, renamed monosymptomatic hypochondriacal psychosis, was revived by Munro (1980). He defined this as a rare disorder characterized by a single hypochondriacal delusion that is sustained over a considerable period, sometimes for many years. As in other forms of paranoia, the state is not secondary to another disorder, and the personality remains otherwise well preserved. According to Munro, the hypochondriacal belief is fundamentally delusional in character, and is only superficially similar to hypochondriasis of a neurotic type. He included delusions of infestation; dysmorphic delusions of ugliness, misshapenness, or overprominence of a feature; the olfactory paranoid syndrome where an individual believes he gives off a foul smell; and also some instances of chronic pain syndromes and anorexia nervosa where the symptom has a recognizably delusional quality. Such patients seek out a succession of medical opinions and are insistent that there is a physical cause for their symptoms. They become angry and disdainful if this is not accepted. Although the patients may give the impression of being hallucinated, for example reporting seeing insects or being able to smell the odour they believe they emit, in most cases the apparent abnormal perception is in reality a delusional misinterpretation. In his own series of patients Munro (unpublished) also stated that around half showed ideas of reference. The prognosis is poor and treatment is usually considered unsatisfactory. However, Munro has claimed that the neuroleptic pimozide produces an excellent or fair response in nearly two-thirds of patients.

The concept of hypochondriacal paranoia or monosymptomatic hypochondriacal psychosis provides an exceptionally clear illustration of the difficulties that are run into when attempts are made to separate psychotic and non-psychotic forms of paranoia. Hypochondriacal delusions are commonly encountered in schizophrenia. Hypochondriacal beliefs which are firmly held but not necessarily bizarre or fantastic are also seen in manic-depressive psychosis, depressed type. Finally, as hypochondriasis (Merskey 1979), dysmorphophobia (Hay 1970; Andreasen and Bardach 1977), and parasitophobia (Hopkinson 1973) isolated disorders have been described which are similar, if not identical to those identified by Munro, except that the beliefs are not considered to be delusional in nature. When confronted with a hypochondriacal conviction, the clinician has to fall back on one of two not fully satisfactory approaches: either he or she must try and determine whether the patient holds the belief with an intensity and non-understandability which qualifies it as a delusion — a hazardous and highly subjective undertaking — or he or she can fall back on invoking the concept of an overvalued idea in all cases where there is no other evidence of psychosis, in particular referential delusions — a strategy which under-estimates the complexity of the presentations and probably will not predict very well whether or not the patient will respond to neuroleptic drugs.

Conclusion

In 1912 Kraepelin (cited by Lewis 1970) considered whether, in view of its shabby record, the disease classification of paranoia should be dropped altogether. Over 50 years later, Lewis concluded emphatically that the term should only be retained in psychiatric usage in its descriptive sense and not as a diagnostic category. A paranoid syndrome was merely one in which there were delusions which could not be immediately derived from a pre-vailing abnormal mood state; it carried no implications about chronicity, permanence, curability, presence of hallucinations, integrity of personality or aetiology; its recognition was a preliminary to diagnosis, and this would invariably turn out to be one of the major categories of mental disorder.

The conclusion of this chapter is rather different. It is that, in the clinical sense at least, paraphrenia and paranoia both exist. Patients showing the kinds of initial presentation first described by Kraepelin certainly seem to be encountered from time to time. Some, although not all of these patients go on to pursue a course which is uncharacteristic of schizophrenia. For paraphrenia, it seems clear that the cross-sectional and longitudinal dif-ferences from schizophrenia are merely quantitative; but in paranoia they edge towards the qualitative. Aetiologically, the picture is undoubtedly more muddy. While a case can be made that neither paraphrenia nor paranoia is separable from schizophrenia, a more honest conclusion would have to be that in paraphrenia there is probably some modification of the underlying pathological process, and that in paranoia the weight of the evidence points to a separate cause altogether.

11

Schizoaffective and other atypical psychoses

While it is widely accepted that the boundaries of schizophrenia are not well defined, when it comes to its relationship to the other main variety of functional psychosis, manic-depressive psychosis, the border is positively disputatious. The orthodox view, still held by many, is that schizophrenia and manic-depressive psychosis are entirely separate entities. There have also, as described in Chapter 4, always been some who have regarded the two presentations merely as points along a continuum of psychosis, and this is currently a respectable, even fashionable position. What both sides in the argument would accept, however, is that patients exist who show combinations of schizophrenic and affective symptomatology, sometimes simultaneously, sometimes at different points in the same episode of illness, and sometimes at widely separated points in time.

A comprehensive list of what it might mean when a patient presents with a combination of schizophrenic and affective symptoms has been compiled by Kendell (1986). It could be that the patient is suffering from schizophrenia with some incidental affective symptoms — that is, the mood colourings described in Chapter 1. Alternatively, he or she could have manic-depressive psychosis with some incidental schizophrenic symptoms — for example the mood congruent delusions and hallucinations which can complicate both phases of this disorder. Or the patient could have been unlucky enough to have developed both schizophrenia and affective psychosis; there is no reason to suppose that this should not occasionally happen as a chance combination. Another possibility is that there exists a third psychosis, unrelated to schizophrenia or manic-depressive psychosis which shows combinations of schizophrenic and affective symptoms, perhaps among other features. Conversely, it might be that the disorder is a genuine 'interform', reflecting unknown aetiological interactions between schizophrenia and manic-depressive psychosis. Finally, it is quite possible that some combination of the preceding five factors might be operating; the answer does not have to be simple.

Historically, the concept of schizoaffective psychosis, the term normally applied to patients who present with both schizophrenic and affective symptoms, has had two main themes. On the one hand it has described a disorder which has been more appropriatedly named cycloid psychosis, an alleged third form of functional psychosis, in which there are fluctuating schizophrenic and affective symptoms, and others besides. It also encompasses what might be referred to as schizoaffective psychosis proper, disorders characterized purely and simply by combinations of both schizophrenic and affective symptoms, either simultaneously or at different times. There are also a number of other atypical psychoses which have sometimes attracted the label schizoaffective. But before a critical evaluation of any of these disorders can be mounted, the discussion has to be informed by some understanding of the limits of the two main psychoses—how far schizophrenia can be complicated by affective symptoms and still be regarded as unquestionably schizophrenia, and vice-versa for manic-depressive psychosis.

The limits of schizophrenia and manic-depressive psychosis

The natural starting point for this exericise is, as usual, the writings of Kraepelin and Bleuler. As the architects of the concepts of schizophrenia and manic-depressive psychosis, not only did these authors give the relevant issues careful consideration, but their views also had the benefit of observations which were made and refined over a number of years.

Affective symptoms in schizophrenia

In 1913, as described in Chapter 2, Kraepelin (1913*a*) came to the conclusion that his earlier division of schizophrenia into paranoid, hebephrenic, and catatonic subtypes was inadequate. One reason for this was the incorporation of simple schizophrenia. Another was his separation of mild and severe forms of paranoid schizophrenia and also a form characterized principally by confusion of speech. But perhaps the most important reason was Kraepelin's recognition of five new forms of schizophrenia in which there were severe, long-lasting intercurrent affective symptoms: he introduced two depressive forms (*simple depressive* and *delusional depressive dementia praecox*) and three where there were states of excitement as well (*circular, agitated*, and *periodic dementia praecox*). In all of these, the disorder was ushered in and subsequently characterized by pronounced depression and elevation of mood, and it ran a notably periodic course.

In the depressive forms of schizophrenia, anxiety, tearfulness, lack of interest, and dejection formed a long introductory phase. These symptoms could be accompanied by poor appetite and disorders of sleep, as well as by hypochondriasis, suicide attempts, and delusions of sin, guilt, and worthlessness; sometimes they were interrupted by stupor (and occasionally also brief periods of excitement). However, many delusions and hallucinations which were unrelated to the depressed mood were invariably also present, and the patients' objective emotional attitude and behaviour were out of keeping with the usual picture of depression. The common feature of the three excited forms was progression via one or more phases of elation and overactivity. As with the depressive forms, the mood change could be distinguished from that of manic-depressive psychosis by the presence of many florid delusions and hallucinations; speech which was completely incoherent or verbigerative rather than showing distractibility and flight of ideas; and behaviour which was bizarre, divorced from the surroundings, and in which catatonic phenomena abounded. In both the depressive and excited forms, a characteristic impoverishment of thought was evident from an early stage, and ultimately—sometimes after one or more periods of good remission—a typical state of schizophrenic deterioration was reached.

Under the headings of 'melancholic' and 'manic' conditions, Bleuler (1911) gave what is perhaps the definitive phenomenological analysis of depression and elation in schizophrenia. Depression, he stated, was one of the most frequent symptoms of acute schizophrenia. In many cases, this was an essentially normal reaction of unhappiness in the face of distressing experiences, or a painful subjective awareness of the effects of deterioration. Bleuler also considered that there were depressive states which stemmed from the disease process itself: sometimes these were easily identifiable as 'the usual schizophrenic melancholias'—that is schizophrenic mood colourings. In other cases, though, they showed all the features of depression seen in other disorders. But even when this was the case, schizophrenic depression was characterized by a strange lack of pervasiveness, a failure of the whole personality to be engaged: some patients criticized or laughed about their own depressive thoughts; others, even though apparently extremely distraught, carried on activities which were incompatible with depression: smearing faeces, interfering with the care of other patients, engaging in indiscriminate sexual intercourse, etc.. Even when the depressive affect seemed overwhelming, it still had something of the typical schizophrenic stiffness, superficiality, and exaggeratedness about it—one could not quite believe that deep painful feelings were present. Florid delusions and hallucinations, as accompaniments, were rarely absent. Sometimes depression and depressive delusions existed side by side with grandiose delusions, the patient being unhampered by the logical contradictions.

Likewise Bleuler described 'manic' states in schizophrenic patients, which could appear alone, or alternate with 'melancholic' conditions; they were often also seen in combination with mild catatonic features. In many cases, rather than being elated, the mood was one of hebephrenic-like capriciousness, such patients teasing, engaging in silly pranks, and making stupid puns and jokes; in these patients little real euphoria was seen. Often the mood was stilted, the patient was 'cheerful in a mechanical way'. Other cases, often those in transition to full-blown catatonic excitement, could

---

Fish's view on the presence of manic and depressive
symptoms in schizophrenia
(from Fish 1962/Hamilton 1984)

Elevated mood of the hypomanic variety is not common in schizophrenia,
although some chronic fantastic schizophrenics have a hypomanic mood.
These patients are cheerful, with marked pressure of talk, but the
fantastic content of their speech makes the diagnosis obvious. The
elevated mood in schizophrenia usually has none of the infectious gaiety
of true mania, but is one of exaltation and ecstasy. The patient has an
ecstatic transfigured look and the examiner is impressed by the lack of
rapport. Often the patient is not willing to talk about his feelings, but if
he does so he will talk about being in a state of grace, of an indescribable
happiness, or even use the word 'ecstasy'. Usually he believes that he has
been in a special type of relationship with the Almighty and may express
this by saying that God has spoken to him.

Depression is extremely common in the early stages of schizophrenia.
Sometimes a classical melancholia ushers in the illness and this is not
uncommon in the so-called paraphrenias in middle age . . . Sometimes the
depression seems to be a natural reaction to the distress caused by
schizophrenic symptoms. Since some intelligent young schizophrenics have a
painful realization of the inner change which is taking place, they may
justifiably be afraid that they are going mad, and may attempt suicide. In other
patients the sudden onset of auditory hallucinations seems to produce marked
depression and anxiety. Although disorders of emotional expression rather
than disorders of mood are prominent in chronic schizophrenics, nevertheless
depressive moods are met with in chronic schizophrenia, so that some
hebephrenics appear to be depressed and patients with marked bodily
hallucinations are usually depressed and morose.

Fig. 11.1

---

show flight of ideas, elated mood, and make unrealistic plans; however they
did little and showed a striking tendency to ignore their surroundings.

Beyond Kraepelin's and Bleuler's accounts, little further thought has been
given to the nature and extent of depressive and manic mood changes in
established schizophrenia. The nearest thing to a contemporary authoritative statement has been the view expressed by Fish (Fish 1962/Hamilton
1984); this is reproduced in Fig. 11.1. In stating that depression was common in the early stages of schizophrenia, but that true depression and elation were uncommon in chronic patients, he echoed the views of Kraepelin
and Bleuler. However, he also made the important point that an apparently
typical depressive state could be the beginning of a schizophrenic illness,
particularly in later life.

In short, the orthodox view has consistently been that while depression and less commonly elation are certainly encountered in schizophrenia, they are generally distinguishable from manic-depressive mood change, by virtue of being incomplete, bizarre, distorted in form, and having a superficial quality. Put in contemporary terminology, depression and elation in schizophrenia do not show the features of a full affective syndrome: depression is unaccompanied by the biological and the other accessory symptoms which define its manic-depressive nature; likewise mania is stripped of its richness and the hallmark accompaniments of distractibility, overactivity, and overspending are not seen. Nevertheless, no matter how distorted or deprived of their customary associations, there is no doubt that mood changes — sometimes striking and in both directions — may form part of the the clinical picture of otherwise unexceptional schizophrenia.

Schizophrenic symptoms in manic-depressive psychosis

Here, Kraepelin had a great deal to say, whereas Bleuler, not having written an account of manic-depressive psychosis comparable to his work on schizophrenia, was virtually silent. In his account of manic-depressive psychosis, Kraepelin (1913b) distinguished four increasingly severe subtypes of mania, and four corresponding subtypes of depression; he also included two more presentations of depression which had no counterparts in mania, stupor and paranoid melancholia. The features of these are summarized in Fig. 11.2; the important point is that with the exception of *hypomania* and melancholia simplex, all types were accompanied by delusions and hallucinations, and to a lesser extent disturbances of speech and behaviour.

According to Kraepelin, the delusions of mania were, for the most part, grandiose and those of depression were the familiar ones of sin, guilt, and hypochondriasis. He only described persecutory delusions in paranoid depression where, however, they could be quite florid. Hallucinations on the other hand, were considered to be frequent in both mania and depression. Verbal auditory hallucinations, in particular, could be quite extensive and sometimes had a bizarre quality, for example being perceived as emanating from the patient's own body. Invariably, though, the voices had a close connection to mood: in depression they were unpleasant and derogatory; in mania they praised, took the form of communication of sacred knowlege, etc.. In delirious mania and melancholia they could take on truly spectacular, apocalyptic, or revelatory qualities.

The next historically important account of schizophrenic symptoms in manic-depressive psychosis was the study of Lewis (1934) on their occurrence in depression. He described 61 cases of 'melancholia'. Patients were excluded if the mood change was secondary to other symptoms of ill health or organic brain disease, and none showed any evidence of schizophrenia beyond the 'slight or subordinate'. The diagnosis was made after final

Kraepelin's subtypes of mania and depression
(from Kraepelin 1913b)

Mania

Hypomania: Characterized by increased liveliness, busyness, and restlessness. Mood is predominantly cheerful with jocularity and subjective feelings of heightened capabilities. There is garrulousness, overactivity, and increased sexual drive. Flight of ideas is slight.

Acute mania: All the symptoms seen in hypomania are present in increased severity. The patient cannot sit or lie still, and behaviour is unrestrained, disturbed, and occasionally destructive. Speech is distractible and disconnected. Mood is merry or exultant, but fluctuates to irritability or tearfulness. Delusions, generally of a grandiose nature, may be present fleetingly, and there may be isolated hallucinations.

Delusional mania: The patient is restless and interfering, sings and preaches. Excitement is not usually very marked, and the patient may appear to be relatively well ordered in behaviour. However, there are florid and often relatively fixed grandiose delusions: these are often of a religious nature, or concern immense wealth, being of royal descent, etc.. Auditory, visual, and somatic hallucinations may be present.

Delirious mania: The patient shows marked excitement and senseless raving. Mode fluctuates between unrestrained merriment, tearfulness, and erotic or ecstatic states, occasionally with brief periods of stupor. Consciousness is dreamy or clouded and the patients often show an almost complete amnesia for the episode. There are many confused delusions and hallucinations: the patients think they are in a palace, see angels and spirits, have revelations, see heaven open, hear the voice of God announce the day of judgement, believe that a great battle with the antichrist is being fought. Catatonic phenomena may be present.

Depression

Melancholia simplex: A state of simple depression without hallucinations and with no marked delusions. Obvious lowering of mood is accompanied by anxiousness, hopelessness, and gloominess. Everything is disagreeable, and the patient lacks all energy and enthusiasm. There may be obsessions, and ideas of guilt and unworthiness which border on the delusional.

Stupor: The patient is deeply apathetic, and lies in bed, mute or nearly mute with a peculiar vacant strained expression. Depressive delusions may be alluded to in occasional detached utterances.

Melancholia gravis: Similar to simple melancholia but complicated by delusions and hallucinations. Patients see figures, spirits, corpses; and hear abusive language, or voices inviting them to commit suicide; there may also be olfactory, gustatory, and somatic hallucinations. Nihilistic delusions are invariably present.

Paranoid melancholia: Persecutory delusions and auditory hallucinations are to the foreground of the picture. At the same time mood is gloomy and despondent; occasionally the patients appear good humoured and even cheerful in regard to their delusions. Anxiousness and restlessness may also be seen. Depressive delusions can be present.

Fantastic melancholia: Hallucinations are abundant, the patient sees evil spirits, crowds of monsters, hears his tortured relatives screaming. There are many extraordinary depressive delusions, the patient believes he has caused an epidemic, laid waste to cities, his family are being crucified by a mob, his head is as large as Palestine. Mood is characterized by a dull despondency. Consciousness may be impaired.

Delirious melancholia: Characterized by a profound visionary clouding of consciousness. Patients see the room stretch out into infinity, feel they are in prison or purgatory. They appear perplexed and confused and are hardly capable of saying a word. Catatonic phenomena are evident.

Fig. 11.2

discharge of the patient and usually represented the consensus view of several psychiatrists. Lewis found that persecutory and referential ideas ranging from attitudes to full-blown delusions were present in 70 per cent of his patients. Disorders of perception, including in some cases second and third person verbal auditory hallucinations were present in 34 per cent. 'Schizophrenic features' were observed in 38 per cent—these were as a rule isolated, and included patients showing delusions of reference and misinterpretation, bizarre delusions with or without auditory hallucinations, mystical ideas, odd, impulsive behaviour, and in one case grimacing.

A corresponding detailed phenomenological account of mania was provided somewhat later by Winokur *et al.* (1969). From a group of 61 patients with manic-depressive psychosis diagnosed according to strict criteria (later to become the Feighner criteria), these authors obtained detailed decriptions of 36 manic episodes. Grandiose delusions (religious, political, or of wealth) were present in 64 per cent. Other delusions, with sexual and other themes, were present in 26 per cent. What were described as delusions of control were present in 22 per cent (it is not clear how many of these represented true passivity experiences). Usually, these other delusions also had a grandiose flavour. However, 19 per cent showed persecutory delusions and 28 per cent delusions of reference and misinterpretation; unlike the other delusions these did not typically have grandiose qualities. In all cases the delusions tended to be evanescent, appearing and disappearing during the course of a day. At times the patients could be talked out of their delusions, and in some cases they gave the impression of holding the ideas playfully rather than being truly deluded. Auditory hallucinations were present in 21 per cent and visual hallucinations in 9 per cent. Once again these tended to be closely related to the elevated mood, taking the form of hearing choirs of angels, hearing God's voice, seeing Heaven in all its glory, and so on. Visual hallucinations, in particular, tended to be fragmented and fleeting.

The last word on schizophrenic symptoms in manic-depressive psychosis was provided by Pope and Lipinski (1978). In an article which proved to be highly inflential in America, they subjected Kraepelin's, Lewis', Winokur *et al.*'s, and a number of subsequent studies of the phenomenology of manic-depressive psychosis to a critical review. As shown in Table 11.1, it was clear that, even after exclusion of all cases where the clinical features, outcome, family history, or response to treatment was equivocal, delusions and hallucinations could be found in 20–50 per cent. Certainly, some of the delusions reported could be seen as mood-congruent, but several studies gave detailed examples of such symptoms which were difficult to construe as related to the prevailing mood. This also applied to auditory and visual hallucinations which, without obvious mood-congruence, were reported in three or more studies. While persecutory and referential delusions were common, the largest and most rigorous studies suggested that more characteristically schizophrenic delusions and hallucinations were relatively uncommon, occurring in around a fifth to a quarter of cases. Some of the studies (for example Lewis 1934) found that schizophrenic symptoms formed a relatively inconspicuous part of the overall clinical picture. Others (for example Carlson and Goodwin 1973) suggested that they tended to be transient. The frequency of formal thought disorder and catatonic phenomena was not clear from these studies, but the impression is that they were uncommon.

The question of whether first rank symptoms could be seen in otherwise typical mania and depression was also considered by Pope and Lipinski, who concluded that they were. This conclusion was based on some, but not all, of the studies which have already been described in Chapter 4.

This work leaves no room for doubt that delusions and hallucinations which go considerably beyond what can be understood as mood-congruent are regularly encountered in both phases of manic-depressive psychosis. At the same time it is reasonable to draw the conclusion that these phenomena are relatively uncommon, in the background, or transitory. In short, something approximating to the same overall conclusion reached for affective symptoms in schizophrenia seems to be justifiable: while individual schizophrenic symptoms occur in manic-depressive psychosis, a florid syndrome with multiple symptoms which are to the forefront of the clinical picture for long periods is not typical of the disorder.

Armed with the information that typical schizophrenia is not assocatied with a full affective syndrome, and that manic-depressive psychosis does

Table 11.1 Studies of schizophrenic symptoms in manic-depressive psychosis (from Pope and Lipinski 1978)

Study	Sample	Findings
Lange (1922)	700 cases of manic-depressive psychosis.	Formal thought disorder in 7.5%, hallucinations in 6.6%, other symptoms including catalepsy, stereotypy, passivity, extreme regression in 27%.
Bowman and Raymond (1931)	1009 cases of manic-depressive psychosis.	Delusions of persecution in 20%.
Lewis (1934)	61 cases of melancholia.	'Schizophrenic' symptoms in 20%.
Rennie (1942)	Initially, 307 cases of manic-depressive psychosis; discarded 99 because 'wished to include only clear-cut manic-depressive reactions'; data reported for remaining 208 cases.	24% of 66 manics had persecutory or passivity delusions; 22% had hallucinations; depth of psychosis unrelated to status follow-up.
Astrup *et al.* (1959)	96 cases of manic-depressive psychosis with 7–19 years of follow-up.	Auditory hallucinations in 24%, delusions of passivity in 9%, of persecution in 13%, ideas of reference in 5%; none of these symptoms significantly differentiated patients who recovered completely from those with a chronic course.

Table 11.1 *contd.*

Study	Sample	Findings
Clayton *et al.* (1965)	31 manics diagnosed by structured interview; prior good social functioning required; most had past history and family history of manic-depressive psychosis.	Delusions recorded for 73%, ideas of reference in 77%, passivity in 47%. 2 year follow-up in the 7 cases with unequivocal passivity and other 'schizophrenic' symptoms revealed no differences from remaining 24 'typical' manics.
Winokur *et al.* (1961)	100 manic episodes, 14 mixed episodes, and 33 depressive episodes in 61 rigorously diagnosed cases of manic-depressive psychosis.	Passivity in 22%, delusions of persecution in 19%, and auditory hallucinations in 21% of manic episodes; also auditory hallucinations in 6% of depressive episodes and 14% of mixed episodes.
Beigel and Murphy (1971)	12 patients with 'unequivocal diagnosis of manic-depressive illness' on two research in wards.	'Paranoid-destructive' subtype of mania in 33% of cases, all with paranoid delusions.
Mendlewicz *et al.* (1972)	60 bipolar patients at lithium clinic; 30 with family history, 30 without this.	'Psychotic symptoms' in 70% of patients, appearing in mania or depression, and equally in patients with and without a family history.

Carlson and Goodwin (1973)	20 bipolar patients on two research wards, screened on admission to exclude equivocal cases.	'Schizophrenic' symptoms in 70% of cases.
Ianzito *et al.* (1974)	47 unipolar depressed patients with diagnosis confimed by 1½ to 2 year follow-up and by prior exclusion of cases contaminated by a second diagnosis.	Formal thought disorder in 19% of cases; thought broadcasting, thought control, hallucinations, or systematized delusions in 45% of cases.
Murphy and Beigel (1974)	30 highly screened manic-depressive patients on two research wards.	Expanded on 1971 paper to again demonstrate, 'paranoid-destructive' subtype of mania in 23% of cases.
Guze *et al.* (1975)	139 unipolar and 19 bipolar patients diagnosed by research criteria.	'Psychotic symptoms' (delusions, hallucinations, ideas of reference) in 53% of bipolars and 31% of unipolars. None of 37 demographic, family history, premorbid function, or parental home variables distinguished patients with psychotic symptoms from those without.

not commonly feature a full — or rather florid and sustained — schizophrenic syndrome it becomes possible to lay down the minimum requirements for schizoaffective psychoses, as states which present with a roughly equal admixture of schizophrenic and affective symptoms.

Cycloid psychosis

The curious tradition which culminated in the contemporary concept of cycloid psychosis goes back a long way and has been recounted by Fish (Fish 1964; Fish 1962/Hamilton 1984), Leonhard (1961), Brockington *et al.* (1982*a*), and especially Perris (1974, 1986). The clearest point of origin was an early classification of psychosis developed by Wernicke. He rejected Kraepelin's dichotomization of schizophrenia and manic-depressive psychosis, and, drawing on an earlier French tradition of degeneration psychoses — disorders which ran in families which were prone to evolve through a rapid succession of forms — proposed a more finely differentiated categorization. Wernicke died in 1905, but his ideas were kept alive in the work of Kleist, who postulated the existence of more than ten discrete psychotic disorders which were neither schizophrenic nor manic-depressive, and which he considered to be the manifestations of different focal brain dysfunctions. Later he grouped some of these together as 'cycloid marginal psychoses'.

Kleist's follower Leonhard was sceptical about the neuropathological basis of cycloid psychoses, but considered the clinical distinction to be valid in itself. Over time, he elaborated Kleist's classification into three bipolar psychoses. The core of each of these was the conjunction of two opposing symptoms, which the patient alternated between in a similar way to manic-depressive psychosis. The *anxiety — elation* psychosis had poles in an all-pervasive anxiousness (angst) and ecstatic happiness; the *motility* psychosis moved between hypo- and hyperkinesia; and the *confusion* psychosis had its extremes in inhibition and acceleration of thought. In addition to these features, it was clearly evident from Leonhard's description that manic-depressive type mood disturbance, delusions and hallucinations, and something resembling catatonic phenomena could be present in the background. Cycloid psychoses also had other distinctive features, including fluctuations and oscillations between the two poles within a single episode, and full recovery was considered to take place between episodes.

Perris took the bold step of synthesizing Leonhard's three forms of cycloid psychosis into a single entity. He felt justified in doing this on two grounds. In the first place, he noted that each of the three forms was not sharply delimited from the others: in any one form minor symptoms of one of the other two were sometimes seen, and occasionally there was a combination of the symptomatology of all three. Secondly, he argued that

---

*Some of the different names proposed for psychotic syndromes
quite similar to cycloid psychosis
(from Perris 1974)*

America and Canada

Bell's mania	(Bell)
Homosexual panic	(Kempf)
Schizoaffective psychosis	(Kasanin)
Benign stupor	(Hoch)
Oneirophrenia	(Meduna)

Scandinavia

Schizophreniform psychosis	(Langfeldt)
Psychogenic psychosis	(Faergeman, Stromgren)

France

Degeneration psychoses	(Magnan)
Schizomania	(Claude)
Bouffée délirante	(Magnan, Ey)

Japan

Atypical psychosis	(Mitsuda, Asano, Kaij)

Germany

Expansive psychosis with autochthonous ideas	(Wernicke)
Motility psychosis	(Wernicke)
Mixed psychoses	(Gaupp)
Metabolic psychosis	(Schroeder)
Phasophrenia	(Kleist)
Acute exhaustive psychosis	(Adland)

Russia

Periodic (recurrent) schizophrenia	(Schnevnesky)

Fig. 11.3

---

states showing some or all of the features of cycloid psychoses had been described again and again under different names for nearly a century. Perris' list of these disorders is shown in Fig. 11.3. Noteworthy inclusions are the French bouffée délirante; Kasanin's schizoaffective psychosis (although this was the first use of the term schizoaffective, it was clearly a cycloid-like state that was described); oneirophrenia, a dream-like psychotic state described by von Meduna the discoverer of convulsive therapy; and not least, that culture-bound American syndrome, homosexual panic — in its original description by Kempf this described a sudden-onset state of feverish agitation or rage sometimes amounting to temporary insanity (see Chuang and Addington 1988). Finally, it is clear that Kraepelin's delirious mania and delirious melancholia could also be included in the list.

The clinical features of cycloid psychosis as described by Perris (Perris 1974, 1986; Brockington *et al*. 1982*a*) can be outlined as follows. The onset of the disorder is typically abrupt: there is a rapid change from a state of complete health to full blown psychosis within hours or less commonly over a few days. A small minority have a less acute onset and in some there is prodromal period of non-specific symptoms like irritability or poor sleep.

The presentation of the psychosis is marked, above all, by its polymorphousness and kaleidoscopic shifts from one set of symptoms to another. Delusions, hallucinations, first rank symptoms, pananxiety, happiness or ecstasy, motility disturbances, catatonia-like symptoms, and confusion are jumbled together without any discernible pattern. Affective, schizophrenic, and delirium-like presentations fluctuate in and out of the picture from day to day, or even from hour to hour, with none being persistent or dominant. The overall intensity of the state may also wax and wane.

In Perris' series of patients confusion was the most common symptom and was often prominent; it varied from perplexity, through dream-like states, to frank disorientation which could at times be gross. Anxiety was also a frequently recorded symptom, and was sometimes accompanied by depersonalization and derealization; typically it was bound up with ideas about death or catastrophe. The ecstasy seen in cycloid psychosis was considered to be distinguishable from the elation of mania, in that it tended to occur in a setting of unassertive calmness and tranquillity and often had religious or mystical overtones. In addition to the characteristic anxiety depressive moods occurred, but generally these were not severe and did not last any length of time. Motor disorder consisted mainly of overactivity or retardation; the former was considered to have a characteristic fluid and 'pseudoexpressive' quality.

Perris found that the length of an episode of cycloid psychosis could vary greatly; the average duration was two to four months, but he knew of cases which remitted after a few days. There was a strong tendency for episodes to recur, but even after many attacks schizophrenia-like deterioration did not supervene. Some of Perris' patients had experienced more than 30 episodes with complete recovery every time. Between episodes, most patients showed no abnormalities, but in some minor residual symptoms could be detected, such as anxiety, depression, emotional lability, or increased vulnerability to stress.

The salient features of Perris' cycloid psychosis are thus a clinical picture which takes the form of unstable, pleomorphic symptoms; a short-term course characterized by full recovery but a risk of further similar episodes; and a long term outcome distinguished by a lack of deterioration. The concept is a purely clinical one, and its validity therefore depends on how well

---

Perris' criteria for cycloid psychosis
(from Brockington *et al.* 1982*a*)

The patient must have affective symptoms (mood swings) and two of the following five symptoms:

(i)   confusion (ranging from slight perplexity to gross disorientation) together with agitation or retardation;

(ii) delusions of reference, influence, or persecution and/or mood-incongruent delusions;

(iii) motility disturbances of the type described by Leonhard;

(iv) ecstasy as described by Leonhard and others;

(v)   pananxiety, that is anxiety associated with ideas of self-reference and persecution.

Fig. 11.4

---

these requirements are met. Are convincing examples of such states encountered? Do they run a course which is true to form? And, despite showing symptoms which go considerably beyond what could be considered manic-depressive, is the final outcome different from that seen in schizophrenia? Each of these questions has been addressed in a different study.

Cutting *et al.* (1978) examined the case notes of all first admissions to a psychiatric hospital over ten years to see if any patients fitted Perris' description of cycloid psychosis. To establish this they used a set of criteria for the disorder developed by Perris, which are shown in Fig. 11.4. The authors were able to find 73 patients (3 per cent of the total admissions for the ten year period and around 8 per cent of psychotic admissions) who showed such characteristics. Twenty nine of these had been given a case-note diagnosis of schizoaffective or atypical psychosis, and the rest had been diagnosed as either schizophrenic or affective. In these latter cases, however, hints of clinical uncertainty were often betrayed in the use of terms like 'schizophrenia with depressive features', or 'mixed affective state'. While acute onset was common in these patients – 44 per cent seemed to have had symptoms for less than a month prior to admission – this was not an invariable finding. In terms of immediate outcome, 90 per cent were described either as having made a full recovery or as showed a good outcome (these latter patients were free of psychotic symptoms but showed some lowering of mood). This rate was higher than that in a comparison group of manic patients.

Information on the course of patients identified as cycloid was obtained by Maj (1988). In a prospective study, he followed-up 18 patients meeting Perris' criteria for the disorder three years after initial diagnosis; their course was compared with that of 22 patients meeting Research Diagnostic Criteria for depression and 21 meeting the same criteria for mania. The cycloid group showed between no and five further episodes during the three year follow-up, slightly but not significantly higher than the manics and depressives. In 50 per cent of cases, criteria for cycloid psychosis were met in further episodes, with the remainder meeting criteria for major depression or schizoaffective (depressed) disorder. In contrast, none of the manic or depressed patients experienced subsequent episodes diagnosable as cycloid (or schizoaffective for that matter). Interestingly, Maj also included in his follow-up a group of 41 patients meeting Research Diagnostic Criteria for schizoaffective disorder. Fifteen of these subsequently had episodes which met criteria for cycloid psychosis.

The long term outcome of cycloid psychosis was examined in a study by Brockington *et al.* (1982*b*). This utilized a series of 242 psychotic patients who had formed part of the diagnostic studies described in Chapter 4. Extremely detailed history and mental state information was available on these patients and they had all been subjected to a follow-up examination several years later. Perris personally selected 30 cases he considered met his criteria for cycloid psychosis at the time of their initial presentation, and their outcome was compared with the psychotic sample as a whole, and also with those patients diagnosed as schizophrenic and manic-depressive. Although the cycloid patients had as many subsequent admissions as the group as a whole, on every other measure of outcome they fared significantly better. Twenty seven (90 per cent) were considered to be completely well at the time of follow-up. This figure was much higher than that for the schizophrenic patients, but differences from manic-depressive patients were not clearly evident.

As a clinical concept, cycloid psychosis thus seems to withstand fairly close scrutiny. Patients presenting with the requisite polymorphous clinical picture can be identified among acute admissions, where they tend to be difficult to categorize in conventional ways. They usually make an excellent recovery, and go on to run an episodic course in which subsequent episodes frequently show the same atypical characteristics. The disorder does, however, show a few signs of strain: an acute onset was found in less than half of the cases in Cutting *et al.*'s study. A large proportion later have episodes of depression which are not obviously atypical in any way. Finally, there is a suspicion in one of the above studies that the lack of ultimate development of deterioration is relative rather than absolute. This is also evident in the literature on disorders considered to be more or less synomymous with cycloid psychosis by Perris, particularly bouffée délirante (see Ey *et al.* 1960) and schizophreniform psychosis (see Chapter 3).

Aetiological factors in cycloid psychosis

The meagre information here relates principally to the two time-honoured avenues of investigation in psychiatric disorders, family history and premorbid personality. In addition, there is a hint of a further, specific aetiological factor in the shape of EEG abnormalities.

Family history studies: Perris (1974) obtained information on 349 first degree relatives of his 60 patients with cycloid psychosis. He found that 25 (7.2 per cent) suffered from similar cycloid psychoses, 2 (0.6 per cent) from schizophrenia, and 12 (3.4 per cent) from affective disorders. Second degree relatives also showed similar (if anything even higher) rates of psychotic morbidity. Perris concluded that cycloid psychosis showed a significant familiality, that it 'bred true', and that there was little to suggest that the risk of schizophrenia and manic-depressive psychosis was increased. Although a replication of Perris' findings under more rigorous conditions is needed to be sure that cycloid psychosis is truly genetically independent from the other two functional psychoses, provisionally it seems to be a third unrelated psychosis which happens to show combinations of schizophrenic and manic-depressive symptoms among other more characteristic manifestations—in short it conforms to the fourth of the six possibilities outlined by Kendell at the beginning of the chapter.

Premorbid personality: Perris (1974) found that the a majority of his 60 patients were emotionally warm, not obviously abnormal individuals, and the minority who were described as sensitive, suspicious, anxious, insecure, or rigid were matched by a similar number who were happy, hard working, self assertive, etc.. Cutting *et al.* (1978) compared descriptions of personality traits in the case notes of their 73 cycloid patients with those of 66 patients with manic-depressive psychosis, under blind conditions. No significant differences were found, with half the patients in each group being described as normal.

EEG abnormalities: In his own study, Perris (1974) commented that the EEG showed runs or paroxysms of slow (theta) waves in 19 of his 60 patients. In Japan, the idea that there might be an underlying epileptiform EEG disturbance in certain atypical forms of psychosis has been taken further. (This tradition was one of the main reasons behind the introduction of carbamazepine as a treatment for manic-depressive psychosis.) In a series of studies carried out by Mitsuda and co-workers (see Mitsuda 1967) the EEGs of patients with typical schizophrenia and manic-depressive psychosis were compared with those of patients with psychoses that were considered atypical, by virtue of showing unusual clinical features and running a fluctuating and episodic course. It was found that there was a pronounced over-representation of all types of EEG abnormality in the atypical psychoses.

When the EEG was activated with an analeptic agent such as bemegride, the EEG disturbance in the atypical patients tended to become enhanced — often to the point of appearance of clear-cut spike discharges. Monroe (1982) and Tucker *et al.* (1986) in America, have also reported roughly comparable findings in similar naturalistic studies.

Treatment of cycloid psychosis

No treatment studies, controlled or otherwise, have been carried out in cycloid psychosis. In these circumstances, it is not possible to do better than to present the observations of Perris (1974, 1986; Brockington *et al.* 1982*a*). In his own and others' experience, Perris found that ECT was useful in acute episodes, consistently producing a dramatic improvement after only a few treatments. Relapse, however, was frequent and treatment needed to be continued for a minimum of 6–8 applications. Subsequently, Perris has used neuroleptics as the treatment of choice, finding that this was followed by complete remission within a few weeks in most cases. He has tended to combine these drugs with lithium, but has been uncertain whether or not this made a significant contribution to shortening the episode.

Long-term treatment with lithium gave the strong impression of reducing relapses, generally by about half. Usually it was effective alone, but exceptionally combined therapy with neuroleptics needed be undertaken. Neuroleptic treatment alone, however, was not found to be effective as a prophylactic treatment.

Schizoaffective psychosis proper

The term 'schizoaffective' was coined in the USA by Kasanin in 1933, although, as noted above, he was clearly describing cycloid psychosis. Nevertheless, schizoaffective psychosis proper continued to be largely the preserve of American psychiatry. The evolution of the concept is not easy to trace, and probably the most successful attempt to do so has been made by Pichot (1986) who charted its course through successive editions of the Diagnostic and Statistical Manual (DSM) produced by the American Psychiatric Association. The first edition of this in 1952 included a schizoaffective type of schizophrenia. This specified cases showing admixtures of schizophrenic and affective symptomatology. The mental content could be predominantly schizophrenic, but with pronounced depression or elation, or alternatively predominantly affective, but with pronounced schizophrenic-like thinking or bizarre behaviour. It was added that the premorbid personality might be at variance with expectations, and also that, on prolonged observation, such cases usually proved to be basically schizophrenic in nature.

By the second edition, DSM II, published in 1968, the definition had become considerably more terse. Schizophrenia, schizoaffective type was described as referring to 'patients showing a mixture of schizophrenic symptoms and pronounced elation or depression'. Although by this time it was widely appreciated that American psychiatry was going its own way with the diagnosis of schizophrenia (see Chapter 4), a schizoaffective subtype of schizophrenia was nevertheless incorporated into the eighth and ninth editions of the International Classification of Diseases. According to Pichot, this was probably because there were a number of American psychiatrists on the relevant expert committees of the World Health Organization.

In 1978, an American Psychiatric Association task force on nomenclature and classification produced a draft version of DSM III. In this it was noted that the term schizoaffective had been used in many different ways, and that it was controversial whether the disorder represented a variant of affective disorder, or of schizophrenia, or was a third independent nosological entity, or formed part of a continuum between pure forms of the two functional psychoses. Accordingly a special category was created for schizoaffective disorders, which were defined as states in which a depressive or manic syndrome preceded or developed concurrently with certain psychotic symptoms thought to be incompatible with a purely affective diagnosis. Two years later, in the final published version of DSM III, the category had practically disappeared (it lingered on, but as the only major disorder without criteria). The reasons why the members of the task force made the decision to do this are not known, but it is possible that the influential review of Pope and Lipinski (1978) played a part; this argued that the presence of schizophrenic symptoms in otherwise affective presentations had little significance in determining diagnosis, prognosis, and response to treatment. In any event, the original operational criteria for schizoaffective disorder entered the public domain in the Research Diagnostic Criteria (Spitzer *et al.* 1978) whose development was closely linked to that of DSM III. These criteria are shown in Fig. 11.5.

Between the bald statement that schizoaffective psychoses are characterized by combinations of schizophrenic and affective symptoms, and the elaborate operational criteria of Spitzer *et al.* (1978), there has been very little actual description of the clinical features of the disorder. One of the very few authors who has taken on this task is Guze (1980) and his description, with a few additions, is presented below.

Typically, according to Guze, schizoaffective psychoses begin abruptly. The affective and schizophrenic symptoms may appear more or less simultaneously, but in some cases the affective symptoms precede the schizophrenic ones for some days or weeks. Occasionally patients are encountered in whom there has been a lengthy prodrome of isolated delusions without any obvious mood disturbance, who then flare up into depression or mania (such a presentation has already been alluded to in Chapter 10 as paranoia which gives way to manic-depressive psychosis on follow-up).

Research Diagnostic Criteria for Schizoaffective disorder
(from Spitzer *et al.* 1978)

(a) Criteria for schizoaffective mania

(A through E are required)

A. One or more distinct periods with a predominantly elevated, expansive, or irritable mood. The elevated, expansive, or irritable mood must be relatively persistent and prominent during some part of the illness or occur frequently. It may alternate with depressive mood. If the disturbance in mood occurs only during periods of alcohol or drug intake or withdrawal from them, it should not be considered here.

B. If mood is elevated or expansive, at least three of the following symptoms must be definitely present to a significant degree, four if mood is only irritable.

1. More active than usual—either socially, at work, at home, sexually, or physically restless.

2. More talkative than usual or feeling a pressure to keep on talking.

3. Flight of ideas or subjective experience that thoughts are racing.

4. Inflated self-esteem (grandiosity, which may be delusional).

5. Decreased need for sleep.

6. Distractibility, that is attention is too easily drawn to unimportant or irrelevant external stimuli.

7. Excessive involvement in activities without recognizing the high potential for painful consequences, for example buying sprees, sexual indiscretions, foolish business investments, reckless driving.

C. At least one of the following symptoms suggestive of schizophrenia is present during the active phase of the illness.

1. Delusions of being controlled (or influenced) or of thought broadcasting, insertion, or withdrawal (as defined in this manual).

2. Non-affective hallucinations of any type throughout the day for several days or intermittently throughout a 1 week period.

3. Auditory hallucinations in which either a voice keeps up a running commentary on the subject's behaviours or thoughts as they occur, or two or more voices converse with each other.

4. At some time during the period of illness had more than 1 week when he exhibited no prominent depressive or manic symptoms but had delusions or hallucinations.

5. At some time during the period of illness had more than 1 week when he exhibited no prominent manic symptoms but had several instances

of marked formal thought disorder, accompanied by either blunted or inappropriate affect, delusions, or hallucinations of any type, or grossly disorganized behaviour.

D. Signs of the illness have lasted at least 1 week from the onset of a noticeable change in the patient's usual condition (current signs of the illness may not now meet criteria A, B, or C and may be residual affective or residual schizophrenic symptoms only, such as mood disturbance, blunted or inappropriate affect, extreme social withdrawal, mild formal thought disorder, or unusual thoughts or perceptual experiences).

E. Affective syndrome overlaps temporally to some degree with an active period of schizophrenic-like symptoms (delusions, hallucinations, marked formal thought disorder, bizarre behaviour, etc.).

(b) Criteria for schizoaffective depression

(A through E are required)

A. One or more distinctive periods with dysphoric mood or pervasive loss of interest or pleasure. The disturbance is characterized by symptoms such as the following: depressed, sad, blue, hopeless, low, down in the dumps, 'don't care anymore' or irritable. The disturbance must be *a major part of the clinical picture* during some part of the illness and relatively persistent or occur frequently. It may not necessarily be the most dominant symptom. It does not include momentary shifts from one dysphoric mood to another dysphoric mood, for example anxiety to depression to anger, such as are seen in states of acute psychotic turmoil. If the symptoms in C occur only during periods of alcohol or drug use or withdrawal from them, the diagnosis should be unspecified functional psychosis.

B. At least five of the following symptoms are required for definite and four for probable.

1. Poor appetite or weight loss or increased appetite or weight gain (change of 1 lb per week over several weeks or 10 lb per year when not dieting).

2. Sleep difficulty or sleeping too much.

3. Loss of energy, fatiguability, or tiredness.

4. Psychomotor retardation or agitation (but not mere subjective feeling of restlessness or being slowed down).

5. Loss of interest or pleasure in usual activities, including social contact or sex (do not include if limited to a period when delusional or hallucinating). (The loss may or may not be pervasive.)

6. Feelings of self-reproach or excessive inappropriate guilt (either may be delusional).

Fig. 11.5

7. Complaints or evidence of diminished ability to think or concentrate, such as slowed thinking, or indecisiveness (do not include if associated with obvious formal thought disorder, or preoccupation with delusions or hallucinations).

8. Recurrent thoughts of death or suicide, or any suicidal behaviour.

C. At least one of the following is present:

1. Delusions of being controlled (or influenced) or of thought broadcasting, insertion, or withdrawal.

2. Non-affective hallucinations of any type throughout the day for several days or intermittently throughout a 1 week period.

3. Auditory hallucinations in which either a voice keeps up a running commentary on the subject's behaviours or thoughts as they occur, or two or more voices converse with each other.

4. At some time during the period of illness had more than 1 month when he exhibited no prominent depressive or manic symptoms but had delusions or hallucinations (although typical depressive delusions such as delusions of guilt, sin, poverty, nihilism, or self-deprecation, or hallucinations of similar content).

5. Definite instances of marked formal thought disorder accompanied by either blunted or inappropriate affect, delusions or hallucinations of any type, or grossly disorganized behaviour.

D. Signs of the illness have lasted at least 1 week from the onset of a noticeable change in the patient's usual condition (current signs of the illness may not now meet criteria A, B, or C and may be residual affective or residual schizophrenic symptoms only, such as mood disturbance, blunted or inappropriate affect, extreme social withdrawal, mild formal thought disorder, or unusual thoughts or perceptual experiences).

E. Affective syndrome overlaps temporally to some degree with the active period of schizophrenic-like symptoms (delusions, hallucinations, thought disorder, bizarre behaviour).

Fig. 11.5 *contd.*

All patients present with a mixture of affective features amounting to a more or less fully formed affective syndrome, together with clearly evident delusions and/or hallucinations which are either characteristic of schizophrenia (for example first rank symptoms), or which are unusual for affective disorder in that they bear no apparent relation to the abnormal mood. The affective and schizophrenic symptoms may parallel each other in intensity, or fluctuate independently, or one may wax and wane while the other holds steady; a common sequence is for both sets of symptoms to begin more or less coincidentally, then the schizophrenic symptoms subside leaving the patient with a typical depression or mania. The overall presentation tends to be dramatic with considerable social and behavioural disturbance. Individual catatonic symptoms may be present and there may be brief episodes of catatonic stupor or excitement. Suicidal thinking and attempts (which may be successful) are also common.

The duration of the episode may be brief, but more usually it lasts weeks to months. The course of the illness tends to be episodic, with recurrences separated by months or even years. Some patients experience subsequent schizoaffective episodes separated by months or years of full remission. In others, the picture of mixed schizophrenic and affective symptoms is followed, after several attacks, by simple manic or depressive episodes. In yet others, periods of acute illness are eventually supplanted by a state which is indistinguishable from chronic schizophrenia, against the background of which mood disturbance may re-appear from time to time. The outcome is variable but on average it seems to be significantly better than for schizophrenia.

A range of clinical pictures is subsumed under the term schizoaffective, and it is widely suspected that the category contains more than one type of disorder. At one 'mainly affective' end of the spectrum are presentations which can be considered as schizoaffective only in a technical sense. Such cases show an unexceptional manic or depressive picture, but in addition one or two first rank symptoms are elicited on questioning. At the other 'mainly schizophrenic' extreme are patients who, in the course of a hitherto unremarkable schizophrenic illness, unexpectedly develop a degree of depression or mood elevation (or alternations between the two); this seems to go beyond what is acceptable as mood colouring, but the overall schizophrenic character of the illness nevertheless cannot be doubted. A final variety of schizoaffective psychosis is where patients present with purely schizophrenic and purely affective syndromes in different episodes: patients have been described in whom an initial schizophrenic illness subsequently becomes manic-depressive (Sheldrick *et al.* 1977), and depression with typical associated features including mood-congruent delusions and hallucinations is not uncommon in the initial stages of an illness which subsequently becomes schizophrenic (Fish 1962/Hamilton 1984).

To many British psychiatrists, the diagnosis of schizoaffective psychosis is to be frowned upon, a faintly distasteful label that should only be applied provisionally until the true nature of a psychosis declares itself with the passage of time. In America, on the other hand, the disorder seems to be accepted as an everyday clinical reality. Clearly, the validity of the concept requires to be properly established. As with cycloid psychosis, this can only be done clinically. In the first place, it depends on demonstrating that patients with schizoaffective presentations can be found among the population of functionally psychotic patients; this has to be done convincingly and in a way which avoids the possible pitfalls of schizophrenic mood colourings, reactive depression, mood-congruent psychotic symptoms in mania and depression, and so on. Secondly, it is necessary to show that such patients follow a distinctive course and have an outcome which is different from that of either schizophrenia or manic-depressive psychosis. This is a more difficult undertaking since, in order to be distinguishable from both disorders, schizoaffective psychosis is constrained to show an outcome intermediate between the two. In both cases there is an obvious need to employ proper diagnostic criteria for schizoaffective psychosis: the most stringent of these (and also the most sophisticated) are the Research Diagnostic Criteria described above.

The definitive examination of the cross-sectional bona fides of schizoaffective psychoses was carried out by Brockington *et al.* (1980*a*, *b*). They screened the case notes of nearly 4000 admissions to four psychiatric hospitals for presentations which might possibly show a combination of schizophrenic and affective features. Any such patients were then interviewed and required to meet a preliminary, intentionally broad definition of schizoaffective psychosis. This required enough signs of mania or depression to approximate to a full affective syndrome, plus one or more schizophrenic symptoms from a checklist which included persecutory delusions, first rank symptoms, catatonic phenomena, affective flattening or incongruity, and formal thought disorder. After 600 patients were interviewed in this way, 76 'schizodepressive' and 32 'schizomanic' patients were identified (approximately 10 per cent and 4 per cent of all psychotic admissions respectively). These patients were subjected to a more intensive mental state examination (using the Present State Examination) and various diagnostic criteria were applied to them. Sixty of the 76 schizodepressive patients met Research Diagnostic Criteria for schizoaffective disorder, depressed type. Among the 32 schizomanic patients, 8 met RDC criteria for schizoaffective disorder, manic type.

It can thus be concluded that patients showing genuine combinations of schizophrenic and manic-depressive psychosis are encountered in clinical practice. These form something less than 15 per cent of all admissions with a diagnosis of functional psychosis. This percentage is decreased to around 10 per cent by adopting a rigorous diagnostic approach, but it is likely that this figure would be increased again if patients presenting with successive rather than simultaneous combinations of symptoms were to be included.

There have been numerous follow-up studies of patients diagnosed as schizoaffective. These have variously found the outcome to be intermediate between that of schizophrenia and manic-depressive psychosis (Tsuang and Dempsey 1979), similar to schizophrenia (Welner *et al.* 1977; Himmelhoch *et al.* 1981), similar to manic-depressive psychosis (Pope *et al.* 1980) or heterogeneous (Brockington *et al.* 1980*a*, *b*; Berg *et al.* 1983). These studies utilized a wide range of definitions of schizoaffective disorder, ranging from clinical impression or little more than this to formal diagnostic criteria. Only three studies, however, used the Research Diagnostic Criteria. These also had prospective designs and they all assessed outcome in a multi-dimensional way similar to that of the two contemporary outcome studies of schizophrenia described in Chapter 3. These are arguably prerequisites for detecting what are likely to be small differences in outcome from schizophrenic and manic-depressive patients.

Grossman *et al.* (1984) identified at the time of admission 39 patients meeting Research Diagnostic Criteria for schizoaffective disorder, 47 meeting criteria for schizophrenia, and 81 meeting criteria for affective disorder (33 with mania and 48 with depression). All patients were followed-up by means of personal interview after a year; no attempt was made to control the medication received by the different groups over this period. At this time a battery of clinical and social interview schedules was administered, and a measure of overall outcome was obtained from these. The findings are shown in Table 11.2. In terms of overall outcome, the schizoaffective patients did not differ significantly from the schizophrenics, and both these groups had significantly less favourable outcomes than the affective patients. However, the proportion of schizoaffective patients in the poor outcome group was considerably less than for the schizophrenic patients.

A more detailed breakdown of the findings revealed a trend for the schizoaffective patients to have psychotic symptoms less frequently than the schizophrenics at follow-up, but at the same time they showed a trend to more frequent rehospitalization than the affective patients. The schizoaffective patients also had a significantly better work performance than the schizophrenics. No differences were found between the schizoaffective patients classified as 'mainly affective' or 'mainly schizophrenic' at the time of initial assessment. The overall impression was that the majority of schizoaffective patients had an intermediate outcome, showing substantial difficulties in some areas, but not the very favourable outcome of a number of the manic-depressive patients nor the very poor outcome in almost all areas of many schizophrenic patients.

The findings have been roughly similar in the two other studies. Coryell *et al.* (1984) compared the outcome of 24 schizoaffective depressed patients with groups of 56 and 274 patients with diagnoses of psychotic and non-psychotic major depression respectively. At six months, the schizoaffective patients were found to score significantly more poorly than the non-psychotic depressed patients on all clinical and social measures. However, they were not significantly worse on any of these measures than the psychotically depressed group. By two years, the outcome in the psychotically depressed patients had improved to match that of the nonpsychotically

Table 11.2 One year outcome in schizoaffective psychosis, schizophrenia, and manic-depressive psychosis (from Grossman *et al.* 1984)

Group	Overall outcome (%)		
	Good	Intermediate	Poor
Schizoaffective ($n = 39$)	10	59	31
Schizophrenic ($n = 47$)	9	40	51
Manic-depressive ($n = 81$)	36	32	32

depressed patients, but there was no corresponding improvement in the schizoaffective patients; the differences, however, only showed a trend towards significance. Maj (1985) compared 36 schizoaffective patients and 39 patients with manic-depressive psychosis after a three year follow-up period. The outcome for patients presenting initially with schizoaffective mania was not significantly different from those with pure mania. However, schizoaffective depressives were found to be significantly more socially isolated, to have poorer occupational performance, and to show significantly more emotional flattening than the pure depressive group.

Instead of having to search for quantitative differences, it is possible to examine the course and outcome of schizoaffective disorder in a more qualitative way. Brockington *et al.* (1979) and Kendell (1986) used discriminant function analysis to examine whether their group of schizomanic and schizodepressive patients remained homogeneous in the long term or whether they tended to split into groups of more schizophrenia-like and affective-like patients. All the patients were re-assessed between one and four years after they were first examined. An outcome function was then applied, which was made up of eight variables established in previous studies as giving the best discrimination between schizophrenic and affective patients (see Chapter 4); this gave a convenient measure of how far each patient's symptomatology and course during the follow-up period had been schizophrenic or affective in character. When the distributions of the schizoaffective patients were plotted on this function, as shown in Fig. 11.6, no evidence of bimodality was found, either for the group as a whole or for the schizomanics and schizodepressives taken separately. This failure to find heterogeneity lends weight to the concept of schizoaffective

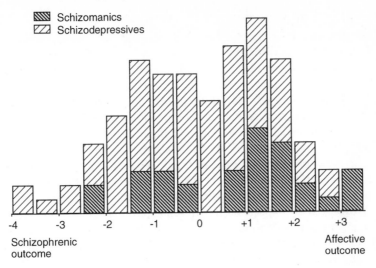

Fig. 11.6 Discriminant function analysis of the course and outcome of schizoaffective patients (from Kendell 1986).

psychosis as a disorder which is longitudinally distinctive. Of course, the patients in this study met a broad definition of schizoaffective psychosis rather than the stricter Research Diagnostic Criteria, but this should if anything have increased the tendency for two groups to segregate at follow-up.

The studies cited here make it clear that schizoaffective psychosis has an unquestionable cross-sectional existence. Around 15 per cent of cases of functional psychosis show both schizophrenic and affective symptoms, and a substantial proportion of these—by virtue of meeting the rigorous RDC criteria—exhibit combinations of the two which go beyond what is attributable to the mood colourings of schizophrenia or the psychotic symptoms of manic-depressive psychosis. Longitudinally, however, the reality of schizoaffective psychosis is more questionable: the outcome studies establish that the course of the disorder is significantly worse than that of manic-depressive psychosis, but not that it is better than schizophrenia—although there are broad hints that this is the case. Discriminant function analysis provides an elegant way round the difficulties inherent in these studies, but perhaps not one which permits an incontestable answer. Overall, the evidence that schizoaffective disorder is a valid clinical entity remains tantalizing, but inconclusive.

Aetiological factors in schizoaffective psychosis

Rather surprisingly, only one aspect of this has been investigated; this is the heredity of the disorder. This has been approached from the viewpoint of trying to establish whether the disorder is genetically related to schizophrenia, to manic-depressive psychosis, to both, or to neither.

Coryell (1986) reviewed 14 family history studies of schizoaffective psychosis. All of these studies included comparison groups of manic-depressive patients, and in eight there were also comparison groups of schizophrenic patients. Ten of the 14 studies found that the first degree relatives of schizoaffective patients had rates of manic-depressive psychosis which were comparable with (or slightly lower than) the rates seen for manic-depressive psychosis itself. Eight of the studies also found that schizoaffective patients had a higher than expected rate of schizophrenia among their relatives. Finally, four studies found the risk of schizoaffective psychosis among relatives to range from 2.2 per cent to 6.1 per cent—a rate that can be presumed to be above the general population rate. At first pass, therefore, schizoaffective psychosis appears to be associated with all kinds of psychotic pathology in the family.

In these studies, a range of diagnostic criteria for schizoaffective psychosis were employed, ranging from the stringent to the very loose indeed: some seem to have conceptualized the category broadly, to include schizophreniform psychoses, manic-depressive psychosis with mood incongruent delusions, or atypical psychosis (not otherwise specified). Six of the studies, however, employed Research Diagnostic Criteria for schizoaffective disorder and their findings are summarized in Table 11.3. All found rates of affective disorder in first degree relatives which were as high as or higher than the rates found in the relatives of manic-depressive patients. Two of the six also found the rates for schizophrenia to be increased two to three times over the population rate (or higher given that, as described in Chapter 5, the rate of schizophrenia diagnosed according to modern criteria is lower than the generally cited figure of around 1 per cent).

What these findings mean is open to several interpretations, and it is probably easier to say what they do not mean. The hypothesis that schizoaffective disorder is genetically separate from both the other two functional psychoses and 'breeds true' can be ruled out with certainty. The hypotheses that the disorder is genetically a variant of schizophrenia, or genetically a variant of manic-depressive psychosis could also be excluded if it could be assumed that these disorders themselves breed true. Unfortunately it is not entirely clear that this is the case: while the majority of investigators have concluded that schizophrenia and manic-depressive psychosis do not show overlapping patterns of inheritance, the studies themselves are not always unequivocal and some studies have suggested otherwise (see Crow 1986).

Table 11.3 Family history studies of patients meeting RDC criteria for schizoaffective disorder (from Coryell 1986)

| Study | Numbers of schizoaffective patients | Percentage of relatives with | | | Comment |
		Schizophrenia	Affective psychosis	Schizoaffective psychosis	
Abrams and Taylor (1976)	7	0	13.9	—	No details of method of assessing relatives given.
Rosenthal et al. (1980)	25	0	24.6 (MR)	—	Diagnosis in relatives made using criteria which did not include schizoaffective psychosis.
Pope et al. (1980)	52	0	40.4	—	9.6% of relatives had psychotic disorders which could not be specified. Diagnosis in relatives made using criteria which did not include schizoaffective psychosis.

Table 11.3 contd.

| Study | Numbers of schizoaffective patients | Percentage of relatives with | | | Comment |
		Schizophrenia	Affective psychosis	Schizoaffective psychosis	
Baron et al. (1982)	50	2.2 (MR)	18.9 (MR)	2.2 (MR)	Mainly 'schizophrenic' and 'mainly affective' subgroups had higher rates of schizophrenia and affective disorder respectively.
Gershon et al. (1982)	11	3.6 (MR)	31.0 (MR)	6.1 (MR)	—
Andreasen et al. (1987)	55	1.4	24.2	0.9	Higher rates of schizophrenia and psychosis not otherwise specified were found when a larger sample of relatives (not interviewed personally) was used.

*MR = morbid risk.

The remaining, and possibly the likeliest, hypothesis is the fifth of the six outlined by Kendell at the beginning of the chapter—that schizoaffective psychosis is the manifestation of an unknown aetiological interaction between schizophrenia and manic-depressive psychosis.

Treatment of schizoaffective psychosis

In treatment studies, the term schizoaffective loses all diagnostic precision. Treatment of schizoaffective psychosis tends to be the treatment of schizoaffective psychosis proper, cycloid psychosis, schizophreniform psychosis, atypical manic-depression, and probably other types of illness as well.

No studies of neuroleptic treatment versus placebo have ever been carried out in schizoaffective psychosis. Of a handful of controlled trials of neuroleptic versus other treatments, two of the largest have been those of Prien *et al.* (1972) and Brockington *et al.* (1978*b*), which were carried out on schizomanic and schizodepressed patients respectively. Prien *et al.* treated 83 patients with schizoaffective disorder, excited type, the diagnosis being made by clinical consensus. These were randomly assigned to treatment with lithium (in dosages determined by serum levels) or chlorpromazine (up to 3000 mg/day) for three weeks. At the start of the study the patients were divided into two subgroups, 'highly active' and 'mildly active', on the basis of psychomotor symptoms. Both drugs were found to be equally effective in the mildly active patients, but chlorpromazine was significantly superior for those in the highly active group. However, this latter finding was due almost entirely to patients on lithium who dropped out of the study because of poor control of symptoms such as hostility and and overactivity. When these were excluded from the analysis the differences between the two treatments became insignificant. Both lithium and neuroleptic treated patients showed significant improvement in both schizophrenic and affective symptoms. However, as there was no placebo group the possibility that this was due to factors other than medication cannot be excluded.

Brockington *et al.* (1978*b*) randomly assigned 36 acute admissions meeting their broad definition for schizodepression to treatment with either chlorpromazine (up to 750 mg/day), amitriptyline (up to 250 mg/day), or both. Treatment was administered under double-blind conditions and continued for a month. The overall recovery rate was low, at 20 per cent. With improvement categorized into full recovery, partial recovery, or no change, it was found that there was no statistically significant difference between the three groups, although the patients on chlorpromazine gave a strong impression of having fared rather better.

Neuroleptic drugs are very often combined with other drug treatments in acute episodes of schizoaffective psychosis, in circumstances where the justification is not very clear. Other than that of Brockington *et al.*, the only study which has examined the rationale of this procedure is that of Johnstone *et al.* (1988). They examined the response to treatment of patients with any form of functional psychosis to neuroleptics, lithium, or the combination of the two drugs. The sample consisted of 105 patients who showed one or more definite psychotic symptoms (as rated on the Present State Examination) in the absence of any organic brain disease. (In fact, nearly all the patients showed delusions and hallucinations.) DSM III diagnoses included schizophrenia, mania, major depression, schizoaffective disorder, atypical psychosis, and paranoid disorder. Twenty six were rated as having predominant elevation of mood, 34 predominant depression, and 60 no predominant mood disturbance (these judgements were made clinically—however, reclassifying patients as schizophrenic, schizoaffective, or affective according to two systems (CATEGO and DSM III) made no difference to the results of the analysis). All patients were randomly assigned to treatment for four weeks with either neuroleptic (pimozide), lithium, both drugs, or placebo under double-blind conditions. Analysis revealed that neuroleptic treatment had a highly significant beneficial effect on psychotic symptoms (that is summed scores on delusions, hallucinations, and formal thought disorder), and also on incongruity of affect, irrespective of whether these were associated with elevation or depression of mood. At the same time, neuroleptic treatment had no demonstrable effect on elevated and depressed mood themselves. Lithium treatment showed the reverse pattern of effects. It had no significant effect on delusions, hallucinations, and formal thought disorder, but produced a significant reduction in elevation of mood; it did not show a significant effect on depression. There was no evidence of any significant interactive effect between lithium and neuroleptic.

Carbamazepine has been advocated as an acute treatment for schizoaffective psychosis. This conclusion depends on the inclusion of patients with schizoaffective states, usually defined loosely, in several of the trials of this drug in affective disorder (see Post *et al.* 1984). Accordingly, it cannot be regarded as being established beyond any doubt. ECT has also been claimed to be effective: Ries *et al.* (1981) found that a good reponse to this mode of treatment had been recorded in nine patients meeting Research Diagnostic Criteria for schizoaffective disorder.

Miscellaneous atypical psychoses

Puerperal psychosis

The study of psychotic states which develop in the weeks or months following childbirth was founded by Marcé (1858). He considered these to be important for two reasons, first by virtue of the frequency with which they seemed to occur, and secondly because they appeared to have symptoms which marked them out as different from psychoses occurring at any other time of life. Puerperal psychosis, according to Marcé and some subsequent authors (see

Hamilton 1962), formed a syndrome characterized by dreaminess, perplexity, confusion, or delirium, superimposed on which were panic, nightmarish hallucinations, delusional misidentifications, and also stupor and excitement. Variability of symptoms was the rule, with patients rarely conforming to simple textbook patterns but instead moving unpredictably from one syndrome to another and relapsing and remitting unpredictably.

More recent work has given credence to the concept of puerperal psychosis by establishing that the incidence of functional psychosis is greater following childbirth than at any other time of life (Pugh *et al.* 1963; Kendell *et al.* 1976). However, the view that such states have their own set of distinctive features has not fared so well. In 1979 the term puerperal psychosis was discarded from the International Classification of Diseases, and it was recommended that functional psychotic states developing in the postnatal period should be classified as schizophrenia or manic-depressive psychosis according to their salient features. This conclusion appears to have been based on the findings of two diagnostic studies (Foundeur *et al.* 1957; Protheroe 1969), neither of which pointed to such a conclusion in any very direct way. In any event, psychiatrists have continued to be make the observation that, while it may be possible to diagnose puerperal psychoses along conventional lines, such states tend to be marked by their similarities as much as their differences (for example Snaith 1983).

The question of whether puerperal psychosis shows features distinguishing it from other forms of psychosis has been investigated by Brockington *et al.* (1981). They examined the clinical features of 58 psychoses in 56 patients with psychoses which began within two weeks of childbirth. These were compared with non-puerperal functional psychoses (of all types) in 52 female patients who were of childbearing age. The main symptomatic difference between the two groups concerned the presence of confusion, ratings of which were nearly twice as high in the puerperal group. Ratings related to behavioural incompetence were also more common in the puerperal group, especially the item 'needs supervision in tasks'. Manic symptoms were also more common, and characteristic symptoms of schizophrenia (odd affect, bizarre delusions, social withdrawal, auditory hallucinations, etc.) were less common. Thus, as a group patients with puerperal psychosis do seem to show certain differences from other patients with functional psychosis.

Even when puerperal psychosis is classified according to its main presenting symptoms, atypical features continue to show up. Dean and Kendell (1981) compared 33 patients meeting Research Diagnostic Criteria for major depression whose illnesses developed within three months of childbirth, with 33 age-matched patients with major depression unrelated to childbirth. Nearly half of the puerperal depressives were deluded or hallucinated, a similar proportion were agitated or retarded, and over two thirds were perplexed; in all cases these rates were two or three times higher than in the non-puerperal group.

Eighteen per cent were also disoriented, compared with none of the controls. Other features shown significantly more frequently by the puerperal depressives included lability of mood, other organic signs, and miscellaneous psychotic symptoms such as delusional mood, minor auditory and visual hallucinations, and perceptual distortions.

Schizophrenia has come to be considered to be uncommon as a puerperal presentation, and so the question of whether this shows atypical features is difficult to examine. One relevant study has, however, been carried out by Hays (1978). He collected clinical, demographic, and other details on 147 patients with a clinical diagnosis of schizophrenia and subjected the data to three different kinds of cluster analysis. In every case this isolated a small group of patients whose illnesses began within a few days of childbirth and which were characterized by 'thought disorder, catatonic symptoms, hectic mood changes, visual misrecognition, auditory hallucinations and varying delusions'. The aftermath if any tended to be depressive rather than apathetic. Two patients whose illnesses were not puerperal also appeared in this cluster; however, the mother of one of these had a history of puerperal psychosis and the other subsequently had a recurrence during the puerperium.

These studies all point to a conclusion which can be stated weakly or strongly. In its weak form, Dean and Kendall (1981) considered that, while most puerperal psychoses are similar to those occurring at other times, the possibility that some cases show specific features cannot be ruled out. Rather more strongly, Brockington *et al.* (1981) argued that there was no case for classifying puerperal psychoses (or at least the vast majority of these) within the group of schizophrenias, and that there was also evidence for significant differences from manic-depressive illnesses. In any event, it seems clear that puerperal psychoses sometimes, although by no means always, show atypical features. When these are present, the picture may be startlingly reminiscent of cycloid psychosis, as has been noted by Brockington *et al.* (1981).

Benign and periodic catatonia

Almost as soon as Kraepelin had placed catatonia firmly within the diagnostic category of schizophrenia, some authors began to suggest that it was not always correct to do so. Kirby (1913) described five patients who developed stuporose states which were unequivocally catatonic in nature. These all recovered spontaneously after several months (or in one case six years), and then went on to remain well for follow-up periods of up to seven years. He noted that the attacks tended to have an acute onset and were not preceded by the typical prodromal symptoms of schizophrenia; in some of the patients there had also been an earlier history of depression. In addition, the periods of stupor were often followed or interrupted by episodes of excitement which were more manic than catatonic in character. Later, Hoch (1921) collected a series of 19 similar patients (in fact the patients were drawn from the same hospital and at least one of the patients was the same as Kirby's). He introduced the term 'benign stupor' for such cases. Both authors argued that the course of these illnesses, as well as certain of their clinical features, betrayed their essentially manic-depressive nature.

Benign or manic-depressive catatonia soon became part of the tradition of atypical psychosis, finding its way, for example, into Perris' list of disorders resembling cycloid psychosis. In a rather similar way, Gjessing (1938; see also Fish 1962/Hamilton 1984) described a series of patients in whom catatonic states developed and remitted abruptly; his term for this presentation, periodic catatonia, also became absorbed into the same tradition. Seemingly forgotten, however, were Kraepelin's original observations on catatonic schizophrenia (see Chapter 2): in his experience around a third of cases showed periods of considerable improvement, sometimes to the point of apparent full recovery. These remissions frequently lasted two or three years, sometimes a decade or more, and rarely as long as 30 years. Nevertheless, sooner or later deterioration – often of a particularly malignant type – invariably supervened. An ultimately schizophrenic outcome was certainly evident in Gjessing's cases of periodic catatonia: he described his patients as being dull, apathetic, and showing no insight between episodes, and eventually a state characterized by poverty of ideation, lack of critical faculty, emotional flattening, and mannerisms set in.

Partly to resolve these uncertainties, Rachlin (1935) carried out a follow-up study of Hoch's original series of patients with benign stupor. He found that six had become chronically hospitalized, and all of these showed unexceptional severe schizophrenic deterioration. Three were alive and out of hospital; two of these, however, were obviously chronically psychotic. Four patients had died in the intervening period: in one, residual catatonic symptoms had been documented and it was clear that recovery had not been complete, in another no information was available, but the remaining two appeared to have had excellent remissions of symptoms lasting 9 and 11 years. In short, only three of the patients followed a course which was not unequivocally schizophrenic, and two of these had died before all of the follow-up period had elapsed.

Two contemporary studies are also commonly cited as supporting the view that catatonia is a feature of manic-depressive psychosis. In the first of these (Abrams and Taylor 1976b), 34 of 123 acute admissions meeting the authors' own criteria for mania were found to exhibit two or more catatonic phenomena. In the second (Taylor and Abrams 1977), 39 of 55 acute admissions showing one or more catatonic phenomena met the same criteria for affective psychosis. These studies, however, are open to criticism. In both, the authors used their own criteria for affective disorder which are easy to fulfil. Some of the patients, in fact, also exhibited first rank schizophrenic symptoms.

The current widely propagated belief that catatonia is a feature of manic-depressive psychosis and may even be more characteristic of this disorder than of schizophrenia (for example Mahendra 1981; Magrinat *et al.* 1983; see also Rogers 1992), turns out not to rest on firm foundations. Certainly, individual catatonic symptoms are occasionally seen in both manic and depressed patients, as was originally described by Kraepelin (1913*b*) and Bleuler (1911). It is also true that catatonic features can form a part of schizoaffective psychosis: stupor and excitement have been described in both cycloid psychosis and schizoaffective psychosis proper. But whether a full catatonic syndrome can occur in otherwise typical manic-depressive psychosis does not yet appear to have been convincingly demonstrated.

Tropical schizophrenia?

A number of authors, notably German (1972) and Stevens (1987), have drawn attention to the frequent occurrence of short-lived, self-limiting episodes of psychosis in Africa. These disorders were considered to be distinguishable from acute confusional states and accounted for up to 30 per cent of admissions to hospital in Senegal. They appeared to be uncommon or rare in the better-off, literate classes, but were endemic in rural settings where there was poverty, poor nourishment, and disease. Such brief psychoses could occur at any age but predominantly affected healthy young men and women.

The psychoses were commonly preceded by a definite environmental stress. The onset was typically abrupt, but there could be a prodromal period of up to several weeks in which there were, for instance, delusions. Most commonly, the picture was one of extreme restlessness, insomnia, confusion, auditory and visual hallucinations, delusions of being controlled, incoherent, rambling, pressured speech, and disturbed behaviour including undressing, tearing or burning clothes, destroying property, or violent attacks. Less commonly, the predominant symptoms were extreme withdrawal, mutism and negativism, or dreaminess. Without treatment, spontaneous remission took place in one to four weeks. Use of neuroleptics and ECT generally halved the length of the episodes. With or without treatment recovery was usually complete. However, the patient usually claimed amnesia for the episode.

With respect to the causative factors of these states, German favoured organic factors such as perinatal trauma, brain damaging illnesses in infancy, and chronic poor nutrition. He speculated that there was a large reservoir of subclinical cerebral dysfunction in Africa which facilitated the appearance of psychosis in response to physical or mental stress. Stevens, on the other hand, was impressed by the fact that investigations for underlying physical disease were generally negative, and that the disorder typically followed in the wake of some definable life stress.

If these descriptions are to believed, something very similar to cycloid psychosis seems to be extremely common in some tropical countries. Stevens suggested that these presentations might account for the variation in the prevalence of schizophrenia found in the International Pilot Study of Schizophrenia: while the rate of a core schizophrenic syndrome was found to be similar in all the countries studied, there was an obvious excess of psychoses which were both functional and non-affective in most of the tropical countries that took part (see Jablensky 1987).

Conclusion

It seems reasonable to accept that cycloid psychosis and schizoaffective psychosis proper both exist as valid clinical entities. On a combination of cross-sectional clinical picture and longitudinal course, they are discernibly different from both schizophrenia and manic-depressive psychosis, and also from each other. Such a conclusion may have no implications for the classification of functional psychosis beyond that it is a more complicated affair than might be wished. Some contemporary authors, notably Kendell and Crow, have, however, taken it to mean that the separation of schizophrenia and manic-depressive psychosis is invalid, and that a continuum view of functional psychosis should be accepted – a revival of the concept of unitary psychosis (Berrios and Beer 1994).

In the hands of Kendell (1987, 1991), the continuum of psychosis has purely clinical implications. The fact that there are functional psychotic states which share the features of the two major syndromes means that neither schizophrenia nor manic-depressive psychosis can be properly regarded as disease entities: they have only a provisional existence and clinicians will almost certainly have to modify their beliefs in the future. Unfortunately, it is not clear that schizoaffective psychosis – with a maximum frequency of 15 per cent of psychotic admissions – provides a convincingly large enough conduit for schizophrenia to merge imperceptibly into manic depressive psychosis. Cycloid psychosis, in addition, fits no better into a continuum concept than it does into a binary concept of psychosis.

For Crow (1986, 1991), the implications are mainly aetiological; he argues that it is the genetics of manic-depressive psychosis and schizophrenia that are on a continuum. However, although he is able to adduce evidence that these two disorders do not always breed true, it is not clear that the existence of schizoaffective and cycloid psychosis has anything particular to add to his argument. In the case of schizoaffective psychosis the genetic argument can be taken a certain distance, in as much as the evidence suggests that the disorder has links with both main forms of functional psychosis. On the other hand, in cycloid psychosis the evidence such as it is points to it being aetiologically distinct from both schizophrenia and manic-depressive psychosis.

12

Schizophrenia and organic brain disease

States bearing an at least passing resemblance to schizophrenia sometimes develop in the course of disorders affecting the brain, in circumstances where the suspicion of a causal relationship is raised. Such presentations are customarily designated as 'organic schizophrenia' or 'organic schizophrenia-like state', somewhat confusingly in view of the presumptive biological aetiology of schizophrenia itself. A large part of this confusion arises from two different meanings that the term organic has acquired: these are organic as symptomatic of underlying brain disease, and organic as opposed to functional in the clinical classification of mental disorder.

The term symptomatic schizophrenia refers to the occurrence of states similar to schizophrenia in association with obvious neurological disease of the brain. The existence of such presentations is not universally accepted, and their exact nature is a subject of dispute. As Mayer-Gross *et al.* (1969) noted, although some would consider these forms of organic schizophrenia to be genuine examples of what is in all probability an aetiologically heterogeneous disorder, others would regard them as distinguishable from true schizophrenia and merely offering a temporary illusion of the disorder. Still others would argue that they were examples of ordinary schizophrenia being triggered off in a predisposed individual.

Although the distinction between organic and functional is fundamental to the classification of mental disorders, what the terms should actually mean — especially the latter — has never been made entirely clear (see Trimble 1982; Berrios and Dening 1990). In current usage, organic disorders encompass two main disorders whose common denominator is obvious cognitive impairment: dementia and the acute confusional state. Functional tends to be defined by exclusion, in a process which has two stages: if there is no evidence of cognitive impairment, and no 'organicity' in the sense of evidence of underlying physical disease — that is the presentation is not symptomatic as defined above — then the disorder is functional, or primary and idiopathic. It is important to note that this does not mean that there is no underlying biological cause, but merely that any pathological lesion is subtle to the point that it cannot be detected by current methods.

Ambiguity and unanswered questions continue to surround both the terms organic and schizophrenia-like. Can a psychosis be functional in the presence of organic brain disorder? Should the accompanying brain disease always be identifiable? Does the psychosis have to occur in clear consciousness? Should a schizophrenia-like state be diagnosed cross-sectionally or longitudinally? Does the full syndrome need to be present, or will, say, isolated delusions or hallucinations be sufficient to qualify for the diagnosis? Where does cognitive impairment fit into the picture? Some of these questions are easy to answer, others raise questions which go to the heart of what is meant by schizophrenia. In this chapter the evidence that symptomatic schizophrenia-like states can complicate certain distinct types of brain disease is first reviewed. Following this an attempt will be made to try and disentangle some aspects of the considerably more knotty problem of what the occurrence of schizophrenic symptoms in dementia and in acute confusional states means. Finally, there are a small number of disorders in which neurological and psychiatric symptoms are inextricably intertwined, one of which, encephalitis lethargica, seems to be especially intimately related to schizophrenia.

Symptomatic schizophrenia

To make explicit what has almost always been left implicit in the literature, symptomatic schizophrenia refers to the occurrence, in a patient with brain disease or systemic disease which can affect brain function, of symptoms which in other circumstances would qualify for a diagnosis of schizophrenia. The clinical picture is quasi-functional, that is, there should be no evidence of cognitive impairment in the form of either clouding of consciousness, subtle or otherwise, or in the form of dementia, early or otherwise. Although the presentation needs to resemble primary schizophrenia, it only has to do this qualitatively – that is be diagnosable as this rather than any other form of psychosis – and not quantitatively – there is no necessity to insist that the clinical features and course conform to any stereotype of schizophrenia.

Symptomatic schizophrenic states meeting none, some, or all of these requirements have been documented for a variety of different brain diseases in a steady stream of case reports, series, and epidemiological surveys dating from the end of the last century. To examine these with a view to determining whether the associations are more than coincidental would be an enormous task, one which would probably be considered impossible were it not for the fact that it has already been achieved. Davison and Bagley (1969), in a 71 page, 782 reference article, critically reviewed the entire English and European language literature on the occurrence of what they termed schizophrenia-like psychosis in 13 classes of organic disease

---

Davison and Bagley's criteria for symptomatic schizophrenia
(from Davison and Bagley, 1969)

1. The presence of an unequivocal disorder of the central nervous system.

2. The presence, at some stage, of at least one of the following characteristic features of schizophrenia:

   Thought disorder, defined as bizarre statements, abnormal syntactical, grammatical, or other linguistic usages; incapacity to pursue a sustained train of thought; use of private symbols.

   Shallow or incongruous affect.

   Hallucinations and delusions.

3. The absence, at the stage when these psychotic features are displayed, of features which would reasonably lead to a diagnosis of affective psychosis, dysmnesic syndrome, delirium, or significant dementia.

Fig. 12.1

---

of the central nervous system. They used diagnostic criteria for schizophrenia which were, for the time, commendable; these are shown in Fig. 12.1. They took pains to exclude the presence of significant concurrent cognitive impairment, either in the form of acute confusion or dementia. They considered whether the association with schizophrenia was genuine mainly from a statistical standpoint, relying on figures for annual incidence of schizophrenia of 0.01–0.5 per cent, lifetime risk of 0.8–1.2 per cent, and prevalence of 0.2–0.5 per cent. However, where possible they also considered this question from the viewpoint of predisposition to schizophrenia, as gauged by presence of a schizoid premorbid personality or a family history of schizophrenia.

Davison and Bagley's monumental work is not easy to précis. Some sections went beyond strict clinical considerations, for instance discussing abnormal EEG findings in schizophrenia. In others, only an informal review of mainly anecdotal data could be made, for example in the cases of Friedrich's ataxia and motor neurone disease. At times poorly charted territory was strayed into, such as metabolic brain diseases and sleep disorders. In such circumstances, an approach which preserves the spirit and contains the highlights of their review will be taken. First, their findings in four principal categories of brain disease will be summarized, presenting an illustrative study in each case. This will be followed by a review of more recent studies where these have subsequently become available.

Epilepsy

As befitting a disorder which has aroused much controversy and supplied the theoretical basis for one of the most effective treatments in psychiatry, Davison and Bagley gave epilepsy pride of place in their review. Tracing the history of views on the relationship between epilepsy and schizophrenia, they noted that the occurrence of paranoid-hallucinatory psychoses in epileptic patients was increasingly reported in the latter half of the nineteenth century. The early years of the twentieth century saw the 'affinity' view become widely accepted (among others, Kraepelin (1909) commented on the association). A little later, however, another view which also dated from the last century became dominant; this was the 'antagonism' hypothesis, that epilepsy and schizophrenia were biological opposites. This was at least partly responsible for the introduction of convulsive therapy into psychiatry (see Chapter 9).

A number of studies carried out between 1925 and 1958 examined the rate of schizophrenia in patients with a diagnosis of epilepsy. These had large numbers (between 487 and 2000 patients), and they produced a measure of agreement, the figures for schizophrenia clustering around 0.7 per cent. They thus did little to support the view that the two disorders might be related. However, as a group they contained so many methodological shortcomings — in most the examination was clearly superficial — and there were so many factors which were not controlled for, that Davison and Bagley concluded that little weight could be attached to their findings.

Against this background, one study virtually singlehandedly established the modern view that epilepsy and schizophrenia are clinically associated. Over an 11-year period, Slater *et al.* (1963) collected and meticulously analysed a series of 69 patients who suffered from a combination of both disorders.

In all patients the diagnosis of epilepsy was based on EEG findings or occurrence of unequivocal clinical seizures. It was noted that 55 of the 69 patients had temporal lobe epilepsy or evidence of a temporal lobe EEG focus. The diagnosis of schizophrenia was made clinically, but was rigorous and easily satisfied Davison and Bagley's criteria: all but two cases cases showed delusions with or without hallucinations and these two had formal thought disorder accompanied by other symptoms. In all the patients psychotic symptoms had lasted for weeks or months in the absence of any cognitive impairment.

The authors collected all their cases from two hospitals in London. Based on lifetime expectancy rates of 0.8 per cent for schizophrenia and 0.5 per cent for epilepsy, they calculated that chance association of the two disorders could give rise to at most 33–55 cases over the 11-year study period. They acknowledged that the two hospitals concerned were both prestigious national referral centres and contained neuropsychiatric units, but they argued that even allowing for selective referral it was inconceivable that they could have so easily ascertained so many cases in only two out of the many general and psychiatric hospitals scattered throughout the area. They concluded that a statistically significant association existed between the two disorders.

Slater *et al.* considered that all the cardinal symptoms of schizophrenia were exhibited by their patients. As well as delusions and auditory hallucinations in the vast majority, visual, somatic, olfactory, and gustatory hallucinations were found in descending order of frequency. Formal thought disorder was present in 31 of the patients and affective flattening or inappropriateness in 28. Catatonic phenomena were surprisingly prevalent, one or more of these being seen in 40 patients, most commonly mannerisms. Various first rank symptoms were also evident in the case descriptions. These clinical features are summarized in Table 12.1.

The outcome of the psychosis was variable. Most typically, it ran a stormy course. A third of the series underwent remission of florid symptoms, and a further third showed improvement. Almost all patients showed some degree of negative symptoms which, however, were unusually mild in many cases; nearly half the patients were in full-or part-time work at follow-up. Slater *et al.* remarked that 'loss of affective response did not occur so early or become so marked in the great majority of these patients, as in the typical schizophrenic. . . . The psychosis from which they suffered tended to leave them preoccupied with old delusional ideas or with the remnants of thought disorder, but not with bleached, washed out or vacuous personalities'. Twenty nine of the patients also developed impairments of a more organic type, rather like these seen in the late stages of severe epilepsy. Perseverativeness, dullness, circumstantiality, or loss of memory were noted in such patients, but the state did not amount to dementia. These findings are also shown in Table 12.1.

Family history was thoroughly examined, with a relative being interviewed in 62 of the 69 patients. Only one first degree relative had a definite diagnosis of schizophrenia. Another had been given a diagnosis of paranoid psychosis. One suffered from the combination of epilepsy and psychosis, and one more had an unspecified psychiatric illness. Based on the first two cases, the familial rate of epileptic schizophrenia was calculated to be 0.7 per cent, not obviously different from that of the general population.

Examination of premorbid personality was limited, being based on previous case notes. Shyness and unsociability were recorded in 23 of the patients, and two more were described as schizoid personalities. A further 9 had paranoid traits (touchy, sensitive, or suspicious). Rather surprisingly, Slater *et al.* reached the conclusion that this did not represent an excess of schizoid or paranoid traits.

Table 12.1 Characteristics of schizophrenia in epilepsy (from Slater *et al.* 1963)

Onset	
Acute	16%
Episodic	29%
Subacute	13%
Insidious	42%
Course	
Towards improvement	32%
Fluctuating	23%
Towards chronicity	48%
Symptomatology	
Delusions	97%
Auditory hallucinations	67%
Other hallucinations	45%
Formal thought disorder	45%
Affective flattening/inappropriateness	41%
Catatonic phenomena	58%
Outcome	
Recovered	35%
Improved	33%
Unchanged	32%
At follow-up	
Employed	39%
No further admissions	47%
Some social interests	22%
Good preservation of personality	14%
Signs of organicity at follow-up	
Epileptic/organic personality change	48%
Handicapping memory impairment	9%

Based on Slater *et al.*'s study, Davison and Bagley concluded that schizophrenia was clinically associated with epilepsy. This conclusion was, however, qualified by a statement that the question should be settled by long term follow up of a cohort of unselected patients with epilepsy. In the years following their review more epidemiologically satisfactory studies have appeared. As reviewed by McKenna *et al.* (1985) and Lishman (1987), evidence from studies of the prevalence of psychosis in epilepsy, the prevalence of epilepsy in psychosis, and one incidence study of schizophrenia in epilepsy leaves little doubt that there there is an association between

epilepsy and persistent functional psychotic states. The risk of schizophrenia may be increased as much as 6–12 times, although this figure is
based on only a single, not very large survey. It has also become accepted,
as proposed by Slater *et al.* that schizophrenia in epilepsy is certainly preferentially, and possibly exclusively, associated with temporal lobe epilepsy.
This conclusion is based on a small number of generally rather poor studies,
but they at least have the virtue of according with the clinical impression
of most clinicians. Finally, schizophrenia in epilepsy has continued to be
considered to show unusual clinical features. A preponderance of paranoid-
hallucinatory presentations has been observed, as well as the lack of negative symptoms and the tendency to run a benign course noted by Slater *et al.*

Cerebral trauma

Insanity as a complication of head injury was first noted, according to
Davison and Bagley, in studies carried out after the Franco-Prussian war
of 1870. The view that there was a clinical association acquired authority
from a review of the literature between 1900 and 1921 by the German
psychiatrist Wilmans. It is worth noting, however, that neither Kraepelin
(1913*a*) nor Bleuler (1911) felt that head injury was a significant cause of
schizophrenia. Some decades later, a review by Elsasser and Grunewald
(1953) cast further doubt on the association.

Determination of whether or not an association exists between head
injury and schizophrenia faces a number of methodological difficulties.
One of these is the wide range in the severity of sequelae of head injury,
from mild concussion with full recovery to states of dementia and/or severe
neurological disability. Another difficulty concerns the interval between the
trauma and the onset of psychosis—how long this can be before the head
injury is no longer regarded as aetiologically relevant. A further complicating factor is the frequent development of post-traumatic epilepsy following head injury, which is independently implicated in the development of
schizophrenia-like psychoses. Davison and Bagley adopted a policy of
reviewing studies which followed patients who were unselected for severity
over a long period. Their table is reproduced in Table 12.2.

It can be seen that of six studies which had follow-up periods of 10 to
20 years, the risk of developing schizophrenia was found to range from 0.7
per cent to 9.8 per cent. On average, compared with an risk of 0.8 per cent
in the general population over 25 years, the rate seemed to be increased
two to three times. One study which found no increase (Liberman 1964)
included only cases with a diagnosis of concussion. Two further studies
(Aita and Reitan 1948; Poppelreuter 1917) found low rates of development
of schizophrenia, but their findings are difficult to judge as the follow-up
period was very short.

Probably the best of these studies was that of Hillbom (1960). He

Table 12.2 Incidence of schizophrenia in patients with head injury (from Davison and Bagley 1969)

Study	Number of patients	Mean observation period	Percentage developing schizophrenia
Poppelreuter (1917)	3000	2 years	0.07
Feuchtwanger and Mayer-Gross (1938)	1564	15 years	1.7
Aita and Reitan (1948)	500	3 months	0.4
Hillbom (1951)	1821	10 years	1.2
Meinertz (1957)	1110	15 years	1.5
Lobova (1960)	1168	15 years	9.8
Hillbom (1960)	415	20 years	2.6
Liberman (1964)	4807	15 years	0.7

examined the clinical case material on 415 individuals randomly selected from the records of 3552 Finnish men who had received brain injuries during military service, and in whom this was not complicated by other injuries, for example to the eyes or spinal cord. Both penetrating and closed injuries were included. Severity was judged on the degree of permanent work disability, and was classified as mild, moderate, or severe. The follow-up period was long, with a mean of 20 years. Psychiatric disturbances of various types were common in Hillbom's sample, and he found 11 cases of psychosis 'more or less reminiscent of schizophrenia'. These cases were all described, and in nine the diagnosis was fairly clear: there were delusions and/or auditory hallucinations with or without other florid symptoms in all but one case (who probably had formal thought disorder and affective flattening). Only one of the core group of nine cases definitely also suffered from epilepsy, with two more showing uncertain evidence of this. Of the two more doubtful cases, one developed a clear-cut psychosis characterized by multiple persecutory delusions; the other was stated to suffer from an episodic paranoid disorder, but decisive evidence of psychosis was not presented. A number of further cases were diagnosed as suffering from psychosis, of which two might possibly have been schizophrenic. Three of these latter four cases also suffered from epilepsy. Psychosis was found in patients with mild, moderate, and severe head injuries, but was most common in those in the last group.

The incidence of schizophrenia following head injury can thus be estimated from this study to range from 1.9 per cent (defined narrowly in patients without definite epilepsy) to 3.1 per cent (defined broadly and including cases with epilepsy).

The two features suggestive of a predisposition to schizophrenia, family history and schizoid premorbid personality, did not seem to be operative in schizophrenia following head injury, according to Davison and Bagley. In one large study of 240 patients with schizophrenia and a definite history of brain injury, the rate of schizophrenia in parents, siblings, and children was found to be 0.4 per cent, 1.3 per cent, and 0.7 per cent respectively—a frequency not obviously greater than that of the general population. Based on rather more anecdotal evidence, Davison and Bagley concluded that there was no excess of schizoid premorbid personality traits among head-injured patients who developed schizophrenia. In the absence of any clear indications of predisposition, they concluded that 'the trauma therefore is of direct aetiological significance rather than merely a precipitating factor'.

The clinical features of schizophrenia following head injury were noted to have attracted comment. The general tenor of these was that, while all the symptoms of schizophrenia could be encountered and the disorder could be indistinguishable from 'true' schizophrenia, there was a tendency to paranoid forms, hallucinations were often the most conspicuous feature, formal thought disorder tended to be absent, and there was a relative preservation of affect.

Since Davison and Bagley's review appeared, there has been one further study of schizophrenia as a complication of head injury. Achte *et al.* (1969) extended Hillbom's study to the whole sample of 3552 men and followed them up 22–26 years later. The proportion who developed schizophrenia was found to be much the same at 2.1 per cent; a further 2 per cent, however, were considered to have paranoid psychoses. Additionally, four patients (1.3 per cent) developed an isolated hallucinosis and seven (2.2 per cent) were considered to have 'reactive psychogenic psychoses', disorders which might well be diagnosed as schizophrenia outside Scandinavia. Schizophrenic psychoses appeared to be more frequent among those with mild injuries than those with severe ones. The interval could be very long, longer than ten years in a substantial proportion of cases. The younger the patient at the time of the trauma, the more commonly schizophrenia was found to be a sequel.

In summary, the frequency of schizophrenia as a complication of head injury seems clearly to exceed chance expectation. Ancillary evidence that the association is genuine comes from the failure of Davison and Bagley to find any evidence of family history or premorbid personality disposition among the cases they reviewed. It seems unlikely that epilepsy is a mediating factor in the development of psychosis.

Disseminated sclerosis

Psychosis was originally considered to be a rare complication of this disorder by nineteenth-century authors such as Gowers. By the early part of the twentieth century, however, a significant number of case reports had accumulated which documented the development of a psychosis resembling schizophrenia. More recently, it has been claimed that a psychotic episode may herald the onset of the disease, or appear as an early symptom, especially in cases which turn out to be neurologically severe.

Altogether, Davison and Bagley were able to collect 39 case reports of schizophrenia in disseminated sclerosis which satisfied their criteria. They noted that the psychosis usually presented early in the course of the disorder, although this was not an invariable feature: in eight cases it preceded the onset by up to five years, and in ten it developed five years or more after the neurological diagnosis had been made. Davison and Bagley also found three series which investigated the psychiatric aspects of disseminated sclerosis, which had sample sizes of 544, 63, and 330 patients. Only one case of schizophrenia was found in each of these. This rate was, if anything, low.

Reviewing the 39 individual case reports, Davison and Bagley noted that when schizophrenia occurred in the context of disseminated sclerosis it was invariably felt to resemble primary schizophrenia very closely. Paranoid, hebephrenic, and catatonic forms were all described. As far as could be determined, the course was equally unexceptional: some cases recovered spontaneously, others followed a relapsing and remitting course and in some deterioration (or dementia) supervened. There was little to suggest a predisposition to schizophrenia from the family histories of the patients. There was essentially no evidence either way bearing on the question of schizoid premorbid personality.

Later studies have tended to support the first of Davison and Bagley's conclusions, that disseminated sclerosis is not associated with an increased risk of schizophrenia. Surridge (1969), in a thorough survey, found only one case of schizophrenia (diagnosed clinically) among 108 cases of the disorder. More recently, Ron and Logsdail (1989) investigated 116 consecutive attenders at a neurological hospital with disseminated sclerosis, diagnosed according to established criteria. They took lifetime psychiatric histories and assigned DSM IIIR criteria where this was possible. Their findings are shown in Table 12.3. Six patients were found to have developed a non-affective functional psychosis after the disease had become established; however, none of these met DSM IIIR criteria for schizophrenia. The diagnosis was delusional disorder in four cases, and two qualified for a classification as atypical psychosis; to some extent this reflected the fact that full retrospective information was not available. One further patient

Table 12.3 DSM IIIR diagnoses in 116 patients with disseminated sclerosis (from Ron and Logsdail 1989)

Diagnosis	Relationship to onset of physical illness		
	before	after	at interview
Adjustment disorder	11	22	17
Bipolar disorder	1	5	2
Depressive disorder	4	12	18
Somatoform disorder	1	1	1
Anxiety disorder	4	1	0
Delusional disorder	0	4	4
Atypical psychosis	1	3	1
Organic disorders*	0	1	7

*At interview three patients were markedly elated in the presence of cognitive impairment, three were demented, and one had a hypomanic episode related to steroid treatment.

also received a diagnosis of atypical psychosis, but had experienced a previous episode more than three years prior to the onset of the neurological disorder. Organic, affective psychotic (depressive and bipolar), and a variety of neurotic disorders were also found, in all cases considerably more frequently than the delusional and atypical psychoses.

Davison and Bagley were ambivalent about whether schizophrenia was a significant complication of disseminated sclerosis. On the one hand, they accepted that the statistical evidence suggested that the association of the two conditions was no greater than chance expectation. On the other, they speculated that the high rate of other mental disorders, especially dementia might have reduced the opportunity to observe schizophrenia in a recognizable form. They were also impressed by the tendency of psychosis, when it was seen, to have its onset at around the same time as neurological symptoms first appeared, as well as the absence of family history in the reported cases. The more recent findings of Logsdail and Ron do not provide much support for this view. Psychosis seems to be a relatively frequent complication of disseminated sclerosis, but not schizophrenic psychosis in particular, and there is still no indication that the overall incidence of this disorder exceeds chance expectation.

Basal ganglia disorders

Davison and Bagley introduced this section of their review by noting that the points of contact and areas of overlap between schizohrenia and basal ganglia disorders were many and varied. Psychosis was accepted as an important sequel of encephalitis lethargica (see below), and there were long-standing traditions of schizophrenia-like psychoses occurring in other basal ganglia disorders, including torsion dystonia, Wilson's disease, and Huntington's chorea. In addition, the similarity between catatonic symptoms in schizophrenia and the hyper- and hypo-kinetic phenomena of basal ganglia disease had been noted many times. All in all, they felt that basal ganglia disease often had a prominent mental component, and then went on to review whether this could take a psychotic form in the following disorders.

Parkinson's disease: Case reports documenting the combination of schizophrenia and idiopathic or arteriosclerotic Parkinsonism have been extremely sparse (the position is quite different for post-encephalitic Parkinsonism, which is discussed later). Two formal series consisting of 146 and 200 patients also failed to document any cases of schizophrenia.

The most detailed survey of patients with Parkinson's disease was carried out by Mjones (1949). He collected a series of 250 patients with a diagnosis of idiopathic Parkinson's disease (194 cases) or arteriosclerotic Parkinsonism (32 cases); 24 patients with unclassifiable Parkinsonian symptoms were also included. Patients with a history of encephalitis or who showed typical sequelae of post-encephalitic Parkinsonism such as oculogyric crises were excluded. All patients were then interviewed personally and examined physically and psychiatrically. He found 4 (2.1 per cent) cases of schizophrenia, paranoid psychosis, or psychosis not otherwise specified among the 194 patients with idiopathic Parkinson's disease.

Davison and Bagley concluded that it was not possible, on the basis of the available findings, to extend the conclusions of clinicians such as Wilson, who stated that 'mental symptoms are limited to a depression of mood, the natural outcome perhaps of an incurable disease, and to an irritability also explicable by the nature of the ailment; anything beyond these is to be ascribed either to a concomitant arteriosclerosis or to some incidental condition'. There has been very little further work on schizophrenia as a complication of Parkinson's disease.

Wilson's disease: Two of Wilson's original cases (who were siblings) developed psychosis; one showed auditory hallucinations and passivity 18 months before neurological symptoms appeared. Subsequently, an association with schizophrenia was reported several more times, and it became dogma that the disorder could be the presenting feature of Wilson's disease—so much so that psychotic patients who develop early or severe involuntary movement disorders are still routinely tested to exclude the disorder. The reality of the association was, however, questioned by Beard

(1959), who argued that the diagnosis was poorly substantiated in many of the recorded cases.

Davison and Bagley reviewed the 520 case reports of Wilson's disease in the literature up to 1959. These contained 8 (1.5 per cent) acceptable cases of schizophrenia, according to their criteria, and 11 (2.1 per cent) doubtful ones. In most cases the psychosis and the neurological abnormalities appeared at around the same time, but in two cases the psychiatric symptoms preceded development of organic signs by 8 years and 20 years respectively. They compared this with the general population prevalence of schizophrenia of 0.2–0.5 per cent, and concluded that the evidence pointed to an association between the two disorders.

The absence of a detailed survey of psychiatric disorder in Wilson's disease at the time of Davison and Bagley's review has since been rectified by Dening and Berrios (1989). They examined detailed case material that existed on 195 patients under the care of a neurologist who had a special interest in the disorder. Although psychiatric disturbance was found to be common, with 20 per cent of the sample having seen a psychiatrist before the diagnosis of Wilson's disease was made, psychotic symptoms were distinctly unusual. At most three patients showed delusions (two definite and one possible) and only two patients (one definite and one probable) experienced hallucinations. On the basis of this, the authors argued that only of the order of 1 per cent of the sample could have been psychotic at the time of their presentation. It is possible that the retrospective nature of the study meant that this figure could have been an underestimate, but it seems unlikely that the prevalence of schizophrenia is greatly increased in Wilson's disease.

Huntington's disease: Psychosis, sometimes schizophrenic and sometimes unspecified, was repeatedly described in this disorder in the studies reviewed by Davison and Bagley. The frequency was stated as 5 per cent to 11 per cent, and the psychosis presented as the initial feature in at least a third of cases. Although these rates are many times higher than expected on the basis of chance, these series were lacking in psychiatric detail and it is not clear that the cases met Davison and Bagley's criteria for schizophrenia. Overall, however, they concluded that it seemed reasonable to include schizophrenia among the many psychiatric manifestations of Huntington's disease.

There has since been little to add to or alter Davison and Bagley's conclusion. Folstein (1989) found ten cases of schizophrenia meeting DSM IIIR criteria over eight years, out of a sample of around 200 patients. When Caine and Shoulson (1983) subjected a group of 30 patients to a detailed psychopathological evaluation, they found that three met DSM III criteria for schizophrenia, one more had experienced a brief schizophrenic episode, and one was diagnosable as suffering from a paranoid disorder. In both studies other forms of psychiatric disorder were observed, and in particular Folstein (Folstein *et al*. 1983; Folstein 1989) documented an extremely high frequency of manic-depressive psychosis: 43 per cent with depression and 10 per cent with hypomania.

The conclusions of this updated and compressed account of Davison and Bagley's work can be summarized as follows. Schizophrenia is over-represented in some central nervous system disorders, but not in all of them. In temporal lobe epilepsy, the risk appears to be increased as much as 6–12 times; after cerebral trauma it is approximately doubled; in other disorders including disseminated sclerosis, Wilson's disease, and Parkinson's disease, notwithstanding numerous anecdotal reports of association, the evidence is that the risk is no greater than in the general population. When schizophrenia does occur, there is little evidence to support the widely perpetuated view that the cerebral disorder has merely precipitated schizophrenia in a predisposed individual. A more durable finding is that the clinical picture of schizophrenia complicating organic brain disease shows differences from 'true' schizophrenia: the presentation may be dominated by delusions and hallucinations, there may be a lack of affective flattening, and the disorder may run a relatively benign course. Often, the impression is that the states correspond to a paranoid or paraphrenic form of schizophrenia. These observations have invariably been impressionistic, it is clear that the differences from true schizophrenia are quantitative rather than qualitative, and overall they are not gross.

This greater than chance occurrence of something essentially indistinguishable from schizophenia raises a number of questions. Any theory to account for the development of schizophrenia in conjunction with organic brain disease also has to account for the comparative rarity of the development, and why it is seen in some disorders but not others. It should also be able to account for increases in manic-depressive psychosis and other psychiatric disorders which have been claimed in at least some of the above conditions. As yet, there has been no attempt to answer any of these questions.

Schizophrenic symptoms in dementia and acute confusional states

Symptomatic schizophrenia, as defined in the previous section, refers to schizophrenia-like states accompanying brain disease in the absence of any impairment of cognitive function. This definition precludes consideration of two important and common classes of brain disorder, dementia and the acute confusional state. In both of these symptoms which bear an at least superficial resemblance to some of those seen in schizophrenia are regularly encountered. In addition, there are grounds for suspecting that something approximating to a full-blown schizophrenic picture may sometimes complicate them—dementia routinely figures in the differential diagnosis of any psychiatric disorder occurring in old age, and there are undoubted instances where acute confusional states have been misdiagnosed as schizophrenia. The fact that these disorders are by definition accompanied by cognitive impairment makes the consideration of what is meant by schizophrenic and schizophrenia-like considerably more difficult than in the case of symptomatic schizophrenia. For both conditions the literature analysing the questions is also small.

Dementia

Lishman (1987) defined dementia (with its many synonyms such as chronic brain syndrome, chronic organic reaction, and chronic psycho-organic syndrome) as a disorder which may result from many different pathological processes, but in which the clinical picture shows a large measure of similarity from one disease entity to another. The majority of dementias are due to diffuse and widespread disease of the brain, but some are the manifestation of focal pathology. Most are slowly progressive, but static or gradually improving pictures can be seen, for example in treated tertiary syphilis or following head injury or encephalitis.

The mode of presentation of dementia is well known, beginning with memory impairment or a change in personality which gives way to a state of global intellectual decline. In a setting of clear consciousness, the patient becomes unable to perform cognitive tasks which were previously well within his or her grasp. Attention is diminished with loss of concentration and distractibility. The content of thought is impoverished and thinking becomes concrete and inflexible. As the disorder progresses, abnormalities in emotion, speech, general behaviour, become increasingly obvious until the entire personality and all intellectual faculties are lost.

In the classical picture of dementia there is little that could be mistaken for the symptoms and signs of psychosis. According to Lishman (1987), perception is not affected to any great extent, and not in a way that gives rise to hallucinations. In the later stages speech may become grossly disorganized and fragmented, and so be incoherent; however, this incoherence is very different in character from formal thought disorder. Disorders of the content of thought are recognized in dementia, but these typically take the form of paranoid ideas and attitudes rather than delusions. The only apparent exception is the occurrence of stereotypies and mannerisms in the advanced dementia, usually as an accompaniment of the grossly deteriorated behaviour characteristic of this stage of the disorder.

Going beyond this, most authors accept that abnormal beliefs can be seen in a minority of patients with dementia, usually as an isolated phenomenon.

Commonly, these are considered to be crude, transient, and poorly systematized—'paranoid ideas', 'false ideas', beliefs that are only delusional 'in the technical sense' (for example Mayer-Gross *et al*. 1969; Raskind and Storrie 1980; Lishman 1987). In one study (Rubin *et al*. 1988) ideas of this type were found in a quarter of patients with Alzheimer's disease. Closely related to these are abnormal ideas dementing patients entertain about the presence or identity of individuals around them. These may involve the belief that people are in the house, or that people on television are really in the room. Alternatively the patient may fail to recognize his or her own reflection in the mirror and converse with the alleged other person. Such ideas were seen in nearly a quarter of Rubin *et al*.'s sample of Alzheimer's disease patients. Some examples of these phenomena are described in Fig. 12.2.

Some authors have also expressed the view that a florid schizophrenic syndrome can occasionally be superimposed on dementia. Lishman (1987) considered that dementia could rarely initially present with the picture of a functional psychotic illness, in which the underlying intellectual deterioration was inconspicuous. The occurrence of delusions and hallucinations with a bizarre quality and revolving around plots to molest or harm the patient was also recognized by Raskind and Storrie (1980). But the author whose name is most associated with this view is Post (1966, 1982): as described in Chapter 9, he was able to collect 16 cases out of his total sample of 93 who showed paraphrenic states in the setting of what turned out to be definite dementing diseases; these were not usually distinguishable from similar states occurring in the absence of organic brain disease. He concluded that 'some patients suffering from dementing illnesses of late life exhibit well structured and persistent paranoid pictures which are only later erased by the increasing dementia'.

A number of studies examining the frequency of psychotic symptoms in dementia—invariably Alzheimer's disease—were reviewed by Wragg and Jeste (1989). Delusions were reported in 10–73 per cent of patients at some stage of the illness, but in most studies the rates clustered around 33 per cent. Often, but not always, these were of a simple 'organic' form. These studies also found appreciable rates of hallucinations, the median frequency of these being 28 per cent. Visual hallucinations were somewhat more common than auditory ones. In the largest study to date, Burns *et al*. (1990) found rather lower rates of delusions (16 per cent) and hallucinations (visual 13 per cent and auditory 10 per cent) in 178 patients with Alzheimer's disease. Delusions were commonly of the simple 'organic' type, but about a quarter of the time they were complex and/or bizarre (for example one patient believed that people were cutting his throat at night, and another that a tape machine was giving him messages). It was clear that the occurrence of both types of phenomena was not restricted to periods of

Descriptions of typical abnormal ideas in dementia

Judgement is impaired early as a result of these various changes [loss of intellectual flexibility, becoming tied to the immediate aspects of situations, and loss of abililty to make abstract interpretations]. The patient's insight into his defects is characteristically poor and sometimes there is little awareness of illness at all. False ideas readily gain ground and and paranoid ideation is particularly common. Ideas of reference may partly reflect an exaggeration of premorbid tendencies, likewise the specific form which delusions may take. Characteristically the delusions are poorly systematized and evanescent, though occasionally they become entrenched and unshakeable. . . . They may be delusions in the technical sense, in that the beliefs are held in the face of evidence of their falsehood, but this is largely because the evidence fails to be understood, not because it is rejected. Delusional themes are often crude and bizarre, typically of being robbed, poisoned, threatened,or deprived. Delusions of influence and other frankly schizophrenic phenomena may appear, perhaps by virtue of special premorbid vulnerability in this respect.

(Lishman 1987)

Some paranoid phenomena are closely related to memory loss. The patient will forget the location of some object or forget having eaten a meal. When the misplaced object is perceived as missing or the food eaten is discovered to be absent from the refigerator, accusations of theft result. Such delusions of theft are quite common and are a frequent cause of interpersonal turmoil.

(Raskind and Storrie 1980)

The imagined people could be either relatives or strangers. A subject might imagine that a stranger had entered the house and hidden in the closet or that an unknown person was hiding in the bedroom with the subject's wife. . . . [Other] subjects were unable to recognize their faces in a mirror. These subjects would converse with the person in the mirror and might try to open the door to which the mirror was attached to invite the person in. The subject would ask others why a person was being kept in a mirror. One subject became agitated because the person in the mirror was always following him. . . . The final subgroup is characterized by the inability to recognize that people on television were not real. . . . One subject did not want the people on television watching her undress and left the room to change. Another was frightened by television violence and thought that 'they' were shooting at him. While watching a ballgame one subject was convinced that the players were in the room with him.

(Rubin *et al.* 1988)

Fig. 12.2

supperadded acute confusion. Delusions and hallucinations have been found to co-occur in many cases (Drevets and Rubin 1989; Rosen and Zubenko 1991).

In short, there is no doubt that individual schizophrenic symptoms in the shape of delusions and hallucinations can be seen in dementia. These may occur in combination so that a full schizophrenic syndrome is sometimes diagnosable. While the former are fairly common, the latter is less frequently seen, and there are no reliable estimates of its prevalence. Nevertheless, the rate of schizophrenia-like psychosis would appear to be at least as great as that in some of the brain diseases described in the previous section.

Acute confusional states

Like dementia, acute confusional states (delirium, acute organic psychosis, and various other synonyms) are in the words of Lishman (1987) called forth by a great number of different pathological processes affecting the brain, from trauma to anoxia and from metabolic derangements to the toxic effects of drugs and alcohol. The clinical picture is due to a widespread disruption of brain function (or perhaps more accurately of higher brain functions such as thinking, perception, and emotion) by means of a biochemical, electrical, or mechanical disturbance. As in dementia, the symptomatology tends to follow a surprisingly similar pattern whatever the underlying cause.

As described by Lishman (1987), the mode of onset of acute confusional states is abrupt, although this might not always be detectable, for example when the state is subtle. The hallmark symptom is impairment of consciousness, which is universal in some degree. This ranges from the barely perceptible ('clouding of consciousness'), through more obvious degrees of muddling and disorientation ('confusion') to a state of torpidity or somnolence. The most extreme expression is coma. The conscious level characteristically fluctuates and is typically worse at night. Occasionally there is a state of hyper-arousal or hyper-alertness, although a defective grasp of the environment is still evident. Acute confusional states normally remit with recovery from the underlying physical illness. However, this potential for reversibility may not always be realized if the underlying cause cannot be remedied.

Acute confusional states may be simple, or be complicated by the intrusive appearance of abnormalities in thought, perception, affect, and psychomotor behaviour. When this occurs the state is usually referred to as delirium in Britain, whereas in the USA this term is used to refer to the syndrome as a whole. As described by Lishman (1987), perceptual abnormalities classically take a visual form, from misinterpretations or illusions, for example window panes are seen as bars on a cell or a table as a coffin, to hallucinations proper. These latter range from simple flashes of light to geometrical patterns, to fully-formed animals, people, and whole scenes, sometimes depicting bizarre or apocalyptic events. A particularly common presentation in the elderly is the phenomenon of 'silent boarders'—seeing full-sized figures in the house who do not speak. Speech also becomes disorganized in a characteristic and easily recognizable way: trains of thought become isolated and chaotic and in severe cases there may be no more than incoherent muttering. Thinking may be speeded up, slowed down, or slurred; underneath, however, it is concrete, banal, and impoverished. Usually, overall activity diminishes in acute confusional states. When left alone the patient does little and when asked to do things is slow, hesitant, and often perseverative. In some cases, however, the reverse is seen with restless hyperactivity and noisy disturbed behaviour. Other changes include picking at bedclothes, ransacking them for imaginary objects, and so-called occupational delirium, where the patient re-enacts a complex series of movements, driving an imaginary car, performing his work activity, etc.. Many emotional changes are seen, from depression, anxiety or irritability, to perplexity, lability, and elation, to anger and fear. Typically, affect is shallow and the most common accompaniment of severe states is indifference and withdrawal.

It is clear that despite the presence of florid mental phenomena the typical picture of delirium is quite different from schizophrenia. However, as in dementia, it is also accepted that more schizophrenia-like phenomena can be part of the pattern of symptomatology. According to Lishman (1987), clear-cut delusions may well up suddenly and be expressed with full conviction; these may be persecutory, grandiose, referential, or hypochondriacal in nature. Usually they betray their organic origin in being vague, shallow, poorly elaborated, transient, and inconsistent. When consciousness is relatively clear, however, they can be coherent and systematized. Rarely, delusions have been known to persist after full recovery from an acute confusional state: Mayer Gross *et al.* (1969) gave the example of a soldier who became delirious after being wounded in battle, and during the course of the disorder formed the belief that he had received a decoration. This was obstinately clung on to after all the other symptoms had cleared up. As well as the classical delirious visual hallucinations, auditory hallucinations may also occur, and also bizarre somatic sensations: body parts may feel shrunken, enlarged, misplaced, or even disconnected.

The only attempt to examine the phenomenology of delirious acute confusional states with particular reference to their relationship to the symptoms of schizophenia has been made by Cutting (1980, 1987). He carried out detailed mental state examinations, using the Present State Examination and Andreasen's scale for the assessment of formal thought disorder, on 74 patients who showed one or more psychotic symptoms which were secondary to some clearly identifiable organic cause. In 62 of the 74

(84 per cent) there was clinical evidence of clouding of consciousness, and most showed some evidence of poor cognitive test performance at times.

Cutting found that 35 of these 74 delirious patients showed delusions. In eight, these were simple and similar to the 'organic' delusions described above for dementia. In 18, however, the beliefs were complex or bizarre; these are shown in Table 12.4. Nine patients also showed delusions which were congruent with an elated, depressed, or mixed mood-state. Hallucinations were also common: visual hallucinations were present in 25 patients and verbal auditory hallucinations were found in 9 cases; in two cases these were in the third person. Formal thought disorder was evident clinically in 47 patients. However, in many cases this was either restricted to slowness and poverty of speech, or it reflected illogicality—this was typically observed when the patients attempted to give explanations for their disorientation. Leaving these aside, 18 patients showed tangential or irrelevant replies to questions, circumstantiality, distractibility, flight of ideas, incoherence, or poverty of content of speech. First rank symptoms were not seen, apart from possible passivity (thoughts controlled) in one case.

Cutting also observed that the psychotic phenomena seen in acute confusional states showed qualities which set them apart from their counterparts in schizophrenia. Thus in half the deluded patients, the content of the beliefs revolved around imminent misadventure to others or bizarre happenings in the immediate vicinity; such themes were only apparent in 6 out of a comparison group of 67 schizophrenic patients. Similarly, in the organic patients visual hallucinations were twice as common as auditory hallucinations, whereas in the schizophrenic group the proportions were reversed. While something that technically had to be called formal thought disorder was present in a majority of patients, the typical schizophrenic phenomena such as derailment, neologisms, and poverty of content of speech were encountered very uncommonly. Cutting's conclusion was that, although psychotic phenomena of equivalent complexity to those of schizophrenia are found in acute confusional states, their pattern is quite distinct in the two disorders.

Drawing together the findings on schizophrenic symptoms in dementia and acute confusional states, the conclusions that emerge seem to be as follows. In the first place, both disorders, as well as presenting with *deficits* in higher cognitive functioning, are quite commonly accompanied by *productive* phenomena, including delusions and hallucinations; these tend to be simple, isolated, and to carry a distinctive 'organic' stamp. Secondly, in some cases there is instead a more florid syndrome made up of psychotic symptoms which are comparable in form and complexity to those of schizophrenia. Details of these states are sketchy, but it seems clear that any alleged differences—for example in the content of the delusions—are relative rather than absolute. Finally, it seems highly probable that the

Table 12.4 Complex, bizarre, or multiple delusions in patients with acute confusional states (from Cutting 1987)

Case	Cause	Content of delusion
Female, age 70	Right parietal CVA	When people washed in sink they scrubbed her back; things shown to her became muddled up in pillow; carrot in windpipe
Female, age 69	Drugs	Thoughts controlled; something funny going on; she was dying; woman in next bed being harmed
Male, age 58	Cardiac failure	Irish Catholics from Streatham driving to Brixton and harming locals by transmitting decomposed matter into their and his own necks by affecting circulatory system parellel to bloodstream called 'man's money'
Male, age 76	Respiratory failure	Wife had left him
Male, age 59	Drugs	X-ray girls involved in sexual misdemeanours; wife outside curtain; something in head turning to dust
Female, age 40	Carcinoma	Mother, sister, and herself dying; relatives in ward; nurses going to kill her
Female, age 76	Myxoedema	Relatives and herself had died; doctor on ward going to marry a beautiful person
Female, age 69	Electrolyte imbalance	Husband eaten by cannibal; drunken nurses obtaining money from patients by doing unspeakable things; she had VD
Female, age 48	Electrolyte imbalance	Fire in hospital; children coming to Casualty choking; husband and friend underneath bed, moving it; psychologist testing her

Case	Cause	Content of delusion
Male, age 68	Carcinoma	Unpleasant incidents on ward blamed on him; all the excrement in ward is his; hospital floating on water; daughter to be shot
Female, age 27	Alcohol	Doctor taking blood out of her and putting it back into her neck; brother out to kill her, her dog, and old ladies
Male, age 81	Respiratory failure	People exporting illicit material, giving dummy drugs; he was substitute patient for someone else
Male, age 62	Cardiac failure	About to die; nurse moving things around in bags, possibly dynamite and involving IRA; doctors not real doctors
Male, age 27	Epilepsy	About to die; people changing things to test him; discrepancy between his thoughts and what he expected to think
Female, age 28	SLE	Something bad going to happen; mother dying
Male, age 63	Cardiac failure	Building bombarded; police all around
Female, age 57	Drugs	Son down road taking drugs; men out to kill husband
Female, age 37	Carcinoma	Baby taken away; nurses met daily to decide who was worst patient on the ward

dividing line between these two presentations is not hard and fast. In dementia, in particular, some patients are seen with one or two crude 'organic' delusions; others show delusions which are more schizophrenia-like but which are still relatively isolated; yet others develop a combination of delusions and hallucinations; and a few present with a paraphrenia-like picture whose underlying organic basis may not declare itself for some time.

There seems to be a gradation from organic to functional presentations rather than an all-or-none transition.

Encephalitis lethargica

Having established that something very similar to schizophrenia can complicate certain brain diseases, and that the relationship of schizophrenia to dementia and acute confusional states is altogether more complicated, the links with organic disorders are not quite exhausted. A number of brain diseases exist in which the combinations of psychiatric and neurological phenomena are so close that they are, in fact, usually referred to as neuro-psychiatric disorders. These include epilepsy, particularly temporal lobe epilepsy, which is almost certainly associated with a number of other psychiatric syndromes besides schizophrenia (Reynolds and Trimble 1981); and Gilles de la Tourette's syndrome, into the fabric of which are woven a range of striking mental and behavioural abnormalities (Lees 1985; Comings 1991). There is, however, one disorder which has affiliations with schizophrenic symptoms above all others, and where the relationship is so intimate that it can almost be regarded as schizophrenia's organic next of kin. This is encephalitis lethargica.

As he pointed out in the foreword to his book, von Economo (1931) was the first author to describe encephalitis lethargica, giving an account of a small local epidemic of cases in Austria in 1917. Initially met with some scepticism, von Economo's claims to have discovered a new illness were soon verified by an outbreak which started in London a year later and spread through Europe over the next two years. As recounted by Sacks (1983), this pandemic attacked nearly five million people worldwide— killing a third of them and sooner or later disabling the majority of the rest—before it disappeared as mysteriously as it appeared in 1927. Earlier epidemics were subsequently recognized to have occurred from the sixteenth century onwards, and cases continued to occur throughout the 1930s. Since then there have been no further outbreaks. However, it remains uncertain whether the disorder can now be consigned to history.

The acute phase of encephalitis lethargica

The vast majority of cases were ushered in by a short prodromal period of fever and pharyngitis, which could be slight. This subsided after a few days or occasionally a few weeks and was replaced by a series of neuro-logical (and psychiatric) symptoms, which though very diverse and haphazard, tended to be classifiable into one of three main forms.

According to von Economo, the most common presentation was the *somnolent-ophthalmoplegic* form. This set in with a deceptively normal appearing sleepiness, but with the patient falling asleep while sitting, standing, eating, or even walking. This could resolve, or go on to more or less permanent sleep from which the patient could only be roused with difficulty, or progress to coma. In the *hyperkinetic* form the prodromal malaise and fever, which tended to be more severe and prolonged than in other forms, was gradually replaced by general mental unrest and ceaseless motor activity. Initially, this appeared normal in form, but became increasingly interfered with by chorea. The involuntary movements could be extremely severe, more severe than in any other form of chorea, the patients rolling about continuously, jerking themselves up, throwing themselves down, and often requiring restraint. Typically, this was accompanied by severe and treatment-resistant insomnia, or alternatively by reversal of the sleep–waking cycle. The least common, *Parkinsonian* form (called the amyostatic-akinetic form by von Economo) began with the usual prodromal signs, after which a state of general weakness supervened: the patient lay in bed with closed eyes but not really asleep, and a slowness and paucity of all movements and speech became obvious. This quickly blurred into Parkinsonian akinesia. All the signs of Parkinsonism could be present, but sometimes the akinesia was marked and there was very little increase in tone. The symptoms often showed marked diurnal variation with the patients improving, becoming normal, or even exhibiting a little psychomotor excitement as the day wore on, only to revert to immobility the next morning.

The three basic forms could occur in any combination, shade into each other, or follow one another in successive phases. All the forms developed against a background of a much wider set of neurological signs. These included particularly ophthalmic signs: one or more of ptosis, ophthalmoplegia, absent pupillary responses, or nystagmus were 'almost regularly present'. Almost every other neurological sign could also be seen—trismus, hiccuping, headache, other cranial nerve palsies, seizures cerebellar signs, neuralgias, aphasias—but sensory disturbances were uncommon. These signs tended to be mild, although they were not always so, and they were sometimes fleeting.

It is evident from von Economo's account that all three varieties of acute encephalitis lethargica were apt to be complicated by psychotic phenomena. The most striking group of symptoms were openly referred to as catatonic: in the Parkinsonian form, patients were reported as showing blocking, psychological pillow, and persistence of postures which could amount to full waxy flexibility; sometimes there was an apathy and failure to take nourishment which reminded one of catatonic stupor. In the hyperkinetic form, the motor unrest was sometimes expressed mainly or wholly as 'a general, curious restlessness of an anxious or hypomanic type, which may occasionally reach a state bordering on frenzy . . . the patient tosses about in bed, pushes the blankets back, pulls them up again, sits up, throws himself back again in a wild sort of haste, jumps out of bed, strikes out aimlessly, talks incoherently, clucks his tongue, and whistles'—surely a description of catatonic excitement.

Psychotic symptoms, according to von Economo, occurred commonly in the initial stage and occasionally dominated the presentation, with neurological signs being subtle or absent. In order of frequency these were as follows: delirium, hypomania-like excitement, dream-like states and apathetic depression. He did not describe schizophrenia-like states, but it seems it was possible that some of the vivid hallucinations described particularly in the hyperkinetic form were accompanied by little or no clouding of consciousness. Hall (1924) and Wilson (1940) considered that euphoria, hypomania, depression, stupor, hallucinations, and paranoia could be all be prominent features. As noted by Lishman (1987) the possibility that the whole course of encephalitis lethargica could be played out as a psychiatric disturbance is attested to by the fact that many patients admitted to mental hospitals with diagnoses of non-specific confusional, delusional, or hallucinatory states later developed typical post-encephalitic symptoms. One such case is shown in Fig. 12.3.

The chronic sequelae of encephalitis lethargica

If schizophrenic phenomena other than catatonic symptoms were not particularly conspicuous in the acute stages of encephalitis lethargica, they certainly became so as part of the late manifestations of the disorder which, in the words of Sacks (1983), rolled in from the 1930s in a great sluggish torpid tide. These sequelae supervened in the majority of survivors, sometimes immediately and sometimes after a delay of years. They comprised Parkinsonism, oculogyric crises, and psychiatric changes, and have been described by von Economo (1931) and Sacks (1983).

Parkinsonism: This constituted the most frequent and serious sequel. In general, the syndrome resembled idiopathic Parkinsonism both in its onset and its constellation of symptoms. However, it also showed a difference, mainly in that it could progress to extremely severe states of immobility, some patients making no movements at all for decades. Post-encephalitic Parkinsonism also differed from the idiopathic form of the disorder in another important respect: it was frequently complicated by repetitive motor phenomena. These took the form of masticatory movements, blepharospasm, torticollis, other dystonic and athetoid movements, and also tics of various kinds, including vocal tics.

In addition, it seems clear that post-encephalitic Parkinsonism was shot through with catatonic phenomena. Blocking and freezing were regularly described by von Economo and other authors. Waxy flexibility, or something closely similar to it, could also be seen. There could also be an overall

Acute encephalitis lethargica dominated by schizophrenic symptoms
(from Sands 1928)

FM, 30, white, married, and has two healthy children. Family history is
negative except for the fact that one brother died from encephalitis at the
age of 30, two years ago. Personal history is normal. Present illness dates
back to February 1st, 1927, when the patient complained of general
weakness and intense headache. From February 5th there was persistent
insomnia. She commenced to act rather strangely, became suspicious and
irritable, and complained that people were talking about her. On
February 7th, she had a generalized convulsion and this was repeated on
the following day. On February 11th she was admitted to hospital
complaining of intense headache, restlessness and irritability, and of
hearing all sorts of voices.

On examination the patient showed definite cervical rigidity and a
moderate Kernig sign. Pupils were decidedly irregular and both reacted
sluggishly. There was bilateral weakness of the external rectus muscles.
There were active abdominal reflexes, generalized hyperreflexia, and
bilateral spontaneous extensor toe phenomena. There was marked
vasomotor instability. Her temperature was 99°F, pulse 104 and
respirations 24. Blood count showed a white cell count of 7800,
68 per cent polymorphs. Clear spinal fluid was obtained under three plus
pressure and showed a trace of globulin, ten cells and no colloidal gold
curve reduction. The blood and spinal fluid Wassermann were negative.

The patient remained in a more or less confused state and was very
evasive and suspicious. She would not permit examination at times. She
asked the nurse repeatedly if someone was going to kill her. She would
not sleep nights. Her temperature remained at 99°F, pulse varied between
88 and 100, and respirations between 16 and 24. She was finally
discharged from the hospital on March 3rd, 1927. I saw her again on
April 4th, 1927. She then showed decided masking of her face with
diminution in her winking reflex. Her gait was decidedly of Parkinson
type. There was impairment of voluntary associative movements. There
was decided left internal rectus weakness. The pupils were equal,
somewhat irregular in outline but very sluggish, both to light and
accommodation. Mentally she admitted auditory hallucinations and
persecutory delusions. She said: 'I hear ear phones telling me that
everything is OK and my husband, my home and my children are well. I
remember you in the hospital. Tell me the truth, didn't you try to kill
me? You wanted to poison me, didn't you? I still hear peculiar voices in
my ears. These voices guide me and tell me what to do. They are human
voices. They advise me what to feed my children and what to do.'

Fig. 12.3

psychic torpor reminiscent, von Economo felt, of catatonia. The hyperkinetic phenomena which accompanied the Parkinsonism sometimes, perhaps characteristically, took complex and intricate forms. Von Economo described patients whose tics which gradually evolved towards repetitions, iterations, and stereotypies; psychological elements associated themselves with the movements increasing them to compulsive actions, often of a grotesque kind. In other patients, passive movements were repeated for a long time. Bellowing, echolalia, and palilalia were also described. One patient repeated the question 'when will I be well again?' over and over again for hours, this always being accompanied by identical compulsive movements.

Oculogyric crises: Nearly half the survivors of the 1924 epidemic became subject to these complex forms of acute dystonic reaction. These could develop as an isolated phenomenon or in association with Parkinsonism; perhaps most typically they heralded the onset of post-encephalitic Parkinsonism, preceding its onset by up to several years. The motor aspects were in themselves unexceptional: the attacks consisted of abrupt onset gaze deviations, usually upwards and often to one side, but occasionally downwards or sideways. This could be the only motor manifestation, but it was frequently accompanied by blepharospasm or blepharoclonus, and dystonic spasms of the neck, trunk, or limbs—the classical presentation was of a patient with his or her head flung back and eyes staring upward.

Von Economo noted that in many patients undergoing oculogyric crises there was a peculiar state of consciousness reminiscent of a fugue, and that other patients always experienced the same compulsive thoughts. A more detailed account was given by Jelliffe (1929, 1932), who made it clear that the dystonic muscle spasms were only one component of what was often a complex neuropsychiatric disturbance. Affective accompaniments were common, such as fear, autonomic arousal, malaise, restlessness, or depression; one of Jelliffe's patients was so tormented by murderous and suicidal thoughts that he attempted to jump through a window. Complex ritualistic behaviour was noted, as were echolalia, palilalia, mutism, and many other speech disturbances (see Lishman 1987; Owens 1990). In some cases there were ruminations and forced thinking, and in others there were visual misperceptions or hallucinations (Jelliffe 1929, 1932; Sacks, 1983). A clear account of schizophrenic symptoms was given by Steck in 1931 (cited by Ward 1986): 'A young man with severe Parkinsonism . . . had oculogyric, crises during which he said he was controlled by . . . evil spirits . . . which spoke ill of God and Jesus Christ, saying, for example, that He was a German. . . . He said that the voices were "on me, in me, in my body, in my mouth" '.

Psychiatric disorders: Personality changes were widely recognized to follow encephalitis lethargica. These often took the form of disinhibition and antisocial behaviour, but other directions — for example hypochondriasis — could be taken (von Economo 1931; Lishman 1987). Children, in particular, often underwent a marked change, becoming wilful, disobedient, lying, stealing, and showing gross swings of mood; sometimes they became so disturbed, violent, and destructive, particularly at night, that they had to be kept in caged cots (Ward 1986). Although felt to be rare by von Economo, depression and mania came to be considered to be relatively common by Lishman.

The evidence that schizophrenia occurred more frequently than expected by chance as a sequel of encephalitis lethargica was reviewed by Davison and Bagley (1969). They noted that reports of schizophrenia developing before, simultaneously with, or after the onset of post-encephalitic Parkinsonism abounded, in marked contrast to the idiopathic and arteriosclerotic forms of the disorder. A number of studies of post-encephalitic patients found rates for schizophrenia in the range of 10–30 per cent. However, these were undoubtedly overestimates of the true rate as they all consisted of patients who were preselected on the basis of showing psychiatric disorder. Nevertheless, Davison and Bagley agreed with the long accepted conclusion that schizophrenia should be considered as one of the sequelae of encephalitis lethargica.

The case that schizophrenic symptoms form an almost integral part of the symptomatology of encephalitis lethargica is strenghthened by an extraordinary postscript which added to the history of the disease by Sacks (1983). In 1969, he began treating a group of patients with severe post-encephalitic Parkinsonism with the then experimental and restricted drug, L-DOPA. The dramatic improvements this treatment produced have been documented in his book *Awakenings* (as well as subsequently in a number of documentaries, a play, and a film). Tragically, this improvement was cut short in the vast majority of cases by the appearance of drastic side-effects. While the most disabling of these took the form of involuntary movements and oculogyric crises, many of the patients also developed extremely florid psychotic symptoms. Catatonic phenomena up to and including excitement were seen, as well as florid delusions and vivid hallucinations. At least sometimes these episodes took place in clear consciousness.

Conclusion

The overrepresentation of schizophrenia in a variety of brain diseases, often cited as evidence of its biological aetiology, seems to be vindicated but contains a few surprises. One of these is the strong probability that the association is not specific for schizophrenia. In particular, in many of the disorders reviewed in the first section of this chapter, there have been indications that associations with manic-depressive psychosis also exist which are at least as strong — or stronger in the case of disseminated sclerosis and Huntington's disease. It might even cross one's mind that the rates of increase of schizophrenia and manic-depressive psychosis in organic brain disease are similar to the respective rates of the disorders in the general population.

The statement that schizophrenia is associated with organic brain disease also turns out to be something of a phenomenological oversimplification. The relationship holds up when a variety of discrete central nervous system disorders is considered, although it should be borne in mind that a recurring theme is that symptomatic schizophrenia shows atypical clinical features. The concept, however, shows definite signs of strain when an attempt is made to apply it to the more generalized brain dysfunctions of dementia and acute confusional states: at this point the idea of schizophrenia as a syndrome starts to lose some of its meaning. When faced with a neuropsychiatric disorder such as encephalitis lethargica, the clinical facts are no longer done justice to: here whole segments of the clinical picture of schizophrenia are incorporated into the neurological presentation — sometimes to be expressed in a distorted fashion — in a way which seems not to be understandable by any simple rules.

13

Childhood schizophrenia, autism, and Asperger's syndrome

The occurrence of schizophrenia in children has become something of an unmentionable topic. It tends to arouse strong emotions in child psychiatrists, who are liable to point out that the term is now reserved for a disorder which is at best rare and at worst misleading or of historical interest only. Adult psychiatrists are characteristically reticent on the subject and, if pressed, may adopt the defensive position that schizophrenia can probably develop before adolescence, but that most alleged cases occurring in early childhood are better regarded as suffering from some other disorder.

The reason why the concept of childhood schizophrenia is emotive is quite simple. In the first half of the twentieth century the term was used, as Rutter (1972) put it, to cover an astonishingly heterogeneous mixture of disorders with little in common other than their severity, chronicity, and occurrence in childhood. Then, in 1943, Kanner described a new syndrome which he first referred to as autistic disturbances of affective contact, later as early infantile autism, and finally just as autism. In 1944, a year after Kanner's description, another disorder with similar, though generally milder features was described which has subsequently become known as Asperger's syndrome. Almost overnight (or more accurately after a lag of eight years), it became recognized the many children who had previously been called schizophrenic were in fact suffering from one of these quite different forms of disorder.

The concept of autism has gone from strength to strength, and rather belatedly that of Asperger's syndrome has also begun to flourish. Meanwhile, childhood schizophrenia seems to have fallen on hard times. Contemporary descriptions are hard to come by: the topic is alluded to more than covered in child and adult psychiatry textbooks and the research literature is exceedingly small—a leading journal in the field recently felt the need to change its name from the *Journal of Autism and Childhood Schizophrenia* to the *Journal of Autism and Developmental Disorders*. In addition, the relationship of schizophrenia, whatever its age of onset, to autism and Asperger's syndrome is not at all clear: while adult psychiatrists may be impressed by certain points of resemblance, their child psychiatric colleagues, having previously been guilty of much phenomenological lack of precision, have become entrenched in the view that the disorders are completely different. The aims of this chapter are therefore first, to attempt to clarify whether and to what extent schizophrenia can develop in childhood, and secondly, to try and settle some of the questions about the relationship — if any — of schizophrenia to autism and Asperger's syndrome.

Schizophrenia in childhood

The first claim that something recognizable as schizophrenia could begin in childhood was made by de Sanctis, who called the disorder dementia praecosissima. In a series of case reports between 1906 and 1909 (cited by Lay 1938) he described a number of young children who, following a period of normal or relatively normal development (one showed some delay), abruptly or insidiously underwent a marked change. Catatonic symptoms including mannerisms, stereotypies, posturing, echolalia, and negativism were the outstanding features; these were accompanied by outbursts of anger and emotional blunting. Some cases recovered, but most progressed to a state of deterioration. De Sanctis emphasized that cognition and memory remained unimpaired, but that there was poor or absent capacity for complex thought. Having observed similar patients of his own, Kraepelin (1913a) accepted that cases existed which resembled adult schizophrenia in their phenomena, course, and outcome to such a degree that there could be no reasonable doubt about the relationship between them.

As a consequence, childhood schizophrenia, which had previously been barely acknowledged as a legitimate topic of interest, became firmly lodged in psychiatric thinking. The concept quickly became overinclusive, with children showing obvious dissimilarities in symptoms and age of onset being lumped together. A few authors, however, continued to adhere to a relatively narrow definition of childhood schizophrenia, requiring the presence of symptoms similar to those seen in the adult form of the disorder. The most phenomenologically minded of these were undoubtedly Potter (1933) and Despert (1968), who described a series of children admitted to a New York hospital in the 1930s. These children all presented with severe symptoms which began after a period of normal or at least not strikingly abnormal early development (it is important to note that only one of these cases would now be regarded as suffering from autism or Asperger's syndrome). The following account is synthesized from the detailed descriptions of these two authors. One of their case histories is reproduced in Fig. 13.1.

The age of onset ranged from 3½ years to 10 years or over. Prior to becoming ill the children appeared normal or at least reasonably well adjusted; in some cases there were hints of abnormality in a tendency to

Schizophrenia in childhood
(from Potter 1933, Despert 1968)

The patient was the eldest of four children. A maternal cousin developed a puerperal psychosis which led to life commitment. Before her marriage the patient's mother suffered from depression.

The patient was born after a prolonged labour but there were no indications of intracranial damage. He was a well nourished infant who walked and talked at the usual ages. He suffered no serious illnesses. He was restless, fretful, and cried a great deal as a baby. At the age of three it was noted that, although he spoke freely, his 'thoughts were not related'. He never appeared to be of a sunny, happy, cheerful disposition but was always a morose irritable child who put on temper tantrums, usually with head banging. He rarely, if ever, displayed the usual amount of affection for his parents. He tended to be indifferent to his brothers and sister, except to one brother who was six years his junior, for whom he showed some affection. His whole life was marked by a generalized indifference. From early childhood he would have periods of marked sullenness and obstinacy.

He started school and made regular progress until about the age of nine when he began to lose all interest in school work and seemed absorbed in his own thoughts. At about the same time his sullenness and irritability increased. At times his talk became so incoherent that it was not possible to understand him. He would have outbursts of anger, laughter, and grimacing. At times he would refuse to eat. He began claiming that things were crawling on his body and that other children made fun of him. He called his mother vile names, would stand for hours before the mirror, stayed in the bathroom for prolonged periods, sat by himself in the dark, and sometimes disappeared from home to be found at a nearby movie. In the two months prior to admission his symptoms increased: he was very antagonistic to his mother, was exceedingly irritable, threatened suicide, and masturbated frequently.

He was hospitalized at the age of 11. During the first 12 months of his stay, he spent the major part of the time gazing fixedly out of the window with a perplexed frown on his face, and at times would be found under the bed or crouched in a corner behind a piece of furniture. At times he would become quite excited and attack the other children. His speech was voluble at times but irrelevant, disconnected, and full of neologisms. His replies to most questions were a stereotyped, colourless 'I don't know'. There was no outstanding mood deviation and his affect was characterized by a combination of disinterest, detachment, and perplexity. He sometimes laughed long and loudly for no reason. He showed somatic delusions making statements like, 'Do you see the bone,' (indicating left shoulder) 'I slept on it and now my bowels moved out

Fig. 13.1

through it', 'I never breathe', 'I have red pulse sores', and 'the inside of my skin is bitten.' He spontaneously referred to voices at times but one could not learn their content.

After approximately a year, he began to show improvement, becoming interested in occupational therapy, and then in people around him, especially the nurses. He became more communicative and went to a summer camp when he made a reasonably good adjustment in a negative, colourless fashion. He returned home and re-entered school where he made mediocre progress. He had to be re-admitted a year later, after which time he went downhill rapidly. When followed up at the age of 18, he showed obvious deterioration and was chronically hospitalized in a state institution.

Fig. 13.1   *contd.*

daydream, poor socialization, or minor anomalies in language development. The disorder could begin acutely, occasionally developing over a matter of days, or alternatively could develop insidiously over months or as long as two years; in a few instances the onset was so gradual that it was impossible to date. In a small number of cases there had been what in retrospect were clear previous episodes of illness which had improved spontaneously after a few weeks or months.

Acute onset cases were commonly preceded by a short prodromal period characterized, for example, by inability to concentrate, a drop in school performance, or vague physical complaints. In the group of insidious onset cases, the earliest signs were withdrawal, quietness, and a progressive loss of interest in activities such as play; alternatively then could be brooding, sullenness, or development of hatred for a parent. These features subsequently gave way to a psychotic state whose features tended to be different in children of different ages.

Cases beginning before the age of seven tended to present principally with disturbances of behaviour and speech. Examples of behavioural abnormalites included staring into space, wandering aimlessly, masturbating continuously, hoarding, spending hours staring into mirrors, crouching under the bed, or peering into empty windows and doorways. Many children were violent or destructive, and some tried to harm themselves: one patient repeatedly beat himself on the head, another tried to choke himself. Catatonic phenomena were also common: examples noted by Potter and Despert included facial grimacing, posturing, marked underactivity, freezing, waxy flexibility, stiff gaits, mutism, playing with fingers, picking up bits of paper and arranging them in rows, taking one step forward and two back while walking, closing drawers, and saying the word 'park' over and over again. In a few cases, simple motor phenomena in the form of blinking and choreiform movements were also noted. Speech sometimes became inarticulate or unintelligible, or took the form of an uninterrupted flow of disconnected utterances, with answers to questions being totally irrelevant; neologisms were also observed. One child who was observed running hot water onto a cut-out picture of a cake said, '. . . to make it hurt, so I should throw it away, so I couldn't make it real, so I couldn't make it a picture. I wouldn't do that to a hungry picture'. Affect was invariably very abnormal, with flattening, inappropriateness, or causeless laughing; perplexity was also a notable feature. In this age group full fledged delusions were not usually noted, but abnormal ideas were alluded to: one child spoke of herself as the girl princess, another seemed to believe that she was an adult and had magical powers. Hallucinations were more clearly evident. One patient stated that she saw 'water balls with keys for eyes' and seemed to hear people in magazines 'talking sassy' to her. Another stopped in the midst of activity and addressed fairies.

Cases beginning from the age of seven onwards tended to be characterized by delusions and auditory hallucinations. Behavioural disturbance could also be prominent, but as a rule catatonic phenomena were only present in the background. At the younger end of this age group, delusions had a naive quality or inclined towards extreme simplicity. Children identified themselves with animals: one patient believed himself at different times to be a rhinoceros, a dog, and a woodpecker; other patients felt they were frightening characters from films, cartoons or fairy tales. After the age of ten or eleven, the delusions became similar to those of adults except that they tended to be simpler and to show a lack of systematization. Several patients first presented with complaints that other children were talking about them. One boy believed he was a philosopher and a genius. A girl gradually came to believe that a 'rip breast team' of 68 men were spying on her and planned to mutilate her. Auditory hallucinations took familiar forms: the voices of children or imagined persecutors were heard talking about the patients, or their parents were heard accusing them of horrible deeds. Visual hallucinations were also described, patients seeing 'spooks', and things crawling on the body. Formal thought disorder, sometimes with neologisms, and inappropriate affect were commonly noted, as were withdrawal and states of dreamy abstraction.

Potter and Despert noted that, as in the adult form of the disorder, the symptoms of childhood schizophrenia could fluctuate. Acute episodes often gradually improved, but left behind greater or lesser degrees of impairment. Further episodes could follow, and led to increasing deterioration. Occasionally there was no real improvement and permanent hospitalization became necessary.

A five year follow-up of Potter's original six cases and eight additional children was carried out by Potter and Klein (1937). It was found that by this time the outcome had become generally poor: only one of the 14 children had made a reasonable social adjustment and the rest had become progressively worse. Thirty years later Bennett and Klein (1966) traced the 10 of these 14 patients who were still alive. Only one patient was living outside hospital; he worked as a dishwasher, was socially isolated, and showed emotional flattening and impoverishment of thought. Two patients were in hospital but showed no evidence of deterioration beyond that noted in the early stages of their illness. One was described as shy and anxious, but followed an active (and consistently successful) pursuit of betting on horse races. The other showed intact self care, but was laconic and extremely passive. The remainder were all on long stay wards, where they did not stand out in any way from their fellow patients with adult-onset schizophrenia.

The graphic accounts of Potter, Despert, and their co-workers have been supplemented by a small number of subsequent formal studies. Kolvin *et al.* (1971) examined 33 children in the age range of 5 to 15 with a diagnosis of schizophrenia which was based on presence of first rank symptoms. Nineteen (57 per cent) showed delusions; 27 (81 per cent) showed auditory hallucinations; 10 (30 per cent) and 9 (27 per cent) showed visual or somatic hallucinations respectively. Twenty (61 per cent) showed at least one element of formal thought disorder. Flattening and incongruity of affect were described in many cases. Interestingly, nearly all the sample showed one or more catatonic phenomena: mannerisms were most common, and grimacing, ambitendence, and abnormal jerkiness of movement were also frequent. In two similar studies, Green *et al.* (1984) and Russell *et al.* (1989) examined groups of 24 and 35 children who met DSM III criteria for schizophrenia. Their ages of onset ranged from 3 to 11 and 5 to 13 respectively. Delusions, auditory hallucinations, and formal thought disorder were present in the majority of cases, regardless of age. In Russell *et al.*'s series, first rank symptoms were also commonly noted: between a quarter and a third showed third-person auditory hallucinations, 11 per cent had thought insertion, 6 per cent showed passivity and 6 per cent thought broadcasting. Catatonic phenomena were recorded in a quarter of Green *et al.*'s patients, but were not commented on by Russell *et al.*.

In the only formal study of the outcome of childhood schizophrenia, Eggers (1978) followed-up 57 children who had been so diagnosed 6 to 40 years (mean 15 years) earlier. He excluded cases with an onset of symptoms before the age of five, and required the presence of clear schizophrenic symptoms as found in 'conservatively diagnosed adult schizophrenia'; in practice, the cases conformed closely to the kind of presentation described by Potter and Despert. Fifteen of the 57 cases pursued a chronic course, going on to develop permanent deterioration which could be mild, moderate, or severe. The remaining 42 followed an episodic or fluctuating course; of these 15 (20 per cent of the whole sample of 57) were considered to have undergone a full remission after up to 11 episodes (however in at least 4 of these there were personality changes described as being 'so slight that they can hardly be called defects'). In a further 9, the deterioration was mild. The rest of the patients who followed an episodic course eventually progressed to a state of severe deterioration. Poor outcome was frequent when there had been an age of onset before age 10, but was not obviously associated with any particular clinical features. Three patients committed suicide.

Altogether, it is reasonable to conclude, as Rutter (1972) did, that a disorder bearing an unmistakable resemblance to adult schizophrenia in clinical picture, course, and outcome can begin in childhood. When this disorder begins in later childhood its identification as schizophrenia is unquestionable: even when it begins earlier it is recognizable – surprisingly so given the widely held view that children cannot verbalize their feelings, hold complicated beliefs, or engage in sophisticated symbolization. Although reliable incidence and prevalence figures are not available, it is clear that presentation in the pre-adolescent period is uncommon or rare, and it is rarer still in young children.

Aetiological factors in childhood schizophrenia

Only the sketchiest information is available on the contributions made by factors usually cited in the adult form of the disorder. To some extent this is undoubtedly a function of the rarity of the disorder. To a minor degree it may also reflect the low profile the disorder has been obliged to take in recent years, eclipsed as it has been by the extensive research interest in autism. What little data there are can be summarized as follows.

Sex ratio: According to Despert (1968), there was a noticeable excess of boys over girls in most early accounts, which decreased with increasing age of onset. Among her own cases there were eight boys and one girl who were aged seven or less on admission, and 15 boys and 5 girls whose first admission was between 7 and 13 years of age. An excess of male cases was evident in the series of Green *et al.* (1984) (19 boys, 9 girls) and Russell *et al.* (1989) (24 boys, 11 girls), but this was not found in the series of Eggers (1978) (25 boys, 32 girls).

Hereditary predisposition: Early writers (see Despert 1968) invariably alluded to the presence of serious psychiatric disorder in the relatives of the majority of children with schizophrenia. Among Potter's and Despert's own cases a family history of psychosis was common among the first and second degree relatives, and was most marked among insidious onset cases.

One formal study has been carried out. Kallman and Roth (1956) screened admisssions to mental hospitals aged 15 or less and managed to find 102 who could be diagnosed as schizophrenic. They excluded very young children, and required a description of a distinct change in a child who had previously seemed to develop normally. The diagnosis relied heavily on diminished interest in the environment, blunted or distorted affect, peculiar motor activity or behaviour, hallucinations, and bizarre thinking with a tendency towards exaggerated fantasies. Seventeen cases were members of a monozygotic twin pair: 12 (71 per cent) of the co-twins of these patients were also diagnosed as schizophrenic before adolescence, with a further 2 (12 per cent) acquiring this diagnosis later in life. Eight (23 per cent) co-twins of 35 dizygotic twins were diagnosed as schizophrenic, and the rate among first degree relatives was in the range of 9–14 per cent. Although clearly unsatisfactory by modern standards, this study certainly suggests that the inheritance of childhood schizophrenia is not markedly different from that of its adult counterpart.

Premorbid personality: It is of course hazardous to try and decide to what extent personality traits are present or absent in children, particularly young children. Even so, Potter and Despert noted that various oddities had been recorded by the parents of their schizophrenic children. These included shyness, unsociability, being a loner, living in a world of their own, being an avid reader with interests in archaeology and astrology — traits clearly suspicious of a schizoid personality type. Other children were described as morose, irritable, aggressive, hyperactive, fearful, or showing indifference and lack of affection.

The only systematic examination of the personalities of schizophrenic children was made by Kolvin *et al.* (1971): they found that 29 (87 per cent) of their 33 children with an onset of psychosis after five years of age had been reported as being odd by their parents, or had been noted to show unusual features at medical or psychiatric clinics attended before overt schizophrenic symptoms developed. The main traits ascribed to the children were shyness, withdrawal, timidity, and sensitivity, these being found in just over half the group.

Treatment of schizophrenia in childhood

The few available data on this subject have been briefly reviewed by Tsiantis *et al.* (1986). They noted that the most emphatic views had been expressed by Kolvin (1972), who stated that neuroleptic drugs often led to the rapid disappearance of florid symptoms. He also considered that these drugs could bring about an arrest of the disease process. This conclusion was shared by the majority of other authors who had written on the subject. However, there has been at least one claim that drug treatment is of little use. Most authors have recognized the need for supportive psychotherapy, but not, at least in Kelvin's view, of an interpretative type.

Schizophrenia in infancy?

In 1908, Heller (see Hulse, 1954) described a number of cases of children between the ages of three and four, who after a period of normal development, began to show signs of personality change, then lost their speech, and ultimately deteriorated to a state of extreme idiotic regression. He called this disorder dementia infantilis; subsequently it has become referred to as disintegrative psychosis or Heller's syndrome.

According to Heller, the earliest changes were in mood and character: having been previously lively or placid, the children became moody, negativistic, disobedient, whining, and prone to attacks of rage and destructiveness; more rarely the onset was quiet and without affective change. In many cases anxiety symptoms were prominent, these occasionally being considered to have 'a hallucinatory character'. Over a period of around nine months, the children then underwent a catastrophic mental decline. Speech became progressively impoverished, words were distorted, sentences could no longer be repeated, and finally language was lost altogether. The capacity to understand speech was also lost except for some primitive remnants. At the same time, motor abnormalities frequently appeared: the children developed tic-like movements, grimaced, or posed in peculiar positions. From then on, they typically remained in a state of complete idiocy which, however, was stationary. This was characterized by severe motor restlessness accompanied by stereotypies and tic-like movements; another striking feature was the retention of an intelligent facial expression, a clear-eyed look, and a deceptive attentiveness to the environment. Many children became incontinent, and required to be fed, but with intensive nursing some could be trained to eat and keep themselves clean.

By 1930 Heller had collected 28 such cases in whom physical diseases — including especially encephalitis lethargica — had allegedly been carefully excluded. Other authors described similar cases and added their own observations, notably that motor function was maintained and that there was a complete absence of focal neurological signs. Even after speech was lost, it was also noted that the ability to sing or hum melodies could be retained. Some of the children were followed-up after several years, and occasionally into adult life. They remained in the same state and continued to show restlessness and abnormal movements (rocking, tics, and stereotypies). It was implied that none had undergone further deterioration or died from the disorder.

Almost immediately thereafter, however, the status of the disorder became controversial. The conflict was ushered in by Corberi (cited by Lay 1938) who carried out brain biopsies on three affected children, two of whom were siblings. He found evidence of degenerative brain disease resembling that seen in lipid storage diseases. Subsequently, other authors described cases which at post-mortem revealed evidence of one or another form of organic neuropathology. The most well known study of this type is that of Malamud (1959). He described the post-mortem findings in four patients who had been diagnosed as suffering from dementia infantilis in life; two of these were a brother and sister and the other two also had affected siblings. Two were found to have been suffering from a neuro-lipidosis (amaurotic family idiocy) and the two related patients both showed marked but unclassifiable subcortical degenerative disease. Unfortunately, it is clear that these patients' disorders were not typical of Heller's syndrome, starting at a later age, being accompanied by obvious neurological signs, and showing a continuously progressive course. Darby (1976) later reviewed 17 cases which conformed clinically to Heller's syndrome and in which biopsy or necropsy findings were available. Some showed obvious pathologies such as neurolipidoses, Pick's disease, metachromatic leuco-dystrophy, tuberose sclerosis, or other often undiagnosable neurological disease. Four showed only gliosis or other non-specific changes. In another four there were no significant findings. Most recently, Evans-Jones and Rosenbloom (1978) documented several cases which showed the clinical features of Heller's syndrome and in which neurological disease (with the possible exception of epilepsy) could be reasonably confidently excluded.

Thus, while some, perhaps the majority of cases of typical Heller's syndrome can be shown to have organic brain disease, it is clear that not all do so. A reasonably recent case showing many of the classical features of the disorder in circumstances where progressive neurological brain disease seems unlikely is described in Fig. 13.2.

Kraepelin (1913a) inclined to the view that some cases of dementia infantilis were genuinely forms of schizophrenia. By 1930, Heller had come to the conclusion that the two disorders were entirely different. The argument for some cases of the disorder (that is those where there is no organic pathology) representing a very early presentation of schizophrenia rests on the presence of catatonic phenomena and development of deterioration which is distinctive, not progressive and unaccompanied by organic signs. The loss of speech and presence of marked intellectual deficits are not typical of schizophrenia, but a developmental explanation can be invoked to account for these. Less easy to deal with are the absence of episodicity and lack of variability in outcome, both of which are features of childhood as well as adult schizophrenia. On balance the similarities are intriguing and the differences can just about be explained away; however, a definitive answer to the question of whether Heller's syndrome is a very early form of schizophrenia cannot be given.

Schizophrenia in infancy? A case of Heller's syndrome
(from Lay 1938)

The patient was an only child. Pregnancy and birth were normal. He was a healthy baby, who sat up at nine months, and began to talk at about 12 months of age. Although heavy he could walk at 15 months. He was difficult to wean on to solid foods; later he was 'finicky' and disliked meat, and on the whole was a fretful child. Thumb-sucking was noticed. Toilet training was achieved early, but there was a temporary relapse at the age of about 18 months. In early life there were no illnesses of importance, and none on which a suspicion of encephalitis might rest.

At the age of three he was taken to see a film, during which he was terrified by the accompanying animal noises, and for some time afterwards repeated the phrase 'noises of animals' as if he were remembering them. He also disliked dogs; after seeing a dog at a friend's house, he woke up from sleep in a great fear, screaming that there were dogs on the ceiling. He never played much with other children, partly as a result of parental regime.

The patient was first seen psychiatrically at the age of 4½ years because of an inability to talk. At the age of four he had had an illness in which he was delirious for one night and spent two days in bed. After this there occurred fits of temper, in which he screamed and threw himself on the ground, and also delusions that his mother was cutting him. About this time he was said to have acquired quite a large vocabulary, but deterioration had occurred in his speech. At the time of coming to hospital he used only single words, and then only if he could not make his wants attended to by other means. Physically he was normal, but his gait was a little uncertain.

At the age of six, he talked in an unintelligible way, uttered cries at intervals, fell on the floor and did not get up for several minutes. He laughed occasionally for no apparent reason. His attacks of violent screaming and crying continued. At home, he took knives from the table and thrust them into the jam dish. He stood in front of a visiting social worker making curious stiff clutching movements with his raised arms, and giving high squeaking cries; he also tried to cram paper into her mouth. Usually he slept well in a bed to himself in the parents' room. About fortnightly, however, there would be nights of frequent screaming.

Between the ages of six and seven, he was described as a tall well-built boy, who entered the consulting-room reluctantly. He played quietly at first, but later cried loudly. He behaved very much as a child of 18 months, turning the pages of a book quickly, and speaking only odd words. His glance was restless, his movements uncontrolled, and constant except when interested. Occasionally he would follow one occupation for

Fig. 13.2

as long as 35 minutes. He hummed to himself and rocked to and fro when only partly occupied, and jumped and shouted from time to time. Often he would stare into the fire, humming and repeating short rhymes, and singing a few words from popular songs. His curiosity was marked and easily stimulated.

Seen again at the age of eight he was well grown and healthy, giving the impression that his real age was 11. In the playroom he was neat with his fingers. He turned over the pages of a book without looking at them; later he tore the book and, when prevented from doing this, took to biting plasticine and spitting bits from his mouth. There were frequent screams which stopped when he was ignored.

The patient was seen again by a social worker at the age of 12. On the whole he was reported to be unchanged. It was noticed that he made no response to anything that was said. He once put his face close to the social worker's and laughed in an inane way. His mother said that he was prone to periods of violence, but was in general somewhat easier to manage.

Fig. 13.2   *contd.*

Autism

Out of the profusion of nomenclature and uncertainties of classification that dogged the early nosology of childhood psychosis, Kanner (1943) extracted a distinctive syndrome. He described 11 children whose common characteristic was what he termed extreme autistic aloneness, an inability to relate to people and situations. This could be seen at as early as four months of age when the child failed to assume the normal anticipatory posture preparatory to being picked up. Later, terms like 'self-sufficient', 'in a shell', 'acting as if people weren't there', and 'perfectly oblivious to everything about him' were employed by the parents. Other features (Kanner and Eisenberg 1956) included an obsessive desire for the preservation of sameness, as manifested by monotonously repetitive activities and distress on changes in routine; a fascination with objects, which were handled with dexterity; mutism or abnormal language with echolalia, pronoun reversal, and other characteristics; and finally an intelligent physiognomy, with latent cognitive potential being manifested in unusual feats of memory or skill. Subsequently, with only a little modification, all Kanner's points have been incorporated into the modern definition of autism.

Autism is a rare disorder: all the epidemiological surveys indicate that it has a prevalence of around 2 per 10 000 children, this rate rising to 5–10 per 10 000 when milder cases or those not showing the core features of aloofness and resistance to change are included (see Zahner and Pauls 1987).

Autism was originally considered by Kanner to be present from birth, but he later accepted that the typical patterns of behaviour could begin after up to 20 months of apparently normal development (Kanner and Eisenberg 1956). Other authors have documented ages of onset of up to three years, and occasionally later (some such cases follow viral infection or other cerebral insults) (Wing and Attwood 1987; Frith 1989). There is a well accepted excess of cases among boys, of the order of 2–3:1.

In addition to the classic descriptions of Kanner, there have been numerous clinical accounts of autism, most of which have been of a high standard (Rimland 1965; Victor 1984; Frith 1989; Gillberg and Coleman 1992). Some of the most graphic and concise of these have been contributed by Wing (Wing 1980; Wing and Attwood 1987), from which the following summary is taken.

The two core features of autism (that is those which are found in all cases) are first, absent or severely impaired two-way social interaction accompanied by abnormal non-verbal communication and imagination; and secondly, a pattern of behaviour which is dominated by repetitive, stereotyped routines. The abnormal social interactions recognized in autism take multiple forms, and patients are currently considered to fall into *aloof*, *passive*, or *active-but-odd* groups. The *aloof* form corresponds most closely to the classical picture of autism: here the child rejects physical or social contact, becomes distressed when in close proximity to others, especially other children, and lacks most or all of the normal attachment behaviours displayed by young children, for example following parents, running to greet them, seeking comfort from them when in pain. Non-verbal communication in the form of eye contact, bodily movements, and gestures is absent or obviously abnormal. There is a marked lack of pretend play. *Passive* cases do not make spontaneous social approaches, except to obtain needs, but accept the approaches of others without protest and even with some appearance of enjoyment. The *active-but-odd* subgroup do make spontaneous approaches to others but in these are peculiar and even embarrassing in their one-sidedness and persistence.

The repetitive, stereotyped behaviours of autism range from the very simple to the complicated and elaborate. Some simple behaviours are self-directed and include rocking, teeth grinding, grunting, eye poking, flicking fingers, waving hands, and twirling around. Others involve objects, such as flicking pieces of string, tapping or shaking objects, turning wheels of toy cars, or dextrously spinning toys and other objects. Equally characteristic are more elaborate routines which the child insists on following: making repetitive patterns from leaves, stones, kitchen utensils, etc.; insisting on taking particular routes around the house or on walks, making everyone in a room sit with their right leg crossed over their left, demanding to have certain foods presented in certain ways, or eaten in a special fashion; showing a fascination with and collecting objects like empty detergent packets, tin lids, shoes, umbrella handles, and all manner of peculiar and useless things. Sometimes the phenomenon takes the form of a single-minded interest, in having a bath, in rooms with yellow curtains, or in books, but only those with red covers. In the most able children these may blur into academic interests in esoteric subjects, large numbers of facts about which are learnt by rote with little regard for their significance.

First and foremost among the other symptoms of autism are abnormalities of language. Depending on the diagnostic criteria used, up to half of all autistic children are mute, or nearly so. In most of the remainder speech is abnormal: there may be echolalia, or a peculiar variant of this in which words, phrases, or whole texts (for example of television adverts) are reproduced verbatim, sometimes in the original intonation. Reversal of pronouns, and stereotyped and idiosyncratic use of words and phrases are particularly characteristic. Sometimes speech is—or becomes—grammatically correct but is noticeably odd, pedantic, or otherwise stilted. Literalness, concreteness, and an inability to handle the nuances of language are ubiquitous. Even when relatively normal in form, speech tends to be used not as a means of social interaction or to exchange knowledge, but rather as a vehicle for the patient to obtain his or her wants or describe his or her circumscribed interests.

A variety of other symptoms are seen in autism which, like the language disturbance, are not seen in all cases. These include abnormal responsiveness to sensory stimuli: the child may ignore some sounds (often he or she first comes to medical attention because of the suspicion of deafness), while being distressed or delighted by others. There may be fascination with bright lights, shiny objects, particular textures, or the smells and tastes of things. Motor abnormalities like grimacing, writhing, and peculiar hand and finger movements are well-known. The gait is often abnormal, with walking on tiptoe, lack of arm swing, or other peculiarities. There may be a tendency to adopt odd postures while standing. Some movements are clumsy while others are graceful and finely executed. Perhaps the most unusual symptom of all is the phenomenon of savantism: often in the setting of overall subnormal IQ, particular abilities—mathematical, musical, or artistic—stand out from the background, and may be exceptional by any standards.

Concerning the course of autism, the essential point is its developmental quality. As described particularly well by Frith (1989), autistic children tend to speak more as they grow older, have better contact with adults, and become more disciplined in their behaviour. They acquire intellectual skills such as reading and writing, and even some social skills. While they remain discernibly different as adults and their intellectual attainments never catch up, autistic children are perhaps no more like autistic adults than normal children resemble normal adults. All or almost all, however, remain obviously handicapped, completely naive, and show obvious peculiarities in speech and behaviour. A few are able to work, but many more live uncomplicated lives at home, doing odd jobs, and helping out their parents in small ways. A substantial proportion end up in sheltered accommodation or institutional care.

The aetiology of autism is unknown. Psychodynamic theories having been originally advocated, not least by Kanner, the disorder has subsequently come to be considered completely or almost completely biologically determined. This about face has been made inescapable by a number of findings, which have been reviewed in detail several times (for example DeMyer *et al.* 1981; Cohen and Donnellan 1987; Frith 1989; Gillberg and Coleman 1992). The first of these is the association of autism with mental retardation: 70–90 per cent of autistic children show some degree of mental handicap and only 10 per cent are of average or above average intelligence (Gillberg and Coleman 1992). Secondly, there is the fact that autism is frequently complicated by another disorder which is undoubtedly organic, epilepsy. This has been reported in between one in seven and one in three autistic children and it becomes even more common in adult life — when up to 42 per cent of patients develop seizures (Golden 1987; Frith 1989; Gillberg and Coleman 1992). Other relevant findings include the strong suspicion that a proportion of cases of autism are associated with chromosomal abnormalities, particularly the fragile-X syndrome; and also the probability that a variety of prenatal, perinatal, and neonatal hazards increase the risk of the disorder. Nevertheless, while this evidence is compelling, no structural, functional, or neurochemical abnormalities have so far been demonstrated in the autistic brain.

There is also convincing evidence for a genetic factor in autism. As reviewed by Pauls (1987) and Gillberg and Coleman (1992), rates for autism in the siblings of autistic children have been found to cluster around 2–3 per cent; although this is low, it is in fact 15–100 times more common than the general population rate (depending on whether narrow or broad criteria are used). A number of twin studies have found a concordance of 36 per cent to 89 per cent for monozygotic twins, compared with nil for dizygotic twins.

The inheritance of autism in relation to other psychiatric disorders is somewhat more complicated. Hanson and Gottesman (1976) reviewed five studies which examined the prevalence of schizophrenia among the parents of children with a diagnosis of childhood psychosis beginning before the age of five. Leaving aside one study which was hopelessly flawed, the mean rate for schizophrenia was 0.5 per cent, a value not significantly different from the risk for the general population. In the single more recent study, Gillberg *et al.* (1992) examined the parents and siblings of 35 children with a DSM III diagnosis of autism (12 of these also had additional diagnoses ranging from fragile-X syndrome to congenital hydrocephalus). There were no cases of schizophrenia among the relatives, but three mothers had suffered from schizoaffective psychosis. Two of these, however, were mothers of children with autism in association with fragile-X syndrome. This study also revealed an unexpectedly high rate of affective disorder in the mothers: major depression (three cases) and bipolar disorder (one case).

The relationship between autism and schizophrenia

It should be evident from the above description that autism and schizophrenia — even childhood schizophrenia — are quite different conditions. At the same time, it is also apparent that now and again they seem to strike similar chords in their presentations. These points of apparent resemblance have not been widely discussed in the literature, and when they have, the debate has not been sober. In what seems to be a reaction against the position before Kanner, where all severe, chronic disorders of childhood were lumped together, the differences between the two disorders are emphasized whereas any similarities are glossed over or dismissed out of hand. Sometimes the impression is gained that authors go out of their way to avoid describing phenomena in autism in the way that seems most natural, because this would involve using terms that have already been used for schizophrenic symptoms. In trying to take a more even-handed approach, the first step is to distinguish two separate questions, that of similarities in the clinical features of the two disorders, and that of similarities in their course and outcome.

Similarities in clinical picture: The similarities between the core affective disorder of autism and that of schizophrenia certainly impressed Kanner, to the extent that he named the disorder after one of Bleuler',s fundamental schizophrenic symptoms. It is not easy to take this observation further, however, because the affective styles of normal children and adults are so obviously different.

One way round this difficulty is to examine the affect of autistic patients in adulthood. Rumsey *et al.* (1986) assessed 14 autistic adults, all of whom met DSM III criteria for the disorder (six had, in fact, been diagnosed by Kanner). Ratings of affect were made by Andreasen, using a rating scale which was a forerunner of her Schedule for the Assessment of Negative Symptoms. None of the patients was taking medication at the time of the study. The findings are shown in Table 13.1. Nine of the patients scored significantly on at least one of a cluster of motor and behavioural expressions of affective flattening, including unchanging facial expression, decreased spontaneous movements, and paucity of expressive gestures. A somewhat smaller proportion showed evidence of the corresponding syn-

Table 13.1 Affective flattening and inappropriateness in adult autistic patients (from Rumsey *et al.* 1986)

	Numbers showing abnormality*	
	Autistic patients (*n* = 14)	Normal controls (*n* = 14)
Unchanging facial expression	9	1
Decreased spontaneous movements	4	0
Paucity of expressive gestures	6	0
Poor eye contact	2	3
Affective non-responsivity	4	0
Inappropriate affect	3	0
Lack of vocal inflections	6	0
Slowed speech	1	0
Increased latency of response	2	0
Global rating of affective flattening	8	1

*Scores of greater than 2 (mild but definite impairment) were required for abnormality to be considered present.

drome in speech (that is lack of inflection, slowed speech, and increased latency of responding). Four were considered to show affective unresponsiveness, and three showed clear instances of inappropriate affect.

A second area where autistic and schizophrenic phenomena might overlap is in the realm of abnormalities of speech. In autism, when the patient is not mute, speech is almost always abnormal to some extent. Leaving aside pronoun reversal, which has no counterpart in schizophrenia, and echolalia and the stereotyped and inflexible use of words and phrases (whose counterparts in schizophrenia would be classified as catatonic speech disorders), there remain abnormalities like long-windedness, over-literalness of meaning, repetitiveness, neologisms, and idiosyncratic word usage. One or two of these, neologisms and ungrammatical speech, are also important features of formal thought disorder in schizophrenia. Several more (for example long-windedness, repetitiveness) also crop up in descriptions of schizophrenic thought disorder, although they are not central to it.

Rumsey *et al.* (1986) also assessed disorders of thought, language, and communication in their 14 adult autistic patients. Once again, the ratings were made by Andreasen, using her own scale (see Chapter 1). The commonest abnormality found was poverty of speech which was present in ten of the patients, and perseveration which was present in eight. Seven patients were rated as showing poverty of content of speech; three showed incoherence; and two showed derailment and tangentiality respectively. One

Table 13.2 Thought, language, and communication disorders in adult autistic patients (from Rumsey *et al.* 1986)

	Numbers showing abnormality*	
	Autistic patients (*n* = 14)	Normal controls (*n* = 14)
Poverty of speech	10	1
Poverty of content of speech	7	0
Pressure of speech	1	0
Distractible speech	0	0
Tangentiality	2	0
Derailment	2	2
Incoherence	3	0
Illogicality	0	0
Clanging	0	0
Neologisms	0	0
Circumstantiality	1	1
Loss of goal	0	3
Perseveration	7	1
Echolalia	3	0
Stilted speech	0	0
Blocking	0	0
Global rating	14	1

*Scores of greater than 2 (mild impairment) were required for abnormality to be considered present.

patient exhibited pressure of speech which was marked. The findings are summarized in Table 13.2.

The richest vein of all for tapping similarities between autism and schizophrenia lies in the area of motor, volitional, and behavioural disorders. Virtually every account of autism has made some reference to phenomena which seem on the face of it to be strikingly similar to the catatonic symptoms of schizophrenia. The occurrence of simple repetitive movements, gait abnormalities, and complex ritualistic behaviour has been repeatedly noted, but typically such disorders have been categorized under some blatantly interpretative heading such as 'insistence on sameness' or 'fascination with objects'. Recently, however, a tacit return to a more phenomenological approach is discernible, for example in the accounts of Wing and Attwood (1987) and Frith (1989).

The most detailed tabulation of the motor, volitional, and behavioural disorders of autism has been provided by Victor (1984). These are repro-

Table 13.3 Motor volitional and behavioural disorders in autism (from Victor 1984)

Whirling
Whirling when given a turn of the head
Running to and fro
Bouncing
Walking on toes or in other peculiar ways
Banging or rolling head
Grinding teeth
Mouthing and licking things
Blinking
Wiggling fingers near eyes
Grimacing
Allowing moulding by others (waxy catalepsy)
Moving fingers as if double jointed or made of dough
Moving constantly
Sitting or standing in one place for hours
Dancing round an object
Making strange repetitive dance steps
Making body gyrations
Making intricate hand movements

duced, using the author's original terminology, in Table 13.3. It is clear from this that virtually every catatonic phenomenon described in schizophrenia is also encountered in autism. Certainly, some of the abnormalities seen in autism have their own distinctive stamp—for example, whirling, fanning hand movements, and walking on tiptoes—but phenomenologically, it does not seem reasonable to distinguish them from other catatonic symptoms.

Similarities in course and outcome: One of the striking features of childhood schizophrenia is that it follows the same variety of episodic and insidious courses to reach much the same range of good and poor outcomes as the adult form of the disorder. Autism, on the other hand, is a disorder with a strictly developmental trajectory: the picture does change with time, but this is usually in the direction of improvement as skills like language, reading, and writing are acquired and some degree of social adaptation is gradually achieved.

This view of autism may, however, be something of an oversimplification. Rutter (1970), Wing and Attwood (1987), and particularly Gillberg (1991*a*) have documented the fact that a proportion of autistic children undergo temporary or permanent deterioration around the time of adolescence. According to Gillberg this is often, but by no means always associated with the onset of epilepsy. In cases where permanent deterioration takes place, there is a return of symptoms seen in early childhood, such as repetitive behaviours. Superimposed on these may be hyperactivity, aggressiveness, and destructive behaviour, which then gives way to inertia, loss of language skills, and slow intellectual decline.

A small literature has also described the occasional development of something very like schizophrenia in autistic patients. Howells and Guirguis (1984) examined 10 children with early onset child psychosis (using a definition which conformed closely to autism, although it may have included some cases of disintegrative psychosis) on average 20 years later. None showed any first rank symptoms of schizophrenia, but two were noted to adopt hallucinatory attitudes or to express vague, bizarre ideas. Delusions and/or hallucinations were suspected in a few other cases. In another study Petty *et al.* (1984) described three patients who clearly had autistic symptoms prior to 30 months of age and who all met DSM III criteria for autism. By school age or early adolescence, all three had also developed symptoms which led to an additional diagnosis of schizophrenia. The first described hearing 'parrotlike voices' at the age of nine. By the age of 12 he was experiencing auditory hallucinations giving commands and keeping up a running commentary, delusions of control, and showed marked formal thought disorder. The second patient held the apparently literal belief that he was a car from the age of five, and also expressed the idea that his thoughts were falling out of his head. At the age of 13 he started to believe that other children were talking about him and persecuting him. He described hearing a voice which said things that 'piled up' in his head. The third patient developed increasing evidence of formal thought disorder from the age of seven, and this was associated with probable delusions and auditory hallucinations. None of the patients suffered from epilepsy. All three patients showed some improvement with neuroleptic treatment.

Rutter (1970) commented that very few autistic children developed delusions and hallucinations in adult life, and Wing and Attwood (1987) stated that they had never seen a convincing case of autism in which schizophrenia developed. The above findings, particular those of Petty *et al.* suggest otherwise. A description of a further case is given in Fig. 13.3. Nevertheless, at the present time a decisive answer to the question of whether there is a causal association between autism and schizophrenia cannot be given. Additionally, nothing so far cited indicates that there is an exclusive relationship with schizophrenia; it could be that autism is associated with various different kinds of additional psychopathology. This possibility assumes significance in the discussion of Asperger's syndrome.

Autism complicated by the development of schizophrenia
(author's own case)

The patient was the illegitimate child of an African prostitute who was adopted by English parents at the age of six weeks. As a baby he was healthy, but behavioural difficulties were noted from the time of adoption. He typically slept all day and was awake most of the night, and he could not bear to be handled, screaming and shuddering when touched. He acquired toilet training at the normal times. Between the ages of two and three he fell into the habit of refusing to defecate until he could hardly walk. He began to speak at the age of 2½, but for the first 6–8 months spoke only in a self-invented language: this had no grammar and consisted of nouns which referred only to objects and not to people. At the age of three he suddenly started using English, understanding it well, but not always expressing himself properly. He was described as having some echolalia and his tone of voice was very flat.

During childhood, he rarely asked questions, and showed very little natural curiosity. He was described by his parents as 'obsessive': his play centred almost exclusively on toy farmyard animals which he would place in particular positions, becoming distressed if they were moved. Between the ages of 5 and 14 he wrote single words or phrases up to hundreds of times on any available scraps of paper. Later, he became obsessed with football, watching games and collecting cards. He never cried except sometimes when in pain. He continued to try and avoid being touched, withdrawing if someone accidentally touched him. He disliked women, to the extent that he would not sit in a chair that a woman had been sitting in or had put her coat on. He spoke little to his parents, and was completely socially isolated.

Other features of the patient during childhood were laughing and talking to himself and to inanimate objects, for example hedges — if confronted with this he would deny that he had been doing it. He also clicked his teeth. He was unusually good at sports like table tennis, and had excellent hand–eye co-ordination. However, he was completely unable to play as part of a team. He taught himself Swahili, acquiring a several hundred word vocabulary. However, he never spoke this language.

From the age of 11 the patient improved intellectually, being described as starting to 'shine' and 'flourish' at school. His social isolation became less of a problem, but he remained odd. For example, for several months after a teacher jokingly threatened to 'bounce a wall off his head', the patient repeatedly asked his parents which wall he was going to be hit with.

At the age of 13, around the time of puberty, the patient began to undergo a gradual change. He spoke less, and laughed and talked to

Fig. 13.3

himself more. His educational performance fell off dramatically, and his ability to relate to others disappeared. He became lazy, unkempt, and stopped changing his clothes. He spent more and more time by himself, much of it in bed. His parents became unable to cope and at the age of 17 he was transferred to a residential facility for mentally handicapped adults. Around this time he started expressing the ideas that everyone hated him because he was 'rude', and that his feet were making a noise and getting him into trouble. He told his parents that he could hear the voice of a staff member shouting at him, even though he was on leave at home at the time. He also heard the wife of a staff member shouting at him and telling him she loved him. Later he stated he could hear people shouting in Bradford, Edinburgh, and London, and repeatedly heard Leeds football fans saying they were going to kill him. After innumerable instances of antisocial behaviour including entering other residents' bedrooms, urinating in public, stealing and making unprovoked attacks on people, he was admitted to hospital at the age of 21.

Mental state examination revealed an unkempt appearance with torn clothes, marked poverty of speech, and obvious flattening and shallowness of affect, accompanied by inappropriate laughter. In addition to experiencing auditory hallucinations, he stated that someone was pulling his neck round. Cognitive status was difficult to test but the patient has remained more or less fully oriented and knows recent facts, both concerning his family and world events. Full scale IQ at age 15 (WISC-R) was 80 (verbal IQ 96, performance IQ 67). All investigations, including chromosomal analysis and screening for inherited disorders of metabolism have been normal. CT scan revealed an empty sella turcica; this was not associated with endocrine abnormality. The patient remains in hospital. His mother commented that there was 'almost nothing of the child I once knew'.

Fig. 13.3   *contd.*

In summary, it can be concluded that autism and schizophrenia, while being aetiologically different as far as is known, share features of their phenomonology to a greater extent than child psychiatrists have been prepared to admit. Autism is also sometimes—it is not known how commonly—complicated by the development of a state closely resembling schizophrenia. Nevertheless, it is clear that the two disorders are not co-extensive in their clinical features: delusions and hallucinations are not features of autism, and there are many phenomena seen in autism which have never been described in schizophrenia. Nor does the former disorder evolve into something assembling the latter with any regularity; on the whole adult autistic patients do not resemble patients with chronic schizophrenia.

Asperger's syndrome

The year following Kenner's description of autism, Asperger (1944) independently gave a detailed account of a childhood disorder which, by complete coincidence, he named using closely similar terminology. What he called autistic psychopathy of childhood referred to a lifelong pattern of abnormal behaviour which showed broadly similar features to autism, but which was milder and which did not usually become apparent until after three years of age.

Asperger's syndrome as it has since become known currently occupies an uncertain nosological position. It has been argued to be distinct from autism and closely related to schizoid personality disorder (Van Krevelen 1971; Wolff and Chick 1980). Alternatively, it is regarded by many as an attenuated form of autism (Bosch, 1970; Kerbeshian *et al.* 1990). Most recently, there has been a tendency to subsume Asperger's syndrome partly or wholly under the *active-but-odd* variety of autism (Wing and Attwood 1987). A balanced and considered account of the classificatory arguments has been provided by Wing (1991).

The clinical features of Asperger's syndrome have once again been succinctly described by Wing (1981). The disorder is very much more common in boys than girls, and is not usually recognized before the third year of life. Speech develops at the normal time, or is at worst somewhat delayed. Pronoun reversal and other autistic-like disturbances may be present in a minor form but a full command of language is generally developed sooner or later. Speech is abnormal, however, being long-winded and pedantic, impoverished, and featuring stereotyped repetitions of words and phrases, and sometimes also neologisms. The non-verbal accompaniments of speech are also abnormal: intonation is monotonous, exaggerated, or otherwise aprosodic; gestures are limited, or excessive but clumsy; and there is often a lack of facial expression. Although there is no aloofness or desire to avoid others, two-way interaction is handicapped by a marked inability to grasp the rules governing social behaviour: patients stare, stand too close, wear inappropriate clothes, even attempt to touch or kiss strangers. Posture is odd and movements are ill-coordinated; the vast majority of patients are poor at games and show impairments in other activities requiring motor skills, for example writing and drawing. Many patients show the stereotypies and rituals typical of autism but to a less marked extent. They tend to become intensely attached to particular personal possessions and are often very unhappy when away from their familiar surroundings. Finally, in contrast to autism, intelligence may be normal or sometimes high, and many patients show savant-type skills, having exceptional memories, musical abilities, or developing absorbing interests in narrowly defined fields. It has been said that the patients are often original and creative in their chosen fields, although this view is not shared by Wing.

Asperger's syndrome is currently believed to be rare. Wing and Gould (1979) could identify only two unequivocal cases and four more where autism was a possible alternative diagnosis in a survey of 35 000 children under the age of 15. Little is known about the aetiology of the disorder. There is a clinical impression (Wing 1981) that a significant proportion of the parents of patients with Asperger's syndrome show some of the same behaviours; it has been suggested that 50 per cent of cases have a close relative who also has Asperger's syndrome or something approximating to this. Recently, a number of family studies (Bowman 1988; Gillberg, 1991*b*) have documented pedigrees where there is a spectrum of disabilities in affected family members, ranging from autism, through Asperger's syndrome, to mild autistic traits. Pre- and post-natal cerebral damage or evidence of neurological dysfunction is quite commonly found in affected children (Wing 1981; Gillberg 1991*b*).

One of the main points of interest of Asperger's syndrome is the frequency with which it appears to be complicated by development of other psychiatric disorders. Anxiety and depression are frequently reported (for example Wing 1981). Whereas Asperger (1944) reported that only one of his 200 cases developed schizophrenia, the occurrence of states to a greater or lesser extent resembling schizophrenia have been documented in virtually every subsequent series. One of Wolff and Chick's (1980) 19 patients developed florid schizophrenia, and one more was chronically hospitalized with a diagnosis of simple schizophrenia. Wing (1981) noted that of 18 patients seen in adult life, one had a psychosis with delusions and hallucinations, one had had an episode of catatonic stupor, 3 had bizarre behaviour but with no clear psychiatric diagnosis, and 4 had become increasingly odd and withdrawn, perhaps related to underlying depression.

The most accurate information on the prevalence of schizophrenia in Asperger's syndrome is to be obtained from the study of Tantam (1988, 1991). He accumulated a sample of 85 patients which he personally diagnosed as suffering from Asperger's syndrome (he appears to have used a combination of his own and other criteria). Thirty (35 per cent) were diagnosed as having a secondary psychiatric diagnosis. The diagnostic breakdown is shown in Table 13.4. Three carried a diagnosis of schizophrenia, four had isolated hallucinosis (not further specified), and one was considered to have a psychosis associated with epilepsy. Two more held complex and extremely bizarre beliefs: one believed that he was really asleep (in a 'missage') between two periods of existence ('boating lines'), and that he was only conscious because a witch had made him have a bad dream. The other believed that he had been abducted from a heavenly home by the people who called themselves his parents, was afraid that he might turn into a skeleton, and may also have believed he was in contact with the Holy Ghost. These

Table 13.4 Psychiatric diagnoses in 85 adults with Asperger's syndrome (from Tantam 1991)

Schizophrenia	3 (3.5%)
Hallucinosis	4 (4.7%)
Epileptic psychosis	1 (1.1%)
Mania	4 (4.7%)
Mania alternating with depression	4 (4.7%)
Depressive psychosis	2 (2.4%)
Depression	5 (5.9%)
Depression and anxiety	2 (2.4%)
Anxiety	4 (4.7%)
Obsessive-compulsive disorder	2 (2.4%)
Total	30 (35.3%)

All diagnosis were made according to ICD-9.

patients' symptoms were not considered to be evidence of psychosis by Tantam, but rather were seen as attempts to rationalize their differences from other people.

Excluding these last two cases, but none of the others, 9.4 per cent suffered from a psychosis broadly resembling schizophrenia. As Tantam noted, this proportion was likely to be higher than in an unselected community sample, since the superimposed psychiatric disorder may have predisposed to the original psychiatric referral.

Conclusion

There can be no doubt that schizophrenia sometimes develops in childhood. When it does, it clearly resembles adult schizophrenia much more than it resembles anything else, and, as far as the evidence permits any conclusions to be drawn, the same aetiological factors appear to be operative. Childhood schizophrenia is not just a disorder of late childhood, but can occur at ages ranging down to five years or earlier, albeit increasingly rarely.

Life becomes a bit more complicated when autism and Asperger's syndrome are brought into the picture. Nevertheless, it is possible to avoid the excesses of the early part of the century without falling prey to a tendency to throw the baby out with the bathwater which seems to characterize much of the recent literature. There can be little doubt that the phenomena of autism and schizophrenia overlap, particularly with respect to catatonic symptoms, but also to some extent as far as disorders of affect and thought form are concerned. This conclusion is not, however, as provocative as it might first appear. Symptoms which are often considered to be characteristic of schizophrenia can also be seen in mania, depression, and organic brain disease. It would be curious if autism, with its putative biological basis and outward expression in the realms of behaviour and mental functioning, were to form an exception. In any case the overlap is not worryingly great—delusions and hallucinations, the two features on which the diagnosis of schizophrenia most commonly rests, are conspicuous by their absence in autism.

It also seems overwhelmingly likely that autism is complicated by the development of schizophrenia in a small but significant proportion of cases. If it is accepted that Asperger's syndrome is a subtype of autism, and schizophrenia develops in Asperger's syndrome at several times the general population rate, then it is difficult to resist this conclusion. Once again this should not raise fears that autism and schizophrenia are in imminent danger of being recombined into a single entity. It is highly likely that the relationship with schizophrenia is not exclusive, and it seems plausible to suppose that the association is merely another example of schizophrenia complicating an organic central nervous system disorder—albeit one that is developmental in this case.

References

Abbott, R.J. and Loizou, L.A. (1986). Neuroleptic malignant syndrome. *British Journal of Psychiatry*, **148**, 47–51.

Abrams, R. and Taylor, M. (1973). First-rank symptoms, severity of illness, and treatment response in schizophrenia. *Comprehensive Psychiatry*, **14**, 353–5.

Abrams, R.A. and Taylor, M.A. (1976a). Mania and schizo-affective disorder, manic type: a comparison. *American Journal of Psychiatry*, **133**, 1445–7.

Abrams, R. and Taylor, M.A. (1976b). Catatonia: a prospective clinical study. *Archives of General Psychiatry*, **33**, 579–81.

Abrams, R. and Taylor, M.A. (1978). A rating scale for emotional blunting. *American Journal of Psychiatry*, **135**, 226–9.

Abrams, R. and Taylor, M.A. (1983). The genetics of schizophrenia: a re-assessment using modern criteria. *American Journal of Psychiatry*, **140**, 171–5.

Achte, K.A. (1967). On prognosis and rehabilitation in schizophrenic and paranoid psychoses. *Acta Psychiatrica Scandinavica*, Supplement, **196**, 1–217.

Achte, K.A., Hillbom, E., and Aalberg, V. (1969). Psychoses following war brain injuries. *Acta psychiatrica Scandinavica*, **45**, 1–18.

Ackner, B., Harris, A., and Oldham, A.J. (1957). Insulin treatment of schizophrenia: a controlled study. *Lancet*, **i**, 607–9.

Addonizio, G. and Susman, V.L. (1991). *Neuroleptic malignant syndrome: a clinical approach*. Mosby, St Louis.

Adler, L., Angrist, B., Peselow, E., Corwin, J., Maslansky, R., and Rotrosen, J. (1986). A controlled assessment of propanolol in the treatment of neuroleptic-induced akathisia. *British Journal of Psychiatry*, **149**, 42–5.

Aita, J.A. and Reitan, R.M. (1948). Psychotic reactions in the late recovery period following head injury. *American Journal of Psychiatry*, **105**, 161–9.

Alberts, J.L., François, F., and Josserand, F. (1985). Etude des effets secondaires rapportes a l'occasion de traitements par dogmatil. *Semaine Hôpital Paris*, **61**, 1351–7.

Al-Khani, M., Bebbington, P., Watson, J., and House, F. (1986). Life events and schizophrenia: a Saudi Arabian study. *British Journal of Psychiatry*, **148**, 12–22.

Allderidge, P. (1974). *Richard Dadd*. Academy Editions, London.

Almeida, O.P., Howard, R., Forstl, H., and Levy, R. (1992). Should the diagnosis of late paraphrenia be abandoned. *Psychological Medicine*, **22**, 11–4.

Altschuler, L.L., Conrad, A., Kovelman, J.A., and Scheibel, A. (1987). Hippo-campal pyramidal cell orientation in schizophrenia: a controlled neurohistologic study of the Yakovlev Collection. *Archives of General Psychiatry*, **44**, 1094–8.

Altschuler, L.L., Casanova, M.F., Goldberg, T.E., and Kleinman, J.E. (1990). The hippocampus and parahippocampus in schizophrenic, suicide and control brains. *Archives of General Psychiatry*, **47**, 1029–34.

Andersen, P.H., Nielsen, E.B., Gronvald, F.C., and Braestrup, C. (1986). Some atypical neuroleptics inhibit [3-H]SCH 23390 binding in vivo. *European Journal of Pharmacology*, **120**, 143–4.

Andreasen, N.C. (1979a). Thought, language and communication disorders: I. Clinical assessment, definition of terms and evaluation of their reliability. *Archives of General Psychiatry*, **36**, 1315–21.

Andreasen, N.C. (1979*b*). Affective flattening and the criteria for schizophrenia. *American Journal of Psychiatry*, **136**, 944–7.

Andreasen, N.C. (1982). Negative symptoms in schizophrenia: definition and reliability. *Archives of General Psychiatry*, **39**, 784–8.

Andreasen, N.C. and Bardach, J. (1977). Dysmorphophobia: symptom or disease. *American Journal of Psychiatry*, **134**, 673–6.

Andreasen, N.C. and Olsen, S. (1982). Negative v. positive schizophrenia: definition and validation. *Archives of General Psychiatry*, **39**, 789–94.

Andreasen, N.C., Rice, J., Endicott, J., Coryell, W., Grove, W.M., and Reich, T. (1987). Familial rates of affective disorder. *Archives of General Psychiatry*, **44**, 461–9.

Andreasen, N.C., Swayze, V.W., Flaum, M., Yates, W.R., Arndt, S., and McChesney, C. (1990*a*). Ventricular enlargement in schizophrenia evaluated with computed tomographic scanning. *Archives of General Psychiatry*, **47**, 1008–15.

Andreasen, N.C., Ehrhardt, J.C., Swayze, V.W., Alliger, R.J., Yuh, W.T.C., Cohen, G., and Ziebell, S. (1990*b*). Magnetic resonance imaging of the brain in schizophrenia: the pathophysiologic significance of structural abnormalities. *Archives of General Psychiatry*, **47**, 35–44.

Andreasen, N.C., Rezai, K., Alliger, R., Swayze, V.W., Flaum, M., Kirchner, P., Cohen, G., and O'Leary, D.S. (1992). Hypofrontality in neuroleptic-naive patients and in patients with chronic schizophrenia. *Archives of General Psychiatry*, **49**, 943–58.

Andreasson, S., Allebeck, P., Engstrom, A., and Rydberg, U. (1987). Cannabis and schizophrenia: a longitudinal study of Swedish conscripts. *Lancet*, **ii**, 1483–5.

Angrist, B.M. and Gershon, S. (1970). The phenomenology of experimentally induced amphetamine psychosis—preliminary observations. *Biological Psychiatry*, **2**, 95–107.

Angrist, B. and Sudilovsky, A. (1978). Central nervous system stimulants: historical aspects and clinical effects. In *Handbook of Psychopharmacology*, Vol. 11, stimulants, (ed. L.L. Iversen, S.E. Iversen, and S.H. Snyder), pp. 99–166. Plenum, New York.

Angst, J. (1986). The course of schizoaffective disorders. In *Schizoaffective psychoses*, (ed. A. Marneros and M.T. Tsuang), pp. 63–93. Springer-Verlag, Berlin.

American Psychiatric Association (APA) Task Force (1979). *Tardive diskinesia: report of the American Psychiatric Association task force on the late neurological effects of antipsychotic drugs*. American Psychiatric Association, Washington, DC.

Arevalo, J. and Vizcarro, C. (1989). 'Emocion expresada' y curso de la esquizofrenia en una muestra española. *Analisis y Modificacion de Conducta*, **15**, 3–23.

Ariel, R.N., Golden, C.J., Berg, R.A., Quaite, M.A., Dirksen, J.W., Forsell, T., *et al.* (1983). Regional cerebral blood flow in schizophrenics. *Archives of General Psychiatry*, **40**, 258–63.

Arieti, S. (1974). *Interpretation of schizophrenia*, (2nd edn). Crosby Lockwood Staples, London.

Arndt, S., Alliger, R.J., and Andreasen, N.C. (1991). The distinction of positive and negative symptoms: the failure of a two dimensional model. *British Journal of Psychiatry*, **158**, 317–22.

Arthur, A.Z. (1964). Theories and explanations of delusions: a review. *American Journal of Psychiatry*, **121**, 105–15.

Asperger, H. (1944). Die 'Autistic Psychopathen' im Kindesalter. *Archiv für Psychiatric und Nervenkrankheiten*, **117**, 76–136. (Translated by U. Frith as 'Autistic Psychopathy' in childhood. In *Autism and Asperger syndrome* (ed. U. Frith), pp. 37–93. Cambridge University Press.)

Astrup, C. (1979). *The chronic schizophrenias*. Universitetsforlaget, Oslo.

Astrup, C. and Noreik, K. (1966). *Functional psychoses: diagnostic and prognostic models*. Thomas, Springfield, Illinois.

Astrup, C., Fossum, A., and Holmboe, R. (1959). A follow-up study of 270 patients with acute affective psychoses. *Acta Psychiatrica et Neurologica Scandinavica*, **34**, supplement, **135**, 11–65

Astrup, C., Fossum, A., and Holmboe, R. (1962). *Prognosis in functional psychoses*. Thomas, Springfield, Illinois.

Ayd, F.J. (1961). A survey of drug-induced extrapyramidal reactions. *Journal of the American Medical Association*, **175**, 1054–60.

Ayd, F.J., Coyle, J.T., Hollister, L.E., Simpson, G.M., Carpenter, W.T., Casey, D.E., *et al.* (1984). Tardive dyskinesia and thioridazine. *Archives of General Psychiatry*, **41**, 414–16.

Baddeley, A.D. (1986). *Working memory*. Clarendon, Oxford.

Baddeley, A. (1990). *Human memory: theory and practice*. Erlbaum, Hove.

Bajc, M., Medved, V., Basic, M., Topuzovic, N., and Babic, D. (1989). Cerebral perfusion inhomogeneities in schizophrenia demonstrated with single photon emission computed tomography and Tc99m-hexamethylpropyleneamineoxim. *Acta Psychiatrica Scandinavica*, **80**, 427–33.

Barnes, T.R.E. and Braude, W.M. (1985). Akathisia variants and tardive dyskinesia. *Archives of General Psychiatry*, **42**, 874–8.

Baron, M., Gruen, R., Asnis, L., and Kane, J. (1982). Schizoaffective illness, schizophrenia, and affective disorders: morbidity risk and genetic transmission. *Acta Psychiatrica Scandinavica*, **65**, 253–262.

Baron, M., Gruen, R., Rainer, J.D., Kane, J., Asnis, L., and Lord, S. (1985). A family study of schizophrenia and normal control probands: implications for the spectrum concept of schizophrenia. *American Journal of Psychiatry*, **142**, 447–55.

Barrelet, L., Ferrero, F., Szigethy, L., Giddey, C., and Pellizzer, G. (1990). Expressed emotion and first-admission schizophrenia: nine-month follow-up in a French cultural environment. *British Journal of Psychiatry*, **156**, 357–62.

Barrowclough, C. and Tarrier, N. (1992). *Families of schizophrenic patients*. Chapman and Hall, London.

Baruk, H. (1959). Delusions of passion. In *Themes and variations in European psychiatry*, (ed. S.R. Hirsch and M. Shepherd, 1974), pp. 375–84, Wright, Bristol.

Bateson, G., Jackson, D.D., Haley, J., and Weakland, J. (1956). Toward a theory of schizophrenia. *Behavioral Science*, **1**, 251–64.

Beard, A.W. (1959). The association of hepatolenticular degeneration with schizophrenia. *Acta Psychiatrica et Neurologica Scandinavica*, **34**, 411–28.

Bebbington, P. and Kuipers, L. (1988). Social influences on schizophrenia. In *Schizophrenia: the major issues,* (ed. P. Bebbington and P. McGuffin), pp. 201–25. Heinemann/Mental Health Foundation, Oxford.

Bebbington, P., Wilkins, S., Jones, P., Foerster, A., Murray, R., Toone, B., and Lewis, S. (1993). Life events and psychosis: initial results from the Camberwell Collaborative Psychosis Study. *British Journal of Psychiatry*, **162**, 72–9.

Beigel, A. and Murphy, D.L. (1971). Assessing clinical characteristics of the manic state. *American Journal of Psychiatry*, **128**, 688–94.

Benes, F.M. (1988). Post-mortem structural analyses of schizophrenic brain: study designs and the interpretation of data. *Psychiatric Developments*, **6**, 213–26.

Bennett, D.H. (1978). Community psychiatry. *British Journal of Psychiatry*, **132**, 209–20.

Bennett, D. (1983). The historical development of rehabilitation services. In *Theory and practice of psychiatric rehabilitation*, (ed. F.N. Watts and D.H. Bennett), pp. 15–42. Wiley, Chichester.

Bennett, S. and Klein, H.R. (1966). Childhood schizophrenia: 30 years later. *American Journal of Psychiatry*, **122**, 1121–4.

Benson, D.F. (1973). Psychiatric aspects of aphasia. *British Journal of Psychiatry*, **123**, 555–66.

Benson, D.F. (1979). *Aphasia, alexia and agraphia*. Churchill Livingstone, Edinburgh.

Berg, E., Lindelius, R., Patterson, U., and Salum, I. (1983). Schizoaffective psychoses: a long-term follow up. *Acta Psychiatrica Scandinavica*, **67**, 389–98.

Berrios, G.E. (1982). Tactile hallucinations: conceptual and historical aspects. *Journal of Neurology, Neurosurgery and Psychiatry*, **45**, 285–93.

Berrios, G.E. (1985). Positive and negative symptoms and Jackson. *Archives of General Psychiatry*, **42**, 95–7.

Berrios, G.E. (1986). Presbyophrenia: the rise and fall of a concept. *Psychological Medicine*, **16**, 267–75.

Berrios, G.E. and Beer, D. (1993). The notion of unitary psychosis: a conceptual history. *Psychological Medicine*. In press.

Berrios, G.E. and Dening, T.R. (1989). Biological and quantitative issues in organic psychiatry. *Behavioural Neurology*, **3**, 247–59.

Biehl, H., Maurer, K., Schubart, C., Krum, B., and Jung, E. (1986). Prediction of outcome and utilization of medical services in a prospective study of first-onset schizophrenics: results of a five-year follow-up study. *European Archives of Psychiatry and Neurological Science*, **236**, 139–47.

Biel, J.H. and Bopp, B.A. (1978). Amphetamines: structure-activity relationships. In *Handbook of psychopharmacology*, Vol. 11, stimulants, (ed. L.L. Iversen, S.E. Iversen, and S.H. Snyder), pp. 1–40. Plenum, New York.

Bilder, R.M., Mukherjee, S., Rieder, M.D., and Pandurangi, A. (1985). Symptomatic and neuropsychological components of defect states. *Schizophrenia Bulletin*, **11**, 409–17.

Birchwood, M.J., Hallett, S.E., and Preston, M.C. (1988). *Schizophrenia: an integrated approach to research and treatment*. Longman, London.

Bird, E.D., Barnes, J., Iversen, L.L., Spokes, E.G.S., MacKay, A.V.P., and Shepherd, M. (1977). Increased brain dopamine and reduced glutamic acid decarboxylase and choline acetyl transferase activity in schizophrenia and related psychoses. *Lancet*, **ii**, 1157–9.

Bird, E.D., Spokes, E.G.S., and Iversen, L.L. (1979). Increased dopamine concentrations in limbic areas of brain of patients dying with schizophrenia. *Brain*, **102**, 347–60.

Bird, E.D., Langais, P.J., and Benes, F.M. (1984). Dopamine and homovanillic acid in postmortem schizophrenic brain. *Clinical Neuropharmacology*, **7**, supplement, **1**, 910–11.

Birley, J.L.T. and Brown, G.W. (1970). Crises and life changes preceding the onset or relapse of acute schizophrenia. *British Journal of Psychiatry*, **116**, 327–33.

Blair, D. (1940). Prognosis in schizophrenia. *Journal of Mental Science*, **86**, 378–477.

Bland, R.C. and Orn, H. (1978). 14 year outcome in early schizophrenia. *Acta Psychiatrica Scandinavica*, **58**, 327–38.

Blashfield, R.K. (1984). *The classification of psychopathology: neo-Kraepelinian and quantitative approaches.* Plenum, New York.

Bleuler, E. (1911). *Dementia praecox or the group of schizophrenias*, (trans. J. Zinkin, 1950). International Universities Press, New York.

Bleuler, E. (1926). *Textbook of psychiatry*, (trans. A.A. Brill). George Allen and Unwin, London.

Bleuler, M. (1974). The long-term course of the schizophrenic psychoses. *Psychological Medicine*, **4**, 244–54.

Bleuler, M. (1978). *The schizophrenic disorders: long-term patient and family studies*, (trans. S.M. Clemens). Yale University Press, New Haven.

Boeringa, J.A. and Castellani, S. (1979). Reliability and validity of emotional blunting as a criterion for diagnosis of schizophrenia. *American Journal of Psychiatry*, **139**, 1131–5.

Bogerts, B., Meertz, E., and Schoenfeldt-Bausch, R. (1985). Basal ganglia and limbic system pathology in schizophrenia: a morphometric study of brain volume shrinkage. *Archives of General Psychiatry*, **42**, 784–91.

Bonner, H. (1951). The problem of diagnosis in paranoic conditions. *American Journal of Psychiatry*, **107**, 677–83.

Borison, R.L., Hitri, A., Blowers, A.J., and Diamond, B.I. (1983). Antipsychotic drug action: clinical, biochemical and pharmacological evidence for site-specificity of action. *Clinical Neuropharmacology*, **6**, 137–50.

Bosch, G. (1970). *Infantile autism.* Springer, New York.

Bourne, H. (1953). The insulin myth. *Lancet*, **ii**, 964–8.

Bowers, M.B. (1974). Central dopamine turnover in schizophrenic syndromes. *Archives of General Psychiatry*, **31**, 50–4.

Bowers, M.B. and Van Woert, M.H. (1972). 6-hydroxydopamine, noradrenergic reward and schizophrenia. *Science*, **175**, 920–1.

Bowman, E.P. (1988). Asperger's syndrome and autism: the case for a connection. *British Journal of Psychiatry*, **152**, 377–82.

Bowman, K.M. and Raymond, A.F. (1931). A statistical study of delusions in the manic-depressive psychoses. In *Proceedings of the association for research in nervous and mental diseases*, Vol. 11. Williams and Wilkins, Baltimore.

Boyle, M. (1990). *Schizophrenia: a scientific delusion?* Routledge, London.

Bradbury, T.N. and Miller, G.A. (1985). Season of birth in schizophrenia: a review of evidence, methodology, and etiology. *Psychological Bulletin*, **98**, 569–94.

Brandon, S., Cowley, P., McDonald, C., Neville, P., Palmer, R., and Wellstood-Eason, S. (1985). Leicester ECT trial: results in schizophrenia. *British Journal of Psychiatry*, **146**, 177–83.

Breier, A., Schreiber, J.L., Dyer, J., and Pickar, D. (1991). National Institute of Mental Health longitudinal study of chronic schizophrenia: prognosis and predictors of outcome. *Archives of General Psychiatry*, **48**, 239–46.

Bridge, T.P. and Wyatt, R.J. (1980). Paraphrenia: paranoid states of late life. *Journal of the American Geriatrics Society*, **28**, 193–205.

Bridge, T.P., Kleinman, J.E., Karoum, F., and Wyatt, R.J. (1985). Postmortem central catecholamines and antemortem cognitive impairment in elderly schizophrenics and controls. *Neuropsychobiology*, **14**, 57–61.

Broadbent, D.E. (1958). *Perception and communication*. Pergamon, London.

Brockington, I.F., Kendell, R.E., and Leff, J.P. (1978a). Definitions of schizophrenia: concordance and prediction of outcome. *Psychological Medicine*, **8**, 387–98.

Brockington, I.F., Kendell, R.E., Kellett, J.M., Curry, S.H., and Wainwright, S. (1978b). Trials of lithium, chlorpromazine and amitriptyline in schizoaffective patients. *British Journal of Psychiatry*, **133**, 162–8.

Brockington, I.F., Kendell, R.E., Wainwright, S., Hillier, V.F., and Walker, J. (1979). The distinction between the affective psychoses and schizophrenia. *British Journal of Psychiatry*, **135**, 243–8.

Brockington, I.F., Kendell, R.E., and Wainwright, S. (1980a). Manic patients with schizophrenic or paranoid symptoms. *Psychological Medicine*, **10**, 73–83.

Brockington, I.F., Kendell, R.E., and Wainwright, S. (1980b). Depressed patients with schizophrenic or paranoid symptoms. *Psychological Medicine*, **10**, 665–75.

Brockington, I.F., Cernik, K.F., Schofield, E.M., Downing, A.R., Francis, A.F., and Keelan, C. (1981). Puerperal psychosis: phenomena and diagnosis. *Archives of General Psychiatry*, **38**, 829–33.

Brockington, I.F., Perris, C., and Meltzer, H. (1982a). Cycloid psychoses: diagnostic and heuristic value. *Journal of Nervous and Mental Disease*, **170**, 651–6.

Brockington, I.F., Perris, C., Kendell, R.E., Hillier, V.F., and Wainwright, S. (1982b). The course and outcome of cycloid psychosis. *Psychological Medicine*, **12**, 97–105.

Brown, G.W. (1985). The discovery of expressed emotion: induction or deduction? In *Expressed emotion in families: its significance for mental illness*, (ed. J. Leff and C. Vaughn), pp. 7–25. Guildford Press, London.

Brown, G.W. and Birley, J.L.T. (1968). Crises and life changes and the onset of schizophrenia. *Journal of Health and Social Behavior*, **9**, 203–14.

Brown, G.W., Carstairs, G.M., and Topping, G.C. (1958). The post hospital adjustment of chronic mental patients. *Lancet*, **ii**, 685–9.

Brown, G.W., Monck, E.M., Carstairs, G.M., and Wing, J.K. (1962). The influence of family life on the course of schizophrenic illness. *British Journal of Preventative and Social Medicine*, **16**, 55–68.

Brown, G.W., Bone, M., Dalison, B., and Wing, J.K. (1966). *Schizophrenia and social care*, Maudsley Monograph, No. 17. Oxford University Press, London.

Brown, G.W., Birley, J.L.T., and Wing, J.K. (1972). Influence of family life on the course of schizophrenic disorders: a replication. *British Journal of Psychiatry*, **121**, 241–58.

Buchkremer, G., Stricker, K., Holle, R., and Kuhs, H. (1991). The predictability of relapses in schizophrenic patients. *European Archives of Psychiatry and Clinical Neurosciences*, **240**, 292–300.

Buchsbaum, M.S., DeLisi, L.E., Holcomb, H.H., Cappelletti, J., King, A.C., Johnson, J., *et al*. (1984). Anteroposterior gradients in cerebral glucose use in schizophrenia and affective disorders. *Archives of General Psychiatry*, **41**, 1159–66.

Buhrich, N., Crow, T.J., Johnstone, E.C., and Owens, D.G.C. (1988). Age disorientation in chronic schizophrenia is not associated with pre-morbid intellectual impairment or past physical treatments. *British Journal of Psychiatry*, **152**, 466-9.

Burns, A., Jacoby, R., and Levy, R. (1990). Psychiatric phenomena in Alzheimer's disease. *British Journal of Psychiatry*, **157**, 72-85.

Burt, D.R., Creese, I., and Snyder, S.H. (1977). Antischizophrenic drugs: chronic treatment elevates dopamine receptor numbers. *Science*, **196**, 326-8.

Cade, J.F.J. (1970). The story of lithium. In *Discoveries in biological psychiatry*, (ed. F.J. Ayd and B. Blackwell), pp. 230-43. Lippincott, Philadelphia.

Caine, E.D. and Shoulson I. (1983). Psychiatric syndromes in Huntington's disease. *American Journal of Psychiatry*, **140**, 728-33.

Caldwell, A.E. (1970). *Origins of psychopharmacology: from CPZ to LSD*. Thomas, Springfield, Illinois.

Calev, A. (1984*a*). Recall and recognition in mildly disturbed schizophrenics: the use of matched tasks. *Psychological Medicine*, **14**, 425-9.

Calev, A. (1984*b*). Recall and recognition in chronic nondemented schizophrenics: use of matched tasks. *Journal of Abnormal Psychology*, **93**, 172-7.

Calev, A., Berlin, H., and Lerer, B. (1987*a*). Remote and recent memory in long hospitalised chronic schizophrenics. *Biological Psychiatry*, **22**, 79-85.

Calev, A., Korin, Y., Kugelmass, S., and Lerer, B. (1987*b*). Performance of chronic schizophrenics on matched word and design recall tasks. *Biological Psychiatry*, **22**, 699-709.

Calloway, P. (1993). *Soviet and western psychiatry: a comparative study*. Wiley, New York.

Cameron, N. (1938). Reasoning, regression and communication in schizophrenics. *Psychological Monographs*, **50**, 1-34.

Cameron, N. (1939). Schizophrenic thinking in a problem-solving situation. *Journal of Mental Science*, **85**, 1012-35.

Cameron, N. (1944). Experimental analysis of schizophrenic thinking. In *Language and thought in schizophrenia*, (ed. J.S. Kasanin), pp. 50-64. University of California Press, Berkeley.

Canton, G. and Fraccon, I.G. (1985). Life events and schizophrenia: a replication. *Acta Psychiatrica Scandinavica*, **71**, 211-16.

Carlson, G.A. and Goodwin, F.K. (1973). The stages of mania: a longitudinal analysis of the manic episode. *Archives of General Psychiatry*, **28**, 221-8.

Carlsson, A. (1977). Does dopamine play a role in schizophrenia? *Psychological Medicine*, **7**, 583-97.

Carlsson, A. and Lindqvist, M. (1963). Effect of chlorpromazine and haloperidol on formation of 3-methoxytyramine and normetanephrine in mouse brain. *Acta Pharmacologica et Toxicologica*, **20**, 140-4.

Caroff, S.N. (1980). The neuroleptic malignant syndrome. *Journal of Clinical Psychiatry*, **41**, 79-83.

Carone, B.J., Harrow, M., and Westermeyer, J.F. (1991). Posthospital course and outcome in schizophrenia. *Archives of General Psychiatry*, **48**, 247-53.

Carpenter, W.T., Jr., and Strauss, J.S. (1974). Cross-cultural evaluation of Schneider's first-rank symptoms of schizophrenia: a report from the International Pilot Study of Schizophrenia. *American Journal of Psychiatry*, **131**, 682-7.

Carpenter, W.T., Jr., Strauss, J.S., and Muleh, S. (1973). Are there pathognomonic symptoms in schizophrenia? An empiric investigation of Kurt Schneider's first-rank symptoms. *Archives of General Psychiatry*, **28**, 847-52.

Carpenter, W.J., Bartko, J.J., Carpenter, C.L., and Strauss, J.L. (1976). Another view of schizophrenic subtypes. *Archives of General Psychiatry*, **33**, 508–16.

Carpenter, W.T., Jr., Kurz, R., Kirkpatrick, B., Hanlon, T.E., Summerfelt, A.T., Buchanan, R.W., *et al.* (1991). Carbamazepine maintenance treatment in out-patient schizophrenics. *Archives of General Psychiatry*, **48**, 69–72.

Casey, D.E. (1989). Clozapine: neuroleptic-induced EPS and tardive dyskinesia. *Psychopharmacology*, **99**, supplement, S47–S53.

Cazzullo, C.L., Bressi, C., Bertrando, P., Clerici, M., and Maffei, C. (1989). Schizophrenie et expression emotionelle familiale: étude d'une population italienne. *Encephale*, **15**, 1–6.

Chaika, E. (1974). A linguist looks at 'schizophrenic' language. *Brain and Language*, 257–76.

Chaika, E. and Lambe, R.A. (1989). Cohesion in schizophrenic narratives, revisited. *Journal of Communication Disorders*, **22**, 407–21.

Chapman, L.J. and Chapman, J.P. (1973). *Disordered thought in schizophrenia.* Appleton-Century-Crofts, New York.

Chiu, L.P.W. (1989). Transient recurrence of auditory hallucinations during acute dystonia. *British Journal of Psychiatry*, **155**, 110–13.

Christison, G.W., Casanova, M.F., Weinberger, D.R., Rawlings, R., and Kleinman, J.E. (1989). A quantitative investigation of hippocampal pyramidal cell size, shape, and variability of orientation in schizophrenia. *Archives of General Psychiatry*, **46**, 1027–32.

Chuang, H.T. and Addington, D. (1988). Homosexual panic: a review of its concept. *Canadian Journal of Psychiatry*, **33**, 613–17.

Chung, R.R., Langeluddecke, P., and Tennant, C. (1986). Threatening life events in the onset of schizophrenia, schizophreniform psychosis and hypomania. *British Journal of Psychiatry*, **148**, 680–5.

Ciompi, L. (1980). The natural history of schizophrenia in the long term. *British Journal of Psychiatry*, **136**, 413–20.

Clare, A. (1980). *Psychiatry in dissent*, (2nd edn). Tavistock, London.

Clark, D. (1981). *Social therapy in psychiatry*, (2nd edn). Churchill Livingstone, Edinburgh.

Clayton, P., Pitts, F.N., Jr., and Winokur, G. (1965). Affective disorder: IV. Mania. *Comprehensive Psychiatry*, **6**, 313–22.

de Clérambault, G. (1942). *Œuvre psychiatrique*. Presses Universitaires de France, Paris.

Cobb, J. (1979). Morbid jealousy. *British Journal of Hospital Medicine*, **21**, 511–18.

Cohen, D.J. and Donnellan, A.M. (ed.) (1987). *Handbook of autism and pervasive developmental disorders*. Winston, Silver Spring, Maryland.

Cohen, R.M., Semple, W.E., Gross, M., Nordahl, T.E., DeLisi, L.E., Holcomb, H.H., *et al.* (1987). Dysfunction in a prefrontal substrate of sustained attention in schizophrenia. *Life Sciences*, **40**, 2031–9.

Cohen, W.J. and Cohen, N.H. (1974). Lithium carbonate, haloperidol, and irreversible brain damage. *Journal of the American Medical Association*, **230**, 1283–7.

Comings, D.E. (1991). *Tourette syndrome and human behavior*. Hope Press. Duarte, California.

Connell. P. (1958). *Amphetamine Psychosis*, Maudsley Monograph, No. 5. Oxford University Press, London.

Conrad, A.J., Abebe, T., Austin, R., Forsythe, S., and Scheibel, A.B. (1991).

Hippocampal pyramidal cell disarray in schizophrenia as a bilateral phenomenon. *Archives of General Psychiatry*, **48**, 413-17.

Cooper, A.F., Garside, R.F., and Kay, D.W.K. (1974). A comparison of deaf and non-deaf patients with paranoid and affective psychoses. *British Journal of Psychiatry*, **129**, 532-8.

Cooper, J.E., Kendell, R.E., Gurland, B.J., Sharpe, L., Copeland, J.R.M., and Simon, R. (1972). *Psychiatric diagnosis in New York and London*, Maudsley Monograph, No. 20. Oxford University Press, London.

Coryell, W. (1986). Schizoaffective and schizophreniform disorders. In *The medical basis of psychiatry*, (ed. G. Winokur and P. Clayton), pp. 102-14. Saunders, Philadelphia.

Coryell, W., Lavori, P., Endicott, J., Keller, M., and vanEerdewegh, M. (1984). Outcome in schizoaffective, psychotic, and nonpsychotic depression. *Archives of General Psychiatry*, **41**, 787-91.

Costall, B. and Naylor, R.J. (1981). The hypothesis of different dopamine receptor mechanisms. *Life Sciences*, **28**, 215-29.

Coward, D.M. (1992). General pharmacology of clozapine. *British Journal of Psychiatry*, **160**, supplement, **17**, 5-12.

Cramond, W.A. (1987). Lessons from the insulin-story in psychiatry. *Australian and New Zealand Journal of Psychiatry*, **21**, 320-6.

Crane G.E. (1972). Pseudoparkinsonism and tardive dyskinesia. *Archives of Neurology*, **27**, 426-30.

Crawley, J.C., Crow, T.J., Johnstone, E.C., Oldland, S.R.D., Owen, F., Owens, D.G.C., *et al.* (1986). Dopamine D2 receptors in schizophrenia studied in vivo. *Lancet*, **ii**, 224-5.

Creese, I., Burt, D.R., and Snyder, S.H. (1976). Dopamine receptor binding predicts clinical and pharmacological potencies of antischizophrenic drugs. *Science*, **192**, 481-3.

Critchley, M. (1964). The neurology of psychotic speech. *British Journal of Psychiatry*, **110**, 353-64.

Crow, T.J. (1980). Molecular pathology of schizophrenia: more than one disease process? *British Medical Journal*, **280**, 66-8.

Crow, T.J. (1986). The continuum of psychosis and its implication for the structure of the gene. *British Journal of Psychiatry*, **149**, 419-29.

Crow, T.J. (1991). The failure of the Kraepelinian binary concept and the search for the psychosis gene. In *Concepts of mental disorder: a continuing debate*, (ed. A. Kerr and H. McClelland), pp. 31-47. Gaskell/Royal College of Psychiatrists, London.

Crow, T.J. and Mitchell, W.S. (1975). Subjective age in chronic schizophrenia: evidence for a sub-group of patients with defective learning capacity. *British Journal of Psychiatry*, **126**, 360-3.

Crow, T.J., Deakin, J.F.W., and Longden, A. (1977). The nucleus accumbens— possible site of antipsychotic action of neuroleptic drugs. *Psychological Medicine*, **7**, 213-21.

Crow, T.J., Owen, F., Cross, A.J., Lofthouse, R., and Longden, A. (1978). Brain biochemistry and schizophrenia. *Lancet*, **i**, 36-7.

Crow, T.J., Baker, H.F., Cross, A.J., Joseph, M.H., Lofthouse, R., Longden, A., *et al.* (1979). Monoamine mechanisms in chronic schizophrenia: post-mortem neurochemical findings. *British Journal of Psychiatry*, **134**, 249-56.

Crow, T.J., MacMillan, J.F., Johnson, A.L., and Johnstone, E.C. (1986). The Northwick Park study of first episodes of schizophrenia I. A randomised controlled trial of prophylactic neuroleptic treatment. *British Journal of Psychiatry*, **148**, 120-7.

Crow, T.J., Ball, J., Bloom, S.R., Brown, R., Bruton, C.J., Colter, N., *et al.* (1989). Schizophrenia as an anomaly of development of cerebral asymmetry: a postmortem study and a proposal concerning the genetic basis of the disease. *Archives of General Psychiatry*, **46**, 1145-50.

Cutting, J. (1980). Physical illness and psychosis. *British Journal of Psychiatry*, **136**, 109-19.

Cutting, J. (1985). *The psychology of schizophrenia*. Churchill Livingstone, Edinburgh.

Cutting, J. (1987). The phenomenology of acute organic psychoses: comparison with acute schizophrenia. *British Journal of Psychiatry*, **151**, 324-32.

Cutting, J. (1990). *The right cerebral hemisphere and psychiatric disorders*. Oxford University Press.

Cutting, J. and Dunne, F. (1989). Subjective experiences of schizophrenia. *Schizophrenia Bulletin*, **15**, 217-31.

Cutting, J. and Shepherd, M. (ed.) (1987). *The clinical roots of the schizophrenia concept*. Cambridge University Press.

Cutting, J.C., Clare, A.W., and Mann, A.H. (1978). Cycloid psychosis: an investigation of the diagnostic concept. *Psychological Medicine*, **8**, 637-48.

Dalby, M.A. (1975). Behavioral effects of carbamazepine. In *Complex partial seizures and their treatment*, Advances in Neurology, Vol. 11, (ed. J.K. Penry and D.D. Daly). Raven, New York.

Dale, R. (1991). *Louis Wain: the man who drew cats*, (2nd edn). Michael O'Mara, London.

Darby, J.K. (1976). Neuropathological aspects of psychosis in childhood. *Journal of Autism and Childhood Schizophrenia*, **6**, 339-52.

David, G.B. (1957). The pathological anatomy of the schizophrenias. In *Schizophrenia: somatic aspects*, (ed. D. Richter), pp. 93-130. Pergamon, Oxford.

Davidson, M. and Davis, K.L. (1988). A comparison of plasma homovanillic acid concentrations in schizophrenic patients and normal controls. *Archives of General Psychiatry*, **45**, 561-3.

Davis, J.M. (1975). Overview: maintenance therapy in psychiatry: I. Schizophrenia. *American Journal of Psychiatry*, **132**, 1237-45.

Davis, J.M. (1985). Antipsychotic drugs. In *Comprehensive textbook of psychiatry*, (4th edn), (ed. H.I. Kaplan and B.J. Sadock), pp. 1481-1512. Williams and Wilkins, Baltimore.

Davison, K. and Bagley C.R. (1969). Schizophrenia-like psychoses associated with organic disorders of the central nervous system: a review. *British Journal of Psychiatry*, special publication, **4**, 113-83.

Day, R. (1981). Life events and schizophrenia: the 'triggering' hypothesis. *Acta Psychiatrica Scandinavica*, **64**, 97-122.

Dean, C. and Kendell, R.E. (1981). The symptomatology of puerperal illness. *British Journal of Psychiatry*, **139**, 128-33.

Debray, Q. (1975). A genetic study of chronic delusions. *Neuropsychobiology*, **1**, 313-21.

Delay, J. and Deniker, P. (1955). Hibernotherapies et cures neuroleptiques en psychiatrie. *Bulletin de la Academie Nationale de Medicin*, **139**, 145-7.

Delay, J. and Deniker, P. (1968). Drug-induced extrapyramidal syndromes. In *Handbook of clinical neurology*, Vol. 6, diseases of the basal ganglia, (ed. P.J. Vinken and G.W. Bruyn), pp. 248–66. Wiley, New Nork.

Delay, J., Deniker, P., and Harl, J.-M. (1952). Traitement des états d'excitation et d'agitation par une methode medicamenteuse derivée de l'hibernotherapie. *Annales Medico-Psychologique*, **110**, 267–73.

Delay, J., Deniker, P., Ropert, R., Beek, H., Barande, R., and Eurieult, M. (1959). Syndromes neurologiques experimentaux et therapeutiques: effets neurologiques d'un nouveau neuroleptique majeur le 7843 RP. *Presse Medicale*, **67**, 123–6.

DeLisi, L., Buchsbaum, M.S., Holcomb, H.H., Dorling-Zimmerman, S., Pickar, D., Boronow, J., *et al.* (1985). Clinical correlates of decreased anteroposterior gradients in positron emission tomography (PET) of schizophrenic patients. *American Journal of Psychiatry*, **142**, 78–81.

Delva, N.J. and Letemendia, J.J. (1982). Lithium treatment in schizophrenia and schizo-affective disorders. *British Journal of Psychiatry*, **141**, 387–400.

DeMyer, M.K., Hintgen, J.N., and Jackson, R.K. (1981). Infantile autism reviewed: a decade of research. *Schizophrenia Bulletin*, **7**, 388–451.

Dencker, S.J., Lepp, M., and Malm, U. (1980). Do schizophrenics well adapted in the community need neuroleptics? A depot withdrawal study. *Acta Psychiatrica Scandinavica*, supplement, **279**, 64–6.

Deniker, P. (1960). Experimental neurological syndromes and the new drug therapies in psychiatry. *Comprehensive Psychiatry*, **1**, 92–102.

Dening, T.R. and Berrios, G.E. (1990). Wilson's disease: psychiatric symptoms in 195 cases. *Archives of General Psychiatry*, **46**, 1126–34.

Despert, J.L. (1968). *Schizophrenia in children*. Brunner/Mazel, New York.

Diem, O. (1903). The simple dementing form of dementia praecox. In *The clinical roots of the schizophrenia concept*, (ed. J. Cutting and M. Shepherd, 1987), pp. 25–34. Cambridge University Press.

DiSimoni, F.G., Darley, F.L., and Aronson, A.E. (1977). Patterns of dysfunction in schizophrenic patients on an aphasia test battery. *Journal of Speech and Hearing Disorders*, **42**, 498–513.

Done, J.D., Johnstone, E.C., Frith, C.D., Golding, J., Shepherd, P.M., and Crow, T.J. (1991). Complications of pregnancy and delivery in relation to psychosis in adult life: data from the British perinatal mortality survey sample. *British Medical Journal*, **302**, 1576–80.

Dose, M., Apelt, S., and Emrich, H.M. (1987). Carbamazepine as an adjunct of antipsychotic therapy. *Psychiatry Research*, **22**, 303–10.

Dousse, M., Mamo, H., Ponsin, J.C., and Tran Dinh, H. (1988). Cerebral blood flow in schizophrenia. *Experimental Neurology*, **100**, 98–111.

Dove, H.W. (1984). Phencyclidine: pharmacologic and clinical review. *Psychiatric Medicine*, **2**, 189–209.

Drevets, W. and Rubin, E.H. (1989). Psychotic symptoms and the longitudinal course of senile dementia of the Alzheimer type. *Biological Psychiatry*, **25**, 39–48.

Dulz, B. and Hand, I. (1986). Short-term relapse in young schizophrenics: can it be predicted and affected by family (CFI), patient and treatment variables? An experimental study. In *Treatment of schizophrenia: family assessment and intervention*, (ed. M.J. Goldstein, I. Hand, and K. Hahlweg), pp. 59–75. Springer, Berlin.

Eggers, C. (1978). Course and prognosis of childhood schizophrenia. *Journal of Autism and Childhood Schizophrenia*, **8**, 21–36.

Eitinger, L., Laane, C.L., and Langfeldt, G. (1958). The prognostic value of the clinical picture and the therapeutic value of physical treatment in schizophrenia and the schizophreniform states. *Acta Psychiatrica et Neurologica Scandinavica*, **33**, 33–53.

Ekbom, K., Lindholm, H., and Ljungberg, L. (1972). New dystonic syndrome associated with butyrophenone therapy. *Journal of Neurology*, **202**, 94–103.

Ellingson, R.J. (1954). The incidence of EEG abnormality among patients with mental disorders of apparently nonorganic origin: a critical review. *American Journal of Psychiatry*, **111**, 263–75.

Ellis, A.W. and Young, A.W. (1988). *Human cognitive neuropsychology*. Erlbaum, Hove.

Elsasser, G. and Grunewald, H.-W. (1953). Schizophrene oder schizophrenieähnliche Psychosen bei Hirntraumatikern. *Nervenarzt*, **190**, 134–40.

Enoch, M.D. and Trethowan, W.H. (1979). *Uncommon psychiatric syndromes*, (2nd edn). Wright, Bristol.

Esquirol, J.E.D. (1838). *Les maladies mentales*. Baillière, Paris.

Essen-Moller, E. (1941). Psychiatrische Untersuchungen an einer Serie von Zwillingen. *Acta Psychiatrica*, supplement 23.

Evans-Jones, L.G. and Rosenbloom, L. (1978). Disintegrative psychosis in childhood. *Developmental Medicine and Child Neurology*, **20**, 462–70.

Everitt, B.S., Gourlay, J., and Kendell, R.E. (1971). An attempt at validation of traditional psychiatric syndromes by cluster analysis. *British Journal of Psychiatry*, **119**, 399–412.

Ey, H. (1952). *Etudes psychiatriques*, Vol. 1. Desclee de Brouwer, Paris.

Ey, H., Bernard, P., and Brisset, C. (1960). Acute delusional psychoses (*bouffées délirantes*). In *Themes and variations in European psychiatry* (ed. S.R. Hirsch and M. Shepherd, 1974), pp. 395–404, Wright, Bristol.

Faber, R. and Reichstein, M.B. (1981). Language dysfunction in schizophrenia. *British Journal of Psychiatry*, **139**, 519–22.

Faber, R., Abrams, R., Taylor, M.A., Kasprison, A., Morris, C., and Weisz, R. (1983). Comparison of schizophrenic patients with formal thought disorder and neurologically impaired patients with aphasia. *American Journal of Psychiatry*, **140**, 1348–51.

Faergeman, P.M. (1963). *Psychogenic psychoses*. Butterworth, London.

Farde, L., Wiesel, F.-A., Hall, H., Halldin, C., Stone-Elander, S., and Sedvall, G. (1987). No D2 receptor increase in PET study of schizophrenia. *Archives of General Psychiatry*, **44**, 671–2.

Farde, L., Wiesel, F.-A., Nordstrom, A.-L., and Sedvall, G. (1989). D1- and D2-dopamine receptor occupancy during treatment with conventional and atypical neuroleptics. *Psychopharmacology*, **99**, supplement, S28–S31.

Farde, L., Wiesel, F.-A., Stone-Elander, S., Halldin, C., Nordstrom, A.-L., Hall, H., and Sedvall, G. (1990). D2 dopamine receptors in neuroleptic-naive schizophrenic patients: a positron emission tomography study with [^{11}C]raclopride. *Archives of General Psychiatry*, **47**, 213–19.

Farde, L., Nordstrom, A.L., Wiesel, F.-A., Pauli, S., Halldin, C., and Sedvall, G. (1992). Positron emission tomographic analysis of central D1 and D2 dopamine receptor occupancy in patients treated with classical neuroleptics and clozapine. *Archives of General Psychiatry*, **49**, 538–44.

Farkas, T., Wolf, A.P., Jaeger, J., Brodie, J.D., Christman, D.R., and Fowler, J.S. (1984). Regional brain glucose metabolism in chronic schizophrenia: a positron emission transaxial tomographic study. *Archives of General Psychiatry*, **41**, 293–300.

Farmer, A.E., McGuffin, P., and Gottesman, I.I. (1987). Twin concordance for DSM-III schizophrenia: scrutinizing the validity of the evidence. *Archives of General Psychiatry*, **44**, 634–41.

Feighner, J.P., Robins, E., Guze, S., Woodruff, R.A., Winokur, G., and Munoz, R. (1972). Diagnostic criteria for use in psychiatric research. *Archives of General Psychiatry*, **26**, 57–62.

Feuchtwanger, E. and Mayer-Gross, W. (1938). Hirnverletzung und Schizophrenie. *Schweizer Archiv für Neurologie und Psychiatrie*, **41**, 17–99.

Fink, M. (1984). Meduna and the origins of convulsive therapy. *American Journal of Psychiatry*, **141**, 1034–41.

Fischer, M. (1973). Genetic and environmental factors in schizophrenia. *Acta Psychiatrica Scandinavica*, supplement, **238**, 1–158.

Fish, F.J. (1957). The classification of schizophrenia: the views of Kleist and his co-workers. *Journal of Mental Science*, **103**, 443–63.

Fish, F. (1958*a*). Leonhard's classification of schizophrenia. *Journal of Mental Science*, **104**, 943–71.

Fish, F.J. (1958*b*). A clinical investigation of chronic schizophrenia. *Journal of Mental Science*, **104**, 34–54.

Fish, F. (1960). Senile schizophrenia. *Journal of Mental Science*, **106**, 938–46.

Fish, F.J. (1962). *Schizophrenia*. Wright, Bristol.

Fish, F. (1964). The cycloid psychoses. *Comprehensive Psychiatry*, **5**, 155–69.

Folstein, S.E. (1989). *Huntington's disease: a disorder of families*. Johns Hopkins University Press, Baltimore.

Folstein, S.E., Abbott, M.H., Chase, G.A., Jensen, B.A., and Folstein, M.F. (1983). The association of affective disorder with Huntington's disease in a case series and in families. *Psychological Medicine*, **13**, 537–42.

Foundeur, M., Fixsen, C., Triebel, W.A., and White, M.A. (1957). Post-partum mental illness: a controlled study. *Archives of Neurology and Psychiatry*, **77**, 503–12.

Frangos, E., Athenassenas, G., Tsitourides, S., Katsanon, N., and Alexandrakou, P. (1985). Schizophrenia among first-degree relatives of schizophrenic probands. *Acta Psychiatrica Scandinavica*, **72**, 382–6.

Freeman, H.L. (1978). Pharmacological treatment and management. In *Schizophrenia: towards a new synthesis*, (ed. J.K. Wing), pp. 167–88. Academic Press, London.

Frith, C.D. (1973). Abnormalities of perception. In *Handbook of abnormal psychology*, (ed. H.J. Eysenck), pp. 284–308. Pitman, London.

Frith, C.D. (1979). Consciousness, information processing and schizophrenia. *British Journal of Psychiatry*, **134**, 225–35.

Frith, C.D. (1987). The positive and negative symptoms of schizophrenia reflect impairments in the perception and initiation of action. *Psychological Medicine*, **17**, 631–48.

Frith, C.D. and Done, D.J. (1988). Towards a neuropsychology of schizophrenia. *British Journal of Psychiatry*, **153**, 437–43.

Frith, C.D., Leary, J., Cahill, C., and Johnstone, E.C. (1991). IV. Performance on psychological tests. Demographic and clinical correlates of the results of these tests. *British Journal of Psychiatry*, **159**, supplement, 13, 26–9.

Frith, U. (1989). *Autism: explaining the enigma*. Blackwell, Oxford.

Fromm-Reichmann, F. (1948). Notes on the development of treatments of schizophrenics by psychoanalytic psychotherapy. *Psychiatry*, **2**, 263–73.

Funding, T. (1961). Genetics of paranoid psychoses of later life. *Acta Psychiatrica Scandinavica*, **37**, 267–82.

Gardos, G. and Cole, J.O. (1980). Public health issues in tardive dyskinesia. *American Journal of Psychiatry*, **137**, 776–81.

Garety, P. (1991). Reasoning and delusions. *British Journal of Psychiatry*, **159**, supplement, 14, 14–18.

Garnett, E.S., Firnau, G., and Nahmias, C. (1983). Dopamine visualized in the basal ganglia of living man. *Nature*, **305**, 137–8.

Gattaz, W.F., Waldmeier, P., and Beckmann, H. (1982). CSF monoamine metabolites in schizophrenic patients. *Acta Psychiatrica Scandinavica*, **66**, 350–60.

Gaupp, R. (1914). The scientific significance of the case of Ernst Wagner. In *Themes and variations in European psychiatry*, (ed. S.R. Hirsch and M. Shepherd, 1974), pp. 121–33. Wright, Bristol.

Gaupp, R. (1938). The illness and death of the paranoid mass murderer, schoolmaster Wagner: a case history. In *Themes and variations in European psychiatry*, (ed. S.R. Hirsch and M. Shepherd, 1974), pp. 134–52. Wright, Bristol.

Gerlach, J. (1979). Tardive dyskinesia. *Danish Medical Bulletin*, **46**, 209–45.

Gerlach, J., Behnke, K., Heltberg, J., Munk-Anderson, E., and Nielsen, H. (1985). Sulpiride and haloperidol in schizophrenia: a double-blind cross-over study of therapeutic effect, side effects and plasma concentrations. *British Journal of Psychiatry*, **147**, 283–8.

German, G.A. (1972). Aspects of clinical psychiatry in sub-Saharan Africa. *British Journal of Psychiatry*, **121**, 461–79.

Gerner, R.H., Fairbanks, L., Anderson, G.M., Young, J.G., Scheinin, M., Linnoila, M., *et al.* (1984). CSF neurochemistry in depressed, manic and schizophrenic patients compared with normal controls. *American Journal of Psychiatry*, **141**, 1533–40.

Gershon, E.S., Hamovit, J., Guroff, J.J., Dibble, E., Leckman, J.F., Sceery, W., *et al.* (1982). A family study of schizoaffective, bipolar I, bipolar II, unipolar, and normal control probands. *Archives of General Psychiatry*, **39**, 1157–67.

Giannini, A.J., Loiselle, R.H., Giannini, M.C., and Price, W.A. (1987). Phencyclidine and the dissociatives. *Psychiatric Medicine*, **3**, 197–217.

Gillberg, C. (1991*a*). Outcome in autism and autistic-like conditions. *Journal of the American Academy of Child and Adolescent Psychiatry*, **30**, 375–82.

Gillberg, C. (1991*b*). Clinical and neurobiological aspects of Asperger syndrome in six family studies. In *Autism and Asperger syndrome*, (ed. U. Frith), pp. 122–46. Cambridge University Press.

Gillberg, C. and Coleman, M. (1992). *The biology of the autistic syndromes*, (2nd edn), Clinics in Developmental Medicine, No. 126. Mac Keith Press, London.

Gillberg, C., Gillberg, I.C., and Steffenburg, S. (1992). Siblings and parents of children with autism: A controlled population-based study. *Developmental Medicine and Child Neurology*, **34**, 389–98.

Gjessing, R. (1938). Disturbances of somatic functions in catatonia with a periodic course and their compensation. *Journal of Mental Science*, **84**, 608–21.

Gold, D.J., Jr. (1984). Late age of onset schizophrenia: present but unaccounted for. *Comprehensive Psychiatry*, **25**, 225–37.

Goldberg, S.C. (1985). Negative and deficit symptoms in schizophrenia do respond to neuroleptics. *Schizophrenia Bulletin*, **11**, 453–6.

Goldberg, S.C., Klerman, G.L., and Cole, J.O. (1965). Changes in schizophrenic psychopathology and ward behaviotir as a function of phenothiazine treatment. *British Journal of Psychiatry*, **111**, 120–33.

Goldberg, T.E., Weinberger, D.R., Berman, K.F., Pliskin, N.H., and Podd, M.H. (1987). Further evidence for dementia of prefrontal type in schizophrenia? A controlled study of teaching the Wisconsin Card Sorting Test. *Archives of General Psychiatry*, **44**, 1008–14.

Goldberg, T.E., Kelsoe, J.R., Weinberger, D.R., Pliskin, N.H., Kirwin, P.D., and Berman, K.F. (1988). Performance of schizophrenic patients on putative neuropsychological tests of frontal lobe function. *International Journal of Neuroscience*, **42**, 51–8.

Goldberg, T.E., Weinberger, D.R., Pliskin, N.H., Berman, K.F., and Podd, M.H. (1989). Recall memory deficit in schizophrenia: a possible manifestation of prefrontal dysfunction. *Schizophrenia Research*, **2**, 251–7.

Golden, G.S. (1987). Neurological functioning. In *Handbook of autism and pervasive developmental disorders*, (ed. D.J. Cohen and A.M. Donnellan), pp. 133–47. Winston, Silver Spring, Maryland.

Goldman, P.S. and Galkin, T.W. (1978). Prenatal removal of frontal association cortex in the fetal rhesus monkey: anatomical and functional consequences in post-natal life. *Brain Research*, **152**, 451–8.

Goldstein, K. (1944). Methodological approach to the study of schizophrenic thought disorder. In *Language and thought in schizophrenia*, (ed. J.S. Kasanin), pp. 17–40. University of California Press, Berkeley.

Goodwin, K. (1971). Psychiatric side effects of levodopa in man. *Journal of the American Medical Association*, **218**, 1915–20.

Gottesman, I.I. (1991). *Schizophrenia genesis: the origins of madness*. Freeman, New York.

Gottesman, I.I. and Shields, J. (1963). Schizophrenia in twins: sixteen years' consecutive admissions to a psychiatric clinic. *British Journal of Psychiatry*, **112**, 809–18.

Gottesman, I.I. and Shields, J. (1982). *Schizophrenia: the epigenetic puzzle*. Cambridge University Press.

Gottfries, C.G., Gottfries, I., Johansson, B., Olson, R., Person, T., Roos, B.-E., and Sjostrom, R. (1971). Acid monoamine metabolites in human cerebrospinal fluid and their relations to age and sex. *Neuropharmacology*, **10**, 665–72.

Gould, L.N. (1948). Verbal hallucinations and activity of vocal musculature. *American Journal of Psychiatry*, **105**, 367–72.

Gould, L.N. (1949). Auditory hallucinations and subvocal speech. *Journal of Nervous and Mental Disease*, **109**, 418–27.

Gould, L.N. (1950). Verbal hallucinations as automatic speech. *American Journal of Psychiatry*, **107**, 110–19.

Grahame, P.S. (1982). Late paraphrenia. *British Journal of Hospital Medicine*, **27**, 522-7.

Gray, J.A., Rawlins, J.N.P., Hemsley, D.R., and Smith, A.D. (1991). The neuropsychology of schizophrenia. *Behavioral and Brain Sciences*, **14**, 1-84.

Green, M.F. and Kinsbourne, M. (1990). Subvocal activity and auditory hallucinations: clues for behavioral treatments? *Schizophrenia Bulletin*, **16**, 617-25.

Green, P. and Preston, M. (1981). Reinforcement of vocal correlates of auditory hallucinations by auditory feedback: a case study. *British Journal of Psychiatry*, **139**, 204-8.

Green, W.H., Campbell, M., Hardesty, A.S., Grega, D.M., Padron-Gayol, M., Shell, J., Erlenmeyer-Kimling, L. (1984). A comparison of schizophrenic and autistic children. *Journal of the American Academy of Child and Adolescent Psychiatry*, **23**, 399-409.

Greysmith, D. (1973). *Richard Dadd: the rock and castle of seclusion*. Studio Vista, London.

Griffith, J.D., Cavanaugh, J., and Oates, J. (1968). Paranoid episodes induced by drug. *Journal of the American Medical Association*, **205**, 39, 46.

Grossman, L.S., Harrow, M., Fudala, J.H., and Meltzer, H.Y. (1984). The longitudinal course of schizoaffective disorders. *Journal of Nervous and Mental Disease*, **172**, 140-9.

Gruzelier, J., Seymour, K., Wilson, L., Jolley, A., and Hirsch, S. (1988). Impairment on neuropsychological tests of temporohippocampal and frontohippocampal function in remitting schizophrenia and affective disorders. *Archives of General Psychiatry*, **45**, 623-9.

Gur, R.E., Skolnick, B.E., and Gur, R.C. (1983). Brain function in psychiatric disorders: I. Regional cerebral blood flow in medicated schizophrenics. *Archives of General Psychiatry*, **40**, 1250-4.

Gur, R.E., Gur, R.C., Skolnick, B.E., Caroff, S., Obrist, W.D., Resnick, S., and Reivich, M. (1985). Brain function in psychiatric disorders: III. Regional cerebral blood flow in unmedicated schizophrenics. *Archives of General Psychiatry*, **42**, 329-34.

Gur, R.E., Resnick, S.M., Alavi, A., Gur, R.C., Caroff, S., Dann, R., *et al.* (1987). Regional brain function in schizophrenia: I. A positron emission tomography study. *Archives of General Psychiatry*, **44**, 119-25.

Gutierrez, E., Escudero, V., and Valero, J.A. (1988). Expresion de emociones y curso de la esquizofrenia: II. Expresion de emociones y curso de la esquizofrenia en pacientes en remision. *Analisis y Modificacion de Conducta*, **14**, 275-316.

Guze, S.B. (1980). Schizoaffective disorders. In *Comprehensive textbook of psychiatry*, (3rd edn), (ed. H.I. Kaplan, A.M. Freedman, and B.J. Sadock), pp. 1301-4. Williams and Wilkins, Baltimore.

Guze, S.B., Woodruff, R.A., and Clayton, P.J. (1975). The significance of psychotic affective disorders. *Archives of General Psychiatry*, **32**, 1147-50.

Guze, S.B., Cloninger, R., Martin, R.L., and Clayton, P.J. (1983). A follow-up and family study of schizophrenia. *Archives of General Psychiatry*, **40**, 1273-80.

Hadju-Gaines, L. (1940). Contributions to the etiology of schizophrenia. *Psychoanalytic Review*, **27**, 421-38.

Hakim, R.A. (1953). Indigenous drugs in the treatment of mental diseases. VIth Gujarat and Saurashtra provincial medical conference, Baroda, 1953. *Journal of the Indian Medical Association*, **22**, supplement, 85.

Hakola, H.P.A. and Laulumaa, V.A. (1982). Carbamazepine in treatment of violent schizophrenics. *Lancet*, **ii**, 1358.

Hakola, H.P.A. and Laulumaa, V.A. (1984). Carbamazepine in violent schizophrenics. In *Anticonvulsants in affective disorders*, (ed. H.M. Emrich, T. Okuma, and A.A. Miller), pp. 204–7. Excerpta Medica, Amsterdam.

Hall, A.J. (1924). *Epidemic encephalitis*. Wright, Bristol.

Hamilton, J.A. (1962). *Post-partum psychiatric problems*. Mosby, St Louis.

Hamilton, M. (1984). *Fish's schizophrenia*, (3rd edn). Wright, Bristol.

Hanson, D.R. and Gottesman, I.I. (1976). The genetics, if any, of infantile autism and childhood schizophrenia. *Journal of Autism and Childhood Schizophrenia*, **6**, 209–34.

Harding, C. (1988). Course types in schizophrenia: an analysis of European and American studies. *Schizophrenia Bulletin*, **14**, 633–44.

Hare, E.H. (1973). A short note on pseudohallucinations. *British Journal of Psychiatry*, **122**, 469–76.

Hare, E.H. (1980). Seasonal variations in psychiatric illness. *Trends in Neurosciences*, **3**, 295–8.

Hare, E. (1982). Epidemiology of schizophrenia. In *Handbook of psychiatry*, Vol. 3, Psychoses of uncertain aetiology, (ed. J.K. Wing and L. Wing), pp. 42–8. Cambridge University Press.

Hare, E.H., Price, J., and Slater, E. (1974). Mental disorder and season of birth: a national sample compared with the general population. *British Journal of Psychiatry*, **124**, 81–6.

Harnryd, C., Bjerkenstedt, C., Gullberg, G., Oxenstierna, G., Sedvall, G., and Wiesel, F.-A. (1984). Clinical evaluation of sulpiride in schizophrenic patients – a double-blind comparison with chlorpromazine. *Acta Psychiatrica Scandinavica*, **69**, supplement, **311**, 7–30.

Harrison, G. and Mason, P. (1993). Schizophrenia – falling incidence and better outcome? *British Journal of Psychiatry*, **163**, 535–41.

Harrow, M. and Quinlan, D.M. (1985). *Disordered thinking and schizophrenic psychopathology*. Gardner Press, New York.

Hassett, A.M., Keks, N.A., Jackson, H.J., and Copolov, D.L. (1992). The diagnostic validity of paraphrenia. *Australian and New Zealand Journal of Psychiatry*, **26**, 18–29.

Haug, O.J. (1962). Pneumoencephalographic studies in mental disease. *Acta Psychiatrica Scandinavica*, supplement, **165**, 1–114.

Hay, G.G. (1970). Dysmorphophobia. *British Journal of Psychiatry*, **116**, 399–406.

Hays, P. (1978). Taxonomic map of the schizophrenias, with special reference to puerperal psychosis. *British Medical Journal*, **ii**, 755–7.

Heaton, R.K., Baade, L.E., and Johnson, K.L. (1978). Neuropsychological test results associated with psychiatric disorders in adults. *Psychological Bulletin*, **85**, 141–62.

Heckers, S., Heinsen, H., Heinsen, Y.C., and Beckmann, H. (1990). Limbic structures and lateral ventricle in schizophrenia: a quantitative postmortem study. *Archives of General Psychiatry*, **47**, 1016–22.

Heh, C.W.C., Potkin, S.G., Pickar, D., Costa, J., Herrera, J., and Sramek, J. (1989). Serum homovanillic acid concentrations in carbamazepine-treated chronic schizophrenics. *Biological Psychiatry*, **25**, 639–41.

Hemsley, D.R. (1975). A two stage model of attention in schizophrenia research. *British Journal of Social and Clinical Psychology*, **14**, 81–9.

Hemsley, D.R. (1977). What have cognitive deficits to do with schizophrenic symptoms? *British Journal of Psychiatry*, **130**, 167–73.

Hemsley, D.R. and Garety, P.A. (1986). The formation and maintenance of delusions: a Bayesian analysis. *British Journal of Psychiatry*, **149**, 51–6.

Hemsley, D.R. and Richardson, P.H. (1980). Shadowing by context in schizophrenia. *Journal of Nervous and Mental Disease*, **168**, 141–5.

Herbert, M. and Jacobson, S. (1967). Late paraphrenia. *British Journal of Psychiatry*, **113**, 461–9.

Heritch, A.J. (1990). Evidence for reduced and dysregulated turnover of dopamine in schizophrenia. *Schizophrenia Bulletin*, **16**, 605–15.

Herman, E. and Pleasure, H. (1963). Clinical evaluation of thioridazine and chlorpromazine in chronic schizophrenia. *Diseases of the Nervous System*, **24**, 54–9.

Heston, L.L. (1966). Psychiatric disorders in foster home reared children of schizophrenic mothers. *British Journal of Psychiatry*, **112**, 819–25.

Hillbom, E. (1951). Schizophrenia-like psychoses after brain trauma. *Acta Psychiatrica et Neurologica Scandinavica*, supplement, **60**, 36–47.

Hillbom, E. (1960). After-effects of brain-injuries. *Acta Psychiatrica et Neurologica Scandinavica*, supplement, **142**, 1–195.

Himmelhoch, J.M., Fuchs, C.Z., May, S.J., Symons, P.H.B.J., and Neil, J.F. (1981). When a schizoaffective diagnosis has meaning. *Journal of Nervous and Mental Disease*, **169**, 277–82.

Hirsch, S.R. and Leff, J.P. (1971). Parental abnormalities of verbal communication in the transmission of schizophrenia. *Psychological Medicine*, **1**, 118–27.

Hirsch, S.R. and Leff, J.P. (1975). *Abnormalities in parents of schizophrenics*, Maudsley monograph, No. 22. Oxford University Press, London.

Hirsch, S.R. and Shepherd, M. (1974). *Themes and variations in European psychiatry*. Wright, Bristol.

Hoch, A. (1921). *Benign stupors: a study of a new manic-depressive reaction type*. MacMillan, New York.

Hoenig, J., (1983). The concept of schizophrenia: Kraepelin-Bleuler-Schneider. *British Journal of Psychiatry*, **142**, 547–56.

Hogarty, G.E., Anderson, C.M., Reiss, D.J., Kornblith, S.J., Greenwald, D.P., Javna, C.D., and Madonia, M.J. (1986). Family psychoeducation, social skills training and maintenance chemotherapy in the aftercare treatment of schizophrenia. I: One-year effects of a controlled study on relapse and expressed emotion. *Archives of General Psychiatry*, **43**, 633–42.

Hogarty, G.E., Anderson, C.M., and Reiss D.J. (1987). Family psychoeducation, social skills training and medication in schizophrenia: the long and short of it. *Psychopharmacology Bulletin*, **23**, 12–13.

Hogarty, G.E., Anderson, C.M., Reiss, D.J., Kornblith, S.J., Greenwald, D.P., Ulrich, R.F., and Carter, M. (1991). Family psychoeducation, social skills training and maintenance chemotherapy in the aftercare treatment of schizophrenia. II: Two-year effects of a controlled study on relapse and adjustment. *Archives of General Psychiatry*, **48**, 340–7.

Holden, N.L. (1987). Late paraphrenia or the paraphrenias? A descriptive study with a 10-year follow-up. *British Journal of Psychiatry*, **150**, 635–9.

Holmboe, R. and Astrup, C. (1957). A follow-up study of 255 patients with acute schizophrenia and schizophreniform psychoses. *Acta Psychiatrica et Neurologica Scandinavica*, **32**, supplement, **115**, 1–61.

Hopkinson, G. (1973). The psychiatric syndrome of infestation. *Psychiatria Clinica*, **6**, 330–45.

Howells, J.G. and Guirguis, W.H. (1984). Childhood schizophrenia 20 years later. *Archives of General Psychiatry*, **41**, 123–8.

Huber, G. (1967). Symptomwandel der Psychosen und Pharmakopsychiatrie. In *Pharmakopsychiatrie und Psychopathologie*, (ed. H. Kranz and K. Heinrich), pp. 78–89. Thieme, Stuttgart.

Huber, G., Gross, G., and Schuttler, R. (1975). A long-term follow up study of schizophrenia: Psychiatric course of illness and prognosis. *Acta Psychiatrica Scandinavica*, **52**, 49–57.

Huber, G., Gross, G., Schuttler, R., and Linz, M. (1980). Longitudinal studies of schizophrenic patients. *Schizophrenia Bulletin*, **6**, 593–605.

Hulse, W.C. (1954). Dementia infantilis. *Journal of Nervous and Mental Disease*, **119**, 471–7.

Huq, S.F., Garety, P.A., and Hemsley, D.R. (1988). Probabilistic judgments in deluded and non-deluded subjects. *Quarterly Journal of Experimental Psychology*, **40A**, 801–12.

Huston, P.E. and Locher, L.M. (1948). Involutional psychosis: course when untreated and when treated with electric shock. *Archives of Neurology and Psychiatry*, **59**, 385–404.

Hyde, L., Bridges, K., Goldberg, D., Lowson, K., Sterling, L., and Faragher, B. (1987). The evaluation of a hostel ward: a controlled study using modified cost-benefit analysis. *British Journal of Psychiatry*, **151**, 805–12.

Hymas, N., Naguib, M., and Levy, R. (1989). Late paraphrenia—a follow-up study. *International Journal of Geriatric Psychiatry*, **4**, 23–9.

Hyttel, J., Larsen, J-J., Christensen, A.V., and Arnt, J. (1985). Receptor-binding profiles of neuroleptics. In *Dyskinesia—research and treatment*, Psychopharmacology Supplementum, No. 2, (ed. D.E. Casey, T.W. Chase, A.V. Christensen, and J. Gerlach), pp. 9–18. Springer, Berlin.

Ianzito, B.M., Cadoret, R.J., and Pugh, D.D. (1974). Thought disorder in depression. *American Journal of Psychiatry*, **131**, 703–7.

Illowsky, B.P., Juliano, D.M., Bigelow, L.B., and Weinberger, D.R. (1988). Stability of CT scan findings in schizophrenia: results of an 8 year follow-up study. *Journal of Neurology, Neurosurgery and Psychiatry*, **51**, 209–13.

Ingvar, D.H. and Franzen, G. (1974). Abnormalities of cerebral blood flow distribution in patients with chronic schizophrenia. *Acta Psychiatrica Scandinavica*, **50**, 425–62.

Inouye, E. (1961). Similarity and dissimilarity of schizophrenia in twins. In *Proceedings of the third world congress of psychiatry*, Vol. 1, pp. 524–30. University of Toronto Press, Montreal.

Itil, T.M. (1977). Qualitative and quantitative EEG findings in schizophrenia. *Schizophrenia Bulletin*, **3**, 61–79.

Ivanovic, M. and Vuletic, Z. (1989). Expressed emotion in families of patients with frequent types of schizophrenia and influence on the course of illness: nine months' follow-up. Unpublished study presented at 19th congress of the European association for behaviour therapy, Vienna.

Iversen, L.L. (1978). Biochemical and pharmacological studies: the dopamine hypothesis. In *Schizophrenia: towards a new synthesis*, (ed. J.K. Wing), pp. 89–116. Academic Press, London.

Iversen, S.D. and Fray, P.J. (1982). Brain catecholamines in relation to affect. In *The neural basis of behaviour*, (ed. A.L. Beckman), pp. 229–69. Spectrum, New York.

Jablensky, A. (1987). Multicultural studies and the nature of schizophrenia: a review. *Journal of the Royal Society of Medicine*, **80**, 162–7.

Jacobs, S. and Myers, J. (1976). Recent life events and acute schizophrenic psychosis: a controlled study. *Journal of Nervous and Mental Disease*, **162**, 75–87.

Jaspers, K. (1959). *General psychopathology*, (trans. J. Hoenig and M.W. Hamilton, 1963). Manchester University Press.

Javitt, D.C. and Zukin, S.R. (1991). Recent advances in the phencyclidine model of schizophrenia. *American Journal of Psychiatry*, **148**, 1301–8.

Jelliffe, S.E. (1929). Psychological components in postencephalitic oculogyric crises. *Archives of Neurology and Psychiatry*, **21**, 491–532.

Jelliffe, S.E. (1932). *Psychopathology of forced movements and the oculogyric crises of lethargic encephalitis*. Nervous and Mental Disease Publishing Co., Washington, DC.

Jenner, P. and Marsden, C.D. (1984). Multiple dopamine receptors in brain and the pharmacological action of substituted benzamide drugs. *Acta Psychiatrica Scandinavica*, **69**, supplement, **113**, 125–38.

Jernigan, T.L., Zatz, L.M., Moses, J.A., and Berger, P.A. (1982). Computed tomography in schizophrenics and normal volunteers: I. Fluid volume. *Archives of General Psychiatry*, **39**, 765–70.

Jeste, D.V. and Caligiuri, M.P. (1993). Tardive dyskinesia. *Schizophrenia Bulletin*, **19**, 303–15.

Jeste, D.V., Lohr, J.B., Clark, K., and Wyatt, R.J. (1988). Pharmacological treatment of tardive dyskinesia in the 1980's. *Journal of Clinical Psychopharmacology*, **8**, supplement, 38S–48S.

Jilek, W.G. (1968). The residual dimension. A study of residual syndromes in veterans with chronic psychiatric illness. *Psychiatria Clinica*, **1**, 175–218.

Johanson, E. (1958). A study of schizophrenia in the male. *Acta Psychiatrica et Neurologica Scandinavica*, **33**, supplement, **125**, 1–132.

Johanson, E. (1964). Mild paranoia. *Acta Psychiatrica Scandinavica*, supplement, **177**, 1–100.

Johnson, K.M., Jr. (1987). Neurochemistry and neurophysiology of phencyclidine. In *Psychopharmacology: the third generation of progress*, (ed. H.Y. Meltzer), pp. 1581–8. Raven, New York.

Johnstone, E.C. (ed.), (1991). Disabilities and circumstances of schizophrenic patients—a follow-up study. *British Journal of Psychiatry*, **159**, supplement, **13**, 4–46.

Johnstone, E.C., Crow, T.J., Frith, C.D., Husband, J., and Kreel, L. (1976). Cerebral ventricular size and cognitive impairment in chronic schizophrenia. *Lancet*, **ii**, 924–6.

Johnstone, E.C., Crow, T.J., Frith, C.D., Carney, M.W.P., and Price, J.S. (1978). Mechanism of the antipsychotic effect in the treatment of acute schizophrenia. *Lancet*, **i**, 848–51.

Johnstone, E.C., Crow, T.J., Frith, C.D., and Owens, D.G.C. (1988). The

Northwick Park 'functional' psychosis study: diagnosis and treatment response. *Lancet*, **ii**, 119-25.

Joyce, J.N. (1983). Multiple dopamine receptors and behavior. *Neuroscience and Biobehavioral reviews*, **7**, 227-56.

Jus, A., Pineau, R., Lachance, R., Pelchat, G., Jus, K., Pires, P., and Villineuve, R. (1976). Epidemiology of tardive dyskinesia: part I. *Diseases of the Nervous System*, **37**, 210-14.

Kahlbaum, K.L. (1874). *Catatonia*, (trans. Y. Levij and T. Priden, 1973). Johns Hopkins University Press, Baltimore.

Kalant, O.J. (1966). *The amphetamines: toxicity and addiction*, Brookside Monographs, No. 5. University of Toronto Press.

Kallman, F.J. (1938). *The genetics of schizophrenia*. Augustin, New York.

Kallman, F.J. (1946). The genetic theory of schizophrenia: an analysis of 691 schizophrenic twin index families. *American Journal of Psychiatry*, **103**, 309-22.

Kallman, F.J. and Roth, B. (1956). Genetic aspects of preadolescent schizophrenia. *American Journal of Psychiatry*, **112**, 599-606.

Kane, J.M. and Smith, J.M. (1982). Tardive dyskinesia: prevalence and risk factors, 1959-79. *Archives of General Psychiatry*, **39**, 473-81.

Kane, J.M., Woerner, M., and Lieberman, J. (1985). Tardive dyskinesia: prevalence, incidence and risk factors. In *Dyskinesia: research and treatment*, (ed. D.E. Casey, T.N. Chase, and A.V. Christensen), pp. 72-8. Springer, Berlin.

Kane, J.M., Honigfeld, G., Singer, J., and Meltzer, H. (1988). Clozapine for the treatment resistant schizophrenic. *Archives of General Psychiatry*, **45**, 789-96.

Kanner, L. (1943). Autistic disturbances of affective contact. *Nervous Child*, **2**, 217-50.

Kanner, L. and Eisenberg, L. (1956). Early infantile autism 1943-1955. *American Journal of Orthopsychiatry*, **26**, 55-65.

Kant, O. (1940). Types and analyses of the clinical pictures of recovered schizophrenics. *Psychiatric Quarterly*, **14**, 676-700.

Kant, O. (1941*a*). Study of a group of recovered schizophrenic patients. *Psychiatric Quarterly*, **15**, 262-83.

Kant, O. (1941*b*). A comparative study of recovered and deteriorated schizophrenic patients. *Journal of Nervous and Mental Disease*, **93**, 616-24.

Karno, M., Jenkins, J.H., and de la Selva, A. (1987). Expressed emotion and schizophrenic outcome among Mexican-American families. *Journal of Nervous and Mental Disease*, **175**, 143-51.

Kasanin, J. (1933). The acute schizoaffective psychoses. *American Journal of Psychiatry*, **13**, 97-126.

Katz, M.M., Cole, J.O., and Lowery, H.A. (1969). Studies of the diagnostic process: the influence of symptom perception, past experience and ethnic background on diagnostic decisions. *American Journal of Psychiatry*, **125**, 109-19.

Kavanagh, D.J. (1992). Recent developments in expressed emotion and schizophrenia. *British Journal of Psychiatry*, **160**, 601-20.

Kay, D.W.K. (1959). Observations on the natural history and genetics of old age psychoses: a Stockholm survey, 1931-1937. *Proceedings of the Royal Society of Medicine*, **52**, 791-4.

Kay, D.W.K. (1963). Late paraphrenia and its bearing on the aetiology of schizophrenia. *Acta Psychiatrica Scandinavica*, **39**, 159-69.

Kay, D.W.K. and Roth, M. (1961). Environmental and hereditary factors in the schizophrenias of old age ('late paraphrenia') and their bearing on the general problem of causation in schizophrenia. *Journal of Mental Science*, **107**, 649–86.

Kay, D.W.K., Cooper, A.F., Garside, R.F., and Roth, M. (1976). The differentiation of paranoid from affective psychoses by patients' premorbid characteristics. *British Journal of Psychiatry*, **129**, 207–15.

Kay, S.R., Opler, L.A., and Fiszbein, A. (1986). Significance of positive and negative syndromes in chronic schizophrenia. *British Journal of Psychiatry*, **149**, 439–48.

Kebabian, J.W. and Calne, D.B. (1979). Multiple receptors for dopamine. *Nature*, **277**, 93–6.

Kelsoe, J.R., Cadet, J.L., Pickar, D., and Weinberger, D.R. (1988). Quantitative neuroanatomy in schizophrenia: a controlled magnetic resonance imaging study. *Archives of General Psychiatry*, **45**, 533–41.

Kemali, D., Maj, M., Galderisi, S., Milici, N., and Salvati, A. (1989). Ventricle-to-brain ratio in schizophrenia: a controlled follow-up study. *Biological Psychiatry*, **26**, 756–9.

Kendell, R.E. (1975). *The role of diagnosis in psychiatry*. Blackwell, Oxford.

Kendell, R.E. (1981). The present status of electroconvulsive therapy. *British Journal of Psychiatry*, **139**, 265–83.

Kendell, R.E. (1986). The relationship of schizoaffective illness to schizophrenic and affective disorders. In *Schizoaffective psychoses*, (ed. A. Marneros and M.T. Tsuang), pp. 18–30. Springer, Berlin.

Kendell, R.E. (1987). Diagnosis and classification of functional psychoses. In *Recurrent and chronic psychoses*, British Medical Bulletin, 43, No. 3, (ed T.J. Crow), pp. 499–513. Churchill Livingstone, Edinburgh.

Kendell, R.E. (1991). The major functional psychoses: are they independent entities or part of a continuum? Philosophical and conceptual issues underlying the debate. In *Concepts of mental disorder: a continuing debate*, (ed. A. Kerr and H. McClelland), pp. 1–16. Gaskell/Royal College of Psychiatrists, London.

Kendell, R.E. and Gourlay, J. (1970). The clinical distinction between the affective psychoses and schizophrenia. *British Journal of Psychiatry*, **117**, 261–6.

Kendell, R.E., Wainwright, S., Hailey, A., and Reed, R.S. (1976). The influence of childbirth on psychiatric morbidity. *Psychological Medicine*, **6**, 297–302.

Kendell, R.E., Brockington, I.F., and Leff, J.P. (1979). Prognostic implications of six alternative definitions of schizophrenia. *Archives of General Psychiatry*, **36**, 25–31.

Kendler, K.S. (1980). The nosologic validity of paranoia (simple delusional disorder). *Archives of General Psychiatry*, **37**, 699–706.

Kendler, K.S. (1988). Kraepelin and the diagnostic concept of paranoia. *Comprehensive Psychiatry*, **29**, 4–11.

Kendler, K.S. and Tsuang, M.T. (1981). Nosology of paranoid schizophrenia and other paranoid psychoses. *Schizophrenia Bulletin*, **7**, 594–610.

Kendler, K.S., Gruenberg, A.M., and Tsuang, M.T. (1985). Psychiatric illness in first-degree relatives of schizophrenic and surgical control patients: a family study using DSM III criteria. *Archives of General Psychiatry*, **42**, 770–9.

Kendler, K.S., Masterson, C.C., and Davis, K.L. (1985). Psychiatric illness in first-degree relatives of patients with paranoid psychosis, schizophrenia and medical illness. *British Journal of Psychiatry*, **147**, 524–31.

Kerbeshian, J., Burd. L., and Fischer, W. (1990). Asperger's syndrome: to be or not to be? *British Journal of Psychiatry*, **156**, 721–5.

Kerr, A. and McClelland, H. (ed.), (1991). *Concepts of mental disorder: a continuing debate*. Gaskell/Royal College of Psychiatrists, London.

Kidron, R., Averbuch, I., Klein, E., and Belmaker, R.H. (1985). Carbamazepine-induced reduction of blood levels of haloperidol in chronic schizophrenia. *Biological Psychiatry*, **20**, 219–28.

King, J.K. (1985). A visit to the home of lithium. *Bulletin of the Royal College of Psychiatrists*, **9**, 90–1.

Kirby, G.H. (1913). The catatonic syndrome and its relation to manic-depresssive insanity. *Journal of Nervous and Mental Disease*, **40**, 694–704.

Kirch, D.G. and Weinberger, D.R. (1986). Anatomical neuropathology in schizophrenia: post-mortem findings. In *Handbook of schizophrenia*, Vol. 1, the neurology of schizophrenia, (ed. H.A. Nasrallah and D.R. Weinberger) pp. 325–48. Elsevier, Amsterdam.

Klawans, H.L. and Weiner, W.J. (1976). The pharmacology of choreatic movement disorders. *Progress in Neurobiology*, **6**, 49–80.

Klawans, H., Tanner, C.M., and Goetz, C.G. (1979). Psychiatric reactions to ergot derivatives. In *Dopaminergic ergot derivatives and motor function*, (ed. K. Fuxe and D.B. Calne), pp. 405–14. Pergamon, Oxford.

Klein, E., Bental, E., Lerer, B., and Belmaker, R.H. (1984). Carbamazepine and haloperidol v. placebo and haloperidol in excited psychotics: a controlled study. *Archives of General Psychiatry*, **41**, 165–70.

Kleist, K. (1914). Aphasie und Geisteskrankheit. *Münchener Medizinische Wochenschrift*, **61**, 8–12.

Kleist, K. (1943). Die Katatonien. *Nervenarzt*, **16**, 1–10.

Kleist, K. (1960). Schizophrenic symptoms and cerebral pathology. *Journal of Mental Science*, **106**, 246–55.

Kline, N.S. (1954). Use of Rauwolfia serpentina Benth. in neuropsychiatric conditions. *Annals of the New York Academy of Sciences*, **59**, 107–32.

Knight, J.G. (1982). Dopamine-receptor-stimulating autoantibodies: a possible cause of schizophrenia. *Lancet*, **ii**, 1073–5.

Koehler, K. (1979). First rank symptoms of schizophrenia: questions concerning clinical boundaries. *British Journal of Psychiatry*, **134**, 236–48.

Koehler, K., Guth, W., and Grimm, G. (1977). First rank symptoms in Schneider-oriented German centers. *Archives of General Psychiatry*, **34**, 810–13.

Kokkinides, L. and Anisman, H. (1981). Amphetamine psychosis and schizophrenia: a dual model. *Neuroscience and Biobehavioral Reviews*, **5**, 449–61.

Kolb, B. and Whishaw, I.Q. (1983). Performance of schizophrenic patients on tests sensitive to right or left frontal, temporal or parietal function in neurological patients. *Journal of Nervous and Mental Disease*, **171**, 435–43.

Kolle, K. (1931). *Die primäre Verrücktheit*. Thieme, Leipzig.

Kolvin, I. (1972). Late onset psychosis. *British Medical Journal*, **3**, 816–17.

Kolvin, I., Ounsted, C., Humphrey, M., and McNay, A. (1971). Studies in the childhood psychoses. II. The phenomenology of childhood psychoses. *British Journal of Psychiatry*, **118**, 385–95.

Korboot, P.J. and Damiani, W. (1976). Auditory processing speed and signal detection in schizophrenia. *Journal of Abnormal Psychology*, **85**, 287–95.

Kraepelin, E. (1896). Dementia praecox. In *The clinical roots of the schizophrenia concept*, (ed. J. Cutting and M. Shepherd, 1987), pp. 13–24. Cambridge University Press.

Kraepelin, E. (1905). *Lectures on clinical psychiatry*, (3rd English edn), (trans. T. Johnstone, 1917). W. Wood, New York.

Kraepelin, E. (1907). *Clinical psychiatry*, (7th edn), (trans. A.R. Diefendorf, 1915). Macmillan, New York.

Kraepelin, E. (1909). *Lehrbuch der Psychiatrie*, (7th edn), Vol. 1, pp. 1025, 1040–68. Barth, Leipzig.

Kraepelin, E. (1913a). *Dementia praecox and paraphrenia*, (trans. R.M. Barclay, 1919). Livingstone, Edinburgh.

Kraepelin, E. (1913b). *Manic-depressive insanity and paranoia*, (trans. R.M. Barclay, 1921). Livingstone, Edinburgh.

Kreiskott, H. (1980). Behavioral pharmacology of antipsychotics. In *Handbook of experimental pharmacology*, Vol. 55, psychotropic agents, part 1: antipsychotics and antidepressants, (ed. F. Hoffmeister and G. Stille), pp. 59–88. Springer, Berlin.

Kretschmer, E. (1925). *Physique and character: an investigation of the nature of constitution and of the theory of temperament*, (2nd edn), (trans. W.J.H. Sprott). Kegan Paul, Trench, Trubner and Co. Ltd., London.

Kretschmer, E. (1927). The sensitive delusion of reference. In *Themes and variations in European psychiatry*, (ed. S.R. Hirsch and M. Shepherd, 1974), pp. 153–96. Wright, Bristol.

Kringlen, E. (1967). *Hereditary and environment in the functional psychoses*. Heinemann, London.

Kuipers, L. and Bebbington, P. (1988). Expressed emotion research in schizophrenia: theoretical and clinical implications. *Psychological Medicine*, **18**, 893–909.

Kulhara, P., Kota, S.K., and Joseph, S. (1986). Positive and negative subtypes of schizophrenia: a study from India. *Acta Psychiatrica Scandinavica*, **74**, 353–9.

Kurachi, M., Kobayashi, K., Matsubara, R., Hiramatsu, H., Yamaguchi, N., Matsuda, H., *et al.* (1985). Regional cerebral blood flow in schizophrenic disorders. *European Neurology*, **24**, 176–81.

Laborit, H., Huguenard, P., and Alluaume, R. (1952). Un nouveau stabilisateur vegetatif (le 4560 RP). *Presse Medicale*, **60**, 206–8.

Laing, R.D. (1964). *Sanity, madness and the family*, (2nd edn). Tavistock, London.

Laing, R.D. (1965). *The divided self: a study of sanity and madness*. Penguin, Harmondsworth.

Laing, R.D. (1967). *The politics of experience*. Penguin, Harmondsworth.

Laing, R.D. and Esterson, A. (1964). *Sanity, madness and the family*, (2nd edn). Tavistock, London.

Lange, J. (1922). *Katatonische Erscheinungen in Rahmen manischer Erkrankungen*. Springer, Berlin.

Langfeldt, G. (1937). The prognosis in schizophrenia and the factors influencing the course of the disease. *Acta Psychiatrica et Neurologica Scandinavica*, supplement, **13**, 7–228.

Langfeldt, G. (1956). The prognosis of schizophrenia. *Acta Psychiatrica et Neurologica Scandinavica*, supplement, **110**, 1–143.

Lantos, P. (1988). The neuropathology of schizophrenia: a critical review of recent work. In *Schizophrenia: the major issues*, (ed. P. Bebbington and P. McGuffin), pp. 73-89. Heinemann/Mental Health Foundation, Oxford.

Larsen, C.A. and Nyman, G.E. (1970). Age of onset in schizophrenia. *Human Hereditary*, **20**, 241-7.

Lay, R.A.Q. (1938). Schizophrenia-like psychoses in young children. *Journal of Mental Science*, **84**, 105-133.

Lee, T. and Seeman, P. (1980). Elevation of brain neuroleptic/dopamine receptors in schizophrenia. *American Journal of Psychiatry*, **137**, 191-7.

Lee, T., Seeman, P., Tourtellotte, W.W., Farley, L.J., and Hornykiewicz, O. (1978). Binding of ^{3}H-neuroleptics and ^{3}H-apomorphine in schizophrenic brains. *Nature*, **274**, 897-900.

Lees, A.J. (1985). *Tics and related disorders*. Churchill Livingstone, Edinburgh.

Leff, J.P. and Wing, J.K. (1971). Trial of maintenance therapy in schizophrenics. *British Medical Journal*, **3**, 599-604.

Leff, J., Wig, N.N., Ghosh, A., Bedi, H., Menon, D.K., Kuipers, L., et al. (1987). Influence of relatives' expressed emotion on the course of schizophrenia in Chandigarh. *British Journal of Psychiatry*, **151**, 166-73.

Leonhard, K. (1961). Cycloid psychoses — endogenous psychoses which are neither schizophrenic nor manic-depressive. *Journal of Mental Science*, **107**, 633-48.

Leonhard, K. (1979). *The classification of endogenous psychoses*, (5th edn), (trans. R. Berman). Irvington, New York.

Letemendia, F.J.J. and Harris, A.D. (1967). Chlorpromazine and the untreated chronic schizophrenic. *British Journal of Psychiatry*, **113**, 950-8.

Levenson, J.L. (1985). Neuroleptic malignant syndrome. *American Journal of Psychiatry*, **142**, 1137-45.

Lewine, R.R.J. (1980). Sex differences in age of onset and first hospitalization in schizophrenia. *American Journal of Orthopsychiatry*, **50**, 316-22.

Lewine, R.J., Fogg, L., and Meltzer, H.Y. (1983). Assessment of positive and negative symptoms in schizophrenia. *Schizophrenia Bulletin*, **9**, 368-76.

Lewis, A.J. (1934). Melancholia: a clinical survey of depressive states. *Journal of Mental Science*, **80**, 277-378.

Lewis, A. (1936). Patterns of obsessional illness. *Proceedings of the Royal Society of Medicine*, **29**, 325-36. (Reprinted 1967, in *Inquiries in psychiatry*, pp. 141-56. Routledge and Kegan Paul, London.)

Lewis, A. (1970). Paranoia and paranoid: a historical perspective. *Psychological Medicine*, **1**, 2-12.

Lewis, S.W. (1989). Congenital risk factors for schizophrenia. *Psychological Medicine*, **19**, 5-13.

Lewis, S.W. (1990). Computerised tomography in schizophrenia 15 years on. *British Journal of Psychiatry*, **157**, supplement, **9**, 16-24.

Lewis, S.W. and Murray, R.M. (1987). Obstetric complications, neurodevelopmental deviance and risk of schizophrenia. *Journal of Psychiatric Research*, **21**, 413-21.

Liberman, J.I. (1964). The influence of head injury in peace time on the development of schizophrenia: a statistical investigation. *Zhournal Nevropatologii Psikhiatrii I.M.S.S. Korsakova*, **64**, 1369-73.

Liddle, P.F. (1987). The symptoms of chronic schizophrenia: a re-examination of the positive-negative dichotomy. *British Journal of Psychiatry*, **151**, 145-51.

Liddle, P.F. and Crow, T.J. (1984). Age disorientation in chronic schizophrenia is associated with global intellectual impairment. *British Journal of Psychiatry*, **144**, 193–9.

Liddle, P.F. and Morris, D.L. (1991). Schizophrenic symptoms and frontal lobe performance. *British Journal of Psychiatry*, **158**, 340–5.

Liddle, P.F., Friston, K.J., Frith, C.D., Hirsch, S.R., Jones, T., and Frackowiak, R.S.J. (1992). Patterns of cerebral blood flow in schizophrenia. *British Journal of Psychiatry*, **160**, 179–86.

Lidz, T. and Blatt, S. (1983). Critique of the Danish-American studies of the biological and adoptive relatives of adoptees who became schizophrenic. *American Journal of Psychiatry*, **140**, 426–34.

Lidz, T., Cornelison, A.R., Fleck, S., and Terry, D. (1957*a*). The intrafamilial environment of the schizophrenic patient: I. The father. *Psychiatry*, **20**, 329–42.

Lidz, T., Cornelison, A.R., Fleck, S., and Terry, D. (1957*b*). The intrafamilial environment of the schizophrenic patient: II. Marital schism and marital skew. *American Journal of Psychiatry*, **114**, 241–8.

Lidz, T., Blatt, S., and Cook, B. (1981). Critique of the Danish-American studies of the adopted-away offspring of schizophrenic parents. *American Journal of Psychiatry*, **138**, 1063–8.

Lindstrom, L.H. (1985). Low HVA and normal 5-HIAA CSF levels in drug-free schizophrenic patients compared to healthy volunteers: correlations to symptomatology and family history. *Psychiatry Research*, **14**, 265–73.

Linn, M.W., Caffey, E.M., Klett, J., Hogarty, G.E., and Lamb, H.R. (1979). Day treatment and psychotropic drugs in the aftercare of schizophrenic patients. *Archives of General Psychiatry*, **36**, 1055–66.

Lipinski, J.F., Zubenko, G.S., Cohen, B.M., and Barriers, P.J. (1983). Propanolol in the treatment of neuroleptic induced akathisia. *Lancet*, **i**, 685–6.

Lishman, W.A. (1987). *Organic psychiatry*, (2nd edn). Blackwell, Oxford.

Lobova, L.P. (1960). The role of trauma in the development of schizophrenia. *Zhournal Nevropatologii Psikhiatrii I.M.S.S. Korsakova*, **60**, 1187–92.

Lohr, J.B., and Wisniewski, A.A. (1987). *Movement disorders: a neuropsychiatric approach*. Wiley, Chichester.

Lorr, M., Klett, C.J., and McNair, D.M. (1963). *Syndromes of psychosis*. Pergamon, Oxford.

Lorr, M., Klett, C.J., and McNair, D.M. (1966). Acute psychotic types. In *Explorations in typing psychotics*, (ed. M. Lorr), pp. 33–75. Pergamon, Oxford.

Lund, C.E., Mortimer, A.M., Rogers, D., and McKenna, P.J. (1991). Motor, volitional and behavioural disorders in schizophrenia. 1: assessment using the modified Rogers scale. *British Journal of Psychiatry*, **158**, 323–7.

Luxenburger, H. (1928). Vorläufiger Bericht über psychiatrische Serienuntersuchtingen an Zwillingen. *Zeitschrift für die gesamte Neurologie und Psychiatrie*, **116**, 297–326.

McCreadie, R.G. and Phillips, K. (1988). The Nithsdale schizophrenia survey: VII. Does relatives' high expressed emotion predict relapse? *British Journal of Psychiatry*, **152**, 477–81.

McGhie, A. (1969). *Pathology of attention*. Penguin, Harmondsworth.

McGhie, A. and Chapman, J. (1961). Disorders of attention and perception in early schizophrenia. *British Journal of Medical Psychology*, **34**, 103–6.

McGuffin, P. (1988). Genetics of schizophrenia. In *Schizophrenia: the major issues*, (ed. P. Bebbington and P. McGuffin), pp. 107–26. Heinemann/Mental Health Foundation, Oxford.

McGuffin, P., Farmer, A.E., Gottesman, I.I., Murray, R.M., and Reveley, A.M. (1984). Twin concordance for operationally defined schizophrenia. *Archives of General Psychiatry*, **41**, 541–5.

Mackay, A.V.P. (1982). Clinical controversies in tardive dyskinesia. In *Movement disorders*, (ed. C.D. Marsden and S. Fahn), pp. 249–62. Butterworth, London.

Mackay, A.V.P., Doble, A., Bird, E.D., Spokes, E.G.S., Quik, M., and Iversen, L.L. (1978). ^{3}H-spiperone binding in normal and schizophrenic postmortem brain. *Life Science*, **23**, 527–32.

Mackay, A.V.P., Iversen, L.L., Rossor, M., Spokes, E., Bird, E., Arregui, A., *et al.* (1982). Increased brain dopamine and dopamine receptors in schizophrenia. *Archives of General Psychiatry*, **39** 991–7.

McKenna, P.J. (1984). Disorders with overvalued ideas. *British Journal of Psychiatry*, **145**, 579–85.

McKenna, P.J. (1987). Pathology, phenomenology and the dopamine hypothesis of schizophrenia. *British Journal of Psychiatry*, **151**, 288–301.

McKenna, P.J. (1991). Memory, knowledge and delusions. *British Journal of Psychiatry*, **159**, Supplement, **14**, 36–41.

McKenna, P.J. and Bailey, P.E. (1993). The strange story of clozapine. *British Journal of Psychiatry*, **162**, 32–7.

McKenna, P.J., Kane, J.M., and Parrish, K. (1985). Psychotic syndromes in epilepsy. *Americal Journal of Psychiatry*, **142**, 895–904.

McKenna, P.J., Tamlyn, D., Lund, C.E., Mortimer, A.M., Hammond, S., and Baddeley, A.D. (1990). Amnesic syndrome in schizophrenia. *Psychological Medicine*, **20**, 967–72.

McKenna, P.J., Lund, C.E., Mortimer, A.M., and Biggins, C.A. (1991). Motor, volitional and behavioural disorders in schizophrenia. 2: the 'conflict of paradigms' hypothesis. *British Journal of Psychiatry*, **158**, 328–36.

MacMillan, J.F., Gold, A., Crow, T.J., Johnson, A.L., and Johnstone, E.C. (1986). The Northwick Park study of first episodes of schizophrenia IV. Expressed emotion and relapse. *British Journal of Psychiatry*, **148**, 133–43.

Magrinat, G., Danziger, J.A., Lorenzo, I.C., and Flemenbaum, A. (1983). A reassessment of catatonia. *Comprehensive Psychiatry*, **24**, 218–28.

Mahendra, B. (1981). Where have all the catatonics gone? *Psychological Medicine*, **11**, 669–71.

Maher, B. (1972). The language of schizophrenia: a review and interpretation. *British Journal of Psychiatry*, **120**, 3–17.

Maher, B.A. (1974). Delusional thinking and perceptual disorder. *Journal of Individual Psychology*, **30**, 98–113.

Maher, B. and Ross, J.S. (1984). Delusions. In *Comprehensive handbook of psychopathology*, (ed. H.E. Adams and P.B. Sutker), pp. 383–410. Plenum, New York.

Maj, M. (1985). Clinical course and outcome of schizoaffective disorders. *Acta Psychiatrica Scandinavica*, **72**, 542–50.

Maj, M. (1988). Clinical course and outcome of cycloid psychotic disorder: a three-year prospective study. *Acta Psychiatrica Scandinavica*, **78**, 182–7.

Malamud, N. (1959). Heller's disease and childhood schizophrenia. *American Journal of Psychiatry*, **116**, 215–8.

Malamud, W. and Render, N. (1938). Course and prognosis in schizophrenia. *American Journal of Psychiatry*, **95**, 1039-57.

Malzacher, M., Merz, J., and Ebnother, D. (1981). Einschneidende Lebenserreignisse im Vorfeld akuter schizophrener Episoden: Erstmals erkrankte Patienten im Vergleich mit einer Normalstichprobe. *Archiv für Psychiatrie und Nervenkrankheiten*, **230**, 227-42.

Mann, S.C., Caroff, S.W., Bleier, H.R., Welz, W.K.R., Kling, M.A., and Hayashida, M. (1986). Lethal catatonia. *American Journal of Psychiatry*, **143**, 1374-81.

Marcé, L.V. (1858). *Traite de la folie des femmes enceintes des nouvelles accouchées et des nourrices*. Baillière et fils, Paris.

Marengo, J., Harrow, M., Sands, J., and Galloway, C. (1991). European versus U.S. data on the course of schizophrenia. *American Journal of Psychiatry*, **148**, 606-11.

Margo, A., Hemsley, D.R., and Slade, P.D. (1981). The effects of varying auditory input on schizophrenic hallucinations. *British Journal of Psychiatry*, **139**, 122-7.

Marsden, C.D. and Jenner, P. (1980). The pathophysiology of extrapyramidal side-effects of neuroleptic drugs. *Psychological Medicine*, **10**, 55-72.

Marsden, C.D., Tarsy, D., and Baldessarini, R.J. (1975). Spontaneous and drug induced movement disorders in psychiatric patients. In *Psychiatric aspects of neurologic disease*, (ed. D.F. Benson and D. Blumer), pp. 219-66. Grune and Stratton, New York.

Marsden, C.D., Mindham, R.H.S., and Mackay, A.V.P. (1986). Extrapyramidal movement disorders produced by antipsychotic drugs. In *The psychopharmacology and treatment of schizophrenia*, (ed. P.B. Bradley and S.R. Hirsch), pp. 340-402. Oxford University Press.

Martinot, J.L., Peron-Magnan, D., Huret, J.D., Mazoyer, B., Baron, J.-C., Boulenger, J.-P., *et al.* (1990). Striatal D2 dopaminergic receptors assessed with positron emission tomography and [76]Br bromospiperone in untreated schizophrenic patients. *American Journal of Psychiatry*, **147**, 44-50.

Martinot, J.L., Paillere-Martinot, M.L., Lich, C., Hardy, P., Poirier, M.F., Mazoyer, B., *et al.* (1991). The estimated density of D2 striatal dopamine receptors in schizophrenia. A study with [76]Br bromolisuride. *British Journal of Psychiatry*, **158**, 346-51.

Mason, S.T. (1984). *Catecholamines and behaviour*. Cambridge University Press.

Mathew, R.J., Duncan, G.C., Weinman, M.L., and Barr, D.L. (1982). Regional cerebral blood flow in schizophrenia. *Archives of General Psychiatry*, **39**, 1121-4.

Mathew, R.J., Wilson, W.H., Tant, S.R., Robinson, L., and Prakash, R. (1988). Abnormal resting regional blood flow patterns and their correlates in schizophrenia. *Archives of General Psychiatny*, **45**, 542-9.

May, P.R. (1968). *Treatment of schizophrenia*. Science House, New York.

Mayer, W. (1921). Über paraphrene Psychosen. *Zentralblatt für die gesamte Neurologie und Psychiatrie*, **26**, 78-80.

Mayer-Gross, W. (1932). Die Schizophrenie. In *Handbuch der Geisteskrankheiten*, Vol. IX (ed. O. Bumke), pp. 534-78. Springer, Berlin.

Mayer-Gross, W., Slater, E., and Roth, M. (1954). *Clinical psychiatry*. Cassell, London.

Mayer-Gross, W., Slater, E., and Roth, M. (1969). *Clinical psychiatry*, (3rd edn). Baillière, Tindall, and Cassell, London.

Mednick, S.A. and Cannon, T.D. (1991). Fetal development, birth and the syndromes of adult schizophrenia. In *Fetal neural development and adult schizophrenia*, (ed. S.A. Mednick, T.D. Cannon, C.E. Barr, and M. Lyon), pp. 3–13. Cambridge University Press.

Meehl, P.E. (1962). Schizotaxia, schizotypy, schizophrenia. *American Psychologist*, **17**, 827–38.

Meinertz, F. (1957). Schizophrenieähnliche Psychosen und Grenzzustände bei Hirnverletzten. In *Report of second international congress of psychiatry*, Vol. 4. Zurich.

Mellor, C.S. (1970). First-rank symptoms of schizophrenia. *British Journal of Psychiatry*, **117**, 15–23.

Mendlewicz, J., Fieve, R.R., Rainer, J.D., and Fliess, J.L. (1972). Manic-depressive illness: a comparative study of patients with and without a family history. *British Journal of Psychiatry*, **120**, 523–30.

Merskey, H. (1979). *The analysis of hysteria*. Baillière, Tindall, London.

Mettler, F.A. (1955). Perceptual capacity, function of the corpus striatum and schizophrenia. *Psychiatric Quarterly*, **29**, 89–111.

Mettler, F.A. and Crandell, A. (1959). Neurologic disorders in psychiatric institutions. *Journal of Nervous and Mental Disease*, **128**, 148–59.

Mitsuda, H. (ed.) (1967). *Clinical genetics in psychiatry*, bulletin of the Osaka medical school, supplement XII. Osaka medical college.

Mjones, H. (1949). Paralysis agitans: a clinical and genetic study. *Acta Psychiatrica et Neurologica Scandinavica*, supplement, **54**, 1–195.

Moline, R.E., Singh, S., Morris, A., and Meltzer, H.Y. (1985). Family expressed emotion and relapse in schizophrenia in 24 urban American patients. *American Journal of Psychiatry*, **142**, 1078–81.

Monroe, R.R. (1982). Limbic ictus and atypical psychoses. *Journal of Nervous and Mental Disease*, **170**, 711–16.

Montero, I., Gomez-Beneyto, M., and Ruiz, I. (1990). Emotional expressiveness and development of schizophrenia: a reply to the work of Vaughn. *Actas Luso-Españolas de Neurologia, Psiquiatria y Ciencias Afines*, **18**, 387–95.

Moore, K.E. (1978). Amphetamines: biochemical and behavioral actions in animals. In *Handbook of psychopharmacology*, Vol. 11, stimulants, (ed. L.L. Iversen, S.E. Iversen, and S.H. Snyder), pp. 41–98. Plenum, New York.

Morice, R. (1990). Cognitive inflexibility and and pre-frontal dysfunction in schizophrenia and mania. *British Journal of Psychiatry*, **157**, 50–4.

Mortimer, A.M., McKenna, P.J., Lund, C.E., and Mannuzza, S. (1989). Rating of negative symptoms using the HEN scale. *British Journal of Psychiatry*, **155**, supplement 7, 89–92.

Mortimer, A.M., Lund, C.E., and McKenna, P.J. (1990). The positive: negative dichotomy in schizophrenia. *British Journal of Psychiatry*, **156**, 41–9.

Mozny, P., Petrikovitsova, A., and Lavicka, Z. (1989). Expressed emotions, relapse rate and utilization of psychiatric hospital care in schizophrenia. Unpublished study presented at 19th congress of the European association for behaviour therapy, Vienna.

Munro, A. (1980). Monosymptomatic hypochondriacal psychosis. *British Journal of Hospital Medicine*, **24**, 34–8.

Murphy, D.L. and Beigel, A. (1974). Depression, elation, and lithium carbonate responses in manic patient subgroups. *Archives of General Psychiatry*, **31**, 643-8.

Murray, R.M., Lewis, S.W., and Reveley, A.M. (1985). Towards an aetiological classification of schizophrenia. *Lancet*, **i**, 1023-6.

Murray, R.M., Lewis, S.W., Owen, M.J., and Foerster, A. (1988). The neuro-developmental origins of dementia praecox. In *Schizophrenia: the major issues*, (ed. P. Bebbington and P. McGuffin), pp. 90-106. Heinemann/Mental Health Foundation, Oxford.

Naguib, M. and Levy, R. (1987). Late paraphrenia: neuropsychological impairment and structural brain abnormalities on computed tomography. *International Journal of Geriatric Psychiatry*, **2**, 83-90.

Nasrallah, H.A., Olsen, S.C., McCalley-Whitters, M., Chapman, S., and Jacoby, C.G. (1986). Cerebral ventricular enlargement in schizophrenia: a preliminary follow-up study. *Archives of General Psychiatry*, **43**, 157-9.

Neale, J.M. and Oltmanns, T.F. (1980). *Schizophrenia*. Wiley, New York.

Nelson, H.E., Pantelis, C., Carruthers, K., Speller, J., Baxendale, S., and Barnes, T.R.E. (1990). Cognitive functioning and symptomatology in chronic schizophrenia. *Psychological Medicine*, **20**, 357-65.

Neppe, V.M. (1982). Carbamazepine in the psychiatric patient. *Lancet*, **ii**, 334.

Neppe, V.M. (1983). Carbamazepine as adjunctive medication in nonepileptic chronic inpatients with EEG temporal lobe abnormalities. *Journal of Clinical Psychiatry*, **44**, 326-31.

National Institute of Mental Health (NIMH) Psychopharmacology Service Center Collaborative Study Group (1964). Phenothiazine treatment in acute schizophrenia. *Archives of General Psychiatry*, **10**, 246-61.

Nuechterlein, K.H., Snyder, K.S., Dawson, M.E., Rappe, C.R., Gitlin, M., and Fogelson, D. (1986). Expressed emotion, fixed-dose fluphenazine decanoate maintenance, and relapse in recent-onset schizophrenia. *Psychopharmacology Bulletin*, **22**, 633-9.

Nyback, H., Berggen, B.M., Hindmarsh, T., Sedvall, G., and Wiesel, F.-A. (1983). Cerebroventricular size and cerebrospinal fluid monoamine metabolites in schizophrenic patients and healthy volunteers. *Psychiatry Research*, **9**, 301-8.

O'Grady, J.C. (1990). The prevalence and diagnostic significance of Schneiderian first-rank symptoms in a random sample of acute psychiatric in-patients. *British Journal of Psychiatry*, **156**, 496-500.

Owen, F., Crow, T.J., Poulter, M., Cross, A.J., Longden, A., and Riley, G.J. (1978). Increased dopamine-receptor sensitivity in schizophrenia. *Lancet*, **ii**, 223-5.

Owens, D.G.C. (1990). Dystonia—a potential psychiatric pitfall. *British Journal of Psychiatry*, **156**, 620-34.

Owens, D.G.C. (1992). Imaging aspects of the biology of schizophrenia. *Current Opinion in Psychiatry*, **5**, 6-14.

Owens, D.G.C. and Johnstone, E.C. (1980). The disabilities of chronic schizophrenia—their nature and the factors contributing to their development. *British Journal of Psychiatry*, **136**, 384-93.

Owens, D.G.C., Johnstone, E.C., and Frith, C.D. (1982). Spontaneous involuntary disorders of movement: their prevalence, severity and distribution in chronic schizophrenics with and without treatment with neuroleptics. *Archives of General Psychiatry*, **39**, 452-61.

Owens, D.G.C., Johnstone, E.C., Crow, T.J., Frith, C.D., Jagoe, J.R., and Kreel, L. (1985). Lateral ventricular size in schizophrenia: relationship to the disease process and its clinical manifestations. *Psychological Medicine*, **15**, 27-41.

Owens, H. and Maxmen, J.S. (1979). Mood and affect: a semantic confusion. *American Journal of Psychiatry*, **136**, 97-9.

Parker, G., Johnston, P., and Hayward, L. (1988). Parental 'expressed emotion' as a predictor of schizophrenic relapse. *Archives of General Psychiatry*, **45**, 806-13.

Paulman, R.G., Devous, M.D., Gregory, R.R., Herman, J.H., Jennings, L., Bonte, F.J., *et al.* (1990). Hypofrontality and cognitive impairment in schizophrenia: dynamic single-photon tomography and neuropsychological assessment of schizophrenic brain function. *Biological Psychiatry*, **27**, 377-99.

Pauls, D.L. (1987). The familiality of autism and related disorders: a review of the evidence. In *Handbook of autism and pervasive developmental disorders*, (ed. D.J. Cohen and A.M. Donnellan), pp. 192-7. Winston, Silver Spring, Maryland.

Payne, R.W. (1973). Cognitive abnormalities. In *Handbook of abnormal psychology*, (ed. H.J. Eysenck), pp. 420-83. Pitman, London.

Payne, R.W. and Caird, W.K. (1967). Reaction time, distractibility and over-inclusive thinking in psychotics. *Journal of Abnormal Psychology*, **72**, 112-21.

Payne, R.W., Caird, W.K., and Laverty, G. (1964). Overinclusive thinking and delusions in schizophrenic patients. *Journal of Abnormal and Social Psychology*, **68**, 562-6.

Payne, R.W., Matussek, P., and George, E.I. (1967). An experimental study of schizophrenic thought disorder. *Journal of Mental Science*, **105**, 627-52.

Peroutka, S.J. and Snyder, S.H. (1980). Relationship of neuroleptic drug effects at brain dopamine, serotonin, alpha-adrenergic, and histamine receptors to clinical potency. *American Journal of Psychiatry*, **137**, 1518-22.

Perris, C. (1974). A study of cycloid psychosis. *Acta Psychiatrica Scandinavica*, supplement **253**, 1-76.

Perris, C. (1986). The case for the independence of cycloid psychotic disorder from the schizoaffective disorders. In *Schizoaffective psychoses*, (ed. A. Marneros and M.T. Tsuang), pp. 272-308. Springer-Verlag, Berlin.

Petty, L.K., Ornitz, E.M., Michelman, J.D., and Zimmerman, E.G. (1984). Autistic children who become schizophrenic. *Archives of General Psychiatry*, **41**, 129-35.

Pichot, P. (1982). The diagnosis and classification of mental disorders in French-speaking countries: background, current views and comparison with other nomenclatures. *Psychological Medicine*, **12**, 475-92.

Pichot, P. (1986). A comparison of different national concepts of schizoaffective psychosis. In *Schizoaffective psychoses*, (ed. A. Marneros and M.T. Tsuang), pp. 8-17. Springer-Verlag, Berlin.

Pilowsky, L.S., Costa, D.C., Ell, P.J., Verhoeff, N.P.L.G., Murray, R.M., and Kerwin, R.W. (1994). D2 dopamine receptor binding in the basal ganglia of antipsychotic-free schizophrenic patients: a [123]IBZM single photon emission tomography (SPET) study. British Journal of Psychiatry, **164**, 16-26.

Pogue-Geile, M.F. and Harrow, M. (1985). Negative symptoms in schizophrenia:

their longitudinal course and prognostic significance. *Schizophrenia Bulletin*, **11**, 427–39.

Pogue-Geile, M.F. and Oltmanns, T.F. (1980). Sentence perception and distractibility in schizophrenic, manic and depressed patients. *Journal of Abnormal Psychology*, **89**, 115–24.

Pollin, W., Allen, M.G., Hoffer, A., Stabeneau, J.R., and Hrubec, Z. (1969). Psychopathology in 15,909 pairs of veteran twins: evidence for a genetic factor in the pathogenesis of schizophrenia and its relative absence in psychoneurosis. *American Journal of Psychiatry*, **126**, 597–610.

Pope, H.G. and Lipinski, J.F. (1978). Diagnosis in schizophrenia and manic-depressive illness: a re-assessment of the specificity of 'schizophrenic' symptoms in the light of current research. *Archives of General Psychiatry*, **35**, 811–28.

Pope, H.G., Lipinski, J.F., Cohen, B.M., and Axelrod, D.T. (1980) 'Schizoaffective disorder': an invalid diagnosis? A comparison of schizoaffective disorder, schizophrenia and affective disorder. *American Journal of Psychiatry*, **137**, 921–7.

Pope, H.G., Jonas, J.M., Cohen, B.M., and Lipinski, J.F. (1982). Failure to find evidence of schizophrenia in first-degree relatives of schizophrenic probands. *American Journal of Psychiatry*, **139**, 826–8.

Poppelreuter, W. (1917). *Die psychischen Schadingungen durch Kopfschuss im Kriege, 1914–1916*. Leipzig.

Post, F. (1966). *Persistent persecutory states in the elderly*. Pergamon, Oxford.

Post, F. (1982). Functional disorders: I. Description, incidence and recognition. In *The psychiatry of late life*, (ed. R. Levy and F. Post), pp. 176–96. Blackwell, Oxford.

Post, R.M., Fink, E., Carpenter, W.T., Jr., and Goodwin, F.K. (1975). Cerebrospinal fluid amine metabolites in acute schizophrenia. *Archives of General Psychiatry*, **32**, 1063–9.

Post, R.M., Uhde, T.W., and Wolff, E.A. (1984). Profile of clinical efficacy and side effects of carbamazepine in psychiatric illness. *Acta Psychiatrica Scandinavica*, supplement, **313**, 104–17.

Potter, H.W. (1933). Schizophrenia in children. *American Journal of Psychiatry*, **12**, 1253–70.

Potter, H.W. and Klein, H.R. (1937). An evaluation of the treatment of problem children as determined by a follow-up study. *American Journal of Psychiatry*, **17**, 681–9.

Povlsen, U.J., Noring, U., Fog, R., and Gerlach, J. (1985). Tolerability and therapeutic effect of clozapine. *Acta Psychiatrica Scandinavica*, **71**, 176–85.

Prien, R.F., Caffey, E.M., and Klett, C.J. (1972). A comparison of lithium carbonate and chlorpromazine in the treatment of excited schizo-affectives. *Archives of General Psychiatry*, **27**, 182–9.

Priest, R.G. (1976). The homeless person and the psychiatric services: an Edinburgh survey. *British Journal of Psychiatry*, **128**, 128–36.

Procci, W.R. (1976). Schizo-affective psychosis: fact or fiction? *Archives of General Psychiatry*, **33**, 1167–78.

Protheroe, C. (1969). Puerperal psychosis: a long term study. *British Journal of Psychiatry*, **115**, 9–30.

Pugh, T.F., Jerath, B.K., Schmidt, W.M, and Reed, R.B. (1963). Rates of mental disease relating to childbearing. *New England Journal of Medicine*, **268**, 1224–8.

Rabins, P., Pearlson, G., Jarayan, G., Steele, C., and Tune, L. (1987). Increased ventricle-to-brain ratio in late-onset schizophrenia. *American Journal of Psychiatry*, **144**, 1216–18.

Rachlin, H.L. (1935). A follow-up study of Hoch's benign stupor cases. *American Journal of Psychiatry*, **92**, 531–58.

Ram, R., Bromet, E.J., Eaton, W.W., Pato, C., and Schwartz, J.E. (1992). The natural course of schizophrenia: a review of first admisssion studies. *Schizophrenia Bulletin*, **18**, 185–207.

Rappaport, M. (1967). Competing voice messages: effects of message load and drugs on the ability of acute schizophrenic patients to attend. *Archives of General Psychiatry*, **17**, 97–103.

Raskind, M.A. and Storrie, M.C. (1980). The organic mental disorders. In *Handbook of geriatric psychiatry*, (ed. E.W. Busse and D.L. Blazer), pp. 305–28. Van Nostrand Reinhold, New York.

Rathod, N.H. (1975). Cannabis psychosis. In *Cannabis and man: psychological and clinical aspects and patterns of use*, (ed. P.H. Connell and N. Dorn), pp. 90–106. Churchill Livingstone, Edinburgh.

Rennie, T.A.C. (1942). Prognosis in manic-depressive psychoses. *American Journal of Psychiatry*, **98**, 801–14.

Retterstol, N. (1966). *Paranoid and paranoiac psychoses*. Thomas, Springfield, Illinois.

Retterstol, N. (1970). *Prognosis in paranoid psychoses*. Thomas, Springfield, Illinois.

Reveley, M.A., Chitkara, B., and Lewis, S.W. (1988). Ventricular and cranial size in schizophrenia: a 4 to 7 year follow-up. *Schizophrenia Research*, **1**, 163.

Reynolds, E.H. and Trimble, M.R. (ed.) (1981). *Epilepsy and psychiatry*. Raven, New York.

Reynolds, G.P. (1983). Increased concentrations and lateral asymmetries of amygdala dopamine in schizophrenia. *Nature*, **305**, 527–9.

Ries, R.K., Wilson, L., Bokan, J.A., and Chiles, J.A. (1981). ECT in medication resistant schizoaffective disorder. *Comprehensive Psychiatry*, **22**, 167–73.

Rimland, B. (1965). *Infantile autism: the syndrome and its implications for a neural theory of behaviour*. Methuen, London.

Rimon, R., Stenback, A., and Achte, K. (1965). A sociopsychiatric study of paranoid psychoses. *Acta Psychiatrica Scandinavica*, **40**, supplement, **180**, 335–47.

Rimon, R., Roos, B.E., Rakkolainen, V., and Alanen, Y. (1971). The content of 5-HIAA and HVA in the CSF of patients with acute schizophrenia. *Journal of Psychosomatic Research*, **15**, 275–8.

Roberts, G.W. (1991). Schizophrenia: a neuropathological perspective. *British Journal of Psychiatry*, **158**, 8–17.

Robins, E. and Guze. S.B. (1970). Establishment of diagnostic validity in psychiatric illness: its application to schizophrenia. *American Journal of Psychiatry*, **126**, 983–7.

Rochester, S. and Martin, J.R. (1979). *Crazy talk: a study of the discourse of schizophrenic speakers*. Plenum, New York.

Rogers, D. (1985). The motor disorders of severe psychiatric illness: a conflict of paradigms. *British Journal of Psychiatry*, **147**, 221–32.

Rogers, D. (1992). *Motor disorder in psychiatry*. Wiley, Chichester.

Rollin, H.R. (1981). The impact of ECT. In *Electroconvulsive therapy: an appraisal*, (ed. R.L. Palmer), pp. 11–18. Oxford University Press.

Ron, M.A. and Logsdail, S.J. (1989). Psychiatric morbidity in multiple sclerosis: a clinical and MRI study. *Psychological Medicine*, **19**, 887–96.

Rosanoff, A. (1914). A study of brain atrophy in relation to insanity. *American Journal of Insanity*, **70**, 101–32.

Rosanoff, A.J., Handy, L.M., Plesset, I.R., and Brush, S. (1934). The etiology of so-called schizophrenic psychoses with special reference to their occurrence in twins. *American Journal of Psychiatry*, **91**, 247–86.

Rosen, J. and Zubenko, G.S. (1991). Emergence of psychosis and depression in the longitudinal evaluation of Alzheimer's disease. *Biological Psychiatry*, **29**, 224–32.

Rosen, W.G., Mohs, K.S., Johns, C.A., Small, N.S., Kendler, K.S., Horvath, T.B., and Davis, K.C. (1984). Positive and negative symptoms in schizophrenia. *Psychiatry Research*, **13**, 277–84.

Rosenhan, D.L. (1973). On being sane in insane places. *Science*, **179**, 250–8.

Rosenthal, D., Wender, P.H., Kety, S.S., Schulsinger, F., Welner, J., and Ostergaard, L. (1968). Schizophrenics' offspring reared in adoptive homes. In *The transmission of schizophrenia*, (ed. D. Rosenthal and S.S. Kety), pp. 1377–92. Pergamon, Oxford.

Rosenthal, D., Wender, P.H., Kety, S.S., Welner, P.H., and Schulsinger, F. (1971). The adopted-away offspring of schizophrenics. *American Journal of Psychiatry*, **128**, 307–11.

Rosenthal, N.E., Rosenthal, L.N., Stallone, F., Dunner, D.L., and Fieve, R.R. (1980). The validation of RDC schizoaffective disorder. *Archives of General Psychiatry*, **37**, 804–10.

Rostworowska, M., Barbaro B., and Cechnicki, A. (1987). The influence of expressed emotion on the course of schizophrenia: a Polish replication. Unpublished study presented at 17th congress of the European association for behaviour therapy, Amsterdam.

Roth, M. (1955). The natural history of mental disorder in old age. *Journal of Mental Science*, **101**, 281–301.

Roth, M. and Morrissey J.D. (1952). Problems in the diagnosis and classification of mental disorders in old age. *Journal of Mental Science*, **98**, 66–80.

Rowlands, M.W.D. (1988). Psychiatric and legal aspects of persistent litigation. *British Journal of Psychiatry*, **153**, 317–23.

Rubin, E.H., Drevets, W.C., and Burke, W.J. (1988). The nature of psychotic symptoms in senile dementia of the Alzheimer type. *Journal of Geriatric Psychiatry and Neurology*, **1**, 16–20.

Rubin, P., Holm, S., Friberg, L., Videbach, P., Andersen, H.S., Bendsen, B.B., *et al.* (1991). Altered modulation of prefrontal and subcortical brain activity in newly diagnosed schizophrenia and schizophreniform psychosis: a regional cerebral blood flow study. *Archives of General Psychiatry*, **48**, 987–95.

Rudin, E. (1916). *Zur Vererbung und Neuentstehung der Dementia Praecox*. Springer, Berlin.

Rumsey, J., Andreasen, N.C., and Rapaport, J. (1986). Thought, language, communication, and affective flattening in autistic adults. *Archives of General Psychiatry*, **43**, 771–7.

Rupniak, N.M., Kilpatrick, G., Hall, M.D., Jenner, P., and Marsden, C.D. (1984).

Differential alteration in striatal dopamine receptor sensitivity induced by repeated administration of clinically equivalent doses of haloperidol, sulpiride or clozapine. *Psychopharmacology*, **84**, 512–19.

Rupniak, N.M., Jenner, P., and Marsden, C.D. (1986). Acute dystonia induced by neuroleptic drugs. *Psychopharmacology*, **88**, 403–19.

Russell, A.T., Bott, L., and Simmons, C. (1989). The phenomenology of schizophrenia occurring in childhood. *Journal of the American Academy of Child and Adolescent Psychiatry*, **28**, 399–407.

Rutter, M. (1970). Autistic children: infancy to adulthood. *Seminars in Psychiatry*, **2**, 435–50.

Rutter, M. (1972). Childhood schizophrenia reconsidered. *Journal of Autism and Childhood Schizophrenia*, **2**, 315–37.

Rylander, G. (1972). Psychoses and the punding and choreiform syndromes in addiction to central stimulant drugs. *Psychiatrica, Neurologica, Neurochirurgica*, **75**, 203–12.

Sacks, O.W. (1982). Acquired tourettism in adult life. In *Gilles de la Tourette syndrome*, (ed. A.J. Friedhoff and T.N. Chase), pp. 89–92. Raven, New York.

Sacks, O. (1983). *Awakenings*. Dutton, New York.

Sands, I.J. (1928). The acute psychiatric type of epidemic encephalitis. *American Journal of Psychiatry*, **7**, 975–87.

Sarbin, T.R. and Mancuso, J.C. (1980). *Schizophrenia: medical diagnosis or moral verdict?* Pergamon, New York.

Sagawa, K., Kawakatsu, S., Shibuya, I., Oiji, A., Morinobu, S., Komatani, A., *et al.* (1990). Correlation of regional cerebral blood flow with performance of neuropsychological tests in schizophrenic patients. *Schizophrenia Research*, **3**, 241–6.

Sartorius, N., Leff, J., Jablensky, A., Anker, H., Korten, A., Gulbinat W. *et al.* (1987). The international pilot study of schizophrenia: five-year follow-up findings. In *Search for the causes of schizophrenia* (ed. H. Hafner, W.F. Gattaz, and W. Janzarik), pp. 110–28. Springer, Heidelberg.

Saykin, A.J., Gur, R.C., Gur, R.E., Mozley, P.D., Mozley, L.H., Resnick, S.M., *et al.* (1991). Neuropsychological function in schizophrenia: selective impairment in memory and learning. *Archives of General Psychiatry*, **48**, 618–24.

Scheibel, A.B. and Kovelman, J.A. (1981). Disorientation of the hippocampal pyramidal cell and its processes in the schizophrenic patient. *Biological Psychiatry*, **16**, 101–2.

Schilder, P. (1920). Über Gedankenentwicklung. *Zeitschrift für die gesamte Neurologie und Psychiatrie*, **59**, 250–63.

Schiorring, E. (1981). Psychopathology induced by 'speed drugs'. *Pharmacology, Biochemistry and Behavior*, **14**, supplement 1, 109–22.

Schneider, C. (1930). *Die Psychologie der Schizophrenen*. Thieme, Leipzig.

Schneider, K. (1949). The concept of delusion. In *Themes and variations in European psychiatry*, (ed. S.R. Hirsch and M. Shepherd, 1974), pp. 33–9. Wright, Bristol.

Schneider, K. (1950). *Psychopathic personalities*, (9th edn), (trans. M.W. Hamilton, 1958). Cassell, London.

Schneider, K. (1958). *Clinical psychopathology*, (5th edn), (trans. M.W. Hamilton, 1959), Grune and Stratton, New York.

Schofield, W., Hathaway, S.R., Hastings, D.W., and Bell, D.M. (1954). Prognostic factors in schizophrenia. *Journal of Consulting Psychology*, **18**, 155–66.

Schonecker, M. (1957). A strange syndrome in the oral area with application of chlorpromazine. *Nervenarzt*, **28**, 35.

Schulsinger, F., Parnas, J., Petersen, E.T., Schulsinger, H., Teasdale, T.W., Mednick, S.A., *et al.* (1984). Cerebral ventricular size in the offspring of schizophrenic mothers: a preliminary study. *Archives of General Psychiatry*, **41**, 602-6.

Schulz, S.C., Koller, M.M., Kishore, P.R., Hamer, R.M., Gehl, J.J., and Frieder, R.O. (1983). Ventricular enlargement in teenage patients with schizophrenia spectrum disorder. *American Journal of Psychiatry*, **140**, 1592-5.

Schwartz, S. (1982). Is there a schizophrenic language? *Behavioral and Brain Sciences*, **5**, 579-626.

Sedler, M.J. (1985). The legacy of Ewald Hecker: a new translation of 'die Hebephrenie'. *American Journal of Psychiatry*, **142**, 1265-71.

Sedman, G. (1970). Theories of depersonalization: a reappraisal. *British Journal of Psychiatry*, **117**, 1-14.

Seeman, P. (1980). Brain dopamine receptors. *Pharmacological Reviews*, **32**, 229-313.

Seeman, P. (1987). Dopamine receptors and the dopamine hypothesis of schizophrenia. *Synapse*, **1**, 133-52.

Seeman, P., Wong, M., and Lee, T. (1974). Dopamine receptor-block and nigral fiber impulse blockade by major tranquillizers. *Federation Proceedings*, **33**, 246.

Seeman, P., Lee, T., Chau-Wong, M., and Wong, K. (1976). Antipsychotic drug doses and neuroleptic/dopamine receptors. *Nature*, **261**, 717-19.

Seeman, P., Ulpian, C., Bergeron, C., Riederer, P., Jellinger, K., Gabriel, E., Reynolds, G.P., and Tourtellotte, W.W. (1984). Bimodal distribution of dopamine receptor densities in brains of schizophrenics. *Science*, **225**, 728-9.

Shagass, C. (1977). Twisted thoughts, twisted brain waves? In *Psychopathology and brain dysfunction*, (ed. C. Shagass, S. Gershon, and A.J. Friedhoff). Raven, New York.

Shalev, A. and Munitz, H. (1986). The neuroleptic malignant syndrome: agent and host interaction. *Acta Psychiatrica Scandinavica*, **73**, 337-47.

Shallice, T. (1988). *From neuropsychology to mental structure*. Cambridge University Press.

Shallice, T., Burgess, P.W., and Frith, C.D. (1991). Can the neuropsychological case-study approach be applied to schizophrenia. *Psychological Medicine*, **21**, 661-73.

Sheldrick, C., Jablensky, A., Sartorius, N., and Shepherd, M. (1977). Schizophrenia succeeded by affective illness: a catamnestic study and statistical enquiry. *Psychological Medicine*, **7**, 619-24.

Shepherd, M., Watt, D., Falloon, I., and Smeeton, N. (1989). The natural history of schizophrenia: a five-year follow-up study of outcome and prediction in a representative sample of schizophrenics. *Psychological Medicine*, monograph supplement, **15**, 1-46.

Shur, E. (1988). The epidemiology of schizophrenia. *British Journal of Hospital Medicine*, **40**, 38-45.

Sibley, D.R. and Monsma, F.J. (1992). Molecular biology of dopamine receptors. *Trends in Pharmacological Sciences*, **13**, 61-9.

Siegel, B.V., Buchsbaum, M.S., Bunney, W.E., Gottschalk, L.A., Haier, R.J.,

Lohr, J.B., *et al.* (1993). Cortical-striatal-thalamic circuits and brain glucose metabolism in 70 unmedicated male schizophrenic patients. *American Journal of Psychiatry*, **150**, 1325–36.

Siever, L.J. and Davis, K.L. (1985). Overview: towards a dysregulation hypothesis of depression. *American Journal of Psychiatry*, **142**, 1017–31.

Sigwald, J., Bouttier, D., and Courvoisier, S. (1959*a*). Les accidents neurologiques des medications neuroleptiques. *Revue Neurologique*, **100**, 553–95.

Sigwald, J., Bouttier, D., Raymondeau, C., and Piot, C. (1959*b*). Quatre cas de dyskinesie facio-bucco-linguo-masticatrice à evolution prolongée secondaire à un traitement par les neuroleptiques. *Revue Neurologique*, **100**, 751–5.

Silverberg-Shalev, R., Gordon, H.W., Bentin, S., and Aranson, A. (1981). Selective language deterioration in schizophrenia. *Journal of Neurology, Neurosurgery and Psychiatry*, **44**, 547–51.

Simon, W. and Wirt, R.D. (1961). Prognostic factors in schizophrenia. *American Journal of Psychiatry*, **117**, 887–90.

Simpson, G.M., Lee, J.H., Zoubok, B., and Gardos, G. (1979). A rating scale for tardive dyskinesia. *Psychopharmacology*, **64**, 171–9.

Sims, A. (1988). *Symptoms in the mind*. Baillière, Tindall, London.

Singer, M.T. and Wynne, L.C. (1965). Thought disorder and family relations of schizophrenics III. Methodology using projective techniques. *Archives of General Psychiatry*, **12**, 187–212.

Singer, M.T. and Wynne, L.C. (1966). Principles for scoring communication defects and deviances in parents of schizophrenics. Rorschach and T.A.T. scoring manuals. *Psychiatry*, **29**, 260–8.

Slade, P.D. (1976*a*). Hallucinations. *Psychological Medicine*, **6**, 7–13.

Slade, P.D. (1976*b*). Towards a theory of auditory hallucinations: outline of an hypothetical four-factor model. *British Journal of Social and Clinical Psychology*, **15**, 415–23.

Slade, P.D. and Bentall, R.P. (1988). *Sensory deception: a scientific analysis of hallucination*. Croom Helm, London.

Slater, E. (1953). *Psychotic and neurotic illness in twins*. HMSO, London.

Slater, E. (1968). A review of earlier evidence on genetic factors in schizophrenia. In *The transmission of schizophrenia*, (ed. D. Rosenthal and S.S. Kety), pp. 15–26. Pergamon, Oxford.

Slater, E., Beard, A.W., and Glitheroe, E. (1963). The schizophrenia-like psychoses of epilepsy. *British Journal of Psychiatry*, **109**, 95–150.

Smith, G.N. and Iacono, W.G. (1986). Lateral ventricular size in schizophrenia and choice of control group. *Lancet*, **i**, 1450.

Smith, J.M., Kuchanski, L.T., and Eblen, C., (1979). An assessment of tardive dyskinesia in schizophrenic outpatients. *Psychopharmacology*, **64**, 99–104.

Smythies, J.R. (1983). The transmethylation and one-carbon cycle hypothesis of schizophrenia. *Psychological Medicine*, **13**, 711–14.

Snaith, P. (1983). Pregnancy-related psychiatric disorder. *British Journal of Hospital Medicine*, **29**, 450–6.

Snaith, P. (1992). Anhedonia: exclusion from the pleasure dome. *British Medical Journal*, **305**, 134–5.

Soni, S.D. and Freeman, H.L. (1985). Early clinical experiences with sulpiride. *British Journal of Psychiatry*, **146**, 673.

Spitzer, R.L., Endicott, J., and Robins, E. (1978). *Research diagnostic criteria for a selected group of functional disorders*. Biometric Research, New York State Psychiatric Institute, New York.

Sponheim, S.R., Iacono, W.G., and Beiser, M. (1991). Stability of ventricular size after the onset of psychosis in schizophrenia. *Psychiatry Research: Neuroimaging*, **40**, 21–9.

Sramek, J., Herrara, J., Costa, J., Heh, C., Tran-Johnson, T., and Simpson, G. (1988). A carbamazepine trial in chronic, treatment-refractory schizophrenia. *American Journal of Psychiatry*, **145**, 748–50.

Steck, H. (1954). Le syndrome extrapyramidal et diencephalique au cours des traitements au largactil et au serpasil. *Annales Medico-Psychologique*, **112**, 737–43.

Stephens, J.H. (1970). Long-term course and prognosis in schizophrenia. *Seminars in Psychiatry*, **2**, 464–85.

Stephens, J.H. (1978). Long-term prognosis and followup in schizophrenia. *Schizophrenia Bulletin*, **4**, 25–47.

Stephens, J.H. and Astrup, C. (1965). Treatment outcome in process and non-process schizophrenics treated by 'A' and 'B' type therapists. *Journal of Nervous and Mental Disease*, **140**, 449–56.

Stern, Y., Mayeux, Y., Ilson, J., Fahn, S., and Lote, L. (1984). Pergolide therapy for Parkinson's disease: neurobehavioral changes. *Neurology*, **34**, 201–4.

Stevens, J. (1987). Brief psychoses: do they contribute to the good prognosis and equal prevalence of schizophrenia in developing countries? *British Journal of Psychiatry*, **151**, 393–6.

Stevens, M., Crow, T.J., Bowman, M.J., and Coles, R.C. (1978). Age disorientation in schizophrenia: a constant prevalence of 25 per cent in a chronic mental hospital population? *British Journal of Psychiatry*, **133**, 130–6.

Stirling, J., Tantam, D., Thomas, P., Newby, D., Montague, L., Ring, N., and Rowe, S. (1991). Expressed emotion and early onset schizophrenia: a one year follow-up. *Psychological Medicine*, **21**, 675–86.

Straube, E.R. and Germer, C.K. (1979). Dichotic shadowing and selective attention to word meaning in schizophrenia. *Journal of Abnormal Psychology*, **88**, 346–53.

Strauss, J.S., Carpenter, W.T., and Bartko, J.J. (1974). The diagnosis and understanding of schizophrenia: III. Speculations on the processes that underlie schizophrenic symptoms and signs. *Schizophrenia Bulletin*, **1**, 61–9.

Surridge, D. (1969). An investigation into some psychiatric aspects of multiple sclerosis. *British Journal of Psychiatry*, **115**, 749–64.

Swett, C. (1975). Drug-induced dystonia. *American Journal of Psychiatry*, **132**, 532–4.

Szasz, T.S. (1960). The myth of mental illness. *American Psychologist*, **15**, 113–18.

Szasz, T. (1971). *The manufacture of madness*. Routledge and Kegan Paul, London.

Szechtman, H., Nahmias, C., Garnett, S., Firnau, G., Brown, G.M., Kaplan, R.D., and Cleghorn, J.M. (1988). Effect of neuroleptics on altered cerebral glucose metabolism in schizophrenia. *Archives of General Psychiatry*, **45**, 523–32.

Tamminga, C.A., Thaker, G.K., Buchanan, M., Kirkpatrick, B., Alphs, C.D., Chase, T.N., and Carpenter, W.T. (1992). Limbic system abnormalities identified in schizophrenia using positron emission tomography with fluorodeoxyglucose and neocortical alterations with deficit syndrome. *Archives of General Psychiatry*, **49**, 522–30.

Tamlyn, D., McKenna, P.J., Mortimer, A.M., Lund, C.E., Hammond, S., and Baddeley, A.D. (1992). Memory impairment in schizophrenia: its extent, affiliations and neuropsychological character. *Psychological Medicine*, **22**, 101–15.

Tantam, D. (1988). Lifelong eccentricity and social isolation. I. Psychiatric, social and forensic aspects. *British Journal of Psychiatry*, **153**, 777–82.

Tantam, D. (1991). Asperger syndrome in adulthood. In *Autism and Asperger syndrome* (ed. U. Frith), pp. 147–183. Cambridge University Press.

Tarrier, N., Barrowclough, C., Vaughn, C., Bamrah, A., Porceddu, K., Watts, S., and Freeman, H. (1988). The community management of schizophrenia: a controlled trial of a behavioural intervention with families to reduce relapse. *British Journal of Psychiatry*, **153**, 532–42.

Tatetsu, S. (1964). Methamphetamine psychosis. *Folia Psychiatrica et Neurologica Japonica*, supplement **7**, 377–80.

Taylor, M.A. (1972). Schneiderian first-rank symptoms and clinical prognostic features. *Archives of General Psychiatry*, **26**, 64–7.

Taylor, M.A. and Abrams, R. (1973). The phenomenology of mania: a new look at some old patients. *Archives of General Psychiatry*, **29**, 520–2.

Taylor, M.A. and Abrams, R. (1977). Catatonia: prevalence and importance in the manic phase of manic-depressive illness. *Archives of General Psychiatry*, **34**, 1223–5.

Taylor, M.A. and Abrams, R. (1984). Cognitive impairment in schizophrenia. *American Journal of Psychiatry*, **141**, 196–201.

Taylor, P. (1981). ECT: the preliminary report of a trial in schizophrenic patients. In *Electroconvulsive therapy: an appraisal*, (ed. R.L. Palmer), pp. 214–25. Oxford University Press.

Taylor, P. and Fleminger J.J. (1980). ECT for schizophrenia. *Lancet*, **i**, 1380–2.

Thornicroft, G. (1990). Cannabis and psychosis: is there epidemiological evidence for an association? *British Journal of Psychiatry*, **157**, 25–34.

Thornton, A. and McKenna, P.J. (1994). Acute dystonic reactions complicated by psychotic phenomena. *British Journal of Psychiatry*, **164**, 115–18.

Tienari, P. (1963). Psychiatric illness in identical twins. *Acta Psychiatrica Scandinavica*, **39**, supplement, **171**, 1–195.

Tienari, P. (1975). Schizophrenia in Finnish male twins. In *Studies of schizophrenia* (ed. M.H. Lader), pp. 29–35. Headley Brothers, Ashford, Kent.

Toru, M., Nishikawa, T., Mataga, N., and Takashima, M. (1982). Dopamine metabolism increases in postmortem schizophrenic basal ganglia. *Journal of Neural Transmission*, **54**, 181–91.

Tramer, M. (1929). The biological significance of the birth month, with special reference to psychosis. *Schweizer Archive für Neurologie und Psychiatrie*, **24**, 17–24.

Trimble, M.R. (1982). Functional diseases. *British Medical Journal*, **285**, 1768–70.

Tsiantis, S., Macri, I., and Maratos, O. (1986). Schizophrenia in children: a review of European research. *Schizophrenia Bulletin*, **12**, 101–19.

Tsuang, M.T. and Dempsey, M. (1979). Long-term outcome of major psychoses. *Archives of General Psychiatry*, **36**, 1302–4.

Tsuang, M.T., Woolson, R.F., and Fleming, J.H. (1979). Long-term outcome of major psychoses I: Schizophrenia and affective disorders. *Archives of General Psychiatry*, **36**, 1295–1301.

Tsuang, M.T., Winokur, G., and Crowe, R.R. (1980). Morbidity risks of schizophrenia and affective disorders among first degree relatives of patients with schizophrenia, mania, depression and surgical conditions. *British Journal of Psychiatry*, **137**, 497–504.

Tucker, G.J., Price, T.R.P., Johnson, V.B., and McAllister, T. (1986). Phenomenology of temporal lobe dysfunction: a link to atypical psychosis—a series of cases. *Journal of Nervous and Mental Disease*, **174**, 348–56.

Tune, L.E., Wong, D.F., and Pearlson, G.D. (1992). Elevated dopamine D2 receptor density in 23 schizophrenic patients: a positron emission tomography study with [^{11}C]N-methylspiperone. *Schizophrenia Research*, **6**, 147.

Turner, S.W., Toone, B.K., and Brett-Jones, J.R. (1986). Computerised tomographic scan changes in early schizophrenia: preliminary findings. *Psychological Medicine*, **16**, 219–25.

Turner, T.H., Cookson, J., Wass, J.A.H., Drury, P.L., Price, P.A., and Besser, G.M. (1984). Psychotic reactions during treatment of pituitary tumours with dopamine agonists. *British Medical Journal*, **289**, 1101–3.

Tyrer, P., Casey, P., and Ferguson, B. (1988). Personality disorder and mental illness. In *Personality disorders: diagnosis, management and course*, (ed. P. Tyrer), pp. 93–104. Wright, London.

Ungvari, G.S. and Hollokoi, R.I.M. (1993). Successful treatment of litigious paranoia with pimozide. *Canadian Journal of Psychiatry*, **38**, 4–8.

Vaillant, G.F. (1962). The prediction of recovery in schizophrenia. *Journal of Nervous and Mental Disease*, **135**, 534–43.

Van Krevelen, D.A. (1971). Early infantile autism and autistic psychopathy. *Journal of Autism and Childhood Schizophrenia*, **1**, 82–6.

Van Putten, T. (1975). The many faces of akathisia. *Comprehensive Psychiatry*, **16**, 43–7.

Vardy, M.M. and Kay, S.R. (1983). LSD psychosis or LSD-induced schizophrenia: a multimethod inquiry. *Archives of General Psychiatry*, **40**, 877–83.

Vaughan, K., Doyle, M., and McConaghy, N. (1994). The relationship between relatives' expressed emotion and schizophrenic relapse: an Australian replication. *Social Psychiatry and Psychiatric Epidemiology*. In press.

Vaughn, C.E. and Leff, J.P. (1976). The influence of family and social factors on the course of psychiatric illness. *British Journal of Psychiatry*, **129**, 125–37.

Vaughn, C.E., Snyder, K.S., Jones, S., Freeman, W.B., and Falloon, I.R.H. (1984). Family factors in schizophrenic relapse: replication in California of British research on expressed emotion. *Archives of General Psychiatry*, **41**, 1169–77.

Victor, G. (1984). *The riddle of autism*. Gower Publishing/Lexington Books, Lexington.

Volavka, J. (1985). Late onset schizophrenia: a review. *Comprehensive Psychiatry*, **26**, 148–56.

Volkow, N.D., Wolf, A.P., Van Gelder, P., Brodie, J.D., Overall, J.E., Cancro, R., and Gomez-Mont, F. (1987). Phenomenological correlates of metabolic activity in 18 patients with chronic schizophrenia. *American Journal of Psychiatry*, **144**, 151–8.

von Economo, C. (1931). *Encephalitis Lethargica: its sequelae and treatment*, (trans. K.O. Newman). Oxford University Press/Humphrey Milford, London.

Waddington, J.L. (1984). Tardive dyskinesia: a critical re-evaluation of the causal role of neuroleptics and of the dopamine receptor supersensitivity hypothesis.

In *Recent research in neurology*, (ed. N. Callaghan and R. Galvin), pp. 34–48. Pitman, London.

Waddington, J.L. (1989). Functional interactions between D-1 and D-2 dopamine receptor systems: their role in the regulation of psychomotor behaviour, putative mechanisms, and clinical relevance. *Journal of Psychopharmacology*, **3**, 54–63.

Waddington, J.L. (1993). Mechanisms of action of typical and atypical antipsychotic drugs in the treatment of schizophrenia. *Clinician*, **11**, 45–54.

Waddington, J.L., Cross, A.J., Gamble, S.J., and Bourne, R.C. (1983). Spontaneous orofacial dyskinesia and dopaminergic function in rats after six months of neuroleptic treatment. *Science*, **220**, 530–2.

Walker, C. (1991). Delusion: what did Jaspers really say? *British Journal of Psychiatry*, **159**, supplement, **14**, 94–101.

Ward, C.D. (1986). Encephalitis lethargica and the development of neuropsychiatry. *Psychiatric Clinics of North America*, **9**, 215–23.

Weinberger, D.R. (1987). Implications of normal brain development for the pathogenesis of schizophrenia. *Archives of General Psychiatry*, **44**, 660–9.

Weinberger, D.R., Torrey, E.F., Neophytides, A.N., and Wyatt, R.J. (1979). Lateral cerebral ventricular enlargement in schizophrenia. *Archives of General Psychiatry*, **36**, 735–9.

Weinberger, D.R., DeLisi, L.E., Perman, G.P., Targum, S., and Wyatt, R.J. (1982). Computed tomography in schizophreniform disorder and other acute psychiatric disorders. *Archives of General Psychiatry*, **39**, 778–83.

Weinberger, D.R., Berman, K.F., and Zec, R.F. (1986). Physiological dysfunction of dorsolateral prefrontal cortex in schizophrenia. *Archives of General Psychiatry*, **43**, 114–35.

Welner, A., Croughan, J., Fishman, R., and Robins, E. (1977). The group of schizoaffective and related psychoses: a follow-up study. *Comprehensive Psychiatry*, **18**, 413–22.

West, L.J. (1962). A general theory of hallucinations and dreams. In *Hallucinations*, (ed. L.J. West). Grune and Stratton, New York.

West, L.J. (1975). A clinical and theoretical overview of hallucinatory phenomena. In *Hallucinations: behavior, experience and theory*, (ed. R.K. Siegel and L.J. West), pp. 287–312. Wiley, New York.

Whitlock, F.A. (1967). The Ganser syndrome. *British Journal of Psychiatry*, **113**, 19–29.

WHO (World Health Organization) (1973). *Report of the international pilot study of schizophrenia*. World Health Organization, Geneva.

WHO (World Health Organization) (1979). *Schizophrenia: an international follow-up study*. Wiley, Geneva.

Wielgus, M.S. and Harvey, P.D. (1988). Dichotic listening and recall in schizophrenia and mania. *Schizophrenia Bulletin*, **14**, 689–700.

Wilson, M. (1993). DSM-III and the transformation of American psychiatry: a history. *American Journal of Psychiatry*, **150**, 399–409.

Wilson, S.A.K. (1940). *Neurology*. Edward Arnold, London.

Wing, J.K. (1963). Rehabilitation of psychiatric patients. *British Journal of Psychiatry*, **109**, 635–41.

Wing, J.K. (1978). Clinical concepts of schizophrenia. In *Schizophrenia: towards a new synthesis*, (ed. J.K. Wing), pp. 1–30. Academic Press, London.

Wing, J.K. and Brown, G.W. (1970). *Institutionalism and schizophrenia: a comparative study of three mental hospitals, 1960–1968.* Cambridge University Press.

Wing, J. and Nixon, J. (1975). Discriminating symptoms in schizophrenia. *Archives of General Psychiatry*, **32**, 853–9.

Wing, J.K., Cooper, J.E., and Sartorius, N. (1974). *The measurement and classification of psychiatric symptoms.* Cambridge University Press.

Wing, L. (1980). *Early childhood autism,* (2nd edn). Pergamon, Oxford.

Wing, L. (1981). Asperger's syndrome: a clinical account. *Psychological Medicine*, **11**, 115–29.

Wing, L. (1991). The relationship between Asperger's syndrome and Kanner's autism. In *Autism and Asperger syndrome,* (ed. U. Frith), pp. 93–121. Cambridge University Press.

Wing, L. and Attwood, A. (1987). Syndromes of autism and atypical development. In *Handbook of autism and pervasive developmental disorders,* (ed. D.J. Cohen and A.M. Donnellan), pp. 3–19. Winston, Silver Spring, Maryland.

Wing, L. and Gould, J. (1979). Severe impairments of social interaction and associated abnormalities in children. *Journal of Autism and Developmental Disorders*, **9**, 11–29.

Winokur, G. (1977). Delusional disorder (paranoia). *Comprehensive Psychiatry*, **18**, 511–21.

Winokur, G., Clayton, P.J., and Reich, T. (1969). *Manic-depressive illness.* Mosby, St. Louis.

Winters, K.C. and Neale, J.M. (1983). Delusions and delusional thinking in psychotics: a review of the literature. *Clinical Psychology Reviews*, **3**, 227–53.

Withers, E. and Hinton, J. (1971). Three forms of the clinical tests of the sensorium and their reliability. *British Journal of Psychiatry*, **119**, 1–8.

Wolfe, T. (1971). *The electric kool-aid acid test.* Bantam, New York.

Wolff, S. and Chick, J. (1980). Schizoid personality in childhood: a controlled follow-up study. *Psychological Medicine*, **10**, 85–100.

Wolkin A., Angrist, B., Wolf, A., Brodie, J.D., Wolkin, B., Jaeger, J., *et al.* (1988). Low frontal glucose utilization in chronic schizophrenia: a replication study. *American Journal of Psychiatry*, **145**, 251–3.

Wong, D.F., Wagner, H.N., Tune, L.E., Dannals, R.F., Pearlson, G.D., Links, J.M., *et al.* (1986). Positron emission tomography reveals elevated D2 dopamine receptors in drug-naive schizophrenics. *Science*, **234**, 1558–63.

Woods, B.T. and Wolf, J. (1983). A reconsideration of the relation of ventricular enlargement to duration of illness in schizophrenia. *American Journal of Psychiatry*, **140**, 1564–70.

Wragg, R.E. and Jeste, D.V. (1989). Overview of depression and psychosis in Alzheimer's disease. *American Journal of Psychiatry*, **146**, 577–87.

Wynne, L.C. (1968). Methodologic and conceptual issues in the study of schizophrenics and their families. In *The transmission of schizophrenia,* (ed. D. Rosenthal and S. Kety), pp. 185–200. Pergamon, Oxford.

Wynne, L.C. (1971). Family research on the pathogenesis of schizophrenia. In *Problems of psychosis: international colloquium on psychosis,* Excerpta Medica congress series, No. 194, (ed. P. Doucet and C. Laurin), Excerpta Medica, Amsterdam.

Wynne, L.C. and Singer, M.T. (1963). Thought disorder and family relations of schizophrenicis. *Archives of General Psychiatry*, **9**, 191–6.

Wynne, L.C., Ryckoff, I., Day, J., and Hirsch, S. (1958). Pseudo-mutuality in the family relations of schizophrenics. *Psychiatry*, **21**, 205-20.

Young, A.H., Blackwood, D.H.R., Roxborough, H., McQueen, J.K., Martin, M.J., and Kean, D. (1991). A magnetic resonance imaging study of schizophrenia: brain structure and clinical symptoms. *British Journal of Psychiatry*, **158**, 158-64.

Young, D. and Scoville, W.B. (1938). Paranoid psychosis in narcolepsy and the possible danger of benzedrine treatment. *Medical Clinics of North America*, **22**, 637-46.

Zahner, G.E. and Pauls, D.L. (1987). Epidemiological surveys of infantile autism. In *Handbook of autism and pervasive developmental disorders*, (ed. D.J. Cohen and A.M. Donnellan), pp. 199-210. Winston, Silver Spring, Maryland.

Zubin, J. (1967). Classification of the behavior disorders. *Annual Review of Psychology*, **18**, 373-406.

Index